To Paul, Becky and Susan
Fond memories of
our trip to the
Yarra Valley
                Ross and Margaret
                5/2/2000.

D1383704

THE AUSTRALIAN WINE
Pictorial Atlas

The creation of this the third such book on Australian Wine I have written is tinged with sadness through the passing of my dear friend, colleague and incredibly gifted photographer Milan Roden in 1996. Fortunately Milan's great work lives on and graces many of the pages of this Pictorial Journey. I have had the great fortune of meeting and working with two tremendous travelling companions and photographers Don Brice, in my home state of South Australia and French born Stephane L'Hostis.

Don's athletic ability was often astounding, capturing images from incredible angles. Stephane was always at the ready with his Grand Prix experience but we never did catch that elusive Kangaroo in the vines although he did get close so many times. When I wrote the Pictorial Guide two years ago and printed a considerable quantity it was with a view that it would sell steadily over 3 years and sufficient changes would occur in the wine industry that a new edition would be warranted then.

The book sold out in under 12 months and a reprint became an option, but once I began the photographic pilgrimage it became so obvious the industry had in two short years gone through revolutionary changes and mind blowing development. Even in the most distant and isolated wine regions we so often fell upon marvelous new wineries both small and large sensational cellar doors with warm inviting winery restaurants and cafes abounding. Alongside all this, beautiful bed and breakfast and other outstanding accommodation houses have mushroomed everywhere.

Certainly wine is the catalyst but the gourmet food industry from Land and Sea is sweeping our Nation. Frequently these food mecca's are in our Wine districts, wherever the vine grows physical beauty is its natural host and the richness of natures produce flows forward, complimenting the liquid sunshine encompassing it.

Australia's mission to reach a billion dollars of wine exports shortly into the new Century

Author - Tom Hardy

is well on target. We have withstood the challenge of the other New World Wine Powers to firmly cement our place as their undisputed leader, our viticultural base is increasing at the rate of some 10% per annum. Most importantly these largely cool climate plantings of the right varieties is improving our current wines constantly. The quality of our next century's wines with our innovative winemakers guiding them will be awesome. Wine Shows around the World attest to the success of our endeavors. Our clean environment and the increasingly organic methods of grape growing and winemaking can only enhance our chance of assured development as a true world wine power.

The pages that follow include some new wine regional chapters and over 120 new detailed winery features added to the many

familiar faces of the industry. Some exciting food, accommodation and hospitality houses accompany you on this truly enlightening and pleasurable journey, whether it be in your own lounge room, imagination in top gear or following the pathways of the accurate atlas maps to enhance your wine knowledge through sharing first hand experiences with its many custodians around our splendid country.

Good luck and cheers,

Tom Hardy

TOM HARDY

Introduction

The Prime Minister - Mr John Howard

It gives me great pleasure to provide the introduction to Thomas Hardy's new Australian Wine Pictorial Atlas. This is Thomas' fourth major wine publication and the third on the wonderful wines of our country which are making such a mark on the discerning wine markets of the world. Thomas comes from a family with a rich history in the wine industry - they have contributed much to the wine industry in Australia. His great, great grandfather, (also Thomas), wrote prolifically on wine, along with founding one of Australia's major wine companies.

Thomas' father, who was awarded an OBE for services to the wine industry, was a friend of mine, as is also his uncle, famous wine-maker, yachtsman and truly great Australian, Sir James Hardy.

I met Thomas only this year, when Janette and I had the pleasure of attending the inaugural "Hunter Thanksgiving Dinner" at the McGuigan Brothers Winery. The night was not only thoroughly enjoyable - particularly Len Evans' unique wine options challenge, in which Janette's palate triumphed - but reinforced to me the dynamic and coherent nature of the Australian wine industry of which we can all be justly proud.

In 1987, wine exports from Australia totalled 21.3 million litres and netted our country $44 million. Over the last year, wine export volume increased to 155 million litres netting Australia $596 million of export income - an increase of more than 1300 percent over the 10 years.

Wine competitions throughout the world have been dominated by Australian wines for a number of years, attesting not only to the skill of our winemakers, but also our superb and diverse climates, soils and our clean environment.

Wine is now successfully grown in many parts of Australia. The beauty of our wine regions and the burgeoning wine tourism network of hospitality, restaurants, accommodation, gourmet food producers, arts and crafts, etc. is astounding. Wine festivals now proliferate through our wine regions showcasing so well our arts and music, along with wine and food. I trust you will find time to participate in one soon.

The pages of Thomas Hardy's Pictorial Wine Atlas that follow, take you on an entrancing journey accompanied by excellent maps and vibrant photography, graphically portraying the beauty and bounty that is Australian wine.

John Howard

(JOHN HOWARD)

Jack Mann (1906 -1989)
Presided over 65 Vintages.
"A winemaker is a humble servant of nature; his role
is to give nature the opportunity to produce the best
possible wine. Nature creates, man only guides."

Introduction - The history of Australian Wines

The history of Australian wine begins with the first settlers. Vine cuttings were brought into the country by Captain Arthur Phillip when he landed at Sydney Cove in 1788. Planted where Sydney's Botanic Gardens now stand, the cuttings, mainly because of unsuitable soil, did not thrive.

It wasn't long, however, before others, such as the great pastoralist and grazier, John Macarthur, moved on to more suitable areas around Parramatta. From there the vineyards extended to the rich, volcanic soils of the Hunter Valley, around the towns of Pokolbin and Cessnock. All southern mainland states had vineyards established within a few years of their founding.

Ethnic groups were a major influence in establishing the various vineyard areas. The Lutherans, having fled religious persecution in Germany, pioneered the Barossa Valley in South Australia. Their influence is still very obvious today. It can be seen in the picturesque churches and local townships, along with the classic Germanic-style rieslings and the unique German mettwursts which are showcased in the Barossa's colourful and exuberant wine festival. This is a traditional German celebration which was imported to the Barossa Valley to become the first of its kind in Australia, and is now held every two years.

Victoria's strong beginnings in the industry date back to the Swiss settlers who were encouraged to come to Australia by the first Governor, Charles LaTrobe and his wife, also Swiss. Victoria went on to become the premier Wine State, having three quarters of the country's total production until the 1890's.

Unfortunately, wine in Australia has always been subject to fashion, changes in taste and economic conditions. Only in the last couple of decades, when wine has become an integral part of the Australian way of life, has some sort of stability and steady growth taken place. Of course stability is also dependent on the forces of nature. The worldwide plague phylloxera swept through most of Australia's vineyards in the 1890's. This tiny vine louse eats into and eventually kills the root of the vine. South Australia was, fortunately, spared this threat and remains one of the very few areas in the world not devastated by this plague. Nevertheless, it still remains a threat.

In the early days winemaking, even at its very best, was a 'hit or miss' affair. With little knowledge worldwide as to the very nature of the process of fermentation from grape juice to wine, many wines were unsound. Some exceptional wines, however, which are now making a comeback, were made in cooler areas such as the Yarra Valley in Victoria.

Heavy fortified wines became increasingly popular as they were protected by blending with high quality grape spirit, thus ensuring their integrity. They could be produced in the warmer and often irrigated areas where crops were often of greater size per hectare than in the cooler, high quality table wine areas. The Great Depression of the 1930ís reinforced the drinking of fortified wines. Not only was it the most affordable beverage, but it was also very palatable in its rich, sweet style.

The dominance of fortified wines lasted 70 to 80 years, only being reversed in the early 1970ís when table wines eventually rose to above 50 percent of wine consumed. Many factors were at work. The heavy post-war immigration of Europeans brought to Australia their century-old tradition of drinking table wine with meals. This influence, along with the growing affluence of the average Australian, brought more leisure time, overseas travel and an interest in the finer things of life, and thus there was an upsurge in wine drinking. The industry accommodated this change with a reasonable price structure, and the introduction of bulk containers such as the flagon, which culminated in the ingenious Australian invention, the 'bag in the box' wine cask. People were now able to enjoy table wine whenever they so desired, without fear of the wine 'going off'. Red wines have certainly made a resurgence in the 1990s and the richness in colour, flavour, and the complexity and balance winemakers today are achieving with their reds is indeed marvelous. The best Australian reds are easily on the top rung of the world's great wines. Much credit for this and the overall outstanding quality of Australian wines, comes right back to the vineyard. Soil selection, the aspect of the new plantings, micro-climates carefully chosen, the clonal selections of grape varieties now available, vine spacing, innovative trellising and pruning, are all contributing to better and better grapes and consequently wines.

Since the '60s, interest and investment have grown in the wine industry, particularly from the multi-national companies rationalisation has continued among the ownership of the bigger wine companies. Alongside this has been the enormous growth in 'boutique vineyards' and the expansion into new viticultural areas. We now have vineyards in all states of Australia and undoubtedly world-class wines.

Australia is the best performed by far in any world wine competitions. During the last decade or so until 1997, Australian wines have taken the wine world by storm. Wine exports have increased more than 12-fold, wine is now one of Australia's main exports, and a very prestigious one at that. To cope with this demand and future plans – among others, a billion dollar Australian wine export goal around the turn of the century – the huge plantings starting some 3 years ago continues at an even more frantic pace but we are still short of quality wine the world is demanding from us.

The health benefits of wine are finally being properly acknowledged and red wine is a particular beneficiary of this although white wine is also healthy in moderation.

Exciting times and challenges are ahead for Australian wines. The Australian wine industry has really come of age. In this book, we look forward to guiding you to wineries and vineyards, large and small; a comprehensive tour which not only provides readily identifiable wine labels, up to the minute maps and sensitive photography, but also experiences that you, the traveller, should seek out.

Wine Festivals and Gourmet Wine Food celebrations in all regions are booming bringing together food, art, music and people. Wine is the magic elixir enhancing our enjoyment of fine civilized living.

AUSTRALIAN WINE PRODUCING AREAS

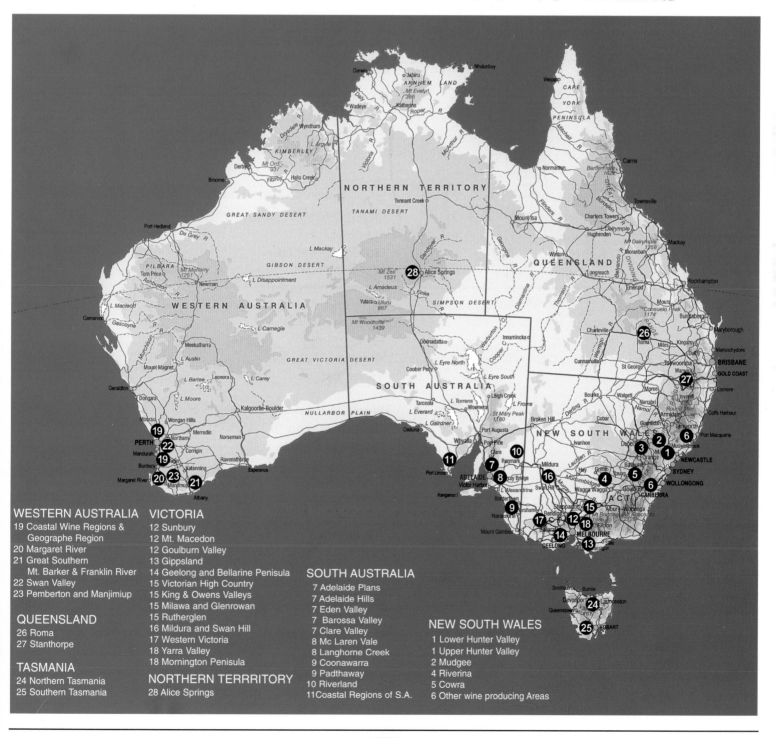

WESTERN AUSTRALIA
19 Coastal Wine Regions & Geographe Region
20 Margaret River
21 Great Southern
    Mt. Barker & Franklin River
22 Swan Valley
23 Pemberton and Manjimiup

QUEENSLAND
26 Roma
27 Stanthorpe

TASMANIA
24 Northern Tasmania
25 Southern Tasmania

VICTORIA
12 Sunbury
12 Mt. Macedon
12 Goulburn Valley
13 Gippsland
14 Geelong and Bellarine Peninsula
15 Victorian High Country
15 King & Owens Valleys
15 Milawa and Glenrowan
15 Rutherglen
16 Mildura and Swan Hill
17 Western Victoria
18 Yarra Valley
18 Mornington Peninsula

NORTHERN TERRRITORY
28 Alice Springs

SOUTH AUSTRALIA
7 Adelaide Plans
7 Adelaide Hills
7 Eden Valley
7 Barossa Valley
7 Clare Valley
8 Mc Laren Vale
8 Langhorne Creek
9 Coonawarra
9 Padthaway
10 Riverland
11 Coastal Regions of S.A.

NEW SOUTH WALES
1 Lower Hunter Valley
1 Upper Hunter Valley
2 Mudgee
4 Riverina
5 Cowra
6 Other wine producing Areas

Contents

Written By: Thomas K Hardy

Photography: Don Brice, Stephane L'Hostis

Publisher: Thomas K Hardy

Project Assistant: Julie Idema

Production: Thomas K Hardy
　　　　　Thomas W Hardy

Finished Art/Film: Image Digital, Adelaide Australia

Printed by: Graphic Print Group, Adelaide Australia

Published by: Vintage Image Productions, 1-57 Sturdee Street, Linden Park SA Australia 5065 Copyright ©. 1997

An introduction to New South Wales

New South Wales was the first State to plant vines; in fact, the first vine cuttings arrived with Governor Phillip and the first fleet in 1788. The vines were planted at Farm Cove, which is now part of Sydney's Botanic Gardens. These vines unfortunately did not fare well due to poor soil conditions.

Vineyards soon sprang up in many areas around Sydney. The first commercial wine came from Gregory Blaxland, a member of the famous pioneering family, from his vineyard at Brush Farm on the Parramatta River, which is now part of metropolitan Sydney. Another included the Rooty Hill 'Minchinbury' Vineyard of Penfolds. None survive today.

Other vineyards sprang up around the State but it was not until vines were planted in the Hunter Valley in the late 1820's that the New South Wales wine industry became firmly established. The first vines in the Hunter were planted in the Branxton/Singleton area. This is some 20 kilometres north of the current main grape-growing area around Cessnock, referred to as the Lower Hunter Valley, although Wyndham Estate have a large and very successful vineyard at Branxton. The main pioneers were George Wyndham at Dalwood near Branxton, and James Busby at Kirkton. George Wyndham's classic old home 'Dalwood House', was built in 1828 and had

fallen into disrepair. It was restored in a joint project by Wyndham Estate and the National Trust of Australia for the Australian Bicentenary in 1988. George Wyndham also planted some 10 hectares of vines at Inverell in 1850. This vineyard produced until 1890. (No further vines were planted in the region until the mid 1960ís when Gilgai Vineyard was established). James Busby established his vineyard at Kirkton between Branxton and Singleton in 1825. Mudgee, situated in the northern part of the Great Dividing Range, some 300 kilometres north west of Sydney, was the next wine region to be opened up. It was pioneered in 1858 by Arthur Roth, a vineyard worker from Germany. He named his property Rothweir and his family was still involved in viticulture a century later. He was followed by other Germans, namely Andreas Kurtz and Frederick Bucholtz. As in the Barossa Valley in South Australia, there was a notable German wine growing influence. Other areas of New South Wales planted in the latter part of the 19th century were Junee, Wellington, Molong, Bathurst and Young on the slopes of the Great Dividing Range. Today this area is enjoying a renaissance, with huge areas of vines being planted at Cowra, and other large vineyards such as McWilliam's Barwang property near Young.

By far the largest wine region in New South

Wales is the Riverina area, first planted to vines in 1912, and centered around the towns of Griffith and Leeton. This area produces over 100,000 tonnes of grapes from around 5,000 hectares of vines, representing approximately one-sixth of Australia's total wine production. Some very high quality table wines come from this region with a number of companies crushing from 10,000 to 40,000 tonnes. Until the late 1950's the majority of wine produced in the region was fortified, but since the wine boom of the mid-60's table wine production has risen dramatically in both quantity and quality.

An introduction to the Lower Hunter Valley

The Lower Hunter Valley was the first wine region to really cater for the wine-lover with properly turned out tasting areas, personal service by proprietors and a framework of restaurants, galleries, art and craft outlets and other venues of interest to attract visitors. Probably it was its proximity to Sydney and the fact that Australia's first boutique wineries sprang up here that the Hunter led the way.

The development of these small but very attractive wineries occurred in the early 1960's and their reputation for beauty and quality of produce has spread worldwide. The first such operation was Dr. Max Lake's 'Lake's Folly', established in 1963. Today the Lower Hunter boasts around 50 wineries and many more vineyards. Nearly all are very keen to open their doors and offer hospitality to the visitor.

The larger companies such as McWilliam's, Lindemans, Hungerford Hill, Wyndham Estate, Tyrrells, McGuigan and others have responded by upgrading their facilities and staff, resulting in improved conditions for the visitor. Progress in this area over the last decade has been remarkable and has been augmented by the establishment of some great restaurants and accommodation houses which are fine-tuned to the wine traveller's needs. Peppers, the McGuigan Wine Village, Wandin Valley, Robert and Sally Molines at the Pepper Tree complex and the Casuarina Restaurant are just a few.

If there were an area in Australia that outwardly seemed totally unsuited to viticulture, it would be the Lower Hunter. The climate is very hot. Many vineyards are on poor soil, and the sub-tropical climate can bring rain exactly when it isn't needed, at Vintage time. Why then does the Hunter produce some outstanding table wines? After talking to that great district identity Murray Tyrrell, I believe part of the answer lies with the cool, afternoon sea breezes that seem to concentrate around the vineyard area and then die along the magnificent Brokenback Range, the backdrop to the whole region. This often prevents excessive temperatures, and when coupled with afternoon cloud in summer, results in protecting the grapes from direct heat, thereby conserving flavour components.

There is much feeling within Australia that only areas with cool climates can produce really top quality wines. The Lower Hunter is one of several regions that are certainly exceptions to this rule. After all it is the wine in the bottle that people enjoy (even the wine judges) that is the real proof of the pudding! I am sure it is the great beauty of the region that has attracted many of the winery proprietors to the Hunter despite its difficult climate and low yields from the vineyards. There are now approximately 3,000 hectares of vines planted. The wines that originally put the Hunter on the map were whites made from Semillon (or Hunter River riesling as it was known in the area), and the dry reds from shiraz, often referred to as hermitage. Both are distinctive styles. The semillon, particularly has come back into vogue after spending some years languishing in the shadows of the more 'trendy' varieties such as chardonnay and sauvignon blanc. Hunter semillons age exceptionally well, developing deep golden colour and rich toasty, nutty and honey-like flavours. There is too, a delightful crisp lemon-citrus finish, which stays with them all their life. The older wines of Lindeman, McWilliam, Tulloch, Tyrrell, Drayton and Elliot often show these sought-after characteristics which make Hunter semillons such good food wines.

The late 1960's and early 1970's saw the Australian wine boom at its peak and there was a veritable rush from Sydney to invest in the Hunter Valley. Many co-operative ventures started, including the Rothbury Estate, brainchild of Len Evans, and Brokenwood where James Halliday and other notables were involved.

The Rothbury Estate has endured tough times but is now firmly established. The winery is magnificent with its banquet hall regularly used, and the light delicatessen-style luncheon you can enjoy on the lawns daily is excellent.

Many other regions have challenged the wine tourism strength of the Hunter. The Yarra Valley, Mornington Peninsula, the Barossa and McLaren Vale along with Margaret River in Western Australia, but after a slight hiatus in growth in the mid-nineties. The expansion in multi-million dollar developments such as Cypress Lakes and small wineries with bed and breakfast such as Peacock Hill has once again revitalised the region.

It is a must visit to experience the natural beauty, history, wonderful wines, beautiful wineries and to meet all the regions hospitable folk.

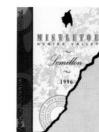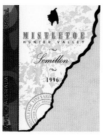

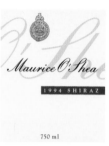

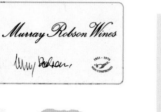

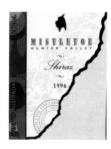

BROKENWOOD WINES PTY LTD
Address: McDonalds Road, Pokolbin NSW 2320
Phone: (02) 4998 7559
Fax: (02) 4998 7893
Established: 1970
Winemakers: Iain Riggs & Dan Dineen
Principal varieties grown: Chardonnay, Shiraz, Cabernet Sauvignon
Ha under vine: 20
Average no. cases produced: 70,000

Principal wines & brands	Cellar Potential
Semillon	7 years
Cricket Pitch Sauvignon Blanc-Semillon Chardonnay	3-4 years
Cricket Pitch Merlot-Cabernet Sauvignon	3-4 years
Shiraz	5-7 years

Public & trade tours: By appointment only
Hours open to public: 10am-5pm, daily
Retail distribution: National Distribution

The Lower Hunter Valley

Lower Hunter - NSW

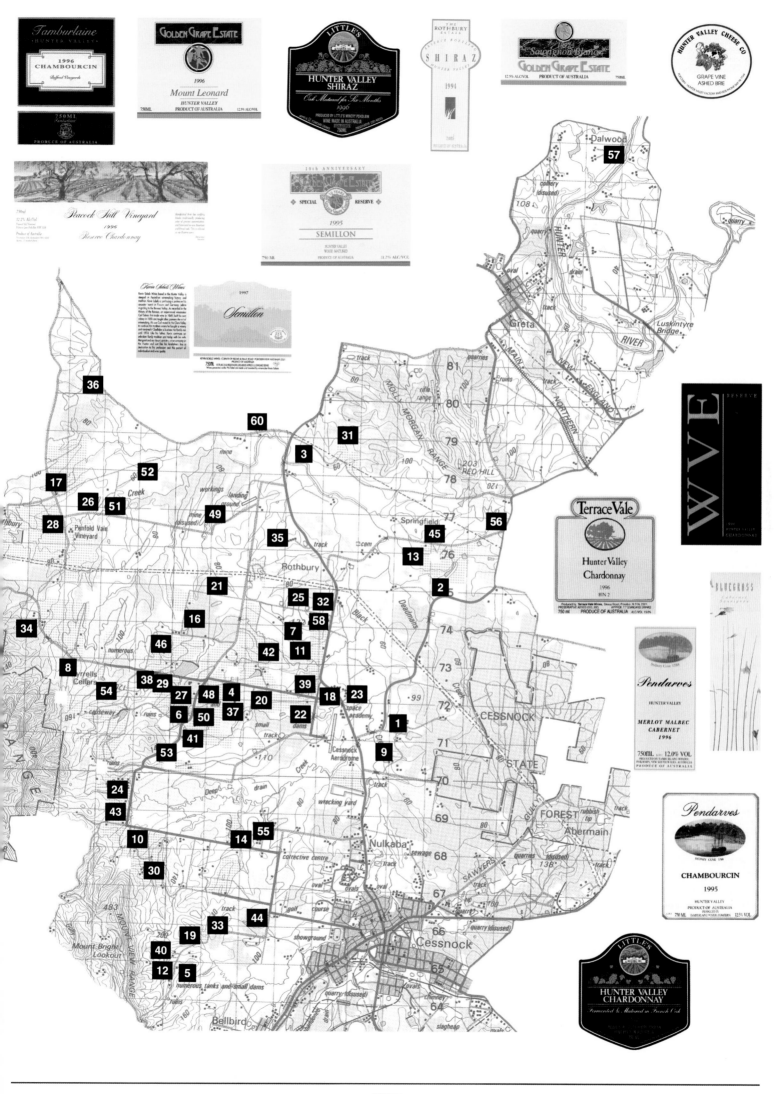

Allandale

ALLANDALE WINERY

Address: Lovedale Road, Pokolbin, NSW 2321
Direction: via Maitland
Phone: (02) 4990 4526 Fax: (02) 4990 1714
Established: 1978 Owner: Villa Villetri (Wines) Pty Ltd
Winemakers: Bill Sneddon & Peter Orr
Principal varieties grown: Pinot Noir, Chardonnay, Semillon
Ha under vine: 7
Average annual crush: 200 tonnes
Average no. cases produced: 12,000

Principal wines & brands	Cellar Potential
Chardonnay	2-5 years
Semillon	5-10 years
Matthew Shiraz	5-10 years

Public & trade tours: By appointment only
Hours open to public: 9am-5pm, Mon-Sat; 10am-5pm Sun
Retail distribution: Restaurants & Bottle Shops

Allandale takes its name from the sub-region of the Hunter so named. This sub-region in turn, is part of the Lovedale area near the Cessnock Airport which in fact was the wine capital of the Hunter Valley during the last century, boasting many vineyards and wineries, including the Hunter's largest, 'Daisy Hill'. This is the capital of the 'friendly boutique winery',
of which 'Allandale' was one of the first, established in 1978.

Allandale is situated on a hill with commanding views of its seven hectares of vines and the Brokenback Ranges.

The tasting area is in the winery itself and you are surrounded by French and American oak barrels quietly maturing the wines. The winery has recently been enlarged, upgraded
and beautifully landscaped and is a must to visit during your next Hunter pilgrimage. Enthusiastic and knowledgeable winemaker Bill Sneddon, a graduate of Charles Sturt University's wine course at Wagga Wagga, has been in charge for the last ten years and makes an excellent range of wines, including a semillon, chardonnay, pinot noir and shiraz which go under the Allandale label.

Allanmere

Allanmere has gone through a real wine renaissance. On a recent visit through the valley I dropped in, it was a rainy Sunday morning, and freezing cold but the wines were spectacular bringing some liquid sunshine into the day all fresh, vibrant and full of great varietal fruit flavours.

For something different try the unoaked verdelho, it is a real fruit salad of flavour or the botrytis semillon-tokay with its luscious and lingering finish.

Four of the Hunter's most dynamic winemakers Greg Silkman, Gary Reed, Steve Allen and Craig Brown-Thomas, all have the zeal of youth but 50 years of winemaking experience between them. Early in 1997 they bought the winery from founder Dr Newton Potter, who with his wife Virginia began the enterprise in 1985 winning two gold medals with his first two wines in the Hunter Wine Show – a cabernet sauvignon and a hermitage (shiraz).

Newton and 'Ginny' have set up a wonderful luxury cottage on the property with three suites, lounge and kitchen where up to six adults can spend a wonderful four days in this charming wine region. Trinity Cottage has an open fire for winter and is fully air-conditioned.

Allanmere, which takes its name "Allan" from the Allandale region and "Mere" from the 10 acre lake in the Estate is just about to undergo major renovations and extensions as I write this article. Included will be an air-conditioned cellar door that will feature cheese and olive oil tastings accompanied by the wineries own home baked bread and of course great wines. Try the two Trinity wines, the red is a cabernet merlot shiraz blend and the white a chardonnay semillon sauvignon blanc blend or the classic 'Durham Chardonnay' or the lesser oaked Gold Label Chardonnay. Soon you will be able to sip them under the shady
verandah looking out over the newly planted vineyard and the beautiful Brokenback Mountains.

ALLANMERE WINERY

Address: Lovedale Road, Pokolbin NSW 2321
Direction: 10kms from Cessnock
Phone: (02) 4930 7387
Fax: (02) 4930 7900
Established: 1985
Owners: Greg Silkman, Gary Reed, Craig Brown-Thomas, Steve Allen
Winemaker: Greg Silkman
Average annual crush: 100 tonnes
Average no. cases produced: 7,000

Principal wines & brands	Cellar Potential
Durham Chardonnay	2-5 years
Trinity White	Now
Trinity Red	Now
Verdelho	2-5 years
Shiraz	3-5 years
Cabernet Sauvignon	3-5 years
Chambourcin	2-5 years

Public & trade tours: By appointment only
Hours open to public: 9am-5pm, weekdays; 9.30am-5pm, weekends
Points of interest: Garden, picnic area and grand views
Retail distribution: Fine wine outlets - Restaurants, Sydney, Brisbane. Sydney agents: Gaubro Wine Agencies. Exports to Thailand, USA, Taiwan, Switzerland. Cellar Door and Wine Club.

Bimbadgen Estate

One of the most striking Wineries in Australia sits on top of a rise on McDonalds Road a kilometre or so north of the Centre of Pokolbin.

An impressive tower visible right around the valley caps off the whitewashed Spanish inspired mission style winery.

The winery, formerly known as Parker Estate, was established by Stan Parker in 1991.

The winery is constructed into the hillside, which provides for an efficient gravity aided operation plus cool and moist conditions in the underground section for barrel maturation of the wines.

Bimbadgen also has a large cellar door with splendid views over the vines and an impressive area set up as a restaurant, which was be re-opened in November 1997.

Mulpha Australia, who are in the process of overhauling the whole property, under the experienced and careful eye of local identity and innovative winemaker Kees Van de Scheur, are well on course to create a great Estate.

The Bimbadgen Estate has 50 hectares of vineyards supplying estate-grown grapes for a classic range of wines – Semillon, Chardonnay, Shiraz and Cabernet Sauvignon.

So far the 1997 wines I have seen are of such excellent quality that I am sure the future augurs well for Bimbadgen. It is great to see this fine Estate being put on track as one of the Hunters best.

BIMBADGEN ESTATE

Address: Lot 21 McDonalds Road, Pokolbin NSW 2321
Phone: (02) 4998 7585
Fax: (02) 4998 7732
Winemakers: Kees van de Scheur, Thomas Jong
Principal varieties grown: Chardonnay, Semillon, Shiraz, Cabernet Sauvignon
Ha under vine: 50
Average annual crush: 500 tonnes
Average no. cases produced: 30,000

Principal wines & brands	Cellar Potential
Semillon	5-7 years
Chardonnay	3-6 years
Shiraz	6-10 years

Public & trade tours: Yes
Hours open to public: Daily
Points of interest: Restaurant
Retail distribution: Grand Liquor Wholesalers, NSW & QLD

Brian Mc Guigan Wines

Brian McGuigan and his wife Fay are two of the loveliest people you'll ever meet. Even with breakneck pace of their super busy lives, their achievements and the wealth they have created, they have time for everyone and for the simple pleasures and family values of life.

This was brought home to me strongly on a visit to the winery. We arrived just as a most beautiful glowing Hunter sunset was starting. We tore Brian away from his business papers spread across his large dining room table and raced up into the vineyards surrounding his Hunter Ridge winery and home. We were thrilled with the conditions and Brian was in his best ebullient form, it was an adrenalin-packed half-hour.

On arriving back at his home, he proudly made us a platter of the cheeses from his new Hunter Valley Cheese Company. They were sensational and we enjoyed washing them down with a glass or two of the McGuigan wines. I noticed Brian was not eating any cheese, I jibed at him that he couldn't stand his own cheeses. On the contrary, a passionate cheese lover, he had given up this passion for Lent. I couldn't believe it - another side to McGuigan had surfaced. As I was explaining that my mother had always done the same thing, my mobile phone rang, my mother in Adelaide and Brian had a great conversation.

When you're around the McGuigans magic things happen. I am sure they have a positive psychic power and it definitely transfers into their wines. At this moment Fay arrived home from a promotion in Sydney in time to pick up wine and food for a Hunter Valley Wine Club meeting. She should have been absolutely stressed out, but no, as she got it all together, she chatted and shared the time she didn't have with us, even enjoying a glass of the sparkling methode traditional named after their equally dynamic daughter Lisa. Lisa runs the newly acquired

"Hermitage Road" Winery, just down the road from their home.

The McGuigan family has long been involved in the wine industry of the Hunter Valley. Brian's father Perc was the long time winemaker and manager for Penfolds at their Dalwood Winery in the northern part of the Lower Hunter Valley, a winery established in 1827 by George Wyndham. Brian and his father bought the run-down winery from Penfolds in 1971. By the mid '80's Brian, who had taken over from his father, owned 3 other Hunter wineries, Hunter Estate, Saxondale and Richmond Grove. Shortly after, he bought Montrose and Craigmoor, the two biggest wineries in Mudgee.

In 1991, Brian who had formed a public company, although unlisted, sold his entire wine empire to the Orlando Wine Group, then owned by the giant French Pernod Ricard Company. Being idle is not Brian McGuigan's favourite pastime and he quickly formed a vineyard investment company. He could see the coming need for more grape supply with export sales booming and the certainty that domestic sales would recover from their slight decline due to the

recession of the late '80's and early '90's. Brian was itching to get back into the mainstream of winemaking and marketing, which saw the formation in 1992 of McGuigan Brothers with his dynamic wife Fay. The company made a public float and Brian in his usual way took the show on the road. I ran into him one day in a leading Melbourne broker's office where he was delivering an address to their leading clients, followed naturally by a wine tasting.

Brian and Fay chose a most unusual symbol for their label, I am sure, inspired by their deep religious convictions. Many of their labels have the likeness of St. Francis Xavier, the patron saint of Australia, carrying his shepherd's crook. After forming the company, Brian and Fay took off to live and work in America for 6 months. They say St. Francis was working hard for them also, particularly in the very religious southern states.

At home since, the main McGuigan Wine Village and Winery have expanded. A fresh Bakery has been included, the "Gift Hunter Boutique" in the Village is thriving and the "Wine Country Souvenir Shop" in the main winery area now with the hugely successful "Hunter Cheese Factory" both are going extremely well.

At a splendid inaugural Thanksgiving Dinner for over 600 guests in April 1997, Prime Minister John Howard sang praises of the wine industry. How suitable it was that Brian McGuigan was host a last minute change of venue, which as usual the great man, his wife and team took in their stride. The McGuigan wines are made for easy drinking by the widest range of people possible world-wide. For my mind, this is a noble goal and one which is making McGuigan liquid sunshine in the bottle, the flavour of Australia.

Hunter Valley Cheese Company

In early 1995 a joint venture was agreed to between dynamic wine producer and gourmet cheese lover, Brian McGuigan, and pioneer specialty cheesemaker, David Brown, from the Milawa Cheese Company, just down the road from Brown Brothers Wines in Victoria.

In quick time, a cheese factory was built into a sealed off section of the main McGuigan Brothers Winery at Pokolbin. It has viewing windows along the long verandah where one can watch the cheeses being made, as you taste and enjoy them with a McGuigan Brothers wine or a cup of the best espresso or cappuccino in the Hunter.

Now under the ownership of David and Anne Brown, Peter Curtis and Rosalia Lambert this cottage factory is now producing a range of fine cheeses, taking their names from the region: Branxton Brie and Busby Blue, an assertive gorgonzola style; Pokolbin White, a fresh acid cheese with a soft texture (great with a McGuigan 'Lisa' Brut Sparkling) a Cessnock Cheddar and a multi-facet Pokolbin Club Blue. Hunter Valley Gold is a washed rind cheese and the Fromage Blanc a farmhouse cheese. Added to this impressive list are three goat's milk cheeses, Hunter Valley Chevre, Hunter Valley Aged Ashed Chevre, Hunter Valley

Table Chevre in a pyramid - delicate and white moulded - and the Hunter Valley Aged Ashed Chevre dusted with grape vine ash - a cheese which ages well.

Master Cheesemaker, Rosalia Lambert has taken the cheeses to an even higher quality level over the last year or so. A visit to the Hunter Valley Cheese Company is a great learning experience. It will help you get to know one of wine's great accompaniments. Why not purchase a plate of their cheeses and other produce and enjoy them on the verandah with a glass or two of McGuigan wines.

Gift Hunter / Wine Country Souvenirs

Gifted Wineman Ken Sloan and his wife Gwen who are proprietors of the boutique winery 'Mistletoe', have two excellent art, craft and wine accessory galleries in the heart of Pokolbin. "Gift Hunter" was the first such boutique in the Hunter, becoming part of the "McGuigan Wine Village". The works of local crafts people feature strongly, paintings, prints, woodcarvings and a large range of pottery accompany souvenirs including clothing. Recently opened is the "Wine Country Souvenir Shop" behind the Hunter Cheese Factory in the McGuigan Winery. This large area has everything a wine lover could want. Whilst in the Hunter Valley why not call in and I am sure you will find something as a souvenir of your pilgrimage to this Wine Mecca.

Briar Ridge

beautiful garden enshrined verandah on a sunny Hunter Thanksgiving weekend. Touché Neil.

The rustic charming winery recently expanded, is built from local timbers and other materials and retains a lovely country boutique nature. The wines are excellent and largely snapped up by the 'Briar Ridge Vintage Club' which is certainly worth joining. Briar Ridge is a good place to start your tour of the Hunter if you're coming from Sydney.

BRIAR RIDGE VINEYARD
Address: Mount View Road, Mount View, Via Cessnock NSW 2325
Direction: 5kms west of Cessnock
Phone: (02) 4990 3670
Fax: (02) 4990 7802
Established: 1972
Owners: John Davis & Neil McGuigan
Winemaker: Neil McGuigan
Principal varieties grown: Chardonnay, Semillon, Cabernet, Shiraz
Ha under vine: 50
Average annual crush: 250 tonnes
Average no. cases produced: 15,000

Principal wines & brands	Cellar Potential
Early Harvest Semillon	3-5 years
Hand Picked Chardonnay	3-5 years
Old Vines Shiraz	3-5 years
Cabernet Sauvignon	3-5 years
Stockhausen Semillon	4-6 years
Stockhausen Hermitage	4-6 years
Chairman's Selection Chardonnay	4-6 years
Chairman's Selection Cabernet Merlot	4-6 years
Shiraz	5-7 years

Public & trade tours: By appointment only
Hours open to public: 10am-5pm, daily
Retail distribution: National Distribution

The Mount View sub-region at the south end of the valley is really in the foothills of the Brokenback Ranges and quite a deal cooler than the vineyard area in the valley proper.

Briar Ridge has won the most successful small wine trophy at the annual Hunter Valley Wine Show several times.

The vineyard and winery was started by the enigmatic but charming Murray Robson back in 1971 and he built a pretty cottage which was available for visitor accommodation. Today, the energetic and enthusiastic Neil McGuigan, younger brother of the human dynamo Brian, runs Briar Ridge. Neil still retains an interest in McGuigan Brothers but was keen to make his own statement. Neil's love of winemaking is at once obvious and his desire to share this with visitors to the winery is most apparent, donít expect a quiet, studious tasting session at Briar Ridge, this is wine in action. You will probably see Neil sprinting around the winery and springing up on top of tanks and wine casks, the contents of which are like children to him. One a recent visit I tasted some 20 different chardonnay's from the 1997 vintage, all complex and interesting wines that have all had caring and individual attention. That was before tasting a dozen or so young, vibrant shiraz wines followed by an equal number of cabernet cubs, all in 20 minutes or so. This lively attitude shows up in Neil's wines not to mention the "Family Recipe" pumpkin soup he ladled out to us and a few other visitors on the

Calais Estate

As one enters the driveway of Calais Estate the impressive winery buildings come into view over the vines. The huge convict-hewn stones, the wide two storied verandahs with their intricate iron lacework trimmings all give a feeling of the Victorian colonial charm or yesteryear.

The winery started off in the 1970s under the name Woolundry Estate that was later changed when Colin Peterson from the dynamic Peterson wine clan became involved.

The cellar door also has much charm inside with huge wooden beams coming from early colonial buildings, giving it a warm solid atmosphere. Calais Estates also runs a corporate wine club and should you wish, would be delighted to send you the details. The restaurant, with its regional cuisine focus, caters only for functions.

The award-winning Calais range includes semillon, chardonnay, pinot noir, shiraz, cabernet sauvignon and sauterne. Specially selected reserve wines are also available. The Calais wines are packaged in splendid tall imposing bottles, which do justice to their exciting quality.

CALAIS ESTATES
Address: Palmers Lane, Pokolbin NSW 2320
Phone: (02) 4998 7654
Fax: (02) 4998 7813
Established: 1987
Winemaker: Colin Peterson
Principal varieties grown: Chardonnay, Cabernet Sauvignon, Shiraz, Semillon
Ha under vine: 10
Average annual crush: 400 tonnes
Public & trade tours: By appointment only
Hours open to public: 10am-5pm, weekends and school holidays
Points of interest: Covered BBQ area
Retail distribution: Cellar Door and Mail Order,

Drayton's Family Wines

Drayton is a famous family wine name in the Hunter Valley with the winery being a real family affair. Max Drayton, a fourth generation member, owns and runs the business with his three sons. Eldest son, John, a giant of a man, returned to the fold in 1989 after tracking around NSW for some 14 years. Trevor, who graduated from Roseworthy Agricultural College as Dux of the course in 1977, is winemaker. Youngest son Greg is vineyard manager, helped along by his father Max. Greg has an Agricultural Diploma from Tocal Agricultural College where he passed all subjects with distinction.

The Drayton story commenced when Joseph Drayton, in his early twenties, set sail from England in 1852 with his wife Anna and two sons. Tragically, during the voyage, he lost his wife, newborn daughter and one of his sons. Undaunted, he and his surviving son Frederick purchased a property in the Hunter in 1853. The dynasty, I am sure retains this solid commitment. The Drayton's are not flashy people - they go about their business producing great wines that they figure do the talking, and more power to them.

DRAYTON'S FAMILY WINES
Address: Oakey Creek Road, Pokolbin NSW 2321
Phone: (02) 4998 7513
Fax: (02) 4998 7743
Established: 1853
Winemaker: Trevor Drayton
Principal varieties grown: Semillon, Chardonnay, Verdelho, Shiraz, Cabernet Sauvignon, Merlot
Ha under vine: 65
Average no. cases produced: 100,000

Principal wines & brands	Cellar Potential
Chardonnay	2-5 years
Verdelho	2-5 years
Semillon	4-7 years
Bin 5555 Shiraz	5-10 years
Cabernet Merlot	5-10 years
Cabernet Sauvignon	5-10 years

Public & trade tours: By appointment only
Hours open to public: 8am-5pm, weekdays; 10am-5pm weekends
Points of interest: Cellar Door and Mail Order sales
Retail distribution: Liquor stores KEVIN SOBELS WINES
Address: Cnr. Halls and Broke Road, Pokolbin NSW 2321
Phone: (02) 4998 7766
Fax: (02) 4998 7475
Email: sobels@ozemail.com.au WWW: http://www.ozemail.com.au/~sobels

Golden Grape Estate

The history of Golden Grape Estate is like a mini history of Pokolbin. The site of the winery, on a prominent hill in the south end of the region, was the original site of the "Clayton Winery". Taking its name from the property, first settled by George Wills in the mid 1800's, grapes were first planted on the property by James Connolly in 1866.

The Estate was purchased by Wesley 'Johnny' Drayton around the end of the First World War and passed onto Barry Drayton who operated it as "Happy Valley" Vineyard. Golden Grape purchased the property in 1985.

The complex, in addition to its cellar door outlet, has a Wine Museum, Gift Shop, Restaurant (winner of the 1996 Hunter Valley Tourism Award for Excellence for the Best Tourism Restaurant), Picnic Areas, a Wine Trail and approximately 15 hectares of vines.

Golden Grape concentrates on sales of wine through tastings on the Estate or at client's own homes or business premises, Australia wide. Golden Grape also offers customised labels for selected premium white, red, sparkling and fortified wines. Why not visit Golden Grape and enjoy a meal at the award-winning Restaurant under the guidance of Stephen Price and Jannelle Pringle or if you cannot make it to the Hunter give the winery a call and arrange for a tasting to come to you.

GOLDEN GRAPE ESTATE

Address: Oakey Creek Road, Pokolbin NSW 2321
Direction: 6km west of Cessnock off Mount View Road
Phone: (02) 4998 7588
Fax: (02) 4998 7730
Established: 1853
Principal varieties grown: Chardonnay, Semillon, Verdelho, Cabernet Sauvignon, Merlot, Shiraz
Ha under vine: 16

Principal wines & brands	Cellar Potential
Semillon	5-8 years
Gew\'fcrztraminer	4-6 years
Chardonnay Reserve	8-10 years
Fum\'e9 Blanc	4-6 years
Verdelho	3-5 years
Botrytis	10-15 years
Shiraz	4-6 years
Cabernet Hermitage	4-6 years
Mount Leonard Cabernet Sauvignon	8-10 years
Merlot	5-8 years

Public & trade tours: By appointment only
Hours open to public: 9am-5pm, daily
Points of interest: Award winning restaurant, wine museum with the oldest winepress in Australia, gift shop, BBQ and picnic grounds.
Retail distribution: Golden Grape Estate Pty Ltd, Sydney.
Promotion Offices: Newcastle, Brisbane, Adelaide, Perth, Melbourne

Hermitage Road Winery

I have long been a fan of the McGuigan Family, their commitment to each other and to wine in the deepest most complete and meaningful sense.

Once again, I am fresh from another fantastic encounter with this unique family whose enthusiasm and zest for living not only reflects in their wines but its infectious nature rubs off on all around them.

The Hermitage Road family of premium wines represent a bright new chapter in one of Australia's most exciting wine stories. Behind the Hermitage Road name is a small but dedicated team of wine professionals who, between them, have nearly half a century of experience in the Australian and International wine industries.

Hermitage Road General Manager is Ms Lisa McGuigan. Lisa is the third generation of her family, the McGuigan's, to enjoy a passion for quality wine. Following a successful career in both the family wine business and the demanding world of International Hotel management, Lisa describes Hermitage Road as the most exciting opportunity of her career.

Working closely with Lisa is Hermitage Road's National Sales Manager Ms Veronica Lourey, a wine marketing graduate of South Australia's Roseworthy Agricultural College. Veronica has nearly a decade of experience in the wine industry both within Australia and abroad.

Lisa and Veronica are joined by Hermitage Road's winemaker Peter Hall. Peter has been making award-winning wine for Australia's leading vineyards for twenty years.

Only the best fruit available from vineyards in South Australia's Barossa Valley, New South Wales' Hunter Valley, Mudgee and Victoria's King Valley have been picked to create the Hermitage Road collection.

Each of these is synonymous with the growing of premium Australian wine ranging from the full flavours of shiraz grown in the rich soil of the Barossa Valley to Hermitage Road's unique rieslings grown in Mudgee. Hermitage Road wines are built on the strengths of Australia's premier wine grown in regions and have been created for one reason – to share the pleasure of quality wine with those who appreciate it.

"Hermitage Road" is actually the largest wine production facility on the eastern seaboard of Australia.

If the sneak preview I saw of the stunning bottles and labels plus the exciting red wines are a sign of the future, it is going to be a great one for the Winery.

Hermitage Road also has a splendid Resort as part of the complex. The Hunter Resort with beautiful bungalow style accommodation set amongst the vines has numerous leisure activities to pursue and if savouring a glass of wine or the lawns between the vines outside your own private unit, leaves you with any other desires.

Mine host Philip Healy, his family and team have won a host of Tourism Awards and can really look after your every need a no-fuss manner. They also manage the Restaurant and Function Facilities in the winery.

A pilgrimage up the hill on Hermitage Road signposted by the striking tower is a wine lovers dream.

Hunter Ridge

The Hunter Ridge Winery began its life in1985 as The Richmond Grove Hunter Winery built by Brian McGuigan under the Wyndham Estate Group banner. Brian unfortunately lost the winery with the Orlando buyout in 1990 but retained the vineyards with a syndicate group. In late 1993 Brian's new company, Brian McGuigan Wines Ltd, bought back the winery relaunching it under the Hunter Ridge name.

The cellars and equipment are state of the art and set in a magnificent vineyard scene. The cool maturation cellars being in the lower half of the expansive buildings.

In 1997 a joint venture between Brian McGuigan and BRL Hardy has seen Hardy's take on the management and marketing of the wine, whilst Brian McGuigans team with input from Hardy winemakers, producing the wines, giving the best of both worlds. I am sure the already excellent wines of Hunter Ridge will improve even further and find their way to the wine markets of the world. The brilliant cellar door is now run by Hardy's adding a new flavour to the Hunter.

Little's Winery

The Little family purchased the vineyard established by the late Dr. Quentin Taperell on Palmers Lane. That was back in 1983. Ian Little studied biochemistry in England and worked at Tooth's Brewery in Sydney on arriving in Australia.

Ian took the wine course at what is now the Charles Sturt University at Wagga Wagga and worked with Geoff Merrill at Chateau Reynella during the 1981 and 1982 vintages. Ian also had some experience at Penfolds, working in their champagne cellars. After buying the vineyard, the Little's quickly established a winery on the property.

I well remember visiting the winery during its early days. I was, and still am, very impressed by their wines and the quiet no-nonsense way they go about producing and promoting them. Ian is meticulous with his picking, and chills all the grapes and fermenting wine in his large cool room.

The wines are all made from their two vineyards in Palmers Lane. The "Winery" and "Homestead" blocks are now expanded to 14 hectares. Look for the distinctive Little's Label for unique styles and lots of flavour.

LITTLES WINERY
Address: Lot 3, Palmers Lane, Pokolbin NSW 2320
Phone: (02) 4998 7626
Fax: (02) 4998 7867
Established: 1983
Owners: Little & Kindred Families **Winemaker:** Ian Little
Principal varieties grown: Chardonnay, Pinot Noir, Semillon, Shiraz
Ha under vine: 16
Average annual crush: 120 tonnes
Average no. cases produced: 8,000 - 9,000

Principal wines & brands	Cellar Potential
Chardonnay	2-5 years
Semillon - Dry F.O.M.	2-5 years
Semillon Sauvignon Blanc	2-5 years
Gewurztraminer	2-5 years
Shiraz	5-10 years
Cabernet Sauvignon	5-10 years
Vintage Port	10+ years

Public & trade tours: By appointment only
Hours open to public: 10am-4.30 pm, daily
Points of interest: Craft products, wine accessories, picnic area, wine club/mail order
Retail distribution: Cellar Door - Mail Order & Club, Restaurants, 2 or 3 Retail Bottle Shops, within 100 kms

Hungerford Hill

A product of the wine boom of the 1960's, Hungerford Hill's first vines were planted in 1967. Over a period of five years, the original area expanded to well over 200 hectares, much of which was shiraz grapes. By the time the first Hungerford Hill reds came onto the market, red wine popularity was in a dramatic decline. A drastic rationalisation program followed, which saw the Hungerford Hill wines back on the rails to success.

In 1990 Hungerford Hill was bought by Seppelt, already part of S.A. Brewing which later became Southcorp. The good reputation of Hungerford Hill, it is becoming a specialist in making wines from the newer grape growing regions of N.S.W. such as Cowra, Young and Tumbarrumba, is now being extended through the winemaking and marketing skills of Southcorp. Hungerford Hill is one of the prestige labels of Southcorp

and can be relied upon to give you a consistent and enjoyable experience.

In 1996 Hungerford Hill found a new home just down the road from Lindemans, a charming old weatherboard church is now resounding in the praises for their fine wines and the French petanque pitch outside resounds to the clatter of this ancient bowls game and happy contented Hungerford Hill fans.

Lindemans Hunter River Winery

This famous winery is a vital part of the Southcorp Wine empire. Formerly known as the Ben Ean Winery, it was purchased to become Lindemans, from John MacDonald in 1912. The company of Lindemans was started at a much earlier date, however, by the famous Dr Lindeman, a Royal Navy surgeon who settled in the Hunter Valley in 1842. With his three sons, Dr Lindeman bought and established vineyards at Cawarra, Coolalta, Catawba, Warrawee and Kirkton.

The Lindemans also purchased the name of 'Porphyry' along with all remaining stock of the wine (the vineyard had ceased to exist) from the Carmichael family. Porphyry had an enviable reputation and had been served to Queen Victoria in 1851. Lindemans still produce Porphyry Sauternes, of which the Carmichael family would have been proud, improving as it does with every year in the bottle.

Lindemans Hunter River Wines are probably Australia's best-known wine 'family', with their simple but bold label and distinctive four figure bin classification. The Hunter Valley whites are made from semillon and chardonnay grapes. The major wines marketed under this label are the Lindemans Hunter River Semillon and the Hunter River Chardonnay. These wines are produced each year and the four figure bin numbers change each vintage. They age exceptionally well and develop into classic and unique wines of world class, which dominate Australian wine shows.

When young, Lindemans Hunter Valley semillons are pleasant, but often simple. They usually have a grassy, herbaceous character both in the aroma and on the palate, with a distinct lemon-citrus flavour in the aftertaste. As they approach ten years of age however, marvellous things begin to happen. Flavours develop which include toast, honey and nuts and the finish is enhanced by the beautiful lemon-citrus character. The colour too, develops into a bright yellow gold, but does not tarnish. The Hunter River Chardonnay has also shown this good ageing potential.

Until 1978, Lindemans chardonnays were not aged in new imported oak casks, as is the trend today, and so the wines exhibited pure, although complex fruit flavours. Since then, however, some wood ageing has become part of the style. This procedure, combined with temperature control and modern white wine making techniques, has produced wines with more fruit and vanilla oak characters. Grape selection has also changed with the times; fruit now comes to

Lindemans from various parts of the Hunter Valley, including vineyards in the Broke Region. These changes were brought about by Karl Stockhausen who made the wines from 1960 until the late 1980's.

The red wines from the Hunter Valley winery have nothing to fear from the reputation of the whites. They are Steven Vineyard Shiraz and various Hunter River Shiraz' with different bin numbers every year. The Hunter River Shiraz develops a silky feel in the mouth as it ages. This wine does not necessarily have a deep colour or heavy body, but it does always have long and interesting flavours combining Hunter River 'leather' and an earthy character. The wine is well balanced, has a soft silky finish and is usually reasonable buying when young. Although it is good drinking while young, this wine improves further with ageing. The 'Steven Shiraz' is a firmer wine with light acid and occasionally more body than the

Lindemans Hunter River Winery

the Hunter River Shiraz. This is a wine to put down for some years.

Early in 1986, Karl Stockhausen took up a senior marketing position with Lindemans. His winemaking position was filled by Gerry Sissingh, who had assisted Len Evans in establishing Rothbury Estate. The current winemaker is Pat Auld, from a famous South Australian winemaking family, who in 1997 completed his twenty-fourth Hunter vintage. Today the Southcorp team are carrying on a fine tradition. Lindemans jealously guard their reputation for premium wines. For as long as the wine's unique quality is maintained, Dr Lindeman will be making us smile.

Mc Williams Mount Pleasant Winery

There are probably very few family-owned companies as proud or as conscious of their heritage as McWilliam's Wines, who are well into their second century of winemaking. In addition to being one of Australia's largest wine producers, the company is entirely family-owned and controlled.

The McWilliams are a close-knit family, and members of the last three generations can be found throughout the company. While most of those involved are working in the managerial area, or the running of one of their huge wineries in the Riverina or at Robinvale, the McWilliams are not above a hard day's work in whatever field demands their attention.

Both the winery itself and the wines from Mount Pleasant are close to the heart of the McWilliam family, not surprising given the outstanding show record of Mount Pleasant's wines over many decades. In what must be an expensive exercise, Mount Pleasant is one of the few remaining wine producers to cellar-age commercial quantities of bottled table wines until they are at their peak. This enlightened policy allows wine lovers to enjoy fully mature, five year old whites and reds at very reasonable prices. There is also a regular release of even older wines. This conscious policy by McWilliam's is to be applauded.

The birth of the winery and vineyards at Mount Pleasant began in 1880 when Charles King planted vines on some of the best red volcanic soil in the region. Exciting things started to happen when the property was

purchased by the O'Shea family. The young Maurice O'Shea was sent to study winemaking at Montpelier in France and upon his return in 1921, quickly established a reputation for himself as perhaps the greatest and most celebrated winemaker of his time. During the most dismal period of the Great Depression in 1932, O'Shea was forced to sell half of the property at Mount Pleasant to the McWilliams, who later completed the purchase by buying the remaining half while allowing Maurice O'Shea to stay on as winemaker and winery manager until his death in 1956.

The wines made by Maurice O'Shea are legendary and their longevity is astonishing, with some wines of more than 40 years of age still drinking magnificently. It was O'Shea who started a tradition, now adopted by McWilliam's, of naming his wines after friends of the family. Some well-known examples are their 'Elizabeth', made from semillon (often referred to in days gone by as Hunter River Riesling), and 'Phillip', (formerly 'Phillip Hermitage') made from shiraz. In recent years McWilliam's have released a 'Maurice O'Shea Chardonnay' and a 'Maurice O'Shea Shiraz'.

Other great wines in Mount Pleasant's Individual Vineyard range are a shiraz from the Rosehill Vineyard and another from the Old Paddock and Old Hill Vineyards. Keep an eye out too for regular re-releases of some of the older vintages of Mount Pleasant Elizabeth under the 'Museum Release Label'.

The current long-serving winemaker at

Mount Pleasant is Phil Ryan, a quiet, astute man who is also a terrific host - if you can track him down. Phil was one of the first graduates from the new winemaking course at Charles Sturt University, and has been with McWilliam's for many years - like the winery name, he is a very pleasant chap. The cellar door has been rebuilt and is delightful

I well remember a tasting at the winery some 12 years ago, I'm not sure my late friend Milan remembered it so well as he kept asking me how I could spit out the exquisite wines. After 23 wines, all more than 15 years old, finishing with a 1946 Maurice O'Shea Sauterne of which McWilliam's at that stage still had over 1,000 dozen, Milan found out why I do spit them out. As we exited the tasting room, the moon was rising. That was our first day working together and I had to help him put the camera on the tripod. He took one of his greatest photos ever.

To Phil Ryan and all his team, and to the great Mount Pleasant Wines, thanks for the memories.

Mistletoe Wines

Tucked away in a pretty northwestern corner of the Hunter Valley just off Hermitage Road is the exquisite "Mistletoe Estate". This romantic name relates to the region, which was famous for its wine in the last century.

Ken and Gwen Sloan have constructed a delightful winery and cellar door. Its glass paneled French doors opening onto a return verandah offering splendid views over the vineyard and the Brokenback Ranges.

Keen on art and memorabilia, the gallery like tasting area is always resplendent with exhibitions. On the day of our visit a superb Photographic Exhibition from the work of famous photographer Max Dupain from the 1930's and 40's graced the walls including Hunter Vineyard scenes

In November 1997 the first Brokenback Trail Fair featured central coast artists at the Mistletoe Gallery. This yearly event will see art, food and entertainment grace the Mistletoe Gallery.

The Mistletoe Vineyard is planted to the Hunter Classics of semillon and shiraz. The yields are low and the concentrated flavours in the wines very evident. A classy chardon-

MISTLETOE WINES	Principal wines & brands	Cellar Potential
Address: 771 Hermitage Road, Pokolbin via Branston NSW 2335	Mistletoe Shiraz	6-10 years
Phone: (02) 4998 7770	Mistletoe Semillon	6-10 years
Fax: (02) 4998 7792	Mistletoe Chardonnay	3-5 years
Established: 1990	**Public & trade tours:** By appointment only	
Winemakers: Jon Reynolds - Consultant	**Hours open to public:** 11am-6pm, Fri-Mon	
Principal varieties grown: Shiraz, Semillon, Chardonnay	**Points of interest:** Ever changing display of quality art, pottery and photography. Two guest rooms, with private facilities, overlooking vineyards, available for rent.	
Ha under vine: 4		
Average annual crush: 25 tonnes	**Retail distribution:** Cellar door, selected specialist wine retailers and restaurants - NSW & ACT.	
Average no. cases produced: 2,000		

nay from the Cock Fighter Creek Vineyard at Broke completes a great range when meandering through the Hunter. Do not miss Mistletoe.

Murray Robson

I had the pleasure of meeting Murray Robson – the squire of the Hunter – some 30 years ago, as he was embarking on his wine adventure after a career in menswear with his exclusive store "The Squire Shop" in Double Bay.

In 1974 he launched his beautiful 'Robson Vineyard' in the Mount view district of the Hunter. Murray and his wife Lynley both have exquisite taste that is well evidenced in

the meticulous and charming restoration of the historic buildings that now form Roberts Restaurant at Pepper Tree in the Pokolbin area.

This skill and Murray's winemaking skills have now been put to work at Old North Road Rothbury ,where they have created a picture perfect winery and tasting room all from historic materials gathered around the valley. It is the perfect place to hold a function and your hosts will add classy and

thoughtful touches that will make for a memorable occasion. As I write the gardens have been planned and laid out and I am sure will grow into true splendour.

Murray handcrafts his wines which are produced in strictly limited quantities. Those I have so far tasted show his mastery particularly with the temperamental merlot, it's a masterpiece.

Touché Murray, you have done it again and more power to you.

MURRAY ROBSON WINES
Address: Old North Road, Rothbury NSW 2335
Phone: (02) 4938 3577
Fax: (02) 4938 3411
Established: 1995, 1970 in the Hunter
Owner: Murray Robson
Principal varieties grown: Semillon, Chardonnay, Gew\'fcrztraminer, Shiraz, Merlot, Pinot Noir, Cabernet Sauvignon, Muscat
Ha under vine: 4.5
Average annual crush: 50 tonnes
Average no. cases produced: 3,500
Principal wines & brands   Cellar Potential
1996 First Vintage
Public & trade tours: Trade tours by appointment only
Hours open to public: All day, every day
Points of interest: Landscaped garden and function facilities
Retail distribution: Very limited. Sydney,Gold Coast, Brisbane, Hunter region and fine restaurants.

Peppertree Wines

V ying for the title of Australia's prettiest winery is Peppertree Wines. Situated amongst ancient pepper trees at the end of Halls road, almost opposite Rothbury, off the main Broke road. The verdant gardens and vines enclose the New England style wooden barns that house a truly great winery.

Media mogul James Fairfax has spared no expense to ensure the wines and winery are world class. Pepper Tree has won a number of New South Wales Tourism Awards. Pepper Tree has the luxury of owning and managing its own vineyards under the watchful eye of Carl Davies, 50 hectares locally at Pokolbin and a further 10 hectares at Coonawarra from where the wines produced in their Hunter winery are marketed under a separate label.

Winemaker and Managing Director Chris Cameron is assisted by Chris Archer in the winery and Wendy Saywell in the Administration. Nothing is left to chance, a

wide range of wine styles and labels are produced and a tasting visit to the cellar door is a real adventure slong with other classic red and white varieties. Merlot, malbec and caberner franc gives assistant winemaker Chris Archer other strings to his bow and their bordeaux style blends are sensational. Gewurztraminer and black muscat are used to produce some wines different to the normal Hunter theme.

All this adds up to a great wine experience when you make your obligatory pilgrimage to Pepper Tree, you should also drop into Roberts for lunch or dinner and finish your trek at the Convent.

PEPPER TREE WINES

Address: Halls Road, Pokolbin NSW 2320
Phone: (02) 4998 7539
Fax: (02) 4998 7746
Email: peppertw@ozemail.com.au WWW:http://www.ozemail.com.au~peppertw
Winemakers: Chris Cameron and Chris Archer
Principal varieties grown: Chardonnay, Semillon, Cabernet Sauvignon, Merlot, Shiraz, Traminer, Verdelho, Malbec, Muscat
Average annual crush: 650 tonnes
Average no. cases produced: 50,000
Principal wines & brands
Reserve Coonawarra Merlot
Reserve Connawarra Classics (Cabernet Blend)
Reserve Hunter Valley Merlot
Reserve Hunter Valley Chardonnay
Reserve Hunter Valley Malbec
Reserve Hunter Valley Shiraz
Reserve Hunter Valley Semillon
Reserve Hunter Valley Traminer
Public & trade tours: By appointment only
Hours open to public: 9am-5pm, weekdays; 9.30am-5pm weekends/Public Holidays
Points of interest: Surrounded by spectacular gardens, the winery and sale barn epitomise the charm and essence of style that are trademarks of this operation

The Convent

"Heaven on Earth in the Hunter". This serene retreat is the perfect place to recharge the batteries to escape to an almost forgotten world of elegant charm in a French baroque style. The Convent began its life in 1909 as the home of the Brigidine Nuns in Coonamble.

In 1990 the wreckers hammer was about to fall, when it was rescued and transported to its current site forming the focal point for the new Peppers complex, opening in 1991. The 17 ensuite rooms are all decorated and furnished with class in a warm country fashion. Whether it is mid week or weekend,

summer, winter, spring or a lazy post vintage autumn, the gardens and charm of The Convent, Pepper Tree Wines and Roberts Restaurant have allure that is irresistible.

Robert's at Peppertree

Since the mid '70's the Hunter Valley has been enriched by the find food and hospitality of Robert and Sally Molines. Roberts a Frenchman, is a chef sleeped in the grand tradition of French cuisine. He is both passionate and painstaking about his work and love – cooking, whether

it be preparing a classic banquet or cooking a barbecue at the back of the Pepper Tree Winery, where we found him during the inaugural thanksgiving weekend this April. Roberts Restaurant is located in the Heritage listed Pepper Tree Cottage built in 1876. Robert and Sally have kept the old cottage as it was meticulously restored by Murray and Lynley Robson. Its charming rooms are used for private gatherings or pre-dinner drinks before entering the main Restaurant built on at the rear – a true "Restaurant du Campagne". Solid French country style with a somewhat baroque feel – all wood with much of the cuisine – au feu de bois – over the wood fire.
The food focuses on game with sensational demi glaze sauces. The rich spicy and earthy Hunter reds and full-bodied whites are right at home at Roberts where the ambience and service are truly special.
The Restaurant is surrounded by vines with the cutest charming Chapel visible over the vineyard. When Roberts caters for functions, private dinners and seminars I always

await my next visit to Roberts with joy in my heart, I am sure you will to.

Reg Drayton Wines

In 1994 an airline tragedy robbed the Hunter Valley of two of the Hunter's true stalwarts, Reg Drayton and his wife Pam, on their way to a well-earned holiday. Happily daughter Robyn, a fifth generation Drayton, has continued the family tradition and is now firmly ensconced as a female vingeron in the Hunter.

Reg Drayton's is a true family winery with the cellar door at the rear of Robyn and Craig's home on a prominent corner travelling between Lindeman's and McWilliam's under the shelter of the spectacular Brokenback Range. Robyn is involved in a more than full-time basis whilst Craig runs the vineyard and also involved in the Mining Industry.

When you visit and take in the warm family hospitality and enjoy the characterful wines, the Lambkin Semillon is a favourite of mine, you can also enjoy the complimentary cheese and biscuits.

Robyn and Craig are continuing a fine family tradition.

REG DRAYTON WINES

Address: Cnr McDonalds and Pokolbin Mountain Roads, Pokolbin NSW 2321
Direction: Pokolbin Hunter Valley. Between McWilliams and Lindemans wineries
Phone: (02) 4998 7523
Fax: (02) 4998 7523
Established: 1989
Owner: Robyn Drayton
Winemaker: Andrew Spinaze
Principal varieties grown: Semillon, Chardonnay, Verdelho, Shiraz
Ha under vine: 12
Average annual crush: 67.9
Average no. cases produced: 2,000

Principal wines & brands	Cellar Potential
Lambkin Semillon	8-10 years
Pokolbin Hills Chardonnay Semillon	4-5 years
Pokolbin Hills Chardonnay	6-7 years
Pokolbin Hills Shiraz	10+ years

Public & trade tours: Mini buses, by appointment only for tasting
Hours open to public: 10am-5pm, Fri-Mon and Public Holidays: Tue-Thu "when the doors are up, we are open"
Points of interest: Specialising in corporate and personal designed port decanters, labels, bottles and gift lines
Retail distribution: Cellar door sales, mail order, local restaurants and at Sydney Airport with 'Down town' Duty Free.

Pendarves Estates

Dr Philip Norrie is a general practitioner in a northern beaches suburb of Sydney. He is also President of the 'Australian Medical Friends of Wine Society' and with his wife Belinda is the owner of the premium wine producer, Pendarves Estate, which they founded in 1986. Philip is one of a long line of doctors, going right back to Dr Henry Lindeman, who have been prime movers in the Hunter Valley wine industry. The roll-call of doctors who have started wineries in Australia is now up to at least 150, proving beyond doubt that medical practitioners at large, believe in the medicinal value of wine.

Dr Norrie has published a booklet entitled "Wine and Health" with the help of McWilliams Wines. This most informative booklet quotes the world's leading Epidemiologist and Oxford Professor, Sir Richard Doll, who states, "The positive affect of wine consumption in moderation has been conclusively proved". Dr Norrie has also published several significant Historical books, two on the most famous of Australia's Wine Doctors. Firstly Dr Henry Lindeman, This book was published in 1993. Secondly Dr Christopher Rawson Penfold, published in 1994. A most enlightening book followed these two on Leo Buring "Australia's First Wine Authority". Dr Norrie is a credit to our great industry to whom I toast "good health".

PENDARVES ESTATE

Address: 110 Old North Road, Belford NSW
Phone: (02) 9913 1088
Fax: (02) 9970 6152
Established: 1986
Owner: Dr P.A. & Mrs B.J. Norrie
Winemaker: Greg Silkman
Principal varieties grown: Verdelho, Sauvignon Blanc, Chardonnay, Pinot Noir, Merlot, Malbec, Chambourcin, Pinot Meunier, Shiraz
Ha under vine: 20
Average annual crush: 150 tonnes
Average no. cases produced: 6,000

Principal wines & brands	Cellar Potential
Cabernet-Merlot-Malbec	5-10 years
Chardonnay	5 years
Shiraz	5-10 years
Semillon	5 years
Pinot Noir	5 years
Verdelho	5 years
Sauvignon Blanc	2-5 years
Chambourcin	2-5 years

Public & trade tours: By appointment only
Hours open to public: 11am-5pm Weekends
Points of interest: Peacocks roam freely, provincial style tasting rooms set in French provincial garden
Retail distribution: Haviland Wine Merchants (NSW), Richard Mackie Fine Wines (SA), Vintage Exports (WA), Primewines (VIC), Coastal Wine and Spirit Merchants (QLD), Australian Wineries (UK), Lyndoc Australia (Asia)

Petersons

The name Mount View is most applicable as a location for one of the Hunter Valley's most revered wineries, Petersons. The cottage-style tasting room in front of the winery opens out to a delightful garden, which has elevated views in all directions over the orderly vines and the rich fertile valleys surrounding them. As a backdrop the steep slopes of the impressive mountains not only add a grandeur to the whole scene, but give a sheltered yet surprisingly cool micro-climate.

Petersons was founded in 1971 and quickly began to collect awards at the Hunter Valley Wine Show, particularly with its chardonnay, and forging an enviable reputation for all the wines in a very short time.

The family is very involved in the operation and are modest, open and friendly people. Son Colin has a definite entrepreneurial flair and is also co-proprietor of the Calais Winery.

Colin, with the assistance of his father and the rest of the family, also put together the exciting 'Petersons Champagne House', a publicly-floated venture to producing outstanding methode champenoise in the French tradition, from a superb 'maison', prominently located on the corner of Branxton and Broke Roads. They have every reason to toast its success. The Petersons are a credit to the Hunter Valley.

PETERSONS
Address: Mount View Road, Mount View NSW 2325
Phone: (02) 4990 1704
Fax: (02) 4991 1344
Established: 1971
Winemaker: Gary Reed
Principal varieties grown: Merlot, Cabernet Sauvignon, Shiraz, Chardonnay, Semillon, Pinot Noir, Malbec
Ha under vine: 20
Average annual crush: 200 tonnes
Hours open to public: 9am-5pm, Mon-Sat; 10am-5pm Sun
Retail distribution: Cellar Door and Mail Order, Classic Wines of Australia

Petersons Champagne House

It seems absolutely right that the gateway to the Hunter should be resplendent with a world class "Champagne House". This, the only sparkling wine production house began in 1995. It provides the ideal tipple to celebrate the beginning or the end of your Hunter adventure.

Colin Peterson is a courageous entrepreneur with a great capacity for coolness under pressure. Not only running the family winery at Mount view and Calais Estates but also bottling wine for many Hunter Wineries, both large and small. I am not sure whether he wears shorts all year round because of the weather or he just does not have the time to pull on a pair of long strides!! Shoes are also optional for Colin. One thing is for sure, true Methode Champenoise – Sparkling Wine made in the true French tradition should have life and vitality, if a wine is a reflection of its maker as I truly believe, then the Petersons Sparkling Wine has an abundance of these vital qualities.

Your essential visit here is accompanied by personal table service and a tutored tasting together with smoked trout pate and bread. Don't miss it!!

PETERSONS CHAMPAGNE HOUSE
Address: Corner Broke and Branxton Roads, Cessnock NSW 2325
Phone: (02) 4998 7881
Fax: (02) 4998 7882
Established: 1994
Winemaker: Gary Reed
Principal varieties grown: Chardonnay, Pinot Noir
Ha under vine: 32
Average annual crush: 30 tonnes
Hours open to public: 9am-5pm, daily

Peacock Hill Vineyard

The Hunters newest winery "Peacock Hill"also has a delightful two-bedroom vineyard cottage available for vineyard visitors.

The history of the vineyard dates back to the beginnings of European settlement. John James Peacock was listed on the 1828 census as owner-farmer, born in the colony, he settled on the "Hill" in 1841. In 1969 Peacock Hill became part of the Rothbury Estate, shiraz and cabernet sauvignon vines were planted shortly afterwards and chardonnay followed in 1984. After a number of owners, in October 1995 charming couple George Tsiros and Sylvia Laumets took over the property and put it on a firm commercial footing.

They have instituted a careful vineyard management program and plan to plant some merlot in 1998. David Lowe, who has followed the vineyard since its Rothbury days, understands the fruit well and continues as contract winemaker. He has won many medals. For both red and white wines from the "Hill" only premium imported oak barrels are used.

The cellar door is now open amongst the gardens and houseguests can use the tennis court. George and Sylvia are great hosts. Avail yourself of their hospitality soon.

PEACOCK HILL
Address: Cnr Branxton Road and Palmers Lane,
Pokolbin NSW 2320
Direction: North of Cessnock
Phone: (02) 4998 7661
Fax: (02) 4998 7661
Established: 1969
Owners: George Tsiros and Sylvia Laumets
Winemaker: Mr David Lowe
Principal varieties grown: Shiraz, Cabernet Sauvignon, Chardonnay
Ha under vine: 5
Average annual crush: 22 tonnes
Average no. cases produced: 1500

Principal wines & brands	Cellar Potential
Cabernet Sauvignon	8+ years
Jaan Shiraz	6+ years
Reserve Chardonnay (oaked)	3-5 years
Absent Friends Chardonnay (unwooded)	1-2 years

Public & trade tours: No
Hours open to public: 9am-5pm, Fri-Mon, other days by appointment only
Points of interest: Picnic area, 2 bedroom accomodation, scenic gardens, tennis court
Retail distribution: Cellar door, Hunter Valley Wine Society

The Rothbury Estate

The brainchild of Wine Guru, Len Evans. Rothbury began its life in the seventies as an opportunity for people to become involved in a true winery operation. The "Rothbury Society" was founded to give hands on involvement in premium wine.

An impressive winery was built on an imposing hill on the main Broke road at Pokolbin. A cathedral like large hall was incorporated in the construction "The Great Hall" and became the venue for legendary Dinners and Celebrations that continue today.

Rothbury also pioneered the Cowra Region, making a chardonnay that quickly captured the wine drinkers imagination.

Today the enterprise is in the hands of the progressive and innovative Mildara Blass Group. A wide range of flavoursome wines are produced and now happily for wine lovers widely distributed.

ROTHBURY ESTATE
Address: Broke Road, Pokolbin NSW 2320
Phone: (02) 4998 7555
Fax: (02) 4998 7553
Established: 1969
Winemaker: Alan Harris
Ha under vine: 260
Average no. cases produced: 150,000

Principal wines & brands	Cellar Potential
Cowra Chardonnay	1-2 years
Mudgee Cabernet Merlot	2-5 years
Mudgee Shiraz	2-5 years
Hunter Valley Semillon	5-8 years
Hunter Valley Verdelho	3-5 years
Hunter Valley Chardonnay	2-3 years
Reserve Chardonnay	4-6 years
Reserve Shiraz	5-10 years

Public & trade tours: Trade Tours, Public tours will be available in the near future. By appointment only
Hours open to public: 9.30am-4.30pm, daily
Points of interest: The Rothbury Café - specialised menus with regional produce. The Cask Hall - function facility for up to 200 visitors

Saddler's Creek

A lively and interesting winery, attracting much interest over recent years, is Saddler's Creek. Located at the beginning of Marrowbone Road, in fact an ideal spot to commence your journey through the Hunter Wineries, as it is not far from the town of Cessnock and gives you a very pleasant start to the day.

A number of enthusiastic partners have put together a great Enterprise. The newly opened Bluegrass Room offers tutored, personal tastings by appointment as well as the normal cellar door tastings.

The winery produces wines on site under the distinctive label names of Bluegrass, Equus and Marrowbone. The wines are increasingly being seen in top restaurants around Australia and the Bluegrass

Cabernet Sauvignon was recently awarded the top accolade of 5 stars from Winestate in their 1996 Hunter feature.

Along with their innovative approach Saddler's Creeks packaging is exquisite. Magnums are offered along with some extraordinary dessert wines in a sensational wax sealed presentation, which is totally in keeping with the wines quality.

These wines along with traditionally fermented sparkling blends and a surprising Sauvignon Blanc contribute to what is an extraordinary range for a Boutique winery. On the first Hunter Thanksgiving weekend a true country style fair enlivened the wineries entrance and the sense of fun and hospitality which typifies Saddler's Creek was well evidenced, but do not be fooled, the wines are seriously good.

SADDLERS CREEK

Address: Marrowbone Road, Pokolbin NSW 2320
Phone: (02) 4991 1770
Fax: (02) 4991 2482
Established: 1991
Winemaker: John Johnstone
Principal varieties grown: Chardonnay, Merlot, Cabernet Sauvignon, Shiraz, Sauvignon Blanc, Semillon
Ha under vine: 15
Average annual crush: 100-125 tonnes
Average no. cases produced: 10,000

Principal wines & brands	Cellar Potential
Unwooded Chardonnay	
Botrytis Semillon	5-8 years
Botrytis Tokay	5-8 years
Semillion Pinot Noir Sparkling	3 years
Bluegrass Cabernet Sauvignon	6-10 years
Bluegrass Merlot	3-5 years
Equus Shiraz	5-8 years
Marrowbone Chardonnay	3-5 years
Reserve Selection Malolactic Semillion	3-5 years
Reserve Selection Sauvignon Blanc	3 years

Public & trade tours: By appointment only
Hours open to public: 10am-5pm, daily
Retail distribution: Saddlers Creek Wines Sydney. 606/20 Bungan St, Mona Vale NSW 2103

Scarborough

Ian and Merralea Scarborough are perfectionists. Their idyllic setting perched on top of a substantial hill looking over Pokolbin with the Brokenback Ranges as a backdrop has been carefully chosen. The vineyard, perfectly tended all year round, is on rich red terra rossa soil, a rarity in the Hunter, but one of the worlds most sought after viticultural soil types. It is ideal for the two wines they produce a rich opulent chardonnay and a regal pinot noir both with definite burgundian styles.

Scarborough's are virtually the only Boutique Winery who give their wines bottle aging. Both are aged for 3 years before their release.

The hilltop winery is meticulously kept and adjoins a charmingly appointed tasting room, delightfully decorated in a provincial style with splendid views in all directions. The Scarborough's are a close family. Son Jerome and daughters Sally and Chloe all pull their weight in the enterprise. This vineyard and winery demands a visit do not leave the Hunter without visiting it!!

SCARBOROUGH

Address: Gillards Road, Pokolbin NSW 2321
Phone: (02) 4998 7563
Fax: (02) 4998 7786
Established: 1987
Winemaker: Ian Scarborough
Principal varieties grown: Chardonnay, Pinot Noir
Ha under vine: 10
Average annual crush: 200
Hours open to public: 9am-5pm, daily
Retail distribution: Cellar Door and Mail Order

Sutherland Wines

SUTHERLAND WINES PTY LTD
Address: Deaseys Road, Pokolbin NSW 2321
Phone: (02) 4998 7650
Fax: (02) 4998 7603
Established: 1979
Winemaker: Neil G. Sutherland
Principal varieties grown: Chardonnay, Semillon, Chenin Blanc, Pinot Noir, Cabernet Sauvignon, Shiraz
Ha under vine: 22
Average annual crush: 100 tonnes
Average no. cases produced: 8,000
Public & trade tours: By appointment only
Hours open to public: 10am-4.30 pm, daily
Retail distribution: Ex Winery

The Sutherland's have established a thoroughly professional vineyard and winery, and a beautiful home, overlooking the Brokenback Range. To sit on their verandah with a glass of their fine wine, enjoying their excellent company, is a delightful experience.

The Sutherlands searched for a small vineyard in the Hunter to develop into a lifetime concern and to make their family's home. Both Neil and Caroline already had a love of wine and were members of Rothbury Estate. In 1977, they purchased part of the McPherson Co-operative vineyard that was badly in need of some attention. For the first few years they sold grapes. Building a winery in 1979, that is both smart and functional, includes a beautiful wood-panelled tasting area on a raised mezzanine. This raised area promotes the feeling of being part of the winemaking process.

The first vintage was produced in the new winery in 1983. As winemaker, Neil draws on his science degree and a number of courses he has completed at the Charles Sturt University at Wagga.

The wines are full of positive fruit flavours and rich varietal character. Sutherland's invest heavily in new French oak but use it with admirable restraint to enhance their wine's character, not dominate them. The early chardonnay's were a revolution in the Hunter and won a number of awards and trophies. Sutherland's winery is an invigorating place to visit and seeing people leave with armloads of wine must be a just reward for the family's hard work. Today, the next generation of the family is involved.

Terrace Vale Wines

It was a syndicate of 20 Sydney businessmen and their families who started Terrace Vale. Most remain, and other than winemaker Alain Le prince and some administrative staff, the rest of the 'workers' are the syndicate members and families. Work, including cellar door sales, is handled on a roster basis and the result of this extraordinary co-operation is a congenial family atmosphere.

The Terrace Vale vineyard was planted in 1971 and the first vintage was produced in 1974 at Tyrrell's Winery. The first vintage to be made in the new winery at Terrace Vale was in 1976. As his name suggests, winemaker Alain Le prince is French and from the Touraine region of the Loire Valley. Alain is a gentle person who cares deeply for his wines.

The Bin 2 Chardonnay was an early success story for the winery when the 1979 vintage won many medals and trophies.

Terrace Vale reds are often big, fruity wines particularly the shiraz which will improve with several years cellaring. The pinot noir is usually a lighter style wine with pronounced fruit, while the cabernet sauvignon is a more elegant wine that develops well in the bottle. There is a stunning view of the Brokenback Ranges from Terrace Vale and this, combined with lovely wines and warm hospitality, makes it a must for the visitor.

TERRACE VALE WINES PTY LTD	
Address: Deasy Road, Pokolbin, NSW 2320	**Chardonnay, Shiraz, Cabernet, Pinot Noir, Gewurztraminer, Sauvignon Blanc**
Direction: Off Hermitage Road	**Ha under vine:** 36.69
Phone: (02) 4998 7517	**Average annual crush:** 150 tonnes
Fax: (02) 4998 7814	**Average no. cases produced:** 10,000-12,000
Established: 1971	**Public & trade tours:** By appointment only
Winemaker: Alain Leprince	**Hours open to public:** 10am-5pm, daily
Principal varieties grown: Semillon,	**Retail distribution:** NSW - Simsed Pty Ltd

Van de Scheur

Kees Van de Scheur and his partner in life Helen Palmer have created a piece of paradise in Pokolbin. A delightful cluster of historic old buildings on O'Conners lane (formerly the Ingleside Winery founded in 1872) has become a captivating winery complex. Kees is an old hand at the winemaking game whilst his youthful enthusiasm and lively imagination has come up with a great hands on concept. "City Vignerons", he and Helen were faced with the age old dilemma of the wine industry, the large investment it takes to set up a vineyard and winery and finance the aging and packaging of the wine. They floated the idea of an involvement of friends and city dwellers looking for an earthy outlet and to expand their horizons and change their lifestyle.

They have been inundated by keen amateur vignerons. Chatting with Helen this morning by telephone I could hear the winery buzzing with excitement as the five teams involved in their first winemaking challenge labelled their chardonnays (they all made 2 barrels from the same vineyard).

The 1998 vintage will see the chardonnay challenge continue with a level two challenge offered to make any style wine, red or white, from the vineyard they have helped plant. Why not become a City Vigneron contact Van de Scheur, you won't regret it.

VAN DE SCHEUR WINES	
Address: Lot 2 O'Connor Lane Pokolbin NSW 2321	
Direction: Off Oakey Creek Road	
Phone: (02) 4998 7789	
Fax: (02) 4998 7847	
Established: 1994	
Owners: Kees Van De Scheur and Helen Palmer	
Winemaker: Kees Van De Scheur	
Principal varieties grown: Shiraz, Semillon, Cabernet Sauvignon, Chardonnay	
Ha under vine: 10 acres	
Average annual crush: 30 tonnes	
Principal wines & brands	**Cellar Potential**
Shiraz	8-12 years
Semillon	6-10 years
Chardonnay	4-6 years
Cabernet Sauvignon	8-12 years
Hours open to public: 10am-5pm, daily	
Points of interest: City vignerons, Hands-on involvement, Winemaking experience and competition, Vineyard fun. Restored Winery Building.	
Retail distribution: Cellar Door	

Tyrrells Vineyard

T yrrell's has expanded into a very significant Australian Wine Company and is now ably run by fourth generation Bruce Tyrrell. His father Murray is, without doubt, the character of the Hunter Valley. He has been awarded the Order of Australia for his services to the wine industry, and is very outspoken about Australian wine, in particular that of the Hunter Valley. When Murray took over Tyrrell's in 1959, the company sold only bulk wine to other wine companies, such as McWilliam's, where Maurice O'Shea blended them with his own. O'Shea also bottled some of Tyrrell's wines and sold them under the 'Richard' label. As soon as he had taken charge, Murray Tyrrell instigated some

major changes. He developed a label and began exhibiting wines successfully in many shows. Visitors soon flocked to the winery's cellar door and sales boomed. From only several hundred tonnes in the 1960's, Tyrrell's now crush many thousands of tonnes and have invested in vineyards in other regions such as McLaren Vale and Coonawarra in South Australia.

Tyrrell's have a number of traditional labels such as their top selling 'Long Flat' wines and the 'Old Winery' label. The Tyrrell's Vat 47 Chardonnay was really the first commercial chardonnay in Australia and has just celebrated 27 successful vintages, regularly winning gold medals and trophies in wine shows. This 'Vat' series, which includes a number of white and red wines, really put Tyrrell's on the map when they were launched by Murray in the mid-1960's at the start of the wine boom.

Tyrrell's also made some of the first pinot noirs in Australia. Their pinot noir vineyard is planted in rich, red volcanic soil over shale and limestone on the Brokenback Range to the rear of the winery. This is an ideal location for this grape variety and

Tyrrell's have produced some incredible wines. Their 1976 Pinot Noir won an international wine show award in France as the top pinot exhibited. This led to world-wide publicity and acclaim for Tyrrell's, which was further enhanced by Murray's own distinctive way of passing on good news. The history of Tyrrell's Hunter Valley Winery is the longest and most continuous progression of any of the winemakers in the district. In 1993, they celebrated 135 years of operation. The business was begun by Edward Tyrrell who was granted 330 acres of land at Pokolbin in 1858. This property was ideally suited to the vine with its rich volcanic soils on well drained slopes. A slab hut (which is still preserved by the family) was built and vines planted, with the first vintage occurring in 1864. Edward's son Dan took over winemaking in 1885 at the age of 15, and proceeded to make 75 vintages, surely a world record. It was not until a fall from a ladder in 1958 that Dan was forced into retirement.

Murray took the helm in 1959 and his son Bruce is now general manager. While Murray covers the promotional trail for Tyrrell's, Bruce astutely handles the marketing and business side of the company. Tyrrell's also produce some wonderful methode champenois wines from semillon, pinot and chardonnay grapes.

TYRRELL'S VINEYARDS PTY LTD

Address: Broke Road, Pokolbin NSW 2320
Phone: (02) 4993 7000
Fax: (02) 4998 7723
Email: admin@tryrrells.com.au
WWW: http://www.tyrrells.com.au and http://www.winefutures.com.au
Established: 1858
Owners: Murray and Bruce Tyrrell
Winemakers: Andrew Spinaze and Andrew Thomas
Principal varieties grown: Semillon, Chardonnay, Pinot Noir, Shiraz
Ha under vine: 610
Average annual crush: 3180
Average no. cases produced: 650,000

Principal wines & brands	Cellar Potential
VAT 47 Pinot Chardonnay	5-10 years
VAT 1 Semillon	5-15 years
VAT 9 Shiraz	5-10 years
Moon Mountain Chardonnay	5-10 years
Shee-Oak Chardonnay	2-5 years
Stevens Shiraz	5-10 years
Lost Block Semillon	5-10 years
Old Winery Cabernet Merlot	5-10 years
Old Winery Chardonnay	2-5 years

Public & trade tours: By appointment only
Hours open to public: 8am-5pm, Mon-Sat
Retail distribution: Nationwide plus export markets

Tulloch Wines

The year 1996 marked 160 years since the arrival of the first member of the Tulloch family in Australia. It was not until 1883, however, that John Younie Tulloch became the slightly reluctant owner of a vineyard. In settlement of a debt to his store at Branxton, he accepted a 17 hectare property around the corner from Lindemans. Although a devout Methodist, John obviously saw no sin in developing nature's gift of the grape.

After rejuvenating the small shiraz vineyard, Tulloch made his first wine in 1895. By the 1920s, he had bought much surrounding property and had more land under vine than any other local winemaker. Tullochs, like many other winemakers, sold their wine in bulk to large wine merchants in the capital cities, including Rhinecastle with Johnnie Walker and Leo Buring.

John Younie's son Hector succeeded him in 1940 and established the first Tulloch label in the early 1950s. Later, Tulloch was bought out but the family were left in control and upgraded production and cellar door facilities. There was a confusing period for Tullochs with many changes of ownership. The company is now owned by the Southcorp Group and is now managed by Pat Auld whose family are steeped in Wine Tradition, Jay Tulloch having just retired. The recently renovated cellar door, with its beautiful pergola and facade in the shadow of The Brokenbacks, is worth a visit.

Tulloch wines are consistently excellent. They are individual in style and the verdelho is particularly good each year. Tullochs have a reputation for their white wines, which have managed to remain consistently good throughout the company's tumultuous history.

Tullochs also make an excellent Vintage Sparkling wine from chardonnay and semillon under the label "Hunter Cuvee" which has regularly won major wine awards. Their Glen Elgin Estate is a pretty place with vineyards planted over the undulating countryside and now has a very settled happy feeling about it, which is reflected in the characterful wines of recent years.

The cellar door has recently been renovated and upgraded in various timbers. Its location, looking out on the brokenbacks, makes it an ideal stop-off on your trip through the Hunter.

Wandin Valley Estate

The imagination and foresight that led to the long running Australian television series "A Country Practice" is well evidenced at the wonderful Wandin Valley Estate created by James and Philippa Davern.

Flying over the Hunter, with my intrepid photographer Stephane, the planning, capitalising on the natural beauty of Wandin Valley's site was obvious. The winery, high on the hill overlooking the Estate and the Tuscan style villas of two and four bedrooms set in amongst the trees contrasts with the classic English cricket pavilion looking out over the immaculate oval, the imposing gates and the beautifully ordered vineyards. The cellar door is unique, a spacious mezzanine complete with art and jewellery exhibitions sitting happily above the state of the art winery overseen by creative winemaker Geoff Broadfield, who also doubles as a hilariously amusing M.C., as I am sure our esteemed Prime Minister can affirm after his gentle roasting at the Hunter Thanksgiving Dinner.

The wines from Wandin Valley have won many awards and can be often enjoyed in the Ruby Pavilion at the many functions hosted at the Estate and catered for by renowned chef, Peter Meier from Casuarina.

WANDIN VALLEY	
Address: Wilderness Road, Lovedale NSW 2321	**Average annual crush:** 120 tonnes
Phone: (02) 4930 7317	**Hours open to public:** 10am-5pm, daily
Fax: (02) 4930 7814	**Points of interest:** Views of the Brokenback Ranges,. Crafts for sale including pottery, paintings and furniture. Winery café and playground. 2 and 4 bedroom accommodation and function facilities, including cricket ground
Established: 1973	
Winemaker: Geoff Broadfield	
Principal varieties grown: Chardonnay, Cabernet Sauvignon, Shiraz, Ruby Cabernet, Merlot, Malbec	
Ha under vine: 8	**Retail distribution:** Cellar Door and Mail Order

Wilderness Estate

"Out of the Wilderness - into the limelight" would well describe the remarkable partnership that has been welded between Austrian born Hunter grapegrower and winemaker Joe Lesnik and ebullient corporate winemaker John Baruzzi. The Wilderness winery is right at the crossroads of the Hunter on the corner of Broke and Branxton roads. John's long experience as chief winemaker for the Wyndham Estate group stands him in good stead. He is a Roseworthy and Adelaide University Graduate whose career in wine began in the early 70's at Penfolds Magill Cellars. Joe has green fingers and has extensive vineyards on the rich terra rossa style soils on his Wilderness Road Vineyards and on the fertile loams around the winery, which was built in 1985 and is well equipped with the most up-to-date technology.

The Wilderness Wines I have tried lately are full of rich fruit flavours and extremely drinkable along with the main range are Black Creek and Lesnik labels. Look out for them with Wilderness's go get'em attitude. I am certain you will run across them.

WILDERNESS ESTATE	
Address: Branxton Road, Pokolbin NSW 2325	
Phone: (02) 4998 7755	
Fax: (02) 4998 7750	
Established: 1985	
Owners: John Baruzzi and Josef Lesnik	
Winemaker: John Baruzzi	
Principal varieties grown: Merlot, Chardonnay, Verdelho, Semillon, Pinot Noir, Shiraz, Cabernet	
Ha under vine: 40	
Average no. cases produced: 20,000	
Principal wines & brands	**Cellar Potential**
Wilderness Estate Chardonnay	6 years
Wilderness Estate Merlot	4 years
Wilderness Estate Cabernet Merlot	6 years
Wilderness Estate Individual Block Semillon	5 years
Black Creek Verdelho	3 years
Black Creek Chardonnay	4 years
Black Creek Shiraz	3 years
Public & trade tours: By appointment only	
Hours open to public: 9am-5pm, daily	
Retail distribution: Norman Wines, National Distributor. Exports to Canada, UK, USA and Thailand	

Wyndham Estate

Located on the banks of the Hunter River, Wyndham Estate was founded by one of the earliest pioneers in the region, George Wyndham, who planted his first vines in 1828 on a property called "Dalwood". The classic old homestead, Dalwood House has been restored as an official Australian Bicentenary Project as an important part of Australia's Heritage and is now open for tours at 11.30am Wednesday through Sunday.

Vines and winemaking were a large part of George Wyndham's rural interests, however he is also credited with introducing the first Hereford cattle to mainland Australia. George Wyndham purchased property throughout New South Wales and planted vines as far north as Inverell near the Queensland border. Under careful handling by his son, the wine business grew until it was the second largest wine company in the State. Unfortunately with the great 1890s depression and the death of both Wyndhams by 1870, the Wyndham company was reduced to bankruptcy, to be bought by H. Wilkinson in 1901. The vineyards, winery and related interests were bought by Penfolds who kept the Dalwood name and gave it great circulation, with their "Dalwood" series of table wines. The winery was sold to their winemaker Perc McGuigan, whose son Brian began Wyndham Estate Pty Ltd in 1971, and in late 1989 early 1990, was sold to current owners Orlando Wyndham. Wyndham Estate is now one of the largest and perhaps most widely-known winery in the Hunter Valley, with its wines also well known on the international market through the marketing prowess of parent company, Orlando Wyndham.

Wyndham Estate wines reflect the vibrant team that produces them, and always seem to have a liveliness and zest to them along with rich fruit flavours. The Bin TR2 and Bin 222 Chardonnay are amongst Australia's market leaders in their price range and are superb fruit driven wine. In fact, Bin TR2 is a favourite to many consumers being one of the top selling white wines in New South Wales. The Oak Cask Chardonnay is extremely good, and benefits from a few years' bottle ageing. The Wyndham range also includes a verdelho, the grape of the Island of Madeira, which always inhibits beautiful tropical fruit flavours with a crisp dry finish. The Bin 555 Selected Hermitage made from shiraz grapes, is a wine of drinkability, ideal as a lunchtime red. Bin 444 Cabernet Sauvignon is a rich, round wine, full-bodied, but with typical Wyndham approachability.

This historic winery has been brought back to its former glory, with extensive refurbishment and now houses a wonderful cellar door, restaurant, function facilities, wine eduation centre and caters for daily tours. The gardens at Wyndham are also superb, with riverside barbecue and picnic grounds, in fact the whole estate is wonderfully turned out and a must for a visit on your Hunter pilgrimage.

WYNDHAM ESTATE
Address: Dalwood Road, Dalwood NSW 2335
Phone: (02) 4998 3444
Fax: (02) 4998 3422
Established: 1828
Owner: Orlando Wyndam Group Pty Ltd
Principal varieties grown: Shiraz, Semillon, Chardonnay, Cabernet Sauvignon, Traminer, Riesling, Merlot

Principal wines & brands   Cellar Potential
Bin 222 Chardonnay
Bin 555 Shiraz
Bin 444 Cabernet Sauvignon
TR2 Classic White and Classic Red
Oak Cask Chardonnay
Bin 888 Cabernet Merlot
Bin 777 Semillon Chardonnay
Chablis Superior Semillon Sauvignon Blanc
Bin 111 Verdelho
Bin 333 Pinot Noir
Public & trade tours: By appointment only
Hours open to public: 9am-5pm, Mon-Sat; 10am-5pm, Sun
Points of interest: Season's lunches, Opera in the vineyard, Dalwood House, picnic area on the banks of the Hunter River, Historic cellar door and restaurant facilities
Retail distribution: National

Kevin Sobels Wine

Kevin Sobels comes from a family steeped in wine history going back to the founding of the famous Buring & Sobels Quelltaler Estate in the Clare Valley of South Australia in 1865. His wife Margaret comes from a well-known Riverland Wine Family and son Jason is involved in the vineyard and winery operations.

The Sobels have built a unique circular winery and cellar door on the main Broke road at Pokolbin and give the visitor a real family greeting often accompanied by their faithful St Bernard "Plonk", the only thing missing, being the mini barrel of brandy around his neck!!

The Sobels wines are carefully made using minimal amounts of preservatives and include some sweeter table wine styles, sparkling and fortified wines as well as dry reds and whites. You can be sure to find something to suit your palate. Larger groups are welcome and picnic tables and barbecue facilities are freely available.

The Sobels boast on their brochure "open every day whilst the doors are open or the lights are on:" so there is no excuse not to drop in.

KEVIN SOBELS WINES

Address: Cnr. Halls and Broke Road, Pokolbin NSW 2321
Phone: (02) 4998 7766
Fax: (02) 4998 7475
Email: sobels@ozemail.com.au
WWW: http://www.ozemail.com.au/~sobels
Established: 1991
Winemaker: Kevin Sobels
Principal varieties grown: Semillon, chardonnay, shiraz, pinot noir, traminer
Ha under vine: 10
Average annual crush: 90 tonnes
Average no. cases produced: 6,000
Principal wines & brands   **Cellar Potential**

Semillon	5 years
Chardonnay	3 years
Shiraz	5 years
Cabernet-Merlot	3 years
Sparkling Burgundy	5 years

Public & trade tours: By appointment only. Public tours starting in 1998; 10am, 12noon, 2pm
Hours open to public: 9am-6pm, daily
Points of interest: 2 large picnic and bbq areas for customer use. Lunch supplied with prior notice.
Sales room attended by winemaker, family and Saint Bernard Dog.
Retail distribution: From Cellar Door and Mail Order only.

Tamburlaine

Found in the heart of Hunter Wine Country, in the shadows of the Brokenback Mountain Range, Tamburlaine has been evolving since the mid 60ís. It is a privately owned company and has achieved significance amongst Hunter Winemakers, both in terms of innovation and production growth. Over a decade of winemaking continuity has been under the guidance of Chief Winemaker and Managing Director, Mark Davidson.

Grape growing on the Winery site in Pokolbin began before the current day boom, and the cellar maintains some traditional Australian charm.

Tastings at the winery are unhurried and personal, particularly during the week. Informative and enthusiastic staff introduce the wines you would like to know more about as well as those with which you may be familiar.

The wines are not widely available, however the limited releases each vintage are well worth tasting.

TAMBURLAINE WINES

Address: McDonalds Road, Pokolbin NSW 2320
Phone: (02) 4998 7570
Fax: (02) 4998 7763
Established: 1966
Winemaker: Mark Davidson
Principal varieties grown: Syrah, Cabernet Sauvignon, Semillon, Chardonnay, Verdelho
Ha under vine: 10
Average annual crush: 500 tonnes
Average no. cases produced: 28,000
Principal wines & brands   **Cellar Potential**

The Chapel Reserve Red	10+ years
The Chapel Chardonnay Reserve	5-8 years
Cabernet Merlot Malbec	8+ years
Chambourcin	5 years
Semillon	5-10+ years
Verdelho	6-8+ years
Three Parish Chardonnay	5-7 years
Sauvignon Blanc	3-5 years
Botrytis Semillon	8+ years
Frambase Liqueur	3 years

Public & trade tours: By appointment only
Hours open to public: 9.30am-5pm, daily
Points of interest: Private tasting facilities, BBQ area
Retail distribution: Select restaurants only

An introduction to the Upper Hunter Valley

The area loosely called the Upper Hunter Valley surrounds the Hunter and Goulburn Rivers and their tributaries, and the towns of Denman, Muswellbrook, Sandy Hollow and Scone. The landscape is striking and diverse with both rich alluvial plains and steep mountain ranges. It is rich country with deep red and black soils over many coal deposits, this being one of the region's major industries. Vines have been grown in the Upper Hunter since early in the 19th century. One of the first wine growers was George Bowman who established Arrowfield and other properties, and made wine at his property, Archerfield. Other wines in the area were made mostly as a hobby. In 1960, Penfolds bought a large property at Wybong (just north of Sandy Hollow), where they planted several hundreds of hectares of vines of a great variety. The winery and dam were constructed on the property, but there were only limited supplies of water available at times. This property was sold to Rosemount in 1977.

The period of real growth for the Upper Hunter started in 1969 when Arrowfield began a huge development at Jerry's Plains. This became the largest single vineyard in Australia consisting of more than 800,000 vines by 1977. Also in 1969, Bob Oatley bought a large tract of land at the junction of Wybong Creek and Goulburn River, which became Rosemount Estate. The period saw other beginnings for the Upper Hunter with David Hordern beginning a vineyard at Wybong.

Winemaker Simon Gilbert has become a stalwart of the area, first making wines for Arrowfield, and in 1995 when three weeks before vintage, he took over the old Oak Factory at Muswellbrook and converted it to a winery which crushed several hundred tonnes on behalf of clients during the 1995 vintage and has grown much since.

Although the Upper Hunter receives less rain than the Lower Hunter, there is an abundant water supply in the local rivers and nearly all new vineyards rely on drip irrigation to become established. The mature vines in the area seem to be producing better fruit each vintage. The area seems to produce white grape varieties more successfully than red and it was the Rosemount's rieslings and traminers, produced in the '70's by John Ellis, that first brought the area wide acclaim. Since then, the Upper Hunter has become best known for its chardonnays with Phillip Shaw of Rosemount winning accolades worldwide. Other whites such as wood-aged semillons and sauvignon blancs have also brought credit to Rosemount and others.

Red wines in the region are now getting their stripes, particularly those produced from Rosemount's Roxburgh vineyard. The Upper Hunter has seen some large increases in vineyard areas during the last 2 years some under the McGuigan banner, and as the existing vineyards mature the wines are improving each vintage. It is a region with a great depth of winemaking talent and they all seem to work well together, spurring each other on.

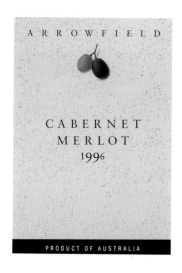

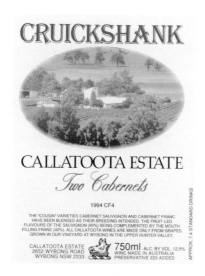

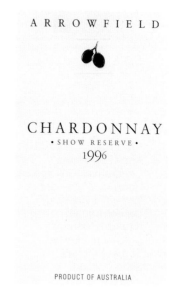

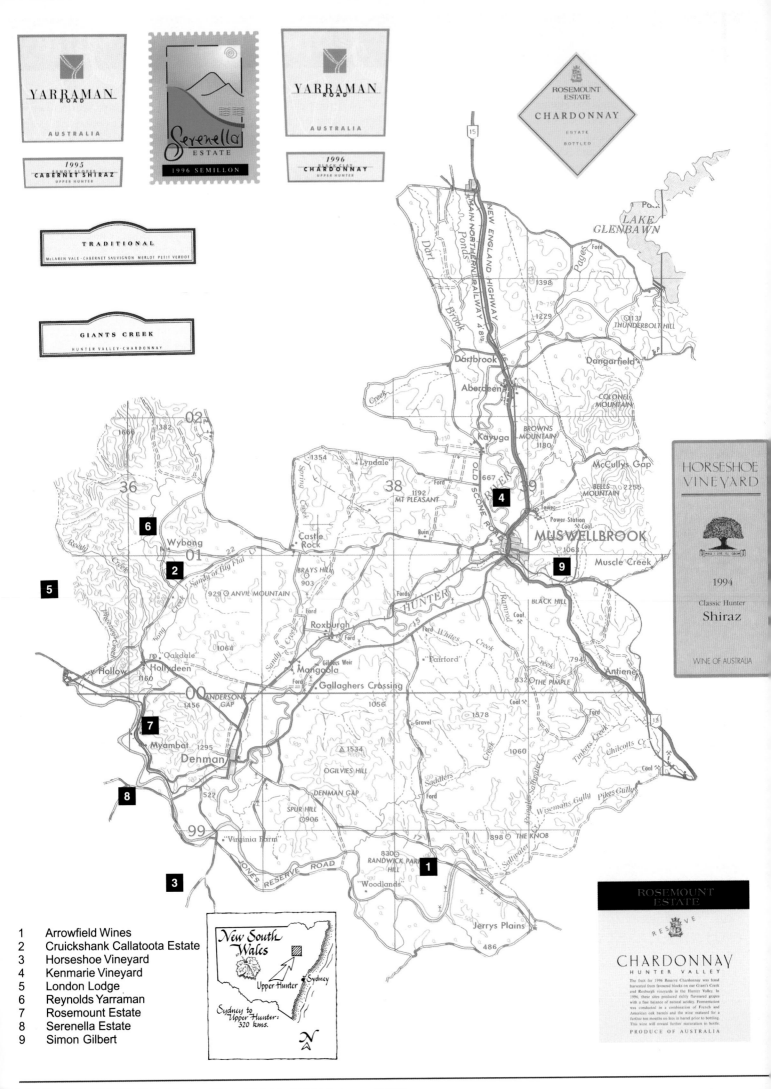

1 Arrowfield Wines
2 Cruickshank Callatoota Estate
3 Horseshoe Vineyard
4 Kenmarie Vineyard
5 London Lodge
6 Reynolds Yarraman
7 Rosemount Estate
8 Serenella Estate
9 Simon Gilbert

Arrowfield Wines

Arrowfield's history dates back from 1824 when George Bowman, one of the first settlers in the Upper Hunter region, received several large land grants from Governor Macquarie. A vineyard was planted and a horse stud and grazing property developed.

In 1969, new owners established a large vineyard and winery and by 1977 it was the largest single vineyard in Australia with 1,200 acres of vines. The collapse of the red wine market in the late 1970's saw a rationalisation of the vineyard keeping only the best plantings on the best soil types and aspects.

The nucleus of Arrowfield Wines now consists of the best 300 acres of this most picturesque valley and this area is now being expanded partly due to the success of Arrowfield's new Hunter Valley Range. The remainder of its grapes are sourced from other premium regions around Australia – semillon from the Barossa Valley, shiraz from McLaren Vale, cabernet sauvignon from the Goulburn Valley and chardonnay from the Cowra region. The Cowra Chardonnay is acknowledged as the best of the region and a leader in the premium chardonnay market.

More than 50% of Arrowfield's sales are from premium wine exports to markets in USA, Germany, Singapore, Japan and New Zealand. The growth in these markets is driven by the "New World" wine styles made in the high tech winery. The artistry of the winemaking team is led by Chief Winemaker Don Buchanan. Don has a wealth of experience from 10 years of winemaking at his own vineyards in the Tamar Valley, just out of Launceston.

In the search for quality and innovation Arrowfield believe there is no finishing line. For a great day out, you should dine at S.J.'S restaurant offering great food with spectacular views over the vine-covered valley with the Hunter River at its base. This innovative café style restaurant is on the wineries top level.

ARROWFIELD WINES PTY LTD

Address: Denman Road, Jerrys Plains, Upper Hunter NSW 2330
Direction: 10kms from Jerrys Plains, 30kms from Denman
Phone: (02) 6576 4041
Fax: (02) 6576 4144
Established: 1969
Winemaker: Don Buchanan
Principal varieties grown: Chardonnay, Semillon, Shiraz, Cabernet Sauvignon, Merlot, Pinot Noir, Ruby Cabernet, Sauvignon Blanc
Ha under vine: 59
Average no. cases produced: 100,000
Principal wines & brands   Cellar Potential
Show Reserve Chardonnay
Show Reserve Shiraz
Show Reserve Cabernet Sauvignon
Hunter Valley Chardonnay
Hunter Valley Shiraz
Hunter Valley Semillon
Cowra Chardonnay
Arrowfield Chardonnay
Arrowfield Semillon Chardonnay
Arrowfield Cabernet Merlot
Public & trade tours: By appointment only
Hours open to public: Cellar door 10am-5pm, daily, SJ's Restaurant - Lunch (Thur-Sun) and by appointment
Points of interest: BBQ; playground and lunch facilities. SJ's restaurant
Retail distribution: All states: Broken Bay Beverages (NSW), Wine 2000 (QLD), Harry Williams (ACT), The Wine Company (VIC), David Johnstone & assoc. (TAS), John Parker Agencies (SA), Moss Stilling (WA)

Yarraman Road Barrington Estate

During the mid 1960ís Penfolds "Dalwood Estate" was the Hunter Valleys largest single vineyard. Jeffery Penfold Hyland, Max Schubert, Percy McGuigan and others had selected the site in 1958.

The property comprises 1,100 acres and at one stage held some 400 acres of vines. This Wybong site was chosen for its ideal soil types, climate and water supply from the Wybong Creek to supplement the original Dalwood vineyards at Branxton.

Rosemount bought the property in 1978 and sold it to current owners, the Blom Family, in 1994. Gary Blom is a man of vision and one of those responsible for the establishment of the incredible giant I-Max Cinema at Darling Harbour.

The vineyards have been expanded with an extra 50 acres of vines in 1994 and another 150 acres being planted now including some merlot.

The Yarraman Road is a famous wine route also including the exciting Reynolds Yarraman. The Blom's have already captured the upper echelon of Sydney wine lovers with their exceptional wines and Gary's wife Karen, a former tea merchant born in the USA, are also exporting wines to a number of countries.

BARRINGTON ESTATE
Address: Yarraman Road, Wybong NSW 2333
Phone: (02) 6527 8118
Fax: (02) 6527 8039
Established: 1967
Owner: Gary Bloh
Winemaker: David Lowe
Principal varieties grown: Merlot, Shiraz, Chardonnay, Semillon
Ha under vine: 80
Average no. cases produced: 10,000

Principal wines & brands	Cellar Potential
Yarraman Road Chardonnay	2-5 years
Yarraman Road Cabernet Shiraz	2-5 years
Yarraman Road Shiraz Cabernet	2-5 years

Public & trade tours: By appointment only
Points of interest: Country cottages, BBQ and picnic areas, bush walking, native flora and fauna
Retail distribution: Australia wide in many of the best restaurants and hotels and select bottle shops featuring premium wines

Cruickshank Callatoota Estate

A true individualist, John Cruickshank has his vineyard planted with only two grape varieties, cabernet sauvignon and cabernet franc. From this unique vineyard only four wines are produced. Two are cabernet sauvignons, one a lighter style than the other, the third a blend of cabernets sauvignon and franc. The fourth wine is a very good cabernet rose.

A very logical approach was taken to set up this vineyard with deep red alluvial soil and good water access. The vines chosen were specially selected clones that have grown beautifully.

The first four hectares were planted in 1974 and the winery in 1981. The most modern equipment was purchased to give total control of fermentation. John and his son Andrew use American Oak and the resulting wines are of a high quality that will age very well in the bottle. A further 4 hectares of vines were planted. The cabernet franc is released as a straight varietal wine in some years and in others blended with the cabernet sauvignon.

John Cruickshank, involved in engineering and management consulting, approached the vineyard as a factory producing the best possible material for the finished product - the wine.

The unique industrially designed trellises presenting the strong vines in the form of a giant glass with four arms holding the bowl. This gives great exposure to the leaves and fruit as helps prevent disease.

Two eagles protect the vineyard from small grape-eating birds.

The winery visitor's centre was rewarded by winning the 1995 Hunter Tourism Award For Excellence as "The Most Significant Local tourism Attraction" for the entire region, a fine achievement and yet another reason to visit this have of natural beauty and great wine.

CRUICKSHANK CALLATOOTA ESTATE
Address: Wybong Road, Wybong NSW 2333
Phone: (02) 6547 8149
Fax: (02) 6547 8144
Established: 1973
Winemakers: Andrew Cruickshank and Hartley Smithers
Principal varieties grown: Cabernet Sauvignon, Shiraz, Cabernet Franc
Ha under vine: 10
Average annual crush: 100 tonnes
Hours open to public: 9am-5pm, daily
Points of interest: BBQ area, children's playground. Winery tours and winemaking talks
Retail distribution: Cellar Door and Mail Order. Estate Wine Distributors, NSW

Horseshoe Vineyard

This small vineyard, owned and operated by the Hordern family, was established in the late 1960's. However, it was not until 1987 that the first commercial Horseshoe wines were released on the market.

John Hordern is one of the few winemakers in the Upper Hunter who was raised in the region, developing his interest in wine from his father, who first planted the classic Hunter stalwarts semillon and shiraz on the family property.

John's philosophy that 'specialisation is one of the most important elements for success in the wine industry' has certainly proven very successful for Horseshoe. Aside from a swag of gold medals for their semillon and chardonnay, the 1987 Horseshoe Vineyard Chardonnay was selected by wine writer James Halliday as one of the top wines released in 1988. Small amounts of Horseshoe wines have been exported to the United Kingdom, USA and Japan. In 1993 the Horseshoe Vineyards 1991 Chardonnay Semillon was awarded the UK Critics

Choice for the best imported dry white wine. The Horseshoe wines are full flavoured with both elegance and complexity and will age gracefully with cellaring.

HORSESHOE VINEYARD	
Address: Horseshoe Road, Horseshoe Valley, Denman NSW 2328	
Direction: 16km south of Denman	
Phone: (02) 6547 3528	
Fax: (02) 6547 3542	
Established: 1969	
Owner: Anthony Hordern and Sons Pty Ltd	
Winemaker: John Hordern	
Principal varieties grown: Shiraz, Semillon, Chardonnay	
Ha under vine: 10	
Average no. cases produced: 3,000	
Principal wines & brands	**Cellar Potential**
Classic Hunter Semillon	10 years
Classic Hunter Chardonnay	5 years
Unwooded Semillon	10 years
Classic Hunter Shiraz	10 years
Cabernet Sauvignon	10 years
Public & trade tours: By appointment only	
Retail distribution: Fine Wine Specialist (02) 9365 4845 Sydney, Australia Boutique Wine (08) 8296 3228 Adelaide	

Reynolds Yarraman

Jon Reynolds is a consummate winemaker who has had long experience making wines for some of Australia's largest, most progressive and dynamic companies. Although originally from the Maitland area he began his winemaking career in South Australia, then a stint in Western Australia, where he oversaw a renaissance of the wines at the famous Houghton Winery. Jon then returned to the Hunter and became chief winemaker for the Wyndham Empire of Brian McGuigan. Jon and Jane were looking for their own domain. Good fortune smiled on them. They bought a property at Wybong on a sandstone ridge with majestic views over the valley and with the Yarraman

Range in the background. A beautiful old sandstone building that was part of the Bengala Homestead near Musswelbrook, built in 1837, was dismantled in the mid 1970ís and rebuilt at Yarraman. The winery is housed in the building and a cellar is dug into the hillside underneath, which gives ideal cool conditions. The massive ironbark beams came from the old Dalgety Woolstores at Darling Harbour, the rafters from the old Resch's Brewery, and the ceiling is old red cedar. Reynolds have created an extraordinary open plan house on the top floor.

Jon and Jane's wines are handcrafted masterpieces and now also include some from

the promising new Central NSW Highlands, district of 'Orange'. These and all the great Reynolds range can be enjoyed weekends in their open-air café "Limbo" which has a stunning view over their vine-covered valley.

REYNOLDS YARRAMAN	
Address: Yarraman Road, Wybong, Upper Hunter Valley NSW 2333	
Direction: 25km from either Denman or Muswellbrook Phone: (02) 6547 8127	
Fax: (02) 6547 8013	
WWW: http://www.winetitles.com.au/reynolds.html	
Established: 1967	
Owners: Jon and Jane Reynolds	
Winemaker: Jon Reynolds	
Principal varieties grown: semillon, chardonnay, merlot, shiraz	
Ha under vine: 19	
Average no. cases produced: 10,000	
Principal wines & brands	**Cellar Potential**
Semillon	15 years
Chardonnay	8 years
Shiraz	15 years
Cabernet Merlot (Hunter/Orange)	7 years
Chardonnay (Orange)	10 years
Cabernet Sauvignon (Orange)	15 years
Hours open to public: 10am-4pm, Mon-Sat; 11am-4pm Sunday and Public Holidays	
Points of interest: Café Limbo, on the verandah at the winery. Open 11am-3pm Sat-Mon and Public Holidays	
Retail distribution: Cellar door and the Top 500	
Club mailing list. Otherwise national distribution through Negociants Australia.	

Rosemount Estate

Rosemount Estate stands out as one of the great success stories of the modern Australian wine industry. During a recent visit to their head office in Sydney, I posed the question, "What does the Latin expression under your crest mean?" Founder Bob Oatley's son Ian replied, "We always land on our feet." Certainly the family was blessed by a great premonition when they chose these words.

Rosemount Estates has excelled in all areas. They have managed to select the best areas of the Upper Hunter for planting and obtain very good grape yields of exceptional quality.

Although John Ellis was young and without great experience when he was appointed as Rosemount's first winemaker, he proved himself more than capable and produced some white wines of extraordinary quality

at Roseglen on the banks of the Goulburn and planted fifteen hectares at the Edinglaissie homestead. With a greater amount of fruit each vintage and demand for its wines exceeding supply, the Rosemount winery was soon bursting its seams. In 1977, the Penfolds Wybong winery and vineyard were purchased and the pressure was alleviated. In 1983, Rosemount purchased a further 400 hectares at Mt. Danger,

which excited the wine drinking public and got Rosemount off to a flying start. His use of modern equipment and techniques saw these early rieslings, traminer and chardonnay capture instant market acclaim.

The vineyard began as a small and successful operation planted by Carl Brecht in the 1860's. It was bought by Bob Oatley in 1969 and a winery was built in 1975. The first wines were successful on the show circuit which generated great publicity for Rosemount, and in combination with a powerful advertising campaign brought the wines to both Australian and International wine drinkers.

Spurred on by this success, Rosemount expanded their home vineyard, planted vines

where now more than 100 hectares are under vine.

The prize purchase by Rosemount has proved to be their Roxburgh vineyard. Bought from Denman Estate as a small planting of chardonnay with some cabernet sauvignon, semillon and rhine riesling, the company have also added shiraz, pinot noir and sauvignon blanc. The wines produced from Roxburgh grapes all exhibit rich varietal fruit characters, and the chardonnay is fermented in wood and left to mature on its lees for three months.

The Roxburgh Chardonnay is the top of the company's range and is of the richest style of chardonnay produced in Australia. The wine has a full feel derived from a combination of glycerol compounds in the grapes, strong vanilla character and some tannin from the wood ageing and intense peach apricot flavours inherent in the Roxburgh fruit. The wine is not as soft as some people suggest, it does have quite high acid levels which help to balance its weight and flavour. It is an extraordinary wine.

Rosemount also produces other chardonnays. The Show Reserve has achieved world-wide acclaim as the best wine of its variety, both in price and quality. The Yellow Label Chardonnay is also of a similar rich style and as such is incredibly popular with wine drinkers.

Although John Ellis got the wines at Rosemount off to a flying start, Rosemount Wines however, really came of age under current winemaker Philip Shaw, who has made the wines at Rosemount for the last 16 vintages. Philip is definitely one of the three or four most gifted winemakers in Australia. After graduating from Roseworthy College, he spent two years working for Lindemans where he was in charge of developing their range of premium wines. He is a laconic character who takes his position very seriously.Philip also makes the wine from Rosemount's various vineyard interests in Victoria and Coonawarra as well as other NSW regions, a challenging job which he takes in his stride. He also has overall responsibility for the Ryecroft winery in McLaren Vale, now owned by Rosemount and producing a good deal of red wine for the Rosemount label as well as it's own full range of Ryecroft wines. The Rosemount Black Label Shiraz has been a huge success, several times being awarded the World's Best Shiraz accolade by the American Wine Spectator Magazine, beating wines at many times its modest price. Philip also consults for a Chinese wine venture and at Rosemount at vintage time there are often a few Chinese winemakers in the vintage team along with Californian and French winemakers.Over the last few years Rosemount have invested heavily in premium vineyards in both traditional and new cool climate Australian wine regions. At Mudgee they have now planted sixty hectares mainly to shiraz and cabernet sauvignon, whilst at Orange in the Central Highlands of NSW thirty hectares have gone in, chardonnay cabernet sauvignon, merlot and pinot noir being the varieties planted. In South Australia a massive vineyard of 300 hectares has been planted at Langhorne Creek to shiraz and cabernet sauvignon with a little chardonnay grenache, merlot and pitit verdot. Another vineyard has also been planted in the new exciting area of Kuitpo in the Southern Adelaide Hills, thirty-two hectares to the white varieties of sauvignon blanc and chardonnay. Rosemount has created a truly great international feel to its whole operation. The great success of Rosemount on the export market, particularly in the USA, has been hard won. Rosemount has taken tough and expensive individual initiatives that other wine exporters would do well to note, but in the long run, it is the consistently high quality of its whole wine range that has gained it fame and outstanding sales results. At Rosemount, they always land on their feet and keep running!

ROSEMOUNT ESTATE

Address: Rosemount Road, Denman NSW 2328
Phone: (02) 6549 6400
Fax: (02) 6549 6499
Email: rosemount@winery.com
WWW: http://www.winery.com
Established: 1969
Owner: Mr Robert Oatley
Winemaker: Philip Shaw
Principal varieties grown: Chardonnay, Semillon, Shiraz, Cabernet Sauvignon, Gewurztraminer, Pinot Noir, Merlot, Petite Verdot, Grenache, Mouverdre

Ha under vine: 700
Average no. cases produced: 700,000
Public & trade tours: By appointment only
Hours open to public: 10am-4pm, Mon-Sat; 10am-4pm, Sun (Summer); 12pm-4pm, Sun (Winter) (Closed Christmas Day & Easter Friday)
Points of interest: Rosemount Vineyard Brasseriese open Tuesday to Sunday lunches. Tuesday to Sunday for dinners.
Retail distribution: National Distribution

Serenella Estate

Serenella is an exciting wine venture of the Cecchini Family in the Upper Hunter. The property was established by Giancarlo Cecchini. I think these heartfelt notes from his daughter Tish say it all!! Serenella Estate 1993 Bin GCC Chardonnay is our most special wine, grown and bottled on this estate. Bin GCC is named after Giancarlo Cecchini. Giancarlo founded and established Serenella Estate, his dream come true. He purchased this remote acreage with his wife, Maria, in 1968. He worked the land from a bushy aspect to a fine pastoral property, at Baerami in the Uppermost Hunter Valley.

A highly regarded engineer, he ëretiredí in 1990 to finally realise his most special dream, to establish his own family winery, alongside his family. A winery which has become highly regarded within the wine industry as first rate in construction, technology, wine quality and integrity. He employed a little known winemaker as the Serenella winemaker and maintained his faith in the ability and potential of this unknown quantity, much to the surprise of some more established industry people. His confidence in this winemaker never flinched. This winemaker is his daughter, Letitia (Tish).

Giancarlo died suddenly and quietly at Serenella Winery early on a Tuesday morning, 23 March, 1993. He worked full-time and over-time during vintage, he operated the crane, did varied cellar work, helped run cellar door wine-tastings and most importantly, put his winemaker constantly in her place! Some of his old workmates came along to lend a hand at vintage; he left them

with many wonderful and amusing memories.

Tish's reputation as a winemaker and the quality of her wines are growing with each vintage and the new labels certainly reflect this.

SERENELLA ESTATE	
Address: 951 Rylstone Road, Baerami NSW 2333	
Direction: 20kms NW of Denman	
Phone: (02) 6547 5168	
Fax: (02) 6547 5164	
Established: 1989	
Owner: Cecchini Family	
Winemaker: Letitia "Tish" Cecchini	
Principal varieties grown: Cabernet Sauvignon, Shiraz, Chardonnay, Merlot, Sylvaner, Pinot Noir	
Ha under vine: 35	
Average no. cases produced: 5,000	
Principal wines & brands	**Cellar Potential**
Shiraz	10+ years
Chardonnay	8+ years
Semillon	8+ years
White Hunter	5+ years
Public & trade tours: By appointment only	
Hours open to public: 10am-4pm, Weekends and Public Holidays	
Points of interest: BBQ facilities, lunches and functions can be organised with bookings only	
Retail distribution: Serenella Pastoral Co. Pty Ltd - Sydney & Queensland	

Simon Gilbert

Simon Gilbert, a fifth generation winemaker, was christened in the Chapel at the Pewsey Vale Vineyard in the Barossa Ranges. His great-great-grandfather Joseph Gilbert, a well respected Adelaide identity, first planted this vineyard in the 1840's.

Joseph also established other vineyards, the grapes of which were sold to Leo Buring until 1950. Ironically, it was there that Simon began his first hands-on winemaking experience during his studies in winemaking at Roseworthy Agricultural College, from which he graduated in 1977.

Subsequently he worked for the Lindemans Group at Karadoc, the Barossa, the Hunter and Coonawarra. In 1985 he became Chief Winemaker at Arrowfield in the Hunter. In January 1994, Simon established his own company, Simon Gilbert Wine Services Pty Ltd (SGWS).

Since then, SGWS has grown significantly, now processing in excess of 1500 tonnes and located in the former Hunter Valley Dairy Coop building on the outskirts of Muswellbrook.

SGWS is a custom winemaker and consultant to the wine industry and has become recognised as a personalised producer of the highest quality premium wines, after just three years of operation. SGWS is managed by an experienced professional management and winemaking team and employs current best practice technologies.

On behalf of itsí clients, SGWS has produced tailor-made wines which have received eight trophies and over 300 medals at National and International Wine Shows. SGWS client-base regions include: The Hunter Valley, Southern Queensland, Cowra, Orange and Mudgee.

While Simon has plans to develop his own label in the distant future, the core business of custom winemaking and consultancy will remain unchanged.

An introduction to Mudgee

all the other wineries are small individual boutiques.

The sense of the 1960's and '70's wine renaissance is still strong in Mudgee. Many locals are pioneering organic grape-growing and winemaking, learning every day the wonderful balance in nature. I am sure this work will reap its rewards as our world becomes ever more conscious of our fragile, precious environment, our own health and the health of future generations.

Mudgee grapes are much sought-after due to their rich flavours. Although on the same latitude as the Hunter Valley, vintage in Mudgee is almost a month later. The district is 500-1,000 metres above sea level and therefore has some cold nights from spring through to early summer while the vines are flowering. This extends the growing season and, in combination with the warm climate

Like the Barossa Valley in South Australia, the viticultural roots of the Mudgee area were planted by German immigrants. In the case of Mudgee, the Germans were invited to Australia by William Macarthur to tend his vineyard at Camden, now part of outer Sydney.

Vines were first planted at Mudgee by one of these 'vine dressers', Adam Roth, who was given a grant of 37 hectares in 1858. Although gold was discovered in the area in 1872, Roth was not tempted to change his interests. By 1880, six out of the thirteen wineries in the area were operated by Roth and his sons.

Andreas Kurtz, another of the German immigrants, planted the second vineyard in the area. The largest vineyard of 80 hectares was planted by Fredrich Bucholz, and later bought by the Roth family. The Australian Surgeon General of the time, Thomas Fiaschi, purchased the Augusine Vineyard from the Roth Family in 1917. By 1930, Jack Roth had bought out his brother at Rothview, the original winery, and was the only surviving winemaker in the area, although several growers remained. He also consolidated winemaking at the Craigmoor winery and there made a dry white wine containing a nameless grape variety. The wine fared very well. The same nameless variety was planted by a descendant of Andreas Kurtz, with great success. Eventually, it was identified by a French viticulturist as a chardonnay, one of the best

disease-free clones he had seen. In this way, Mudgee became the first wine-growing area in Australia to grow chardonnay, and other areas used this stock to start their own chardonnay vineyards.

Two more wineries were established in Mudgee in 1969, the Botobolar Winery by Gil Wahlquist and Huntington Estate by Bob Roberts. The 1970's saw a number of new wineries open, including Mirimar and Pieter Van Gent. There are now over 20 wineries in the region; outside of the large Montrose and Craigmoor operations and the impressive new Winery Estate of Andrew Harris,

and rich soil, the grapes have a long ripening period. As a result, local table wines average 13, 14 and even 15 percent alcohol. The well-made wines of the area, particularly the whites, exhibit well-defined varietal flavours. It was the first region in Australia to introduce a wine appellation scheme. This occurred in 1979, and all wines are guaranteed free of defects and of 100 percent Mudgee fruit.

Mudgee is undergoing a large vineyard expansion. Rosemount are currently planting 60 hectares and Asian interests many hundreds of hectares more.

Mudgee

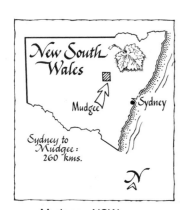

New South Wales

Mudgee ● Sydney

Sydney to Mudgee: 260 kms.

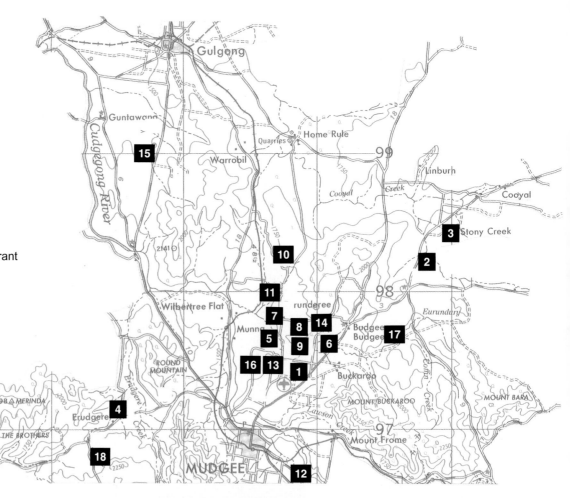

Mudgee - NSW

1. Augustine Vineyard & Restaurant
2. Botobolar Vineyard
3. Britten's Vineyard
4. Burnbrae Wines
5. Craigmoor Winery
6. Huntington Estate
7. Knight's Vines
8. Lawson Hill Estate
9. Mansfield Wines
10. Miramar Wines
11. Montrose Wines
12. Mount Vincent Mead & Wines
13. Mudgee Wines
14. Pieter Van Gent Winery
15. Platt's Winery
16. Seldom Seen Vineyard
17. Stein's Wines
18. Thistle Hill Vineyard

MIRAMAR

1995

Shiraz

MUDGEE

MIRAMAR WINES
Henry Lawson Drive, Eurunderee
Mudgee, 2850 Australia

14.0% by Volume

Product of Australia

750mL

The wine growing area of Mudgee is located high on the slopes of the Australia Great Dividing Range in New South Wales Central Tablelands. The wines of the district are known for their fullness and depth of flavour.
Made from Shiraz grapes grown at Andreas Estate and from our own vineyards, this full bodied wine has a rich chocolaty aroma and a soft tannin finish. It may be enjoyed as a young wine but will repay further cellaring.

Preservative (222) Added Approx. 8.3 STD Drinks

Ian MacRae, R.D. Oen

NON OAKED

PIETER VAN GENT

Chardonnay 1996

MUDGEE CHARDONNAY 1996

Made from Australia's oldest Chardonnay rootstock. With a bouquet full of ripe passionfruit and splashes of lime, this 100% Chardonnay had no need for oak maturation. On the palate it is full with a crisp dry finish. An ideal wine with light meats, seafood and vegetables. Enjoy now or cellar for 2 to 5 years.

GROWN AND MADE AT PIETER VAN GENT WINERY MUDGEE NSW 2850

750 mL PRODUCT OF AUSTRALIA

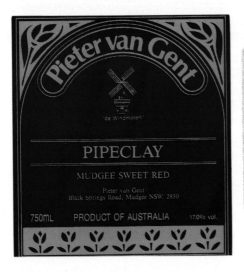

Pieter van Gent

"de Windmolen"

PIPECLAY

MUDGEE SWEET RED

Pieter van Gent
Black Springs Road, Mudgee NSW 2850

750ML   PRODUCT OF AUSTRALIA   17.0% vol.

MONTROSE

Mudgee

CABERNET SAUVIGNON

1995

PRODUCE OF AUSTRALIA
750ml

MONTROSE

POET'S CORNER

SEMILLON SAUVIGNON BLANC CHARDONNAY

1996

750 mL

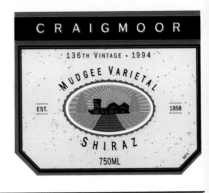

ENCORE

GROWN & BOTTLED AT MIRAMAR WINES MUDGEE. PRODUCT OF AUSTRALIA.
Miramar Wines, Henry Lawson Drive, Eurunderee, Mudgee NSW Australia 2850

CRAIGMOOR

136TH VINTAGE • 1994

MUDGEE VARIETAL

EST.   1858

SHIRAZ

750ML

Craigmoor

Craigmoor is the oldest established winery in Mudgee and planted its first vineyards over 135 years ago, by the then owners, the Roth Family who ran the winery for 100 years.

From these historic origins Craigmoor is also known as the birthplace of chardonnay in Australia as it was Jack Roth who planted cuttings of a particularly fine clone of chardonnay given to him indirectly from either William Busby or William Macarthur. This small planting was to become the sourceblock for much of Australia's chardonnay. Craigmoor released a chardonnay from the 1971 vintage making it a pioneer of the variety in Australia. This great wine is still the flagship of the Craigmoor range.

Orlando Wyndham took over the Craigmoor Winery in late 1989 early 1990, happily supporting capital and quality investments in both the vineyards and the winery and producing fantastic varietal wines under chief winemaker Robert Paul, who maintains their traditional full-bodied style.

The facilities for visitors are first class with a rustic ambience including an excellent restaurant, banquet hall, new tasting area, museum containing old winemaking and viticultural equipment, a picnic area and even a cricket pitch.

Craigmoor has a delightful unspoiled historic Australiana feel about it, with sweeping lawns and a picnic area going down to the creek in front of the winery and the ranges in the distance.

CRAIGMOOR WINES
Address: Craigmoor Road, Mudgee NSW 2850
Phone: (02) 6372 2208
Fax: (02) 6372 4464
Established: 1858
Owner: Orlando Wyndham Group Pty Ltd
Winemaker: Robert Paul Principal varieties grown: Chardonnay, Cabernet Sauvignon, Shiraz, Semillon, Merlot, Pinot Noir, Sauvignon Blanc
Principal wines & brands   Cellar Potential
Craigmoor Mudgee Chardonnay
Craigmoor Mudgee Cabernet Sauvignon
Craigmoor Mudgee Shraz
Craigmoor Sparkling Chardonnay Vintage Brut
Craigmoor Rummy Port
Public & trade tours: By appointment only
Hours open to public: 10am-4pm, daily
Points of interest: Unique restaurant and cellar door, cricket pitch/oval, BBQ and picnic area
Retail distribution: National

Montrose

The Montrose Winery, overlooking the picturesque Cudgegong Valley is situated in an area that has long been a source of inspiration.

The beautiful setting inspired Aboriginals to name it Mudgee, "nest in the hills".

It is a region that inspired the poet Henry Lawson. Today it has also inspired a range of premium Montrose table wines. The winery was established in 1974 and upgraded in 1989 to incorporate the latest technology in winemaking practices.

At Montrose, under the guidance of the extremely talented wine craftsman, Robert Paul, the philosophy is to produce wines with well-defined varietal characters and freshness of fruit. The wines are subtle and show finesse, exhibiting elegance and restraint, especially when young. The emphasis is on fruit flavour but superbly complemented by high quality oak treatment and varietal integrity.

Australia's greatest "poet of the bush", Henry Lawson spent much of his life near the site of Montrose winery. Local mythology tells how the tranquil beauty of the landscape here inspired some of his greatest works. The popular Poet's Corner wines were named in his honour.

These wines have carved out a nice niche in the value for money premium market. The cellar door at Montrose is extensive and often features wines from older vintages. The winery exudes an atmosphere of quiet strength and stability and this must reflect the confidence the management places in their recent releases and successes. The facilities have been greatly expanded in recent years with an even greater emphasis on technology to produce the best possible wines.

MONTROSE
Address: Henry Lawson Drive, Mudgee NSW 2850
Phone: (02) 6373 3853
Fax: (02) 6373 3795
Established: 1974
Owner: Orlando Wyndham Group Pty Ltd
Winemaker: Robert Paul
Principal varieties grown: Chardonnay, Cabernet Sauvignon, Shiraz, Semillon, Sauvignon Blanc, Cabernet Franc, Merlot
Principal wines & brands   Cellar Potential
Poet's Corner Semillon Chardonnay Sauvignon Blanc
Poet's Corner Cabernet Sauvignon Cabernet Franc
Montrose Mudgee Cabernet Sauvignon
Montrose Mudgee Black Shiraz
Montrose Mudgee Chardonnay
Public & trade tours: By appointment only
Hours open to public: 10am-4.30pm, daily
Points of interest: Large winery and cellar door. BBQ and picnic grounds

Miramar

I an McRae is a talented and resourceful individual in control of all the operations of his Estate in the rolling hills north of the township of Mudgee. Being at an altitude of 570 metres he enjoys a unique microclimate with vintage often several weeks behind some of the region. The deep red soils at Miramar also adds character to the wines which can be very full-bodied but with elegance and balance.

Ian, an honors graduate from Roseworthy, worked for giants of the industry Penfolds and Hardys before branching out into a winery design consultancy, designing a number of well-known wineries.

In 1975 Ian arrived in Mudgee as winemaker for Montrose. He began establishing Miramar making his first vintage there in 1977. He has won numerous National and International awards over the years and has a large range of wines providing a great cellar door tasting area in his rustically charming cellars adjoining his home.

Happily on my last visit we arrived to a newly sealed bitumen driveway laid that very day. Well done Ian.

MIRAMAR

Address: Henry Lawson Drive, Mudgee NSW 2850
Phone: (02) 6373 3874
Fax: (02) 6373 3854
Established: 1977
Winemaker: Ian Macrae
Principal varieties grown: Chardonnay, Semillon, Sauvignon Blanc, Riesling, Shiraz, Pinot Noir, Cabernet Sauvignon
Ha under vine: 25
Average annual crush: 150 tonnes
Average no. cases produced: 8,000
Principal wines & brands   Cellar Potential

Chardonnay	10 years
Semillon	10 years
Fumé Blanc	5 years
Sauvignon Blanc	5 years
Riesling	15 years
Cabernet Sauvignon	10 years
Shiraz	10 years
Encore (Sparkling)	5 years
Rosé	2 years
Poux Blanc (Botrytis)	10 years

Public & trade tours: Trade Tours
Hours open to public: 9am-5pm, daily
Retail distribution: Limited Distribution

Pieter Van Gent

P ieter Van Gent is one of the strong characters of the Mudgee region. He arrived in the area in 1970 to work for Craigmoor Wines, after previously spending eleven years at Penfolds working with champagne and fortified wines.

Fortified wines are a favourite of Pieter's and he is the only winemaker in Mudgee to make them consistently. His Pipeclay Port is a rich, unique style with intense flavours and a smooth quality. It is a hit with visitors to the winery.

The winery is charming with wide verandahs, wooden vats and casks and a warm friendly atmosphere. There is an earthen floor and the furnishings include pews from an old church. Pieter was one of the first chardonnay makers in Australia, producing award winners for Craigmoor. He now makes his own, the best known wine being Mudgee White Port along with a range of

unusual wine varieties. Pieter has just expanded his production and cellar door sales areas in the same characterful style. Pieter Van Gent and his family are delightful hosts. Their approach to winemaking and visitors is a sincere, honest and no-fuss one, which makes you feel right at home. Pieter has many fans in his own Dutch homeland and some of his wines find its way there too.

PIETER VAN GENT WINERY & VINEYARD

Address: 141 Black Springs Road, Mudgee NSW 2850
Phone: (02) 6373 3807
Fax: (02) 6373 3910
Established: 1979
Winemaker: Pieter van Gent
Principal varieties grown: Cabernet Sauvignon, Shiraz, Chardonnay, Müller Thurgau, Semillon, Verdelho, Muscat á petits grains
Ha under vine: 12
Average annual crush: 150 tonnes
Average no. cases produced: 9,000
Hours open to public: 9am-5pm, Mon-Sat; 11am-4pm Sun
Points of interest: 20 x 1000 gallon oval shaped wine casks and 100 year old choir stalls from the Nun's Chancel at Singleton. Lots of atmosphere.
Retail distribution: Arquilla, Leichhardt NSW; Coastal Wine and Spirit Merchants, Kunda Park QLD

Rosemount

Rosemount have always been the innovative individual company self-motivated and self-assured on the leading edge of Australian Wine. They have put a tremendous effort into marketing and promoting premium Australian wines overseas together with the fact that they have been extremely successful in the 28 years or so of their existence are self-evident. The Rosemount policy over the last few years has been to expand their vineyard holdings into the leading Australian Wine region. This they have accomplished with gusto. Firstly, Coonawarra followed by vineyards and a winery in McLaren Vale. Now Mudgee has joined the push and 60 hectares have been planted to shiraz cabernet sauvignon, chardonnay and pinot noir. The property is on rich red soils on a westerly sloping site almost opposite Montrose. The 1998 vintage should see a small crop with the vineyard coming on stream in 1999. As ever the family crests motto the Latin version of "we always land on our feet"seems sure to echo loudly through this well thought out venture.

Andrew Harris Vineyards

Andrew Harris has performed in an impressive way, rising with great vision from small beginnings in 1991 to a massive vineyard and new multi-million dollar winery that saw its first vintage in 1997.
Andrew's family had been in cotton and soyabeans in a substantial way. During the late 1980's two significant things happened for Andrew. He met his bride to be at the Lightening Ridge Races and embarked on a vinous path purchasing a 730 acre sheep station south of Mudgee on rich clays over limestone and with plentiful water from the Cudgegong River. It seemed ideal.
I well remember visiting the property in 1995, its splendid vineyards and majestic views were inspiring and a complete surprise as we arrived in Mudgee at sunset. 1994 was the first vintage and Simon Gilbert then continued through until 1996 producing the wines at his own winery facility and then in 1997 at the new Andrew Harris winery.

As a trial 14 entries were exhibited in wine shows from the 1994 vintage, 11 medals and a trophy the result. This outstanding result has even been eclipsed by the 1995 vintage. The 1995 Andrew Harris Shiraz-Cabernet Sauvignon took all before it at the 1997 Royal Sydney Easter Show. The Rudy Kornon Memorial Trophy for the best medium bodied red wine of the show and the Leslie Kemeny Memorial Trophy for the best 1995 red table wine of the show. The Andrew Harris label, a painting of Andrew surveying his Estate and new plantings from high on the hill where his winery now stands surrounded by vines, captures well his vision.

An introduction to Riverina

Centred on the thriving towns of Griffith and Leeton in the Murrumbidgee Irrigation Area, the Riverina is the largest winemaking region in NSW and one of the largest in Australia. With more than 100,000 tonnes of grapes produced by 500 growers in a normal year, the region has the highest proportion of premium varietal fruit of any of the major inland grapegrowing regions.

Semillon and shiraz are widely planted as well as large plantings of chardonnay, cabernet sauvignon, sauvignon blanc, while newer varieties such as merlot, marsanne and verdelho represent an increasing proportion of the Riverina's varietal portfolio.

was dominated by McWilliam's and Penfolds, the Riverina is the home of many of Australia's larger remaining family wine companies including De Bortoli, Miranda, Rossetto and Toorak, with the growing enterprises of Riverina Wines, Cranswick Estate and the new enterprise of Casella. While in the past much of the wine produced was bulk white and red destined for the cask market, increased interest in Australian wine overseas over the past decade now sees much of the region's wine exported. Improved viticultural and winemaking techniques have seen the overall quality of bottled varietal wine improve dramatically, with the region's semillon –

at Hanwood and still bear fruit!), the area now produces almost every style of wine from the more than forty grape varieties. Following the First World War, the area became the new home for returned soldiers, followed in the 1920ís by many Italian immigrants who contributed greatly to the wine industry's development. The Riverina's cultural heritage is still prominent today.

The area is probably the most efficient wine producer in Australia, with its large yields approaching an average of twenty tonnes of grapes per hectare. The area pioneered the use of mechanical harvesting which enables picking of fruit at optimum ripeness and in

Being as efficient, low cost producer, the Riverina's grapes are now keenly sought for Australiaís burgeoning export market, and in the past five years there has been considerable investment in new broad acre viticulture on the adjacent rice farms.

There are a dozen wineries in the region ranging from the large scale of De Bortoli and McWilliam's to the boutique wineries such as Lillypilly in Leeton and West end Wines in Griffith. While in the past the area

chardonnay blends prominent.

By far the region's star is the botrytised semillons that have swept the world by storm taking award after award in International contests. Pioneered by the De Bortoli Family with the 1982 vintage, there are now more than a dozen different botrytised wines produced locally.

Founded in 1912 when John James McWilliam planted his first vines in Hanwood (some of these have been retained

the cool of the night, thus enhancing wine quality. The Riverina was also in the forefront of the development of mechanical pruning. A sense of purpose and a desire to meet the challenges of modern viticulture and winemaking pervades the Riverina – it's an exciting, positive feeling.

For further information on the Riverina write to the Winemakers of the Riverina Promotions Committee, PO Box 2401, Griffith 2680.

Riverina

Riverina - NSW

1. Casella Wines
2. Cranswick Estate
3. De Bortoli Wines
4. Lillypilly Estate
5. Mcwilliams Hanwood Winery
6. Mcwilliams Yenda Winery
7. Miranda Wines
8. Riverina Wines
9. Rossetto's Wines
10. Toorak Wines
11. West End Wines
12. Wilton Estate

New South Wales

Riverina

Sydney

Sydney to Riverina: 600 kms.

Casella Wines

John Casella's parents arrived as Italian immigrants in the 1950's, settling on a small fruit block near Yenda in the Riverina. The Casella's didn't take long to set up a small winery on their vineyard to make the traditional family wine each year. Gradually many of the family friends started to come by to replenish their wine cellars. The family grape and fruit growing business remained the main focus.

Then son John became a trained winemaker and for many years was in charge of the winemaking at the giant Riverina Wine Company, the other side of Griffith. Things began to change rapidly in 1994, when John commissioned a huge modern building to house a large winemaking operation. As the 1995 vintage started, work on the building and the winemaking centre was still in frantic progress. The massive stainless steel tanks holding hundreds of thousands of litres of wine were soon full and John breathed a sigh of relief knowing his dream and vision were fast becoming a reality. The subsequent 1996 and 1997 vintages have been a great success and the winery has tripled in size during this time. Tucked away in the corner of the old family shed is the first fermenting tank of his fathers, proudly shown to us by John.

The Casella wine label has just been released and the wines shape up superbly.

Wine exports of Casella have become a mainstay of the business. Enthusiastic and talented winemaker Alan Johnson works in tandem with John to handle an extremely big crush with very few hands around the cellars.

John Casella well represents the new entrepreneurial wave of young winemakers Australia really needs to satisfy the world-wide thirst for new world wines.

CASELLA WINES

Address: Farm 1471, Wakely Road, Yenda NSW 2681
Phone: (02) 6968 1346
Fax: (02) 6968 1196
Established: 1969
Winemaker: Alan Kennett
Principal varieties grown: Chardonnay, Semillon, Marsanne, Verdelho, Shiraz, Cabernet Sauvignon, Merlot
Ha under vine: 220

Average annual crush: 8,000 tonnes
Average no. cases produced: 600,000

Principal wines & brands	Cellar Potential
Carramar Estate Semillon Sauvignon Blanc	Now
Carramar Estate Shiraz Cabernet	Now
Carramar Estate Chardonnay	3-5 years
Carramar Estate Cabernet Sauvignon	3-5 years
Carramar Estate Shiraz	3-5 years

Public & trade tours: By appointment only
Hours open to public: Not open currently

The Cranswick Estate

Riverina) near Scenic Hill. The property has been named Cocoparra, Aboriginal for Kookaburra. This massive investment on this vineyard of perfect soils and good well-drained slopes and drip irrigation, also a rarity in the Riverina, has already shown great results. Expansion at the winery has seen the ability to give the reds long fermentation, adding to body, flavour and quality.

Cranswick Estate's Managing Director, Graham Smith is also a keen private pilot, a suitable pastime for his high flying style of taking Cranswick Estate to the top. The company also supports local strongly.

In June 1996 at 'Wine Australia', after their export success, Cranswick Estate launched their Australian range of wines. Already the wines have enjoyed incredible success on the show circuit.

The 1996 Semillon won the top gold in that year's Melbourne Wine Show, the 1995 Shiraz was judged one of N.S.W.ís top four red wines at the 1996 N.S.W. Wine Industry Awards and a very highly commended (equivalent to a gold medal) at the 1996 Hobart Wine Show. The 1996 Chardonnay also scored a highly commended award in the same show. The Autumn Gold continues its success with 2 trophies and 4 gold medals during 1996. Qantas have served the last two vintages in their first class cabin.

One of Australia's most progressive and successful wine companies is the Cranswick Estate. They are in the top ten in size, being Australia's seventh largest wine exporter.

The Cranswick Estate is a totally professional operation - its history dates back to 1931 when the Cinzano Family of Italian Vermouth fame began winemaking in Australia. In 1974, they built one of Australia's most modern and best-equipped wineries and began making table wines under contract, as well as their own Vermouths. In 1991 the management team, led by dynamic Managing Director Graham Cranswick Smith, bought out the business. Their immediate focus was on fine-tuning the winemaking and establishing exciting brands to attack the premium bottled wine export market.

Their success speaks volumes for their courage and foresight. One might also say "well done Ken Done" - his uniquely Australian Barramundi design wine labels have flooded the export market. In six short years, sales overseas have rocketed from nothing to a substantial volume.

Barramundi has a distinct Australian feel with its design, and carries graphically the message 'Australian wine - sunshine in the bottle'.

Cranswick also has a more traditional range of varietal wines under the Cranswick Estate label. The 1993 Botrytis Semillon has carried all before it on the wine show scene ñ 'Autumn Gold'.

Cranswick grower Pat Zirilli worked hand in hand with winemaking team to get his botrytised (noble rot) grapes to perfect condition, a risky business in which he could have lost everything, but this sense of trust and teamwork typifies the Cranswick operation. In 1993, Cranswick spent $2 million on a 400 hectare property on the slopes (a rarity in the

---

CRANSWICK ESTATE

Address: Walla Avenue, Griffith NSW 2680
Direction: South West of City Centre
Phone: (02) 6962 4133
Fax: (02) 6962 2888
Email: info@cranswick.com.au
WWW: http://www.cranswick.com.au
Established: 1931
Owner: Graham Cranswick Smith
Winemaker: Ian Hongell
Principal varieties grown: Chardonnay, Shiraz, Merlot, Cabernet Sauvignon, Marsanne
Ha under vine: 150
Average annual crush: 12,000 tonnes
Average no. cases produced: 550,000

Principal wines & brands   Cellar Potential
The Cranswick Estate Unoaked Chardonnay 5 years

The Cranswick Estate Barrel Fermented Semillon 8-10 years
The Cranswick Estate Semillon 5 years
The Cranswick Estate Pinot Chardonnay up to 10 years
The Cranswick Estate Young Vine Chardonnay 6 years
The Cranswick Estate Conlon Block Marsanne 6 years
The Cranswick Estate Cabernet Merlot 7 years
The Cranswick Estate Shiraz   10 years
"Autumn Gold" Botrytis Semillon 10 years

Public & trade tours: Public tours- 10am Mondays (except Public Holidays)
Hours open to public: 10am-4pm, daily
Retail distribution: Retail outlets through Australia

De Bortoli Wines

Victorio De Bortoli arrived in Australia in 1924 and began working at Beelbangera Winery. In 1927 he purchased land, now the site of his winery. His son Deen joined him in the 1950's and has since taken over the management of the company. Deen expanded the winery, increasing its capacity, and developed a bulk sparkling wine system. This system produced the De Bortoli 'Vittorio Spumante' which was an instant success in the market place. 1982 saw the third generation of the De Bortoli family take their place in the company ranks, as Deen's son Darren graduated from Roseworthy College in South Australia.

Darren made his mark on the industry quickly experimenting with semillon grapes which had been left on the vines until two months after vintage and were heavily infected with mould. Unsure as to whether the grapes contained the 'noble rot' (botrytis cinerea) he had to make the wine before he could be sure. The result has passed into Australian wine history. The 1982 De Bortoli Semillon Sauterne has won more gold medals within a relatively short period of time than any other Australian wine, and is sold world wide. The family has also been successful with a bottle-fermented sparkling wine, using mainly chardonnay grapes.

Today the giant winery at Bilbul has a storage capacity of over 30 million litres, producing the equivalent of three million cases of wine annually. More than 100 people are now employed in production, marketing and distribution through branches in Sydney, Melbourne and Brisbane and Darren De Bortoli is in charge of a team of five winemakers. Because of the large varietal mix and the long growing season, the vintage lasts from early February to late May with the picking of the botrytised grapes for the now legendary 'Noble One' Botrytis Semillon.

In 1987 the De Bortoli's purchased Miller's Chateau Yarrinya in the Yarra Valley of Victoria. This adventurous move has been totally successful and the Yarra operation (which is covered in the relevant chapter of this book) makes its own range of wines and has an award winning restaurant and hospitality complex on site. The *'Montage'* label is a blended series of Southern Victorian and Yarra Valley wine. The *'Sacred Hill'* value for money range from the Bilbul winery is of outstanding quality and like everything the De Bortoli's do, reflects great credit on family and the Australian Wine Industry.

DE BORTOLI WINES PTY LTD
Address:
De Bortoli Road, Bilbul NSW 2680
Phone:
(02) 6964 9444
Fax:
(02) 6964 9400
Established: 1928
Winemaker:
Darren De Bortoli
Principal varieties grown:
Shiraz, Cabernet Sauvignon, Pinot Noir, Semillon, Chardonnay, Traminer, Riesling, Colombard, Trebbiano, Sauvignon Blanc
Ha under vine: 200
Average annual crush: 40,000 tonnes

Principal wines & brands	Cellar Potential
Noble One	10+ years
Rare Botrytis	10+ yrs
Deen De Bortoli Vat Range	2-5 years
Willowglen Range	2-3 years
Montage Range	2-3 years
Premium Fortified Wine	
Emeri - Premium Sparkling Pinot Noir Brut	
Sacred Hill	2-3 years

Public & trade tours:
By appointment only
Hours open to public:
9am-5.30pm, Mon-Sat; 9am-4pm Sun
Retail distribution:
Available through most fine wine

McWilliams Hanwood Winery

In 1912, shortly after completion of the Murrumbidgee Irrigation Scheme, J.J. McWilliam arrived with his bullock wagon loaded down with 40,000 cuttings from the family's vineyard at "Markview", near Junee, and planted the area's first vines. The Hanwood winery was built in 1917 and is the centre of McWilliam's operations in the Riverina. They also have a large winery at Yenda.

The Hanwood winery is enormous and its entrance is modelled to appear like a huge barrel. This is the tasting and visitors' entertainment area. Alongside the barrel is a giant bottle on its side, of about 25 metres in length. This houses a museum, which details the history of McWilliam's. The

winery itself produces mainly white and red varietal table wines but is also the wood maturation centre for McWilliam's range of sherries and ports.

Perhaps the best known of these is 10 year old Hanwood Port, one of Australia's most popular and finest tawny ports – a wine that still contains a drop of the original blend of 1926. McWilliam's also make an excellent vintage port at Hanwood. Total storage capacity at Hanwood is a massive 22 million litres, about seven per cent of the Australia's annual wine consumption.

The genius behind this modern set up was Glenn McWilliam who foresaw the swing in popularity away from fortified to table wines, and changed the emphasis in production at McWilliam's accordingly. He was also responsible for building the Robinvale Winery on the Murray River in Victoria in 1961. Glenn McWilliam refurbished and expanded the local McWilliam's wineries with equipment of his own design in the 1950's and my family had many dealings with him. After graduating from an engineering course at Adelaide University in 1948, my father went to work for Glenn at Hanwood, where he picked up valuable information and experience. This was later

utilised when he designed all of Hardy's new winery equipment and additions, over the next few decades.

Glenn's contribution to McWilliam's Wines and the Australian wine industry cannot be underestimated, he was a typical member of an extraordinary family who are not surprisingly well into their second century of winemaking. McWilliam's was one of the first wine companies in the Riverina and Australia, for that matter, to market varietal table wines some 30 years ago. The focus today is on vibrant wines with young fresh obvious varietal character. The Hanwood Range - a chardonnay, semillon/chardonnay shiraz and cabernet sauvignon, have been redressed in a distinctively Australian style with labels featuring Aboriginal dot art from the artists living on the Napperey Station, 200 kms north-west of Alice Springs. These wines at great value prices have already gained a good slice of the export market. Production director in charge of all of McWilliam's wineries is Doug McWilliam, a graduate from the famous Davis University's oenology course in California. Day to day management of the Hanwood Winery itself is in the very capable hands of his cousin, the genial, Brian McWilliam.

McWILLIAMS HANWOOD
Address: Jack McWilliams Road, Hanwood NSW 2680
Phone: (02) 6963 0001
Fax: (02) 6963 0002
Email: mcwines@mcwilliams.com.au
Established: 1913
Winemakers: Simon Crook and Russell Cody
Principal varieties grown: Chardonnay, Merlot, Cabernet Sauvignon, Shiraz, Sauvignon Blanc, Pinot Noir, Riesling, Semillon, Malbec, Gewurztraminer, White Frontignac, Muscadelle, Touriga, Red Frontignac
Ha under vine: 225
Average annual crush: over 10,000 tonnes
Public & trade tours: By appointment only
Hours open to public: 9am-5pm Mon-Sat
Points of interest: Tours of approximately 1.5 hours through the winery, vineyards and wine museum ending in Hanwood barrel antique bottle collection and winemaking memorabilia. Free BBQ facilities to seat 60 people

This impressive Riverina winery is the head office for Miranda Wines. It is at this winery where Sam, Jim and Lou Miranda as the sons of the founder Frank Miranda gather as the Board of Directors.

The winery boasts over 200 stainless tanks and 4,000 French and American oak barrels with the total storage capacity being over 24 million litres.

The modern state-of-the-art administration area houses the sales operations as well as a large cellar door sales complex.

At present the cellar door is being expanded into a hospitality centre. This transformation will encompass the beautification of the existing building and grounds. Miranda Wines premium image will be intensified as all visitors to the hospitality centre will be welcomed into the elegantly designed tourist information bureau, a show case for all Miranda world class wines.

The brothers, with their comprehensive knowledge of the wine industry, have had the foresight to expand their premium areas to include the Barossa Valley of South Australia and the King Valley of Victoria, where they have wineries.

Miranda Wines has not only forged a reputation for being a progressive family owned company but also as a producer of nationally and internationally recognised wines. This was never more true when Miranda Wines received the Mission Hill Trophy for the Best Chardonnay Worldwide at the 1996 London Wine and Spirit competition.

So with such accolades and no doubt more to follow Frank Miranda can be justly proud of his family's achievements.

MIRANDA WINES
Address: 57 Jondaryan Avenue, Griffith NSW 2680
Phone: (02) 6962 4033
Fax: (02) 6962 6944
Established: 1939
Winemakers: Doug Wilson, Luis Simian
Average annual crush: 28,000 tonnes
Average no. cases produced: 2,000,000

Principal wines & brands	Cellar Potential
Miranda Show Reserve	5-15 years
Rovalley Ridge Grey Series	5-15 years
Miranda Estate	5-15 years
High Country	2-10 years
Mirrool Creek	2-5 years
Somerton	2-5 years
Christy's Land	

Public & trade tours: Yes
Hours open to public: Daily
Points of interest: Tours are conducted every Wednesday at 2.15pm. Coach tours by prior appointment only.
Retail distribution: National and international distribution

Frank Miranda came to Australia with his new bride Caterina in 1938 to start a new life. A professor of languages in his homeland, he and Caterina bought a half share in a general store in Kooyoo Street, Griffith. Frank was interned during World War II at the Loveday Camp, Barmera, but not before making his first vintage, three tonnes of grapes crushed with his bare feet in the old Italian tradition

Frank's winemaking career took an unusual turn at the prison camp in Katherine, an unlikely a place to make wine as you could imagine, but not for the innovative Frank. From dried sultanas, re-hydrated and many winemaking books in his hand he became a very popular individual indeed.

Two years after his release in 1944, he began building a winery and in the early 50's employed his first winemaker, the equally innovative Ron Potter.

Frank was totally devoted to his family and friends and in his life expanded Miranda with the help of his three sons and their families, to be one of the largest privately owned wine companies in Australia.

The hospitality flows freely at Miranda and the generously flavoured wines follow this theme.

Lillypilly Estate Wines

Post war immigrant to Australia Pasquale Fiumara brought to his new homeland the expertise of thousands of years of viticultural and winemaking heritage. Vines were planted on Pasquale's property in 1972. With seven sons to keep busy, a winery was the logical choice. Son Robert, a giant of a man, went to Charles Sturt University as one of the first students under wine guru Brian Croser's instruction. The first vintage was made at Lillypilly in the new winery in 1982. Robert coined a name for a wine he made from traminer and semillon, 'Tramillon'. It was an instant hit, not only with the wine-drinking public but also with the wine judges, winning a trophy at the 1983 Royal Sydney Easter Show. It has also proven to age well.

Lillypilly have won many awards since this first success. Robert has definite skill in making the late harvest and botrytised dessert wines. His Noble Semillon, Nobel Riesling, Noble Traminer and Noble Muscat of Alexandria all have similar luscious char-acters. Often, the grapes are not picked until May or June - a risky business, but the rewards to the drinker are high. Lillypilly also win many awards for its chardonnay, sauvignon blanc, shiraz cabernet sauvignon, spatlese lexia and vintage port. I am certain if you visit Lillypilly and enjoy its charming atmosphere, you will also fall in love with at least one of the Fiumara's fine wines.

LILLYPILLY ESTATE WINES
Address: Lillypilly Road, Leeton NSW 2705
Direction: Between Yanco and Leeton
Phone: (02) 6953 4069
Fax: (02) 6953 4980
Email: lillypil@webfront.net.au
Established: 1982
Winemaker: Robert Fiumara
Principal varieties grown: Chardonnay, Cabernet Sauvignon, Traminer, Semillon, Muscat of Alexandria, Riesling, Shiraz, Sauvignon Blanc
Ha under vine: 17
Average annual crush: 180 tonnes
Average no. cases produced: 8,000
Public & trade tours: By appointment only
Hours open to public: 10am-5pm, Mon-Sat; Sun by appointment
Points of interest: Vineyard, we grow all our own grapes
Retail distribution: From the Winery

West End Wines

In 1945 Francesco and Elizabeth Calabria harvested and vintaged their first wine in the Riverina region of Australia. These wines were made in the tradition of their Italian heritage and with the excellent grape growing conditions the Riverina provided, a new boutique winery had emerged.

Westend Wines is now under the guiding had of their son, Bill, who has sought to increase both the quality and range of wines offered. Testimony to his success is the collection of medals won at major Australian and International Wines Shows.

James Ceccato joined the Westend team as Chief Winemaker in 1996 bringing with him further winemaking expertise from years of experience. James' attention to quality has seen Westend Wines continue to excel on the Wine Show circuit and also launch Westend's premium wine label '3 Bridges'. In its first release in 1997, 3 Bridges has been awarded 2 trophies, 4 Gold and 3 Silver medals.

Situated in Griffith, Westend Wines is in the heart of New South Wales' largest grape producing area – The Riverina. The rich agricultural land of the Riverina is a leader in viticultural and winemaking technologies, blending these with the traditional methods to create exquisite, unique wines.

WEST END WINES
Address: 1283 Brayne Road, Griffith NSW 2680
Phone: (02) 6964 1506
Fax: (02) 6962 7512
Established: 1945
Owner: William Calabria
Winemakers: William Calabria and James Ceccato
Principal varieties grown: Shiraz, Semillon, Chardonnay, Cabernet Sauvignon, Merlot
Ha under vine: 22
Average annual crush: 1,580 tonnes
Average no. cases produced: 32,700
Principal wines & brands   Cellar Potential
3 Bridges Cabernet Sauvignon
3 Bridges Chardonnay
3 Bridges Golden Mist Botrytis Semillon

Richland Merlot
Richland Shiraz
Richland Cabernet Merlot
Outback Shiraz
Outback Semillon Colombard Sauvignon Blanc
Outback Traminer Riesling
Public & trade tours: Yes
Hours open to public: 9am-4.30pm, Mon-Sat
Retail distribution: VIC - Camberwell South Cellars, Remano Cellars, Morgan's Tuckerbag, Kendalls Fine Wines, Yarraville Cellars. NSW - Dayles Liquor Store, Oxford St Cellars. ACT - Kemeny's Stores, Port-O-Call Cellars, Narrabundah Liquor Barn. WA - Aussie Liquor Discounts, Balcatta Liquor, La Ulana, Old Bridge Cellar. QLD - Aust. Trade Partners. SA - Eureka Tavern, Tea Tree Gully Hotel

Riverina Wines

Tony Sergi is a hardworking, down to earth man, reflecting his solid Italian roots. He is happiest when working with his men out in his large rural and vineyard holdings, he's much happier at the wheel of his four wheel drive than behind his seldom used desk.

Joe's father who has just turned 85, migrated from his native Italy to the Riverina, he had 9 children, 8 daughters and 1 son.

From small beginnings, Riverina now rates as the eighth biggest winery in Australia. At present, the Sergi's have 140 hectares of vines bearing, but a massive 480 hectares planted, which will ensure they have the varieties and quantities needed for their ambitious expansion programme.

The spread of varieties planted includes a substantial quantity of chardonnay, but also 40 hectares of verdelho, the famous variety of the Island of Madeira which also makes an exciting, fruity, full bodied white wine and is ideally suited to a warm climate like the Riverina, there are also substantial plantings of sauvignon blanc. Tony Sergi also runs a number of vineyards for other members of his family, so Riverina are one of the most self sufficient wineries in the region which also gives them good quality control over the grapes they process.

The winemaker is the young genius Sam Trimboli and their main brand "Ballingal" has an impressive range of wines.

At a recent masked tasting I conducted all the Judges agreed that the "Ballingal" wines shone out, often out-pointing much more expensive wines. The sparkling burgundy made mainly from shiraz recently impressed all the judges.

The hardworking and professional manager is David Hammond, formerly with Hungerford Hill Wines.

The winery has just gone through a 1.2 million dollar upgrade and expansion with the accent on winemaking equipment to enhance quality, a further expansion and bottling hall is on the drawing boards.

The Riverina Winery has a large and attractively appointed tasting area and a pleasant leafy covered outdoor alfresco area, a pleasant place indeed to while away a few moments whilst tasting the impressive range of wines.

RIVERINA WINES PTY LTD
Address: Farm 1305 Hillston Road, Griffith NSW 2680
Phone: (02) 6962 4122
Fax: (02) 6962 4628
Email: rivwines@webfront.net.au
Established: 1969
Owners: Antonio & Angela Sergi
Winemaker: Sam Trimboli
Principal varieties grown: Chardonnay, Semillon, Sauvignon Blanc, Merlot, Verdelho, Shiraz, Cabernet Sauvignon, Pinot Noir, Chenin Blanc, Barbera, Ruby Cabernet

Ha under vine: 1,100
Average no. cases produced: 250,000

Principal wines & brands	Cellar Potential
Ballingal Estate Chardonnay	3 years
Ballingal Estate Semillon	3 years
Ballingal Estate Semillon Chardonnay	3 years
Ballingal Estate Shiraz	3 years
Ballingal Estate Merlot	3 years
Ballingal Estate Cabernet Sauvignon	3 years

Public & trade tours: By appointment only
Hours open to public: 9am-5.30 pm, daily
Points of interest: BBQ area
Retail distribution: Wholesale Warehouses

Rossetto Wines

Although the Rossetto winery was founded in 1930 the founder Angelo Rossetto arrived in the region in 1923 as part of the wave of post World War One Italian immigration. Coming from the Northern Italian town of Treviso, he pur-chased a farm and planted vines in 1928 making his first wine two years later. Today the third generation of the family runs the vastly expanded business, crushing an aver-age of 12,000 tonnes of grapes each vintage. The Family has its own vineyards, known as Beelgara Estate, which adjoins the winery in the Beelbangara district of the Riverina.

The three Rossetto brothers, Garry, Brian and Kevin are a most positive, pleasant and ener-getic team. They run the enter-prise and control everything, from the viticulture, through their modern well-equipped winery, to their own bottling line making the most of the richly flavoured ripe grapes produced from the fertile soils of their region. The Rossetto's, like many long-estab-lished wineries, make a large range of wines - table, fortified, sparkling and even cocktail styles - all representing excellent value for money. At a recent line-up of chardonnays I tasted - masked - the Rossetto Chardonnay was one of the best. Its rich, peachy fruit flavours shone through.

Although the winery is amongst the largest in the Nation, with the ability now to crush up to 15,000 tonnes, all the wines receive individual care and it cer-tainly shows through.

The Rossetto motto 'from the heart of the grape" rings true.

ROSSETTO WINES
Address: Farm 576, Beelbangera NSW 2680
Direction: 7kms from Griffith
Phone: (02) 6963 5214
Fax: (02) 6963 5542
Established: 1930
Winemaker: Eddie Ross. General Manger: Rodney Cope
Principal varieties grown: Semillon, Shiraz, Colombard, Chardonnay, Gordo, Trebbiano, Merlot, Cabernet Sauvignon
Ha under vine: 50
Average annual crush: 11,000 tonnes
Average no. cases produced: 100,000

Principal wines & brands	Cellar Potential
Shiraz	5 years
Cabernet Merlot	5 years
Cabernet Sauvignon	5 years
Chardonnay	3 years
Unwooded Chardonnay	3 years
Rhine Riesling Eden Valley	5 years
Semillon Chardonnay	3 years
Old Liqueur Muscat	10 years
Very Old Tawny Port	10 years
Botrytis Semillon	5 years

Brands: Wattleglen, Rossetto, Promenade, Mitchell Estate
Public & trade tours: By appointment only
Hours open to public: 8.30am-5.30pm, Mon-Sat
Points of interest: BBQ facilities, Picnic Area
Retail distribution: Cellar Door Sales. Wines sold to major wholesalers Australia liquor mar keters, I.L.G., Campbell's Cash Carry national liquor company, Novocatrian wholesale liquor

Toorak Wines

Francesco Bruno Snr migrated from Sicily in 1950. Three years later he purchased a small 18 hectare property that was then planted with fruit trees. In 1963, together with his two sons, Frank Jnr and Vincent, he decided to expand into winegrape growing. In 1965 they established a small winery and produced regional wines. The winery has expanded during the last 30 years to produce approximately 3 million litres of mainly table wines. A percentage of these wines are sold under contract to various customers throughout Australia. Some 80,000 cases of mixed varietal wines, such as chardonnay, semillon, cabernet, shiraz and traminer are sold under the Toorak Estate Label. As well, the company produces a secondary label for the 4 litre wine cask market. Frank Jnr looks after the winemaking productions and

Vincent the administration. They have expanded the Packaging Plant to produce wines for the export market that has become very successful for them.

Toorak wines over the years have won awards at major Australian Shows and they continue to produce wines of exceptional character and flavour.

The Toorak Estate Chardonnay, Semillon Chardonnay, as well as Cabernet Sauvignon display excellent varietal character and are made from 100% Riverina fruit. Also, Frank Snr Port and Liqueur Muscat are well regarded by consumers and the trade.

Frank Snr has now retired and brothers Frank Jnr and Vincent run the business. Cellar door sales are handled by sister Nina and Frank Jnr's son Robert, who is studying at Charles Sturt University for his Bachelor of Applied Science in Winemaking.

TOORAK WINES PTY LTD
Address: Toorak Road, Leeton NSW 2705
Direction: Southwest of Leeton
Phone: (02) 6953 2333
Fax: (02) 6953 4454
Established: 1966
Winemaker: Robert Bruno
Principal varieties grown: Semillon, Chardonnay, Shiraz, Cabernet Sauvignon, Colombard, Sauvignon Blanc, Ruby Cabernet, Fortified and Dessert wines
Ha under vine: 30
Average annual crush: 3,000 tonnes
Average no. cases produced: 150,000

Principal wines & brands	Cellar Potential
Cabernet Sauvignon	3-5 years
Ruby Cabernet	3 years
Semillon Chardonnay	3 years
Headmaster Port	
Liqueur Muscat	

Public & trade tours: Yes Hours open to public: 9am-5pm, Mon-Sat. Tours daily at 10.30am

An introduction to Cowra

Situated in the heart of New South Wales, not far from Orange and the National Capital, Canberra, Cowra is probably best known for the infamous 'Cowra Breakout' of Japanese prisoners from the Cowra Prison Camp during the Second World War. Cowra is a pretty town and features a Japanese War Cemetery Garden and Cultural Centre. The town is built around a huge granite rock; a nesting place for wedgetail eagles. From this lofty view-point, the vine rows seem to stretch into eternity.

The vineyard expansion in recent years has been astounding. Richmond Grove's vineyard alone now covers over 250 hectares, the largest vine-yard venture ever undertaken in Australia in one year. More than 600 hectares are now covered with vines on the fertile soils. These are made up of broken down granite and basalt, with alluvial loam brought down by the Lachlan River, which also provides supplementary irrigation during the rather dry summers.

Five main vineyards dominate the region - Cowra Estate the first established vineyard in 1973, followed by Rothbury and Richmond Grove. The O'Dea Family's Windowrie Estate 15 kms north of town with a large vineyard next door planted by a consortium lead by Brian McGuigan. Arrowfield have had a long association with the region and long-term contracts with some of the few independent growers. Several small wine producers have also sprung up over recent years, whilst Brokenwood have also established vineyard operations adjacent to Windowrie.

Cowra is fast becoming the chardonnay capital of Australia. Rothbury have made a strong statement with this variety in recent years, as have Arrowfield, Cowra Estate and now, Richmond Grove. The chardonnays are ripe, rich and fleshy with strong stone fruit peach-nectarine characters often with some nuttiness in the background, finishing with easy-drinking acids. (Brian Croser helped launch chardonnay from Cowra in his days as lecturer at Wagga Wagga's then Riverina College, now Charles Sturt University). Other varieties, both red and white, seem to thrive in this climate with its good soils and water. Undoubtedly further expansion will see this region as a major player in the Australian wine scene by the turn of the century.

The long established Quarry Restaurant and Cellars and the newly established Cowra Mill Winery and Restaurant in an historic bluestone farmer flour mill add a delightful wine tourism feel to the town.

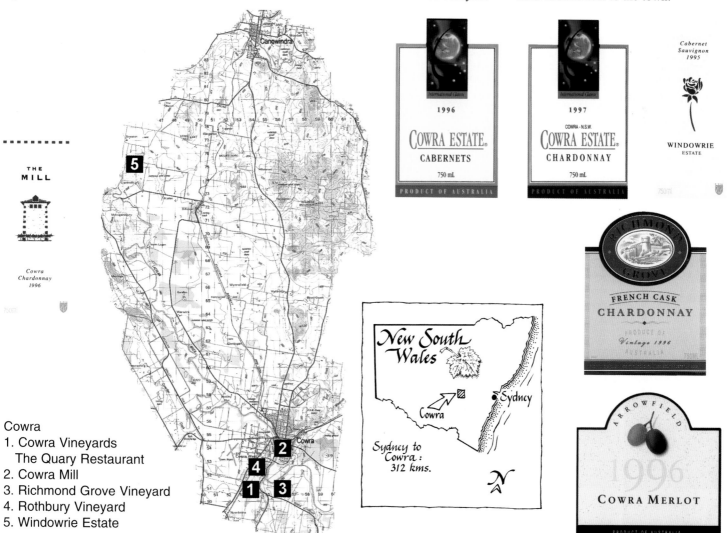

Cowra
1. Cowra Vineyards
   The Quary Restaurant
2. Cowra Mill
3. Richmond Grove Vineyard
4. Rothbury Vineyard
5. Windowrie Estate

Cowra Estate

Cowra Estate Wines is a new, boutique quality, mainstream wine label dedicated to making premium quality wine from Australia's newest and most exciting grape growing region – Cowra. South African born food and beverage entrepreneur John R. Geber took over Cowra Estate Wines in 1995 from the Cowra wine-growing pioneer, the late Tony Gray. Geber relaunched the label with a bold new look and a view to expanding the company's market share, confident in the quality of Australian wines in general and recognising the unique potential of Cowra in particular. Cowra Estate Wines sources its fruit from the original vineyards planted in 1973, which have now expanded to cover 75 hectares under vine. The success of pioneering Cowra Estate has led to a further development of 800 hectares in the region, which will produce in the order of 12,000 tonnes of grapes when mature. This represents around 900,000 cases of wine – approximately 50% of the capacity of the Hunter Valley crop. The Cowra Estate vineyards now produce some highly complex fruit, which allow Cowra Estate Wines to produce wines that rate amongst the finest in the world.

Cowra Estate Wines currently produces three styles of wine: Chardonnay, Cabernets and Cabernet Rosé. Talented wine maker Simon Gilbert has had extensive experience with Cowra fruit; the chardonnay is the best known variety having won numerous awards and countless fans. The Cabernets are a blend of Cabernet Sauvignon and Cabernet Franc and follow the successful track record set by the Cowra Estate Shiraz Cabernet Sauvignon.
The Cabernet Rosé is an ideal summer wine, set to revolutionise the way Australian think about this style. Limited quantities of

Merlot (Director's Reserve), Cabernet Sauvignon (Director's Reserve) and Unwooded Chardonnay are also available. An innovative marketing plan is in place to ensure widespread availability of the magnificent Cowra Estate wines in major liquor chains and top restaurants, offering lovers of good wine a quality product at a surprisingly affordable price.

THE COWRA ESTATE - COWRA WINES	
Address: Boorowa Road, Cowra NSW 2804 **Direction:** 4kms from Cowra on Boorowa/Yass Road **Phone:** (02) 9905 4613 (02) 6342 1136 **Fax:** (02) 9905 4613 (02) 6342 4286 **Established:** 1983 **Owner:** Cowra Wines - John Geber **Winemaker:** Simon Gilbert **Principal varieties grown:** Chardonnay, Pinot Noir, Merlot, Sauvignon Blanc, Cabernet Sauvignon, Cabernet Franc	**Ha under vine:** 75 **Average annual crush:** 985 tonnes **Average no. cases produced:** 20,000 **Public & trade tours:** By appointment only **Hours open to public:** 10am-4pm, Tues-Sun Sales and Tasting **Points of interest:** Quarry Restaurant - Tues-Sun - Lunch At the Vineyard - Thurs-Sat Nights from 7pm **Retail distribution:** PO Box 363, Harbord, NSW

Windowrie Estate/The Cowra Mill

WINDOWRIE ESTATE - COWRA MILL	
Address: *Windowrie Estate:* Windowrie, Canowindra NSW 2804 *Cowra Mill:* 4 Vaux Street, Cowra NSW 2804 **Phone:** *Windowrie:* (02) 6344 3264, *Cowra Mill:* (02) 6341 4141 **Fax:** (02) 6344 3227 **Established:** 1988 **Principal varieties grown:** Chardonnay, Cabernet Sauvignon, Sauvignon Blanc	**Ha under vine:** 44 **Average annual crush:** 550 tonnes - 35 tonne own label **Hours open to public:** At the Mill: 10am-6pm, daily **Points of interest:** Tastings held at Cowra Mill Winery and Restaurant, the oldest building in Cowra (circa 1861)

David O'Dea was early to recognise the potential of Cowra as a viticultural region when he planted his first vines in 1988. Today he has 45 hectares of his own vines and manages almost 200 more hectares of vines adjoining his property for clients such as the respected Brokenwood Wines and a consortium of growers supplying McGuigan Brothers. David's vineyards are located in sweeping valleys between Cowra and Canowindra. His first main client was

Arrowfield Wines who have been largely successful with chardonnay from the O'Dea vineyards.
The O'Dea's are a large family and youngest son Jason is involved in viticulture having worked in vineyards in South America and California's Napa Valley. Daughter Dimity is studying Wine Marketing at Roseworthy in South Australia.
Eldest son Steph has had a different mission, a builder, he has renovated and restored the classic old blue stone flour mill in Cowra, built in 1861, into a splendid Restaurant and Wine Tasting Centre featuring the Windowrie Estate wines from the family's vineyards and a specially launched label "The Mill Wines".
All the Windowrie and Mill wines are from the Estate but made under the watchful eye of New Zealander Kristen Monroe at the Charles Sturt University Winery at Wagga Wagga.
The Windowrie wines have already achieved wine show success, a gold at the highly competitive Chilean Wine Show in South American and a gold medal for their chardonnay in Adelaide. At Windowrie they make sure they're winners.

An introduction to other wine producing areas

Being the first Australian State, and the first wine-producing State, established in Australia with the arrival of vines with the first fleet, New South Wales has vineyards in all areas, including the far west. As well as the main wine-producing regions, excellent wines are found in the cool south near Bega, with Grevillea Estate, and on the mid-south coast near Shoalhaven Heads and Nowra.

The cool and hilly regions around Yass and Young produce excellent table and sparkling wines.

Nearby the Canberra district has vineyards and wineries sited in both NSW and the ACT, where the traditional cabernet-merlot blend has become a hallmark of the region. Emerging regions, with wine quality reputation growing faster than their plantings, demonstrate the potential of NSW wines from regions with higher altitudes or with cooling breezes.

Along the ridges surrounding Young, the appropriately names Hilltops, originally planted to vines almost 100 years ago, is reclaiming its reputation with cabernet sauvignon, shiraz and Riesling. It includes McWilliams Barwang vineyards and the Woodonga Hills Winery.

Further north around Orange, Rosemount have planted a 30 hectare vineyard in this newly planted wine region at altitudes between 600 and 1,000 metres above sea level, wines are already highly sought after for unique and full-flavoured varietal characteristics.

Vineyards stretch to the north through Port Macquarie, where one of the state's most heralded wine producers, Cassegrain, has a large winery and restaurant complex, right up to Tenterfield on the Queensland border. One can only admire the intrepid souls who have so diligently sought out the regional conditions and micro-climates and who prove that, with attention to site and variety, and in caring hands, the vine is a marvellous plant, always able to produce fine wines with the right love and attention applied.

Coolangatta Estate

On the temperate coast a couple of hours south of Sydney the new wine region of Shoalhaven Heads has emerged.

The convict built Coolangatta Estate which dates back to the regions founding in 1822 by Alexander Berry, now encompasses 130 hectares – a vineyard with fine wines, accommodation, Alexander's Restaurant, the Great Hall – banquet centre and a 9 hole gold course. The 6 hectare vineyard planted to chardonnay, semillon, sauvignon blanc,verdelho, shiraz, cabernet sauvignon, merlot and chambourcin already boasts 3 silver and 10 bronze medal winning wines.

This historic pretty estate nestles between the coast and the 'Coolangatta' mountain. If in Sydney the drive to this idyllic escape is truly breathtaking and worthy of the effort.

COOLANGATTA ESTATE

Address: 1335 Bolong Road Shoalhaven Heads NSW
Direction: 14km east of Nowra, 10km southeast of Berry
Phone: (02) 4448 7131
Fax: (02) 4448 7997
Email: coolangatta@shoalhaven.net.au
Established: 1988
Owner: The Bishop Family
Principal varieties grown: Chardonnay, Sauvignon Blanc, Verdelho, Semillon, Cabernet Sauvignon, Shiraz, Merlot, Chambourcin
Ha under vine: 7
Average annual crush: 35 tonnes
Average no. cases produced: 2,500

Principal wines & brands	Cellar Potential
Alexander Berry Chardonnay	6 years
Coolangatta Estate Chambourcin	5 years
Coolangatta Estate Verdelho	5 years
Coolangatta Estate Sauvignon Blanc	4 years
Coolangatta Estate Cabernet-Shiraz-Merlot	5 years

Public & trade tours: By appointment only
Hours open to public: 10am-4pm, daily
Retail distribution: Cellar door, local restaurants and liquor outlets. 'The Wine Boutique' Wollongong

Other Wine Producing Areas.

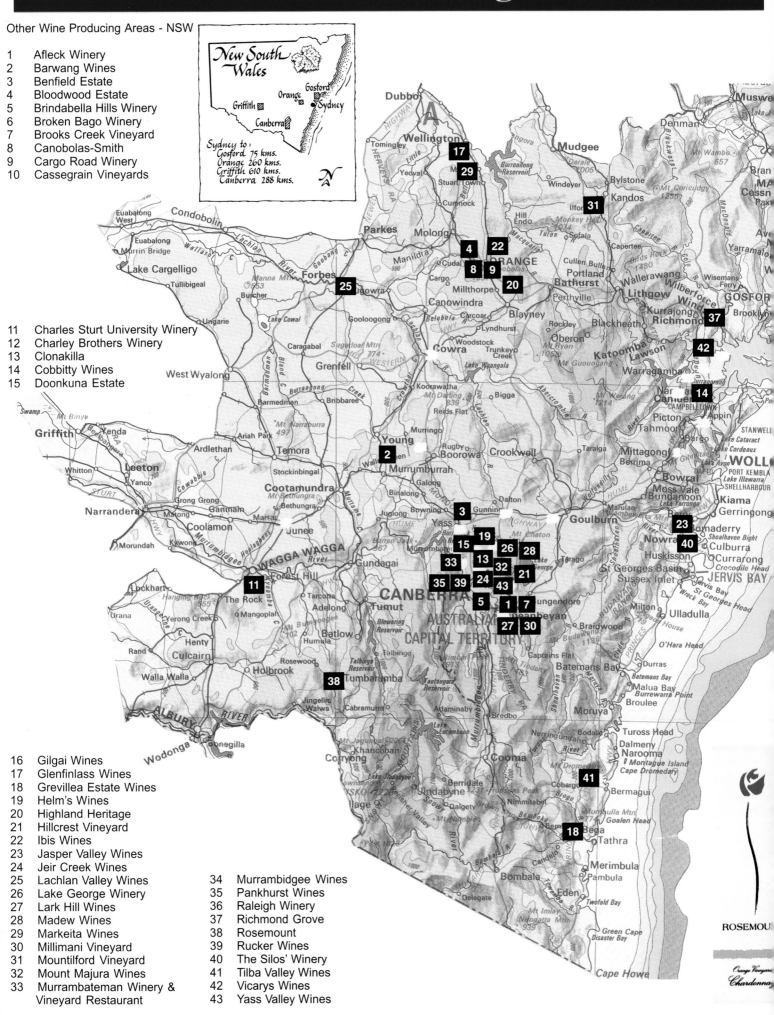

Other Wine Producing Areas - NSW

1 Afleck Winery
2 Barwang Wines
3 Benfield Estate
4 Bloodwood Estate
5 Brindabella Hills Winery
6 Broken Bago Winery
7 Brooks Creek Vineyard
8 Canobolas-Smith
9 Cargo Road Winery
10 Cassegrain Vineyards

11 Charles Sturt University Winery
12 Charley Brothers Winery
13 Clonakilla
14 Cobbitty Wines
15 Doonkuna Estate

16 Gilgai Wines
17 Glenfinlass Wines
18 Grevillea Estate Wines
19 Helm's Wines
20 Highland Heritage
21 Hillcrest Vineyard
22 Ibis Wines
23 Jasper Valley Wines
24 Jeir Creek Wines
25 Lachlan Valley Wines
26 Lake George Winery
27 Lark Hill Wines
28 Madew Wines
29 Markeita Wines
30 Millimani Vineyard
31 Mountilford Vineyard
32 Mount Majura Wines
33 Murrambateman Winery & Vineyard Restaurant

34 Murrambidgee Wines
35 Pankhurst Wines
36 Raleigh Winery
37 Richmond Grove
38 Rosemount
39 Rucker Wines
40 The Silos' Winery
41 Tilba Valley Wines
42 Vicarys Wines
43 Yass Valley Wines

New South Wales

Sydney to :
Gosford 75 kms.
Orange 260 kms.
Griffith 610 kms.
Canberra 288 kms.

ROSEMOU

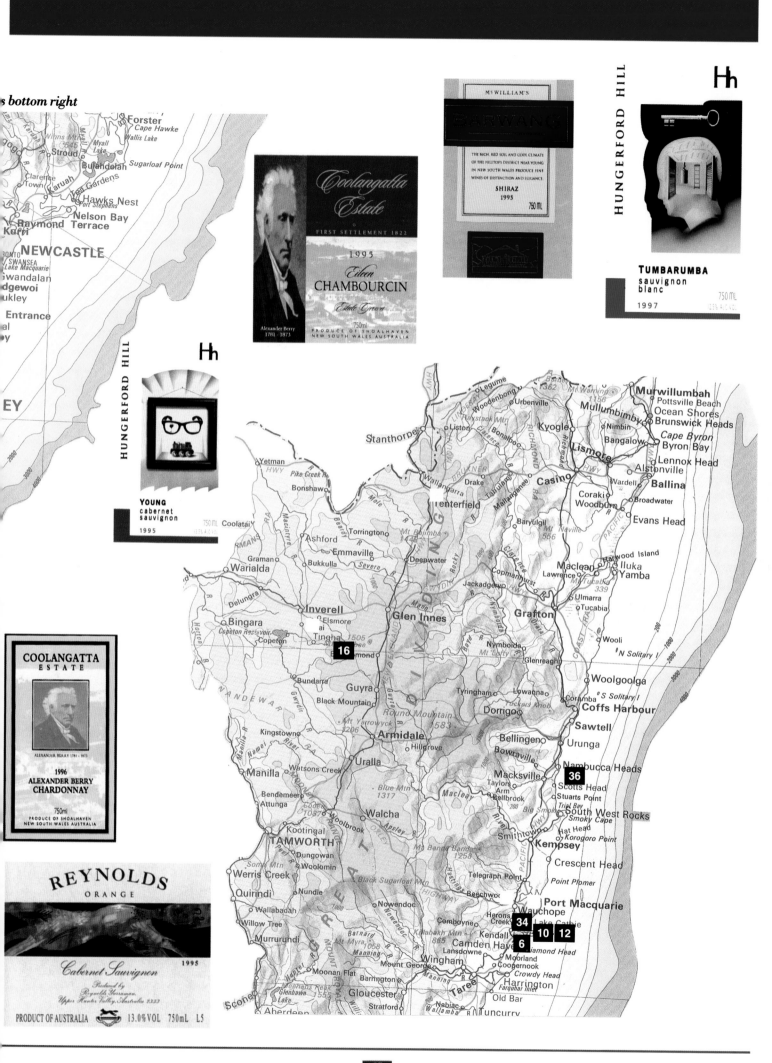

McWilliams – Barwang

On the south-western slopes of the Great Dividing Range some 25 kilometres east of Young, at an average height above sea level of 600 metres, is the impressive McWilliam's Barwang Vineyard. The vineyards covers over 100 hectares of rolling hills of the 400 hectare property and the view over the patchwork quilt of vines from the furthest hill is quite something.

The soils are deep red decomposed granite impregnated with basalt, and I'm sure this comes through in the strength and complexity of the red wines.

This remote cool climate location was first planted back in 1969, 13 hectares along the high ridges to avoid the worst of the frosts that are common in the area.

McWilliam's bought the vineyard in 1989 from the founders, the Robertson family, whom McWilliam's had been supplying with vine cuttings since the vineyard's founding. McWilliam's immediately planted a further 87 hectares, and today it is all bearing. The grapes are crushed on site and then make the three-hour journey as chilled 'must' (grape juice).

The vineyard is chiefly planted to cabernet sauvignon, shiraz and chardonnay with smaller quantities of merlot, pinot noir, semillon, sauvignon blanc and riesling. The wines from Barwang have been spectacularly successful in wine shows and are often confused with those from Coonawarra. The first vintage shiraz, a 1989, has already won five gold medals and the 1991 Cabernet Sauvignon has won two trophies and two gold medals.

In all, the McWilliam's Barwang wines have won more than 100 medals in only seven short years. Qantas and a number of prestigious 5-star hotels have already included Barwang on their wine lists, along with other Australian classics, proving McWilliam's aim of developing fruit-driven wines from the excellent viticultural conditions to be absolutely correct.

Cassegrain

The Hastings River was a viticultural paradise in the last century. During the 1860's, there were no fewer than 33 wineries. John Cassegrain has an organically run vineyard which is doing fine showing his mastery of the sometimes tricky sub-tropical maritime climate.

John's background has more than prepared him for a career in the wine industry. His mother was Countess Francoise de Solere from a wine-making family in Burgundy, and his uncle Count Barignot de Varenne is the head of France's oldest cognac-producing company, Angier Freres & Co. John is a graduate of Roseworthy College in South Australia, who worked for Tyrrellís Wines for 10 years. He has planted pinot noir along with chardonnay, sauvignon blanc, merlot, cabernet sauvignon, chambourcin, semillon, verdelho and shiraz. John was encouraged to plant chambourcin, an unusual French hybrid, by viticultural guru Dr. Antcliff.

John's own family came from the wheat district around Orleans, south of Paris. The name Cassegrain means literally "breaking the grain". His father came to Port Macquarie, and from nothing, built a

huge construction business. He was affectionately known as 'Frog' and well loved by the locals. The trees, parks and gardens he planted around all his properties, pay tribute to his caring good taste. John, together with his brother, has developed 'Le Clos Estates' a French custom where investors get a beautiful building block among the trees surrounding the vineyards, plus a share of the vineyard, a yearly return on their investment and some wine, of course.

The vineyards now cover 170 hectares and the annual crush of 750 tonnes is set to rise to about 1,500 tonnes by the turn of the century. The 'fromenteau' - an old French term for chardonnay, is a very good wine indeed. The 'chambourcin' has a rich dark cherry character - soft,

with mouth-filling flavours. The 'Cassae', a version of the famous Pineau-des-Charentes of Cognac, literally grape juice fortified with brandy chilled, it makes a delicious pre- or after-dinner drink.

Cassegrain also have a splendid Terrace Cafe in the French tradition, looking out on the vineyards and the gardens which boast 2,500 roses. If any winery has a claim to paradise in Australia, it's Cassegrain.

Rosemount - Mt Canoblas

Centred 280 kms west of Sydney the Orange Region has long been an important horticultural area supplying Sydney with much of its apples, pears and cherries.

The choice of the Mt Canoblas site in 1989 nearly 900 metres above sea level for the Rosemount Vineyard was the culmination of a 20 year search by winemaker Philip Shaw and the Oatley Family, owners of Rosemount.

The very cool climate combined with the red volcanic soils over limestone on the slopes of this extinct volcano has proved a great vineyard site.

The first wine a 1992 chardonnay is being followed by red wines from cabernet sauvignon, merlot and pinot noir.

Whilst a new wine region, grapes have been grown around Orange since the turn of the century and some twenty vineyards now grow around 250 tonnes of premium wine grapes. Look out for the distinctive Rosemount "Orange" label and its existing wines.

Charles Sturt University Winery

Australia's first degree course in winemaking, Bachelor of Applied Science (Wine), was introduced by the Riverina College of Advanced Education, (now the Charles Sturt University) at Wagga Wagga in 1975. The course can be studied full-time or by external studies and there are currently 600 students enrolled. The winery has since been expanded and now processes around 800 tonnes each vintage, producing 20,000 cases under their own C.S.U. Label. Some of the multiple award winning wines are their Sparkling from Tumbarumba fruit, a Chardonnay from Cowra grapes and a Cabernet dominant red from the University Vineyard at Wagga Wagga.

Brian Croser was the first winery director and the first crush was in 1977. Today wine-making is in the capable control of New Zealander, Kirsten Munro. The winery enterprise demonstrates an accountable commercial operation and provides stimulating training for those students fortunate enough to be employed (winery scholarship). In association with the formal teaching, the practical experience the students obtain will prepare them for challenging careers in the wine industry.

CHARLES STURT UNIVERSITY

Address: Boorooma Street, Wagga Wagga NSW 2678
Phone: (02) 6933 2435
Fax: (02) 6933 2107
Winemaker: Kirsten Munro
Principal varieties grown:
Chardonnay, Cabernet Sauvignon, Merlot, Cabernet Franc, Traminer, Semillon, Shiraz
Ha under vine: 15
Average annual crush: 300 tonnes
Average no. cases produced: 10,000
Public & trade tours:
By appointment only
Hours open to public:
10am-4pm, weekdays, 11am-4pm Weekends
Points of interest:
Charles Sturt University Wagga Wagga is one of only two Wine Science Schools in Australasia - Experimental Vineyards
Retail distribution:
Cellar Door, Sydney, Melbourne, Adelaide, Brisbane

Cobbitty Wines

The Cogno's arrived in Australia in 1950 and planted their vineyard of 5.6 hectare vineyard at Cobbitty in 1964. The Cobbitty vineyard is planted with barbera, shiraz, trebbiano, grenache and muscat with the remainder of grapes purchased from South Australia. John's son Joseph Cogno who runs the Maglieri Winery at McLaren Vale, takes care of the premium end of the market producing wines under the new Cogno Brothers label.

The company has now diversified into the manufacturing of Wine Base Liqueurs that are produced on premise for substitutes of imported Liqueurs. The majority of all wines produced are for exclusive sale through cellar door, local bottle shops and restaurants.

Cobbitty Wines are open every day for tastings and there are barbecue and picnic facilities with a wide range of wines as the family motto states "The best wine is the one you like".

COBBITTY WINES PTY LTD
Address: 40 Cobbitty Road, Cobbitty NSW 2570
Direction: 60kms South West of Sydney
Phone: (02) 4651 2281
Fax: (02) 4651 2671 **Established:** 1964
Owner: Cogno Bros.
Winemaker: John Cogno
Principal varieties grown: Trebbiano, Grenache, Muscat, Barbera, Shiraz
Ha under vine: 5
Average annual crush: 25-30 tonnes
Average no. cases produced: 10,000
Public & trade tours: By appointment only
Hours open to public: 9am-5.30pm, Mon-Sat; 12pm-5.30pm Sun
Points of interest: Picnic Grounds, Large Selection of Fortified Wines and Liqueurs, Free Wine Tasting
Retail distribution: Cellar Door and Mail Orders

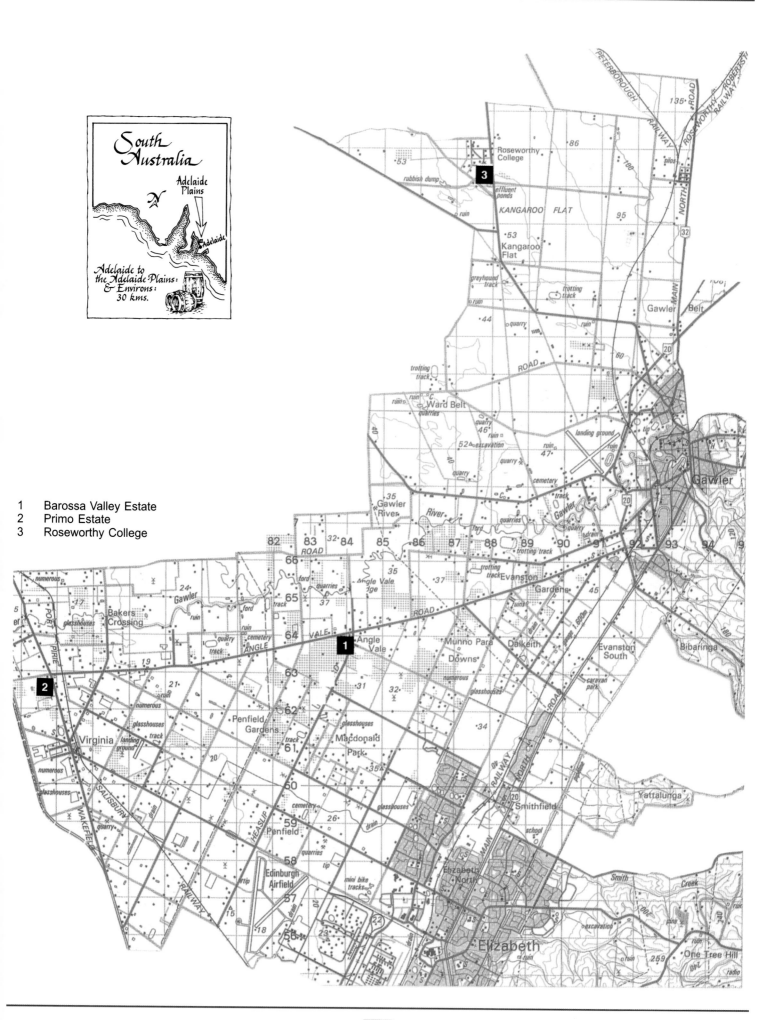

1   Barossa Valley Estate
2   Primo Estate
3   Roseworthy College

Although one of the last settled states in Australia, by 1887 South Australia was leading Australian wine production.

In 1837, only one year after the state's founding, J.B. Hach and George Stevenson planted vine cuttings from Tasmania in North Adelaide. Later that same year Richard Hamilton planted his Ewell vineyards in what is now the suburb of Marion. Shortly afterwards, John Reynell planted his first vines at Reynella.

In 1844 Dr Christopher Rawson Penfold established his Grange vineyard at Magill. The 1840's were the period when the German Lutheran immigrants began arriving in the Barossa Valley and Johann Gramp planted his Jacob's Creek Vineyard. English immigrant and brewer Samuel Smith established Yalumba in 1849.

During the 1850's, the wake of the gold rush saw a flurry of new vineyards, Thomas Hardy, Jesse Norman and the Holbrook family all commenced winemaking and established vineyards in what are now inner suburbs of Adelaide: Woodley's vineyard was established at Glen Osmond in 1858. Back to the Barossa, where Joseph Seppelt commenced planting in 1851 and Samuel Hoffmann even earlier in 1847. The names of the early pioneers of wine in South Australia have lived on and continue to dominate the wine scene in the state. One of these early pioneers, like many others, was a medical practitioner, Dr Alexander Kelly, who planted his Trinity Vineyard at Morphett Vale in 1843. An entrepreneur at heart, he later formed the Tintara Vineyard Company and planted extensive vineyards at McLaren Vale, later to be bought out of bankruptcy by Thomas Hardy.

We must not to forget Clare, where John Horrocks put his first vines in the ground in 1840; he was only 22 years of age, but managed to convince many others to plant vines in this beautiful valley. By the 1860's more than 6,000 acres of vines covered many areas of the state. In fact, the first wine surplus was at hand and the vignerons of the state made their first assault on the English market. The logistics and time involved meant this push had a very limited affect, thus many growers and suppliers to the larger wineries were forced to make their own wine or see their grapes go to waste. Unfortunately there was a flood of cheap, poorly-made wine which affected the industry's reputation badly for a period; however, the earlier established companies and well known names today such as Hardy, Seppelt, Penfold, Orlando and Yalumba continued to focus on quality and grew stronger through the period, although overall production decreased dramatically.

South Australian wine began to secure markets in the other states; this progress was halted somewhat late in the century with tariffs being imposed by NSW and Victoria on South Australian wine, by then the nation's leading producer. At this time the dreaded vine louse phylloxera struck the vineyards in Victoria and to a degree,

New South Wales. South Australia being more remote and on lighter soils, escaped this blight which destroyed other states' vineyards. In fact, South Australia remains one of the few producing regions of the world where phylloxera has never struck; vine quarantine regulations are understandably strict. It was with great interest that I read a collection of contemporary "letters to the editor" contained in a scrapbook kept by my great-great-grandfather at Bankside in Adelaide. Dated 1869-1870 that chronicled the differences of opinion in certain matters pertaining to wine and vines between Messrs. Hardy and Seppelt of South Australia and Messrs. Morris and Chambers of Victoria. By the outbreak of the World War I, South Australia was producing 18 million litres of wine, more half the nation's output. Fortified wines had started to make in-roads in the market; they were easier to keep pure and in good condition and during the next 50 years dominated the wine scene in South Australia.

It was the influx of European immigrants after World War II that started to tip the scales back in favour of table wines and changed our drinking habits; it was only in 1970 when table wine production actually exceeded that of fortified wines, and the culture of nearly universal enjoyment of table wines with meals began. Development over the last two decades in the South East of the state started with Coonawarra in the early 1950's with Samuel Wynn and also Ron Haselgrove from Mildara reviving Coonawarra as a wine region, almost 100 years after John Riddoch had founded the regions' wine industry as part of his 'Penola Fruit Colony'. Padthaway, Cape Jaffa and other parts of this region, from Bordertown down to Mt. Gambier and across to Robe, promise this Limestone coast is set to be a huge world-renowned quality wine region.

Langhorne Creek near the mouth of the mighty Murray River has a cool but mild climate and has had vineyards since the last century. Stonyfell with their Metala and Wolf Blass have shown in the last few decades the capabilities of the region. Huge vineyard plantings are now underway.The resurgence of wine growing in the Adelaide Hills has been quite remarkable with modern day pioneers such as Brian Croser, Stephen Henschke and Tim Knappstein forging the way. South Australia richly deserves its title of "The Wine State", producing more than 60% of Australia's wines. With suitable land and climate, water is really the only problem in the driest state on the world's driest continent. South Australians are determined, inventive and proud of the impact their wines are having on the world market. In 1997 over $300 million in export income was earned by the state's wine industry, with 70% of the nation's wine exports.

The South Australian Government is understandably very supportive of its wine industry and the burgeoning wine tourism industry. The state is fast developing, cheers to South Australia's wine success story.

An introduction to the Adelaide Plains

Although this area saw the birth of South Australia's wine industry, Adelaide's urban sprawl has all but wiped out viticulture within the greater metropolitan area, however vineyards and wineries still remain.

The Magill Cellars and Vineyards, the spiritual home of Grange Hermitage, along with the original home of founder Dr. Christopher Rawson Penfold, remain an active part of Australian wine and are protected by National Trust classification.

Richard Hamilton's original Ewell Vineyards, planted in 1837, a year after the state's settlement, have fallen to housing and a transport depot, but Patritti's in Dover Gardens are still going strong along with Crestview, Hardy's Chateau Reynella and Mt. Hurtle in the Happy Valley regional area, plus Torresans at Flagstaff Hill.

Many changes have occurred in the consolidation of the wine industry of South Australia. Hamilton's moved to the Eden Valley and were taken over by Mildara, Woodleys went to the Barossa and were taken over by Seppelts and Normans have expanded by moving to Angle Vale as well as buying the Coolawin Winery at Clarendon in the Adelaide Hills. Hardys moved from their Bankside Winery after it was destroyed by fire in 1904. They established Mile End Cellars close to the city and Champagne Cellars in Currie Street in the city.

In 1983, Hardys moved lock, stock and barrel to Reynella and the former property of early settler, Walter Reynell. The wonderful old homestead and Chateau were restored and a new winery, bottling and storage facilities were constructed.

So far $8 million has been spent on these improvements, and further developments are planned.

Angoves had extensive vineyards and a winery at Tea Tree Gully, a north-eastern Adelaide suburb. Their Tregrehan vineyard was famed for its red wine but unfortunately, and much to the disgust of the Angove family, it was compulsorily acquired by the State Housing Commission.

Douglas A. Tolley of Pedare fame had an operating winery until 1995.

The significant vineyards of the Adelaide Plains area are now found around Angle Vale near Gawler and around the entrance to the Barossa Valley. There have been grapes grown in this area since the first days of the industry.

Expansion began in 1969, when the Angle Vale winery was built as a consortium venture. However, the business foundered and equipment was virtually sold off piecemeal until a co-operative was formed with the assistance of the Berri-Renmano Consolidated Co-operative.

The new Valley Growers Co-op Ltd took over the winery in 1984, employing Colin Glaetzer who produced some great wines, stylishly packaged.

This operation is now named Barossa Estates.

Norman's also have a large vineyard at Angle Vale called Evanston Estate, where many grape varieties are planted, and in 1973, in the same area, the Grilli family established Primo Estate.

The region is very warm, but with the moderating effects of sea breezes from St. Vincents Gulf the climate is not too harsh.

The soil is the result of a rich alluvial flood plain and fruit picked at the right time, and handled well, produces award-winning wines.

However, with the heat and low rainfall, irrigation is essential. Adelaide Plains is renowned for producing high quality wines. At the northern end of the region lies the famous Roseworthy Agricultural College where so many of Australia's great winemakers have trained.

Barossa Valley Estates

Barossa Valley Estate winery is located on Heaslip Road at Angle Vale. Barossa Valley Estate Wines was formed in 1985 by Valley Growers Co-operative. As the name suggests the Co-operative is a group of Barossa Valley growers who joined together to purchase the winery and produce wines from this famous region. Under the name of Barossa Valley Estate "The Pick of the Barossa" business has flourished and Barossa Valley Estate Wines now produce various ranges of exceptional quality wines. All the fruit that goes into the Barossa Valley Estate wines is sourced from within the co-operative therefore making all the wines 100% Barossa. The labels include the E & E Black Pepper Shiraz and E & E Sparkling Shiraz as well as the Ebenezer range, all of which have been bestowed with awards both nationally and internationally. This gives great testament to the quality of wines made from this premium grape growing area. The other ranges that come under the umbrella of Barossa Valley Estate are the Moculta range of premium selection reds and whites as well as the Barossa Valley Estate Dry White and Barossa Valley Estate Dry Red. The winery crushes approximately 3,000 tonnes of fruit over the vintage and is situated at Angle Vale on the Adelaide Plains amidst extensive lawned parkland and majestic Gawler River gums. Picnic and barbecue facilities are available on the grounds for gatherings with friends and family with the cellar door sales located at the winery and open daily for tastings.

BAROSSA VALLEY ESTATES

Address: Healslip Road, Angle Vale SA 5117
Phone: (08) 8284 7000
Fax: (08) 8284 7219
Established: 1985
Owner: Valley Growers Co-operative
Winemaker: Natasha Mooney
Principal varieties grown: Shiraz, Cabernet Sauvignon, Merlot, Chardonnay, Riesling, Semillon
Average no. cases produced: 90,000

Principal wines & brands	Cellar Potential
E&E Black Pepper Shiraz	15+ years
E&E Sparkling Shiraz	5+ years
Ebenezer Shiraz	10+ years
Ebenezer Cabernet Sauvignon/Merlot	10+ years
Ebenezer Chardonnay	5 years
Ebenezer Sparkling Pinot Noir	now
Moculta Shiraz	3 years
Moculta Cabernet/Merlot	3 years
Moculta Chardonnay	2 years
Moculta Semillon Sauvignon Blanc	4 years

Public & trade tours: Trade tours by appointment only
Hours open to public: 9am-5pm, daily
Points of interest: BBQ's and extensive picnic grounds
Retail distribution: National via BRL Hardy

An introduction to the Adelaide Hills

Adelaide Hills region stretches from Mount Pleasant in the north to Mount Compass in the south. Together with Eden Valley it forms Australia's largest cool climate viticultural region, outside of Coonawarra/Padthaway in the south east of South Australia, with vineyards at a height of more than 400 metres above sea level.

The region is quickly forging a strong reputation worldwide with high profile winemakers such as Brian Croser at Piccadilly, Tim Knappstein, Stephen and Prue Henschke and Geoff Weaver and Nepenthe at Lenswood. Pinot Noir is becoming a shining star for the Hills with Henschke and Knappstein being pressed for supremacy by some great pinots from the small wineries of Ashton Hills, Pibbin and Hillstowe. In the southern Adelaide Hills, Geoff Hardy's large Kuitpo Vineyard is the showpiece vineyard of Australian viticulture, supplying the likes of exclusive wine producer Shaw and Smith along with the large companies. Geoff keeps his favourite little patches of the vineyard to make his stunning Geoff Hardy Kuitpo varietal wines and won the first great Australian Shiraz Challenge in 1995 with his 1993 Kuitpo Shiraz.

This diverse hills region is certainly at the forefront of the quality wine development of Australia. The sky is the limit so to speak. Perhaps one day we will see the hundreds of vineyards in the Hills that the last century boasted.

1   Angroves Tea Tree Gully Winery
2   Ashbourne Stafford Ridge Vineyards
3   Bridgewater Mill
4   Geoff Hardy – Kuitpo
5   Glenara Winery
6   Gumeracha Cellars -
      Chain of Ponds Winery
7   Henschke Cellars – Lenswood
8   Hillstowe Wines
9   Lenswood Vineyards
10   Nepenthe
11   Penfold's Magill
12   Petaluma
13   Pibbin
14   Rosemount – Kuitpo
15   Stonyfell Winery

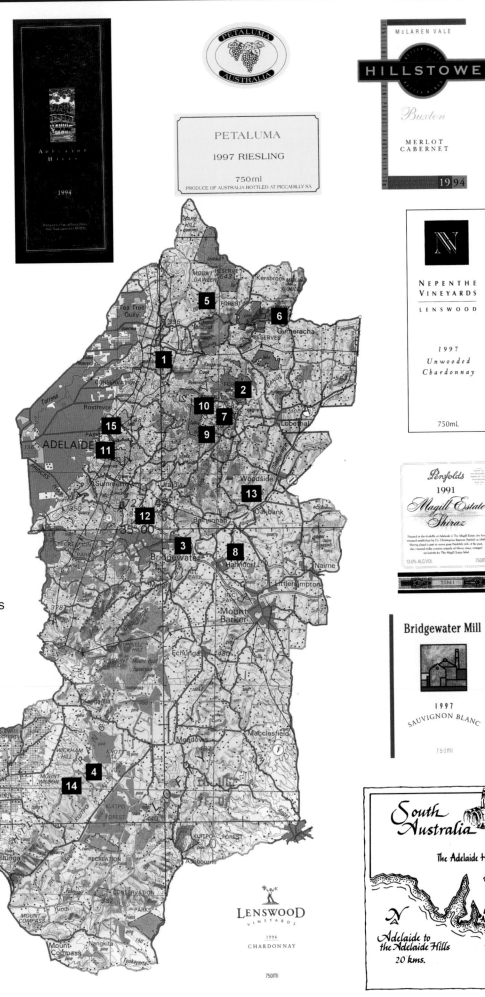

Lenswood Vineyards

Tim Knappstein has always been at the cutting edge of Australian viticulture and winemaking.

During the late 1960's and early 1970's he revolutionised the wines at his family's Stanley wine Company in Clare. The Leasingham Bin5 and Bin 7 Rhine Rieslings took all before them on the show circuits and his Bin Reds, the 56 Cabernet Malbec and Bin 49 Cabernet Sauvignon wine, were benchmarks of the industry.

Stanley was acquired by Heinz and in 1976 he took over the beautiful old Enterprise Brewery in Clare. Enterprise Wines, then to become Tim Knappstein, began its life.

Tim was looking for a way to add another dimension to his wines so in 1981 he purchased a steep sloped property at Lenswood between the Mawson Bike Trail and the Heysen Walking Trail in the cool Adelaide Hills. Tim's was the first vineyard in the region. The chardonnay was planted in October 1981 preceding the Henschke's next door by a year.

The Ash Wednesday bushfires destroyed the remains of the apple orchards on the property and about 50% of the vines.

Tim and his wife Annie, who runs the management and marketing, persevered. The original 18 hectare property was expanded to 45 hectares with the purchase of the next door orchards and now there are some 27 hectares under vine with some merlot being planted at present and some cabernet sauvignon being grafted over to merlot/malbec and pinot noir.

The Lenswood Wines are sensational. The pinot noir by Tim is a knockout (he fully immerses himself in the vats of fermenting wine to mix the skins and juice and keep the temperature even – it's an age-old burgundy tradition).

The chardonnay and sauvignon blanc and cabernet sauvignon blend are also superb, watch out for the merlot.

Annie and Tim are just putting the finishing touches to a private tasting and entertaining area with exquisite views over the vineyards. The have a true paradise and know what to do with it.

LENSWOOD VINEYARDS
Address: Croft's Road, Lenswood SA 5240
Phone: (08) 8365 3733
Fax: (08) 8365 3766
Established: Vineyard 1981, Brand 1991
Winemaker: Tim Knappstein
Principal varieties grown: Pinot Noir, Sauvignon Blanc, Chardonnay, Semillon, Cabernet Sauvignon, Merlot, Malbec
Ha under vine: 27
Average annual crush: 130-200 by 2001
Average no. cases produced: 5,500-10,000 by 2100

Principal wines & brands	Cellar Potential
Lenswood Vineyards	
Sauvignon Blanc	0-2 years
Pinot Noir	5-10 years
Chardonnay	up to 5 years
Cabernet (Warm years only)	8-12 years
Semillon (Warm years only)	up to 10 years

Public & trade tours: Trade tours by appointment only
Retail distribution: Nationwide except ACT

Chain of Ponds Wines

Caj and Genny Amadio are legends in their own time. Following many years of entrepreneurial ventures attacked with remarkable success, and being surrounded by generation of Italian wine-making tradition, it was only a matter of time before they ventured into the wine producing business themselves.

and attention with the ideally cool micro 0climate of Gumeracha in the Adelaide Hills and you have very special wines". Wine judges have agreed by honouring them with many achievements: Best Performer – Adelaide Hills Wine Show '96 – 5 medals and 2 trophies, Best Performer – Australian Boutique Wine Awards '96 – 3 Gold

launched. It has rapidly increased its market share every vintage since. It is a vibrant, young, full flavoured Grenache/Sangiovese blend which is ideal for the Australian/Alfresco environment.
In fact, why not visit the gorgeous Chain of ponds Winery, its only a stone's throw from Adelaide. Grab a bottle of the Novello

After having pioneered the now much sought after subregion of Gumeracha in 1985, this is what they have to say: "We grow our vines on an enhanced trellising system and hand pick all our fruit to ensure fruit quality and flavour is maintained; combine all the personal care

Awards, 1 commendation, "Best New Winery '96" by Vogue Entertaining National Magazine and Nominated for "The 21 Hottest Wineries of the World" by Decanter International Wine Magazine.
In 1995 the enormously successful Italian style light red, "Novello Rosso", was

Rosso and enjoy a picnic in this beautiful part of the hills.
And by the way, they are also helping to develop a world of wine on Kangaroo Island. You can taste the excellent results of that venture at the Cellar Door too – you'll be very pleasantly surprised.

CHAIN OF PONDS

Address: Main Road, Gumeracha SA 5233
Phone: (08) 8389 1415
Fax: (08) 8389 1877
Established: 1985, 1993 (First Vintage)
Winemaker: Caj Amadio
Principal varieties grown: Cabernet Sauvignon, Shiraz, Merlot, Pinot Noir, Chardonnay, Sauvignon Blanc, Semillon, Riesling, Grenache-Sangiovese
Ha under vine: 21
Average no. cases produced: 5,000

Principal wines & brands	Cellar Potential
Cabernet Sauvignon 'Amadeus'	5-10 years
Shiraz	5-10 years
Chardonnay	5-7 years
Semillon	5-7 years
Sauvignon Blanc-Semillon	3-5 years
Riesling	10+ years
Novello Rosso - light red	-2 years
Kangaroo Island Vines	
Cabernet Merlot	3-8 years

Hours open to public:
10.30am-4.30, daily
Points of interest:
Bed & Breakfast on site - 1880 cottage. Regional Food Platters, Strawberry Farm and Birdwood National Motor Museum
Retail distribution:
Cellar Door and Mail Order. NSW, SA, WA and VIC

Chain of Ponds – "Vineyard Cottage"

With the advent of Caj renovating the 1880 stone cottage and converting it into a Bed & Breakfast a visit to Chain of Ponds Wines is a must. Try their widely acclaimed wines; enjoy a lunch of regional food products and stay at their fabulous Vineyard Cottage.

The Cottage is in a very romantic setting and Caj and Genny's building background has ensured it is most comfortable and splendidly appointed. Up to 3 couples are able to be accommodated. The main bedroom has an ensuite bathroom.

The main bathroom includes a spa, spacious living area, has an open log fire and there is a fully equipped kitchen. The Cottage even has a dining room area and a private courtyard with barbecue facilities and if you don't feel like cooking there is a great restaurant just around the corner.

Hillstowe

HILLSTOWE

Address: 104 Main Road, Hahndorf SA 5245
Phone: (08) 8388 1400
Fax: (08) 8388 1411
Established: Hillstowe Vineyards 1980;
Hillstowe Wines 1991
Owner: The Laurie Family
Winemaker: Chris Laurie
Principal varieties grown: Chardonnay, Pinot
Noir, Sauvignon Blanc, Merlot, Shiraz, Cabernet
Sauvignon, Pinot Gris
Ha under vine: 14

Principal wines & brands	Cellar Potential
Adelaide Hills Udy's Mill Chardonnay	8-10 years
Adelaide Hills Udy's Mill Pinot Noir	6-8 years
Adelaide Buxton Sauvignon Blanc	
McLaren Vale Buxton Merlot Cabernet	8-10 years
McLaren Vale Buxton Chardonnay	6-8 years
McLaren Vale Buxton Shiraz	12-15 years

Public & trade tours: Yes
Hours open to public: 10am-5pm, daily
Points of interest: Regional cheese platters;
wines by the glass; petange piste; picnic area;
outdoor eating
Retail distribution: All States, UK and Europe;
Asia, USA and Canada.

The Hillstowe story is a long and enriched tale, beginning with Buxton Forbes Laurie, a pioneer of viticulture in South Australia an ancestor of Dr Chris Laurie and his son Hamish.

In 1853, in the lush foothills near Port Elliot, Buxton laid the foundation of is family home "Southcote" on land chosen for its suitability as a vineyard. The first vines were planted in the winter of 1853 and in 1857 the first vintage was harvested. By 1866 his vineyard produced top quality Shiraz, Cabernet, Grenache and Riesling wines. The legacy of Buxton Forbes Laurie imbued in his descendent the desire to continue the tradition of producing premium quality wines for Australia and export.

Udy's Mill was a 19th century timber mill located in the heart of the Adelaide Hills in bushland at Carey Gully near Lenswood, where the ancient Stringy Bark gums were felled by timber cutters until the 1900's. More than a century later, the clearings left in the forest have been planted to Chardonnay and Pinot grapes by the Laurie family. The Hillstowe label was born in 1991, when Chris Laurie decided to take the best of the fruit the company was growing and make his own wines. The Hillstowe philosophy of 'better vines better wines', its concentration on high quality grapes and focus on wine-making techniques has led to a string on international and national awards. Hillstowe has become a label to watch.

In 1995 Hillstowe Wines opened their cellar door in Hahndorf, in the heart of the Adelaide Hills wine growing region. Hillstowe's complex of stone cottages nestles amongst trees and gardens in this historic township. On the main street is Thiele's Cottage (circa 1845), believed to be the oldest building still standing in Hahndorf: A collection of cottages, in the style of German villages of Thiele's era, cuddle behind ... and here Hillstowe has made its home. Through Thiele's Cottage, past static winemaking displays and wine and associated products retail area, one follows through the connecting walkway to Hillstowe's tasting area. In the Cellar Door, tastings are offered of Hillstowe's award winning single vineyard and wines from both the Adelaide Hills and McLaren Vale. A range of cheese platters are available, for nibbling or a light meal, and all wines are available for purchase by the glass.

A large picnic area beckons from across the creek dividing the grounds. A stroll over a bridge to a large grassy meadow, dappled with stunning Willows and Australian Native Trees, takes you to the perfect spot for throwing a rug, relaxing with a bottle of wine and some local cheeses.

And in 1997, Hillstowe extended their commitment to the Adelaide Hills by establishing their barrel hall and winery in the old cheese factory at Mount Torrens.

Nepenthe Vineyards

Nepenthe (pronounced 'ne-pen-thee' and literally meaning 'no sorrow') is the creative vision of Ed, Sue and son James Tweddell. It nestles in the heart of the Adelaide Hills, on the cool slopes of idyllic Lenswood. Here they are creating the quintissential 'estate' where fine and distinctive regional wines are grown, vintaged and bottled on the property. The Nepenthe journey began in 1994 with the purchase of 144 acres of prime Lenswood orchard land. World class fruit has been grown here for over 100 years and the presence of names such as Knappstein, Weaver and Henschke suggested there was more going on! Exhaustive viticultural research followed and resulted in a meticulously planned vineyard that melds perfectly with the beautiful landscape of the region. In due course the estate will be completed with the building of a spectacular cellar door facility that will sit over the deep waters of the trout filled lake that sits to the front of the winery.

The commitment to quality in all areas of production is evidenced by the attention afforded Nepenthe's facility by some of the country's top makers. The flexibility inherent in the design of the winery allows the winemaker a marvellous range of technical and creative opportunities that may not otherwise be available in a 'standard' operation.

Full time winemaker and creative driving force behind the development of Nepenthe's fine and distinctive regional style is Peter Leske. His extensive Australian and French winemaking experience, coupled with an impressive research and development background, reflects much of what is internationally acclaimed as excellent in the Australian wine industry. A self professed 'Pinot-phile', Peter is adamant that the Adelaide Hills, and Lenswood in particular, will become Australia's pre-eminent Pinot region. 1997 marked the release of the first 100% grown, vintaged and bottled wines to bear the Nepenthe label. Wines from this vintage included an Unwooded Chardonnay and Sauvignon Blanc that were unveiled in September of 1997. Waiting for release in 1998 are the wooded wines.

These include a Pinot Noir, Cabernet Sauvignon, Chardonnay and Semillon. Be aware of the Merlot and small parcels of Zinfandel and Pinot Gris that are on the property, early evidence is that these will be stars of the future!

In keeping with the forward thinking ethos of Nepenthe, the Tweddell family has only

recently acquired a second hills property. It is located in the picturesque hamlet of Charleston, only a short 'glass of Merlot' from Nepenthe Vineyards. Work has already begun on a stunning vineyard development which will see the creation of a new label with its own focus and identity. The addage 'watch this space' could not be more apt! Nepenthe is the essence of the modern Australian wine industry. It combines a vision and commitment to excellence that will see it amongst the leaders of the future.

NEPENTHE
Address: Vickers Road, Lenswood SA 5240
Phone: (08) 8389 8218
Fax: (08) 8389 8140
Email: jtweddell@nepenthe.com.au
WWW: http://www.nepenthe.com.au
Established: 1994
Winemaker: Peter Leske
Principal varieties grown: Chardonnay, Sauvignon Blanc, Merlot, Pinot Noir, Cabernet Sauvignon, Semillon, Zinfandel, Pinot Gris
Ha under vine: 25
Average annual crush: 100-249 tonnes

Principal wines & brands	Cellar Potential
Nepenthe Lenswood Chardonnay	5 years
Nepenthe Lenswood Semillon	4 years
Nepenthe Lenswood Pinot Noir	3 years
Nepenthe Lenswood Cabernet Sauvignon	5 years
Nepenthe Vineyards Zinfandel	3 years
Nepenthe Lenswood Sauvignon Blanc	2 years
Nepenthe Unwooded Chardonnay	2 years

Retail distribution: Mail Order, Internet. Chase Agencies, SA; Wine Source, VIC, NSW

Petaluma

The pursuit of excellence is becoming a well-worn phrase, but when used in reference to Petaluma, it is most appropriate.

Petaluma is the brainchild of the brilliant Brian Croser. Brian Croser graduated with honours from Adelaide University in 1972, and joined the winemaking team at Thomas Hardy and Sons, where he assessed the entire winemaking, bottling and vineyard production areas. In 1973, he went to David University in California for further study and returned in 1974 in time to take over the year's white wine production.

Brian did his best to introduce his philosophy and technique of oxygen exclusion from the time grapes arrive in the winery to the time of bottling. Unfortunately the winemaking equipment at Hardys was not fit for this procedure. Whilst working with Brian, I well remember dragging cylinders of carbon dioxide around the winery at Waikerie at 4.00am, attempting to cover and protect wine being loaded for transport to Adelaide for bottling, the winery workers thinking I had screws loose!!

In 1975, Croser convinced Hardys to invest in new equipment, refrigeration and improved storage facilities. He helped introduce oxygen exclusion, cold settling of wines, filtering before fermentation, careful yeast choice and long slow fermentation at Hardys, and the rest is history. The 1975 white wines took the industry and market by storm. They dominated the white wine classes in every wine show in Australia, and overnight Brian Croser became a legend. Despite an offer of Chief winemaker's position, Brian left Hardys in 1976 and joined the staff at the Riverina College of Advanced Education at Wagga Wagga in New South Wales where he did much to introduce modern winemaking skills which have helped our entire industry so much. The first Petaluma wine, a spaetlese rhine, was made at the College winery in 1976 from Mitchelton fruit.

By 1978, Brian had left the College and begun a wine consultancy business, where he instantly amassed a huge group of clients. In the same year, he constructed a winery and planted a vineyard for champagne, at Piccadilly. Brian brings in his grapes from selected regions which he believes have the potential to best produce the varietal characteristics he is looking for.

Petaluma has large vineyards in the Clare Region specialising in riesling in the high cool Polish Hill River region. The reds largely come from Petaluma's Coonawarra and Sharefarmers vineyards in the cool southeast of South Australia, rich in the famed terra rossa soils. The chardonnay and sparkling wines under the Petaluma and Croser labels largely come from the Adelaide Hills, as does the Bridgewater Mill Sauvignon Blanc.

Petaluma has become a very successful public company and also owns Knappstein Wines of Clare and the Mitchelton Winery in Victoria. Brian is immersed in the maximisation of wine quality and production efficiency of these two additions to Petaluma's wine stable.

The Bridgewater Mill is a beautiful historic mill nearby to Petaluma in the hills. It was a derelict shell when Brian took it over in the early 1980's; today it is a splendid Restaurant and Gallery that also holds concerts. It is also a successful cellar door for Petaluma as well as marketing a Bridgewater Mill Label, encompassing some exciting and different fresh fruit driven wine styles.

Brian Croser has been a true crusader for the wine industry in its fight against the huge increases in wine taxes. Over two years, at least half his working life was devoted to fighting for the industry, creating a plan and blueprint for the Australian wine and grape industry as we approach the 21st Century. Due to his efforts the industry now has the government support and understanding it so richly deserves, considering its employment, export success and tourism multiplier effects. Petaluma and Brian Croser are a credit to wine in Australia.

Brian has just reported a sizeable increase in Petaluma Ltd's profits and been awarded the Annual Maurice O'Shea Award for services to the industry, a richly deserved honour.

PETALUMA'S BRIDGEWATER MILL
Address: Old Mount Barker Road, Bridgewater SA 5152
Phone: (08) 8339 3422
Fax: (08) 8339 5311
Established: 1976; Public Co., 1993
Winemaker: Brian Croser

Principal wines & brands	Cellar Potential
Bridgewater Mill Sauvignon Blanc	2-5 years
Bridgewater Mill Chardonnay	2-5 years
Bridgewater Mill Millstone Shiraz	10+ years

Public & trade tours: By appointment
Hours open to public: 10.30am-5pm, daily
Points of interest: Restaurant, cellar door facility for Petaluma function centre, historical flour mill houses sparkling wine cellar
Retail distribution: Cellar Door sales. Tucker Seabrook,NSW, VIC, QLD, WA; David Ridge, SA; Tim Seats, NT

Bridgewater Mill

In between Aldgate and Mount Barker in the pretty Adelaide Hills lies one of the gems of the wine industry and a monument to good taste and cultural living. The Bridgewater Mill is fully restored even with even its giant wheel quietly ticking over as the tranquil stream flows by. Brian Croser was searching the hills to find a suitable location for a cellar for his methode champenoise; solid, cool and somewhat humid were the basic demands. In the Bridgewater Mill, he found all those things plus a handsome historic building. The cellars hold some of his beloved Croser Sparkling, whilst the internal structure now holds a multi level gallery and restaurant. When Brian and long time friend Len Evans were giving the Mill the once over, Len remarked it would make a marvellous theatre. The cleverly designed internal roof of the tasting area and bar is actually on a hydraulic system and towers to form a genuine stage.

Like the wine, the ambience at the Mill is a real treat. The Bridgewater Mill Sauvignon Blanc is fresh and fruity with a keen exotic oriental edge to its flavour and the finish is a

winner. The Riesling Methode Champenoise is superb and the reds very fruity and

balanced. Put a lunch at the Bridgewater Mill on your must-do list now.

Henschke – Lenswood

During the 1980's Henschke's conducted a search to find vineyard land to produce the highest quality table wines. Their search led them to the heart of the Adelaide Hills, where they purchased an existing 40 acre apple orchard and began establishing a picture book vineyard at Lenswood, which is 50 kms south of their Keyneton vineyards.

Prue and Stephen Henschke met during their studies at Adelaide University on the 1970's, where Prue was then majoring in Botany and Zoology. After marrying, they took off to Germany, where they both studied at the famous Geisenheim Wine Institute. Prue worked closely with the world renowned viticulturist and oenologist Dr Helmut Becker for two years, learning the German's meticulous and rigorous approach to viticulture in particular.

The quality of the grapes Prue is producing is truly world class and the wines of the last few vintages have been truly wonderful and one wonders just how good the Henschke wines of the future will be. I for one await them with keen anticipation.

HENSCHKE - LENSWOOD

Address: Lenswood. Postal Address: PO Box 100, Keyneton SA 5353
Phone: (08) 8564 8223
Fax: (08) 8564 8294
Established: 1981
Winemaker: Stephen Henschke
Principal varieties grown: Chardonnay, Riesling, Pinot Noir, Merlot, Cabernet Sauvignon
Ha under vine: 12

Average annual crush: 65 tonnes
Average no. cases produced: 4,500

Principal wines & brands	Cellar Potential
Abbotts Prayer	5-10 years
Greens's Hill Riesling	2-5 years
Giles Pinot Noir	2-5 years
Croft Chardonnay	2-5 years

Retail distribution: Nationally through Tucker Seabrook

Penfolds Magill Estate

The first Penfold to reach Australia was Dr. Christopher Rawson Penfold. He and his wife Mary arrived in Adelaide in 1844. Being a great believer in the healing powers of red wine (especially when treating anaemia), Dr Penfold planted vine cuttings he had brought from the south of France. He built a solid stone cottage which he called 'The Grange', and which is today classified under the National Trust. The soil at the Magill Estate is rich and red and Dr Penfold's vines thrived. After his death in 1870, his wife, daughter Georgina and son-in-law Thomas Francis Hyland took over the company, opening offices in Melbourne and Sydney.

Penfolds wines were increasingly successful and before 1913, the company had purchased Wyndham's Dalwood vineyards in the Hunter Valley, Pridmore's Southern Vales winery south of Adelaide, the Minchinbury winery and cellars on the outskirts of Sydney, and they had established the Nuriootpa Cellars in the Barossa Valley. In order to process the large crops of grapes being produced by returned soldiers, Penfolds also established a winery at Griffith in New South Wales in 1921. Over the next 40 years the company purchased further properties in the Hunter Valley, Coonawarra and next door to their own winery at Magill, the latter being the old Auldana Cellars and future home of Penfolds' famous St. Henri Claret. By 1950, 95 per cent of Penfolds production

was based on fortified wines. The management decided to change the company's direction and develop a range of table wines. The man chosen to head this project was Max Schubert, who had been with Penfolds since his youth.

As a youngster, Max had worked each night after school, mucking out stables and priming gas lanterns, for the princely sum of 2 shillings and sixpence (25 cents) a week.

Max was sent to Europe to study winemaking and while in France met one of the Bordeaux region's most famous winemakers, Christian Cruse.

After observing his winemaking techniques and tasting some very old Bordeaux wines, Max was determined to create a new style of Australian red wine, one that would age well for decades. The wine he produced in 1951 was the first vintage of Australia's most famous wine, Grange Hermitage. Very few people recognised the quality or potential of the wine and it received some

aggressive criticism. Today, however, Grange's of the early 50's sell for thousands of dollars a bottle at auction.

Sensitive to the criticism, Penfolds revoked their support of the wine, but were forced to capitulate as it grew in popularity and acclaim during the 1960's.

Like Grange Hermitage, Penfolds St. Henri Claret was not instantly accepted by the public. This wine was originally made at the Auldana Winery and is of a rich, full-bodied style, being aged only in old oak casks.

As with Grange, St. Henri was considerably ahead of its time. So were Penfolds Bin 389, a cabernet shiraz blend aged in the previous Grange hogsheads, Bin 28, a soft, full, Kalimna Shiraz and Bin 128, an elegant, Coonawarra Shiraz. Koonunga Hill is a similar style of wine, although more commercial and excellent value for money. In 1985, Penfolds released their 1983 Magill Estate. This special wine was made entirely from the remaining 5 ha shiraz vines at the famous Grange Vineyards. Originally covering 77 ha, the vineyard has been reduced to 5 ha by Adelaide's suburban sprawl.

undergone a major restoration, to make it a splendid showpiece of the wine industry, doing justice to its true heritage.

The complex includes the truly first class "Magill Estate Restaurant" which has panoramic views over the city of Adelaide, a visit is a must as it is less than 15 minutes from the city centre.

The modern day winemaking hub of Penfolds is now the Nuriootpa Cellars which is one of the world's most technically advanced wineries. The world class restaurant at Magill Estate is now a classy addition to Adelaide dining with splendid views over the vineyard, city and St Vincent's (the patron saint of wine) Gulf. I am sure St Vincent and Max Schubert's spirits are now as one.

The wine is made in the old Grange fermenting cellar and aged in new American and French oak hogsheads.

Even in his retirement, Max spent much of his time in his laboratory office which was always open to anyone who wanted to bring in their old Penfolds wines for "Dr" Max to check over and if necessary restore to good health with a top-up or a new cork.

Max was ever generous, a true gentleman, and he is sadly missed by all since his death in early 1994.

John Duval, the chief winemaker for Penfolds, is a protege of Max Schubert and is doing an excellent job with all the Penfolds wines, which cover the whole gambit of styles - reds, whites, the fortifieds - up to the great 'Grandfather Port' and many excellent sparkling wines.

Magill Estate, with Dr Rawson Penfold's old cottage and its vineyards remains the spiritual home of Penfolds and has

"Dr." Max and his baby
"Grange-Schubert's Unfinished Symphony"

Geoff Hardy – Kuitpo

In 1980 a youthful 24 year old, Geoff Hardy, purchased the Old Ryecroft vineyards in the foothills behind McLaren Vale with the then vineyard manager Ian Leask.

They grafted over many of the then unfashionable varieties and started making a reputation as top-flight grapegrowers and viticulturists winning the first South Australian Vineyard of the Year award in 1990.

Geoff was keen to develop a truly cool climate vineyard and chose a site near the Kuitpo pine forests high in the ranges, 7 or so kilometres inland from McLaren Vale in the Adelaide Hills wine region. Today he has some 33 hectares of Australia's most revered vineyards. His grapes are eagerly sought after by the cream of the best winemakers. Geoff selects his favourite rows of the vineyard to make his own few hundred dozen super premium wines.

In 1995 his 1993 Kuitpo Shiraz outpointed 400 of Australia's best shiraz wines from any vintage to win the inaugural Australia Shiraz Challenge sponsored by Qantas and held in the Goulburn Valley, Victoria. All three judges, James Halliday in

Melbourne, Brian Croser at Bridgewater and Geoff Merrill at Reynella chose this wine as Australia's Best Shiraz totally independently.

Geoff also runs a vine nursery at the

vineyard during springtime. In 1997 he supplied four million cuttings to the burgeoning viticultural boom around Australia. Geoff Hardy, who just happens to be my brother, is a credit to our great industry.

Rosemount – Kuitpo

Rosemount's movement into establishing their own vineyards in the premium cool climate areas of Australia took a big step forward a few years ago when managing director Bob Oatley saw Geoff Hardy's Kuitpo vineyards and tasted the wines.

During a dinner between the two friends he made Geoff a very generous offer to buy the vineyard. Geoff gave the offer much thought.

That night he awoke to the realisation he could not part with his gem in the hills, but he did know of a great site on Range Road, so he and Bob worked out a deal and Geoff designed and laid out a picture book vineyard.

Now 32 hectares are about to bear their first crop of sauvignon blanc and chardonnay. Look out for these wines, they are sure to be sensational.

An introduction to Eden Valley

The Eden Valley Region has been in recent years tied in with the Adelaide hills climatically as both regions are in the Mt Lofty Ranges. However, from a wine tourism point of view, traditionally the region has always been aligned with the Barossa Valley and often known as the Barossa Ranges. The climate is cool with most vineyards located 400 metres or more above sea level.

Many vineyards such as Pewsey Vale planted firstly by Joseph Gilbert date back to the 1840's. The development in the region over the last two decades has been astonishing. The Hill-Smith's of Yalumba fame have planted large vineyards at Pewsey Vale, Hill-Smith Estate and Heggies. Southcorp have large vineyards at Tollana-Woodbury and Seppelts Partalunga, on the border with the Adelaide Hills. Mountadam is most impressive and others such as Jim Irvine and Karl Seppelt join with traditional long term vineyards and wineries such as Henschke at Keyneton. The region stretches from Mt Pleasant in the south to Moculta in the north and borders on the Barossa Valley on the west. The main town with long wine traditions are Springton and Keyneton. Riesling thrives and makes exceptional wines but all classic varieties do well in this classic region.

1	Craneford Wine Co.
2	Grand Cru
3	Hamilton's Springton Winery
4	Heggies Vineyard
5	Henschke Cellars - Keyneton
6	Hill Smith Estate
7	Irvine
8	Leo Buring High Eden Estate
9	Mountadam
10	Pewsey Vale Vineyards
11	Seppelt's PartalungaVineyard
12	Tollana Woodbury Vineyard

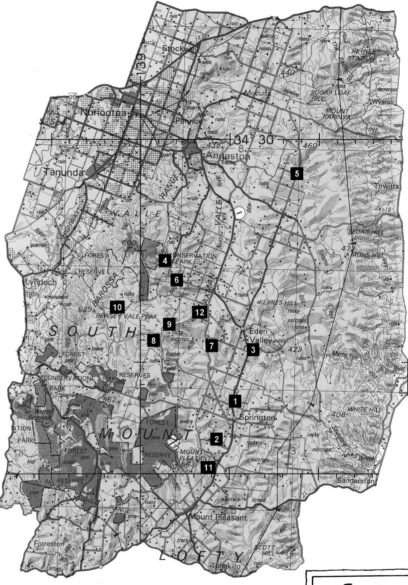

High up in the Eden Valley is the Springhill Manor of Jim and Marjorie Irvine, built in 1860. Jim is a real gentleman and without doubt one of Australia's busiest and most sought-after winemaking consultants.

Over the years Jim has made wine on a consulting basis for some 43 different wineries, all of whom speak highly of his professionalism and ability.

In 1993, he achieved the ultimate accolade when a wine made by him for the Elderton Winery won the Jimmy Watson Trophy. For his own label, Jim has chosen the high ground; he makes an absolute stunner of a merlot. Many years ago when consulting for Normans, at a lunch with the Horlin-Smiths, he tasted the Chateau Petrus, the world's most expensive red wine - a 100% merlot from the Pomerol district near Bordeaux.

Jim has attempted to make his own version of the taste he fell in love with that day. The merlot spends almost four years in wood and yet is still fresh, but so silky smooth and complex. It earns every bit of its regal name 'Grand Merlot' dressed in its regal robes - probably Australia's best-packaged wine. The 1988 Merlot won the World Merlot Competition from hundreds of entrants and he recently repeated the same feat.

Jim also makes several superb methode champenoise wines including a straight meslier, an unusual variety used in the Champagne region of France to help the acidity in the base wines during warm years: its zesty fruit makes it the ideal aperitif drink.

The Irvine Blanc de Blanc Chardonnay normally spends 4-5 years on yeast lees but often longer, his merlot red methode champenoise is exquisite.

For almost 48 years since his first job in the laboratory at Glenloth as a sixteen year old, Jim Irvine has weaved his creative magic with wine, never losing his enthusiasm and zest for life, shared wholeheartedly by his wife Marjorie and their two daughters. The elder, Joanne, traded in her nursing theatre sister's degree to study winemaking. The Irvine wines of the future look assured.

IRVINE
Address: Basil Roeslers Road, Eden Valley S.A. 5235
Phone: (08) 8564 1046
Fax: (08) 8564 1046
Established: 1980
Owners: James and Marjorie Irvine
Winemaker: James Irvine
Principal varieties grown: Merlot, Meslier, Chardonnay, Pinot Gris
Ha under vine: 10
Average annual crush: 100 Tonnes
Average no. cases produced: 7,000

Principal wines & brands	Cellar Potential
Eden Crest Unwooded Chardonnay	5 years
Irvine Grand Merlot	15+ years
Irvine Sparkling Merlot Brut	5 years
Irvine Brut Royale	5 years
Eden Crest Meslier Brut	3 years
Eden Crest Merlot Cabernet	7 years
Eden Crest Petit Merlot	5 years
Eden Crest Pinot Chardonnay Brut	5 years

Public & trade tours: Trade by invitation
Hours open to public: Not open as yet
Points of interest: Only Australian grower of the variety Meslier - from Champagne district of France. Specialist Merlot makers
Retail distribution: Switzerland, NZ, Taiwan, VIC, SA, NSW, WA

Henschke Eden Valley/Keyneton

The Henschke family have a long and rich winemaking history in Australia. They are dignified and private people, who are purposeful and enthusiastic in their desire to produce individual and exceptional wines.

Johann Christian Henschke arrived in South Australia in 1841, initially settled in the Barossa Valley at Bethany, and moved to Keyneton in the Barossa Ranges in 1862. Henschke's is now the only winery in the immediate area but it was once one of many established by German and English settlers in the last century.

The first wine was made at Henschke in 1868 and Johann's grandson Paul Alfred helped his father build substantial cellars at the turn of the century. The wine was sold in bulk until 1951 when Cyril Henschke took over the business, and began bottling and labelling Henschke wine. In 1970 he received a Churchill Fellowship and travelled the world studying wine making. Henschke wines are now made and managed by Stephen Henschke who was educated at Adelaide University and at the Geisenheim Wine Institute in Germany. He has updated and restored much of the winery, and the cellar door area is superb. The winery exudes an air of history and the wonderful 130 year old Henschke home next door is set in a beautiful garden.

Stephen Henschke's white wines are exciting. The improvements to the winery and his study have paid off, producing a range of excellent white varietal wines including a chardonnay, semillon, riesling, sauvignon blanc, gewurztraminer and a magnificent noble riesling. The Henschke reds are still living up to their big reputation with Mt Edelstone and Hill of Grace (from a vineyard near the Church of the same name) being outstanding.

The Henschke's are a real team with research viticulturist Prue Henschke providing Stephen with fantastic grapes for his great wines, which easily ranks the winery in the top ten of Australia's best.

HENSCHKE - KEYNETON
Address: Keyneton. Postal Address: PO Box 100, Keyneton SA 5353
Phone: (08) 8564 8223
Fax: (08) 8564 8294
Established: 1868
Winemaker: Stephen Henschke
Principal varieties grown:
Riesling, Semillon, Shiraz, Cabernet Sauvignon, Chardonnay
Ha under vine: 75
Average annual crush: 510 tonnes
Average no. cases produced: 35,000

Principal wines & brands	Cellar Potential
Hill Of Grace	10+ years
Cyril Henschke Cabernet Sauvignon	5-10 years
Mount Edelstone	5-10 years
Keyneton Estate	5-10 years
Julius Eden Valley Riesling	5-10 years
Eden Valley Semillon	5-10 years
Tilly's Vineyard	2-5 years

Public & trade tours: By appointment
Hours open to public: 9am-4.30pm, weekdays; 9am-12noon, Sat; 10am-3pm, public holidays
Retail distribution: Nationally through Tucker Seabrook

Grand Cru Estate – Karl Seppelt

After a long search Karl and Lotte Seppelt found an ideal property to plant vines and start their own wine enterprise. They purchased 120 hectares in 1981, located a couple of kilometres south of Springton, which originally belonged to George Fife Angas.

The stone buildings are quite special and the Estate has developed remarkably since then. Karl is a meticulous person with a grand plan and the Tower he has built at the entrance to the winery is distinctly reminiscent of Chateau La Tour, the famous French Grand Cru.

Four hectares were planted to chardonnay and cabernet sauvignon in 1981. This was to be a retirement project for Karl and Lotte after his long working life with Seppelts. However things did not stop there, in 1985 a further four hectares were planted and the first vintage from the Estate was made. Expansion continues to this day.

Karl has made wines that are of truly exceptional quality. His Brut Sauvage Methode Champenoise is bone dry and an ideal aperitif style. He also makes a Chardonnay Brut Sparkling and a Shiraz Sparkling also by the Methode Champenoise process.

The table wine range includes a chablis style chardonnay dry and crisp. A rhine riesling and a long living bordeaux style cabernet sauvignon. Added to this is a shiraz from Langhorne Creek grapes. Long a devotee of fortified wines, Karl makes an exquisite dry flor fino sherry which often graces my dinner table – "try it with or in the soup" a vintage and a tawny port. Over 100 medals have been won in major shows.

The Estate has a wonderful cellar door and a function cellar ideal for a dinner or lunch. Karl's son Peter is now involved at Grand Cru. It is an Estate not to be missed on your wine journey.

KARL SEPPELT - GRAND CRU
Address: R. Dewells Road, Springton SA 5235
Direction: 9km north of Mt Pleasant, turn left and proceed 1.5km second road on right
Phone: (08) 8568 2378
Fax: (08) 8568 2799
Email: grandcru@terra.net.au
Established: 1981
Owner: K. J. Seppelt
Winemaker: K. J. Seppelt / Petaluma
Principal varieties grown: Chardonnay, cabernet, meunier, merlot
Ha under vine: 10
Average annual crush: 75 tonnes. Some grapes purchased as well
Principal wines & brands
Brut Sauvage (bone dry sparkling)
Chardonnay Brut (sparkling)
Sparkling Shiraz
Cabernet Sauvignon (Bordeaux style) long living
Chardonnay (lightly wooded) long living
Shiraz (Langhorne Creek) long living
Rhine Riesling (Eden Valley)
Tawny Port
Vintage Port very long living
Flor Fino
Hours open to public: Cellar Door sales: 10am-5pm, 7 days a week
Points of interest: Picnic facilities available.
Retail distribution: Available in selected bottle shops, Sydney, Melbourne and Adelaide, or Cellar Door and Mail Order. Exports to Germany, Canada, Japan and Indonesia

Mountadam

Adam Wynn is a real winner, focused, positive and urbane, his technical skills rank with the world's best, but his creative flair and love of music and art give extra dimensions to his wines that are truly exciting.

His family's achievements in Australian wine have been extraordinary; however, he is one of the most likeable and natural people you would be likely to meet. The Wynn wine saga commenced in Poland just after the turn of the century. Samuel Wynn made a yearly pilgrimage to the Black Sea and returned to Poland with dried raisins which he reconstituted and turned into wine. At 21 years of age, he arrived in Australia keen to pursue a career in wine; this began with a wine bar in Bourke Street Melbourne, where he came up with the classic barrel-design Wynns 2 litre flagon. Samuel lived until 90 years of age, a testament to a life tempered by good wine. Adam's late father David truly put the Wynn family on the wine map. In 1950 he purchased the run down old Coonawarra Estate, featuring its famous three-gabled roof on his Wynn's Coonawarra label. The world recognition of this region bear testament to David's greatness, but he did much more. A very talented artist, he was chairman of the Adelaide Festival Trust for many years and created the concept of the highly successful Barossa Music Festival which he served until his death as its founding chairman.

David had enormous vision; his search for the top viticultural region in Australia ended 600 metres above the Barossa and Eden Valleys. A visit to Mountadam is a rare treat, set high on Eden Ridge in rugged rocky country, habitat for the majestic wedgetail eagle, the symbol of the winery, and prominently displayed in the huge granite sculptures on the impressive stone pillared entrance to the vineyard.

The setting just on the lee side of the ridge gives protection to the vines from harsh winds, and provides an ideal frost-free microclimate; the resultant outstanding fruit is the cornerstone of Adam's Wines. Adam followed a degree in agricultural science with a postgraduate degree in oenology from Bordeaux in France, where he was dux of the course in 1981.

Rarely have I seen so many expensive French oak barrels in any winery, let alone the modestly sized Mountadam. Adam follows a no expense spared philosophy, using French Troncais oak, tight-grained and with subtle but distinct flavour characteristics.

Barrel fermentation, careful selection and individual treatment of the many hundreds of barrels for the chardonnay and the reds, produces complex wines that shine at the top of Australia's wine tree.

Adam produces a 50/50 merlot cabernet wine simply called 'The Red', which is simply superb. The cornerstone of the product range is the Mountadam Chardonnay. The David Wynn range of quality Eden Valley varietals and the Eden Ridge organic range complement the domain-grown Mountadam wines. Adam Wynn has literally taken the high ground of Australian wine.

MOUNTADAM

Address: High Eden Road, Eden Valley SA 5235
Phone: (08) 8564 1101
Fax: (08) 8564 1064
Email: office@mtadam.com
WWW: http://mtadam.com
Established: 1972
Owner: Adam Wynn
Winemaker: Adam Wynn
Principal varieties grown: Chardonnay, Pinot Noir, Cabernet Sauvignon, Merlot
Ha under vine: 40
Average annual crush: 300 tonnes
Average no. cases produced: 40,000

Principal wines & brands	Cellar Potential
Mountadam Chardonnay	2-5 years
Mountadam Pinot Noir	5-10 years
Mountadam The Red	5-15 years
Mountadam Cabernet Sauvignon	5-15 years
Mountadam Merlot	5-15 years

Public & trade tours: By Appointment Only
Hours open to public: 11am-4pm, daily
Retail distribution: Bottle Shops and Restaurants Australia Wide

Tollana – Woodbury Vineyard

Tollana's Woodbury Vineyard is situated down the road from Mountadam in the rugged Barossa Ranges.

It was established in the 1960's when Tolley, Scott & Tolley decided to branch out from distilling into the premium wine market.

The grape varieties already planted in the Barossa Valley were for fortified wine production and thus were unsuitable for premium wine production. New land was required to facilitate the company's expansion and Woodbury Vineyard was the result. The vines planted along certain lines, cover a massive area, even more impressive because from the road you can see over the entire rolling hillsides of vines; it's the largest contour-planted vineyard in Australia and an awesome sight in autumn.

The varieties include, riesling, chardonnay, semillon, sauvignon blanc, shiraz and cabernet sauvignon. The rhine riesling has proved to be the consistent medal winner and the 'T.R.' series of red wines have had a distinguished show career, including several trophies and many gold medals.

The Woodbury roll call of winemakers is also impressive. Wolf Blass, winemaker from 1968-1973, was followed and ultimately joined by John Glaetzer. Alan Hoey gave the Tollana Woodbury whites their real boost and was capably followed by Pat Tocaciu. Today the devoted winemaker and ambassador for Tollana is Neville Falkenberg who has 'Toll' in one eye and 'ana' in the other.

The Tollana range with their bold black labels are all marvellous wines. If you want one of Australia's finest botrytised rieslings for that special dessert, you just cannot go past the Tollana which is also sold at a most reasonable price. Considering the expense involved in making this unique style, search it out!

An introduction to the Barossa Valley

Without doubt the most famous of Australia's wine regions is the Barossa Valley. Something of an institution with Australian wine lovers, the area has a personality all its own.

This character is mainly due to the Barossa's large German population who began to arrive in 1842. Having sought a new start in a new land, not possible in their homeland, many hundreds of German Lutherans were settled on the huge properties of George Fife Angas. Many of these immigrants had already been involved in viticulture in Germany and soon planted vine cuttings they had brought with them to Australia. Significant amongst these first commercial plantings were those made by Johann Gramp at Rowland Flat, which saw the beginning of the Orlando Company and that of Samuel Smith at Angaston which became Yalumba. The Seppelt family company was established with Joseph Seppelt's planting in 1851.

The first wines produced in the Barossa were table wines, but as fortifieds gained in popularity by the turn of the century, wine-makers were forced to alter the emphasis of the production. This transition was easy due to the valley's temperate climate, rich soils and sheltered environment, which enabled new grape varieties, such as grenache and pedro to reach production relatively quickly. Over the last ten years however, popular tastes have reverted to premium table wines. As a result, the area under vine in the Barossa is currently less than its peak, as many vignerons are replanting their vineyards with grapes more suitable for table wine.

Companies such as Peter Lehmann, Basedow, St. Hallett, Rockford and others are producing excellent premium table wines and have recently been joined by newcomers on the boutique arena such as Burge Family, Bethany, Charles Melton, Charles Cimicky, Grant Burge and others. The Barossa Valley is home to many large companies such as Penfold's and Kaiser Stuhl, Orlando, Seppelts, Yalumba, Wolf Blass, Tollana, Krondorf, Leo Buring and Saltram. All these wineries are totally committed to Barossa fruit and have a full recognition of the Barossa's solid viticultural base. Many vineyards have been in the same families and worked by them for five or six generations.

Many vineyards of shiraz, grenache and semillon have 50 year old vines and some over 100 years old, whilst other regions have changed dramatically viticulturally. There has also been a renaissance of quality bottled table wines at such wineries as Chateau Yaldara and Rovalley Estate. The growing emphasis on wine tourism has led to the establishment of the likes of Kaesler Wines with its restaurant, conference and seminar facilities and cottage accommodation. The list goes on, with many fine restaurants and Bed and Breakfast Inns being established during the last decade. Every two years the Barossa Valley is the setting for a wonderful Vintage Festival. Commencing on Easter Monday, the festival runs for a week and is centred around the Tanunda oval. There is a giant fair and all the local wine companies set up marquees for public tastings. A colourful parade passes through the streets and a Vintage Festival Queen is crowned.

The highlights of this celebration are the huge banquets, held in Tanunda's enormous hall, consisting of a sit down Barossa feast for roughly 2,000 people at a time. The entertainment provided at these functions is excellent, particularly the comedian - who is the local undertaker. In addition, the Ledertahl Choir and Tanunda Brass Band usually perform to delighted crowds who, by the end of the evening are usually standing on their tables clapping to the music.

The Festival wine auction is also worth attending and must be the best of its kind held in Australia.

The Spring Barossa Music Festival features two weeks of outstanding concerts at wineries, the valley's beautiful churches and other venues. This event is not only of National but International significance and is already a major South Australian Tourism attraction. Another event, the Annual Barossa Classic Gourmet Weekend in August, where most wineries participate and team up with a leading restaurant and provide live entertainment, is hugely successful. This weekend welcomes more than 30,000 happy visitors each year. The Valley also boasts some of the best bakeries and small goods makers in Australia. Put a trip to the Barossa on your travel agenda. Until then, why not enjoy some of her fine wines.

Kaesler Wines

Toby and Treena Hueppauff are a delightful down to earth couple who have worked very hard indeed to create the charming and multi-faceted Kaesler Estate on the main road, just before the township of Nuriootpa.

The whole complex has a real feel of old Australiana, with its corrugated iron roofs and verandahs; indeed some of the buildings were German pioneers' cottages.

The property was purchased in 1986 to expand Toby's landscaping business, but its potential was soon realised and the restoration process began. In 1990 came the tasting area and the delightful vine and pergola-covered courtyard, then the lake with its mini bridges and landings.

The initial development was followed by an alfresco style restaurant and then a conference and seminar area expanded further in 1997. In 1994 Toby and Treena decided to convert some of the older buildings into high class bed and breakfast accommodation with a superb central lounge area where one can gaze out over the vineyards to the Barossa Ranges beyond.

The Kaesler wines cover the main table wine styles along with some excellent old fortifieds. The flagship if the Old Vine Shiraz with its distinctive oval shaped black and gold label. The vines this wine comes from celebrated their centenary in 1992; it's a wine well worth seeking out. The Kaesler semillon is also a great traditional Barossa white.

Kaesler's laid-back style, its cosy atmosphere and the Hueppauffs' hospitality make a visit here one to look forward to.

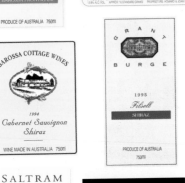
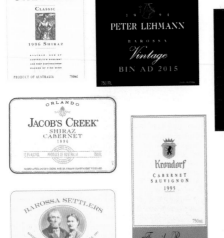

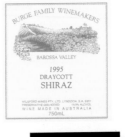

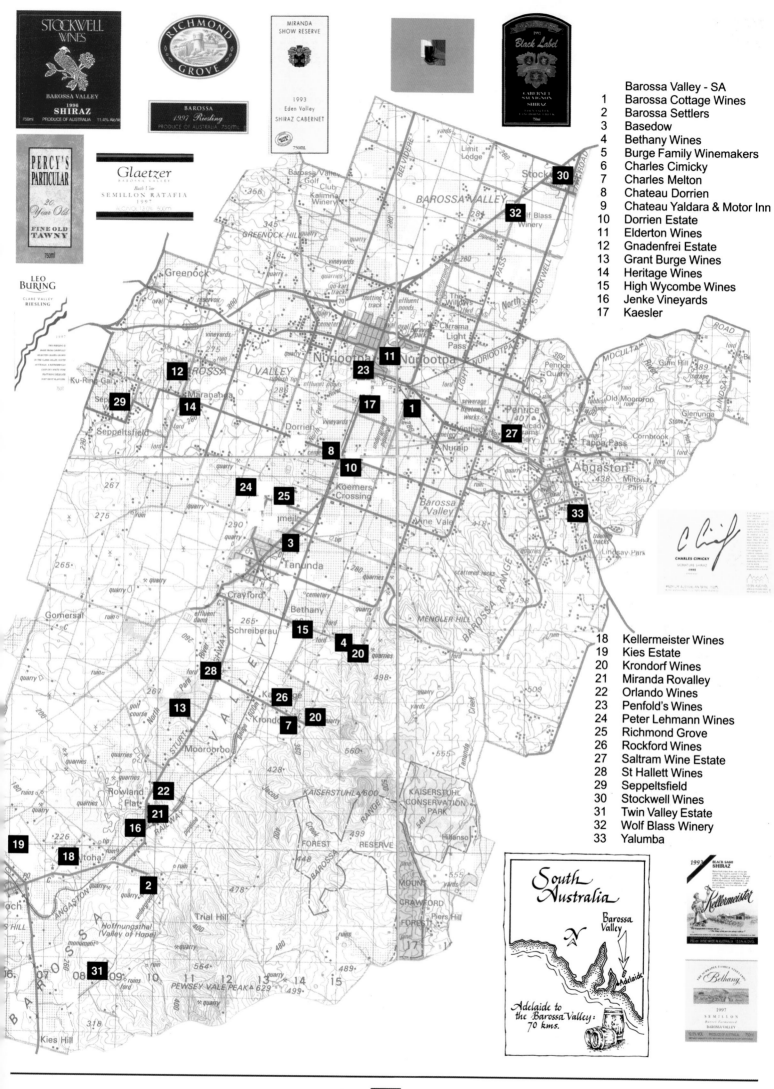

Barossa Valley - SA

1 Barossa Cottage Wines
2 Barossa Settlers
3 Basedow
4 Bethany Wines
5 Burge Family Winemakers
6 Charles Cimicky
7 Charles Melton
8 Chateau Dorrien
9 Chateau Yaldara & Motor Inn
10 Dorrien Estate
11 Elderton Wines
12 Gnadenfrei Estate
13 Grant Burge Wines
14 Heritage Wines
15 High Wycombe Wines
16 Jenke Vineyards
17 Kaesler

18 Kellermeister Wines
19 Kies Estate
20 Krondorf Wines
21 Miranda Rovalley
22 Orlando Wines
23 Penfold's Wines
24 Peter Lehmann Wines
25 Richmond Grove
26 Rockford Wines
27 Saltram Wine Estate
28 St Hallett Wines
29 Seppeltsfield
30 Stockwell Wines
31 Twin Valley Estate
32 Wolf Blass Winery
33 Yalumba

Chateau Tanunda

A significant part of Australia's wine industry and one of the most imposing, beautiful wine and spirit complexes is about to come to life again. Built in 1890 as part of the Seppelt burgeoning Wine Empire, Chateau Tanunda has just acquired only its third owner in over a hundred years.

John Geber is a highly successful wine and food entrepreneur. Several years ago he bought Cowra Estate in New South Wales and has used it as the centrepiece of a co-ordinated effort mainly aimed at the Export Market which has built the turnover up from a few thousand cases of wine to well over 100,000 cases.

John's enthusiasm and imagination were literally flying high as I discussed this grand project with him in the Golden Wings Lounge at the Adelaide airport as he flew out after meetings sealing up the deal as this book was going to press.

John has his feet firmly on the ground though, he sees himself as the custodian and guardian of the Chateau and with a mission to enhance and bring it to life, with the utmost respect for its history and tradition. The Chateau is located on about 13 hectares of prime Barossa land right on the eastern edge of the town of Tanunda literally right in the centre of the valley. The 4 hectares of wines will be expanded to cover much of the property and properly place it in its context as a winery.

A Boutique Winery, a real showpiece processing about 1,000 tonnes of grapes per year will grace half of the main Chateau building. John has a name the wines will carry well under his hat as the Chateau Tanunda brand is still used by Southcorp for brandy. All wines will be very traditional Barossa styles with old vines, basket pressing and such traditions featuring strongly and will be super premium in quality. The other half of the huge main building will become a first class resort type Hotel and Restaurant with rooms taking advantage of the panormaic views across the valley which looks over the first Barossa township of Bethany and the Barossa Ranges. The tall striking Distillery building will house a number of luxury apartments.

The huge old bond store will once again come to life storing wine and spirits for the expanding industry. Chateau Tanunda once crushed Australia's largest vintage of 26,000 tonnes many years ago, so everything is literally on a grand scale. The Adelaide to Angaston railway line which already hosts one tourist train a week skirts the property and the Tanunda Station is situated adjacent to the corner of the Chateau's vineyard.

The famous Bethany track which passes the Chateau will be great for guests. John is also renovating the old Administration Complex which will become very affordable vineyard accommodation.

John lauds the assistance and support he has received from the South Australian Government who share his vision and passion to revitalise this true gem in the crown of the wine industry and the heart of the best known Australian wine region; 'the Barossa'. We the wine lovers of Australia and the world are fortunate indeed. Good luck John – a toast to Chateau Tanunda.

Basedow Wines

In 1996, Basedow celebrated their centenary. The winery, built beside a creek in the centre of Tanunda by brothers Martin and Johann Basedow, was eventually taken over by Martin's son Oscar and renamed O. Basedow and Sons. Basedow's history and reputation had been forged with fortified wines, although John Basedow won the coveted Jimmy Watson Trophy in 1970 with his dry red. The real transformation for Basedow came during the mid 70's when Peter Lehmann's son Doug took over the reins, restoring the lovely old sandstone buildings, and upgrading the facilities, expanding the winery's capacity considerably.

Doug began contract crushing for the likes of Wolf Blass as well as upgrading the Basedow wines. The Basedow White Burgundy was the real pioneer for wood-aged semillons and remains a success story today. In 1993, Grant Burge, who had been using the Basedow winery for most of his fast-growing production, took over the winery, upgrading even further.

In 1996 progressive wine merchant Terry Hill, whose Hill International Wines in Sydney is a highly successful premium wine distributor, took over Basedow. Terry is a long time friend of Grant Burge and Grant remains in charge of the winemaking activities also making wine for Terry's two great McLaren Vale wineries, Marienberg and Fern Hill.

The Basedow wines and label today represent a quality boutique style wine at bargain prices. The underground tasting cellar is one of the best in the valley. Drop in while you are in Tanunda - it's easy to find.

BASEDOW WINES

Address: 161-165 Murray Street, Tanunda SA 5352
Phone: (08) 8563 3666
Fax: (08) 8563 2597
Email: basedow@ozemail.com.au
Established: 1896
Winemakers: Craig Stansborough and Grant Burge (Consulting)
Principal varieties grown: The company has a long term supply contract with independent growers
Average no. cases produced: 75,000

Principal wines & brands	Cellar Potential
White Burgundy (Oscar's Frattennal)	2-5 years
Oscar's Heritage	5-10 years
Chardonnay	5-10 years
Barossa Shiraz	5-10 years
Fine Old Tawny Port	10+ years

Public & trade tours:
By appointment only
Hours open to public:
10am-5pm, weekdays; 11am-5pm, weekends
Retail distribution:
Hill International Wines, Australia; Bibendum Wine Limited, UK;
The Australian Wine Connection, USA.

Bethany Wines

The Schrapel family, with Robert as winemaker and Geoff as marketing/sales/ viticulturist, represent one of the oldest grape-growing families in the region, going back to the German pioneers of the last century.

In 1977 they set up a beautiful winery, with a stunning panoramic view over the entire valley, by building into an old disused quarry. The natural cellar and insulation this has provided at minimal expense shows their good sense.

Like many Barossa wineries, they first made a mark with their riesling and today make a fine range of premium table and fortified wines including the aptly-named 'The Old Quarry Port'.

In 1994, at the Canberra National Wine Show, Bethany Wines won the trophy for the best dry red table wine, shiraz predominant, with its 1992 Bethany Shiraz. If you are ever in the valley for the Barossa Gourmet weekend, don't miss Bethany. The folk there always put on a great show with food, wine and dancing and the location is a knock out.

BETHANY

Address: Bethany Road, Tanunda SA 5352
Direction: 4 Km east of Tanunda
Phone: (08) 8563 2086
Fax: (08) 8563 0046
Established: Vineyard - 1850, Winery - 1981
Owners: Robert & Geoffrey Schrapel
Winemakers: Rob & Geoff Schrapel
Principal varieties grown: Riesling, Chardonnay, Shiraz, Semillon, Cabernet Sauvignon, Grenache
Ha under vine: 25
Average annual crush: 200-250 Tonnes
Average no. cases produced: 18,000

Public & trade tours: By Appointment Only
Hours open to public:
10am-5pm, Monday-Saturday; 1pm-5pm, Sunday
Points of interest:
Tasting area, Picnic area and Great view over-looking the Barossa Valley.
Retail distribution:
Westwood Wine Agencies, VIC; Carol-Ann Martin Classic Wines, NSW; Allied Vitners, ACT; Tasmanian Fine Wines, TAS. Porter and Co, SA, Wine 2000, QLD; Western Wines, WA; Bethany Wines, UK; Vintage Wines and Spirits Ltd, NZ. Also Germany, Switzerland, Ireland, Holland

Burge Family Winemakers

Back in 1928 the Burge family founded Wilsford Wines. Today carrying on that fine tradition is Rick Burge, a big genial fellow with both winemaking and hospitality skills at his fingertips.

I first ran into Rick in Rutherglen some 12 years ago when Milan Roden and I were researching our first book. He was running the Poachers Paradise, an excellent restaurant and tavern in the main street. Rick did a stint as winemaker at St. Leonards but decided home in the Barossa Valley and the family wine business was for him.

Rick has built a beautiful winery on the family's property at Lyndoch, just as you enter the town. Functionally and aesthetically, it is very well done. Rick has also phased in the new name Burge Family Winemakers and runs the Wilsford label for his fortified wines.

The Burge family run a number of wine, food and music events, always innovative, informative, interesting and lots of fun. Rick's great interest in music has translated into the production of a number of CD's which play at the cellar door as you enjoy the wines. The Burge Family's wines certainly have nothing to fear from competition.

BURGE FAMILY
Address: Barossa Highway, Lyndoch SA 5351
Direction: Outskirts of the Lyndoch township towards Adelaide
Phone: (08) 8524 4644
Fax: (08) 8524 4444
Established: 1928
Owners: Rick & Bronwyn Burge
Winemaker: Rick Burge
Principal varieties grown: Shiraz, Cabernet Sauvignon Merlot, Grenache, Touriga, Cabernet Franc, Riesling, Muscat Blanc
Ha under vine: 12
Average annual crush: 60 tonnes
Average no. cases produced: 3,300

Principal wines & brands	Cellar Potential
Draycott Shiraz	5-10 years
Draycott Homestead Blend	5-10 years
Draycott Merlot	2-5 years
"Old Vines" Grenache	2-5 years
Olive Hill Riesling	2-5 years
Muscat Blanc Late Harvest	2-5 years
"Wilsford" Tawny Port (20 years old)	

Public & trade tours: By Appointment Only
Hours open to public: 10am-5pm, daily except Christmas and Good Friday
Points of interest: Magnificent views of the Barossa Ranges. Stylish architecturally designed Cellar Sales & Tasting Room.
Retail distribution: All wine sold direct ex-Cellars & by Vineyard (Mailing List) Newsletters.

Dorrien Estate – Cellarmaster Wines

This impressively large winery is the home to Cellarmaster Wines, Australia's leading mail-order wine merchant. The complex includes a vast temperature-controlled cellar, with capacity for over 350,000 cases, and a purpose-built barrel hall for extended oak-ageing of selected wines. Cellarmaster Wines have over 250,000 members in Australia and New Zealand, and ship a million cases a year direct to members' homes, making them the largest merchant of home-delivered wine in the world.

If you haven't got time to get around to the wine regions, or even if you do, the wine club offers a convenient and competitive alternative to traditional retail outlets.

I have heard nothing but good reports of this organisation.

They are definitely one of the look-ahead players in the wine industry.

If you would like more information, Cellarmaster's toll-free phone number is 1800 500 260.

Charles Cimicky

Charles Cimicky's family came from Czechoslovakia where they had a background in winemaking and grape growing. The family had also been involved in the building trade.

In 1972, Charles built a winery in the Lyndoch region of the Barossa Valley and crushed his first vintage in 1973. Somehow, in between establishing a business and making wine he found time to study winemaking at the Charles Sturt University near Wagga Wagga in New South Wales. The Charles Cimicky winery is a grand-looking building with the air of a European castle, perched on top of a ridge surrounded by a sea of vines. The Charles Cimicky wines are all from their own vines, supplemented by a small quantity from two neighbouring vineyards. The reds of recent times have impressed me considerably. The cabernet sauvignon is a big opulent style, with a little merlot and cabernet franc blended into it in some years when Charles feels it needs it.

The other wines are a shiraz, a very herbaceous, crisp sauvignon blanc and a chardonnay. Occasionally a semillon or a semillon chardonnay are produced, depending on the season. Aided by the cooler climate of the southern Barossa and their own carefully tended vineyard, the Charles Cimicky wines are indeed impressive. Charles purposely keeps the range small to help him in his quest for quality.

Grant Burge Wines

Grant Burge comes from a family long involved in grape-growing in the Barossa Valley. I first met Grant some 25 years ago when, as young lads, we used to travel to wine shows together. Grant was working as a winemaker for the Southern Vales Co-operative in McLaren Vale just across the road from Hardy's where for a couple of years I prepared the show wines for the company.

Grant then, as now, was a quiet but happy sort of fellow, very committed to his quality winemaking. Some years later, he formed a partnership with colleague Ian Wilson - Burge and Wilson. They created a label and made wine together using their good contacts in both McLaren Vale and the Barossa

wine cellars as Gramps Winekeller. This base gave Grant the chance to develop a high profile for his excellent wines. His many talents and the help of his wife Helen in the marketing area, has seen Grant Burge wines through a period of explosive growth. Grant won the Telecom South Australian Small Business of the Year in 1993.

Grant Burge has quietly amassed large vineyard holdings around the Barossa Valley and Barossa Ranges. At present, 750 acres are planted in strategic locations and planting is still underway. Grant's total land holdings are around 2,000 acres, so he has further potential to expand his vineyards.

He is already in fact, one of the largest grape-growers in the valley.

This control of the vineyards is what gives Grant the opportunity to make the styles of wine he wants. For many years Grant has used the Basedow winery for his making which has been expanded and brought up to the absolute state of the art technically speaking. Grant's flagship is the "Meshach" one of Australia's top ten reds, a regal shiraz from 70 year old vines on Grant's Filsell Vineyard and named after his great-grandfather who started the family wine enterprise in the 1860".

Grant pays great credit to all his staff who have pulled together in this remarkable success story. Grant's wines have won many awards and are all very approachable in their rich fruit-driven style.

to source very high quality grapes. This partnership purchased the Krondorf Winery in the Barossa from the Seagram Wine Estates Group. Ironically it was right next door to the old Burge winery, Wilsford. Grant and Ian were highly successful and had been using the winery since 1976, a few years before purchasing it. In 1983, Krondorf went public to help with capital expenditure and expansion and two years later, Mildara purchased it, retaining Burge and Wilson as consultant winemakers.

In 1988, Grant decided to go out on his own and bought the beautiful cellars at Jacobs Creek, which were restored by Colin Gramp in the 1970's and run as a restaurant and

GRANT BURGE WINES PTY LTD
Address: Barossa Valley Way, Jacobs Creek, Tanunda SA 5352
Phone: (08) 8563 3700
Fax: (08) 8563 2807
Email: gbwines@dove.com.au
Established: 1988
Owners: Grant and Helen Burge
Winemaker: Grant Burge
Principal varieties grown: Riesling, Sauvignon Blanc, Chardonnay, Semillon, Shiraz, Cabernet Sauvignon, Merlot
Ha under vine: 400
Average annual crush: 1,200 tonnes
Average no. cases produced: 90,000

Principal wines & brands	Cellar Potential
Meshach	25 years
Shadrach	15 years
Sauvignon Blanc	4 years
Merlot	8 years
Shiraz	10 years
Cabernet Sauvignon	10 years
Chardonnay	7 years
Semillon	7 years
Pinot Noir Chardonnay (Methode Traditionale)	3 years

Public & trade tours: Yes
Hours open to public: 10am-5pm, daily except Christmas Day and Good Friday
Points of interest: Historic winery which has been carefully restored. First established as Moorooroo Estate in 1855
Retail distribution: NT - Aust. Liquor Marketers. SA - Options Wine Merchants. VIC - The Wine Company. NSW - Young and Roshleigh Wine Merchants. QLD - The Wine Tradition. ACT - Horny Willrons Pty Ltd. TAS - David Johnstone and Assoc. WA - David Mullen Wine Agency

Chateau Yaldara

From the visitor's point of view, Chateau Yaldara must be the most impressive winery in Australia. Originally an old flour mill, the building was little more than ruins when purchased and rebuilt along the lines of a European Chateau by Hermann Thumm.

Work commenced in the late 1940's and in addition to the Chateau, Yaldara have since built a stone distillery and a large stone reception and convention centre, seating up to 300 people. The whole complex is surrounded by beautiful gardens and two large lakes.

Hermann arrived in Australia just after the Second World War. He had studied wine-making in his native land. A year or so after his arrival, he bought the old Flour Mill near Lyndoch.

The chateau building proper is filled with European and Australian antiques and works of art.

During the 1970's, Hermann was joined in the business by his two sons, Robert and Deiter. Robert graduated from the Geisenheim College of Oenology in Germany and has made wine at Chateau Yaldara. Deiter is Managing Director of Chateau Yaldara.

Chateau Yaldara also sports a seminar, convention and motel complex - the famous Barossa Motel was completed in 1969. Over the years Chateau Yaldara have gained a reputation for producing many high quality, value for money wine styles.

In 1985 Chateau Yaldara went through a real revolution with the introduction of the "Lakewood" range of premium table wines. The name was inspired by the many lakes and wooded gardens on the property. They created some extraordinary wines, particularly chardonnay as an initial focus.

Chateau Yaldara have expanded their vineyard holdings substantially in the early 1990's, among other purchases they have bought a property known as "The Farms" right next to the winery.

This vineyard is blessed with Terra Rossa soil and produces red wine grapes of extraordinary quality. Chateau Yaldara recently released a super-super premium range of wines in very-very limited quantities called "The Farms". The overall impression one receives from a visit to Chateau Yaldara is that of orderly elegance and prosperity. The Thumms have come a long way with their energy and hard work, Australian wine is the beneficiary.

Kellermeister – Trevor Jones

Trevor Jones is a young winemaker with many years of experience. He and his family established their winery, which is blessed with a wonderful view of the valley from its hilltop location.

KELLERMEISTER WINES AND TREVOR JONES FINE WINES

Address: Barossa Valley Highway, Lyndoch SA 5351
Phone: (08) 8524 4303
Fax: (08) 8524 4880
Established: 1979
Owners: Ralph, Val and Trevor Jones
Winemaker: Trevor Jones
Principal varieties grown: Shiraz, Cabernet Sauvignon, Grenache, Merlot, Chardonnay, Semillon, Riesling, Frontignan, Sauvignon Blanc
Average annual crush: 100 tonnes
Average no. cases produced: 7,000

Principal wines & brands	Cellar Potential
Trevor Jones Riesling	10 years
Trevor Jones Virgin Chardonnay	8 years
Trevor Jones Dry Grown Barossa Shiraz	10-12 years
Kellermeister Black Sash Shiraz	10+ years
Kellermeister Sable	
Kellermeister 'Oregon Brown' Port	

Public & trade tours: By appointment only
Hours open to public: 9am-5.30pm, daily
Points of interest: Cellar door sales building constructed from mud bricks and recycled oregon, redgum and jarrah timber. Espresso Coffee and Café area adjoining cellar door.
Retail distribution: Direct from winery and mail order

In 1979, Trevor had already made wine for the late Ken Kies at Karrawirra, there lies the beginnings of his unique award winning Trevor Jones label with its illustration of a pair of rubber boots. Coming from Canada, Lesley Forsyth began her Australian career working with Trevor at Karrawirra, and now looks after his marketing, long remembers her wet feet from wandering out into the winery looking for Trevor. His promise to buy her a pair of boots, which as a true hands on winemaker, he rarely takes off himself, has never come to pass.

The cellar door at Kellermeister is a real treat with its huge Oregon beams, mud brick construction and large open fire for winter. The Kellermeister range covers all wine types at very good value prices whilst the Trevor Jones labelled wines are amongst the true elite of the Valley. His Virgin Chardonnay was the first chardonnay made specifically without wood back in 1985.

The Adelaide Hills Eden Valley Riesling is superb as are the Cabernet Merlot, made from Barossa plus Adelaide Hills grapes from Upper Hermitage and the Dry Grown Barossa Shiraz is a traditional full bodied style. There is even under cover parking ideal on a hot summers day visit.

Elderton Wines

I well remember the emergence of Elderton onto the wine market in the early 1980's. I was in Melbourne in charge of marketing for a leading wine merchant. Two shiraz wines then labelled as Hermitage, a 1982 and a 1983, captured the wine drinkers imaginations with their rich flavours and velvety textures.

In 1982 the Ashmead family bought the 40 hectare Tolley vineyard and classic old homestead on the rich alluvial river flats of the North Para River on the southern edge of Nuriootpa. The robust old vines, the oldest of which are around 60 years, produce rich complex wines. In 1993 the 1992 Elderton Cabernet Sauvignon won the coveted Jimmy Watson Memorial Trophy at the Royal Melbourne Show. A just reward for 10 years of exceptional red wines. Consummate consultant winemaker Jim Irvine uses all his skill and many years of experience to handcraft all the wines. Eldertonís cellar door is delightfully appointed and is due to be expanded and enhanced in 1998.

ELDERTON WINES

Address: 3 Tanunda Road, Nuriootpa SA 5355
Phone: (08) 8562 1058
Fax: (08) 8562 2844
Established: 1985
Owner: Lorraine Ashmead
Winemaker: James Irvine
Principal varieties grown: Shiraz, Cabernet Sauvignon, Merlot, Chardonnay, Riesling
Ha under vine: 34
Average annual crush: 300-400 tonnes

Principal wines & brands
Command Shiraz
Shiraz
Cabernet Sauvignon
Cabernet Sauvignon-Shiraz-Merlot
Merlot
Riesling
Semillon
Chardonnay
Golden Riesling
Botrytised Golden Semillon (375ml)
Pinot Chardonnay Sparkling

Public & trade tours: Vineyard tours by appointment only
Hours open to public: 8.30am-5pm, weekdays; 11am-4pm, weekends and public holidays
Points of interest: Picnic Grounds by the North Para River

Glaetzer Wines

In 1995 one of Australia's most respected winemakers Colin Glaetzer left his long term position as Chief Winemaker and Manager for Barossa Valley Estates to start his own family winery in the heart of the Barossa. His winery was built by the late Cyril Henschke and had lain idle for many years.

Along with handcrafting his own range of just eight wines, which I found to be of truly exciting quality on my recent visit, he also makes a large vintage in a new 'state-of-the-art' production facility adjacent, owned by an elite group of winemakers including Glaetzer Wines.

Colin has amassed a huge array of medals and trophies in wine show around the world. In 1995 Colin won the prestigious Intervin Black Diamond Award for his Barossa Valley Estates Wines (E & E Ebenezer). I loved Colin's 'Semillon Ratafia', a great aperitif cold or with dessert. His Sparkling Pinot Noir and Sparkling Shiraz are outstanding examples of great Australian sparkling wines..

The Rhone style grenache/mourverdre is scrumptious. Colin also makes a bushvine semillon, soft and full of flavour along with two Classic Barossa Shiraz Wines – Glaetzer Shiraz and Glaetzer Bishop Shiraz. Also a stunning wine is Glaetzer Malbec/Cabernet Sauvignon. The tasting room on the top floor of the winery with windows both into the winery and onto the balcony is a great stop-off on your Barossa tour.

GLAETZER WINES

Address: 34 Barossa Valley Way, Tanunda SA 5352
Phone: (08) 8563 0288
Fax: (08) 8563 0218
Established: 1996
Winemaker: Colin Glaetzer
Principal varieties grown: Shiraz, Malbec, Cabernet Sauvignon, Semillon, Grenache, Mouvedre, Pinot Noir, Pinot Meunier, Chardonnay
Ha under vine: Fruit purchased from BarossaValley Grape Growers

Average annual crush: 35-50 tonnes
Average no. cases produced: 3,500
Principal wines & brands: Glaetzer Barossa Valley
Hours open to public: 10.30am-4.30pm, Mon-Sat; 10.30am-4.30pm, Sunday and public holidays
Points of interest: Breath taking views of the Barossa Valley
Retail distribution: Cellar Door and Mail Order. Selected premium stockists

Krondorf

One of the older, traditional wineries in the valley, Krondorf has had a rich and varied history. The Barossa Valley was settled in the mid 1800's by German Immigrants who brought with them vine cuttings from their homeland. The Krondorf Winery was established by one of these pioneering families – although it was not called Krondorf until the early 1970's. In 1976, a strong partnership emerged between two young and dynamic winemakers, Grant Burge and Ian Wilson. They began their 'Burge and Wilson' label and made their first wines at the Krondorf Winery, which they later purchased. The wine quality, elegant packaging and good promotion saw Krondorf's reputation and sales soar.

In 1983, the company went public and two years later was purchased by Mildara. Burge and Wilson stayed on and continued to create their magic, which was cemented when they won the 1980 Jimmy Watson Memorial Trophy with a 1979 McLaren Vale, Barossa and Coonawarra cabernet sauvignon.

Burge and Wilson went their separate ways, but Krondorf continued upward. Krondorf's main focus, under Mildara's wing now for more than 10 years, is to regionally select grapes available and make top quality consistent styles that remain true to label from year to year. Krondorf is a label to be relied upon always.

KRONDORF

Address: Krondorf Road, Tanunda SA 5352
Phone: (08) 8563 2145
Fax: (08) 8562 3055
Established: Turn of the century
Owner: Mildara Blass Limited
Winemaker: Nick Walker
Principal varieties grown: Cabernet Sauvignon, Chardonnay
Ha under vine: 100
Average no. cases produced: 50,000

Principal wines & brands	Cellar Potential
Krondorf Chardonnay	2-4 years
Krondorf Barossa Valley Semillon	2-4 years
Krondorf Frontignac Spaetlese	2-4 years
Krondorf Shiraz Cabernet	3-5 years
Krondorf Family Reserve Chardonnay	3-5 years

Public & trade tours: Trade tours by appointment only
Hours open to public: 10am-5pm, daily

Leo Buring

Leo Buring was born in 1876 into the winemaking family involved in the Quelltaler Winery in Clare and certainly made his own distinctive mark in the Australian wine industry.

Somehow his innovative style and entrepreneurial spirit always seems to show through in the exciting quality and good-value prices the Buring Label has become known for. Leo graduated at the top of his class from Roseworthy Agricultural College; he was then privileged to travel to Europe and during his extensive travels through the wine regions he visited the respected wine colleges of Geisenheim in Germany and Montpellier in France.

On his return in 1898 he worked several vintages in Quelltaler before joining Minchinburg Cellars in 1902, later to become Penfolds in 1912. During his 17 years there he pioneered many winemaking techniques, including producing the first Penfolds Minchinbury Champagne. In 1919 Leo struck out on his own as Australia's first winemaking consultant and advisor. It was in this capacity that he was called into Lindemans in 1923 at a time they were beset by serious financial problems. Unfortunately these could not be solved, but Buring went on to other successful consulting jobs until forming a partnership, Leo Buring and Company with Reg Mowat from Great Western. They quickly developed Australia's first universally accepted table wine, the famous Burings Rinegold (from the German for pure gold). This semi-sweet wine from Hunter Valley semillon was enormously successful, packaged in its unique squat bottle.

Sales soared and Buring's took over the Melbourne wine merchant Matthew Lang in the 1930ís. By 1945 Buring's were looking for a permanent home and purchased a small winery in the heart of the Barossa Valley, established in 1897 by Gottlieb Hoffman. The property became known as Chateau Leonay and became famous for its unusual round tower and attractive style.

Leo Buring died at 85 in 1961. Ironically, the following year the winery was bought by Lindemans. Even more ironically, Leo Buring came under the Penfolds wing with the Southcorp purchase of Lindemans in the late 1980s. The winemaker extraordinaire who put the Leo Buring white wines at the pinnacle of their class in the 1950's and 60's was John Vickery, whose innovations such as skin cooling and he dedicated attention to detail created so many classic wines, often from Clare and Eden Valley.

Under Southcorp's direction, Leo Buring continues to make fabulous quality and great value wines which are very successful on the local and overseas markets.

If you are looking for some of Australia's best value premium wines, take a look at the Leo Buring label and muse over the incredible exploits of the great Leo Buring and the rich wine heritage he has left us.

Peter Lehmann

Peter Lehmann is a legend - his long and rich winemaking career has spanned five decades and encompasses all the ups and downs of the Australian Wine Industry over the last 50 years. Peter Lehmann Wines Limited, listed on the Australian Stock Exchange 5th August 1993, crowns the success of an extraordinary career in the wine industry. It is a source of great pride to Peter that the Company he founded is now headed by eldest son Doug who as Managing Director is leading the Company into a very bright future indeed.

The winemaking team is headed by Andrew Wigan, now the Company's Chief Winemaker, who joined Peter in 1976. Andrew and his team, Peter Scholz and Leonie Lange have built upon the solid foundations and philosophy of Peter Lehmann to create a string of National and International award winning wines.

It is the only company to win in successive years trophies for "The World's Best Wine" in the UK International Wine & Spirit Competition. 1995 saw the Peter Lehmann 1993 Cabernet Sauvignon scoop the pool, and in 1996, the 1989 'Mentor' blend of Cabernet, Malbec, Merlot, Shiraz was given the nod.

The flagship wine is Stonewell Shiraz. The Barossa is the heartland of the noble Shiraz grape and Stonewell, made from old vine, dry grown, low yielding Shiraz is the distilled essence of Shiraz. Only ever released as a five year old wine, Andrew Wigan describes the grapes selected for Stonewell as 'little black jewels'.

Stonewell Shiraz quickly gained national recognition. In 1994, I enjoyed one of the best wine releases ever held, when the 1989 Peter Lehmann Stonwell Shiraz, winner of the 1990 Jimmy Watson Memorial Trophy was released. More than 70 guests arrived at the winery to be greeted by the growers, then, after a casual stroll up the hill to the Lehmann home where a long table for 70 had been set, we enjoyed a superb meal prepared by Maggie Beer.

Several weeks previously, the Stonewells had absolutely blitzed the other reds at the Royal Adelaide Show. The 1990 won the Montgomery trophy for the Best Full Bodied Red and the Adelaide Trophy for the Best Red of that Show, whilst the 1989 continued its winning ways with the Wally Ware Trophy for the Best Medium Bodied Dry Red.

Peter is staunchly Barossa. He eats, drinks and breathes the Barossa. His winemaking career began at Yalumba where he remained for 13 years before joining Saltram where he spent 20 vintages creating wine history through wonderful wines, notably Mamre Brook dry red, the 1996 winning the Jimmy Watson in 1967. These classics occasionally surface today and are eagerly sought by collectors.

In 1979 during a period of red wine surplus, Peter was so disgusted with the then owners of Saltram which ordered him not to buy grapes from the stalwart growers of the Barossa to whom he had given his word that if they looked after the Saltram, then the Company would look after them, that with partners, he began his own wine company. This he named Masterson Barossa Vignerons, after the famous Damon Runyon character, gambler Sky Masterson.

At that time he said of the company which was the saviour of the independent Barossa grape growers, 'If anything is a gamble, this is it!'

He adopted The Queen of Clubs, the gambler's card, as his logo. However, in his mind he never felt it was such a gamble for he always had utter faith in the quality of Barossa grapes - a faith which has been well and truly vindicated. Recently, the packaging was given a lift. Artists were commissioned to create a Queen of Clubs expressive of each wine style. The wine and their labels are true works of art.

Peter Lehmann Wines still draws much of its fruit from over 200 great Barossa vineyards lovingly tended by those loyal growers he helped nearly twenty years ago. It has the pick of the best Barossa vineyards, meticulously tended by 5th and 6th generation Barossans. Since 1993, the Company has also bought three vineyards, including the famous Stonewell Vineyard.

It has achieved great export success. Over 50% of its bottled wine sales are overseas, the most important markets being the UK, USA and New Zealand, Switzerland and Scandinavia. It has become a world brand with overseas drinkers eagerly seeking the rich Barossa reds and discovering the joys of Barossa Semillon, the top

Peter Lehmann

selling Peter Lehmann white wine.

Throughout these great developments, Peter Lehmann has never changed.

His favourite spot is still the cosy weighbridge building during vintage, where he greets all the growers with a warm welcome, a cold drink or a glass of wine and always a stick of Barossa Mettwurst whilst weighing their grapes and directing them to the appropriate crusher.

Here's a toast to a great winemaking team with their stalwart Barossa growers, and a very special family!

PETER LEHMANN WINES

Address: Para Road, Tanunda SA 5352
Direction: 1km South of the Township
Phone: (08) 8563 2500
Fax: (08) 8563 3402
Established: 1979
Winemakers: Peter Lehmann, Andrew Wigan, Peter Scholz, Leonie Lange. Managing Director: Doug Lehmann
Principal varieties grown: Shiraz, Cabernet Sauvignon, Grenache, Merlot, Semillon, Chardonnay, Riesling, Chenin Blanc

Principal wines & brands	Cellar Potential
Peter Lehmann Stonewell Shiraz	20+ years
Peter Lehmann Mentor	20+ years
Peter Lehmann Barossa Shiraz	8+ years
Peter Lehmann Barossa Semillon	5+ years
Clancy's Gold Preference	5+ years
Clancy's White	2+ years
Peter Lehmann Barossa Cabernet Sauvignon	8+ years
Peter Lehmann Barossa Chardonnay	5+ years
Peter Lehmann Eden Valley Reserve Riesling	10+ years
Peter Lehmann Bin AD 2000 plus	21+ years

Public & trade tours: Trade tours by appointment only

Hours open to public: 9.30am-5pm, daily; 10.30am-4.30pm weekends and public holidays

Points of interest: Special Range Limited Wines exclusive to cellar door, comprising special red and white varietals, old fortifieds. Shaded picnic grounds

Retail distribution: Nationally distributed. Distributor each state, S. Smith & Son

Orlando – Rowand Flat

Johann Gramp, one of the early German Settlers in the Barossa Valley, planted the first grapes back in 1847 at Jacob's Creek. In 1877 Johann's son, Gustav, transferred the winemaking from Jacob's Creek to the more expansive site at Rowland Flat. The name "Orlando" (the German name for Roland) became the Company's Brand name.

During the early 1950's, Colin Gramp went to Germany and brought back with him some German pressure controlled stainless steel fermenting tanks, which started the

Lyndale Riesling, Moorooroo White Burgundy, Fromm's Spaetlese and Jacob's Creek Claret. Although most of the advertising and promotion was directed at Lyndale, it was the Jacob's Creek Claret, named after site of Johann Gramp's original vineyard, which stole the show. Jacob's Creek is an incredible success story; today the red wine, a blend of cabernet, shiraz and malbec is the biggest selling bottled wine in England. The trickle of the creek has turned into a river which is flowing around the world. Jacob's Creek

most significant technological breakthrough yet in the history of the Australian wine industry. The control of the rate, temperature and length of the fermentation produced white wines with much more aromatic, floral and fruit flavours and naturally being sealed, prevented oxidisation of the wines. These radically different and improved white wines quickly gained popularity and set the stage for the white wine boom of the early 1970's.

Colin Gramp also brought to Australia, German winemaking genius Guenter Prass. Guenter spent more than 30 years with Orlando, finishing as Managing Director and overseeing the remarkable development of Orlando into one of the largest and most respected wine companies in Australia. Capital demands and the need to build an international distribution network led to a buyout by world wine and spirit giant, the French Pernod Ricard company.

Orlando have been at the forefront of many winemaking developments. Barossa Pearl in its unique pear-shaped bottle introduced as Australia's first bulk fermented sparkling wine and at a never before seen affordable price, it became "de rigeur" when courting a young lady, to crack a bottle or two of this exciting new wine. Orlando produced Australia's first commercial chardonnay in the late 1970's.

In the mid 70's, Orlando released four premium wines in the popular price bracket,

Chardonnay has also had great success, winning a number of trophies and awards, including a top French honour, quite a

feat for a wine which sells at under $10 Australian.

The Orlando R.F. standing for Rowland Flat, has been most successful in the affordable premium category. Old stalwarts such as the Steingarten Riesling from the "Garden of Stones" vineyard, high on Trial Hill behind the valley, produces incredibly small crops of exceptional wines capturing the wine lovers imagination.

The Orlando Saints - St. Helga Eden Valley Riesling, St. Hugo Coonawarra Cabernet Sauvignon and the more recently released St. Hillary Chardonnay from Padthaway are all rich in flavour and truly great wine bargains in their price bracket.

In the super premium area, Orlando has two individual vineyard red wines, the Lawsons Shiraz from Padthaway and the Jacaranda Ridge Coonawarra Cabernet Sauvignon. These are in the top few of consistently great Australian red wines.

The Russet Ridge Cabernet blend from Coonawarra, first released first in 1993, is already a success in the medium-priced area. Orlando have a very well-balanced and well-rounded range of wines. Their winery and its state of the art packaging centre is world class. One would be remiss not to mention the great sparkling wines – Trilogy, a pinot noir, chardonnay and pinot meunier cuvee and Carrington. Why not toast their success with these fine sparklers?

ORLANDO WINES
Address: Barossa Valley Way, Rowland Flat SA 5352
Phone: (08) 8521 3111
Fax: (08) 8521 3100
Established: 1847
Owner: Orlando Wyndham Group Pty Ltd
Winemaker: Philip Laffer
Principal varieties grown: Riesling, Cabernet Sauvignon, Shiraz, Merlot, Chardonnay, Pinot Noir, Traminer, Cabernet Franc, Crouchen, Gordo, Palomino, Ruby Cabernet, Sauvignon Blanc, Taminga, White Frontignan, Malbec
Principal wines & brands
Jacob's Creek
Saint Range (St Hugo Coonawarra Cabernet Sauvignon, St Hilary Padthaway Chardonnay, St Helga Eden Valley Riesling)
Trilogy
Gramp's Range
Lawson's Padthaway Shiraz
Jacaranda Ridge Coonawarra Cabernet Sauvignon
Steingarten Riesling
Carrington
RF
Russet Ridge Coonawarra Cabernet Shiraz Merlot
Russet Ridge Coonawarra Chardonnay
Public & trade tours: By appointment only
Hours open to public: 10am-5pm, weekdays; 10am-4pm, weekends and public holidays
Points of interest: Barossa Gourmet Weekend, Vintage Festival, Jacob's Creek to Steingarten Challenge, Spinifex Art & Craft Gift Shop, Barossa Opals and Gift Shop, large cellar door tasting facility, picnic and BBQ facilities
Retail distribution: National

Langmeil Winery

Langmeil was the second village settled in the valley after Bethany and is on the western fringe of the town of Tanunda.

The beautiful complex of buildings which form the Langmeil Winery date back to the middle of the 19th century and rumour has it that the old vineyard behind the winery was planted in 1846. Some of the gnarled old vines certainly are truly ancient but still bearing a good crop of characterful grapes. The first winery on the site was established in 1932 by the Hanisch family and operated under the name of 'Paradale Wines' until the late 1960's when it was transferred to Bernkastel Wines.

In February 1996 three friends, Richard Lindner, Chris Bitter and Carl Lindner got together and undertook their first vintage at the winery. This is truly a family operation. Richard's son Paul is in charge of cellar operation while you will find Chris's son Tyson either in the cellar or out in the vineyard.

They have sensitively restored the stone buildings and upgraded the winery. Their wines made in 1996, which I tasted during a vintage visit, were certainly of the highest quality.

Carl Lindner has large vineyard holdings in the valley and through the group's other contacts Langmeil is assured of top class grapes to work with. I am certain great things are afoot at this classic old winery and I applaud this group of Barossa stalwarts.

LANGMEIL WINERY

Address: PO Box 551, Tanunda SA 5352
Direction: Cnr. Para and Langmeil Roads, Tanunda
Phone: (08) 8563 2595
Fax: (08) 8563 3622
Established: 1932, Langmeil since 1996
Winemaker: Paul Lindner
Principal varieties grown: Shiraz
Ha under vine: 5
Average annual crush: 500 tonnes

Average no. cases produced: 4,000

Principal wines & brands	Cellar Potential
Cabernet Sauvignon	10 years
Grenache	5 years
Shiraz	10 years
Selwins Lot (Cabernet Grenache Shiraz)	5 years
Cabernet Rose	3 years
Chardonnay	5 years
Semillon	5 years
White Frontignac	2 years
Tawny Port (Liqueur Shiraz) 375ml	

Public & trade tours: By appointment only
Hours open to public: 10am-4pm, daily (Closed Christmas Day and Good Friday)
Points of interest: Historic buildings and vineyard (1840's). Blacksmithing displays - Coopering displays during festivals
Retail distribution: Cellar Door and Mail Order

Rockford Wines

Robert O'Callaghan has built a winery that captures the spirit of the traditional Barossa.

The original 1850ís stone buildings have been restored and extended in the same style.

Retaining the feel of a Barossan farm yard and winery while the think stone walls provide insulation that makes these buildings ideal for maturing wine in wood.

In 1965 Robert left school to take a 5 year position as an apprentice winemaker with B. Seppelt & Sons at Rutherglen.

This was the last period before modern technology started to change Australian winemaking forever.

Robert's winemaking career with Seppelts took him through their wineries at Rutherglen, Chateau Tanunda, Dorrien and Seppeltsfield. He was part of the modernisation of the Australian wine industry, his grape-growing background and his time with Seppelts are at the heart of what Rockford is today.

Low yielding vineyards, hand pruned and picked, open fermenters, wooden crushers and basket presses are combined with handed down knowledge to produce the rich earthy complex red and white wines for which Rockford are renowned. The Basket Press Shiraz represents this and was one of the first to re-establish this traditional style. The 'coup de grace' of the Rockford range is their Black Shiraz, a sparkling red that is well-named, inky black in colour, with a kaleidoscope of flavours. I know quite a few people who would "kill" to get some, it is swallowed up literally straight away when the small batches are released.

The sales emphasis has always been at the cellar door to encourage people to visit the winery, taste the wines and understand what they represent. The majority of sales are made in South Australia. All interstate sales are direct from the winery via a mailing list with a newsletter once a year.

Rockford value tradition, there is a real sense of family and belonging to all who work there and you get a really good feeling when you walk through the gates into this domain where wine is respected and enjoyed.

ROCKFORD WINES
Address: Krondorf Road, Tanunda SA 5352
Phone: (08) 8563 2720
Fax: (08) 8563 3787
Established: 1984
Winemaker: R. O'Callaghan & Chris Ringland
Principal varieties grown: Grenache, Riesling, Shiraz, Cabernet Sauvignon, Semillon
Average annual crush: 350 tonnes
Average no. cases produced: 15,000
Public & trade tours: Yes
Hours open to public: 11am-5pm, Mon-Sat
Retail distribution: From winery only

Miranda Rovalley Wines

The Miranda's are very close and hardworking. The family's patron, Frank Miranda, affectionately called "Pop", who came to Australia in 1939 loved his adopted land. He didn't waste time, honing his winemaking skills in of all places, Katherine in the Northern Territory, making wine from dried sultanas and raisins.

On returning to Griffith he began making wine commercially. Today, Miranda is Australia's seventh largest winery and becoming a bigger and bigger player in the premium wine market every year.

In 1991, the Miranda's took over the Rovalley Winery from the Leibich family who had founded it in 1919. Likeable Lou Miranda and his wife Val moved over from Griffith to run the winery. Lou has overseen a rejuvenation of the winery in terms of equipment, new oak barrels and a whole new attitude.

Lou is very much hands on and works hard with the winemaker's. For three years running, 1993 - 1995, they won the top Gold Medal in the Royal Sydney Easter Show for their Rovalley Ridge Show Reserve Chardonnay. The Rovalley Ridge Show Reserve Shiraz Cabernet won the trophy at the Royal Perth Show for the best red wine. The "Old Vine Shiraz" has had considerable success winning a trophy in London. Rovalley is fast forging a reputation for top quality wines at very affordable prices. The winery is undergoing a facelift to provide a cellar door and restaurant where the Miranda's can suitably disperse their warm hospitality and give their exceptional wines the environment they deserve.

Richmond Grove

Housed in the old Leo Buring Winery, right across the lawns from the Peter Lehmann Winery, is the Richmond Grove Barossa Winery.

This leading Australian wine label which had its beginnings in the Upper Hunter in New South Wales was taken over some years ago by the Orlando Wyndham Group, who started looking for a home in the Barossa for Richmond Grove. The giant Southcorp conglomerate owned the Leo Buring label and winery but with a number of large, efficient, quality wineries in the region handling their winemaking needs. The beautiful old Chateau Leonay Winery, built around the turn of the century, complete with its turreted tower lay idle. Today the winery is a buzzing beehive of activity. John Vickery, the living legend of Australian white winemaking, who put Buring's on the map in the 1960's and 70's, is back at his beloved Chateau Leonay after a long absence.

The cellar door area has been enlarged and beautifully styled. John's first 'back home' vintage in 1994 produced some great wines, including two exquisite riesling's, one from the Barossa and another from Watervale. The tradition has recommenced.

Richmond Grove has played host to some great cultural events and has been a major sponsor of the Barossa Music Festival and a popular venue during the Barossa Gourmet Weekend. Richmond Grove's success and expansion has breathed life into a great winery. Why not check it out for yourself?

RICHMOND GROVE WINES

Address: Para Road, Tanunda SA 5352
Phone: (08) 8563 2204
Fax: (08) 8563 2804
Established: 1897
Winemaker: John Vickery
Principal varieties grown: Riesling, Cabernet Sauvignon, Shiraz, Semillon, Chardonnay, Verdelho
Principal wines & brands
Richmond Grove Watervale Riesling
Richmond Grove Barossa Riesling
Richmond Grove Barossa Shiraz
Richmond Grove Barossa/McLaren Vale Semillon
Richmond Grove Coonawarra Cabernet Sauvignon
Richmond Grove Pinot Chardonnay NV Brut

Richmond Grove French Cask Chardonnay
Richmond Grove Eden Valley Traminer Riesling
Richmond Grove Cabernet Merlot
Richmond Grove Semillon Chardonnay

Public & trade tours: Trade tours by appointment only
Hours open to public: 10am-5pm, weekdays; 10.30pm-4.30pm, weekends and public holidays
Points of interest: Barossa Gourmet Weekend, Barossa Music Festival, Barossa Under the Stars, Australia's Master Riesling-maker - John Vickery
Retail distribution: National

Saltram

Although now owned by Mildara Blass a strong family tradition continues at Saltram. The winemaker Nigel Dolan is the son of famed Saltram-Stonyfell winemaker Bryan Dolan an industry legend and a former winner of the Jimmy Watson Trophy.

Saltram was founded in 1859 by William Salter who purchased a property on the banks of a creek naming it Mamre Brook. Longtime winemaker for 20 years was Peter Lehmann making famous the Mamre Brook and Metala labels as amongst Australia's best reds.

Saltram is a classic old winery with its open fermenting tanks for the reds but much money has been spent upgrading the white winemaking facilities and barrel ageing cellars.

The characterful cellar door now leads into a classy café style restaurant both of which look out over the splendid stone villa "Mamre Brook House" a fine example of victorian inspired colonial architecture and classified by the National Trust of Australia, where winemaker Nigel Dolan makes his home.

The Saltram wines and winery are a credit to our great industry.

SALTRAM ESTATE WINERY

Address: Salters Gully, Angaston SA 5253
Phone: (08) 8564 3355
Fax: (08) 8564 2209
Established: 1859
Owner: Mildara Blass Limited
Winemaker: Nigel Dolan
Principal varieties grown: Cabernet Sauvignon, Shiraz, Chardonnay, Grenache, Semillon
Ha under vine: 125
Average no. cases produced: 100,000

Principal wines & brands	Cellar Potential
Saltram Classic Chardonnay	2-4 years
Saltram Classic Sauvignon Blanc	2-4 years
Saltram Classic Cabernet Sauvignon	3-5 years
Saltram Classic Shiraz	3-5 years
Mamre Brook Chardonnay	2-4 years

Public & trade tours: Trade tours by appointment only
Hours open to public: 9am-5pm, weekdays; 10am-5pm, weekends and public holidays
Points of interest: The Saltram Bistro - located near the Cellar Door

Stanley Brothers

Lindsay Stanley is undoubtedly one of the true characters of a region that seems to breed such personalities. One should not however be fooled by his laid back laconic nature. He is a really first class winemaker and a deep thinker who has learned well from his 25 years of winemaking experience including working early in his career with the legendary Max Schubert.

Through their many friends and contacts in the valley the Stanley Brothers have access to some of the best dry grown Barossa grapes from very old vines grown in many of the valley's unique sub-regions. Lindsay's interest in horse racing translates into some of his best selling wines. The Thoroughbred Cabernet with its rich, ripple, upfront flavours and the Full Sister Semillon

full bodied and flavoured a real red wine drinkers white.

Stanley Brothers also do great things with the germanic white variety, Sylvaner, fruity and spicy, it is great with Asian dishes.

The fortified Riesling from the 1986 vintage is worth visiting to try as are the 10 year old Tawny Port and Liqueur Tokay. I must admit I love their sparkling red which is rarely available, but a real blockbuster.

If you do happen to corner Lindsay, a reluctant raconteur, get him to tell you of his duck shooting day with Doug Lehmann, I am sure it will be a highlight of your day in the Barossa!!

STANLEY BROTHERS

Address: Barossa Valley Way, Tanunda SA 5352
Phone: (08) 8563 3375
Fax: (08) 8563 3758
Established: 1990
Winemaker: Lindsay Stanley
Principal varieties grown: Chardonnay, Cabernet Sauvignon, Shiraz, Riesling, Grenache, Semillon, Sylvaner
Ha under vine: 23
Average annual crush: 100-150 tonnes
Hours open to public: 10am-5pm, weekdays; 11am-5pm, weekends

Seppeltsfield

Joseph Seppelt arrived in Australia in 1849. Purchasing a large area of land near Tanunda in 1852, he built a homestead which is known as Seppeltsfield. In addition to planting vines, Joseph originally attempted to establish corn, wheat, tobacco as well as grazing cattle. Initially wine facilities were not a priority as is evident in the fact that the first vintage was made in the diary.

With the exception of tobacco, all Joseph's endeavours were successful but the emergence of wine as his main interest can be seen in the encouragement he gave to other landowners to plant vines. In 1867, Joseph commenced work on the magnificent stone buildings which make up Seppeltsfield and by the turn of the century, the company was the largest wine producer in Australia with two million litres of wine being produced annually.

Seppelt purchased another large winery in 1916, this being Chateau Tanunda. Built in 1890, this impressive stone construction was equal to Seppeltsfield in its grandeur. During the early 1900's much of its large output was dedicated to brandy production and so, Seppelt on the purchase of the property not only acquired an historic landmark,

but also inherited large stocks of brandy. The early years of this century saw Seppelt also purchase wineries and vineyards at Great Western in Victoria and Dorrien near Tanunda, both of which were later furnished with the characteristic Seppelt turrets. Throughout the difficult 1930's Seppelt's were most considerate to their staff. Although on reduced wages, the employees not only kept their jobs but also were provided with food and shelter, if necessary. In return, employees were requested to plant date seeds to a set pattern at each of their wineries. This elegant feature has become another distinguishing characteristic of Seppelt wineries. Seppeltsfield is no exception. The impressive family mausoleum stands on a hill overlooking a valley of palm lined avenues, magnificent stone buildings and turreted tanks. This picture is completed by the rolling greens and golds of Australia's first contoured vineyard.

James Godfrey is in charge of the Seppelt range of old fortified wines and in fact of all the fortified wines of the huge Southcorp wine conglomerate that purchased Seppelt several years ago. James is a Roseworthy graduate who worked previously with Wynns at Coonawarra, Tolleys Pedare and

Saxonvale. Having judged fortified wines with James a few times, I can attest to the fact he is as skilled and knowledgeable about fortified wines as any person could be. The winery and ageing fortified wines are in the capable hands of Dean Kraehenbuhl who began his wine career in 1958 and whose family have been in the valley for four generations.

Seppelt winemakers have always been master blenders and their long and successful show record confirms their skills in this area. Recently, the company purchased an historic property near Eden Valley named Partalunga. A huge vineyard development that stretches over the hills, it is managed by Alan Jenkins whose fine work is also evident at the Tollana Woodbury Vineyard in the Eden Valley. Rhine riesling, chardonnay, sauvignon blanc and cabernet sauvignon from Partalunga have all shown real class. Seppeltsfield has always stored huge quantities of ageing top class fortified wines which in the case of the old Seppelt Para Liqueurs go back to the 1878 vintage. Occasionally, these old Para's are bottled for special occasions - they are almost liquid gold, the essence of wine and history in a glass. The Seppelt fortified wines are all superb, right

Seppeltsfield

down to the commercial sherries, ports and muscats. The Mt. Rufus and Old Trafford Ports are particularly good value. The DP 90, a drier style tawny is superb, as is the richer Para Liqueur. The Seppelt old fortified sherries in the DP series, the fino, amontillado and oloroso are a must in the aperitif cabinet or to add that classy zest to a soup or casserole. It's a real myth to use old opened or oxidised wine in cooking. Wine is a food and an ingredient when you cook - you would use limp vegetables or meat that's on the turn so why handicap your cooking with spoiled wine? Anyway, back to the wine; the secret with good fortified wines is to have old stocks in a solero system (ironically the name of the Seppelts range of cherries) where new wine is added to old in a gradual process each year. With more than 15 million litres of old fortifieds in their Seppeltsfield stronghold, Seppelt has this unique asset. The Seppeltsfield buildings are some of the finest and best-kept Australian colonial architecture and a must for a

visit whilst in the Barossa. The palm-lined avenues, the mausoleum, the peaceful grandeur of the place have a special spiritual

feel to it. Seppeltsfield is a winery with soul - I'm certain yours will be enriched by visiting there.

Yalumba

Yalumba is at the forefront of premium wine production in Australia. It is Australia's oldest family owned winery, established in 1849. The Hill Smith family manage their business in an innovative way, encouraging open communication and a team spirit. The relationship between staff and management is also excellent and this harmony has contributed markedly to their success.

Unlike the majority of Barossa Valley Wine companies, which were established by German immigrants, Yalumba was founded by an Englishman, Samuel Smith, a Dorset brewer whose first work in Australia was for George Fife Angas at Angaston. Whilst employed for Angas, Smith bought 14 acres of land on the lower slopes of the Barossa Ranges, which he planted with vines.

He called his property "Yalumba" which is Aboriginal for "all the land around". This was ultimately an auspicious choice as the Yalumba empire grew to cover just that.

In 1852, like many others, Smith headed to the goldfields and with singular luck, struck gold. He returned to the Barossa, purchased a further 30 acres and established a winery. Although he did not live long enough to see it, by the turn of the century Yalumba was one of the most successful wine companies in Australia.

Robert Hill-Smith and his brother Sam are the proprietors of Yalumba, having guided an amicable family buy-out in 1989, assisted by their late father, Wyndham. Robert and Sam are the fifth generation of Smith's at Yalumba.

The Yalumba family have ongoing projects aimed at producing the best possible grapes for their winemaking team to work with. Under the eye of their chief viticulturist Robin Nettelbeck, Yalumba have established a substantial vine grafting operation and vine

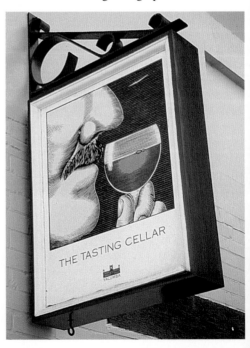

nursery. Their good work is obvious when you visit any of their vineyards in the Eden Valley or the Menzies Vineyard at Coonawarra; these vines are a joy to behold. Needless to say, the Yalumba wine stable since the late 1980's is flawless, each year the wines just keep getting better. Clonal selection, fruit evaluation trials and grafting techniques might all sound a bit obscure and highbrow, but their relevance comes though loud and clear in the finished wines.

Yalumba choose the best possible and most suitable micro-climates for each grape variety they wish to plant. They have developed three individual vineyards in the Eden Valley region being Pewsey Vale, Heggies Vineyard and Hill-Smith Estate. All three vineyards are separate, self sufficient concerns, with wines appearing under their respective names. Common resources are shared at Yalumba's winery, where all of the fruit is processed.

Yalumba owns additional vineyards at Oxford Landing near Waikerie, the "Menzies" and 'Hawthorn's' vineyards in the Coonawarra and vineyards in the emerging winegrowing region of Koppamurra. Yalumba have a unique way of honouring those family members, friends or business associates who have in some way assisted or been very dear to the company. The idea occurred to Wyndham Hill Smith when Sir Robert Menzies described a 1961 Yalumba Special Reserve Stock Galway Claret as 'the finest Australian wine, I have ever tasted!'

Yalumba began holding back the best red each year and releasing them only when they felt the wine had achieved sufficient maturation both in wood and bottle. The flagship wine series became known as 'The Signature'.

I once had the pleasure of tasting every Signature release from the inaugural 1962 to the current 1991; what a wonderful way to imbibe in Australia's wine history. From 1988 onwards, the wines have become richer and more full-bodied, they would be great to put down in the cellar. My pick of the Signatures were the wines commemorating the winemakers of their era's, Rudi Kronberger (1967) and Peter Wall (1990).

In 1990, Yalumba began a new red wine tradition when it released the "Octavius" made from very old vine Barossa Shiraz. These substantial vines are aged in 80 litre casks called Octaves, the smallest casks used commercially for wine maturation. The combination of Missouri oak, seasoned for a minimum of eight years, rich powerful Shiraz fruit and extended maturation in the Octaves, produce wines that are simply awesome.

The pioneering spirit that drove the founder Samuel back in 1849 is as evident today at Yalumba at it was then. Five generations and nearly 150 years later, this family owned company remains innovative and exciting across the broad disciplines of winemaking whilst maintaining a laid back but professional demeanour.

Stockwell Wines

One of the most charming and natural wineries to visit in the valley is Phil and Margie Edwards little Hideaway on the outskirts of the small valley village Stockwell in the northern reaches of the Barossa. Here you get a very personal experience and are guided through a range of hand crafted table and fortified wines.

The tasting room, which was originally the old Stockwell Jail built about 1865, has old low doorways and is like the proprietors, full of character. Adjoining the tasting room is a cute and cosy bed and breakfast suite with its own open fire place. The Duck Ponds Cottage is also next to the winery on the banks of the Stockwell Creek.

Both accommodation facilities provide a romantic and reasonably priced stop over point after a days trip up through the valley from Adelaide. There is also a wine garden picnic facility if you want to cater for lunch, you will be most welcome.

Their Shiraz which comes from 130 year old vines is great, the White Port made from riesling grapes and the Lawsons Port attest to the Edwards skill in making very good fortified wines.

STOCKWELL WINERY
Address: Duckponds Road, Stockwell SA 5355
Phone: (08) 8562 3079
Fax: (08) 8562 3883
Established: 1979
Owners: Phil and Marg Edwards
Winemaker: Phil Edwards
Average annual crush: Under 20 tonnes Barossa grapes

Principal wines & brands	Cellar Potential
"Stockwell Wines"	
Stockwell Shiraz	up to 10 years
Duckponds Creek Riesling	up to 5 years
Stockwell White Port	

Public & trade tours: No
Hours open to public: 10am-4pm, Wed-Sun

Wolf Blass

In a very short space of time, Wolf Blass built one of Australia's most successful wine companies. The company was founded in 1973 and went public in 1984 Wolf was born in East Germany and worked as an apprentice on his grandfather's vineyard. He graduated from university as the youngest ever holder of the Kellermeister Diploma (Master degree) in Oenology.

He came to Australia at the invitation of Kaiser Stuhl in 1960 and it was not long before the industry was sitting up and taking notice of this outspoken new winemaker.

He left to become Australia's first freelance winemaker since Leo Buring made a similar move in 1919. Earning $2.50 per hour, Wolf drove from winery to winery, seven days a week, in his old Volkswagon.

Many small wineries were eased into table wine production with his assistance In the course of his time spent at Tollana, Wolf purchased a couple of hectares on the Sturt Highway north of Nuriootpa. There, he built a large shed which became his winemaking headquarters. Today, it is a magnificent complex, set among gardens and fountains. The first Wolf Blass wine was a red; a shiraz made in 1966.

In 1975, Wolf Blass became the first ever to win the Jimmy Watson Trophy at the Melbourne Show for three consecutive years. The company also won the Montgomery Trophy for the best commercially available red wine at the Adelaide Show six years running, and the best red wine in the Sydney Show for the years 1981 to 1983. Throughout this period, Wolf only produced red wines. Today the company produce a wide range of red, white and sparkling wines. The Black Label Cabernet is one of Australia's most sought after wines and the 100% Langhorne Creek Grey Label red is one of my personal favourites.

Wolf Blass wines continue to please the palates of an ever growing wine drinking public around the world. The Mildara Blass team of winemakers have continued the good work and Wolf Blass Wines are a real cornerstone in this success story.
Ein Prosit Wolfie!!

St Hallett Wines

In 1988, a small band of Barossa producers joined Carl Lindner at the St Hallett winery to create a bolder image and style for St Hallett.

Carl commenced the "revival" through vineyard acquisitions and development with winemaker Stuart Blackwell assigned to upgrade the winery and equipment. The third in this partnership, Bob McLean is niche as "marketer". Applying a very simplistic approach to St Hallett's marketing he criticises others in the industry by saying "too many people lose sight of the fact they are in the business of producing 750 mls of happiness".

How basic it all is. St Hallett believes the Barossa is one of the most unique wine producing regions of Australia. The valley extends over many boundaries, from the extreme heights of the Barossa Ranges to the hot flat plains of the valley floor. Soils differ from dark clay to river loam to sandy and varying micro-climates enable enormous diversity in the wine styles produced.

St Hallett is in a unique position sourcing fruit from its own vineyards and purchasing fruit from growers, this enables greater flexibility and access to some of the best fruit of the Barossa region.

The Old Block Shiraz, was the forerunner of a number of premium Australian reds made from the grapes of very old vines.

A number of traditional Barossa growers produce grapes for The Old Block; the vines vary from around 70 years old to over a century. The wine has been a huge success. Medium-priced wines of exceptional quality include The Poachers Blend, named after the old story involving poachers and the creek at the end of the winery's land, have been most successful additions to the St Hallett stable.

Barossa Cottage Wines

Midway between Nuriootpa and Angaston on the main road right opposite Vintners nestles the Barossa Quilt and Craft Cottage of Ray and Heather Bartsch.

Their vineyard is a little further afield in the Eden Valley and dates back to their ancestor, Godtfried Hartwig who settled there in 1860. The Bartsch's make a selection of their wines from the vineyard under the Hartwig collection banner honouring their forebears and featuring the family's registered European Crest. The range includes a riesling, chardonnay, cabernet sauvignon, a late harvest riesling and a methode champenoise sparkling made from chardonnay, semillon and chenin blanc.

The Quilt and Craft Shop in the restored "Pug" Cottage built in 1888, specialises in quality giftware, unique creative clothing, quilts and hat boxes made to order. Teddy bears and dolls are all handmade. They even conduct craft classes and have a range of over 200 craft instruction and ideas books. Why not stop off at this characterful little cottage when next in the Barossa.

BAROSSA COTTAGE WINES
Address: PO BOX 12, Eden Valley SA 5235
Phone: (08) 8562 3212
Fax: (08) 8562 3243
Established: 1990
Owners: Heather and Roy Bartsch
Winemaker: Contract
Principal varieties grown: Chardonnay, Riesling, Shiraz, Cabernet Sauvignon
Ha under vine: Eden Valley, 16Ha; Angaston, 12Ha

Average no. cases produced: 1,000

Principal wines & brands	Cellar Potential
EV Chardonnay	4-5 years
EV Riesling	4-5 years
EV Shiraz-Cabernet	6 years

Hours open to public: Cellar Door at the Barossa Quilt & Craft Cottage
Points of interest: We promote quilts and wine
Retail distribution: Bailey & Bailey, Adelaide. Various Restaurants in Sydney

---

Barossa Settlers

One of the most beautiful, tranquil, serene and historic winery sites in the Barossa Valley belongs to Howard and Joan Haese's, Barossa Settlers Winery and Vineyards, situated on the site of the Hoffnungsthal settlement, founded in 1847, in the foothills of the Barossa Ranges. The winery is set in the original horsestable and barn built in 1860, the cellar door is resplendent with much memorabilia as both Howard and Joan's families go back to the settlement of the Barossa.

Their magnificent homestead with its splendid gardens and large duck pond forms a delightful setting to taste their excellent wines. The shiraz comes from vines planted in 1887 and is rich and complex. They have two riesling's, the Late Harvest is their flagship wine.

Take a step back in time to a more gracious era and enjoy the Haese's old world hospitality or try one of their fine wines if you cannot make the voyage.

An introduction to the Clare Valley

The region known as the Clare Valley incorporates four main river systems and stretches for 30-35 kilometres in width. There are five sub-divisions within the valley, proceeding south from the northern end, they are the sub-regions of Clare, Sevenhill, Watervale, Polish Hill River and Auburn. Each area has its own geographic and climatic characteristics. Some of the vineyards are quite elevated, and although the general climate could be described as continental, each small area is subject to its own microclimate. Many Clare wines exhibit distinct cool climate characteristics and intense varietal fruit flavours.

Compared to the Barossa Valley, the Clare Valley has a later growing period and vintage, with fruit ripening after the intense heat of summer.

John Horrocks first settled in the area very early in the state's history in 1840. He named his property Hope Farm and planted some vines there. While on a trip to England, Horrocks ordered some South African vine cuttings to be sent back to his property and planted them. Unfortunately Horrocks died in a shooting accident at the age of 28, having set the area on its viticultural course.

Another early settler, Irishman Edward Gleeson, named the Valley after his home, County Clare. Gleeson brought many new vine cuttings into the area, and the industry progressed slowly until the 1890's when planting greatly increased. The Clare Valley was planted largely with red grape varieties such as shiraz, cabernet sauvignon and malbec. These were gradually replaced with higher yielding varieties as the demand for fortified wines grew.

In 1894, the Stanley Wine Company was established and it quickly became one of the largest vignerons in the state.

The four companies still operating in Clare after the depression were Stanley, Buring & Sobels, Sevenhill and Birks Wendouree. During the 1950's, many companies re-established themselves for table wine production by planting high quality grape varieties, particularly riesling. Today, riesling has almost become synonymous with the Clare Valley and recently major wine companies such as BRL Hardy and Petaluma have planted riesling vineyards in the area. Penfolds and Taylors have extensive new vineyards near Sevenhills and Auburn respectively.

The Clare Valley has continued to attract winemakers as an exciting area for premium wine production. Some of the fruit grown in the region however is moved to wineries in other areas for processing. Clare Valley grapes, particularly riesling, are very much in demand all over Australia.

Clare is the spiritual home of the small boutique winery and many great ones have opened in recent years. Today, there are more than 20 wineries in the region and its reputation and new plantings are both rapidly increasing.

In 1984, Clare became the first region to introduce the concept of a gourmet weekend of wine, food, music and art, a celebration of the culture of wine, and each May this most successful event reconfirms the Clare Valley's elevated position in the Australian wine industry.

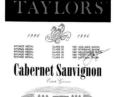

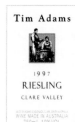

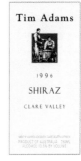

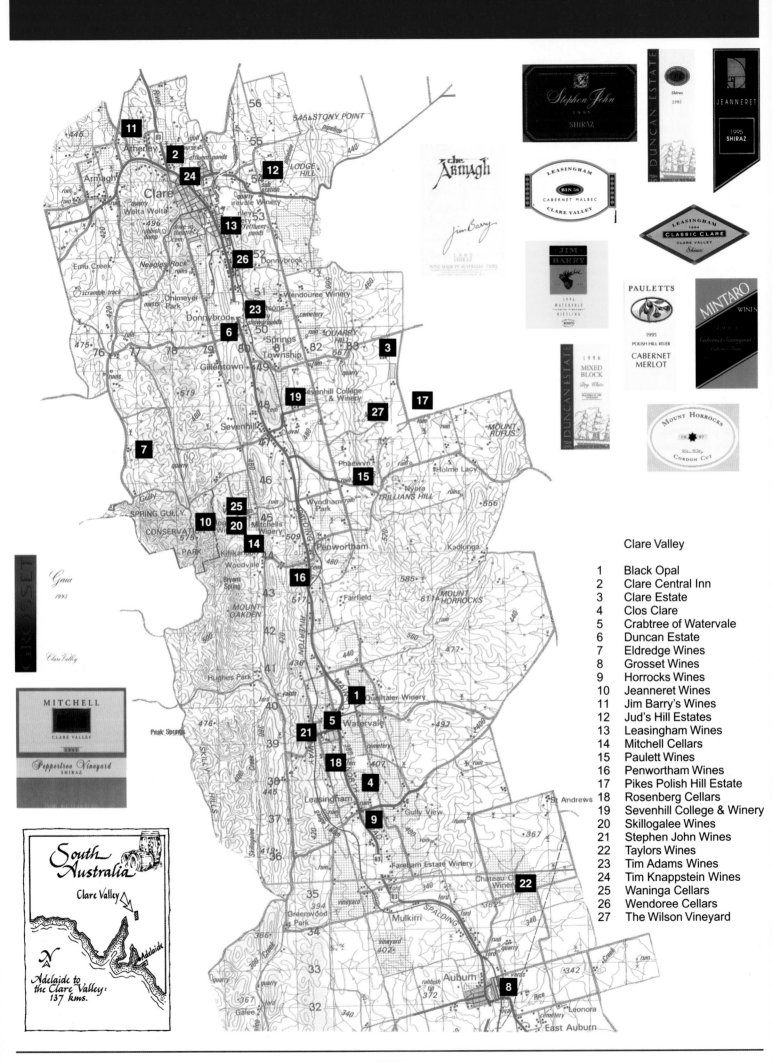

Clare Valley

1   Black Opal
2   Clare Central Inn
3   Clare Estate
4   Clos Clare
5   Crabtree of Watervale
6   Duncan Estate
7   Eldredge Wines
8   Grosset Wines
9   Horrocks Wines
10 Jeanneret Wines
11 Jim Barry's Wines
12 Jud's Hill Estates
13 Leasingham Wines
14 Mitchell Cellars
15 Paulett Wines
16 Penwortham Wines
17 Pikes Polish Hill Estate
18 Rosenberg Cellars
19 Sevenhill College & Winery
20 Skillogalee Wines
21 Stephen John Wines
22 Taylors Wines
23 Tim Adams Wines
24 Tim Knappstein Wines
25 Waninga Cellars
26 Wendoree Cellars
27 The Wilson Vineyard

Jim Barry

Jim Barry is a legendary Clare identity. After graduating from the first post-war Roseworthy course in 1946 he became the first Roseworthy graduate to work in the valley in 1947 and brought with him the first pH (acid meter) used in Clare winemaking when he began his 22 years with the Clarevale Co-operative Winery, many of these as its general manager.

In 1959 Jim began to plant his own vineyards with a view to beginning a family wine business involving his children. Gradually, Jim bought land around the Valley and with his children's assistance planted vines. Their cellar door operations began in 1974 and today four of Jim's six children are directly involved in the business. Peter is general manager, Mark is winemaker, with Julie and John both toiling hard in various areas of the wine business. Jim Barry and his family now have over 100 hectares of their own vines planted throughout the valley – from the northern flats on the edge of town to the high, cool ranges in the east, and the famous 'Florita' vineyard at Watervale where the Jim Barry Watervale Riesling is produced.

With their 1985 vintage the Barry's started a great tradition wine with 'The Armagh', a shiraz of mammoth proportions from their extremely low-yielding Armagh vineyard on the western side of the valley, planted by Jim back in 1968. The name Armagh, which was given circa 1859, to a settlement 4 kms west of Clare, dates back to the County Armagh and was bestowed by the Irish settlers of the region.

Jim Barry has also released a second shiraz from the 1992 vintage called 'McCrae Wood', named after a vineyard planted on land bought by Jim from an old friend, Duncan McCrae Wood. It is like a junior version of the opulent Armagh; both are huge wines, yet balanced, flavoursome and approachable even when young.

The Barry family have also restored to original, a classic FJ Holden. Bought new back at Clare in 1956 by Jim's father, Frederick James Barry, it has travelled only 63,000 miles and is in mint condition.

Jim Barry has enjoyed a prosperous career making wine in Clare a tradition which is being continued by his children.

JIM BARRY WINES

Address: PO Box 394, Clare SA 5453
Direction: 3kms north of post office (Main North Road)
Phone: (08) 8842 2261
Fax: (08) 8842 3752
Established: 1959
Owner: Jim Barry
Winemaker: Mark Barry
Principal varieties grown:
Riesling, Shiraz, Sauvignon Blanc, Chardonnay, Cabernet Sauvignon, Semillon, Pinot Noir, Cabernet Franc, Merlot, Malbec
Ha under vine: 160
Average no. cases produced: 40,000

Principal wines & brands	Cellar Potential
'The Armagh'	5-10 years
Watervale Riesling	2-5 years
Personal Selection Cabernet Sauvignon	5-10 years
Personal Selection Chardonnay	2-5 years
McCrae Wood Shiraz	5-8 years
McCrae Wood Cabernet Malbec	3-5 years
Semillon	3-5 years
Lodge Hill Riesling	3-5 years

Public & trade tours:
No

Hours open to public:
9am-5pm, weekdays; 9am-4pm, weekends and public holidays

Points of interest: Excellent view, well balanced range of table wines, sparkling wine, table wine, dessert wine, port

Retail distribution:
Negociants Australia, NSW, QLD, WA, VIC, SA, NT; Australian Liquor Marketers, Hobart, Launceston

Grosset Wines

Jeffrey Grosset is a deep thinking perfectionist whose wines sell out within days of their release each year. Jeffrey built his winery in the old Auburn Butter Factory in 1981. It has since expanded somewhat but remains a distinctly boutique operation.

Jeff has the highest vineyard in Clare "Gaia" at an altitude of 570 metres. He uses this name for his super premium red wine a bordeaux style blend of cabernet sauvignon, cabernet franc and merlot.

Like many others in the Clare Valley Jeff specialises in riesling and makes two distinct styles. The full flavoured Watervale riesling and an elegant Polish Hill Riesling. He has expanded his range to include wines from the Adelaide Hills, a Piccadilly Chardonnay and an Adelaide Hills Semillon/Sauvignon Blanc.

Jeff's excellent cellar door in the main original stone building serves simple lunches on weekends from September onwards while the wine stocks last. So don't delay your visit.

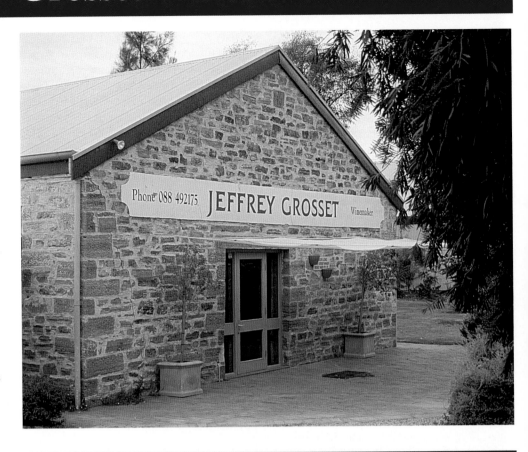

Mount Horrocks

Stephanie Toole has boundless energy, enthusiasm and a vitality that is firmly focussed on creating quality wines. She uses only hand picked, unirrigated fruit to make what Stephanie describes as 'essentially food wines, wines to drink'!

Stephanie's Mount Horrocks Cordon Cut Riesling has become a benchmark wine of this style. It is created by cutting the long cordons that hold the bunches of grapes late in the harvest season, not totally, but restricting the flow of sap to the bunches of grapes causing them to shrivel and concentrate their flavours. The vineyard in Watervale, where these vines grow, is magnificently tended and many of the bunches often get some "botrytis" nobel rot infection, which further concentrates the flavours in the wines. Mount Horrocks also produce a dry riesling, cabernet merlot, shiraz, semillon and chardonnay.

Stephanie is currently in the process of restoring the old Auburn Railway Station as a cellar door which will include a picnic area, a petanque pitch and facilities for private functions. Well done Stephanie, I know it will be a big success and a great thing for the Clare region.

MOUNT HORROCKS

Address: PO Box 72, Watervale SA 5452
Phone: (08) 8849 2243
Fax: (08) 8849 2243
Established: 1982
Owner: Stephanie Toole
Winemaker: Stephanie Toole
Average no. cases produced: 5,000

Principal wines & brands	Cellar Potential
Cordon Cut Riesling	10 years
Watervale Riesling	10 years
Cabernet Merlot	5-8 years
Shiraz	5-8 years
Semillon	10 years
Unwooded Chardonnay	3 years

Hours open to public:
10am-5pm, weekends, public holidays and school holidays from the end of January 1998

Points of interest:
The new cellar door facility will be in the renovated Auburn Railway Station. Picnic areas, parking, petanque and facilities for private functions will be available

Crabtree of Watervale

Having tried his hand at Law and Stockbroking in England, Robert Crabtree felt the need to travel. Pursuing his interest in wine and viticulture, Robert worked in vineyards and wineries in the Dordogne in France, and in New Zealand. In 1981, he finally settled in Auburn in the Clare Valley where he began planting vines. Initially Robert's wines were made at local wineries under his 'Watervale Cellars' label.

Robert and his wife Elizabeth purchased a lovely old stone home in 1985 and converted a front area into a delightful tasting room. In 1987 Robert built a small winery behind their home and after many years making his wine at other wineries did his own thing with excellent results.

CRABTREE

Address: PO Box 164, Watervale SA 5452
Phone: (08) 8843 0069
Fax: (08) 8843 0144
Established: 1978
Winemaker: Robert Crabtree
Principal varieties grown: Cabernet Sauvignon, Shiraz, Riesling, Grenache, Pedro, Cabernet Franc, Semillon, Muscat, Pedro Ximines
Ha under vine: 13
Average annual crush: 50-99 tonnes
Hours open to public: 11am-5pm, daily
Retail distribution: Westwood Wine Agencies, VIC; Barrique Fine Wines, QLD; Regional Liquor, SA; Premium Merchants, WA. Export to UK, Switzerland, NZ

Stephen John Wines

Stephen John is a world class winemaker. For 25 years he worked for large winemakers rising from Laboratory Technician at Seppelts to the Chief Red Winemakers position before joining Wolf Blass Wines as Chief White Winemaker and then finally General Operations Manager which took him often to the Quelltaler Winery. This is only a stones throw from where Stephen and his wife Rita have set up their own winery and cellar door in an 80 year old stable on the 6 hectare vineyard of old dry grown vines, which in Stephen's experienced hands, are producing great wines. Stephen still holds the record of 9 gold medals in one show for his Wolf Blass whites in Brisbane. This skill is obvious in his Watervale Riesling and a very interesting Watervale Pedro Xmenez, a white made in a soft, lightly oaked style. From this Spanish variety I enjoyed this wine a lot and it is very affordably priced.

Stephen also makes a shiraz and cabernet sauvignon as well as a family favourite a shiraz based methode champenoise sparkling called "Traugott Cuvee" a rich, soft and velvety wine ideal with roasts and game dishes. This is one of the great new boutique wineries of recent years.

STEPHEN JOHN WINES

Address: PO Box 345, Government Road, Watervale 5452
Phone: (08) 8843 0105
Fax: (08) 8843 0105
Established: 1994
Owners: Stephen and Rita John
Winemaker: Stephen John
Principal varieties grown: Riesling, Shiraz, Cabernet Sauvignon, Chardonnay, Pedro Ximenez
Ha under vine: 5.5
Average no. cases produced: 3,500

Principal wines & brands	Cellar Potential
Watervale Riesling	10 years
Watervale Pedro Ximenez	4 years
Clare Valley Cabernet Sauvignon	10 years
Clare Valley Shiraz	5-10 years
Traugott Cuvee Sparkling Red	5 years

Public & trade tours: Trade tours
Hours open to public: 10am-5pm, weekdays; 11am-5pm, weekends and public holidays
Retail distribution: Cellar Door sales and Mail Order. Selected Restaurants and Liquor stores SA,VIC and QLD

Mintaro Cellars

Peter Houldsworth is a genuine character with more than an air of a sporting legend about him. He travelled through Mintaro as a visitor from his native England and fell in love with this historic little village. This is an absolute must to visit on your trip to the Clare Valley, it is on the eastern fringes of the region and one travels some 15 kms or so through the Polish River region from the main Clare road to get there.

Whilst Peter makes a traditional range of wines that have won a number of trophies and medals at wine shows during the 1997 vintage he stumbled on something great.

He had a real fruit salad of a white fermenting with its incredibly fragrant bouquet drifting into the tasting room, a young couple came in and were fascinated. The wine made in a late picked style from up to a dozen white varieties including melon de bourgone from France, pinot gris, muscadelle, sylvanner and flora. The lass, an Adelaide nurse, she had the unusual name of Keturah - Hebrew for "Sweet Fragrance", immediately she popped her head over the fermenting vat saying "that's me". Peter now finds it is his biggest seller and having tasted it frosty cold on his verandah late on a gorgeous afternoon I can see why!!

MINTARO WINES

Address: Mintaro Cellars, Leasingham Road, Mintaro SA 5415
Direction: Opposite Mintaro Oval
Phone: (08) 8843 9046
Fax: (08) 8843 9050
Established: 1984
Owner: Peter Houldsworth
Winemaker: Peter Houldsworth
Principal varieties grown: Riesling, Cabernet Sauvignon, Cabernet Franc, Shiraz
Ha under vine: 10
Average annual crush: 50 tonnes

Average no. cases produced: 3,000

Principal wines & brands	Cellar Potential
Shiraz	5 years
Cabernet	7 years
Riesling Dry	4 years
Riesling LP	4 years
Sparkling Cabernet-Shiraz	5 years
Keturah Sweet White	5 years

Public & trade tours: No
Hours open to public: 9am-5pm, daily
Retail distribution: Festival City Wines, Port Road, Albert Park SA

Quelltaler

QUELLTALER

Address: Quelltaler Road, Watervale SA 5452
Phone: (08) 8843 0003
Fax: (08) 8843 0096
Established: 1854
Owner: Mildara Blass Limited
Winemaker: David O'Leary
Principal varieties grown: Cabernet Sauvignon, Shiraz, Chardonnay, Semillon, Riesling

Principal wines & brands	Cellar Potential
Annie's Lane Chardonnay	2-4 years
Annie's Lane Riesling	2-4 years
Annie's Lane Semillon	2-4 years
Annie's Lane Cabernet Merlot	3-5 years
Annie's Lane Shiraz	3-5 years

Public & trade tours: Trade tours by appointment only
Hours open to public: 8.30am-5pm, weekdays; 10am-4pm, weekends and public holidays

Through many changes of name and many great winemakers, this beautiful old winery in the centre of the Clare Valley at Watervale remains as a reminder of the grandeur of days gone by.

Of recent years, the winery has been thoughtfully and thoroughly restored. Quelltaler's history goes back to 1860 when Walter Hughes purchased the property. Vines had already been planted and as these came to bear fruit, Hughes hired Carl Sobels to supervise winemaking and the construction of a winery. After his employer's death, Sobels formed a partnership with Herman Buring and they bought the property in 1890.

To formalise the establishment of this new business, the property was re-named 'Quelltaler' which is derived from the German translation of 'Spring Vale'. The stone houses built at Quelltaler to accommodate Carl Sobels' growing family, are still lived in and beautifully maintained. The Sobels family remained with Quelltaler until the 1960s.

The winery is now owned by the progressive Mildara Blass Company who have invested heavily in the vineyards and re-equipped the winery with the latest state of the art winemaking technology.

Respected winemaker David O'Leary, winner of the 1988 Jimmy Watson Trophy, has wasted no time in re-commissioning the classic old open fermenting tanks to create some classic reds On the day of a recent visit, the first day of the vintage, the dark rich red shiraz grapes and skins were bubbling away in the old fermenters, filling the winery with that indescribable scent of vintage; the whole place had a happy feel as if it was rediscovering it's soul and destiny.

Leasingham

Towards the end of last century, the Clare Valley saw an enormous growth in viticulture. The wine market had been very healthy and many Australian wines were exported, particularly to England.

With so many new vines a grape surplus looked imminent. A syndicate was formed, made up of the valley's leading industry members, including J H Knappstein, the area's largest grower. The new syndicate was called the Stanley Wine Company and purchased the Clare jam factory for conversion into a winery. Stanley's first vintage was in 1895, their first winemaker being Alfred Basedow, of the famous winemaking family.

Alfred had studied at Montpellier in France and after only a few years at Stanley, he was presiding over one of the largest wineries in South Australia.

Due to trouble on the export market however, wine stocks began to build up. By 1911 Knappstein had bought out his partners and owned the company. After much hard work in re-establishing overseas markets, Knappstein left the company in good shape when he died in 1919. By the mid 1940's, under new management, Stanley were selling bulk wine to most major companies. Five years later the company began developing their vineyards at Leasingham, near Watervale. Rhine riesling and cabernet sauvignon were the major grape varieties planted. Stanley developed a unique system with their vineyard employees, who were paid with a share of the value of the crop. In this way, enthusiasm was

generated, and the vineyards were developed quickly and successfully.

Stanley began marketing bottled wine under their own label during the 1960's.

New equipment was acquired for the winery and Leasingham wine grew in stature.

In 1970 the first vintage of the multi-award winning Leasingham Bin 56 Cabernet Malbec was released.

Thomas Hardy & Sons purchased both Leasingham and Stanley in 1988. Hardy's recognised the potential of the Clare Valley and have spent considerable capital on up-grading the winery and vineyards.

In 1993 the winery's centenary saw the re-introduction of the Bin 56 Cabernet Malbec and Bin 37 Chardonnay. A premium limited release range – Classic Clare was also introduced featuring a shiraz and a cabernet sauvignon and more recently a rhine riesling.

Since 1993 the Bin wines have been awarded many accolades, including the 1995 Jimmy Watson Trophy. Demand has outstripped supply. Bin 61 Shiraz and Bin 42 Semillon Sauvignon Blanc have been added to the portfolio.

After 100 years of winemaking Leasingham has survived the test of time and is firmly established as one of Australia's leading wine producers.

LEASINGHAM
Address: 7 Dominic Court, Clare SA 5453
Phone: (08) 8842 2555
Fax: (08) 8842 3293
Established: 1893
Owner: BRL Hardy Limited
Winemaker: Richard Rowe
Principal varieties grown:
Chardonnay, Cabernet Sauvignon, Shiraz,
Sauvignon Blanc, Semillon, Malbec, Riesling
Ha under vine: 250
Average annual crush: 2,500-4,999 tonnes

Principal wines & brands:
Leasingham Bin range
Classic Clare

Hours open to public:
9am-5pm, weekdays; 10am-4pm, weekends
Retail distribution: The Houghton Wine Co.,
WA; BRL Wine Company

Mitchell Winery

The beautiful gates that form the entrance to Jane and Andrew Mitchell's impressive homestead, and also feature on their label, have special significance as they were original to the property. Jane's great-great-grandfather Walter Duffield, a S.A. wine pioneer, owned the Gawler Foundry where they were made as a wedding gift to the original owners of the Mitchell's property – quite a coincidence!!

Andrew and Jane started their wine enterprise back in 1975 in an old stone appleshed, after Andrew resigned from the Public Service.

Andrew completed his winemaking degree from Charles Sturt University by correspondence whilst Jane studied at Roseworthy.

The winery, located in the very picturesque Skillogalee Valley near Sevenhill, is about to undergo expansion again which speaks volumes for their hard work and excellent wines.

The Peppertree Shiraz has become a landmark wine along with their Watervale Riesling in the distinctive silver and blue labels with the famous gateway to enjoyment on the label. The Mitchell's have invested heavily in the vineyards over the last 15 years and have access to great fruit under their own viticultural control. They certainly have their act together.

Make this a stop on the Skillogalee wine trail which now have five excellent boutique wineries. Mitchell's being the first.

MITCHELL WINERY
Address: Hughes Park Road, Sevenhill via Clare SA 5453
Phone: (08) 8843 4258
Fax: (08) 8843 4340
Established: 1975
Owners: Andrew and Jane Mitchell
Winemaker: Andrew Mitchell
Principal varieties grown: Shiraz, Riesling, Cabernet Sauvignon, Grenache, Semillon
Ha under vine: Watervale, 40 ha. Sevenhill, 10 ha
Average annual crush: 300-499 tonnes
Average no. cases produced: 18,000
Principal wines & brands
Watervale Riesling
Peppertree Vineyard Shiraz
Sevenhill Cabernet Sauvignon
Growers Semillon
Growers Grenache
Public & trade tours: By appointment only
Hours open to public: 10am-4pm, daily
Retail distribution: Cellar Door and Mail Order sales. Tucker Seabrook Classic, SA; Fesq Dorado, WA, TAS, NSW, QLD, VIC, ACT; Options, NT. Export to NZ, UK, Canada, USA, Switzerland

Paulett Wines

Neil and Alison Paulett quickly made their mark with their riesling after commencing their well integrated vineyards and winery in 1983. Several years ago they made the bold move of building a new stone winery at the apex of their property. The view from this hilltop winery with its return verandahs looking out over the entire Polish Hill River Valley is awesome. The winery has been cleverly designed to take advantage of gravity to make the wines with a minimum of human and mechanical intervention.

The visitor to the winery also has a birds eye view, not only of the vineyards in the valley, but the working winery as well from the elevated tasting area.

The Paulett wines include riesling both dry and late-picked styles, chardonnay, sauvignon blanc, shiraz and cabernet merlot. They have carved out a solid reputation both in Australia and on several overseas markets. If in the Clare Valley make sure you drop in and catch the view along with tasting the excellent wines. Local artists Murray Edwards and Ian Roberts works grace the tasting room walls and are worth seeing.

PAULETTS

Address: PO Box 50, Sevenhill via Clare SA 5453
Direction: 2.5 kms along Sevenhill Road to Mintaro Road
Phone: (08) 8843 4328
Fax: (08) 8843 4202
Established: 1983
Owners: Neil and Alison Paulett
Winemaker: Neil Paulett
Principal varieties grown: Riesling, Sauvignon Blanc, Shiraz, Cabernet Sauvignon, Merlot, Chardonnay, Mourvedre
Ha under vine: 8.3
Average annual crush: 210 tonnes. 2/3 of crush from grapegrowers in the Polish Valley
Average no. cases produced: 12,500

Principal wines & brands	Cellar Potential
Andreas (Reserve Shiraz)	10-15 years
Riesling	8-10 years
Shiraz	6-8 years
Cabernet Merlot	6-8 years
Sauvignon Blanc	2-4 years
Chardonnay	4-6 years
Late Harvest Riesling	6-8 years
The Quarry (Mourvedre grape)	4-6 years
Trillians - Sparkling Riesling	4-6 years

Public & trade tours: No
Hours open to public:
10am-5pm, daily except Christmas Day and Good Friday
Points of interest:
Magnificent views across the Polish Valley. Nearly always served by the owners. Cellar door and toilets suitable for wheelchair access
Retail distribution:
Cellar Door, Local Restaurants, Hotels, Motels and Bottle shops. Distributed by our wholesale agents in QLD, NSW, VIC, SA. Export to Thailand, UK and NZ

Jeanneret

Denis Jeanneret, a Swiss Chemist, and his wife Pat fell in love with the natural beauty of a property on the edge of the Spring Gully Conservation Park not far from the group of wineries in the Skillogalee Valley.

They planted vines and for a number of years as they grew Denis worked for Robert Crabtree at Watervale honing his winemaking skills.

The first Jeanneret Wines were made in 1992. The winery is on top of a hill in quite dense bushland but the cellar is neatly tucked under the families lovely stone home. On the day of our photographic visit the natural bush gardens were resplendent with thousands of daffodils. The Jeanneret wines are made by son Ben and like the family are generous and open with lots of character. I particularly like their shiraz, resplendent with wild berry flavours and lots of pepper and spice. Jeanneret is a little off the beaten track, but well worth the effort to visit.

JEANNERET

Address: Jeanneret Road, Sevenhill SA 5453
Phone: (08) 8843 4308
Fax: (08) 8843 4251
Email: djeanne@pc.jaring.my
Established: 1992
Winemaker: Ben Jeanneret
Principal varieties grown: Cabernet Sauvignon, Shiraz, Riesling, Semillon, Grenache, Muscat
Ha under vine: 4
Average annual crush: 20-49 tonnes

Principal wines & brands	Cellar Potential
Semillon	5-10 years
Cabernet Sauvignon	5-10 years
Sparkling Grenache	2-3 years
Riesling	5-10 years
Shiraz	5-10 years

Hours open to public: 11am-5pm, daily
Points of interest: Picturesque bushland setting. Picnic settings for visitors
Retail distribution: Cellar Door and Mail Order sales. David Turner Agencies

Stringy Brae Wines

Owned by Donald and Sally Willson, the family's picturesque Stringy Brae property is located at the base of Spring Gully Conservation Park, two kilometres west of Sevenhill.

The first Stringy Brae vintage was produced from Langhorne Creek fruit in 1988. 1991 saw the planting of 6 hectares of vineyard and in 1998 this will be expanded to 9 hectares.

Children are well entertained by the numerous farm animals and 'Bonnie' the amazing 'vineyard' dog, while parents enjoy a well earned taste at the cellar door.

Along with the much sought after Stringy Brae wines the Willson's produce a super premium red of heroic proportions under the Mote Hill label – in magnums only, it is definitely one to 'put away for a decade or two'. The Mote Hill label is reserved for special selections from the Stringy Brae Vineyard so watch out for further editions including the soon to be released 'Sir Lancelot Shiraz'.

The property also boasts two delightful self-contained cottages on the far side of their Stringy Bark tree covered hill overlooking a lake, vineyard and sweeping valleys towards Clare. This combined with the wines and the unforgettable charming hospitality of Donald and Sally makes Stringy Brae an ideal Country getaway retreat.

STRINGY BRAE WINES

Address: Box 35, Sevenhill via Clare SA 5453
Phone: (08) 8843 4313
Fax: (08) 8843 4313
Email: stringy@capri.net.au
WWW: http://www.capri.net.au/~stringy
Established: First Plantings 1991. First Commercial Release 1990
Owners: DB and SM Willson
Winemaker: Contract
Principal varieties grown: Riesling, Shiraz, Cabernet Sauvignon
Ha under vine: 6 (+3 1998)
Average annual crush: 20 tonnes
Average no. cases produced: 1,500

Principal wines & brands	Cellar Potential
Stringy Brae Riesling	Good
Stringy Brae Shiraz	5 years
Stringy Brae Cabernet Sauvignon	5-7+ years
Mote Hill Cabernet Sauvignon	20-25 years

Public & trade tours: Vineyard tours by appointment only
Hours open to public: 10am-5pm, weekends and public holidays. Other times refer road sign, and by appointment
Points of interest: Self contained cottage accommodation. Special tastings, group tastings and vineyard tours by arrangement, dinner presentations and picnic areas
Retail distribution: Local, Adelaide and environs, Mail Order. Export to UK

Knappstein

The Knappstein name has been involved in the wine business in Clare since 1895 when the local brewer, the local doctor, a solicitor and J H Knappstein began the Stanley Wine Company in the premises of the Clare Jam Factory.

The Stanley Wine Company had achieved wine show success second to none, in this early era of the modern premium Australian wine business in Clare. After the sale of the Stanley Wine Company, Tim Knappstein began Enterprise Wines in the old brewery building in the centre of the town, some years later changing it to his own name.

Before leaving the Stanley Wine Company Tim Knappstein selected land high up against the slate hills to the east of Clare on the edge of the Hill River Station. Here he planted 30 hectares of vineyard, mainly cabernet sauvignon, riesling, merlot sauvignon blanc and chardonnay.

Planted in 1972, the Knappstein Vineyard adjoins Petaluma's Hanlin Hill Vineyard and the new 45 hectare Yertabulti Vineyard on rich red soils over limestone planted with premium red varieties to supply Knappstein Wines.

Knappstein's Vineyard on Spring Farm Road, Clare, supplied the core fruit for the development of the Knappstein brand during the 1980's. The riesling, fume blanc and cabernet merlot owe their commercial success to the qualities of these concentrated grapes.

Petaluma Limited purchased the Knappstein Winery in 1992 and the vineyards in 1995. Tim Knappstein left Clare and turned to the Adelaide Hills to develop his Lenswood Vineyard Brand, leaving Petaluma's Chief Winemaker of seven years, Andrew Hardy to take over the reins as manager and wine-maker. Although owned by Petaluma Limited, Knappstein Wines operates as a small independent premium quality winery. Andrew Hardy is doing a great job at Knappstein Wines producing wines that are the "essence of Clare" and most especially the world renowned dry riesling and full bodied ripe fruit reds.

Petaluma Clare

In 1978 Petaluma acquired the Hanlin Hill vineyard on the western slopes of the Clare hills. At some 500 metres above sea level it is the Clare Regions highest major vineyard.

The dry grown vineyard is contoured across the hills clinging to the red-brown slopes littered with grey parent slate material. Hand harvesting of the few bunches from each vine leads to a concentrated and aromatic riesling, loaded with limey and tropical fruit salad flavours. The great style, acid and balance are accentuated by Brian Croser's winemaking teams innovative style, experience and strictly controlled fermentation conditions. This vineyard is undoubtedly one of Australia's very best and his Rolls Royce Riesling says it all.

Neil Pike is a gregarious, happy young man with a very positive attitude to life. His family has long been heavily involved in the beverage industry.

Henry Pike, Neil's great-great-grandfather arrived in South Australia in 1878. He settled in the pretty town of Oakbank in the Adelaide Hills and established a brewing and soft drink business, the symbol of which was the distinctive English pike fish.

In 1972, the business was sold; however by this time Edgar Pike, Neil's father, was vineyard manager for a large wine company and dabbling in his own private winemaking.

Neil and his brother Andrew both studied viticulture and winemaking at Roseworthy Agricultural College. Andrew is involved in viticulture and management, whilst Neil handles the winemaking and marketing and they are a great team.

Their vineyard was established in 1984 and they made wine from the region the following year. The cool Polish Hill River is a genuine sub-region of the Clare Valley, ripening several weeks after most of the valley, giving the wines that extra depth of flavour and keen cool climate edge.

All the Pikes wines will age well; the only problem is they just haven't been able to keep up with demand, particularly from the restaurant trade. The riesling led the way and runs out each year, as does their succulent shiraz with its approachable Rhone Valley character.

Pikes have just released a reserve shiraz, a rigorously selected wine from the best few barrels of the year. The first wine is a 1992 vintage. The 1993, although excellent, didn't rate a reserve selection, but the 1994 and 1995 have been sensational. Neil and Andrew dedicated the first reserve to their hardworking inspirational parents, Edgar and Merle.

Look for the pike fish and make sure he's not the one that got away and was served on someone else's table! After the shiraz and riesling, try the sauvignon blanc and the cabernet with a touch of merlot and cabernet franc.

PIKES WINES PTY LTD

Address: Polish Hill River Road, Sevenhill, Clare Valley SA 5453
Phone: (08) 8843 4370
Fax: (08) 8843 4353
Established: 1984
Winemaker: Neil Pike
Principal varieties grown: Riesling, Sauvignon Blanc, Chardonnay, Shiraz, Cabernet Sauvignon, Merlot, Cabernet Franc, Semillon, Sangiovese
Ha under vine: 25
Average annual crush: 300-400 tonnes
Average no. cases produced: 25,000

Principal wines & brands	Cellar Potential
Clare Valley Riesling	7-10 years
Clare Valley Sauvignon Blanc	1 year
Clare Valley Chardonnay	2-5 years
Clare Valley Shiraz	5-8+ years
Clare Valley Cabernet Sauvignon	5-10+ years
Reserve Shiraz	7-12+ years
Reserve Merlot	5-10 years
Reserve Riesling	10+ years

Public & trade tours: By appointment only
Hours open to public: 10am-4pm, daily
Points of interest: BBQ facilities and Picnic area
Retail distribution: National distribution by Tucker Seabroook Classic Group

Tim Adams

Tim Adams is a man on a mission and is already amongst the very top echelon of Australia's winemakers. Tim is very serious about his viticulture and winemaking and his wines which have already been very good since his first vintage in 1985 seem to be getting better with each year.

Tim has a long connection with the Clare Valley and spent a number of years working with valley legend the late Mick Knappstein, and his nephew Tim, at Stanley Leasingham. He and partner Pam Goldsack run an excellent cellar door and also serve bistro lunches on weekends and public holidays. Tim's Aberfeldy Shiraz is definitely in the top rung of this variety in Australia and his Botrytis Semillon is a classy wine indeed with the sweetness varying with the conditions of the vintage.

This is a winery where one should spend a little time and taste all the wines as there is sure to be more than one that suits your palate.

From Left: Tim Adams, Garry Pink, Stephen McDermid and Pam Goldsack

TIM ADAMS

Address: Warenda Road, Clare SA 5453
Phone: (08) 8842 2429
Fax: (08) 8842 3550
Established: 1987
Owners: Tim Adams and Pam Goldsack
Winemaker: Tim Adams
Principal varieties grown: Shiraz, Cabernet, Cabernet Franc, Grenache, Malbec, Riesling, Semillon
Ha under vine: 0.5 + 13 growers
Average annual crush: 250 tonnes
Average no. cases produced: 15,000

Principal wines & brands	Cellar Potential
Aberfeldy (Shiraz)	15 years
Shiraz	10 years
Semillon	10 years
Riesling	10 years
Cabernet	10 years
Fergus (Grenache)	7 years
Vintage Port	15 years
Botrytis Riesling	10 years
Botrytis Semillon	10 years

Public & trade tours: Trade tours by appointment only
Hours open to public: 11am-5pm, daily
Points of interest: Restaurant (Lunches), weekends and public holidays
Retail distribution: Adelaide, Melbourne, Sydney, Canberra, Brisbane and Perth

Duncan Estate

John Duncan's background as an engineer is well evidenced in his well ordered and arranged boutique winery. He and his family bought an existing vineyard in 1968 and commenced planting a wide range of classic varieties including malbec, merlot, pinot noir, cabernet sauvignon, riesling, grenache and traminer. After a number of years, just supplying grapes to others, they decided to commence their own winemaking enterprise.

The first wines to appear under the Duncan Label were made in 1984. Petit Verdot has been added to the vineyard in recent years. The Duncan wines have won many gold and silver medals in Australian wine shows which is a credit for such a genuinely small family enterprise.

If you are looking for interesting and different styles to try and buy Duncan Estate is an ideal place to visit. You will also receive very personal attention and warm family hospitality.

DUNCAN ESTATE

Address: PO Box 5003, Clare SA 5453
Direction: West of Clare Caravan Park along Spring Gully Road
Phone: (08) 8843 4335
Fax: (08) 8843 4335
Established: 1968
Owner: Duncan Family
Winemaker: John Duncan
Principal varieties grown: Riesling, Chardonnay, Sauvignon Blanc, Traminer, Semillon, Grenache, Cabernet Sauvignon, Shiraz, Merlot, Malbec, Pinot Noir, Petit Verdot
Ha under vine: 8.2

Average annual crush: 30 tonnes
Average no. cases produced: 2,500

Principal wines & brands	Cellar Potential
Pinot Noir Clare Valley	3-7 years
Chardonnay	2-5 years
Mixed Block Traminer Riesling Dry	2-5 years
Mixed Block Traminer Riesling Sweet	2-10 years
Semillon/Sauvignon Blanc	2-5 years
Riesling Clare Valley	2-5 years
Shiraz	5-10 years
Cabernet Sauvignon/Merlot	5-10 years

Public & trade tours: By appointment only
Hours open to public: 10am-4pm, daily
Retail distribution: SA, VIC, Japan

Taylors Wines

The Taylor Family established their vineyard and winery at Auburn in the Clare Valley in 1969. The site was carefully chosen for the red brown loam over limestone soils and the cool climate of the Clare Valley. The initial planting consisted of 178 hectares of which 149 hectares were cabernet sauvignon. Today the vineyard has grown over 500 hectares making it one of the largest contiguous vineyards in Australia with the addition of three white varieties, riesling, chardonnay and crouchen and two red varieties, shiraz and pinot noir. In 1973 the first Taylors Estate grown and bottled cabernet sauvignon received a gold medal in every National Wine Show in Australia. Since then every vintage has won awards at National and International Wine Shows. This is reflected by the long list of medals on each Taylors label.

The unique feature of Taylors is that all the wine is made from the single vineyard at the Winery Estate. This provides the solid base of excellent fruit that produces some of the finest and most consistent wines in Australia. The vineyard is well managed by George Finn and Ken Noack and the winemaking is in the capable hands of Andrew Tolley.

Bill Taylor, who was one of the founding Directors of the company, is the present Managing Director. His son Mitchell is the Export Director and also assists in the winemaking. On the far north western corner of Taylors Estate, on the banks of the Wakefield River is the historic old stone winery St Andrews. Built in 1896 and operating until the 1930's, Taylors have bought the property and the huge old mansion. Plans are underway to develop the superb property, so watch out!!

The philosophy at Taylors is to make soft, easy drinking wines and to hold them back from the market until they are ready to drink. This fact, together with an obsession for quality, sparing no expense, make Taylors one of the best value wines in the country.

TAYLORS WINES PTY LTD
Address: Mintaro Road, Auburn SA 5451
Phone: (08) 8849 2008
Fax: (08) 8849 2240
Established: 1969
Owner: Taylor Family
Winemaker: Andrew Tolley
Principal varieties grown: Chardonnay, Merlot, Cabernet Sauvignon, Shiraz, Pinot Noir, Riesling, Semillon, Crouchen
Ha under vine: 550
Average annual crush: 2,500-4,999 tonnes

Principal wines & brands	Cellar Potential
Taylors Cabernet Sauvignon	5-10 years
Taylors Chardonnay	2-5 years
Taylors Shiraz	5-10 years
Taylors White Clare	2-5 years
Taylors Clare Riesling	2-5 years
Taylors Pinot Noir	2-5 years

Public & trade tours: By appointment only
Hours open to public: 9am-5pm, weekdays; 10am-5pm, Saturday and public holidays; 10am-4pm, Sunday
Retail distribution: Taylors Wines Pty Ltd, NSW, VIC, QLD, WA; Tucker Seabrook Classic, SA; Oak Barrel Wines, ACT. Export to NZ, UK, Malaysia, Hong Kong, Thailand, Singapore, Germany, Holland, Switzerland, Fiji

After making a fortune selling supplies to gold prospectors and running stores in Ballarat and Geelong, John Riddoch and his family moved to Coonawarra in 1861. Riddoch purchased 200 acres (80 ha), but within 20 years he owned the extensive property Yallum Park, which covered tens of thousands of hectares.

On the advice of a local gardener, Riddoch subdivided much land into 25-75 ha blocks, forming the Penola Fruit Colony. This land was bought by 'blockers' as they came to be known, who planted and later sold grapes to Riddoch. Until the bank crash in 1893, the Fruit Colony prospered, due to the magic 'terra rossa' soil of the area. This soil covers about 4,800 ha of land in a strip about 1.6 km wide and 14.5 km long. With 140 ha under vine at Yallum Park, Riddoch built substantial cellars in which to store the wines made from the blockers' fruit. These were largely shiraz, cabernet sauvignon, malbec and some pinot noir. The cellars were built with three distinct gables and have come to be very well known as the building on the Wynns Coonawarra Estate woodcut labels. The cellars were designed to store 340,000 litres of wine, but with the depressed market and large vintages, they soon became inadequate. The Yallum shearing sheds at Katnook provided further storage space for Riddoch's wine.

John Riddoch died in 1901 at a time when fortified wines were becoming increasingly popular. The property was taken over by trustees, who gradually disposed of the land, vineyards and wine. Bill Redman arrived in Coonawarra the year of Riddoch's death and started work at Yallum Park. By 1907, at 20 years of age, he had reached the position of head cellarman and was able to purchase a 16 ha block from Riddoch's estate. Redman's first wine was made using an old cheese press and was fermented in hogsheads purchased from Douglas A. Tolley who had agreed to buy the wine for one shilling per gallon (4.5 litres).

After Yallum Park was purchased by Chateau Tanunda in 1919, Redman became the only winemaker in the area, as the wine remaining from Riddoch's estate was distilled into fortifying spirit and brandy - a shocking waste of excellent reds.

In 1945 Woodleys bought the Yallum Estate, winery, distillery and vineyards and renamed the property Chateau Comaum. Bill Redman and family were commissioned to run the winery. Wynns purchased the property in 1951, renaming it Wynns Coonawarra Estate. There are now more than 20 wineries in the region and many more wine companies around Australia either own vines or purchase grapes or wine from the region.

The climate in Coonawarra is cool and occasionally frosts and ripening are problems. There is a constant underground water supply, but there is limestone between it and the terra rossa. This makes establishing vines both difficult and expensive, as the limestone must be ripped through under each row of vines to enable their roots to reach the water source. Once established, vines are protected from the vagaries of annual rainfall by a constant water supply. Internationally, Coonawarra is the first region in Australia to have a reputation for its wines and their style as distinct from just being an Australian wine. The south east of South Australia now has wines growing far and wide, new multi-million dollar wine planting schemes seem a dime a dozen, but the name Coonawarra still has the magic which has been hard-earned and deserved.

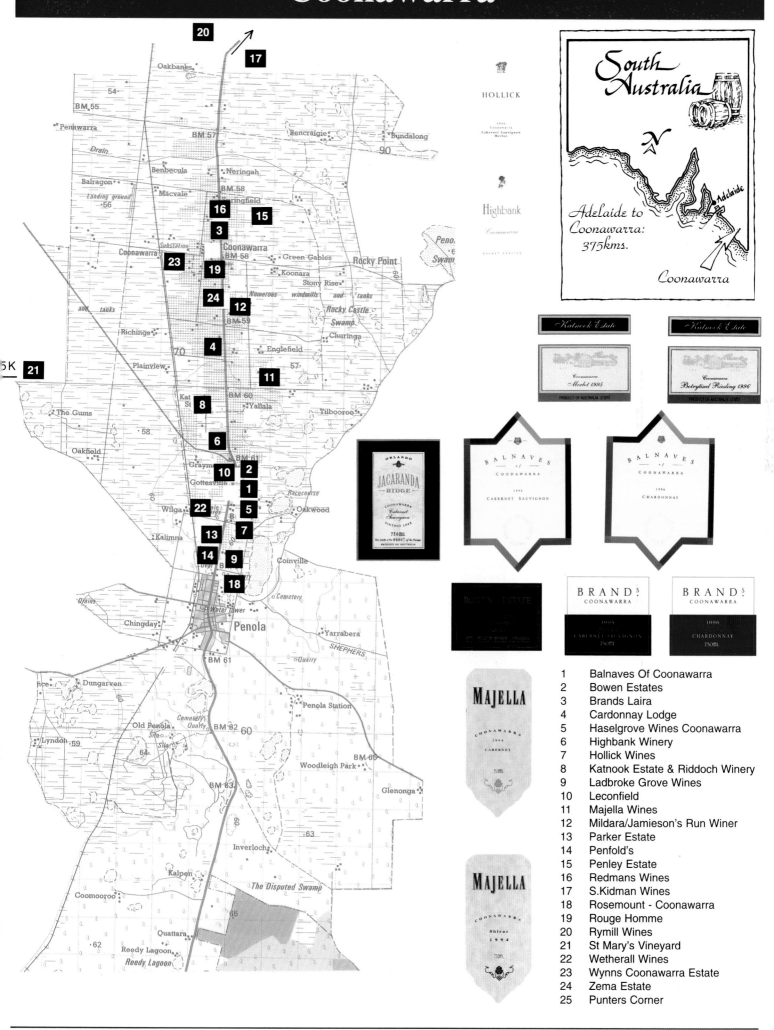

Coonawarra

South Australia

Adelaide to Coonawarra: 375kms.

1 Balnaves Of Coonawarra
2 Bowen Estates
3 Brands Laira
4 Cardonnay Lodge
5 Haselgrove Wines Coonawarra
6 Highbank Winery
7 Hollick Wines
8 Katnook Estate & Riddoch Winery
9 Ladbroke Grove Wines
10 Leconfield
11 Majella Wines
12 Mildara/Jamieson's Run Winer
13 Parker Estate
14 Penfold's
15 Penley Estate
16 Redmans Wines
17 S.Kidman Wines
18 Rosemount - Coonawarra
19 Rouge Homme
20 Rymill Wines
21 St Mary's Vineyard
22 Wetherall Wines
23 Wynns Coonawarra Estate
24 Zema Estate
25 Punters Corner

Coonawarra

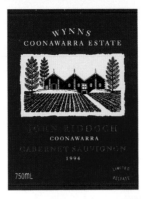

Bowen Estate

Doug Bowen's nonchalant manner is deceptive; he is actually a very dedicated, talented winemaker and viticulturist.

His love for the Coonawarra region grew out of his student days at Roseworthy, when he wrote his thesis on the area. At the first opportunity Doug and Joy purchased 16 ha of land at the region's southern end and began planting immediately. The winery, a grand looking, yet very functional building of local Mount Gambier stone, was built in 1980, and has been extended to include a residence for the family. The firm establishment of this winery was achieved in less than a decade, an indication of the dedication of the Bowen family.

On completion of his studies in 1971, Doug began work for Lindemans Rouge Homme winery and remained there until his own winery's first vintage in 1975. Since then, Bowen's reds have become among the best and most consistent in the region.

Mechanisation now dominates the pruning of vines in Coonawarra but the traditional hand pruning at Bowen Estate has created a style of wines being consistently richer and more opulent and with greater depth of flavour and body. The shiraz exhibits the peppery and spicy cassis flavours much sought after in this variety. The cabernet sauvignon is a little more intense and in addition shows a herbaceous cool climate character, an effect produced by the cooler conditions experienced in the southern part of the region. Vintage here is usually a week or two later, a delay which only increases the superb flavours of the wines.

The Bowen Estate Chardonnay is a blend of stainless steel and barrel fermented fruit to encapsulate the positive aspects of both fermentation styles. The rich peach/melon flavours of chardonnay combined with the subtle french oak flavours make for a very strong complex style. Doug spends much of his time in the vineyard or winery, and it is not an easy task to drag him out of either, which is as it should be.

BOWEN ESTATE
Address: Riddoch Highway, Coonawarra SA 5263
Phone: (08 8737 2229
Fax: (08 8737 2173
Established: 1972
Owners: Doug and Joy Bowen
Winemaker: Doug Bowen
Principal varieties grown: Chardonnay, Shiraz, Merlot, Cabernet Sauvignon
Ha under vine: 33

Principal wines & brands	Cellar Potential
Bowen Estate 0Chardonnay	2 years
Bowen Estate Shiraz	4-6 years
Bowen Estate Cabernet Sauvignon/Merlot/Cabernet Franc	2-6 years
Bowen Estate Cabernet Sauvignon	5-7 years
Bowen Estate Sanderson	Current

Hours open to public: 10am-5pm, daily except Christmas Day and Good Friday
Retail distribution: All Australian capital cities and major regional centres

Balnaves of Coonawarra

Doug Balnaves commenced his career in the Wine Industry when he developed and managed the Hungerford Hill Vineyards in Coonawarra. In 1975, the family began planting their own vineyards and today they have a magnificent 100 acre vineyard at the southern end of the cigar shaped terra rossa strip, in the heart of Coonawarra.

The predominant variety at Balnaves is cabernet sauvignon, but other varieties include shiraz, merlot, cabernet franc and chardonnay. In 1991 the Balnaves launched their own wine label and opened a state of the art tasting and cellar door sales area overlooking a small lake, always resplendent with native bird life.

Doug's wife, Annette, is a great photographer and the cellar door sales area often feature some of her excellent work.

Balnaves of Coonawarra uses only about 20% of the grapes for his own wines.

The wines include the flagship cabernet sauvignon, a wine called 'The Blend', a superb merlot/cabernet franc blend, shiraz, chardonnay and a sparkling burgundy made from cabernet sauvignon.

Kirsty Balnaves is responsible for the office administration and cellar door and sales and Peter Balnaves manages the vineyards.

In 1996 major additions were made to the winery making it one of the most striking in Australia. Its tower is well visible from the main road and the distinctive Australiana flavour and colours of the buildings are aesthetically most pleasing. Balnaves is a high quality family wine business and a great addition to Coonawarra.

BALNAVES OF COONAWARRA

Address: Main Road, Coonawarra SA 5263
Phone: (08) 8737 2946
Fax: (08) 8737 2945
Email: balnaves@dove.net.au
Established: 1975
Winemaker: Peter Bissell
Principal varieties grown: Cabernet Sauvignon, Shiraz, Chardonnay, Merlot, Cabernet Franc, Chardonnay
Ha under vine: 43
Average annual crush: 500 tonnes
Average no. cases produced: 7,500

Principal wines & brands	Cellar Potential
Sparkling Cabernet	5 years
Cabernet Sauvignon	10 years
Shiraz	8 years
Merlot/Cabernet Franc (The Blend)	5 years
Chardonnay	5 years
Cabernet-Merlot	10 years

Public & trade tours: Trade tours by Appointment Only
Hours open to public:
9am-5pm, weekdays; 10am-5pm, weekends and public holidays
Retail distribution:
Cellar Door, Mail Order, Selected Restaurants and Bottle shops

Brand's Laira Wines

Eric Brand married into the wine industry in 1950 when he wed Nancy Redman, Owen's sister. He bought a small property from Redman, which was mostly orchards, but which also included several hectares of vines, some of which were amongst the first planted in Coonawarra in 1896.

There are still walnut trees along the drive and visitors can buy pickled walnuts from the cellar door. The original vineyard, with its one hundred year old vines, continues to produce outstanding red wines, but the early fruit orchards have long since given way to Brand's expanding vineyards. Eric Brand sold his grapes to local wine-makers for many years but began making his own wine in 1966. After many meetings with Hardy's winemaker Dick Heath, Brand's were supplied with a crusher and other necessary equipment. The resulting wine was sold to Hardy's directly after vintage. Redman's also made wine at Brand's winery before completion of their own.

During the late '60's, Brand's began bottling and selling some wine under the 'Laira' label, from their cellar door. 'Laira' was the ship owned by Captain Stentiford, the first owner of Brand's property. The red wines released under this label have developed a legendary reputation, and since Eric's sons, Bill and Jim have joined the company, some interesting new wines and styles have evolved. Brand's made steady progress in the market place and were, in fact, innovators in some areas - they produced Coonawarra's first pinot noir in 1982, and were one of Australia's first wineries to produce straight merlot.

The demand for cash to fund expansion and the challenge of marketing and distributing their wines meant more capital was needed if Brand's were to reach all their goals. This led to an arrangement with McWilliam's, the strong family wine company from New South Wales. The balance was perfect; McWilliam's were looking to expand into a number of premium table wine regions, Brand's fitted the bill, so in 1990 they took a half share in the company. Brand's Wines leapt ahead and in 1994 McWilliam's purchased the remaining half of the company. At the same time McWilliam's purchased an additional 200 hectares immediately adjacent to Brand's existing vineyards making it one of the largest landholders in the Coonawarra area. Sensibly McWilliam's have let Jim and Bill Brand stay on and manage things in their very thorough, diligent style. The Brand's wines are consistently among the best in Coonawarra and remain great value for money.

BRANDS LAIRA

Address: Riddoch Highway, Coonawarra SA 5263
Phone: (08) 8736 3260
Fax: (08) 8736 3208
Established: 1965
Winemakers: Jim Brand and Bruce Gregory
Principal varieties grown: Chardonnay, Merlot, Cabernet Sauvignon, Shiraz, Pinot Noir, Cabernet Franc, Malbec, Riesling
Ha under vine: 180
Average annual crush: 500-999 tonnes

Principal wines & brands	Cellar Potential
Brand's Laira	
Cabernet Merlot	0-4 years
Cabernet Sauvignon	7-8 years
Shiraz	5+ years
Chardonnay	2-4 years

Hours open to public: 9am-4.30pm, weekdays; 10am-4pm, weekends and public holidays
Retail distribution: Cellar Door and Mail Order Sales. McWilliam's Wines Pty Ltd. Export to NZ, UK

Chardonnay Lodge

Set among the vines, bordering the main road in the heart of Coonawarra, is the impressive Chardonnay Lodge. It was built in 1984 by the Yates, Coop and Giles families.

Approaching the main arched doorway, visitors are impressed by the magnificent leadlight glass panelled entrance produced by Barry Mulligan of the districtís St. Mary's Vineyard.

The classic Victorian Australian inspired complex spreads out comfortably, surrounded by the poplar trees traditionally used in Coonawarra as wind breaks. The rooms are spacious with high timber ceilings; a family can happily spread out here.

Partners, James and Anne Yates have managed the establishment for more than ten years and managed it most efficiently.

The food in the restaurant is creative and uses many local ingredients and the seminar and function facilities are large and beautifully appointed. Chardonnay Lodge was a pioneer in terms of offering the wine traveller a truly wine integrated experience.

The addition of more suites and expanded function and seminar facilities is currently underway and is a welcome development for the region. Open every day of the year, Chardonnay Lodge provides an ideal stopover for visitors to Coonawarra.

Highbank Vineyards

Right in the heart of Coonawarra is the pretty two storey house of Highbank, whose gardens and glowing ambience drags one from the long straight road like a magnet.

Highbank is the creation of the most charming, warm and enthusiastic couple, Dennis and Bonnie Vice. Denis is a tall American hailing form San Diego, Bonnie hails from Hawaii.

Dennis' work brought him often to Australia and he and Bonnie saw it as a great place to settle down and raise their family. Denis grows great grapes and wanted them to be made into the best possible wine. Many times each vintage he makes the three hour drive to Trevor Mast's winery at Langi Ghiran near Ararat in Victoria. Trevor is a true master winemaker and the Highbank cabernet sauvignon and chardonnay rank in the top flight of Australian wine.

Beside the winery, under an enormous red gum, is the Highbank Honeysuckle Rise Cottage, a stunning country stone building with a high vaulted ceiling and open plan living, one of the nicest vineyard bed and breakfasts you could find, with an open log fire to keep you cosy in winter. Above the winery, with the same romantic decor of old colonial times, is the 'Room with a view' with its expansive views over the vineyards. In both venues the fridge is stocked with goodies, from bacon and eggs to foie gras - most on the free list.

You can call the free number to book and find out more details on 1800 653 311. Highbank Honeysuckle Rise hospitality is second to none.

HIGHBANK VINEYARDS	
Address: Riddoch Highway, Warners Corner SA	**Principal wines & brands Cellar Potential**
Phone: (08) 8736 3311	Highbank Coonawarra
Fax: (08) 8736 3122	Cabernet Sauvignon 10 years
Email: vice@dove.com.au	Highbank Chardonnay 2-5 years
Established: 1986	**Public & trade tours:** By appointment only
Winemakers: Dennis Vice, Trevor Mast	**Hours open to public:** 10am-5pm, holiday weekends or by appointment
Principal varieties grown: Cabernet Sauvignon, Merlot, Cabernet Franc, Chardonnay	**Points of interest:** Organically grown grapes. Guest Accomodation, Honeysuckle Rise, Room with a View
Ha under vine: 4	**Retail distribution:** Select Vineyards, Melbourne; John Tolley, SA; Karen Hunter, NSW; Australian Premium Wine Collection, USA
Average annual crush: 25 tonnes	
Average no. cases produced: 700	

Punters Corner

The newest addition to this great wine region is Punters Corner. Located on the corner of V & A Lane and the main Coonawarra road. There is a little conjecture as to how the name arrived but V & A Lane leads to the local race track. Timbercorp Securities from Melbourne purchased the 43 hectare vineyard which has cabernet sauvignon, merlot, shiraz, chardonnay planted. The best of each variety is used in the classy contract made Punters Corner range and the remainder of the grapes are sold to leading wineries of the region.

The cellar door is cute and extremely well managed by Sue Hood. The 1996 Chardonnay has already won several awards and is an excellent aperitif style with melon and grapefruit flavours with some subtle oak in the background. The 1994 Shiraz impressed me greatly with lots of wild berry and peppery characters coming through. The 1994 Cabernet is a big complex wine in the gold medal league, deep mauve in colour with lovely licorice and truffle like overtones behind the masses of fruit. The 1995 Cabernet just released is equally as good but a little lighter due to vintage conditions.

It is certain that you will be taking a good punt to pop into Punters Corner, the wines are great.

PUNTERS CORNER

Address: PO Box 28, Coonawarra SA 5263
Phone: (08) 8737 2007
Fax: (08) 8737 2007
Owner: Timbercorp Securities Pty Ltd
Winemaker: Contract
Principal varieties grown: Cabernet Sauvignon, Merlot, Shiraz, Chardonnay
Ha under vine: 28
Average annual crush: 200 tonnes, 60 tonnes used by Punters Corner
Average no. cases produced: 4,000

Principal wines & brands	Cellar Potential
Punters Corner	
Coonawarra Cabernet Sauvignon	5-8 years
Coonawarra Shiraz	3-5 years
Coonawarra Cabernet Sauvignon	2-3 years
Coonawarra Chardonnay	2-3 years

Public & trade tours: Yes
Hours open to public: 10am-5pm, daily except Christmas Day and Good Friday
Retail distribution: Small amounts are available in selected retail outlets in SA, VIC, NSW, QLD and WA

Leconfield

The Leconfield vineyard was planted in 1974 and the winery built in 1974 by Sydney Hamilton at the age of 76. Syd was a fourth generation descendant of Richard Hamilton, South Australia's first vigneron ca. 1837.

After retiring from Hamilton Ewell in the mid 50's, Syd searched the Australian continent for the site to make the classic Australian Red table wine. He decided on Coonawarra to achieve this ambition.

In 1974 planted his vineyard of 12 hectares mainly to cabernet sauvignon and the following year used his engineering skills to build the Leconfield winery. Syd created a legend with his early vintages, the 1978 and 1980 Leconfield Cabernets.

In 1981 Leconfield was purchased by Syd's nephew, Dr Richard Hamilton, a plastic surgeon. Dr Hamilton also has a winery and vineyards at McLaren Vale established in 1972. The Leconfield Cabernets have all been superb wines. The inclusion of merlot and petit verdot into the cabernet blend by respected winemaker, Ralph Fowler, has made Leconfield Cabernet one of Australia's great red wines. Leconfield, an imposing Romanesque style building, constructed of limestone, is situated right on the main road. It strikes me, as some other Coonawarra wineries do, with its similarity to a Bordeaux chateau. Certainly its cabernets are in the mould of the best Bordeaux.

LECONFIELD

Address: Penola - Naracoorte Road, Coonawarra SA 5263
Direction: 3km north of Penola township
Phone: (08) 8737 2326
Fax: (08) 8737 2285
Established: 1974
Owner: Dr Richard Hamilton
Winemaker: Ralph Fowler
Principal varieties grown: Cabernet Sauvignon, Shiraz, Merlot, Cabernet Franc, Petit Verdot, Chardonnay, Riesling
Average no. cases produced: 15,000

Principal wines & brands	Cellar Potential
Riesling	5-8 years
Chardonnay	5-8 years
Botrytis Riesling	5-10 years
Merlot	8-10 years
Shiraz	8-10 years
Cabernets	10-15 years

Public & trade tours: Yes
Hours open to public: 10am-5pm, weekdays; 10am-4pm, weekends and public holidays
Points of interest: Established by industry pioneer Sydney Hamilton. Only lyre trellis system in Coonawarra
Retail distribution: All discerning stockists of Fine Wines and Leading Restaurants

Hollick Wines

Ian and Wendy Hollick purchased 40 acres of land at the southern end of Coonawarra in 1974. At the time, Ian was employed by one of the larger Coonawarra wine companies, and in their spare time the couple began developing a vineyard.

Cabernet sauvignon, riesling, merlot, chardonnay and pinot noir were planted during the following six years, until in 1983 the decision was made to build a winery. The winning of the Jimmy Watson Trophy in 1985, with only their third vintage, gave the Hollick's further incentive to expand and in 1987 they purchased the nearby 'Wilgha' vineyard, which is connected to their original property by Ravenswood Lane, a name used for their super premium cabernet sauvignon.

The Hollick's have a most beautiful home and tasting area for their wines, right in front of the winery in the form of a cottage that was the home of the poet, John Shaw Nielson. The cottage has been lovingly restored and the Hollicks take delight in dispensing their warm hospitality along with their wines. A recent edition to their fine stable of reds is 'Terra', a great Coonawarra blend at a real value price, its name alluding to the rich terra rossa soils that nurtured it.

HOLLICK WINES
Address: Racecourse Road, Coonawarra SA 5263
Phone: (08) 8737 2318
Fax: (08) 8737 2952
Email: hollick@dove.net.au
Established: 1983
Winemakers: Ian Hollick and Matt Pellew
Principal varieties grown: Cabernet Sauvignon, Cabernet Franc, Merlot, Shiraz, Pinot Noir, Petit Verdot, Chardonnay, Sauvignon Blanc, Riesling, Semillon
Ha under vine: 50
Average annual crush: 400 tonnes

Principal wines & brands	Cellar Potential
Ravenswood Cabernet Sauvignon	12+ years
Cabernet Sauvignon Merlot Blend	8+ years
Shiraz Cabernet Sauvignon Blend	3-5 years
Pinot Noir	3-5 years
Reserve Chardonnay	3-8 years
Wilgha Vineyard Unoaked Chardonnay	1-3 years
Sauvignon Blanc Semillon	2-3 years
Sparkling Merlot	2-7 years
Botrytis Riesling	10+ years

Public & trade tours: By appointment
Hours open to public: 9am-5pm, daily
Points of interest: Historic cottage, birth place of John Shaw Neilson (Lyric Poet) has been restored for cellar sales area

---

Rosemount Coonawarra

In line with the Oatley family philosophy of growing their own grapes in each region, Rosemount established their Kirri Billi vineyard at Coonawarra in 1980. Rosemount specialise in what they believe Coonawarra does best - cabernet sauvignon. After crushing, the wine is made at the main winery in the Upper Hunter Valley.

Hand pruning and hand picking of Rosemount's premium fruit, a rarity in Coonawarra, shows Rosemount's determination to make a no expense spared classic Coonawarra Cabernet.

The concern that the Oatley family takes in the selection, planting and management of this vineyard is at the heart of this remarkable company's rapid success.

Rosemount, have for their size been the most successful exporter and ambassador for Australian wines overseas, particularly in North America. With Coonawarra's growing reputation far from our shores, Rosemount have put their Coonawarra Show Reserve Cabernet Sauvignon, well and truly on the world wine map.

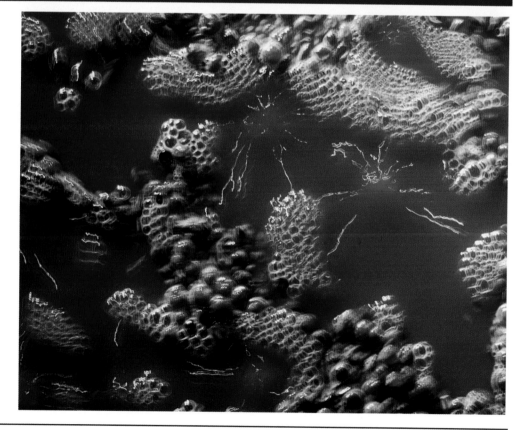

Katnook Estate

atnook is a winery with a history that goes back to the early settlement of Coonawarra. John Riddoch was lured to Australia in the early 1850's by the prospect of gold He did make his fortune, but as a trader, finally arriving in the Coonawarra in 1861. He named his first Coonawarra property 'Yallum Park', Yallum being derived from an aboriginal word meaning grassy.

Riddoch began by constructing a magnificent sandstone mansion surrounded by splendid gardens and a deer park. He was elected to the South Australian Parliament in 1865 and his land holdings quickly grew to 250 square kilometres. Riddoch became known as the 'Squire of Penola' and his restored home, 'Yallum Park' can be visited when you are in Coonawarra.

Riddoch's first enterprises in Coonawarra were grazing and wool, to this end, he built a woolshed calling it 'Katnook'. Today, it is an historic monument and the winery for Katnook wines.

In 1890 Riddoch decided Katnook could support closer settlement and horticulture, and he formed the Coonawarra Fruit Colony at Katnook and from the office set up there, sold off 10 acre blocks at 10 pounds per acre, a considerable sum in those days.

Twenty six colonists began planting fruit and vines on their blocks. The second vintage in 1896 was made at Katnook in the woolshed. During the 1960's, Melbourne businessman, Peter Yunghaans purchased the property, replanting vines and building a high-tech state of the art winery, within the historic old woolshed. The first Katnook wines, made with the help of oenology's dynamic duo Brian Croser and Dr. Tony Jordan, were sensational and the reds particularly, gained instant acceptance in the premium wine market. Katnook today is vastly expanded and a further 250 acres of wines have been planted in 1995 and 1996.

Wayne Stebbens is the capable, affable winemaker, and his lovely wife Michelle, looks after promotion and the cellar door sales. Katnook also produce Riddoch label; these wines are great examples of the best Coonawarra can produce. Katnook produces Coonawarra's best sauvignon blanc, which has won many gold medals and trophies. John Riddoch would indeed be proud to see the way his old woolshed winery has been restored and the great wines it is producing.

KATNOOK ESTATE AND RIDDOCH

Address: Riddoch Highway, Coonawarra SA 5263
Phone: (08) 8737 2394
Fax: (08) 8737 2397
Email: katnook@seol.net.au
Established: 1978
Owner: Wingara Wine Group
Winemaker: Wayne Stehbens
Principal varieties grown:
Cabernet Sauvignon, Shiraz, Merlot, Chardonnay, Sauvignon Blanc, Riesling
Ha under vine: 160
Average annual crush: 850
Average no. cases produced: 35,000

Principal wines & brands	Cellar Potential
Katnook Estate 'Odyssey' Cabernet Sauvignon	10-20 years
Katnook Estate Sauvignon Blanc	8-15 years
Katnook Estate Cabernet Sauvignon	10-18 years
Katnook Estate Merlot	8-15 years
Katnook Estate Chardonnay	10-18 years
Katnook Estate Chardonnay Brut	8-12 years
Katnook Estate Riesling	10-18 years
Katnook Estate Botrytis Riesling (375ml)	8-15 years
Riddoch Sauvignon Blanc	3-8 years
Riddoch Chardonnay	5-10 years
Riddoch Shiraz	8-15 years
Riddoch Cabernet Shiraz	8-15 years

Public & trade tours: No
Hours open to public:
9am-4.30pm, daily; 10am-4.30pm, Saturday; Noon-4.30pm, Sunday
Points of interest:
Historic woolshed built by John Riddoch in 1862. Historic Coonawarra Headquarters - Established in 1890
Retail distribution:
National distribution by Tucker Seabrook Pty Ltd

Mildara – Jamieson's Run Winery

Jamieson's Run has taken the wine world by storm. Mildara launched the name along with an exciting new red wine, back in 1987. The wine, a 1985 vintage, was a blend of cabernet sauvignon, shiraz, merlot and cabernet franc and in some years a little malbec is added for balance. The aim with Jamieson's Run is to produce a rich, smooth style that is consistent and recognisable year after year.

The choice of the name Jamieson's Run is particularly apt as it was the name of the property at Mildura where the Chaffey Brothers built their original winery, 'Chateau Mildura', back in 1888. This became the forerunner of Mildara Wines. The connection is even more appropriate because of Mildara's investment in the early 1950's through long time technical and managing director, Ron Haselgrove who, along with David Wynn, rediscovered Coonawarra and really put it on the wine map.

a dynamic character who was vineyard manager for Wynns Coonawarra for many years. Jamieson's Run chardonnay is no slouch either, a very drinkable wine showing good barrel fermented complexity. In fact, any wine bearing the Mildara Coonawarra label is a guarantee of real enjoyment; long-time winemaker Gavin Hogg has got it right.

The proof of the pudding came in 1989 when the 1988 Jamieson's won the golden urn in the form of the Jimmy Watson Memorial Trophy, the grand prix of Australian wines. After this victory, Jamieson's Run became a truly recognised Australian wine.

They are extremely well served in the viticultural area by the experienced Vic Patrick,

---

MILDARA JAMIESONS RUN
Address: Main Road, Coonawarra SA 5263
Phone: (08) 8736 3380
Fax: (08) 8736 3307
Established: 1995
Owner: Mildara Blass Limited
Winemaker: Gavin Hogg
Principal varieties grown: Cabernet Sauvignon, Shiraz, Merlot
Average no. cases produced: 200,000

Principal wines & brands	Cellar Potential
Jamiesons Run Chardonnay	2-4 years
Jamiesons Run Sauvignon Blanc	2-4 years
Jamiesons Run Pinot Noir	2-5 years
Jamiesons Run Coonawarra Dry Red	2-5 years
Robertson's Well Chardonnay	3-5 years
Robertson's Well Cabernet Sauvignon	3-5 years
Mildara Coonawarra Cabernet Sauvignon	5-10 years
Mildara Alexanders	5-10 years
Black Rock Coonawarra Red	8-10 years

Public & trade tours:
Trade tours by appointment only
Hours open to public:
9am-5pm, weekdays; 10am-4pm weekends and public holidays
Points of interest: Coonawarra's world renowned Terra Rossa soil

---

Petaluma – Coonawarra

Some years ago when Brian Croser was designing the elite Petaluma range and thinking of red he could not go past "Coonawarra". So that is exactly what he did, he called it just that "Petaluma Coonawarra", securing a cabernet sauvignon vineyard on the main road naming it "The Evans Vineyard" after a director of the company at the time, Wine Legend Len Evans. The "Petaluma Coonawarra" is undoubtedly amongst the top dozen Australian red wines, always a fully weighted style, it carries the pedigree of its maker Brian Croser who always strives for balance, interest and complexity in his wines through his winemaking innovations and clever use of top quality French oak. Do not be fooled by the silky texture and approachable style of this wine it will age also gracefully for many years. An exquisite merlot is also released once a year on a futures basis and is snapped up overnight. Well done once again Brian and your team at Petaluma.

S. Kidman Wines

Sid and Susan Kidman have one of the most charming cellar doors in Coonawarra, on the northern fringes of the region. It is in former stables on their property, built in the 1860's.
Their lovely sprawling old colonial Australian home behind the winery dates back even further, to the 1840's. The 'paradise lost' garden behind the homestead would do 'Home and Garden' proud and is lovingly tended by Susie.
The Kidman's have been landowners and farmers in the region since pioneering days. Even during his school years, Sid used to love jumping on the tractor to do some work on the property and, in fact, he still occasionally drives the old 1960 tractor he learnt on. Sid helped his father establish a large vineyard across the road from 'The Ridge' in partnership with Melbourne wine merchant, Dan Murphy, in the 1970's. In 1984 Susie and Sid went their own way, changing their vineyard from grape production to wine production.
The Ridge rieslings are excellent, often showing fruit flavours in the mandarin fruit spectrum and quite full-bodied. Sid has planted more shiraz and has been very successful with the variety, with complex and characterful wines that live on for many years. Why not drop into S. Kidman Wines and share the history and warm hospitality of the Kidman's.

S. KIDMAN
Address: Riddoch Highway, Coonawarra SA 5263
Phone: (08) 8736 5071
Fax: (08) 8736 5070
Established: 1984
Owners: Suzie and Sid Kidman
Winemaker: Sid Kidman
Principal varieties grown: Cabernet Sauvignon, Shiraz, Sauvignon Blanc, Riesling
Ha under vine: 17
Average annual crush: 139 tonnes
Average no. cases produced: 8,000

Principal wines & brands	Cellar Potential
S. Kidman Cabernet Sauvignon	15 years
S. Kidman Shiraz	10 years
S. Kidman Riesling	6 years
S. Kidman Sauvignon Blanc	6 years

Public & trade tours: Trade tours by appointment only
Hours open to public: 9am-5pm, daily
Retail distribution: David Turner Agencies, 20 Hannaford Road, Blackwood SA 5051, (08) 8278 3899. Flinders Wholesale, 3 Wandarri Court, Cheltenham VIC 3192, (03) 9584 5233

Majella

Brian and Anthony Lynn began planting vines back in 1969 when modern day Coonawarra was in its infancy. The two brothers are third generation farmers whose main specialisation was wool; their father named the property Majella after Saint Gerard Majella, a Spanish saint and the patron saint of motherhood. All the produce of the large property goes out under the brand of Majella.
Up until 1991 all the crop from their 85 acres of vines was sold to winemakers in the region. In 1991, they decided to produce a Majella red wine at Brand's Wines by Bruce Gregory. The vineyard has been expanded to around 100 acres, all red grape varieties, about one half cabernet sauvignon and one half shiraz.
The Lynn's are a gregarious family and you can now share their hospitality at their new cellar door in the state of the art winery finished for the 1997 vintage. If you cannot get to Coonawarra go out and get yourself a succulent steak and wash it down with a Majella red with its striking label and great flavour.

MAJELLA WINES
Address: Lynn Road, Coonawarra SA 5263
Phone: (08) 8736 3055
Fax: (08) 8736 3057
Email: prof@a012.aone.net.au
Established: 1967
Owner: The Lynn Family
Winemaker: Bruce Gregory
Principal varieties grown: Shiraz, Cabernet Sauvignon, Merlot
Ha under vine: 42
Average no. cases produced: 4,000

Principal wines & brands	Cellar Potential
Shiraz	7-10 years
Cabernet	10-15 years
Sparkling Shiraz	10-12 years

Public & trade tours: Public tours
Hours open to public: 10am-4.30pm, daily except Christmas Day and Good Friday
Points of interest: Situated on the eastern edge of the famous Coonawarra "red strip", Majella specialises in Classic Coonawarra wines, especially Shiraz and Cabernet Sauvignon
Retail distribution: Selected Bottle shops

Redman Winery

Fourteen year old Bill Redman arrived in Coonawarra in 1901 and began working for Riddoch's winery, thus beginning a long and distinguished career in the wine industry. In 1908, having gained experience in winemaking and cellar management, Bill gained his independence by forming a partnership with his family in the acquisition of established vineyards, later known as Rouge Homme. After 1910, when winemaking all but ceased in Coonawarra, he remained the area's only producing winemaker for many decades.

During the 1940's, Bill was joined in the business by his son Owen, and this alliance lasted until the sale of Rouge Homme to Lindemans in 1965. Owen then decided to establish his own winery. He purchased a vineyard as well as extra land where he mainly grew shiraz vines; until his own winery was built in 1969. Owen's first wines were made at Brand's Laira Winery. Today, Redman's winery is very well set up with the tasting area having picturesque views of the vineyard and the winery.

Bill Redman died in 1979 at 92 years of age, having presided over 65 vintages. His contribution to the wine industry was enormous and he can be truly called one of the fathers of Coonawarra. His grandsons Bruce and Malcolm Redman are continuing this heritage, having not only taken over the management of their father's winery, but also expanding its size and reputation.

Redman's wines had traditionally produced only two wines, a shiraz and a cabernet sauvignon (they're real red men); recently they have introduced a third wine, a cabernet merlot. I tried several vintages at the cellar door and it is a lovely wine, showing some lifted floral characters and soft plummy flavours; a certain percentage of the wine is barrel fermented.

For many years, Bruce and Malcolm persisted in the lighter claret style their father made famous, but in recent years, they have beefed up the colour and body in their wines and used more small oak. The Redman's vineyards, some of which date back to before the turn of the century, produce superb fruit. The wines I have seen in recent years are certainly doing these fine vineyards justice.

REDMAN WINES

Address: Riddoch Highway, Coonawarra SA 5263
Phone: (08) 8736 3331
Fax: (08) 8736 3013
Established: 1966
Winemakers: Bruce and Malcolm Redman
Principal varieties grown: Merlot, Cabernet Sauvignon, Shiraz
Ha under vine: 35
Average annual crush: 250-300 tonnes

Principal wines & brands   Cellar Potential
Redman Shiraz   5-7 years
Redman Cabernet Sauvignon   7-10 years
Redman Cabernet Merlot 6-8 years

Hours open to public:
9am-5pm, weekdays; 10am-4pm, weekends
Retail distribution:
BRL Hardy Limited

Wynns Coonawarra Estate

Late last century, orchardists in the far south east of South Australia noticed the particular fertility of the soil around Penola. The Wynns Coonawarra Estate story began in 1890 when John Riddoch, who had vast landholdings in the area, developed the Coonawarra Fruit Colony, selling off 10 acre blocks of this land to hopeful farmers.

Riddoch himself planted vines and built a large stone winery, which was completed in 1895. It is the facade of this building that has adorned Wynns Coonawarra Estate Estate wine labels since the 1950's.

Riddoch's venture failed to prosper and Coonawarra languished for the first half of the 1900's. Were it not for David Wynn, who purchased the estate in 1951, the winery would almost certainly have become a woolshed and the vineyards a sheep run.

One of the two flagship reds of today's

Wynns Coonawarra Estate is John Riddoch Cabernet Sauvignon, a majestic wine that wins trophies and gold medals in Australian and International Wine shows with monotonous regularity.

The first John Riddoch was the 1982, a wine of such incredible richness, mouthfeel and velvet-like texture that it almost defied description.

I first encountered it in a lineup of the celebrated 1982 Bordeaux first and second growth wines. All were masked and to my mind it was at the top of the class. If anything, the John Riddochs of the 1990's are even better.

If John Riddoch Cabernet commemorates the founder of Coonawarra, the second Wynns Coonawarra Estate flagship red links us with the family that re-established Coonawarra in our own time.

Michael Hermitage, a best-of-vintage Shiraz,

takes its name from the legendary wine of 1955, created by David Wynn as a memorial to his young son who had died suddenly the previous year.

This wine was introduced – or reintroduced – with the 1990 vintage and has quickly become one of Australia's most talked-about wines. Wynns most widely-available reds are the black label Coonawarra Estate Cabernet Sauvignon, the white label Coonawarra Estate Shiraz and the Coonawarra Estate Cabernet-Shiraz-Merlot blend with its black and single red-striped label.

All are fine-textured, full-flavoured wines of the region. Often displaying a minty, herbaceous character over the fruit flavours, they have great appeal to the wine lover and have grown in stature both domestically and internationally through the 1980's and 90's.

They are, as a group, widely regarded as pre-eminent among Coonawarra reds.

The estate also produces whites of great quality.

Wynns Coonawarra Estate Riesling is exceptional value and always exhibits very good floral and fruity aromas and flavours.

In recent years the Wynns Coonawarra Estate Chardonnay has also consolidated its following. This buff-labelled wine shows excellent peach/apricot flavours, beautifully integrated with subtle oak. It explodes in the mouth and is ideal with poultry and other white meats.

The 1990's perspective makes it difficult to imagine that the name Coonawarra was virtually unknown when David Wynn set himself the task of rebuilding the estate. From their beginnings as Melbourne wine merchants, the Wynn's had gained much experience in wine marketing. Their advertising campaigns stressed the Coonawarra origins of the wines and one of David

Wynn's first steps was to commission a new label. Simple and striking, it soon became the best-known in Australia.

During the 1960's the popularity of red wine and the establishment of the label's image was consolidated, with the result that Wynns Coonawarra Estate and 'claret' became synonymous.

Some of the top names in Australian wine helped raised Coonawarra's stocks.

Ian Hickinbotham was the first winemaker to work under Wynns' management and his early efforts to improve facilities laid a firm foundation for success. Another who contributed to the credibility of the estate was John Wade. Winemaker from 1978 to 1985, he introduced new techniques and created that first John Riddoch Cabernet. The winemaker since 1985 has been Peter Douglas, under whose leadership the estate's reputation has continued to grow. Each year

on a Wednesday a special tasting release if held at the winery with top wine, food, personalities and beamed by satellite to functions in major cities where tastings and dinners are held. Wynnsday is a world famous wine event and Peter Douglas's performances each year are legendary.

Both the underground cellars at Wynns, and the newer, air-conditioned, ground-level facilities, are brimming with great wines in a forest of the world's finest oak; it's one of the great liquid assets of Australia.

John Riddoch's vision has finally been fulfilled, a century after its beginnings, but sadly, David Wynn, who masterminded this red wine revolution in Australia, died early in 1995.

If they could, I am sure both would happily raise a glass of John Riddoch, or Michael, to toast Wynns Coonawarra Estate's hard-won success.

Rouge Homme

Right in the heart of Coonawarra are the Rouge Homme vineyards. Their history dates back to 1908 when the Redman family purchased part of John Riddoch's Penola Fruit Colony. For half a century, Rouge Homme supplied wine to other companies and merchants which brought great fame to Coonawarra. But it was not until the release of the 1954 Cabernet Sauvignon, wearing the first Rouge Homme label, that the brand itself began to attract some of that fame.

The translation of the name 'Rouge Homme' – French for 'red man' – signified the similarity of the wines to the red wines of Bordeaux. The 'Richardson's' label was introduced with the 1992 vintage and named in honour of henry Richardson – one of Coonawarra's pioneer settlers. In 1892 Richardson purchased land offered for sale by Riddoch's Coonawarra Fruit Colony and established a vineyard and winery on the property.

In 1965 the Redman family sold the vineyards and winery which, with the original Richardson property, became Rouge Homme as it is today. Occupying about 60 hectares, the vineyards are planted to classic varieties including shiraz, cabernet sauvignon, cabernet franc, merlot and pinot noir, with a small amount of chardonnay. The Rouge Homme winery is now of the most modern and sophisticated in Coonawarra. A climate of cold, wet winters and mild to warm, dry summers, allows slow ripening of the grapes, with excellent development of sugar levels and flavour, and the retention of good acidity. Because of the cold winters and springs, the vines at rouge Homme are trained over especially high trellises, with overhead mist sprinklers to protect them from frosts during spring. Five Rouge Homme wines are produced today in contemporary labels reflecting the earthy colours of the Coonawarra.

The original claret which forged Rouge Homme's early reputation is still made but is today varietally labelled as a shiraz cabernet. This was followed by the straight cabernet sauvignon, a wine of power and presence. Later, Rouge Homme began to produce a pinot noir which consistently exhibits good colour and varietal character. 'Richardsons Red Block' is a blend of the classic Bordeaux varieties of cabernet sauvignon, malbec, merlot and cabernet franc. The chardonnay also shines in the white arena.

Winemaker, Paul Gordon, has been with rouge Homme since 1989. As custodian of the winery's great Coonawarra tradition he continues to produce a range of distinctive, approachable wines which have the potential to develop great complexity with bottle ageing over many years.

With a considerable reputation as classic Coonawarras, Rouge Homme wines are frequent gold medal winners – particularly the reds. In 1994, Rouge Homme received what is regarded by many to be the wine industry's greatest accolade – the Jimmy Watson Memorial Trophy.

Robertson's Well

Mildara were keen to expand their vineyard holdings in the general south eastern South Australian wine regions, which led them to purchase land some 15 kms north of the tiny township of Coonawarra. They have planted a large vineyard here mainly to cabernet sauvignon. The property borders the main road from Penola to Naracoorte, a couple of kilometres north of the impressive old Victorian inspired homestead 'Struan'.

Now converted into a centre for the Department of Agriculture, 'Struan' was built for the Robertson family, wealthy Scottish immigrants, who arrived in the region via Portland in Victoria. Robertson purchased a huge tract of land north of Coonawarra, becoming the neighbour of John Riddoch, the only other large landholder in the region.

Mildara chose the site because its terra rossa soil and the north-westerly aspect of the long ridge supporting the vineyard is ideal in its soil structure aspect and drainage to grow absolutely first class cabernet.

Mildara released a cabernet sauvignon featuring the old windmill and tank from the vineyard on the label. The wine is entirely made from fruit grown in the best vineyards of the Coonawarra region and is the premier cabernet sauvignon to be produced each year by Mildara. Their aim is to make a cabernet sauvignon so chock-full of fruit, rich cassis flavours, with the mintiness and herbaceous characters to typical of Coonawarra, that even a martian landing on earth could pick up a glass and recognise it.

I am no Martian, but I love a good cabernet and Robertson's Well has got the depth.

Sharefarmers Vineyard

In his search of the general Coonawarra region for further good terra rossa soils and an ideal location for further vineyards, Brian Croser found just what he was looking for to provide great grapes for a label "Sharefarmers" which draws its name from the vineyard investment scheme which assisted in this project.

The Sharefarmers plantings were begun on the site in 1983. The site is some 11 kms north of the main Coonawarra plantings. Development to the extent of 3 million dollars has turned it into a showplace of bordeaux varieties.

The elegance of the merlot and cabernet franc components of the sharefarmers blend balance out the concentration and power of the cabernet sauvignon and malbec. The manicured vineyard with its sheltering wind breaks and rigorous canopy management gives evenly ripened fruit with traditional soft coonawarra tannins and a silky, fruit sweet textures and flavour.

The wines are made at Petaluma's Piccadilly winery and aged in top class french oak barriques .

The wines coming from Sharefarmers are of exciting quality and do the general region proud with all the hallmarks of a great vineyard and the consummate winemaking skills of Brian Croser and his team.

An introduction to Padthaway

When land in Coonawarra became increasingly scarce and expensive, many of Australia's major wine companies were forced to search for an alternative area to develop for the production of premium wine.

The Padthaway region, 80 kilometres north of Coonawarra, proved to be the most suitable. Made up of a similar terra rossa soil over limestone, the strip of rich, red soil is 16 kms long and 1 to 1.5 kms wide. The area has a slightly warmer climate, providing a stability that produces less variation in vintages.

Rainfall is lower, but like Coonawarra, there is a good supply of underground water, and, once established, the vines grow very well. Before Seppelts established the vines in 1963, the region was divided into seven large grazing-oriented properties, the most famous being Padthaway House, home of the Lawson family, descendants of Henry Lawson.

Padthaway House was refurbished in the late 1920's; it is one of the most beautiful old colonial homes where you can stay in Australia.

Padthaway has been developed largely by the bigger companies namely Seppelts, Hardy's, Lindemans, Wynns and Orlando, but with others such as the Brown family, who opened a winery in 1994, after many years as a major grape grower in the region. Andrew Garrett and Tolleys moving in in more recent years, along with the Padthaway Estate vineyards and winery.

Although originally envisaged as a red wine area, this region has proved to be extremely versatile, producing white wines of many styles. Rhine riesling, chardonnay and sauvignon blanc along with pinot noir have been successful grape varieties, producing excellent results. Padthaway now has a comparable area under vine to Coonawarra. The intense varietal character found in the high grade fruit of the area, will certainly see Padthaway become of increasing importance to the industry. New areas further south and east of Naracoorte in the hundreds (an old land measure - 10 miles x 10 miles) of Joanna and Jessie are being planted at present, mainly by the large companies. Along with the existing Koppamurra Vineyard, this will provide a huge resource of top quality grapes for the future of wine in Australia, particularly for export.

PADTHAWAY ESTATE

Address: Riddoch Highway, Padthaway SA 5263
Direction: Naracoorte to Keith Road, 90km north of Coonawarra
Phone: (03) 9205 9467
Fax: (03) 9205 9410
Established: 1980 (1847 founded by Robert Lawson)
Owners: Dale Baker and Ian Gray
Winemaker: Nigel Catt
Principal varieties grown: Pinot Noir, Chardonnay, Cabernet Sauvignon, Pinot Meunier
Ha under vine: 41
Average annual crush: 175 tonnes
Average no. cases produced: 7,000 cases

Principal wines & brands	Cellar Potential
Pinot Noir/Chardonnay Cuvee	2-3 years
Unwooded Chardonnay	1-2 years
Sauvignon Blanc/Semillon	1-2 years
Chardonnay	5 years
Cabernet Sauvignon	5 years

Public & trade tours: Yes
Hours open to public: 10am-5pm, daily except Christmas Day and Good Friday
Points of interest: Historic 1880 Homestead converted B&B with silver service dining room. Only operational French Champagne press in Australia. Site of original settlement of Padthaway region
Retail distribution: VIC - Philip Murphy, Bedelis Liquor, King and Godfrey. NSW - Balmain Village Cellars, Toohey Brothers, Newport Bottler. SA - Baily and Baily, Walkerville Cellars, Edinburgh Cellars

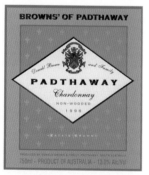

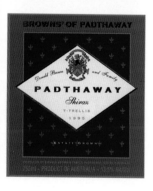

Keppoch/Padthaway - Map Index
1   Browns Padthaway Glendon Park
2   Lindemans Padthaway
3   Padthaway Estate & Homestead
4   Seppelts
5   Thomas Hardy & Sons LTD

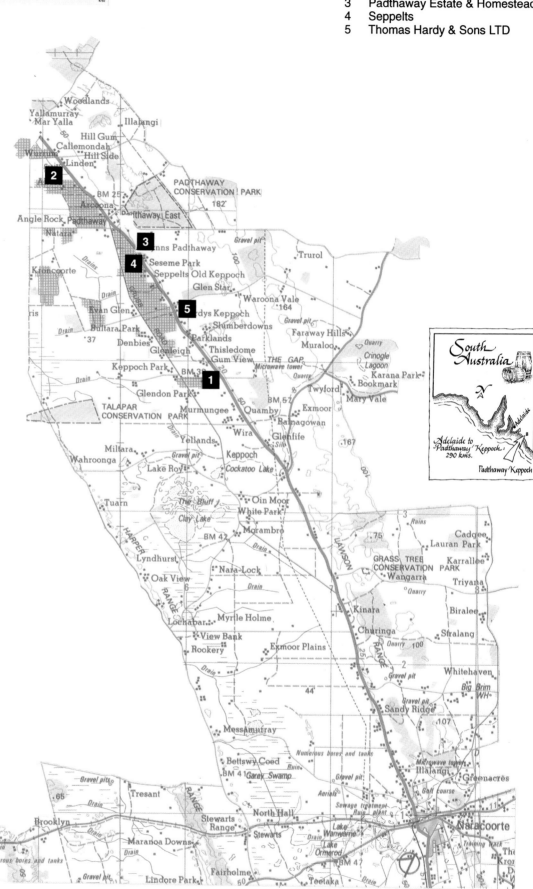

Brown's of Padthaway

In 1959, fourth generation Yorke Peninsula farmer, Don Brown purchased a 290 hectare property at Padthaway. Yorke Peninsula is very dry and famous for its barley, much of it ending up in beer and in some instances, Scotch whisky. The Browns' were looking for land which could be irrigated for their Border Leicester and Southdown stud sheep. Padthaway is actually derived from an Aboriginal word for 'Good Water'. Don and his wife Glenda named the property 'Glendon Park' and gradually they have expanded it to more than 2,500 hectares. The original 4 hectares of irrigation has been expanded drastically. During the 1960's Don developed his 'small seed production' business before planting vines in 1970. Today the vineyard has expanded to 150 hectares. Don also began a contracting company specialising in grape harvesting and transportation.

For many years his eagerly sought after grapes were purchased by large companies such as Orlando, then in 1993, the Browns' launched their own label beginning with a riesling and a unwooded chardonnay.

They have more than enough vines to supply their needs.

Their three children all live and work on the property. Andrew and David both have degrees in farm management from Roseworthy, whilst daughter Sue has the Roseworthy wine marketing diploma. Daughter-in-law Lisa, has a business degree and son-in-law Michael, an agricultural degree. All in all it's a pretty formidable team at Browns' and the wines so far have reflected this. Expect great things from Browns' of Padthaway, I'm sure they won't let you down.

BROWNS' OF PADTHAWAY

Address:
PMB 196, Naracoorte SA 5271
Direction:
15 km South of Padthaway
Phone:
(08) 8765 6063
Fax:
(08) 8765 6083
Established:
1970
Principal varieties grown:
Chardonnay, Riesling, Shiraz, Malbec, Cabernet Sauvignon, Sauvignon Blanc, Verdelho
Ha under vine:
150
Average annual crush:
400 tonnes
Average no. cases produced:
30,000

Principal wines & brands	Cellar Potential
Browns' of Padthaway	
"Myra" Family Reserve Cabernet Sauvignon	5+ years
"T-trellis" Shiraz	3+ years
"Redwood" Shiraz/Malbec	2+ years
Non-wooded Chardonnay	Drink now
"Redwood" Verdelho Sauvignon Blanc Riesling	Drink now
Sparkling Shiraz	2+ years
Sauvignon Blanc	1+ years
Verdelho	1+ years

Public & trade tours:
Wines available cellar door at the Padthaway Estate
Retail distribution:
Hill International Wines, (02) 9630 1311

Hardy's Padthaway

BRL Hardy have a major investment in this exciting wine region. The beginnings of the vineyard go back to 1968 when the vineyard director, David Hardy, found 240 hectares of prime terra rossa land nearby the original Seppelts Keppoch Estate. The 1974 Keppoch Riesling, made by Brian Croser, was the first wine released and won many medals. Three 1993 reds, a shiraz and two different cabernetís were also successful. Other varieties followed, most notably chardonnay in the early 1970.'s. The success of the venture led to a doubling of the land holdings to 480 hectares.

The collection wines were very successful and recently the Padthaway Unwooded Chardonnay and a Cabernet Sauvignon have captured the markets imagination.

A single crushing facility was built in the mid 1970's. Recently BRL Hardy commenced an $18 million winery development. This state of the art winery is the largest development of its kind in Australia for many years. The winery follows a $50 million vineyard acquisition and expansion program undertaken by the company in recent years involving thousands of acres in a number of premium wine-growing regions. The Padthaway vineyard now has some 400 hectares under vine. The new winery will be operating for the 1998 vintage.

An introduction to Langhorne Creek

Situated some 80 kms south-east of Adelaide, along the banks of the River Bremer, lies the grape-growing region of Langhorne Creek.

The rich alluvial plain is periodically flooded by the Bremer River, an event that the local growers look forward to each year, as it brings much needed water and fertile silt to the vineyards.

Planting of vines at Langhorne Creek began in the middle of the last century. The oldest and largest winery in the region is Bleasdale, established by Frank Potts back in 1850. Today the Potts family still manage this historic winery.

Many of the great winemakers from around Australia have used Langhorne Creek grapes in their winemaking. The first wine to acknowledge this on the label was the famous Stonyfell Metala with its distinctive label explaining its origins.

During the late 60's and early 70's, Wolf Blass relied heavily on Langhorne Creek fruit, a significant ingredient of his trio of Jimmy Watson trophies. Today, four excellent wineries share the region with many grape-growers, including a recent influx of larger companies. Orlando Wyndham are in the process of establishing a huge $15 million vineyard development and Rosemount have just completed the planting of 750 acres of vines in one single vineyard. It is a spectacular sight and will have its first crop in 1998.

The wine industry and the State Government have just implemented a massive irrigation scheme, bringing water in a large pipeline from Lake Alexandrina; this sense of co-operation in South Australia's future is welcome. Why not visit the region and see the historic Bleasdale and the fast developing family wineries, Lake Breeze, Temple Bruer and the delightful Bremerton Lodge with its excellent restaurant.

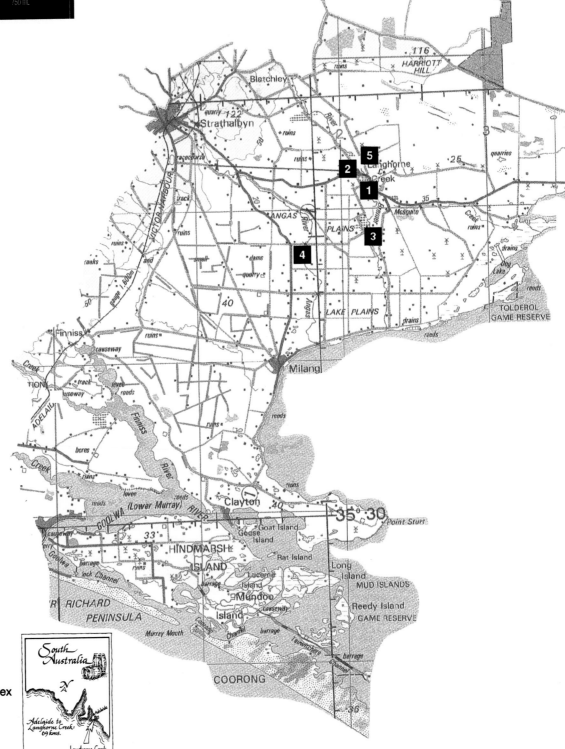

Langhorne Creek - Map Index
1 Bleasdale Wines
2 Bremerton Lodge
3 Lake Breeze Wines
4 Temple Bruer Winery
5 Temple Bruer Cellar Door

Bleasdale

Bleasdale is one of Australia's oldest family owned and operated wineries. Little has changed in parts of the winery since it was established by Frank Potts in 1850. Potts was one of the State's original settlers, landing in Adelaide from H.M.S. Buffalo in 1836. An energetic and entrepreneurial chap, he also built 3 large paddle steamers which plied the Murray River for many years. The old part of the winery is on the National Trust and National Heritage register and makes a fascinating visit; the huge old red gum lever press is truly incredible.

Until the late 1950's, Bleasdale produced only fortified wines, including a number of ports and sherries and a madeira, still produced, made from the rare grape variety, verdelho. Bleasdale still makes great fortifieds but today their table wines form the greater part of their business.

Winemaker is Roseworthy graduate and family member, Michael Potts. Michael has continued installing modern winemaking equipment and increased oak barrel storage. The reds, the chardonnay and the verdelho (table wine) have really shown the benefit of this investment and Michael's skill, combined with the superb fruit from the Langhorne Creek vineyards, has seen some sensational wines.

The winery's tasting room is full of old photographs by family member, Diddy Potts, and paintings by his brother, A.B. Potts. Drop in to Bleasdale and immerse yourself in our wine history. Plans are afoot for a new cellar and hospitality area which will sensitively combine the historic past with the needs of the wine tourist.

BLEASDALE VINEYARDS
Address: Wellington Road, Langhorne Creek SA 5255
Phone: (08) 8537 3001
Fax: (08) 8537 3224
WWW: http://www.wineaustralia.com.au
Established: 1850
Winemaker: Michael Potts
Principal varieties grown: Cabernet Sauvignon, Shiraz, Malbec, Verdelho
Ha under vine: 50
Average annual crush: 1,500 tonnes
Average no. cases produced: 100,000

Principal wines & brands	Cellar Potential
Cabernet/Malbec/Merlot	5-10 years
Cabernet Sauvignon	5-10 years
Special Vintage Shiraz	5-10 years
Verdelho	2-5 years
Pioneer Port (Tawny Port)	10+ years
Madeira (Verdelho)	10+ years
Public & trade tours: Yes	

Hours open to public: 9am-5pm, weekdays; 11am-5pm, Sunday
Points of interest: Historic Winery (Redgum Lever Press, Redgum Vats etc.), Picnic Area nearby
Retail distribution: National Distribution - Carlton S.B.C.

Bremerton Wines

Craig Willson and has delightful wife, Mignonne, (it's French for cute) have restored a beautiful century-old stone building on their property and turned it into a showplace of good taste as a winery and charming restaurant, where Mignonne serves her mood food for lunch, at weekends.

The tasting area of Bremerton Lodge features many historic items from the region and opens out to an outdoor patio which is delightful on a summer's day.

The sweeping circular driveway adds to the beautifully-balanced overall impression. In the winery with its high roof, the eating area is on a mezzanine above the cellars where the wine quietly ages.

The care and aesthetic understanding of the Willson's shows through in their wines which are beautifully balanced and good examples of the top quality that Langhorne Creek is famous for.

Why not wend your way around Langhorne Creek one weekend and then breeze into Bremerton Lodge. I'm sure Mignonne's mood food will suit your mood.

BREMERTON WINES
Address: Strathalbyn Road, Langhorne Creek SA 5255
Phone: (08) 8537 3093
Fax: (08) 8537 3109
Email: bremwine@lm.net.au
Owners: Craig and Mignonne Willson
Winemaker: Rebecca Willson
Principal varieties grown: Cabernet Sauvignon, Shiraz, Merlot, Verdelho, Sauvignon Blanc, Semillon
Ha under vine: 40
Average no. cases produced: 7,000

Principal wines & brands	Cellar Potential
Bremerton 'Old Adam' Shiraz	8+ years
Bremerton Cabernet Sauvignon	5+ years
Bremerton Young Vine Shiraz	5+ years
Bremerton Cabernet/Shiraz/Merlot	5+ years
Bremerton Sauvignon Blanc/Semillon	1 year
Bremerton Verdelho	2 years
Bremerton Ciel Fortified Chenin Blanc	

Public & trade tours: No
Hours open to public: From 10am, daily
Points of interest: Cheese platters daily, Home Made produce, Marinated Olives. Lunch by booking on most weekends
Retail distribution: SA, Perth, Melbourne, UK, Hong Kong

Lake Breeze

Like their wines, the Follett family are youthful, exuberant and dynamic. Father Ken still hasn't hung up his Aussie Rules footy boots and is one of the fittest men of his age you're ever likely to meet. Quietly spoken Ken is a fastidious hard-toiling farmer, whose superb vineyard and the wonderful fruit it produces is respected by winemakers from near and far. After many years supplying grapes to Australia's leading winemakers, Ken decided to start a small winery to put his growing family to work. His three sons are the driving force of the winery - Roger is a viticulturist and assists his father in the vineyard, Tim helps in the vineyard and Greg is the highly successful winemaker. Greg also handles the marketing. Lake Breeze uses only the top ten percent of their crop for their own wines and sell the rest. Greg in his short winemaking career has won a truckload of wine show trophies. His lightning rise to fame began when he graduated from Roseworthy in 1991. He followed this with a vintage at Hardy's, and then a vintage at Geyser Peak winery in California. Then he worked in France at Domaine du Vaissiere for the world famous winemaking Lurton family in the Minervois region south of Bordeaux.

Ken Follett is the epitome of a truly supportive parent and his sons are doing him proud.

LAKE BREEZE WINES

Address: Step Road, Langhorne Creek SA 5255
Phone: (08) 8537 3017
Fax: (08) 8537 3267
Established: 1991
Winemaker: Greg Follett
Principal varieties grown: Cabernet Sauvignon, Shiraz, Chardonnay, small amounts White Frontignac & Grenache
Ha under vine: 70
Average annual crush: 120 Tonnes
Average no. cases produced: 6,000-8,000

Principal wines & brands	Cellar Potential
Cabernet Sauvignon	5-10 years
"Bernoota" Shiraz/Cabernet	5-10 years
Winemaker's Selection Shiraz	10+ years
Winemaker's Selection Cabernet	10+ years
Grenache	3-5 years
Chardonnay	3-5 years
White Frontignac	0-2 years

Hours open to public: 10am-5pm, daily
Points of interest: Friendly Family Atmosphere, Panoramic Views
Retail distribution: Mail Order

Rosemount Langhorne Creek

In three short years Rosemount have planted a massive 750 acres of vines on a huge panoramic site on the western banks of the Bremer River, mainly shiraz and cabernet sauvignon. The first vintage was in 1997 but from 1998 onwards a truly massive quality of absolutely top quality grapes will flow into the Rosemount Ryecroft winery at McLaren Vale. The whole Rosemount range of reds will benefit, from the Super Premium Balmoral GSM, Traditional, the Diamond label Shiraz and the Diamond label Cabernet Sauvignon.

In the hands of chief winemaker, Philip Shaw and the McLaren Vale winemaker Charles Whish, who are both amongst the top rung of the industries winemen, I am sure the exceptional Langhorne Creek fruit will make superb wines.

An introduction to McLaren Vale

The McLaren Vale wine region stretches from the southern suburbs of Adelaide including Reynella in the north to Aldinga and Willunga in the south. The region is bordered by the Adelaide Hills to the east and the Gulf of St Vincent to the west.

John Reynell planted the first vines of the region at Reynella in 1838. He was followed by Dr Alexander Kelly, who founded the Tintara Vineyard Company and developed a considerable property covering 285 hectares.

The first vines planted by Dr Kelly are still bearing fruit, which has traditionally been used in a fortified dessert wine. In 1850 George Manning established the Hope Farm Vineyard, which is now Seaview. By late 1880 wine industry development was booming throughout Australia.

In McLaren Vale, new businesses were founded by J.G. Kelly with the Tatachilla Vineyard, the Kay family with their Amery winery, the Johnstons' Pirramimma Wines and Robert Wigley with Wirra Wirra.

Much of the wine produced in McLaren Vale/Reynella was exported to England.

The area was subject to export market vagaries and grew slowly until the table wine boom of the 1960's.

Larger companies such as Lindemans and Penfolds started purchasing McLaren Vale red wines for blending and many existing local companies began to bottle and market their own wine. Towards the end of the decade and through the early 70's new companies blossomed throughout McLaren Vale. There are now more than 50 wineries in the area and the 1980's and 1990's have seen the area under vines expand dramatically. More importantly, the awareness of McLaren Vale Wines and their reputation for quality has grown even more dramatically.

I can well imagine how the beauty of the region would have captured the heart of my own great-grandfather, Thomas Hardy, as he drove his horse and buggy over the final rise of the southern Adelaide Hills and saw the peaceful Valley spread out before him, the time-worn fingers of the hills holding its final exit into St. Vincents Gulf (by coincidence, St. Vincent is the patron saint of winemakers). The gentle undulating hills have traditionally supported vines,

olives and almonds. The almonds in blossom around the first week or so in August gives the Valley a special glow. During the 1870's, the area had fallen on hard times, the over-cropping of cereals and over-grazing leading to diminishing rural returns. Thomas Hardy set about promoting the vine and educating farmers in its cultivation. He also bought the grand, but bankrupt, Tintara Vineyard Company and the disused Flour Mill, soon having the region well on its feet, with his own flourishing enterprise.

McLaren Vale is one of the world's best-placed wine regions, being only 45 minutes drive south of the Adelaide city centre. This, combined with its physical beauty, has led to a boom in tourism through which, fortunately, the region has lost none of its charm or individual character of its winemakers.

Forerunner among this development was David Hardy, great-grandson of pioneer Thomas, along with renowned artist, David Dridan. They set up the wine-inspired restaurant, The Barn, in 1970 with its vine-covered courtyard and 'choose your

own' wine cellar. It was an innovative and welcome addition to Australia, let alone McLaren Vale.

David also founded the Wine Bushing Festival in 1974, based on the old Elizabethan tradition of hanging a bush outside the inn when the new wine was ready. In October each year, this tradition continues. The makers of the best commercially available McLaren Vale wine are crowned "Bushing King and Queen" at the annual Winemakers' Luncheon. The month kicks off with the McLaren Vale Continuous Picnic on the October long weekend, a Sunday and Monday celebration of wine and food. Some 30 wineries all have a guest restaurant cooking, and all manner of entertainment.

Bushing Week usually starts with the McLaren Vale Wine Show, a varietal workshop and the Winemakers' Luncheon which showcases the show's award winning wines, complemented by regional produce from the Fleurieu Peninsula. All awards from the wine show are presented during the luncheon, the highlight being the crowning of the "Bushing King and Queen".

The festival culminates with the Bushing Festival Street Procession and Fair Day when the whole town stops and stall and entertainment reign supreme. In between,

wineries have dinners, concerts, theatre pieces and all manner of other music, art and cultural experiences.

McLaren Vale has long been known for its full-bodied red wines, aided by the complex soils and mild temperate climate. These rich round generous wines can really warm the soul. The region also produces great whites and although its chardonnays led the way, they have latterly been joined by sauvignon blancs, which are becoming a regional speciality and highly regarded by the wine cognoscenti.

Much of the industry's success originally was based on fortified ports and sherries and while sherry making has ceased, the ports of the region are outstanding; both the vintage and tawny styles excel. The number of winery restaurants, bed and breakfasts and regional eating houses is growing daily and they are superb. The Barn has been joined by The Salopian Inn at the other end of town and the McLarens on the Lake restaurant, function and accommodation centre is splendid, indeed. Woodstock has a superb large restaurant and function centre, The Coterie, a Sunday lunch here is compulsory. Middlebrook has a restaurant and a David Dridan run gallery and art and craft showcase.

Chapel Hill has a splendid gallery in its old

chapel and outdoor eating facilities. Wirilda Creek features a casual restaurant and great bed and breakfast, while closer to town St. Francis has accommodation and a restaurant and conference centre at Reynella. Geoff Merrill's historic Mt. Hurtle Winery also has a restaurant and function area and the Cellar Bistro at Haselgrove is famous for its vineyard platter. The new cellar door at d'Arenberg and Darry's Verandah Restaurant with its spectacular views over the vines, hills and the water of St Vincents Gulf is one of the very best wine hospitality centres in Australia.

"Magnums" at the Hotel McLaren and Pipkins BYO restaurant are located near the Almond Train at the entrance to Hardy's Tintara Winery in McLaren Vale's main street.

The new Fleurieu Regional Visitor Centre (opened in late 1996) is located near the McLaren Vale township's western entrance. The centre offers visitors a glimpse of what they can discover in the McLaren Vale region and beyond on the Fleurieu Peninsula.

Any visitors to Adelaide with an interest in wine should spend a day or two exploring the magnificent scenery, beaches, wines and food of the McLaren Vale Wine Region – Adelaide's playground.

McLaren Vale - South Australia

McLaren Vale - Map Index
1. Aldinga Bay Winery
2. Andrew Garrett Wines
3. The Barn
4. Chapel Hill Winery
5. Chateau Reynella Winery
6. Coriole Vineyards
7. Crestview Wines
8. d'Arenberg Wines
9. Dennis of McLaren Vale
10. Dyson Maslin Beach
11. Fern Hill Estate
12. Hardy's Tintara
13. Haselgrove Wines
14. Hillstowe Wines at Salopian Inn
15. Hugo Winery
16. Ingoldby Cellar Door at Andrew Garrett Wines
17. Kay Bros - Amery
18. Luong Rice Wines
19. Maglieri Winery
20. Manning Park Winery
21. Marienberg Winery
22. Wayne Thomas Wines
23. McLaren Vale Olive Grove
24. McLaren's on the Lake

25. Merrivale Winery
26. Middlebrook Winery
27. Mount Hurtle Vineyards
28. Noon's Winery
29. Normans Wines
30. Old Clarendon Winery
31. Oliverhill Wines
32. Pertaringa Vineyards
33. Pirramimma Winery
34. Richard Hamilton Wines
35. Ryecroft Vineyards
36. St Francis Winery
37. Scarpantoni Estate Wines
38. Seaview Winery
39. Shottesbrooke Vineyards
40. Stevens Cambrai
41. Tanami Red Wines
42. Tatachilla Winery
43. Tinlins
44. Torresans Happy Valley Wines
45. Wirilda Creek Winery
46. Wirra Wirra Vineyards
47. Woodstock Winery & Coterie
48. Fox Creek Wines
49. Maxwell Wines
50. McLaren Vale & Fleurieu Visitors Centre

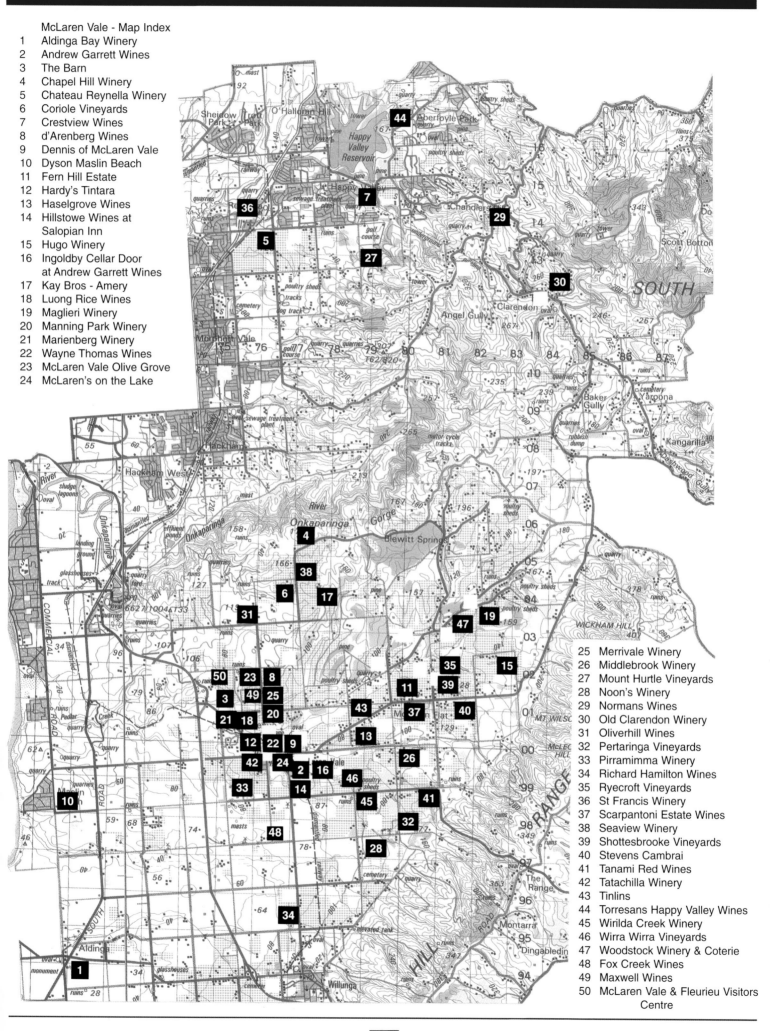

McLaren Vale - South Australia

McLaren Vale and Fleurieu Visitors Centre

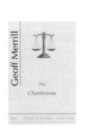

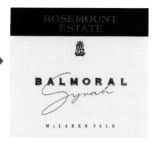

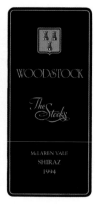

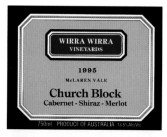

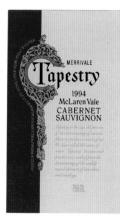

ST FRANCIS

Address: Bridge Street, Old Reynella SA 5162
Phone: (08) 8381 1925
Fax: (08) 8322 6655
Email: StFrancs@ctel.com.au
WWW: http://www.SaintFrancis.com.au
Established: 1856
Winemaker: Various depending on variety
Average no. cases produced: 10,000

Principal wines & brands	Cellar Potential
Grenache	3-5 years
Classic Dry White	3-5 years
Shiraz/Cabernet Sauvignon	5-10 years
Chardonnay	
Late Harvest Frontignac	
Ports	10+ years
Bulk Port	10+ years
Cleanskins	

Public & trade tours: Yes
Hours open to public: 8.30am-5pm, weekdays; 10am-5pm, weekends
Points of interest: Miniature ports for corporate, wedding and convention purposes
Retail distribution: Mailing list, selected bottle shops and restaurants

ALDINGA BAY VINEYARDS

Address: Main South Road, Aldinga SA 5173
Phone: (08) 8556 3179
Fax: (08) 8556 3350
Established: 1979
Winemaker: Nick Girolamo
Principal varieties grown: Chardonnay, Cabernet Sauvignon, Sauvignon Blanc, Merlot, Cabernet Franc, Rhine Riesling, Shiraz, Grenache
Ha under vine: 30
Average no. cases produced: 8,000
Public & trade tours: No
Hours open to public: 10am-5pm, daily
Points of interest: BBQ area, 2.5 km from beach
Retail distribution: Cellar Door and Mail Order, Selected Restaurants and Bottle shops

Beresford Wines

Robert Dundon is a very well credentialled winemaker, completing his studies in Bio-chemistry at Adelaide University and gaining his batchelor in Agricultural Science in 1974.

His wine career began at Hardy's Mile End Cellars as a quality control chemist, but he soon rose to red winemaker for the company and moved to McLaren Vale in 1976.

During his time at Hardy's he accumulated more than 650 medals and 19 trophies for the company's reds.

Rob and his wife Bronwyn formed their own wine enterprise in 1985. Rob chose the name Beresford as he had spent some time as a youth scaling the rock cliffs of Beresford Dales in Derbyshire on the Dove River hence the dove on the Beresford label. Rob has scaled other heights since, in 1989 with a group of investors they bought the magnificent old Horndale Winery built in 1896 and run by a great wine pioneer a Mr Cholmondely and French winemaker Hubert Percival Bosanquet. Today Beresford is Australia's 23rd largest producer marketing some 145,000 cases of wine under various labels.

Rob has won over 350 medals with his wines since 1985. They range from the top of the range Beresford, the Beresford Highwood range and three wines Beresford, St Estelle, St Yvette and St Helene named after the three 'Little Angels' that were Hubert Bosanquets' daughters.

All the wines are not only top quality but exceptional value for money.

The winery is in the outer suburbs of Adelaide and well worth visiting.

BERESFORD

Address: 49 Fraser Avenue, Happy Valley SA 5159
Phone: (08) 8322 3611
Fax: (08) 8322 3610
Established: 1985
Winemaker: Rob Dundon
Principal varieties grown: Cabernet Sauvignon, Petit Verdot, Shiraz, Merlot, Sangiovese, Chardonnay, Pinot Noir
Ha under vine: 96
Average annual crush: 1,900 tonnes
Average no. cases produced: 150,000

Principal wines & brands	Cellar Potential
Beresford Cabernet Merlot	5-8 years
Beresford Chardonnay	3-5 years
Beresford Semillon Sauvignon	1-2 years
Highwood Chardonnay	2-4 years
Highwood Sauvignon Blanc	1-2 years
Highwood Shiraz	3-5 years
Beresford St. Estelle Semillon Chardonnay	3-5 years
Beresford St. Yvette Chardonnay	2-4 years
Beresford St. Helene Cabernet Shiraz	3-5 years

Hours open to public: 11am-5pm, daily
Points of interest: BBQ entertaining, century old magnificent stone cellars excavated into hillside
Retail distribution: National plus 16 countries worldwide including UK, Holland, France, USA, NZ, Japan, Canada and South Africa

Andrew Garrett Wines

Andrew Garrett arrived on the wine scene like a whirlwind. Not since the early days of Wolf Blass's arrival a decade earlier had Australia's wine drinkersí imagination been captured so fully. His wines were exciting. A chardonnay packed full of fruit flavour, with good oak treatment, and methode champenoise of exceptional quality, lifting people's sights well above the ordinary. The Garrett reds were also lively and fruit driven. Andrew's flamboyant marketing style also had a Blass-like ring about it.

Andrew Garrett Wines are of absolutely the highest quality and the growth of the brand I am sure will accelerate even further, both domestically and overseas. The Andrew Garrett N.V. Pinot, a Non-Vintage Methode Champenoise Cuvee with its very faint blushing colour and delectable pinot noir nuances, is a rightful market leader.

The Garrett Red Sparkling is a truly regal rich red at the pinnacle of its class. In the table wine area the quality and styles are equally well conceived and created.

The chardonnay and the "bold" shiraz stand out, but all the wines are outstanding.

The setting for Andrew Garrett wines at McLarens on the Lake oasis is idyllic.

ANDREW GARRETT WINERY

Address: Kangarilla Road, McLaren Vale SA 5171
Phone: (08) 8323 8853
Fax: (08) 8323 8271
Established: 1983
Owner: Mildara Blass Limited
Winemaker: Phil Reschke
Principal varieties grown: Chardonnay, Cabernet Sauvignon, Grenache, Sauvignon Blanc, Pinot Noir
Ha under vine: 120
Average no. cases produced: 120,000

Principal wines & brands	Cellar Potential
Garrett Shiraz Cabernet Franc	2-5 years
Andrew Garrett Sauvignon Blanc	2-4 years
Andrew Garrett Bold Shiraz	3-5 years
Andrew Garrett Botrytis Riesling	3-5 years
Andrew Garrett Brut	2-3 years
Andrew Garrett Sparkling Burgundy	2-3 years

Public & trade tours: By appointment only
Hours open to public: 10am-4pm, daily
Points of interest: Situated on picturesque lake. Great picnic area

Chapel Hill

One of McLaren Vales most exciting wineries is the beautiful Chapel Hill. The charming 19th Century Chapel is perched atop one of the highest hills of the region, with awesome views - the hills, the coast, the contoured vines on the surrounding slopes. On a summer's day, with a picnic on the lawns outside the winery, one could indeed imagine oneself in paradise. The Chapel is now a lovely gallery and tasting centre, constructed in the attractive ironstone for which the region is so renowned. The wines of Chapel Hill reflect the serene, sensitive balance of their home. Winemaker, Pam Dunsford drives herself resolutely in her search of perfection in their creation. Pam started with the large Wynns/Seaview organisation, and went on to be one of the most sought-after wine consultants in Australia. Pam was Roseworthy College's first female graduate in winemaking some 20 years ago, and has travelled the world of wine extensively, always seeking self improvement. She spent a year in Champagne, has worked several vintages in France, and has studied in California. Chapel Hill's show successes are already legendary. The state-of- the-art new winery

complex was completed in 1993 and is one of the most advanced in the world.
The Gerard family, one of Adelaide's most innovative business successes, have invested heavily, but wisely in Chapel Hill.
They have some 125 acres of vineyards around the winery and nearby in the hills near Kangarilla.

Chapel Hill also source grapes from Coonawarra, Padthaway and the Eden Valley. The labelling of all their wines is precise. It is hard in fact, to imagine a better set up winery, winemaking philosophy or a more dedicated approach. Somehow, one can sense a little divine inspiration focussed through this beautiful 'Chapel on the Hill'.

Merrivale Wines

Merrivale with its pretty name and picturesque location was always a Cinderella winery searching for the fairy godmother.
Jack Starr started up the winery in the renaissance days of the early 1970's and got off to a flying start. The winery travelled through some troubled waters until its saviour came along in the form of the innovative winemaker Brian Light and his effervescent wife Kay.
Between them, they really rejuvenated Merrivale. Much of the 26 acres has been either revived or replanted. Brian had an illustrious winemaking background, his father Lloyd has a large, highly respected vineyard in the cool Bakers Gully near Kangarilla.
Brian was chief winemaker for many years for Normans wines and in 1988 he was awarded the immense honour of becoming 'Australasian Winemaker of the Year'.
In August 1997 Gerard Industries, who already own the Chapel Hill Winery, purchased Merrivale. The Light's good work will be continued by the team from Chapel Hill, under the very capable leadership of Pam Dunsford. The cellar door at Merrivale is a real treat and the range of Merrivale Wines are worth tasting.

MERRIVALE WINES

Address: Olivers Road, McLaren Vale SA 5171
Phone: (08) 8323 9196
Fax: (08) 8323 9746
Established: 1971
Winemaker: Pam Dunsford
Principal varieties grown: Shiraz, Cabernet Sauvignon, Chardonnay
Ha under vine: 10
Average annual crush: 200 tonnes
Average no. cases produced: 15,000

Principal wines & brands	Cellar Potential
Tapestry Chardonnay	2-5 years
Tapestry Cabernet Sauvignon	5-10 years
Tapestry Spaetlese Muscat of Alexandria	1-3 years
Tapestry Shiraz	5-10 years
Tapestry 10yo Tawny Port	

Public & trade tours: Trade tours by appointment only
Hours open to public: 11am-5pm, daily
Points of interest: Views over McLaren Vale to Coast
Retail distribution: Lionel Samson, SA, NT, WA; Australian Prestige Wines, VIC; Baywine Distributors, NSW; Australian Trade Partners, QLD

d'Arenberg Wines

d'Arenberg is one of the most significant wine companies in McLaren Vale. In 1912 Joseph Osborn, a teetotaller, director of Thomas Hardy and Sons, purchased the well established Milton Vineyards in the hill just north of the townships of Gloucester and Bellvue, now known as McLaren Vale.

Joseph's son Frank left medical school choosing to forsake the scalpel for pruning shears, selling the fruit from 78 hectares of vineyards to local wineries until the construction of his own cellars were completed in 1928. Dry red table and fortified wines were produced in ever increasing quantities to supply the expanding markets of the Empire.

In 1943 Frank's son d'Arry returned from school, aged 16, to help his ill father run the business, eventually assuming full management of d'Arenberg in 1956, bottling the first of the famous diagonal red stripe labelled wines the following year. d'Arry's wines of the 1960's gained immediate cult status amongst imbibers and judges. One cabernet sauvignon won a Jimmy Watson Trophy at the Melbourne Wine Show and another Grenache based wine was awarded 7 trophies and 29 gold medals from Australian Capital City wine shows.

It is understandable that by the 1970's d'Arenberg Wines had become very fashionable, having gained national and international profiles in less than 20 years and were, as they are now, much sought after in the market place. Enter the fourth generation, d'Arry's son Chester.

After graduating from Roseworthy College, visiting other Australian and European wine regions, Chester took over the reigns as chief winemaker in 1984, immediately rejuvenating the then 70 year old cellars and 19th Century vineyards.

Investing in new oak, lots of small stainless steel tanks and refrigeration resulting in immediate white dividends with his Dry Dam Riesling, Dryland Sauvignon Blanc, Olive Grove Chardonnay and botrytis affected Noble Riesling all winning gold medals and trophies at wine shows. In 1990 Chester was crowned McLaren Vale Bushing King for producing the best table wine in the district judged at the McLaren Vale Wine Show and in 1995 d'Arry was invested as a patron of the Wine Industry of Australia, two years after completing his 50th consecutive vintage.

It is not surprising that with a "Red Stripe" in their blood, d'Arry and

Chester's viticultural and oenological talents have ensured that d'Arenberg have continued to win numerous national and international medals, trophies and critical acclaim, non more so than in recent years. d'Arenberg is continuing to produce wines under many unique labels like The Custodian Grenache, The Twentyeight Road Mourvedre, The Coppermine Road Cabernet Sauvignon and The Dead Arm Shiraz underlining d'Arry's commitment to the region that are a credit both to the winery and the region. They have completed renovating the property's 19th Century homestead incorporating cellar door tastings and a restaurant , aptly named "d'Arry's Verandah" both with imperious views overlooking McLaren Vale and Willunga escarpment to the Gulf of St Vincent. d'Arenberg is indeed a McLaren Vale tradition to be proud of.

---

d'ARENBERG

Address: Osborn Road, McLaren Vale SA 5171
Direction: 3km north of the township of McLaren Vale
Phone: (08) 8323 8206
Fax: (08) 8323 8423
Email: darenberg@mclarenvale.sa.com.au
WWW: www.wineaustralia.com.au/darenberg
Established: 1912
Owner: Osborn Family
Winemaker: Chester Osborn
Principal varieties grown: Riesling, Sauvignon Blanc, Chardonnay, Marsanne, Rousanne, Viognier, Chambourcin, Grenache, Shiraz, Mourvedre, Cabernet Sauvignon, Petit Verdot
Ha under vine: 150
Average annual crush: 1,500 tonnes
Average no. cases produced: 100,000
Principal wines & brands   Cellar Potential

d'Arenberg	
White Ochre and Red Ochre	1-4 years
The Dry Dam Riesling	10+ years
The Dryland Sauvignon Blanc	1-4 years
The Olive Grove Chardonnay	5-10 years
The Noble Riesling (375ml)	5-10 years
The Peppermint Paddock Sparkling Chamb.	1-4 years
The High Trellis Cabernet Sauvignon	5-15 years
The Footbolt Old Vine Shiraz	10+ years
d'Arry's Original Shiraz Grenache	10+ years
The Peppermint Paddock Chambourcin	2-5 years
The Twentyeight Road Mourvedre	5-10 years
The Custodian Grenache	10+ years
The Ironstone Pressings Grenache-Shiraz	10+ years
The Dead Arm Shiraz	20+ years
The Coppermine Road Cabernet Sauvignon	20+years
Vintage Fortified Shiraz	
Nostalgia Fine Old Tawny	

Public & trade tours: By appointment only
Hours open to public: 10am-5pm, daily
Points of interest: d'Arry's Verandah, Hilltop Restaurant overlooking the Willunga Escarpment McLaren Flat, McLaren Vale and the Valley Floor to the Gulf of St. Vincent
Retail distribution: Cellar Door and Mail Order sales. Each state and territory. Nationally and two dozen or so countries internationally

Coriole

<table>
<tr><td colspan="2">

CORIOLE
Address: Chaffeys Road, McLaren Vale SA 5171
Phone: (08) 8323 8305
Fax: (08) 8323 9136
Established: 1968
Winemaker: Stephen Hall
Principal varieties grown: Shiraz, Cabernet Sauvignon, Chenin Blanc, Sangiovese, Semillon
Ha under vine: 20
Average annual crush: 350 tonnes
Average no. cases produced: 25,000

Principal wines & brands	Cellar Potential
Shiraz	5-10 years
Redstone Shiraz/Cabernet Sauvignon	5-10 years
Sangiovese	2-5 years
Cabernet Sauvignon	5-10 years
"Mary Kathleen" Cabernet/ Merlot/Cabernet Franc	5-10 years
Lloyd Reserve Shiraz	10+ years
Chenin Blanc	2-3 years
Semillon	3-7 years
Chardonnay	2-5 years

Public & trade tours: By appointment only
Hours open to public: 10am-5pm, weekdays; 11am-5pm, weekends and public holidays
Points of interest: Tastings and Sales are held in the Old Ironstone Barn built in 1860. Casual Picnics and Occasional Functions are held in the well-known Cottage Garden and Original Homestead of the property.
Retail distribution: Cellar Door and Mail Order. Tucker Seabrook Classic Wines, SA; Haviland Wine Co., NSW; David Johnstone and Ass., TAS; Winestock, VIC; Premium Wine Merchants, WA; Wine 2000, QLD; National Capital Fine Wines, ACT

</td></tr>
</table>

Dr Hugh Lloyd purchased Chateau Bonne Sante (ironically French for good health) and surrounding vineyards in 1968.

The property had a long history, with vines planted in 1920 and the ironstone buildings built in 1860.

Now known as Coriole, the property is set on the hill west of the Seaview vineyards and enjoys uninterrupted views of the valley below and St Vincent's Gulf.

The small viticulture region around Coriole is prized for its distinctive red brown loams over ironstone or limestone. The Coriole shiraz is a consistent and impressive wine and the company's flagship. The top of the range wine produced is the Lloyd Reserve Shiraz.

First produced in 1989, it is made from 70 year old vines grown at Coriole. The Lloyd Reserve is very rich with great complexity of flavour and has long cellaring potential. Sangiovese has become a speciality of the winery. Coriole has led the way with this Italian variety in Australia. Sangiovese is a late variety with good acidity that is well suited to McLaren Vale. The lighter bodied style with its savoury characters and gentle grip gives a wine that contrasts with the other reds. Coriole is one of the few Australian wine companies to produce chenin blanc, which was rediscovered in the region by a French ampelographer. Coriole Chenin has become widely popular because of the depth of flavour – tropical, apple and quince characteristics abound.

There are also small quantities of other wines produced including a shiraz cabernet call 'Redstone', a Semillon Sauvignon Blanc grown on a neighbours vineyard, and a top of range Cabernet blend named 'Mary Kathleen', after Mark Lloyd's late mother.

Mark Lloyd and winemaker Stephen Hall are producing wines at Coriole which compare favourably with the best in Australia. The wines are predominantly estate grown. The old cottage and gardens at the winery with its long views of the surrounding countryside, makes Coriole a favourite place to visit.

Dennis of McLaren Vale

Egerton Dennis was one of the real gentlemen of the wine industry who has sadly passed on since my last publication. During the 1960's, he and Jim Ingoldby regenerated the old Ryecroft winery and vineyards – their vision in fact predated the wine boom. In 1973, the same year as Ingoldby, Dennis's Daringa Cellars was born. Egerton had by then established his own vineyards at the eastern side of the valley, although the winery is located right on the edge of town just opposite McLarens on the Lake.

The wines are all made from the family's own vineyards by Peter Dennis who is ably assisted by his wife Margaret.

Dennis was one of the pioneers of chardonnay in the region and their full-flavoured reds are excellent value.

<table>
<tr><td colspan="2">

DENNIS
Address: Kangarilla Road, McLaren Vale SA 5171
Phone: (08) 8323 8665
Fax: (08) 8323 9121
Established: 1970
Owner: Dennis Family
Winemaker: Peter Dennis
Principal varieties grown: Shiraz, Cabernet Sauvignon, Merlot, Chardonnay, Sauvignon Blanc
Ha under vine: 22
Average annual crush: 225 tonnes
Average no. cases produced: 5,000-10,000

Principal wines & brands	Cellar Potential
Shiraz	5-10 years
Cabernet Sauvignon	5-10 years
Merlot	5-10 years
Chardonnay	2-5 years
Sauvignon Blanc	2-5 years

Public & trade tours: Yes
Hours open to public: 10am-5pm, daily
Points of interest: Picnic Grounds, Historic site, Natural Spring
Retail distribution: National Wine Merchants, NSW; Capital Fine Wines, ACT; Westwood Wine Agencies, UK

</td></tr>
</table>

Dyson Wines

It would be hard to find someone more happy with his lot in life than Allan Dyson. Allan started winemaking back in 1965 at Seaview, when Ben Chaffey was still at the helm, after which he travelled over to the Hunter Valley in 1970 and made wine for Hollydene for six years.

By 1977 Allan was back in McLaren Vale making wine at Middlebrook. The same year, he started planting vines on his estate near the coast, not far from Australia's first "naturalist" beach. He planted all the vines by hand himself and knows everyone of them intimately. In fact, in his own words "I've got 9,121 reasons to be happy" – even a few more reasons since my last writing!! Looking extremely young for his years, Allan tends his vines, makes the characterful wines, including a methode champenoise which he ferments in the cellars, and even does his own disgorging.

One would think he was too busy to say 'G'day'; not Allan – he loves people, and it shows in his wines. His lovely garden and tasting cottage also make this a memorable visit.

DYSON

Address: Sherriff Road, Maslin Beach SA 5170
Direction: 7kms west of McLaren Vale Wine Region
Phone: (08) 8386 1092
Fax: (08) 8327 0066
Established: 1977
Owner: Allan Dyson
Winemaker: Allan Dyson
Principal varieties grown: Cabernet Sauvignon, Chardonnay, Sauvignon Blanc, Pinot Noir, Pinot Primeur
Ha under vine: 6
Average annual crush: 30 tonnes
Average no. cases produced: 1,700-2,000

Principal wines & brands	Cellar Potential
"Clarice" Cabernet Sauvignon	5-10 years
"Dyson" Chardonnay	2-5 years
"Dyson" Sauvignon Blanc	2-5 years
"Dyson" Methode Champenoise	2-5 years
"Dyson" Fortified Sauvignon Blanc	10+ years

Public & trade tours: By appointment only
Hours open to public: 10am-5pm, daily
Points of interest: **Vineyard & Winery being** located 2.5kms from Coast. One of the closest Vineyards to the Sea in Australia.
Retail distribution: Cellar Door and Mail Order Sales. Sydney - Roger Brown Wine Agencies, South Australia - Distribution from Winery

Fernhill Estate

In the heady days of the wine boom back in 1975, the gregarious Wayne Thomas and his wife Pat, began a winery opposite Ryecroft and just down the road from Ingoldby. Fern Hill became a much-respected label.

Early in 1994 the Thomas's sold the winery to dynamic Sydney Wine entrepreneur Terry Hill, proprietor of Hill International Wines.

Small scale production, low quantities of super premium wines are being hand-crafted.

At present these include a chardonnay fermented in French oak and a semillon fermented and aged very briefly in American oak. The reds comprise a cabernet sauvignon plus a shiraz both made in a no-compromise fashion from selected vineyards in the McLaren Vale Region.

The accent in the cellar door is also very much on the wine quality with a very personal and educational approach.

The newly restored premises were re-opened on Christmas Eve 1994 with the elegant new labels proudly to the fore. At Fern Hill they have much to celebrate.

FERN HILL ESTATE

Address: Ingoldby Road, McLaren Flat SA 5171
Phone: (08) 8383 0167
Fax: (08) 8383 0107
Established: 1976
Winemaker: Grant Burge
Principal varieties grown: Chardonnay, Semillon, Cabernet Sauvignon, Shiraz
Average annual crush: 100 tonnes
Average no. cases produced: 5,000

Principal wines & brands	Cellar Potential
Chardonnay	2-5 years
Semillon	2-5 years
Shiraz	2-5 years
Cabernet Sauvignon	2-5 years

Public & trade tours: Yes
Hours open to public: 10am-5pm, daily except Christmas Day and Good Friday
Retail distribution: Fine wine stores and restaurants

Fox Creek Wines

One of McLaren Vales newest wineries is fast forging an enviable reputation, particularly with its red wines, notably its Reserve Shiraz.

Fox Creek is owned by a group of medicos and viticulturist Paul Watts. They are joined by exciting young winemakers Sparky and his wife Sarah Marquis.

The first vintage at Fox Creek was in 1994, but the vineyard was already well established. The first vintage Shiraz won the Annual McLaren Vale Bushing Trophy in 1994, making Sparky and Sarah Bushing King and Queen. The wine has since gone on to win a number of other gold medals. Their 1995 Reserve Shiraz was also very successful being the highest pointed one year old shiraz in the prestigious Qantas Great Australian Shiraz Challenge, a National event open to all winemakers and all vintages. The latest, their 1996 Reserve Shiraz has continued the success and has already won two Trophies and has been named the Penguin Wine Guide Shiraz of the Year for 1997.

Fox Creek also has an excellent Reserve Cabernet Sauvignon and other interesting wines including "Vixen", a Sparkling Cabernets/Shiraz.

The attractive 100 year old stone cottage which houses the cellar door has an open fire for winter and glorious views of the vineyards. Come and picnic beside the lake and enjoy the large variety of bird life on the property.

The vineyard with its Scott Henry trellising seems to be making better wines each vintage. Why not become a Fox Creek preferred customer cardholder and receive their regular newsletter and great wine offers?

FOX CREEK WINES
Address: Malpas Road, Willunga SA 5172
Phone: (08) 8556 2403
Fax: (08) 8556 2104
Established: 1995
Owners: Families Watts, MacKinnon, McDonald, Roberts
Winemakers: Sparky and Sarah Marquis
Principal varieties grown: Shiraz, Cabernet Sauvignon, Cabernet Franc, Merlot, Verdelho, Sauvignon Blanc, Chardonnay, Semillon
Ha under vine: 68
Average no. cases produced: 10,000 in 1997 (increasing)

Principal wines & brands	Cellar Potential
Reserve Shiraz	10-15 years
Reserve Cabernet Sauvignon	10 years
Shiraz-Cabernet	5 years
"Vixen" Sparkling Burgundy	5 years
Verdelho	
Chardonnay	
Sauvignon Blanc	

Public & trade tours: By appointment only
Hours open to public: 11am-5pm, daily
Points of interest: Cellar Door in original Malpas Family Cottage of stone/slate floors. Built circa 1891
Retail distribution: All states except Tasmania

Haselgrove Wines

Haselgrove is a winery on the move in McLaren Vale. Nick Haselgrove is the well credentialled winemaker. His grandfather, Ron Haselgrove put Mildara on the map many decades ago and his great uncle Colin was a winemaking legend at Hardy's and then Reynella.

Nick won the 'Bushing King' title in 1993 with his 1992 Futures shiraz. This is Haselgrove's premium wine sourced from their own vineyard in McLaren Vale. Since 1983 this wine has been pre-sold to the winery's mail-order customers. Basically the buyer commits and pays for three dozen bottles whilst the wine is still maturing in oak. "Futures" is only available this way. Reg Wymond is principle and managing director. Haselgrove's have formed a joint venture with Kay Brothers at Amery and have invested into the winery with winemaking equipment. The Haselgrove wines are certainly among the best in the region. At the cellar door, which is situated at the "Futures" vineyard, Haselgrove run a lovely alfresco luncheon from Wednesday through to Sunday each week. During winter, a wood fire makes a warm cosy atmosphere – in the summer the conservatory overlooking the vineyard is a great place to spend a lazy lunch that could happily drift well into the afternoon. A recent strategic alliance with the progressive Alambie Wines company from Mildura and with large vineyard interests at Koppamurra will help Haselgrove's development.

HASELGROVE
Address: Cnr. Kangarilla and Foggo Roads, McLaren Vale SA 5171
Phone: (08) 8323 8706
Fax: (08) 8323 8049
Email: winery@haselgrove.com.au
WWW: http://www.haselgrove.com.au
Winemaker: Nick Haselgrove
Principal varieties grown: Shiraz, Cabernet Sauvignon, Chardonnay, Merlot, Sauvignon Blanc
Ha under vine: 17
Average annual crush: 400 tonnes
Average no. cases produced: 17,500

Principal wines & brands	Cellar Potential
Reserve Shiraz	10+ years
Cabernet Merlot Shiraz	2-5 years
Chardonnay	2-5 years
Sauvignon Blanc	12 months

Hours open to public: 9am-5pm, weekdays; 10am-5pm, weekends
Points of interest: Cellar Door lunches Wednesday to Sunday
Retail distribution: Cellar Door and Mail Order Sales. Sydney, Melbourne, Adelaide, Brisbane, Gold Coast

Chateau Reynella

One of South Australia's first settlers, John Reynell obtained vines in South Africa en-route to Australia and planted them in the rich soil of Reynella in 1838.

By 1845, he had completed the country's first underground cellar, now known as the 'Old Cave', which, due to its historical importance, has been classified by the National Trust.

After the death of John Reynell, the business became a family company but unfortunately, two world wars exacted a toll on the male line that resulted in the appointment, in 1953, of Colin Haselgrove as managing director of the winery. Under Colin's guidance, Reynella released some excellent red and fortified wines. The Reynella Alicante Flor Sherry, in particular, was one of Australia's best. Similarly, the Vintage Reserve clarets and burgundies released during the 1950's were remarkable wines and generally drastically underpriced. Colin Haselgrove remained at Reynella after the take-over by Hungerford Hill in 1970.

The following year he produced what he considered to be his best vintage and indeed the 1971 Vintage Port and Cabernet Sauvignon are today, considered to be great wines.

However, in the following years, many changes were to occur in corporate management at Reynella.

In 1972 Rothmans purchased a half share in the business and in 1976 became full owners.

Thomas Hardy & Sons purchased the company in 1982 and spent millions of dollars restoring the Chateau, winery and other buildings to their former glory. Having moved their head office and bottling cellars to Reynella. In 1992 Berri Renmano Limited and Hardys merged to form BRL Hardy Limited and the old Reynell homestead houses the company's executive offices and boardroom.

In addition to the careful restoration of the buildings, the century-old botanical gardens planted by John Reynell, have also been rejuvenated and this has resulted in Chateau Reynella becoming one of the most beautiful wineries in Australia.

Chateau Reynella has long been known for its exquisite, long-living vintage ports and its mellow tawny port styles (Old Cave Port). These wines continue to be leaders in their styles and successfully promote the name of Reynella throughout the world.

The winery now produces wines made exclusively from McLaren Vale fruit.

The "Basket Pressed" range of reds feature – Shiraz, Cabernet Merlot and Cabernet Sauvignon. The winemakers have worked closely with the viticulturists monitoring cropping, irrigation and trellising methods to obtain the highest quality fruit. Small open fermenters and the ability to maintain small batches of individual vineyard wine until the blending stage gives maximum flexibility in the quest for quality. The basket press is used to press the skins following fermentation, this process results in fine tannin structure without the bitterness sometimes associated with mechanical pressing. Chateau Reynella reds are big, rich, generous wines typical of McLaren Vale style.

There is also an award winning McLaren Vale Chardonnay in the range that is barrel fermented, stored on lees and a portion undergoes malolactic fermentation resulting in a rich, vanillin, buttery chardonnay style.

The Chateau Reynella renaissance has seen not only the restoration of a great winery, but also the development of a new elegant label along with the launching of an excellent range of table wines.

The return to good management and proficient winemaking has seen the restitution of this winery to its well deserved position as one of the country's leading premium wine producers. The beautiful Reynella complex is only 25 minutes drive from the Adelaide GPO.

The winery has catering facilities for large functions, seminars and conventions, the Thomas Hardy room forming part of the complex. A visit whilst you are in Adelaide is virtually obligatory.

Hardy's Tintara Winery

At 20 years of age, Thomas Hardy arrived in the new colony of South Australia in 1850 with thirty pounds in his pocket. Within 40 years he had built Australia's largest wine company. Along the way, he somehow found time to travel overseas several times, write a book on fruit and wine growing in California, keep extensive diaries and scrapbooks, and educate those people with whom he worked.

Within weeks of his arrival in South Australia, Thomas Hardy obtained a year's work with Walter Reynell at Reynella Farm. Later, while employed on a grazing property at Normanville he became gripped with gold fever and left for the Victorian gold fields, where he was promptly arrested for mining without a licence. Deciding there were easier ways of making money, Hardy persuaded his former employer to let him drive 400 head of cattle to the gold fields, where they were butchered and sold to the miners. This venture was so successful that Hardy repeated the exercise and was then able to return to Adelaide and purchase a property on the banks of the Torrens, which he called 'Bankside'. Vines, fruit and olive trees were planted, cellars were constructed and as soon as the vines began to bear fruit, winemaking commenced.

Hardy's wine quickly found ready markets both locally and in England, giving him the necessary assets to purchase the Tintara Vineyard Company in 1876. The cellars of this new property were full of barrels of rich burgundy, which Hardy sold in England, recouping his purchase price in one year. The company steadily expanded with additional purchases of a bottling plant at Mile End, champagne cellars at Currie Street in Adelaide and a disused flour mill in McLaren Vale.

By 1893, Thomas Hardy controlled the largest wine company in Australia. Thomas Hardy died in 1912, leaving his son Robert in charge of the company. Currently, fourth generation member, Sir James Hardy OBE is on the board of directors of the parent company, the successfully merged BRL Hardy. In 1903, fire destroyed the cellars at Bankside. This fire occurred on a Sunday and as no fire brigade was available to attend, the fire was extinguished by pumping wine onto the flames. Some of the charred casks remain and are used in the maturation of fortified wines at McLaren Vale.

In 1968, Hardy's established extensive vineyards in the Padthaway area, which has become a great source of fruit for their premium table wines. The purchase of the Emu Wine Company in 1976 included the Western Australian Houghton Winery and a large winery at Morphett Vale. The next acquisition was Chateau Reynella in 1982 - ironically, a return of the name Hardy to the winery where Thomas Hardy began his working life in Australia more than 130 years before. In 1992 Thomas Hardy & Sons merged with Berri Renmano Limited to form Australia's second largest wine group, BRL Hardy Limited.

Currently, the flagship wine in Hardy's extensive portfolio is Eileen Hardy. Named after the widow of Tom Mayfield Hardy, the first of this wine, a 1970 McLaren Vale Shiraz, was released in 1973 to honour her 80th birthday. Eileen Hardy Chardonnay was launched in 1986 to partner the Shiraz. In 1994 'Eileen' was joined at the Hardy's red wine pinnacle by the Thomas Hardy Coonawarra Cabernet Sauvignon.

The first four vintages have all won at least one trophy and several gold medals. Other Hardy products that are household names in Australia are – Sir James Cuvee Brut and Brut de Brut, Siegersdorf Rhine Riesling and Chardonnay, the Nottage Hill range, Hardys RR, Whiskers Blake Tawny Port and Black Bottle Brandy.

During 1994/95 large sums of capital were spent expanding the Company's premium vineyard holdings. Hoddles Creek vineyard in the Yarra Valley of Victoria was acquired to supply sparkling wine fruit for the Sir James range including the new Sir James Vintage, a premium Australian sparkling wine. New vineyards in Padthaway, Koppamurra, Furner (towards Robe from Coonawarra in the Woak wine ranges), Coonawarra and Langhorne Creek will supply fruit for existing and planned new labels under the Hardy banner. Consumers can also look forward to some superb new wines from these new properties.

New premiums recently introduced are the Bankside range – Shiraz, Grenache and Chardonnay and the Padthaway range of unwooded Chardonnay and Cabernet Sauvignon.

Hardy's are continuing to produce and market wines of which the company founder would be proud.

The beautiful ironstone Tintara winery in the heart of McLaren Vale, incorporating the town's original mill, has been lovingly restored during the last decade and features a superb cellar door tasting area, brimming over with memorabilia from the company's long and rich history. A pilgrimage to this shrine of wine is a must for any visitor to McLaren Vale.

Maglieri

Arriving in Australia in 1964, Steve Maglieri was among the post-war influx of Italian grape growers, who did such good work in developing McLaren Vale as a premium wine region in the 1950's and 60's.

Their hard work, family values and culture, along with their community spirit has enriched the region great deal, witnessed in many ways, such as in the impressive Italian Bocce and Function Centre alongside the McLaren Flat oval, completed in 1994.

The Maglieri's expanded the plantings of premium grape varieties in McLaren Vale by largely supplying their grapes to the bigger wineries such as Hardy's. Being Italian of course, they had to make their own vino for the casa and the multitudes of family and extended family. They could not resist selling some of the wines, which were of excellent quality and value, to passers-by, thus was born Gully Wines in 1972, changing its name to Maglieri Wines in 1979.

A huge success story for Maglieri has been their excellent market-leading Australian Lambrusco, made in the style of this soft, fruity, slightly sweet Italian red wine. Maglieri's, however, make many seriously great table wines and their highest compliment is the respect they are shown by the other winemakers of the region, both for their absolutely top quality and also for the extraordinary value they represent for the wine lover. Maglieri have won hoards of trophies and gold medals and two terms as McLaren Vale wine busing kings for their wines, and deservedly so. The winery is in the beautiful Blewitt Springs area of the Valley, rising up into the foothills of the Adelaide Hills and reminiscent of the rolling countryside of Tuscany, a fact not lost I am sure on the Maglieri's.

John Loxton is the quiet, hardworking and highly skilled winemaker who has been toiling away in his meticulous fashion for many years. They winery is now ultramodern and crushes over 3,000 tonnes of grapes and is blessed with top class oak and stainless steel storage.

On September 10, 1997 Maglieri's celebrated an incredible success, their 1995 Maglieri Shiraz won the Wine Magazine International Wine Challenge Trophy for the red wine of the year.

In a fortunate coincidence some month or so ago we photographed the ebullient Steve in his expansive Willunga vineyards with his award winning shiraz where it was born – two hours later he was on the plane on his way to accept the award.

The four ranges of Maglieri wines start with two lambruscos, Amabile (red) and Bianco (white), followed by the 'Ingleburne Estate' range of affordable premium table wines from the Maglieri's Ingleburne Vineyards and includes a semillon, shiraz and a cabernet sauvignon. The Maglieri Label and the flagship Steve Maglieri Label.

MAGLIERI WINES
Address: Douglas Gully Road, McLaren Flat SA 5171
Phone: (08) 8383 0177
Fax: (08) 8383 0136
Established: 1972
Winemaker: John Loxton
Principal varieties grown: Shiraz, Cabernet Sauvignon, Semillon, Merlot, Riesling, Chardonnay, Traminer, Sauvignon Blanc, Grenache
Ha under vine: 150
Average annual crush: 3,500 tonnes
Average no. cases produced: 250,000

Principal wines & brands	Cellar Potential
Shiraz	5-10 years
Cabernet Sauvignon	5-10 years
Ingleburne Unwooded Semillon	2-5 years
Ingleburne Cabernet	5-10 years
Chardonnay	2-5 years
Semillon	2-5 years
Cabernet Merlot	5-10 years

Public & trade tours: Trade tours by appointment only
Hours open to public: 9.30am-4pm, Mon-Sat; 11am-4.30pm, Sunday
Points of interest: Large Picnic Area, Ample Parking and Facilities. Wine Tasting and Mail Order Service.
Retail distribution: Maglieri Wines, QLD, NSW, WA; Tasmanian Fine Wines, TAS; Alexander & Paterson, VIC; Oak Barrel Wines, ACT; Festival City, SA, NT. Wine exported to Switzerland, Germany, UK, Singapore, America, Hong Kong, Canada, Taiwan, Thailand, NZ

Marienberg

Ursula Pridham became Australia's first woman winemaker back in the late 1960's when she started her own winery at Happy Valley.

After 25 years of excellent winemaking and hard work she decided to step back a little. Sydney wine dynamo, Terry Hill, saw an ideal opportunity and late in 1990 he bought the Marienberg brand.

Coinciding with this move, he also bought the old 'Limeburners Cottage', opposite The Barn Restaurant in McLaren Vale. The Marienberg range has expanded, with six table wines led by a very elegant chardonnay and a rich round cabernet sauvignon. These are complemented by a non-vintage pinot noir/chardonnay methode champenoise under the name 'Nicolle' after one of Terry and Jill Hill's daughters, plus a 12 year old Tawny Port. The wines are from selected vineyards in the McLaren Vale area and made under the watchful eye

of Grant Burge, an old school days chum of Terry's.

The Marienberg labels really stand out with their art deco inspired look. I have been singularly impressed by all the wines, particularly their very approachable style, delivering clean crisp flavours, mouthfilling but extremely well balanced. The restrained use of top quality oak in some of the wines is particularly well handled.

Marienberg is back to stay, why not make her acquaintance when you see her next, or drop into her cute cottage for a taste or two?

MARIENBERG WINE COMPANY

Address: 2 Chalk Hill Road, McLaren Vale SA 5171
Phone: (08) 8323 9666
Fax: (08) 8323 9600
Established: 1966
Winemaker: Grant Burge
Principal varieties grown: Grapes supplied under contract - Chardonnay, Cabernet Sauvignon, Shiraz
Average no. cases produced: 21,000

Principal wines & brands	Cellar Potential
Chardonnay	2-5 years
Shiraz	5-10 years
Semillon/Chardonnay	2-5 years
Classic Riesling	2-5 years
Methode Champenoise	2-5 years
12 YO Tawny Port	2-5 years

Public & trade tours: Yes
Hours open to public:
10am-5pm, weekdays except Christmas Day and Good Friday
Retail distribution:
Fine wine stores and restaurants

Hugo Winery

I might start this expose on Hugo Wines with a few words of philosophy from winemaker John Hugo – "the McLaren Vale region is a region of small winemakers, people who know their craft – ply it well – I firmly believe that we have to be specialists, people who pick a path in wine production and then follow that course". John Hugo's philosophy is basically to use his own grapes from his 30 acre vineyard, established by his father, Colin in 1950. John is a fastidious viticulturist and the quality of his grapes are renowned in the region. He first began work in the family enterprise in 1970 and established the winery in 1982.

He has just planted another 18 acres of vines, which will come into bearing in about 1997. His reds, a cabernet sauvignon and a shiraz, are rich and full-bodied in the tradition of the region and there is also a dry rhine riesling, and more recently, a full-bodied chardonnay. The tawny port from the 'Solero' started by John in the 1970's is worth the trip to the cellar door to find. The winery is the highest in the McLaren Vale and has a wonderful panoramic view.

HUGO WINES

Address: Rsd Elliott Road, McLaren Flat SA 5171
Phone: (08) 8383 0098
Fax: (08) 8383 0446
Established: 1982
Owner: John Hugo
Winemaker: John Hugo
Principal varieties grown: Shiraz, Cabernet Sauvignon, Chardonnay, Sauvignon Blanc, Riesling, Tawny Port
Ha under vine: 20
Average no. cases produced: 5,000

Principal wines & brands	Cellar Potential
Shiraz	4-6 years
Chardonnay	3-5 years
Unwooded Chardonnay	2 years
Cabernet Sauvignon	4-6 years
Riesling	2-5 years
Tawny Port	10+ years
Sauvignon Blanc	3-5 years

Public & trade tours: By appointment only
Hours open to public: 10.30am-5pm, Sun-Fri; Noon-5pm, Saturday
Retail distribution: SA, NSW, VIC, NZ, Hong Kong

Maxwell Wines

Mark and Ken Maxwell established Maxwell Wines in 1979. Maxwellís new home is truly remarkable built into the chalk hill looking over Manning Park towards the southern fringes of the McLaren Vale township. Mark Maxwell have planned this bold move for many years even planting a hedge maze

some seven years ago which should be ready as a visitors amazing entrance in a year or so. The pathway from the maze leads to an ancient mushroom cave which Mark is connecting into the lower level barrel ageing cellars. The winery complex has an impressive function area, terrace and fully-equipped kitchen.

During the nine months of the year between vintages, winery equipment usually remains idle. Maxwell's however, utilise their winery throughout these months for the production of mead (honey wine). Meads are released, including a standard mead which makes a delightful cool mixed drink; a spiced mead which can be served hot; and

a liqueur mead which contains a higher degree of alcohol and is a delicious after-dinner drink.

Mark Maxwell's dynamic drive and innovative style will make Maxwell Wines' future exciting indeed, in their amazing cellars that just seem to have mushroomed from nowhere!!

MAXWELL WINES

Address: Olivers Road, McLaren Vale SA 5171
Phone: (08) 8323 8200
Fax: (08) 8323 8900
Established: 1979
Owner: Maxwell Family
Winemaker: Mark Maxwell
Principal varieties grown: Shiraz, Cabernet Sauvignon, Merlot, Sauvignon Blanc
Ha under vine: 8
Average no. cases produced: 6,000 wine, 6,000 mead

Principal wines & brands	Cellar Potential
Unwooded Semillon	1-10 years
Sauvignon Blanc	now
Chardonnay	1-6 years
Cabernet Merlot	1-3 years
Lime Cave Cabernet Sauvignon	7-10 years
Ellen Street Shiraz	8-15 years
Maxwell Mead (3 Varieties)	

Public & trade tours: Trade tours by appointment only
Hours open to public: 10am-5pm, daily
Points of interest: Function room for groups with resident caterer for Quality Food

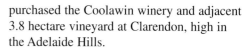

Jesse Norman arrived in Australia from England in 1851 and very soon purchased seven hectares of land near the town of Thebarton, on which he planted vines.

A winery was later established at Underdale and another vineyard planted at Sturt. Both vineyards prospered. Unfortunately with the spread of Adelaide's urban areas the company's land was zoned residential by the South Australian Housing Trust, and compulsorily purchased. As a result, 52 hectares were purchased at Gawler River, and planted to vines. This vineyard still exists today, and is now known as Evanston Estate.

Normans continued to develop slowly until 1982 when the company was bought by the Horlin-Smith family. Having had a century-long association with the hospitality industry, the Horlin-Smiths were already well acquainted with many aspects of wine-making and marketing. Irvine, long-time family friend and creator of Hardys famous Siegersdorf Rhine Riesling, was asked to join the management team.

Following the modernisation of the Underdale winery a new high quality range of wines was developed which quickly won wide acclaim.

Sadly, it was soon discovered that facilities at Underdale were inadequate when coping with greater volumes of fruit and high levels of production.

Following an extensive search, Normans purchased the Coolawin winery and adjacent 3.8 hectare vineyard at Clarendon, high in the Adelaide Hills.

Renamed Normans Clarendon Winery, the new property was soon fitted with the most modern winemaking equipment and ranks with the most efficient wineries in the state. All of Normans wines are now made at Clarendon. The talented and enthusiastic Roger Harbord heads the winemaking staff.

Located near the crest of Chandlers Hill, Normans winery commands magnificent views of the nearby coastline and the rolling hills of Clarendon. High altitude and onshore winds combine to bring the cool climate ideal for the production of premium table wines. Consequently, the vineyard next to the winery is planted with classic grape varieties – cabernet sauvignon, shiraz and chardonnay. Additional fruit is brought in from growers at McLaren Vale.

The range includes sparkling, fortified and table wines.

All the table wines have been consistently of very high quality. The Normans Chandlers Hill range represents great value for money and the exclusive Chais Clarendon range of three wines, a shiraz, a cabernet sauvignon and a chardonnay, rank on the very highest rung of Australia's wines.

On a recent visit I tasted the exciting 1997 Unwooded which has already won 2 gold medals and a 10,000 dozen export order to England. Like its makers it is confident, positive and smiling.

Normans is now a public company. The influx of much needed capital has catapulted the company to even greater heights.

NORMANS CLARENDON WINERY
Address: Grants Gully Road, Clarendon SA 5157
Direction: Adelaide Hills overlooking Adelaide
Phone: (08) 8383 6138
Fax: (08) 8383 6089
Email: info@normans-wines.com.au
WWW: http://www.normans-wines.com.au
Established: 1853
Winemakers: Chief: Roger Harbord. Peter Fraser
Principal varieties grown: Chardonnay, Verdelho, Chenin Blanc, Cabernet Sauvignon, Merlot, Shiraz, Pinot Noir
Ha under vine: 55
Average annual crush: 2,000 tonnes

Principal wines & brands	Cellar Potential
Chais Clarendon Shiraz	10 years
Chais Clarendon Cabernet Sauvignon	10 years
Chais Clarendon Chardonnay	5 years
Old Vine Shiraz	8 years
Unwooded Chardonnay	3 years
Conquest NV Brut	3 years

Public & trade tours: Trade tours by appointment only
Hours open to public: 10am-5pm, Mon-Sat; 11am-5pm, Sunday
Retail distribution: All major retailers

Ingoldby

In May 1995, Mildara Blass Limited purchased Ingoldby Wines of the McLaren Vale and whilst this acquisition was primarily driven by the availability of premium quality fruit, they quickly realised that Ingoldby as a brand presented a great opportunity. Much of this is to the credit of the previous owner and winemaker, Walter Clappis.

Walter is one of those characters who is truly larger than life – his infectious enthusiasm, love of life and the buzz he got from producing great wine is a joy to behold. Walter began working with Jim Ingoldby at Ingoldby Wines in 1981. Jim established the winery in 1971 and the Ingoldby name has been associated with the McLaren Vale region since the turn of the century.

In 1982, Jim was looking at a change in lifestyle and to go and live at his beloved Walker's Flat on the River Murray. Ingoldby became the only winery in the region to win the Dan Murphy Trophy three times for the best Cabernet Sauvignon, awarded each year at the McLaren Bushing Festival. His whites also tended to be rich and round, appealing to the red wine lover. Now under the guidance of Mildara Blass Limited, Ingoldby has been released nationally.

Ingoldby Wines will continue to reflect the individuality and distinctiveness that were their signature under Jim Ingoldby and Walter Clappis – full, rich and round wines of distinct flavour and character.

INGOLDBY WINERY
Address: Kangarilla Road, McLaren Vale SA 5171
Phone: (08) 8323 8853
Fax: (08) 8323 8271
Established: 1973
Owner: Mildara Blass Limited
Winemaker: Phil Reschke
Ha under vine: 7+ long term contract growers
Average no. cases produced: 20,000

Principal wines & brands	Cellar Potential
Ingoldby Chardonnay	2-4 years
Ingoldby Sauvignon Blanc	2-4 years
Ingoldby Grenache	3-4 years
Ingoldby Shiraz	3-5 years
Ingoldby Cabernet Sauvignon	3-5 years

Public & trade tours: Trade tours by appointment only
Hours open to public: 10am-5pm, daily

Pertaringa

Pertaringa is an Aboriginal word meaning "belonging to the Hills".The company, owned by Geoff Hardy and Ian Leask, has extensive vineyards and is one of the area's largest suppliers.

Pertaringa grapes are sold to a number of leading wine companies.

The first parcel of land was purchased in 1981 and was planted mainly with shiraz grapes. Only nine hectares of shiraz still remain, other vines having been grafted with chardonnay, sauvignon blanc, white frontignac, semillon, cabernet sauvignon and cabernet franc.

The 1990 vintage with a cabernet sauvignon was their first commercial effort and an outstanding wine each year a Cabernet Sauvignon, a Shiraz, a Sauvignon Blanc and an exciting 1994 Barrel Fermented Semillon.

Pertaringa won the inaugural South Australian Vineyard of the year in 1990 and their wines have proven to be as successful as the vineyard. Geoff Hardy and Ian Leask have become a welcome and interesting addition the winemaking fraternity of McLaren Vale.

McLaren Vale Olive Groves

Where the vine grows so does the olive. In the traditional wine growing countries of France, Spain, Greece and Italy the olive groves blend happily with the vineyards.
The history of olives in McLaren Vale goes back to my own great great grandfather, Thomas Hardy, who planted olive trees on all the roads and spare land on his property, Tintara, and advised his neighbours to do likewise. The beautiful olives, olive oil and other products were not only a great adjunct to the table but added a welcome extra source of income. Some of these century-old trees can still be seen around the region.
In 1989 Guy and Adele Lloyd bought the olive groves near to the Lloyd family winery, Coriole. David Lloyd has taken over the management and continues to develop the 56 acres of olives so that today the McLaren Vale Olive Groves are producing over 10 different varieties of table and oil olives.
The table olives, principally the Greek Kalamata olives are pickled slowly using a traditional method, whereby fresh water is used to remove the acid, followed by a relatively low salt brine and vinegar mixture. The Kalamata olives are also made into a pesto and flavoured with garlic. This is now used in a number of local restaurants.
The cold pressed extra virgin olive oil is processed in the old oil press using traditional woven mats.
The olive harvest begins in April just as the grape harvest ends and it is in perfect sympathy with wine. The olive grove is now producing vinegar from locally made wines and supplies these through the beautiful Cottage on the property along with locally made jams and preserves, arts and crafts. The health benefits of olives and olive oil, especially when produced in the traditional manner used at the McLaren Vale Olive Groves, are well documented.
During the season, tours are available through the groves and the factory by

previous appointment. The attractive cottage next to the factory also serves morning and afternoon teas along with light lunches.
In front of the cottage is a gorgeous gazebo which is available for groups to book for a barbecue or for "Olive Pickers Lunches", 24 hours notice is required.
Brian Swanson is the caring guardian of the Groves and has real green fingers growing also all the herbs for the products.

Brian made a recent trip through the mediterranean olive capitals of Spain, Portugal and Morocco, he found nothing to come close to his own grove's quality.
Why not complete your visit to McLaren Vale with this unique experience and make that magic connection between the olive and the vine. It will do you the world of good!
Telephone - 08 8323 8792, Fax - 08 8373 5030, Mobile - 0414 323 879

Mount Hurtle – Geoff Merrill

One of the most beautiful old gravity flow wineries of the last century is Mount Hurtle which was built in 1897 by Mostyn Owen. The winery was disused and storing hay when Geoff Merrill, then the high profile winemaker at Chateau Reynella, bought it back in the early 80's. The winery, just down the road from Reynella, was most convenient for making his own wines.

The Mount Hurtle winery is a picture. A small lake reflects the winery as one enters the tree-lined drive. The front section of the winery has been turned into a splendid function area with polished wooden floors and a balcony where one can view the working winery and barrel cellar below. Many weddings and other events now take place in this stunning setting.

Geoff is certainly not the shy and retiring type, with his huge handlebar moustache enhancing his happy smiling face, he is a serious, fastidious winemaker and all his wines reflect this care in their great balance and sophisticated styles. The Mount Hurtle and the super premium Geoff Merrill reds are often in the more herbaceous spectrum, with fine tannins and clean varietal characteristics. The whites are rich and ripe in style, showing classy wood treatments.

Geoff is a passionate cricket fan and a close friend of cricket legends Ian Botham and Bob Willis. Every year they hold a charity cricket event in England, sponsored by Geoff and Mount Hurtle, which raises hundreds of thousands of dollars for charity. Well done Geoff Merrill!

Pirramimma

Situated on the Willunga Plains, the Pirramimma property was purchased by Mr. A.C. Johnston in 1892. Pirramimma is still wholly owned and run by the Johnston family, Alex being the General Manager and Charles Sturt University graduate Geoff, the Winemaker. Pirramimma's first wine was made in 1900, the original cellars being constructed two or three years prior to that date.

The early success of Pirramimma was due to the company's excellent fortified wines and full bodied reds. Their current range illustrates the present day developments of these wines. Geoff has also been building up a commercial vineyard of petit verdot from a small number of original cuttings. The recent bottlings of this distinctive red wine have been successful with gold and silver medals being awarded at recent Australian wine shows.

Most of the Johnston wines until the early 1970's were sold in bulk, a great proportion being exported to England.

Pirramimma released their first rhine riesling in 1979 and their first chardonnay two years later. Both of these wines are full flavoured, well-balanced and splendid examples of the potential of McLaren Vale fruit.

Shortly a semillon produced from Geoff's Kuitpo vineyard will be added to the range showing the delicate fruit intensity from this cool region in the Adelaide Hills.

After experimenting with the various aspects of his craft, winemaker Geoff Johnston has achieved another success with his cabernet sauvignon.

Pirramimma and the Johnston Family have large vineyard holdings in the region and pick the best grapes for their own label before selling the rest of the crop to other premium makers.

Just prior to the 1995 vintage, they completed a large and innovative barrel ageing cellar, cut into the hillside above the winery was constructed with rammed earth.

The very thick walls offer ideal insulation for the cellaring of the wine, its light ochre colour also blends happily into the hillside. The cellars have since been doubled in size and further additions are planned.

In a very sensible move, the family converted a number of 1,000 gallon French oak vats, built by Babidge Coopers in 1904, into 65 gallon hogsheads (the Babidges did this job too). The 1990 Shiraz, bottled to celebrate Pirramimma's centenary, went into these hogsheads. The wine is one of the best reds ever made in McLaren Vale.

Pirramimma are undoubtedly on the move and we the wine drinkers are the beneficiaries.

McLarens on the Lake

In the early 1980's, entrepreneur Jack Weinart built a splendid complex on the outskirts of McLaren Vale, on the road to McLaren Flat, which he called it 'Hazelmere Estate'. The complex included a modern winery, a la carte restaurant, function and souvenir facility along with 30 large attractive accommodation suites. The Victorian/Australian architecture reminds me somewhat of the grand old wineries at Rutherglen, reminiscent of a bygone era.

The whole property is sensitively and beautifully landscaped around a man-made lake, all the huge old redgums have been retained and the cry of the corellas at dawn and dusk is a pleasant reminder that one is among nature in a beautiful country region.

The bird life on the lake is multitudinous, ducks, swans, cygnets, even seagulls happily share this large expanse of water as it blends more naturally into the environment each year.

The name 'Hazelmere' was changed some years ago to 'McLarens on the Lake'.

All this aside, the McLarens on the Lake complex is idyllic and runs like a well-oiled machine. Now once again under the ownership of Andrew Garrett with the assistance of wine marketing guru Brian Miller they are launching an exciting new McLarens On The Lake label and range of wines featuring the famous 'McLarens Duck'. Knowing Andrew's astute judging of the wine consumers mood and tastes, I am sure they will be highly successful. The wines, on previewing them, are chocked full of flavour and with excellent style.

McLarens on the Lake is superb, the Courtyard Conservatory Restaurant, the more formal McLarens Room Restaurant and in the seminar function area weddings abound and businesses almost queue to use the great facilities. Having often stayed in the suites, I can highly recommend them. Do not pass by McLarens whilst in the region.

Seaview

In 1850, George Manning planted vines on his newly purchased Hope Farm in McLaren Vale. A winery and cellars were built 40 years later.

The name Seaview was coined by the owners Ben Chaffey and his partner friend Henry Edwards, who found they could see St Vincents Gulf from various hill crests on the property.

The winery itself sits attractively, surrounded by vines in the centre of a bowl-shaped valley, splendidly landscaped with vines. The Penfold group purchased Seaview in 1985, and Seaview is now in fact the biggest selling wine brand in Australia, a testimony to the value-packed wines constantly streaming out under this prestige label, now under the control of the successful and well-managed Southcorp. The Seaview Cabernet Sauvignon has developed a reputation as the 'value for money' cabernet of Australia, and is also often awarded gold medals in Australian and International wine competitions.

The humble shiraz is also an extraordinarily good wine for its price - look out for it.

The Seaview whites have also added a lustre to the wines of the company in recent times, with the chardonnay winning a prestige International award in 1994. Its rich melon and stone fruit flavours and great balance are consistent from year to year.

The hidden gem of the Seaview whites has been their Seaview Semillon Sauvignon Blanc. Again a wine to look out for, the Seaview Sauvignon Blanc is a definite leader in this growing varietal wine style.

A milestone in 1994 was the release of two super premium reds under the Edwards and Chaffey banner, a shiraz and a cabernet sauvignon and a chardonnay all made by the Seaview winemaking team from the best grapes available in McLaren Vale in an "absolutely no expense spared" style.

They are sensational wines and have been joined by a Pinot Chardonnay Methode Champenoise 'Edwards & Chaffey', the pinnacle of the Seaview sparkling wine stable and Australia's biggest selling sparkling wines.

The Seaview range as value for money premium wines which are a credit to the Australian wine industry, assuring themselves of continued success.

Richard Hamilton

Owner and Manager of wineries and vineyards at Willunga in McLaren Vale and Leconfield in Coonawarra, Dr. Richard Hamilton is both great-great-grandson and namesake to one of the founders of South Australia's wine industry. Richard Hamilton (senior) established the Ewell Vineyard in 1837, one year before John Reynell planted his first vines at Reynella. Hamilton's Leconfield winery and vineyard were founded by Richard's uncle, Syd Hamilton in 1972. Richard's father, Burton, affectionately known as 'Bert', who spent the later years of his life helping Richard, was a vigneron, and from this long family commitment to the industry, Dr. Hamilton has re-established the proud tradition founded by his ancestor.

The vineyard at Willunga was replanted in 1972. The first wines to be released under the 'Richard Hamilton' label, were made in the same year from local fruit. All Richard Hamilton wines are now made exclusively from fruit grown in the company's various vineyards in the McLaren Vale and Willunga area. The range consists largely of table wines, with an excellent Chardonnay leading the way. Richard Hamilton has been instrumental in the revival of Grenache as a premium variety in the region from a very old bush vine Grenache, chiefly from 'Burton's Vineyard one of the old family properties. The Burton's Vineyard also features 40% old vine Shiraz, it's a great drop.

Another vineyard designated wine is the 'Farm Block Semillon" a rich and character-ful white that benefits from a few years in the cellar.

The 'Hut Block' Cabernet Sauvignon from old dry grown Cabernet planted near the Wirra Wirra Winery, is a substantial wine that shows the style of McLaren Vale to perfection. Several fortified wines are also being produced. The star label is Richard Hamilton Chardonnay, which was one of the first wines of this grape variety to be made in McLaren Vale. Like many of the wines, the Chardonnay is aged in small oak casks, imparting it with complex flavours and characters. Other whites comprising the range are: a Rhine Riesling and a sweeter style Auslese Riesling and Sauterne.

Wines are made by Ralph Fowler at Dr. Hamilton's sister winery Leconfield at Coonawarra, and ably marketed by Dr. Hamilton and his team, including the dynamic Darren Gall. Over the years when the demands of Richard's surgical practice became too great, his father Bert lent a hand working right up until his death at 89 years of age in 1994.

As in times gone by, this family is keeping alive the noble traditions of the South Australian wine industry.

RICHARD HAMILTON

Address: Main Road, Willunga SA 5172
Direction: 4km south of McLaren Vale township
Phone: (08) 8556 2288
Fax: (08) 8556 2868
Established: 1972
Owner: Dr Richard Hamilton
Winemaker: Ralph Fowler
Principal varieties grown: Chardonnay, Shiraz, Merlot, Cabernet Sauvignon, Grenache
Average no. cases produced: 30,000

Principal wines & brands	Cellar Potential
Chardonnay	5-8 years
Chenin Blanc	2-5 years
Hut Block Cabernets	5-8 years
Old Vines Shiraz	10-15 years
Burton's Vineyard Grenache Shiraz	10-15 years
Merlot	8-10 years

Public & trade tours: Yes
Hours open to public: 10am-5pm, daily
Points of interest: Museum of Hamilton Ewell history in winemaking since 1837 and our 105 year old Shiraz Vines. Oldest Chardonnay Vines in district (25 years old)
Retail distribution: All discerning stockists of Fine Wine and Leading Restaurant

Ryecroft – Rosemount

Frederick Wilkinson came to South Australia in 1879 from Manchester in England to work for the Bank of South Australia. He decided banking was not for him and in 1884 he purchased 160 acres at McLaren Flat.

Planting began in 1886, with the Cellars in readiness for the 1895 vintage, including a large underground cellar where 800 gallon vats kept the temperature of the fermenting wines in check, long before the days of refrigeration. Much of the original winery remains intact today.

Wilkinson's only son, Lewis, lost his life in the First World War and the winery was sold in 1919 to James Ingoldby, a 23 year old survivor of the war, and his father-in-law T.C. Walker, chairman of the Lion Brewery and the General Navigation Co. They expanded the vineyard area to 65 hectares, with the help of the stalwart Aubrey 'Aub' Chapman who had remained on from Wilkinson's days.

The wines, mainly full-bodied reds from the rich ironstone-riddled clay soils, went from strength to strength.

Ingoldby's eldest son tragically died in the Second World War, but his younger son, Jim, a budding artist, survived several years in the Air Force and came back to finish his arts degree, but the pull of Ryecroft was too strong. In 1970 after building Ryecroft into a specialised premium red producer, Jim Ingoldby junior sold to Reed Consolidated, who subsequently sold to Gilbey's, neither of whom really understood the quality wine business. It was not until Rosemount wines purchased Ryecroft in the early 1990's that the winery's direction was redefined and a program of expansion initiated.

Today, under winemaker, Charles Whish and viticulturist, Paul Buttery, Ryecroft is growing quickly in the making and marketing of the highest possible quality table wines.

During vintage it's a wonderful heady experience seeing and smelling all that fermenting red in the traditional open fermenters. It is the most comforting and uplifting experience any human being could wish for.

RYECROFT - ROSEMOUNT

Address: Ingoldby Road, McLaren Flat SA 5171
Phone: (08) 8383 0001
Fax: (08) 8383 0456
Established: 1888
Owner: Rosemount Estate
Winemaker: Charles Whish

Principal varieties grown: Chardonnay, Cabernet Sauvignon, Shiraz, Merlot, Sauvignon Blanc, Semillon
Ha under vine: 40
Average annual crush: 2,000-5,000 tonnes
Average no. cases produced: 100,000

Principal wines & brands	Cellar Potential
Ryecroft Traditional	5-10 years
Ryecroft Contemporary	5-10 years
Ryecroft Flame Tree Shiraz	5-10 years
Ryecroft Flame Tree Chardonnay	2-5 years
Ryecroft Flame Tree White	2-5 years
Ryecroft Flame Tree Red	2-5 years

Public & trade tours: Trade tours by appointment only
Hours open to public: 10am-5pm, weekdays; 12pm-5pm, weekends
Retail distribution: National Distribution

Scarpantoni

Dom Scarpantoni arrived in Australia as part of the post-war immigration movement into this country. He secured a job at the vineyards of David Hardy and shelter in a shed in the backyard of Bob Hagley, manager of the Hardy's Tintara Winery in the middle of the township of McLaren Vale.

Dom is an incredibly hard worker and blessed with a most helpful and pleasant nature. Gradually, as he established himself in his new land, he also began planting his own vineyards at McLaren Flat. During the 1960's and 70's he supplied grapes to Hardy's and others but as the wheel of fortune of wine accelerated he decided to extend his own family winemaking enterprise and build his own winery which he opened in 1979.

Today Scarpantoni is an expanding premium wine business and Dom has taken a little step back, leaving the day-to-day business to his two sons Michael and Filipo and daughter Mirella, who graduated from the Roseworthy wine-marketing course. All fortunately have inherited the charm and hardworking nature of their parents. Many times I have enjoyed their special brand of sincere hospitality, recently I dropped into the winery for a quick visit, which turned into an impromptu alfresco lunch. A country style veal casserole prepared by Dom's wife Paula, a culinary treat, accompanied by a couple of the most delicious, truly opulent reds I have ever tasted. Their 1996 Shiraz and 1996 Cabernet Sauvignon, both just bottled, they are knockouts. As we talked and reminisced over the renaissance of McLaren Vale over the last few decades, there was a very special feeling and a sense we have all enjoyed something very strong in the welding of the cultures of Europe and Australia, and the richness this has brought to not only our wine industry, but to our whole nation. Long live the Scarpantoni's and all these European families who have enriched our lives in Australia so much.

SCARPANTONI

Address: Scarpantoni Drive McLaren Flat SA 5171
Phone: (08) 8383 0186
Fax: (08) 8383 0490
Established: 1979
Winemakers: Michael and Filippo Scarpantoni
Principal varieties grown: Cabernet Sauvignon, Shiraz, Chardonnay, Sauvignon Blanc, Gamay, Merlot, Riesling
Ha under vine: 32
Average annual crush: 200-250 tonnes
Average no. cases produced: 15,000

Principal wines & brands	Cellar Potential
Cabernet Sauvignon	20 years
Shiraz	20 years
Sauvignon Blanc	1-2 years
School Block	2-12 years
Gamay	2-5 years
Black Tempest Sparkling Burgundy	3-6 years
Botrytis Riesling	10-15 years
Unwooded Chardonnay	2-3 years
Wooded Chardonnay	4-8 years

Hours open to public: 10am-5pm, weekdays; 11am-5pm, weekends
Retail distribution: Cellar Door and Mail Order sales. VIC, NSW, QLD, SA

Shottesbrooke

Nick and Chris Holmes now have a splendid home for their Shottesbrooke wines. This sensitively and cleverly conceived state-of-the-art winery fits beautifully into its vineyard setting towards the hills from McLaren Flat. This is one of the most impressive new wineries I have seen in this country. Nick studied at Roseworthy, graduating in 1971. After five years wine-making in Clare, he took off overseas where he experienced a great deal of winemaking before returning to Australia. In 1981, he purchased a property at Myponga in the southern Adelaide Hills, naming it after the Parish of Shottesbrooke in England, where one of his ancestors had been the vicar. Nick planted 20 acres to vines, including cabernet sauvignon, sauvignon blanc, merlot, malbec and chardonnay. The first wines were released in 1984.Nick was for many years the winemaker at Ryecroft, where he also made the Shottesbrooke wines. Shottesbrooke is now a true boutique winery in its new home. Why not drop in and see the Holmes' and taste their great wine. Don't forget to stock up - their merlot is a knockout.

SHOTTESBROOKE

Address: 1 Bagshaws Road, McLaren Flat SA 5171
Phone: (08) 8383 0002
Fax: (08) 8383 0222
Established: 1981
Owner: Nick Holmes
Winemaker: Nick Holmes
Principal varieties grown: Sauvignon Blanc, Cabernet Sauvignon, Merlot, Chardonnay, Shiraz
Ha under vine: 20

Principal wines & brands	Cellar Potential
Shottesbrooke	
Cabernet/Merlot	5-10 years
Merlot	2-5 years
Shiraz	5-10 years
Sauvignon Blanc	2-3 years
Chardonnay	2-5 years

Hours open to public: 10am-4.30pm, weekdays; 10am-5pm, weekends and public holidays
Points of interest: Creek, Picnic Areas
Retail distribution: All States of Australia, UK

Wayne Thomas Wines

Wayne "Thommo" Thomas and his wife Pat are two real "troupers" of the wine industry. They truly enjoy their vocation and those it brings them in contact with. Their friendly open and gregarious natures definitely shine through in their wines – complete with a star on the label.

Wayne's winemaking career began at Stonyfell in 1961 and led onto studies at Roseworthy in 1964. Stints at Ryecroft and Saltram led to a consultancy business in the mid 1970's.

In 1975 Wayne and Pat set up "Fern Hill" Winery winning 5 trophies and 140 medals over 20 vintages. After selling Fern Hill in 1994 they set up the Wayne Thomas label and have just found a home, the old Maxwell Winery on Kangarilla Road as it leaves McLaren Vale township. They have done a great job in refurbishing and re-enliving the cellar and the cellar door is most tastefully appointed.

The wines, a cabernet sauvignon, shiraz, chardonnay and a sauvignon blanc are all excellent and will be joined soon by a methode champenoise chardonnay. Pat must have her 'elevenses' – and so should you – why not with the Thomas's – I certainly do.

WAYNE THOMAS WINES

Address: 26 Kangarilla Road, McLaren Vale SA 5171
Phone: (08) 8323 9737
Fax: (08) 8323 9737
Established: 1994
Owners: Pat and Wayne Thomas
Winemaker: Wayne Thomas
Average no. cases produced: 5,000

Principal wines & brands	Cellar Potential
Chardonnay	5+ years
Sauvignon Blanc	3-5 years
Shiraz	7-10 years
Cabernet Sauvignon	7-10 years
Premium Brut	

Public & trade tours: Trade tours
Hours open to public: Noon-5pm, daily
Retail distribution: Liquor outlets and Restaurants. Represented by agents in QLD, NSW, VIC, TAS, WA

Tatachilla

Tatachilla has happily gained a new lease of life. During vintage time in 1995, the restored cellars were re-opened by the Premier of South Australia, Dean Brown, and blessed by the Archbishops of Adelaide, Ian George, and Father Paul Cleary.

One could not help feeling that at last, Tatachilla was sailing on the right course. The last two years of exciting wines have born out this fact.

The events that were to create Tatachilla began late in the last century, when Horace Pridmore bought land at McLaren Vale and using wattle slabs built a small cellar in 1901. His brother Cyril joined him from England, they bought a property in the main street of the town and constructed stone cel-

London represent the commitment to excellence in both viticulture and winemaking. Tatachilla Winery has quickly claimed its place in the Australian wine industry earning recognition in many forms. In December 1996 prestigious food and wine magazine Vogue Entertaining nominated Tatachilla as 'Winery of the Year'. Next was a scoop in the pool of medals at the London International Wine Challenge, of the six wines entered all were awarded medals including a Gold Medal for Partners. In September 1997 Tatachilla Winery was named National Winner of the Federal New Exporters awards by the Australian British Chamber of Commerce, a month later Senior Winemaker Michael Fragos was crowned Bushing King for his Tatachilla 1996 McLaren Vale Chardonnay. The wine was judged Best Wine of the Show at the McLaren Vale 1997 Wine Show, winning two trophies and earning Michael the coveted title of McLaren Vale Bushing King.

Michael Fragos was born in McLaren Vale and literally grew up amongst the vines in his father's vineyard. Surrounded by grape growers and winemakers it wasn't a difficult decision to become a winemaker. A Bachelor of Science degree and a Graduate Diploma in Winemaking provided Michael with the technical ability to oversee the entire wine production at Tatachilla. However his passion is for the backbone red varieties of McLaren Vale; Grenache and Shiraz. Careful vineyard selection, small batch ferments and fastidious blending enable him to craft wines that capture the essence of McLaren Vale. Michael is quick to point out the guidance offered by high profile international winemaker Daryl Groom and support from winemaker Justin McNamee, success has not come in isolation.

In chatting with Michael after his crowning as Bushing King this is what he had to say "it is all starting to come together. Two major factors have enabled us to improve the wines; experience over the last four vintages has shown us where the best fruit is, so we spend more time in the vineyards, work with out growers and keep these parcels separate at harvest. We have also spent time setting up trials of small batch ferments. Our aim is to make a wine that has great complexity and flavour rather than pure varietal character. We want to create a wine that the consumers will find challenging".

lars, calling the winery 'The Wattles'. The original foundation stone was unearthed during recent renovations and has been restored to its rightful place.

Since the launch of the modern day Tatachilla in March 1995 the team headed by Vic Zerella and Tatachilla's CEO, Keith Smith have gathered accolades from around the globe. Gold Medals in Australia and

---

TATACHILLA WINERY
Address: 51 Main Road, McLaren Vale SA 5171
Phone: (08) 8323 8656
Fax: (08) 8323 9096
Established: 1901
Winemakers: Michael Fragos and Daryl Groom
Principal varieties grown: Shiraz
Average annual crush: 3925 tonnes
Average no. cases produced: 40,000

Principal wines & brands	Cellar Potential
Sparkling Malbec	2-5 years
Chardonnay	2-5 years
Merlot	5-10 years
Bluestone Brut N.V.	0-1 year
Riesling	2-5 years
Semillon/Sauvignon Blanc	2-5 years
Cabernet Sauvignon	5-10 years
"Keystone" Grenache/Shiraz	5-10 years
"Growers"	2-5 years
"Partners"	2-5 years

Public & trade tours: By appointment only
Hours open to public: 10am-5pm, Mon-Sat; 11am-5pm, Sunday and public holidays
Points of interest: Historic Winery established in 1901, has been renovated to its former glory by the new owners. Tours include a history of McLaren Vale district and the winery and finish in the Barrel Room. In addition to tastings and sales, cellar door offers for sale a large range of regional produce, posters and corporate wear and gifts. Wine purchased in cellar door can be sent anywhere in Australia.
Retail distribution: Chace Agencies, Adelaide, The Wine Company, Melbourne

Wirra Wirra

I first remember strolling into the iron-stone relics, now the heart of the substantial high profile 'Wirra Wirra Winery', way back in 1972. I was searching for red grapes for my family's Tintara Winery and grower Greg Trott was on my hit list.

As I recounted this little bit of trivia to Greg recently, he filled in the details. The man has an incredible memory for detail of the distant past, but ask him what he did yesterday, he'll probably have a few problems filling you in!

Greg Trott is also an acute observer of life and one of the most visionary people I have encountered in the world of wine. Wirra Wirra is in fact a partnership between Greg and his cousin Roger and in recent years they have released a methode champenoise called 'Cousins' to celebrate this connection. This exceptional Pinot Chardonnay Cuvee spends almost four years ageing on the yeast lees in the bottle, and is one of the best sparkling wines you could find in Australia. Greg has a connection also to the Johnston family, large landholders and owners of 'Pirramimma' wines - Greg's mother was a Johnston.

Working life for Greg in McLaren Vale began, in his own words, 'as a mixed-up farmer', growing almonds, grapes, prunes and apricots and producing dried fruits. In 1969, Greg and cousin Roger bought the old ironstone cellars of Wirra Wirra, built in 1893 by Robert Strangways Wigley and disused since his death in 1924.

A big job lay ahead of them. The first grapes were crushed in 1976. By 1979 the rhine riesling had become a mainstay of their business when Greg coined the name 'hand picked' capturing the care and quality concerns always to the fore at Wirra Wirra. The last ten vintages have been made by Ben Riggs, a gentle giant of a man whose enthusiasm and creativity match his physical proportions. Ben deals with the estate grapes from Roger Trott's 'Moray Park' and Greg's 'Bethany' and 'Scrubby Rise' vineyards, along with other premium growers in the region. He now has extra responsibilities as the newly elected McLaren Vale regional Association President.

An outstanding success for Wirra has been their 'Church Block' a cabernet sauvignon, shiraz and merlot blend, named after the vineyard opposite the winery which surrounds an old Methodist Church. Greg has built a large bell-tower outside the winery from which hangs the 'The Angelus'. This enormous bell is rung each year by the winemaker to herald the first crushing of grapes from the region. Wirra Wirra have two super premium wines bottled in exceptional years, 'The Angelus', a cabernet sauvignon and 'RSW Shiraz'. Look out for them. Wirra Wirra have many dinners, concerts and exhibitions at the winery, reflecting Greg Trott's loves, along of course with his beloved Wirra Wirra wines.

WIRRAWIRRA

Address: McMurtrie Road, McLaren Vale SA 5171
Phone: (08) 8323 8414
Fax: (08) 8323 8596
Established: 1969
Winemaker: Ben Riggs
Principal varieties grown: Shiraz, Semillon, Cabernet, Merlot, Riesling, Sauvignon Blanc, Chardonnay, Grenache
Ha under vine: 31
Average annual crush: 748 tonnes
Average no. cases produced: 53,000

Principal wines & brands	Cellar Potential
Church Block	5-10 years
Hand Picked Riesling	2-5 years
The Angelus Cabernet Sauvignon	5-10 years
R.S.W. Shiraz	5-10 years
Chardonnay	2-5 years
Semillon-Sauvignon Blanc	2-5 years
Sauvignon Blanc	2-5 years

Public & trade tours: By appointment only
Hours open to public: 10am-5pm, Mon-Sat; 11am-5pm, Sunday and public holidays
Retail distribution: Cellar Door and Mail Order sales. Available in most Top Restaurants and **Retail Outlets:** Distributor Negociants Australia

Modern McLaren Vale is full of success stories, none more befitting than that of Scott and Anne Collett.

Scott, his brothers Ian and Stephen and their father, wine consultant Doug, established the winery in 1974. Doug bought the property, then named Woodstock, in 1973 and quickly rejuvenated the old vineyard.

Before settling down at Woodstock, Scott had some diverse training in the wine industry. He left Roseworthy with a degree, before making wine at a big Griffith winery for three years, six months of travelling California with a mobile wine bottling line and other visits to winemaking areas of Italy, Germany and France broadened Scott's experience.

Returning to Woodstock in 1982, a young Scott attacked the winemaking with real enthusiasm and a great deal of vision.

Year. His wines have gone on to achieve National distribution as well as International sales to several overseas countries.

On the home front, Scott, his wife Anne and their three children, Max, Peter and Sophia, live in a big home overlooking the Woodstock vineyards. Anne and Scott believe wine should be enjoyed with food, so they built a magnificent restaurant and entertaining venue next to the winery, naming it 'The Coterie'. The Coterie blends superbly into the environment; constructed of ochre-coloured rammed earth by Scott's brother Ian, its clever design is like a giant slice of cake with the full length windows and French doors opening out to a native garden under the stately gums. Across the road,

Scott released high quality McLaren Vale reds and whites under the Woodstock label. In 1986, he won the Wine Bushing Crown for the best Wine of the Region, and was named South Australian Winemaker of the

one can see kangaroos and wallabies peacefully grazing in the Douglas Scrub Sanctuary.

Chef Kay Cazzolato and her young enthusiastic staff run a really top class restaurant,

generally open only for lunch on Sundays and holiday Mondays, but splendid vineyard platters are available everyday if you're a bit peckish. Each Easter Woodstock Coterie hosts a "Food, Wine, Music and Art Affair".

Woodstock

Featuring an art exhibition, sculpture, glassware, music, fine crafts, furniture and a display of exotic roses, along with the food and wine - a real cultural extravaganza superbly staged. Woodstock Coterie also joins the regional food and wine events "From The Sea and The Vines" in early June and "The Continuous Picnic" in early October. The Coterie often invite guest Restaurants to Woodstock. These restaurateurs enjoy a refreshing new kitchen and a visit to McLaren Vale, and the coterie guests enjoy a varied menu from some of Adelaide's better restaurants.

For Scott and Anne Collett, the vision became a reality. They grow and make a range of premium McLaren Vale wines; the "Stocks Shiraz" from Scott's century old vines is a sensation and they offer them with superb food in delightful surroundings at

Scott Collett and McLaren Vale/Fleurieu Visitors Centre he helped Create

Woodstock Winery and Coterie. Scott is a real regional stalwart and has just put in several solid years as the McLaren Vale Winemakers Association Restoration Chairman.

The fabulous McLaren Vale & Fleurieu Visitor Centre at the gateway to the region would be nowhere near as brilliant without his tenacity and capacity for hard work.

Set aside a lazy Sunday to enjoy Woodstock's side of the wonderful McLaren Vale Wine Region.

WOODSTOCK WINES
Address: Douglas Gully Road, McLaren Flat SA 5171
Phone: (08) 8383 0156
Fax: (08) 8383 0437
Email: WOODSTOCK.WINERY@mclarenvale.sa.com.au
WWW: http://www.wineaustralia.com.au/woodstock
Established: 1974
Winemakers: Scott Collett and John Weeks
Principal varieties grown: Cabernet Sauvignon, Shiraz, Grenache, Chardonnay, Riesling, Semillon
Ha under vine: 24
Average annual crush: 250 tonnes
Average no. cases produced: 15,000

Principal wines & brands	Cellar Potential
Cabernet	5-10 years
Shiraz	5-10 years
Chardonnay	2-5 years
Botrytis Sweet White	2-5 years
Sauvignon Blanc	2-5 years
Semillon	2-5 years
Tawny Port	10+ years

Public & trade tours: Trade tours by appointment only
Hours open to public: 9am-5pm, weekdays; 12pm-5pm, weekends and public holidays
Points of interest: Function Centre for group bookings anytime - called Woodstock Coterie. Open to public for Sunday lunch and holiday Monday lunch, Open Easter and Christmas holidays (except Good Friday and Christmas Day)
Retail distribution: National, UK, NZ

Wirilda Creek

Kerry Flanagan and Karen Shertock opened the Wirilda Creek Winery in 1993 and it is really an extension of their lives.

Kerry has a rich and varied background in the wine and hospitality areas. He graduated from Roseworthy in 1980, having spent some time in the Penfolds red wine cellars during his course. He worked at Wirra Wirra during the time Brian Croser and Petaluma were involved in the winemaking. This experience was followed by a stint in the Hunter, then he returned to McLaren Vale and assisted at Hazelmere, Coriole, Woodstock and the old Southern Vales (now Tatachilla).

Kerry has a definite flair in the hospitality side of wine, and saw the Old Salopian Inn as an ideal opportunity to combine the two. Having secured the Salopian, he proceeded to dig out the cellars and launched the McLaren Vale Wine Centre. Kerry and gifted chef Russell Jeavons created a fine reputation for the lovely venue.

Kerry sold the Salopian and took off overseas, travelling the wine regions of Europe and the USA. On returning, he and Karen set about building Wirilda Creek. The building of rammed earth fits discreetly into the vineyards and the casual alfresco dining area is a delight. They also have several excellent rustic style accommodation suites, all tastefully appointed with full facilities including a country kitchen.

The wines are equally as impressive. The first two reds released, the 1993 Shiraz and 1993 Cabernet Merlot, were both trophy winners. In the near future look our for Kerryís Kangaroo Island wines from premium grapes grown at pristine Antechamber Bay.

WIRILDA CREEK
Address: RSD 90 McMurtrie Road, McLaren Vale SA 5171
Phone: (08) 8323 9688
Fax: (08) 8323 9260
Established: 1992/93
Owners: Kerry Flanagan and Karen Sherlock
Winemaker: Kerry Flanagan
Principal varieties grown: McLaren Vale - Shiraz, Cabernet Sauvignon, Malbec, Merlot. Kangaroo Island - , Shiraz, Cabernet Sauvignon, Chardonnay, Verdelho
Ha under vine: McLaren Vale, 3 ha; Kangaropo Island, 3 ha
Average no. cases produced: 2,000-3,000

Principal wines & brands	Cellar Potential
Shiraz	10+ years
Shiraz 'Rare'	10+ years
Cabernet Merlot	5-10 years
Vine Pruners - the blend Cabernet, Merlot, Shiraz	5-10 years
Grape Pickers white blend Verdelho, Semillon, Chardonnay	5+ years
Sauvignon Blanc	2-5 years
Semillon 'Oak Matured'	2-10 years

Public & trade tours: By appointment only
Hours open to public: 11am-5pm, daily
Points of interest: Café, function venue, B&B accomodation, PÈtanque, Local Produce Sales and Seasonal Markets
Retail distribution: Ausvin, San Diego; Wines West, Santa Rosa; Limited in Australia, Cellar Door and Mail Order Sales, Internet

An introduction to the Riverland

The Chaffey brothers, who had pioneered many successful irrigation schemes around Victoria, were asked by the South Australian Government to examine the possibility of implementing such schemes along the course of the Murray River as it wound its way through the state.

During the late 1880's, the brothers set up the scheme with canals and channels, bringing life-giving water to the rich orange-red alluvial soils. With the addition of this magic ingredient, the region began producing excellent quality crops of citrus and stone fruits. Grape growing and winemaking spread quickly and by the beginning of the new century it was already a substantial contributor to the Australian vintage. Today it is Australia's largest wine growing region. The massive Berri Winery, now under the banner of BRL Hardy, and arguably Australia's largest wine producer, is complemented by its sister winery, Renmano. Angove's fast expanding winery and distillery, producing its famous St. Agnes brandies, was the first established in the region in 1910, followed by large Australian companies such as Yalumba, Orlando,

Hardy's, Tollana, Normans, Seppelt and Penfold's all have vineyards in the region. The Riverland, however, is dominated by individual grape-growers, many of whose families took advantage of the soldier settlement program after the First World War to begin a new life planting their blocks with government assistance, a brilliantly conceived and managed scheme. The second major development in the region came with the post- Second World War European immigration flood. The newcomers with their strong link to wine and hard work developed the region quickly, inspiring others by their success.

Such immigrants were the Moularadellis family whose Kingston Estate is a premium wine success story expanding from a 60 tonne crush in 1986 to over 10,000 tonnes in 1997, and winning many trophies and gold medals around the world along the way. Viticultural developments with techniques such as minimal pruning, leading to smaller bunches of berries and increased wine quality, have been most successful. Moisture control and minimum irrigation is also contributing to increased wine quality. Winemaking methods and technology com-

bine with top quality grapes to produce some exciting wines in this important Australian wine region whose future looks bright.

The region offers much to the visitor as it enjoys a very mild-pleasant climate all year round. The attractions of the river with its water sports, houseboat cruises and the many golf courses on its banks beckons one to come and have a break anytime.

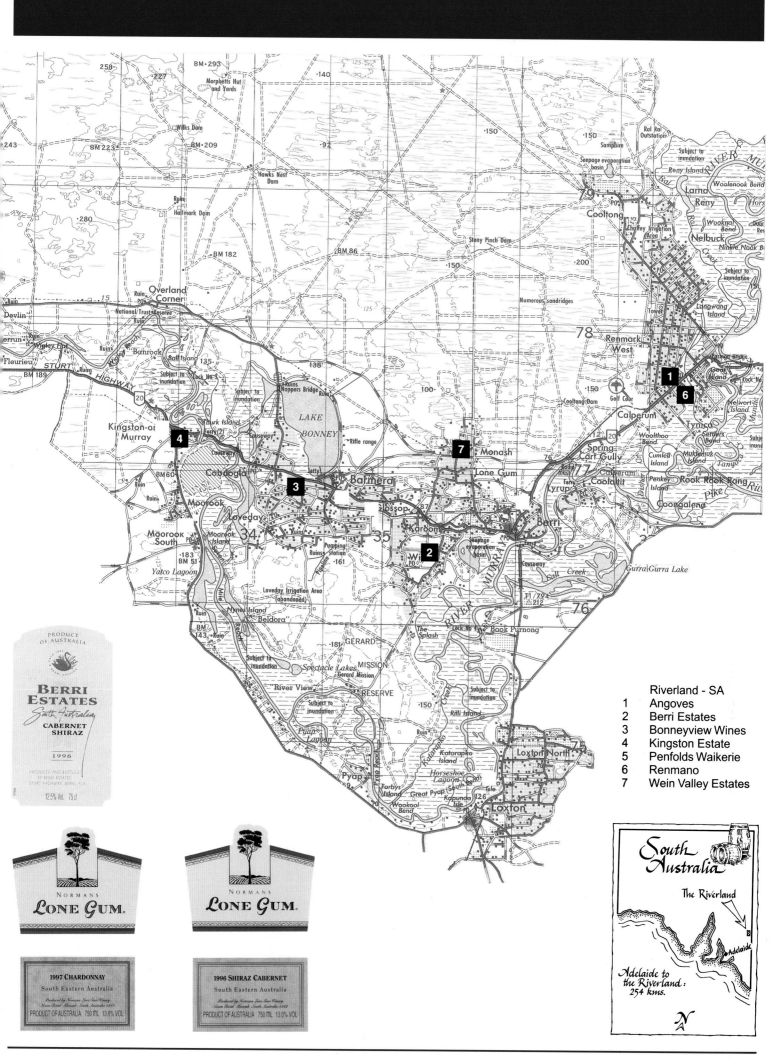

Riverland - SA
1 Angoves
2 Berri Estates
3 Bonneyview Wines
4 Kingston Estate
5 Penfolds Waikerie
6 Renmano
7 Wein Valley Estates

PRODUCT OF AUSTRALIA

BERRI ESTATES
South Australia
CABERNET SHIRAZ

1996

PRODUCED AND BOTTLED BY BERRI ESTATES STURT HIGHWAY, BERRI, S.A.

12.5% Vol. 75 cl

NORMANS
LONE GUM.

1997 CHARDONNAY
South Eastern Australia

Produced by Normans Lone Gum Winery
Nixon Road, Monash, South Australia 6342
PRODUCT OF AUSTRALIA 750 ML 13.0% VOL

NORMANS
LONE GUM.

1996 SHIRAZ CABERNET
South Eastern Australia

Produced by Normans Lone Gum Winery
Nixon Road, Monash, South Australia 6342
PRODUCT OF AUSTRALIA 750 ML 13.0% VOL

South Australia

The Riverland

Adelaide

Adelaide to
the Riverland:
254 kms.

N

Angove's

On July 12, 1986, Angove's celebrated one hundred years of involvement in the Wine & Brandy industry. Dr William Angove planted the company's first vines in 1886 at Tea Tree Gully, near Adelaide.

Dr Angove as well as being a medical practitioner was a highly successful winemaker and marketer and his business thrived. By the turn of the century his wines were well known throughout the country with many show awards to their credit. The company expanded, establishing the first winery and distillery in the Murray Valley, at Renmark, in 1910. Further developments followed, with the construction of another winery at Lyrup, south-west of Renmark in 1913, and the export of large volumes of wine to England during the 1920's.

Angove's continued to expand and consolidate their business and in 1968 plantings commenced at Nanya Vineyard, a few kilometres east of Renmark. Now one of Australia's largest single vineyards, planted with at least 22 different varieties, the Nanya Vineyard produces a large range of varietal table wines including riesling, sauvignon blanc, chardonnay, chenin blanc, colombard and cabernet sauvignon.

The quality of the wines in the different Angove's ranges is exceptionally high and their value extraordinary. A recent new range released by Angove's is their Classic Reserve wines, the best selections of their premium varieties which receive special treatment in the winery in small batches, and in the case of the reds and chardonnay, small barrel fermentation and ageing. The Sarnia Farms label is now the top of the range and named after the original Tea Tree Gully

---

ANGOVES PTY LTD

Address: Bookmark Avenue, Renmark SA 5341
Phone: (08) 8595 1311
Fax: (08) 8595 1583
Established: 1886
Owner: Angove Family
Winemaker: Garry Wall
Principal varieties grown: Chardonnay, Chenin Blanc, Sauvignon Blanc, Cabernet Sauvignon, Rhine Riesling, Shiraz, Colombard, Pinot Noir
Ha under vine: 480
Average annual crush: 16,000 tonnes
Average no. cases produced: 800,000
(Including Export)

Principal wines & brands	Cellar Potential
Sarnia Farm Cabernet	5-10 years
Sarnia Farm Chardonnay	2-5 years
Classic Reserve Chardonnay	2-5 years
Classic Reserve Cabernet Sauvignon	2-5 years
Classic Reserve Sauvignon Blanc	2-5 years
Butterfly Ridge Colombard/Chardonnay	2-5 years

Public & trade tours: By appointment only
Hours open to public: 9am-5pm, weekdays
Points of interest: Largest privately owned vineyard
Retail distribution: Cellar Door and Mail Order sales. Export to NZ, UK, Europe, Canada, Hong Kong, Singapore, Malaysia

properties. The wines are all regionally selected, with the Padthaway region in SA's southeast featuring prominently.

Angove's have a tremendous depth of products of the vine, producing one of Australia's finest brandies under the St Agnes label, along with Australia's best commercial fino sherry, a range of vermouths under the Marko label and the Stone's Green Ginger wine.

Angove's wines are currently produced at Renmark in the Murray Valley. Tea Tree Gully, though originally constructed as a winery, now houses a Cellar Door sales facility as well as the State Branch Office. Vineyards that surrounded the Tea Tree Gully winery no longer exist, as they were compulsorily purchased by the South Australian Government to provide land for housing in the mid 70's.

Having played a major role in establishing the Murray Valley as a wine producing area, Angove's Pty Ltd has not only contributed to the economic welfare of the state but has also furthered the reputation of Australian wine worldwide.

Angove's – St Agnes Brandy

No book on Australian Wine would be complete without a feature on brandy, and important beverage of the wine and grape industry. What is brandy? Brandy is the distilled spirit of wine made from fresh grapes. Australia has some of the world's strictest controls on the production and maturation of this age-old essence of wine.

The first step in the production of brandy is the fermentation of grape juice to produce wine, often referred to as brandy wash. Brandy wash is then distilled, a process that extracts the alcohol and a wide range of volatile flavour components, called congeners, from the wine. It is the mystical distillation process that gives rise to the production of brandy from wine, but before it can be called brandy is must be matured in wood for a period of not less than 2 years. This time of quiet maturation allows the spirit to mellow and soften, and to gain extra interest and complexity of flavour by inter-action with the oak, wood and atmosphere. Longer maturation is not uncommon in order to produce even better quality brandy.

There are two distinct alternative methods of distillation. The first and most important is the classic "pot still" method. This technique has been utilised by the best French cognac houses for centuries. The pot still is "charged" with brandy wash or wine, which is gently heated. As boiling occurs the most volatile components vaporise first. These are called "heads" and are undesirable in the brandy and after condensation are kept separate from the heart of the distillation that follows as the boiling point temperature continues to rise. Towards the end of the distillation the heavier least volatile components are vaporised and condensed and are called "tails" and again are undesirable in the brandy. The heart of this distillation often called "Brandy Low Wine" contains about 50% alcohol by volume. The brandy low wine is returned to the pot still and distilled a second time with the heart of this second distillation being of sufficient purity to be matured in oak barrels for brandy.

A second distillation method utilises a continuous still and as the name implies is a continuous process where wine is constantly fed into the still, the alcohol stripped from the wine by steam generated heat and in a second column the steam alcohol mixture is successively distilled and condensed over a series of specially designed 'plates". Spirit can be extracted from the column at up to 95% alcohol by volume. This is an excellent method for the production of fortifying spirit for addition to ports,

sherries, vermouths etc., but it not the most ideal for production of quality brandy.

St. Agnes Brandy is double distilled pot still brandy, produced by the Angove Family in Renmark, South Australia. St. Agnes has been a flagship of the company for many years and has earned trophies and medals in Australia and Overseas, too numerous to detail. St. Agnes Very Old XO Brandy has been awarded many international honours including the Championship Trophy in France against brandies from around the world.

In the early 1970's the Federal Government severely wounded this important segment of the wine and grape industry with callous ill-conceived tax increases. At this time brandy was on a strong growth curve and Angove's were increasing the size of their distillery to accommodate a new pot still to add to the three existing stills; this space still remains vacant some 25 years later. Recent growth in St. Agnes sales may herald new opportunities for expansion and the fourth pot still may yet find its way into the system.

The age of a brandy is the age in wood of the youngest component of any blend. By this rule, St. Agnes 3 Star Brandy is usually between two and half and three years of age. It is a great value, superb brandy. St. Agnes Old Liqueur 5 Star Brandy has a minimum age of 10 years in wood and St. Agnes Very Old XO Brandy has a minimum age of 20 years in wood. These are superb spirits that the gods would be proud of. Older brandies are very expensive to produce with money tied up in stock for 20 years or more. Additionally, 2-3% of the volume of brandy in each barrel

is lot to evaporation each year. This is called the "angel's share".

The Angove family is led by wine industry stalwart Tom Angove, with more than 60 vintages under his belt and his son John

as Managing Director. This fine family company's commitment to quality wine and brandy production, always seeking to improve and give their customers extra value, is admirable. St. Agnes, the patron saint of purity, would be proud of them.

Banrock Station

Just north of Kingston-On-Murray is the historic Banrock Station, some 4,500 acres within a loop of the majestic River Murray and its magnificent red cliffs encircling three sides with 12 kilometres of river frontage.

The first settlement was made during the last century by a Sydney based drover called Wigley, who fell in love with the property and grazed cattle there.

The ruins of his original homestead remain, but often being flooded, he relocated to a site which became Kingston-On-Murray.

The historic Cobb and Co. Staging Station was just opposite the property which passed through a number of owners gradually turning towards horticulture.

Thirteen acres of vines were planted by the Jackson Family to which legendary identities Jack Warne added a further 20 acres in 1975. Today BRL Hardy are developing 1,000 acres of premium vineyards.

The first wines, a semillon/chardonnay and a cabernet shiraz, proved most successful in both bottles and 2 litre wine casks.

A premium unwooded chardonnay and a premium shiraz were added in 1996.

The property includes a declared conservation protected wetlands which BRL Hardy are helping restore. A royalty on all

Banrock Station Wines is going towards his worthwhile project. Why not let your enjoyment help nature!!

Normans Lone Gum Winery

Situated at Monash, in the upper reaches of South Australia's Riverland, is a large winery formerly known as Wein Valley Estates, and for a number of years under the control of Lionel Krongold a Melbourne wine merchant.

In 1994 Wein Valley merged their operations, including a bottling line in Northgate Victoria, with Normans and floated what has become another successful public wine company, Normans Ltd, of which Lionel Krongold is chairman.

Under winemaker Roger Harbord, the winery has been totally upgraded in a quality sense and expanded with an anticipated crush in 1998 of 18,000 tonnes, putting it in the top league of Australian Wineries.

The Lone Gum and Jesse's Blend, named after the legendary Jesse Norman, labels are focussing on the export and value for money Australian markets. The wine quality is well above average and the prices exceptionally good

value. The sunshine good soils and careful winemaking have once again triumphed, in this, Australia's biggest wine region.

NORMANS LONE GUM WINERY
Address: Nixon Road, Monash SA 5342
Phone: (08) 8583 5255
Fax: (08) 8583 5444
Email: info@normans-wines.com.au
WWW: http://www.normans-wines.com.au
Winemaker: Roger Harbord (Chief) and Otto Konig
Principal varieties grown: Chardonnay, Semillon, Chenin Blanc, Cabernet Sauvignon, Shiraz
Average annual crush: 18,000 tonnes

Principal wines & brands	Cellar Potential
Lone Gum Chardonnay	3 years
Lone Gum Shiraz Cabernet	4 years
Lone Gum Semillon Chardonnay	3 years
Lone Gum Chenin Blanc	3 years
Jesse's Blend Shiraz, Grenache, Mataro	3 years
Jesse's Blend Colombard, Chenin Blanc, Riesling	3 years
Jesse's Blend Gold	3 years
Jesse's Blend Cuvee	
Normans Brut Cuvee	

Public & trade tours: Tours by appointment only
Hours open to public: 9am-5pm, weekdays
Retail distribution: All major retailers

Renmano

In 1915, 130 Riverland grape growers banded together to form the country's first co-operative winery.

They purchased the Chateau Tanunda distillery situated just south of Renmark and produced spirit for twenty years until fortified wines became popular, and production was altered accordingly.

A range of table wines was developed during the late 1950's with Renmano's first varietal release being a cabernet sauvignon in 1962. Other varieties followed in subsequent years, although most wines were sold in bulk to other companies until the 1970's. In addition to Renmano's cask and flagon wines, a premium range of table wines is also produced and marketed under the Chairman's Selection label. This range, cabernet sauvignon, hermitage and chardonnay represent excellent value for money and have been highly successful on the export market. The Chairman's Selection range really came into prominence when the 1988 Chardonnay won 4 trophies including the Tucker Seabrook Caon Trophy for the best show wine over the 1990 Wine Show season.

Renmano also produce a range of premium varietal 2 litre wine casks, these remain among the best and most popular wines in this field.

There is an excellent cellar door at the winery in the heart of Renmark and it makes a good visit if you are passing through the region.

RENMANO WINES
Address: Renmark Avenue, Box 700, Renmark SA 5341
Phone: (08) 8586 6771
Fax: (08) 8586 5939
Established: 1914
Owner: BRL Hardy Limited
Winemaker: Frank Newman
Principal varieties grown: Chardonnay, Merlot, Shiraz, Sauvignon Blanc, Semillon, Riesling, Grenache
Ha under vine: 141
Hours open to public: 9am-5pm, Mon-Sat, by appointment
Retail distribution: Cellar Door sales. Houghton Wine Co., WA; BRL Hardy Wine Company. Export to NZ, UK, Europe, USA, Canada, Japan, SE Asia

Berri Estates

The largest wine producer in Australia has rather humble origins, as a grower co-operative.

The co-operative's first wine, brandy spirit, was produced in a small distillery with make-shift equipment. This brandy spirit was made from a surplus of raisins and sultanas left over after the Riverland harvest of 1918. Within four years, local fruit production had greatly increased with the influx of repatriated soldier settlers to the area. This necessitated the expansion of the distillery, and the Berri Growers Co-operative was formed to manage the business.

Berri's first commercial vintage was made in 1922. The Co-operative continued to enjoy unbridled success and by 1958 a new winery/plant was constructed to cater for the swing in public tastes towards table wines. Wines were marketed in both bottles and flagons with impressive results. Sales figures skyrocketed during the early 1970's with the introduction into the market of the 'bag in the box' wine cask.

Berri quickly developed their five litre cask, one of the largest packaged volumes of wine on the market.

The wine inside the cask if of very high quality and is great value for money.

The Berri cask assured the Co-operative of a large share of the cask market which it has maintained.

Berri also developed a range of premium table wines during the 1970's.

Winemakers Brian Barry and Ian McKenzie built up a range of wines that won more than 1,000 show medals over an eight-year period. These prizes include the illustrious Jimmy Watson Trophy and the 1977 Most Successful Exhibitors Trophy from the National Wine Show in Canberra.

The stars of the Berri range have been their cabernet sauvignons and cabernet blends.

Today Berri Estate is part of the BRL Hardy Wine Company and quality is on a constant improvement curve, with viticultural and winemaking techniques in constant focus.

Kingston Estate

In 1994 Kingston Estate were awarded the South Australian Business of the Year award, an accolade that could not be more deserved.

The winery and its young winemaker, Bill Moularadellis is one of the up and coming success stories of the Australian wine industry. Kingston has carved out a niche in the export market and is well on the way to repeating this success within Australia. Although Bill's parents both came from Greece, they actually met in the Riverland. For many years they ran their fruit and vine block, selling grapes to large wine producers. As their grapes were always among the best in the region and in demand, they decided to build a small winery in 1979. By 1986, the winery was still only crushing 60 tonnes. Today it is one of Australia's largest, crushing over 10,000 tonnes.

Bill attended Roseworthy and graduated with his winemaking credentials in 1985, followed by a vintage in the Hunter Valley. He then returned to Kingston and concentrated on creating a modern winemaking facility with state-of-the-art equipment and expanded capacity.

At the outset the Moularadellis family set quality and value-for-money as the main criteria for their wines to meet and as rapid as the growth of the winery has been, Bill has always had a clear objective to continually improve the quality of the wines being produced and refining this style of winemaking.

Bill liaises strongly with his growers, assisting and encouraging in the pursuit of excellence at every level. To translate this fruit quality into wine Bill has introduced a system based on small tanks and open fermenters enabling him to isolate and personally handle those batches of grapes showing outstanding potential.

Kingston Estate make two main ranges of wine - the elegantly packaged 'Kingston Estate' and the prestige 'Kingston Reserve' range featuring rich, truly powerful wines. In 1994, the 1991 Reserve Chardonnay won the double gold at the San Francisco International Wine Show and the Hyatt Advertiser Award for South Australia's best Chardonnay. Other whites produced are a wood-matured semillon and a semillon/sauvignon blanc blend – both classy wines, full of character. The 'Kingston Estate Cabernet Sauvignon, Merlot and Shiraz' are all award winners. Kingston Estate has pioneered many export markets such as China.

Kingston wines proudly Riverland and Bill pays tribute to the rich sandy loams of the region and the untiring efforts of his grapegrowers.

Bill Moularadellis is a 'new breed' of winemaker, unconstrained by outmoded concepts of winemaking and marketing. Bill's view is global, and he has built a team of young professionals around him who share his passion for excellence in every area of his business. Always in the background and caring for everything, down to keeping the fermentation area clean, are his devoted and proud parents.

KINGSTON ESTATE WINERY

Address: PO Box 67, Kingston-on-Murray SA 5331
Direction: Located on Sturt Highway at turn off to Kingston-on-Murray
Phone: (08) 8583 0244
Fax: (08) 8583 0304
Email: kewines@riverland.net.au
Established: 1979
Winemakers: Bill Moularadellis and Rod Chapman
Principal varieties grown: Chardonnay, Semillon, Sauvignon Blanc, Colombard, Cabernet Sauvignon, Shiraz, Merlot, Grenache, Petit Verdot
Ha under vine: 50
Average annual crush: 1,000 tonnes
Average no. cases produced: 800,000

Principal wines & brands	Cellar Potential
Kingston Estate	
Chardonnay	2-5 years
Shiraz	5-10 years
Cabernet Sauvignon	5-10 years
Semillon/Sauvignon Blanc	1-2 years
Merlot	2-5 years
Reserve Chardonnay	2-5 years
Reserve Shiraz	5-10 years
Reserve Petit Verdot	5-10 years
Reserve Merlot	5-10 years

Public & trade tours: By appointment only
Hours open to public: By appointment only
Retail distribution:
Mail Order. Distributed Nationally by Tucker & Co. Pty Ltd

Bill Moularadellis, Managing Director/Winemaker of Kingston Estate in the barrel maturation cellar at Kingston-on-Murray, South Australia.

An introduction to Currency Creek/Middleton

Some 30 kilometres southwest of Langhorne Creek, close to the resort towns and fishing port of Goolwa and Victor Harbour, lies a distinctive wine region. At present it supports two wineries, but is already supplying grapes to many of South Australia's top winemakers.

The Great Southern Ocean influences the truly maritime climate. In fact, it is one of South Australia's coolest climates overall, but in winter one of its mildest, both ideal for the vine, giving an exceptionally long growing season, building and retaining loads of elegant flavours in the wines.

Wally and Phillip Tonkin's Currency Creek Wines, established in 1969, produces a large range of elegant wines and has a delightful country-style restaurant and six superb vineyard villa's.

Likewise, Middleton Winery, under the experienced and innovative Nigel Catt, makes outstanding wines and has a most pleasant alfresco style holiday and weekend restaurant tucked into the winery itself.

The sandy loams of the area with good drainage also help produce the unique styles this exciting new region will surely become famous for.

Currency Creek/Middleton Beach - Map Index
1   Currency Creek Winery
2   Middleton Winery

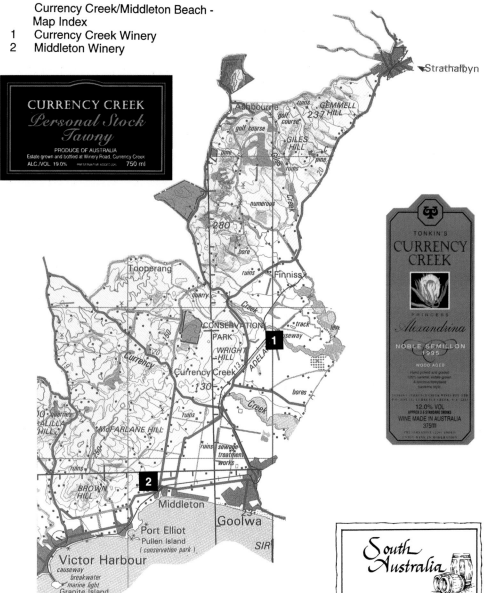

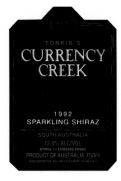

Currency Creek Winery

Wally Tonkin was born and raised in the region, but his bubbling energy and constant search for a new challenge to tackle, led him to Adelaide where he very successfully operated a property development business and a travel business at the same time.His main challenges met, his love for the country of his youth, and animals, led him to purchase a large rural holding on the Finnis and Currency Creeks near Goolwa. Always with a desire to be different, he "ran" a number of unusual animals and birds, from deer to ostriches and peacocks, along with his main love, horses.

He also planted a large vineyard, with most of the grapes being sold to eager winemakers further north, but he set up his own innovative little winery. Today, his son Phillip runs the successful winery, complete with a restaurant and six superb vineyard villas.

The peacocks proudly parade, past the windows, on the expansive lawns as you sip some superb Currency Creek wines with the succulent meals in the casual and charming restaurant. The Currency Creek region is blessed with ideal viticultural conditions, one of the coolest summers and mildest winters in South Australia, providing long growing seasons giving clean and complex fruit flavours in the wines. The sauvignon blanc has been particularly successful, as has their sparkling cabernet and one of Australia's finest botrytised wines, their Noble Riesling, several times the Australian Champion in the small wineries sweet white category.

Whilst Wally is busy winning many races with his self-trained stable of horses, Phillip is forging new markets for the Currency Creek wines around the world. Two new vineyard villas were completed in spring 1997 adding to the four opened in 1996. They are truly magnificently appointed, queen sized beds, spas, a kitchen, dining areas and outdoor courtyards. Set in amongst the dappled white gums, overlooking the Tookayerta Creek within an hour of Adelaide in the heart of the fabulous Fleurieu Peninsula. Why not put this, one of Australia's most colourful and characterful wineries, on your next wine adventure itinerary and stay the night after a sumptuous dinner.

Currency Creek Winery

CURRENCY CREEK WINES

Address:
Winery Road, Currency Creek SA 5214
Direction:
10km north of Goolwa, just off the Goolwa-Strathalbyn Road
Phone:
(08) 8555 4069
Fax:
(08) 8555 4100
WWW: http://www.dove.net.au/~currency
Established: 1969
Owner:
Phillip Tonkin
Winemaker:
Phillip Tonkin
Principal varieties grown:
Chardonnay, Semillon, Sauvignon Blanc, Rhine Riesling, Pinot Noir, Shiraz, Cabernet Sauvignon
Ha under vine: 48
Average annual crush: 300 tonnes
Average no. cases produced: 8,000

Principal wines & brands	Cellar Potential
Currency Creek Sauvignon Blanc	3-6 years
Currency Creek Chardonnay	4-7 years
Currency Creek Cabernet Sauvignon	5-10 years
Currency Creek Shiraz	6-10 years
Currency Creek Methode Tradionale	0-6 years
Currency Creek Sparkling Shiraz	0-6 years
Currency Creek "Princess Alexandria" Noble Semillon	0-5 years
Currency Creek Personal Stock Tawny Port	15 years
Currency Creek Olde Liquer Muscat	
Currency Creek "Old Barrel" White Port	

Public & trade tours:
By appointment only
Hours open to public:
10am-5pm, daily
Points of interest:
Restaurant, a la Carte, can cater for weddings and group bookings. Vineyard villas, 6 self contained villas
Retail distribution: Fine Wine Specialist, NSW; Alepat Taylor, VIC; David Johnstone; TAS; Festival City Wine and Spirits, SA; Oak Barrel Wines, ACT

An introduction to the Coastal Regions

The Coastal Regions of South Australia are generally suitable for viticulture except for the West Coast and Upper Spencers Gulf which are too hot and dry. Others such as Yorke Peninsula would need some supplementary irrigation if they existed, as South Australia is the driest State on the driest continent of the World. This of course has its advantages as vine diseases prove less of a problem with the low humidity. The lighter soils that the State has is probably a factor that phylloxera, the dreaded vine louse that destroyed the vineyard of Europe and the Eastern States of Australia late last Century, has never attacked South Australia, with the advantage the State has many vineyards on their original roots that go back to the mid 1800's.

Odd vineyards have sprung up around the coast over the State's history but it is only since the mid 1980's that wine regions have really emerged, with the exceptions of the McLaren Vale and Langhorne Creek regions, which are quite maritime, and Currency Creek founded in 1969 and Middleton Estate in 1978. The Port Lincoln area now has Boston Bay Wines and Delacolline, both planted in 1984.

Kangaroo Island has a number of vineyards, most small, but with 20 acres currently going in at Emu Bay, Robin Moody from Penfolds being one of the partners in this venture. So far only one wine, a lovely bordeaux blend red, from the Florance family's vines at Cygnet Cove has hit the market. The Mount Benson region near Cape Jaffa is truly exciting with some 180 hectares already planted and some exciting wines from Cape Jaffa, Mt Benson and the Black Wattle brand of Cellarmaster already are

well accepted. Near Robe BRL Hardy have large plantings in the Woak Coastal Ranges and Southcorp are developing large vineyards. The coastal climate with its long temperate growing season is ideal and abundant terra rossa soils completes the quality viticultural picture.

A little further south near Mt Gambier the Winter family and the characterful Sandy Haig have vineyards and wines on the market. The future for the State's Coastal regions viticulturally seems assured with the state's sensational seafoods and the good tourism infrastructure things look rosy indeed, adding another dimension of enjoyment for the intrepid wine lover to seek out!

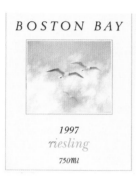

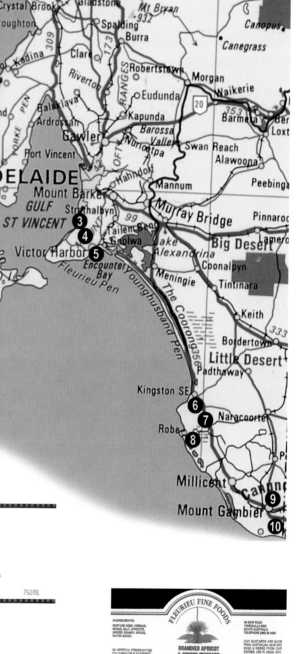

1. Boston Bay Wines
2. Delacolline Wines
3. Twin Bays Wines
4. Fleurieu Fine Foods
5. The Anchorage
6. Cape Jaffa Wines
7. Mt Benson Wines
8. Cellarmaster Mt Benson
9. Haig Wines
10. Winters Wines

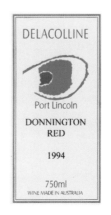

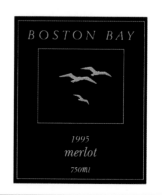

Boston Bay Wines

Graham Ford, a deep sea diver and salvage expert, and his wife Mary came to live at Port Lincoln in the early 1970's and set up in the Abalone business. Loving their new environment they began to think of the future with their young family. The answer came in planting a vineyard, the first in the region.

The climate was ideal with even temperatures due to the surrounding waters of Spencers Gulf and the Great Australian Bite. The French explorer Bawdin recommended viticulture here, undoubtedly seeing the similarity to Bordeaux. He named what is now Boston Bay "Port d' Champagny" referring to the soil type with underlying limestone often the sign of good viticultural country. The Boston Bay vines have flourished and the wines won much acclaim far from their shores.

The vintage of around 2,500 doz. are made by David O'Leary, the renowned winemaker at Quelltaler Wines at Clare, the nearest wine region some 500 kms away.

The riesling and cabernet sauvignon have now been joined by a chardonnay.

The winery is open for visiting on weekends and public holidays and all of December and January. They also have barbecue and function facilities.

BOSTON BAY
Address: Lincoln Highway, Port Lincoln SA 5606
Direction: 6km north of Port Lincoln
Phone: (08) 8684 3600
Fax: (08) 8684 3600
Established: 1984
Owners: Graham and Mary Ford and Family
Winemaker: David O'Leary
Principal varieties grown: Riesling, Chardonnay, Merlot, Cabernet Sauvignon, Shiraz
Average annual crush: 35 tonnes
Average no. cases produced: 2,500

Principal wines & brands	Cellar Potential
Boston Bay Riesling	3-5 years
Boston Bay Chardonnay	3-5 years
Boston Bay Merlot	3-5 years
Boston Bay Cabernet Sauvignon	10 years
Boston Bay Spaetlese Riesling	2-3 years

Public & trade tours: No
Hours open to public: 11.30-4.30, weekends, school and public holidays and each day during December and January
Points of interest: BBQ Facilities and Function Room
Retail distribution: Mail Order sales. We do our own distribution for SA

Delacolline Estate

Literally meaning "Of the Hill" it seems most appropriate that this "Tres Francaise" name should have been chosen for a vineyard and winery that is on the slopes above Boston Bay, or as it was called, "Port de Champagny" by French explorer Baudin, only a matter of days before Mathew Flinders named it Boston Bay in 1803.

Whilst there is a French influence amongst the partners that started the vineyard in 1984, today Delacolline is in the hands of a consortium led by local surgeon, Ian Fletcher.

I first tasted the Delacolline wines some 5 years ago whilst doing a stint at the classic Adelaide wine mecca Chesser Cellars. The Semillon Sauvignon Blanc has a strong bordeaux style as did the Donnington Red, a cabernet dominated wine. The similarity to the bordeaux climate and soils is striking and was certainly not missed by Baudin who would be pleased to see his recommendation of the region for viticulture being taken up in a French Vein. The cellar door awaits your visit at weekends, public holidays and all of December and January – open only in the afternoons. The wines are made by the experienced Andrew Mitchell at Clare, the closest major wine region.

DELACOLLINE ESTATE
Address: PO Box 1624, Whillas Road, Port Lincoln SA 5606
Phone: (08) 8682 4571
Fax: (08) 8683 4195
Email: ifletch@pl.camtech.net.au
Established: 1984
Winemaker: Andrew Mitchell
Principal varieties grown: Riesling, Chardonnay, Cabernet Sauvignon, Sauvignon Blanc
Ha under vine: 5
Average annual crush: 17 tonnes
Average no. cases produced: 2,000

Principal wines & brands	Cellar Potential
Donnington Riesling	5 years
Winter Hill Riesling	1-2 years
Chardonnay	2-3 years
Semillon/Sauvignon Blanc	Drink now

Hours open to public: 1.30pm-4pm, weekends, public holidays and daily during December and January
Retail distribution: Erindale Cellars, Adelaide; Regent Arcade Bottle Shop; Aldgate Pump Hotel; Port Lincoln bottle shops

Cape Jaffa

CAPE JAFFA
Address: PO Box 437, Robe SA 5276
Phone: (08) 8768 5053
Fax: (08) 8768 5040
Email: capejaffawines@picknowl.com.au
WWW:http://www.picknowl.com.au/homepages/
capejaffawines
Established: 1993
Winemaker: Derek Hooper
Principal varieties grown: Chardonnay, Merlot, Cabernet Sauvignon, Shiraz, Sauvignon Blanc, Pinot Noir, Semillon, Cabernet Franc, Petit Verdot
Ha under vine: 18
Average annual crush: 500 tonnes total, 200 tonnes own

Principal wines & brands	Cellar Potential
Chardonnay	5 years
Unwooded Chardonnay	1-2 years
Cabernet Sauvignon	10+ years
Merlot	10+ years
Sauvignon Blanc/Semillon	3-4 years

Hours open to public: 10am-5pm, daily
Points of interest: Barrel storage and cave maturation
Retail distribution: Cellar Door and Mail Order. Australia wide. Export to UK

Kym and Sue Hooper have a long term love of wine. As a stock buyer for the family abattoir he noticed that the sheep coming from around the Cape Jaffa/Mount Benson area had a red tinge in their wool, just like those from Coonawarra. After an exhaustive search the Hooper's, along with partners, highly respected winemaker Ralph Fowler and his wife, bought their vineyard site in the rolling hills in the northern reaches of the new Mount Benson wine region.

The winery was carved into a limestone hillside with the cellar door built from the paddock rocks, picked off the property. 18 hectares are now producing an increasing vintage each year. Son, Derek Hooper, is the innovative and energetic winemaker and vineyard manager. Derek has worked closely with Ralph Fowler spending two vintages at the Leconfield winery.

He has also worked a vintage in a small French Champagne house another at Domaine de Chevalier in Bordeaux and plans to work the 1998 vintage at Chapoutiere in the Rhone region of France. The winery is well designed with its natural rock insulation and gravity flow.

On my first visit the first sauvignon blanc, a 1997, was being bottled. The crisp aromatic characters were most obvious.

The climate is cool like Coonawarra but with some four degrees less seasonal temperature variation. The warmer winters and cooler summers, due to the maritime influence, give a longer more even growing season. I noticed the red wines have very fine velvety tannins.

The 1995 Cabernet Sauvignon to be released soon has just won a gold medal in the Royal Melbourne Show.

The 1997 I found even better with very floral overtones and although a big wine, very supple, which seems to be a desirable regional character.

The 1996 Chardonnay also got gold medal marks from me.

The Cape Jaffa tasting room on top of the hill has panoramic views of the region and the southern ocean in the distance. It is one of the loveliest in Australia.

Cape Jaffa is a truly exciting new winery and vineyard in a great new region that we will hear much more about very soon.

The South Australian Fishing Industry

Like the South Australian Wine Industry the fishing folk of South Australia are a tightly knit bunch. Many families have fished our States waters for numerous generations since the states foundation. Fishing in fact preceded the states official establishment in 1836 as fishing colonies sprang up on Kangaroo Island as early as 1803 just after Flinders and French explorer Baudin charted the coastline.

My own family is very much a seafaring one. Thomas Hardy who arrived in 1850 by ship was a man of the land from Devon and married his cousin Joanna Hardy, my other two great grandfathers were ships captains, Captain William Begg from Scotland and Captain Johannson from Heligoland (now Scandinavia) both whose names appear on a memorial to eight prominent ships captains of those founding days near the Semaphore Jetty. My grandfather, Tom M. Hardy Australia's first Master Yachtsman, met his bride to be Eileen (after whom the Hardy's most prestigious wines are named) at the charming fishing hamlet of Port Vincent where her family ran the historic Ventnor Hotel in the 1920's.

Like wine also South Australia's fishing industry is a major export earner and going through an exciting stage of growth and development, particularly with the advent of agriculture in the tuna and oyster industries. South Australia's first export was three barrels of fish shipped to Tasmania in December 1836 only months after the colony was founded. South Australia is blessed with some 4,000 kms of magnificent coastline. The environment is probably the cleanest in the world helped by the fact, except for the Murray River, that no major river systems flow into its waters, in this the driest state on the driest continent of the world.

Nearly all types of seafood are harvested from the many and varied fisheries of the State and the quality from our cool, clean waters is second to none and now being appreciated in the seafood markets of the world, particularly in Japan and other Asian markets.

Traditional fishing of scale fish by line and net occurs in all waters of the State and accounted for about half the tonnage of the seafood harvest of some tonnes in 1997. The magnificent King George Whiting is a fish to my mind without equal in the world closely followed by the South Australian Snapper. I well remember as a child my first, and thank god only bout of seasickness, as my father put down the pick on the Orantes Bank and pulled in some massive snapper. Port Vincent, though only 10 kms or so away, seemed distant indeed. Those of you who have not tried Snapper head soup have not lived.

Garfish in another South Australian specialty and like many seafood's suits the oriental cuisines now so popular.

Many families fish in these traditional ways and have done so for many years. Women have always played a pivotal role in the fishing industry, often casting and cleaning the catch, keeping the books and doing so many other things a family needs done when the fishermen must be at sea.

June Gill from Yorke Peninsula, a prime mover in the Womens Industry Network (W.I.N.),is a great example of this. Ironically, many names of these fishing families are so appropriate never so evident as the day Kerry Gill will marry David Fisher.

The Rock Lobster or Crayfish as it is so often known in South Australia is now a huge industry, worth some $72 million dollars in 1997. S.A.F.I.C. Immediate past President, Graham Gribble from Robe, the heart of this industry, has done stalwart service for the whole industry over many years.

The King Prawns of South Australian waters are impressive indeed with their size and firm meaty texture and sweet flavour. Management of the prawn fisheries is very delicate and overfishing is now well guarded against. As a whole the fishing industries of the State take a sound long term view in these matters which is in everyone's best interest as demand worldwide for South Australian Seafood is sure to grow and can only be met through good management of all fisheries.

Abalone only started to be fished in the 1960 s and today is a major player in the industry with substantial exports and a value of over $20 million a year in produce.

The aquaculture business is where enormous

growth has taken place and the future seems rosy indeed.

The Tuna Farms near Port Lincoln are already massive export earners and over the last two or three years about 8,000 tonnes of live tuna have been transferred into these ocean farms from the overall tuna catch. The future value of these fish through value adding will be around $200 million.

Several times I have had the opportunity to cook and serve a whole tuna of some twenty kilograms, everything from Japanese style sashimi, tuna tartare to seared tuna steaks, it is sheer heaven to work with.

The resurgence of the South Australian Oyster Industry is nothing short of spectacular. Native oysters, a round variety, were prolific in South Australian waters during the last century and the early 1900's.

In 1870 at Coffin Bay alone, thirty sailing cutters manned by 80 men collected almost 6,500,000 oysters during the year by dredging. Unfortunately by the 1940's native oysters had been all but fished out. The natives took around 4 years to grow to catching size but the pacific oyster, native to Japan, only 2 years. After many attempts finally in the late 1980's a commercial oyster industry began to develop with beds being started in a number of bays on the West Coast and Spenders Gulf.

The first harvest of 1.4 million pacific oysters in 1991 has grown to around 17 million in 1997 with 55 oyster growers in 7 regions contributing. OYSA Limited, the South Australian Oyster Growers Marketing and Infrastructure Organisation has done a superb job, now with not only world class quality and purity of their product, but the worlds most stringent oyster quality assurance program in place. They literally cannot keep up with demand. Every morning at the 1996 Wine Australia Exhibition in Sydney I would drop into the OYSA stand for a few oysters with a glass of Black Velvet Sir James Champagne and Coopers Stout, what better way to start the day!!

The mighty Murray, in days gone by, produced prolific quantities of the majestic Murray Cod and Callop. Unfortunately, the European Carp has upset these native fishes habitat, but if you ever taste a fresh Murray Cod fillet in beer-batter you will know what you have been missing out on in your diet.

I celebrated with the fisher folk a short time ago at the first South Australian Seafood Awards banquet at the Port Dock Station organised by the Womens Industry Network. It was a great night with a train ride from Adelaide station and back.

This brought together all the fishing branches and families with the great processing

families such as the Raptis's and the Angelakis's who have done so much for the industry.

Nick Angelakis, the remaining founder of his huge family business, was crowned "King of the Sea". Fishmongers, restaurateurs, fishermen, they all celebrated together, it was a wonderful night.

The wine industry of the coastal regions of the State is also forging ahead and many of its pioneers are those that pioneered fishing in South Australia. The Wehl family from

Mt Benson, the Winters from Mt Gambier, both former rock lobster fishers, Graham and Mary Ford from Boston Bay Wines, former abalone divers, are bringing together "the sea and the vines" which is also co-incidentally the name of the splendid seafood festival held each year in the McLaren Vale region looking out on that Gulf of St Vincent – the Patron Saint of Winemakers, who I am sure would be smiling on this symbiotic South Australian celebration.

Cellarmasters – Mt Benson

Cellarmaster Wines is the World's second largest direct wine merchant. In recent years Cellarmasters has also become a sizeable producer in its own right with the purchase of a modern winery, Dorrien Estate, in the heart of the Barossa Valley and the planting of vineyards in Eden Valley and Mount Benson. Former chief winemaker Mike de Garis, who is now in charge of Cellarmasters' New Zealand operation, was actively involved in the establishment of the Mount Benson region. As president of the Mount Benson Vignerons Association, Mike prepared the application to the Geographical Indications Committee which saw Mount Benson become the first officially declared region in South Australia.

Cellarmasters' Black Wattle vineyard is a picture book vineyard set on rolling hills under the shadow of Mount Benson. There are some 54 hectares of vines planted on predominantly terra rossa soils. The knowledgable and personable viticulturist Jeff Flint is vineyard manager. Jeff harvested 80 tonnes in 1996 and expects the yield to grow to 1,160 tonnes – or around 25,000–30,000 cases – by the year 2000, making Cellarmasters the largest producer in the region.

I have been most impressed by the Black Wattle wines I have tried to far and I am sure they will only get better.

Mt Benson Vineyards

Bill and Margaret Wehl were the viticultural pioneers of the new exciting Mount Benson wine region.

Bill had long been in the crayfishing industry at the nearby historic town of Robe which provides some 40% of Australia's Rock Lobster for the local and export markets. On arriving at the Wehl's Mount Benson vineyard Bill was busy pruning his original block of cabernet sauvignon planted in 1989. The vines have thrived and are certainly very solid citizens now. Bill is a fastidious fellow and always looking for a way to prune to make the very best wines.

In tasting their first four vintages in the cute, little tasting room adjoining their home, the depth of flavour, colour and character in the wines was a heartening revelation. In reviews by Winestate Magazine they have received the highest honors. The first vintage was in 1992. A smart wine lover would do well to try and put together a collection of all their wines.

Me, I will drink and enjoy them and look forward to their next vintage. The Wehl's are sincere and straightforward people doing exceptional things.

MT BENSON VINEYARDS

Address: RSD 107, via Kingston SE SA 5275	**Cellar**
Phone: (08) 8768 6251	**Principal wines & brands** **Potential**
Fax: (08) 8768 6251	Cabernet Sauvignon 9 years
Established: 1989	
Owners: Bill and Margaret Wehl	**Public & trade tours:** By appointment only
Winemaker: Bruce Gregory	**Hours open to public:** 10am-4pm, daily
Principal varieties grown: Cabernet Sauvignon, Merlot	excepy Christmas Day and Good Friday
Ha under vine: 8	**Retail distribution:** S&V Wholesaler, Stonyfell SA.Yarra Valley Wine
Average annual crush: 10 tonnes	Consultants, Melbourne. Freely available
Average no. cases produced: 600	throught out the SE and C/D sales

Fleurieu Fine Foods

Dropping in on Jill and Tony Chinner at their delightful Fleurieu Fine Foods premises at Yankalilla was a real revelation to me.

The quality and range of their exquisite gourmet food products is a credit to Jill's creative genius and her many years as a teaching Home Economist with T.A.F.E. and the W.E.A.

Jill has more than a touch of flair as witnessed by her 6 years presenting cooking segments on channel sevens "Touch of Elegance".

Fleurieu Fine Foods utilise the bountiful produce of the Peninsula and much other Australian gourmet produce such as macadamia nuts. What started as a cottage industry in Jill and Tony's home, outgrowing this, they moved from Adelaide to Yankalilla to be nearer their source of supply, much of which Tony grows at the rear of their Main Street shop front and production area.

They were at first frightened of the size of the premises, how could they afford it or use it all. Today they are running out of room, a tribute to their success.

Many of their mustards and liqueur jams feature a "drop of the doings". Such as Macadamia and Champagne Mustard, Malt Whisky Mustard, Spiced Brandied Figs and Prunes in Port.

Fleurieu also have a range of excellent herb vinegars using the fruit of the vine.

A tribute to Fleurieu's quality is their foods are served on Qantas and sold in David Jones. Jill also makes Christmas cakes and fruit mince pies in November and December and all their produce is in a myriad of sizes. The Twin Bays Winery is only a couple of kilometres away and the coastal drive from Adelaide to Yankalilla is stunning. A great way to go on the gourmet trail with Fleurieu and a dozen or so other gourmet producers on the Peninsula.

FLEURIEU FINE FOODS
88 Main Road,
Yankalilla,
South Australia
5203
Telephone:
(08) 8558 2436
Facsimile:
(08) 8558 2239
After Hours:
(08) 8558 2271

Twin Bays Vineyard & Winery

The truly captivating view from this well thought out Boutique Vineyard and Winery is spectacular. Set on the slopes above Normanville, the rugged Rapid Bay and the tranquil Lady Bay spread out before you with Kangaroo Island often visible across the gulf waters of St Vincent - the patron Saint of winemakers.

Respected Adelaide Doctor and Specialist Bruno Giorgio gave birth to the venture with plantings in1989. The cool maritime climate, good rainfall and deep soils have proved perfect for the vine giving a long even growing season for building and conserving rich and complex varietal flavours in the grapes.

From his two hectares of vines Bruno produces a range of excellent wines with the help of experienced winemaker Alan Dyson also a maritime grapegrower at Maslins Beach further north.

The Twin Bays Riesling I found exquisite with beautiful floral aromas and flavours, most appropriate on the Fleurieu Peninsula. The shiraz, cabernet sauvignon and grenache all have well defined varietal fruit flavours.

Just over an hour of picturesque coastal driving from Adelaide brings you to Twin Bays where you can taste and buy the fine wines whilst enjoying the sensational view from the cellar door.

Twin Bays also make some gourmet delights such as the Red and White Vinegarís in individually hand painted bottles from a local artist.

To finish off the visit try Bruno's very good Tawny Port, just the shot in front of the cellar door's open fire if itís a cool day.

TWIN BAY

Address: Martin Road, Yankalilla SA 5203	Twin Bays Fleurieu Shiraz 8-10 years
Phone: (08) 8267 2844	Twin Bays Fleurieu Riesling 3-5 years
Fax: (08) 8239 0877	Twin Bays Fleurieu Wild Grenache 5-7 years
Email: twinbays@merlin.net.au	Twin Bays Fleurieu Light Red Current
Established: 1989	Twin Bays Tawny Port
Winemakers: Bruno Giorgio and Alan Dyson (Contract)	
Principal varieties grown: Cabernet Sauvignon, Shiraz, Riesling	**Hours open to public:** 10am-5pm weekends, school and public holidays
Ha under vine: 2	**Points of interest:**
Average annual crush: Less than 20 tonnes	Maritime vineyard overlooking Rapid and Lady Bays
Principal wines & brands **Cellar Potential**	**Retail distribution:**
Twin Bays Fleurieu Cabernet Sauvignon 8-10 years	Cellar Door and Mail Order sales. Selected SA retail outlets and restaurants

B arramundi (lates calcarifer) long prized by leading chefs for its unique texture and flavour, is native to Australia's tropical northern estuaries and possesses the rare quality of being able to thrive in both salt and fresh water.

Yet supply of Barramundi has always been difficult and inconsistent, presenting the restaurant and hospitality industry with a real menu dilemma. Enter innovative entrepreneur Lance Vater, already recipient of many national and international awards, particularly for the export of his creatively devised Australian products.

Some years ago, near the picturesque fishing village of Robe on the southeast coast of South Australia, Lance discovered and purchased, the experimental fish farming programme run by local identity David Stanhope, which together they have since developed to become a unique aquacultural farming operation producing an impeccably pure Barramundi fish of a quality unequalled anywhere in the world.

The secret to this unparalleled operation is the pure sweet, artesian water held fresh by nature for over five million years, which flows freely to the surface and is directed into the pristine and stress free environment of the growout farm.

The sweet spring water is naturally heated hundreds of metres below the surface and maintains a year round temperature of 30.2° C, ideal for the growth of the fingerlings which are raised from day old larvae at Robarra's Adelaide broodstock & hatchery facility in the strictest, sterile conditions. The fingerlings are government certified by the pathology branch of the Department of Primary Industry as 100% virus and disease free before being transferred in specially designed transport tanks to the Robe growout farm.

As the fish grow, the free flowing spring water is continuously passed through each growout tank, thus maintaining the purity of the growing environment.

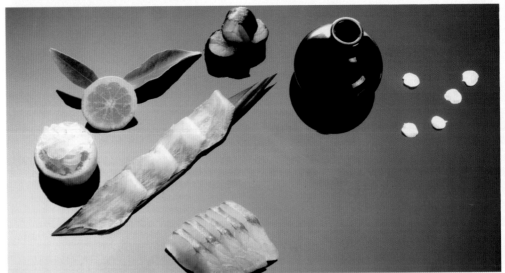

Robarra barramundi are supplied in various sizes ranging from 400 gram whole fish which looks just superb on the dinner plate, to live fish between 700 and 1000 gms, and 1 to 3 kg fish for value adding such as fillets, sugar cured and smoke varieties. The on-site processing facility is truly state of the art, extending the shelf life of the fresh barramundi to approximately ten days.

Live fish are transported in containers, and replenished from the same natural springs that feed the farm. Lance, in his constant pursuit of excellence, has applied his total quality management philosophy to every aspect of Robarra, assuring the highest standards all the way to the restaurant plate. I first met Lance Vater some four years ago at a wonderful seafood cooking presentation

Robarra

by January 1998. Ironically, the Robe Mount Benson wine region has also commenced and is quickly coming of age at the same time as Robarra's development. I salute this truly great concept and the way it has come to such splendid fruition.

by master chef Peter Jarmer, the first Australian chef to be honoured as a member of the international 'Les Disciples d'Auguste Escoffier,' the revered French society of cuisine.

Peter has a real gift as a teaching chef, and his son Christian who was South Australian Apprentice of the Year in 1991, and has represented Australia in international culinary cooking competitions, is Robarra's Executive Chef assisting Lance and David to supervise the processing, as well as developing new mouth-watering recipes. Christian will also be responsible for Robarra's planned International Gourmet Cookbook to be published for world wide distribution in late 1998 featuring barramundi preparation and recipes from some of the world's most recognised chefs, the proceeds benefiting worthy charities.

The Robarra Barramundi with its firm flesh and guaranteed purity also presents a perfect opportunity to the Japanese chef for exquisite raw fish dishes of Sashimi and Sushi. Master chef at the Royal Hyatt Tokyo, Hekaru Orita San is just one of the many devotees offering their personal endorsement of the Robarra product.

1997 also marks the fourth annual presentation of the prestigious Robarra International Epicurean Excellence Trophy. The first was won by Paul Bocuse, a legend of world cuisine, who has used Robarra barramundi in his Melbourne Restaurant continuously for over four years. Once again the Paul Bocuse Restaurant has triumphed, winning the sought after award for the second time.

White wines from the most delicate Rieslings through Sauvignon and Chenin Blancs to full bodied Chardonnays accompany superbly the varying styles of Robarra Home Grown Spring Water Barramundi.

I've even enjoyed a slightly chilled spicy Pinot Noir with the scrumptious smoked variety.

This year the Robe farm has been expanded by 140%, and a further expansion of 100% of the new, increased size is due to be completed

The Anchorage

Bituated on the shores of Encounter Bay at Victor Habor is "The Anchorage" the last bastion of the traditional Bed and Breakfast Guest House – of which Victor Habour boasted some 65 in number during its heydays of the 1920's.

This glorious heritage listed property is ideal, located for a stop over in your Wine Tour of the Fleurieu Peninsula. If coming from Adelaide you can come through McLaren Vale, take a scenic drive from Willunga to Yankalilla. Visit Twin Bays and Fleurieu Fine Foods and its then another short 15 – 20 minutes drive to Victor Harbor. Stay for the night at the Anchorage and travel on to Middleton Winery just up the road, Currency Creek for lunch and on to the Langhorne Creek Wineries for the afternoon.

If coming from Melbourne visit Langhorne Creek first and stay the night at the Anchorage before attacking the Fleurieu Peninsula, up to McLaren Vale refreshed the next day.

The Anchorage café has loads of atmosphere with a whaling boat forming the bar. The progressive Australian Cuisine is complimented by a interesting regional wine list.

I enjoyed a glass of "Black Velvet" stout and champagne with a serve of fresh South Australian Oysters on my recent pitstop. I wish I'd had time to "put the anchor down" for longer.

Why not stop over and enjoy all the old world charm, the polished baltic pine floors, ornate ceilings and antique furnishings.

Mine hosts, Chris and Nina Mortimer and Janis Warren know how to look after you.

An introduction to Victoria

Victoria has been through a wine revolution in the last decade. The number of wineries has exploded - at last count, there were more than 230 wineries in the state, the most of any state in the Australia. However, Victoria accounts for less than 20 per cent of the nation's production.

One important factor is that Victoria is truly a premium wine producer. Well over 90 per cent of the wineries are small, boutique, premium bottled wine producers. No state has such a wide spread of vineyards and virtually no region of the state is without a vineyard, showing how suitable the climate and soil are for vines.

In 1838 William Ryrie planted Victoria's first vines in the Yarra Valley at Yering Station. Within five years many vineyards had been established in Geelong, the Yarra Valley, and in and around metropolitan Melbourne. Suburban vineyards, some as large as 30 acres, were located at South Yarra, Toorak and Brighton. This development was due largely to the arrival of groups of Swiss immigrants who brought both vine cuttings and viticultural knowledge to the new colony. In particular, Paul and Hubert de Castella and the Baron Guillaume de

Pury were influential in establishing a new viticultural industry throughout the Yarra Valley. Swiss settlers also spread winemaking knowledge to Geelong where vines were first planted in 1842.

The gold rush of the late 1800ís encouraged many thousands of people to travel inland in the search for easy wealth. New areas were settled and towns were consequently established. Winemakers travelled also, developing vineyards in Great Western, Avoca, Ballarat, Bendigo, the Goulburn Valley and as far north as Rutherglen.

By the end of the century Victoria was producing more wine than any other colony. Unfortunately this booming industry went into decline owing to a change in public tastes and to an attack from a tiny aphid called Phylloxera Vastatrix which kills vines by eating through their roots. The louse first attacked vines in Geelong in 1875 and gradually spread north through the state. In an attempt to protect Rutherglen, Victoria's principal wine-producing area, affected winemakers were ordered to destroy all vines and chemically sterilize their soil, making replanting financially impractical. By some quirk of fate, the Yarra Valley was spared this parasite, but both here and in

other unaffected areas, production soon ceased due to the growth in popularity of fortified wines and the competitive prices of interstate producers.

The only regions still producing wine by 1921, were the Goulburn Valley and Glenrowan, Great Western, Rutherglen and the North -Western Murray River. With Victoria's wine production thus affected, redevelopment did not begin until the 1960's when table wine again became popular. A few new districts were planted to vines however, such as Drumborg in the south-western corner of the state, the high elevated cool regions in the Central Highlands, King and Ovens Valleys and the Mornington Peninsula. Each of the 11 wine-producing areas of Victoria (with many subdivisions), produces distinctly characteristic wines.

When purchasing a Victorian wine the wine-lover is now confronted with an incredible array of wine styles and varieties. Despite almost total eradication, the wine industry of Victoria has re-asserted itself across the state. Wines currently produced cater for all tastes and compare favourably with those of other states. Generally of a very high quality, Victorian wines are finding a ready market both Australia wide and internationally.

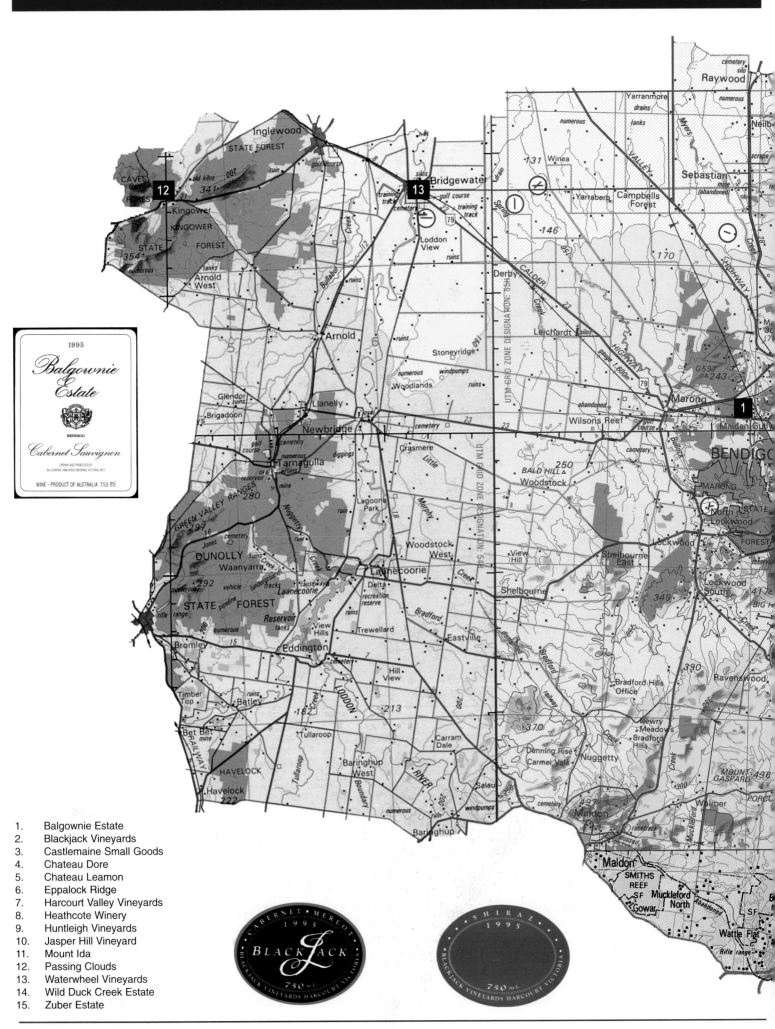

1. Balgownie Estate
2. Blackjack Vineyards
3. Castlemaine Small Goods
4. Chateau Dore
5. Chateau Leamon
6. Eppalock Ridge
7. Harcourt Valley Vineyards
8. Heathcote Winery
9. Huntleigh Vineyards
10. Jasper Hill Vineyard
11. Mount Ida
12. Passing Clouds
13. Waterwheel Vineyards
14. Wild Duck Creek Estate
15. Zuber Estate

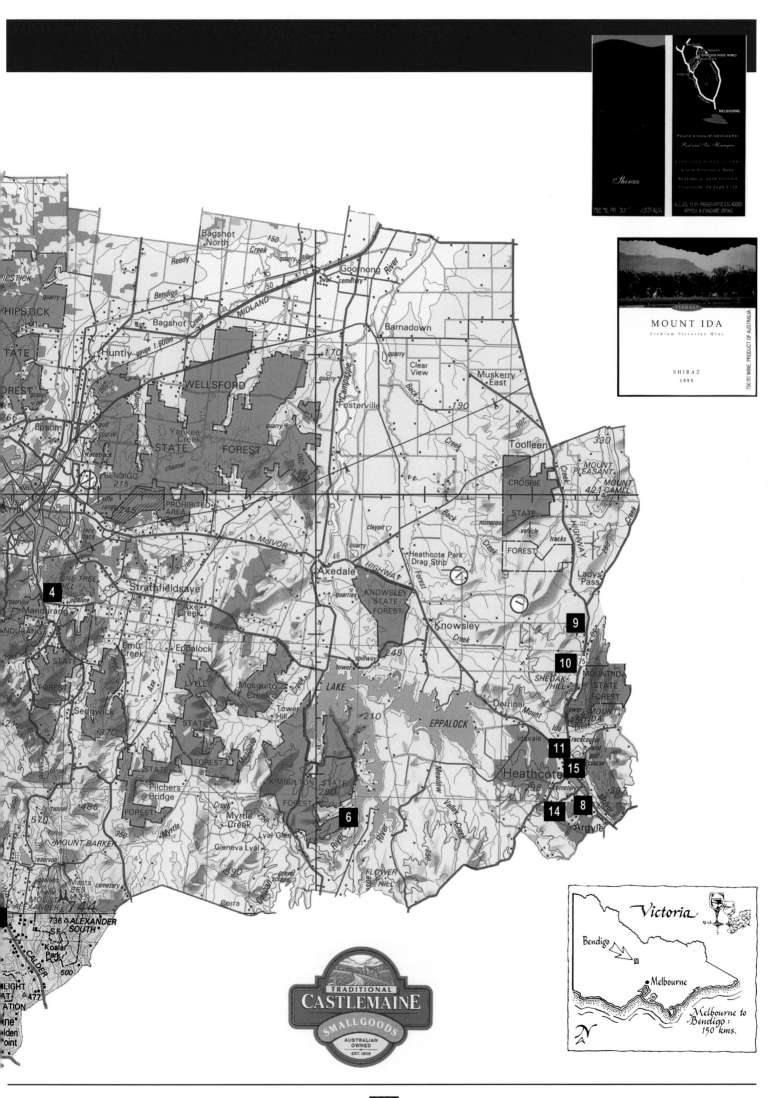

Although a few vineyards existed around Bendigo during the late 1840s the area did not fully develop until gold was discovered in 1851. Within thirty years, there were over one hundred wine producers in the region, manufacturing very high quality wines. Phylloxera, the scourge of Victoria's vignerons, was discovered in Bendigo in 1893, thus bringing a thriving industry to a grinding halt. As in the Geelong district, local winemakers were forced to destroy their vines and the area was not replanted until 1969. In this year, Stuart Anderson established the Balgownie vineyard north east of Bendigo. Since then, the area has once again attracted winemakers, although only a small proportion of the original number (roughly twelve wineries).

While the Bendigo Region produces some premium wines, physical conditions of the area are far from ideal. The average annual rainfall for Bendigo is a low 500-550mm which is compensated for in various ways. Some winemakers irrigate their vineyards, others rely on an underground water supply, while still others depend on clay subsoils to retain what rain does fall. Furthermore, the impervious nature of widespread clay soils can prove to be a problem by restricting growth of vine roots. Once these difficulties have been overcome however, winemakers have followed Stuart Anderson's excellent lead to produce outstanding wines from this colourful region. Innovative winemakers such as Peter Cumming from Waterwheel have done much to conquer the elements and enhance this region's reputation.

EPPALOCK RIDGE WINERY
Address: 633 North Redesdale Road, Redesdale VIC 3444
Direction: 9km north of Redesdale Township
Phone: (03) 5425 3135
Fax: (03) 5425 3135
Established: 1979
Owners: Rod and Sue Hourigan
Winemaker: Rod Hourigan
Principal varieties grown: Shiraz, Cabernet Sauvignon, Merlot, Malbec, Cabernet Franc
Ha under vine: 3
Average annual crush: 25-30 tonnes
Average no. cases produced: 1,500

Principal wines & brands	Cellar Potential
Shiraz	10-12 years

"If every wine could be red ...... it would"

Public & trade tours: No
Hours open to public: 10am-6pm, daily but best to phone first
Retail distribution: Victoria only at the moment

Balgownie

While on a visit to the Bordeaux district of France in 1950, Stuart Anderson fell in love with the region and it's wines. He began a continuing association with the area and in particular, M Louis Vialard of Chateau Cissac from whom he has gained much of his considerable winemaking knowledge. In 1969, Stuart planted approximately 30 acres of vines a short distance north-east of Bendigo. The property was named 'Balgownie' and although only 5,000-6,000 cases of wine were produced annually, these wines have always been of such high quality that they are practically sold before they are on the shelves. The Balgownie Cabernet Sauvignon is the star of the range which also includes a shiraz. The cabernet has great depth with berry/cassis flavours and a beautiful hint of sweet oak and is consistently one of the best wines of this variety in Australia. The Balgownie Shiraz is of a lighter style with a peppery character similar to wines from the Rhone Valley in France. Some years ago, Mildara Wines saw the potential of Balgownie and purchased the vineyard and winery. Balgownie was in fact, the first vineyard to be planted in the rebirth of the Bendigo wine region. This led the way for other winemakers in the region, by producing a range of 100 per cent estate grown varieties. Mildara Blass are carrying on this proud tradition.

BALGOWNIE ESTATE WINERY

Address: Hermitage Road, Maiden Valley VIC 3551
Phone: (03) 5449 6222
Fax: (03) 5449 6506
Established: 1969
Owner: Mildara Blass Limited
Winemaker: Lindsay Ross
Principal varieties grown: Cabernet, Merlot, Shiraz
Ha under vine: 100
Average no. cases produced: 9,000

Principal wines & brands	Cellar Potential
Balgownie Premier Chardonnay	2-4 years
Balgownie Premier Shiraz Cabernet	3-5 years
Balgownie Estate Cabernet Sauvignon	5-8 years
Balgownie Estate Shiraz	5-8 years

Public & trade tours: Trade tours by appointment only
Hours open to public: 10.30am-5pm, Mon-Sat

Blackjack Vineyards

Blackjack is red!! "All wine would be red if it could be" to quote an old wine campaigner and character Colin Richardson, a big man in every way, a little like the reds from Blackjack.

The search for a suitable vineyard site led Ian McKenzie and Ken Pollock to the Old Central Victorian gold fields near Harcourt not far from Castlemaine and only an hour or so up the Calder Highway from Melbourne. They bought the old apple and pear orchard in 1987, commenced planting in 1988 and made their first wines in 1992. Their 1993 Shiraz was voted the Peoples Choice red wine at the 1995 Victorian Wine Exhibition and the 1994 won the trophy for the Best 1994 Shiraz at the 1996 Royal Melbourne Show. Their other mainstay is a cabernet merlot a 70/30 blend. Both the 1993 and 1994 have won medals at the Royal Melbourne Show. When the year suits they also release a full bodied pinot noir.

Blackjack was an American sailor who jumped ship in the 1850's and headed for the gold fields. The vineyard borders on Blackjack road and is certainly producing liquid gold. The vineyard is meticulously managed with high vertical trellising to maximise sun contact with the leaves and grapes giving rich colour and flavour to the wines. Hand pruning and hand picking also adds to this flavour potential.

Why not drop into the cellar door it is near the junctions of three main highways, the Calder, Pyrenees and Midland Highways and is open weekends and public holidays from 11.00am - 5.00pm.

BLACKJACK VINEYARDS

Address: Blackjack Vineyards, Calder Highway, Harcourt VIC 3453
Direction: 2km south of Harcourt
Phone: (03) 5474 2355
Fax: (03) 5474 2355
Established: 1988
Owners: Ian McKenzie and Ken Pollock
Winemakers: Ian McKenzie and Ken Pollock
Principal varieties grown: Shiraz, Cabernet, Pinot Noir, Merlot
Ha under vine: 4

Average annual crush: 36 tonnes
Average no. cases produced: 1,000-2,000

Principal wines & brands	Cellar Potential
Blackjack Shiraz	4-8 years
Blackjack Cabernet/Merlot	

Public & trade tours: By appointment only
Hours open to public: Weekends and public holidays when wine available
Retail distribution: Vintners, Andrew Watts, 176 Rathmings Street, Hawthorn East VIC 3123, (03) 9882 1875

Wallco Ostrich Corporation

Late last summer I went to an evening function organised at the classy Jolley's Boathouse restaurant overlooking the Torrens River in Adelaide. I was a little sceptical and maybe a touch apprehensive because the menu was to be all ostrich.

To say the food was sensational would be an understatement, it came in all shapes, sizes and styles from dim sims, smoked cold to small steakettes, gourmet rissoles, pates, terrines and all manner of other presentations that one could think off. Through all of it the texture, like fillet steak and the fine flavours shone through, refined and not overpowering. That was my first introduction to a very serious and professional company WALLCO who are breeding and farming ostriches in Northern Victoria.

The farming of ostriches is an age old industry mainly tied to South Africa. Apart from the splendid meat, which is a dark red colour and has only 0.5% fat, compared with up to three times this much for lean chicken or beef, there is also the use of the hide for top class leather products, highly sought after. Oil derived from the ostrich is used in cosmetics and other products, not to mention the feathers, which have long been part of the fashion and entertainment business, they even have some uses in industry as the best dust collecting agents possible.

Recently I was lucky enough to secure some fan fillets of ostrich which I seared quickly in a hot griddle pan whole, followed by a quick roasting after flambéing in brandy. The meat really needs to be cooked quickly to be at its best. At the dinner I prepared, out of almost 40 people and a choice of fish, 35 chose ostrich and the comments were most complimentary. Many likening it to beef fillet but with a slightly finer texture and some extra flavour. I also arranged to have a fan fillet hot smoked and this really came out well with marvellous soft even texture and a lovely balance of meat and smokehouse characters.

Ostriches fit in well to our modern food ethics being extremely kind to the environment with their large soft feet. They do not break up our "oldest continents" soil like hooved cattle or sheep. The ostrich is a prehistoric animal belonging to the flightless bird family known as Ratites, they grow to a height of more than two metres at maturity. The secret to the ostrich as a meat producer is that it reproduces through eggs each weighing about 1.5 kilograms. The female lays an average of 45 – 50 eggs during the mating season which lasts from August until March in Australia. 20 – 35 live chicks usually result, this compares with the yearly average of a cow having one offspring and sheep an average of 1.5 offspring per year. Ostriches need little land and have a very efficient metabolism, converting grass to body mass at a rate of 2 to 1, compared with cattle needing much more land and only converting feed to mass on a 5 to 1 ratio. The total meat yield of a breeding ostrich is some 700 kilograms of lean meat per year versus beef at 240 kilograms.

Ostrich is now becoming a very sought after delicacy in France and also in top Los Angeles restaurants.

British Airways are serving it in first class on their Trans Atlantic flights. Even a large supermarket chain in the UK is selling ostrich fillets but just cannot keep up. Here in Australia a number of leading restaurants have ostrich on the menu and it is being very well accepted. The other evening I had a char grilled fillet at the Red Ochre Grill in Adelaide, it was the best meat meal I have ever tasted!!

As far as which wine to enjoy with ostrich, a fairly wide range of wines is possible due to the many and varied dishes which can be prepared.

I enjoyed a full bodied semillon from Henschke with the lighter dishes and feel a good wooded chardonnay or a lighter pinot noir slightly chilled would also be a good companion to the more delicate dishes. For the roast or grilled meats a full bodied gamey pinot noir or a rhone style shiraz or cool climate cabernet or merlot is great. You make the choice, but try this exceptional meat it's a healthy and environmentally sound way to enjoy a wonderful new experience.

Castlemaine Bacon Company

Whilst Castlemaine began its life in this picturesque country Victorian town in 1905 producing mainly bacon, today the company produces more than 500 individual smallgoods of every shape, style and size.

Cured and fermented meat products have long accompanied the wines in European countries. Most wine-growing families in countries such as France, Italy, Spain and Germany make their own cured hams, salamis, terrines and pates. I well remember helping my neighbours each year in the Cognac region of France to turn a complete pigs carcass into an astonishing array of delicacies.

My favourite was the cured prosciutto style ham, I even pressed a couple of legs myself and cured them in the smoke filled tower of my chateau – a slight accident as the grand fireplace was not working too well. The next year my neighbours all wanted to hang their's there also French oak smoked ham – it

was a winner a little secret was massaging them with "Eau de Vie" (70% alcohol cognac) first, but back to Castlemaine.

In 1882 John Weetman arrived in Melbourne from his native England. He set up 3 or 4 small pork shops in the cosmopolitan St Kilda area. He produced his own bacon and smallgoods.

In 1905, with his daughter and prospective son-in-law Wright Harris, he set up business in Castlemaine curing and processing 5 pigs a week in the old Castlemaine Butter Factory. In 1913, with business expanding, he moved to the current site in Richards Road.

After Weetman's death in 1922 Wright Harris carried on the business.

By 1930, 500 pigs a year were being processed. In 1946 Harris formed the Castlemaine Bacon Company with his seven sons, by the 1950's Castlemaine became the first company in Australia to install a vacuum packaging machine. Production had expanded to 15,000 pigs a year by 1967 and the workforce was up to 80 people and much new machinery had been installed.

1979 saw a large world class abattoir installed with a capacity of 1700 pigs a day. A little like wine, to ensure supply of quality meat, Castlemaine set up their own pig raising facilities at Girgarree and Bears Lagoon. 45,000 animals are now housed at these facilities.

Castlemaine purchased Otto Wurth in 1991 to assist in the production and marketing of European delicacies. Castlemaine has remained a family business, operated by five successive generations of the Harris family. Their dedication and quality focus has seen the company grow to employ 900 people. Like the specialist little German sausage and smallgoods makers in the Barossa Valley, Castlemaine are proud of their product and I am sure you can find one of their 500 or more superb products to suit the wine you like!!

An introduction to the Macedon Ranges

The Macedon viticultural region, closer to Melbourne than some parts of the Yarra Valley, stretches from North of the Sunbury Region to Boynton and from Mt William, west to Malmsbury. It is really divided into two separate regions, the wineries grouped around the central Lancefield-Woodend-Macedon area then further north.

Initial development in the region started with the gold rush in the 1850's.

Within 60 years however, due to the phylloxera plague and changes in wine drinking tastes, the industry had faded from existence.

The 1970's saw a renaissance of the area when the Knight family at Granite Hill and Tom Lazar at Virgin Hills established vineyards in the area. Other winemakers who followed were Flynn and Williams at Kyneton, Gordon and Judy Cope-Williams at Romsey, John and Ann Ellis at Hanging Rock, Keith and Lyn Brien at Cleveland Estate and many others. There are now more than 30 grape-growers in the region, supplying about a dozen wineries.

To play such a major role in the production of high quality fruit in such a short period of time is an attribute to the endeavours of all who have been involved in the re-establishment of the area as a viticultural region. The French-based champagne house, Móet and Chandon with their Australian offshoot, Domaine Chandon, have shown great interest in the potential of this district.

Subsequently, most grape growers have planted and are planting chardonnay and pinot noir vines for the production of fruit suitable for methode champenoise wines which are an obvious strength of the region. The Northern District is also renowned for its red wines, with Virgin Hills, Knight's, Hanging Rock and many others making extremely long-living wines.

Shiraz particularly, does extremely well in the cool climate and granite soils.

Some great rieslings, sauvignon blancs and chardonnays are also made, particularly in warmer years.

Vying for the title of Australia's coolest viticultural region with its volcanic and granite soils, the tough conditions challenge the vignerons' and viticulturists' skills to the limit, but great wines are the result.

Wine tourism is fast becoming a way of life for many of the region's producers.

Cope-Williams at Romsey has an extraordinary spread-eagled, but superbly planned hospitality complex, complete with a cricket ground, pavilion and large 'Clubroom' restaurant - you can feel like a lord for the day. The beautifully restored Cleveland Mansion of Keith and Lyn Brien is an absolute gem and they also have bed and breakfast accommodation, while Hanging Rock has a casual eatery, Pam and Don Ludbey's Mt Macedon Winery has a charming Tea Room tasting area.

The list continues, it's so close to Melbourne and yet has a majestic isolated feel that touches the soul.

Macedon Ranges

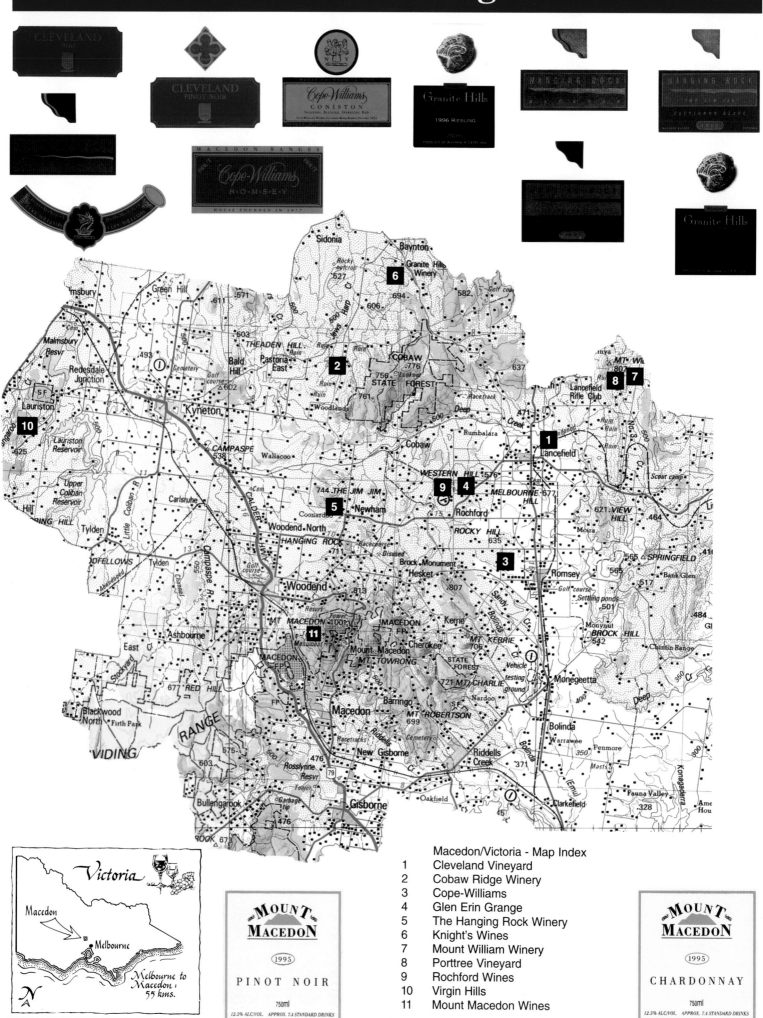

Macedon/Victoria - Map Index
1   Cleveland Vineyard
2   Cobaw Ridge Winery
3   Cope-Williams
4   Glen Erin Grange
5   The Hanging Rock Winery
6   Knight's Wines
7   Mount William Winery
8   Porttree Vineyard
9   Rochford Wines
10 Virgin Hills
11 Mount Macedon Wines

Cleveland

When I first met Keith Brien more than 20 years ago as a fellow member of the Shiraz Club in Melbourne, he was a keen wine connoisseur and a full-time airline pilot, he is now a full-time vigneron. Keith and his charming wife Lynette have enough energy and enthusiasm for 10 people, coupled with extraordinary good taste.

Aside from their award-winning Cleveland Brut Methode Champenoise, which won the Sommelier's Trophy at the 1994 Victorian Winemakers Exhibition on its first outing, they produce a chardonnay beginning with their first vintage in 1988. A cabernet sauvignon and a pinot noir have been added to their stable.

Alongside and above their winery the Brien's have restored the old historic wool shed and stables complex which now incorporates a function area for 50 people. Two delightful bed and breakfast units have panoramic views over the vineyard and ranges as does the attic gallery room. If you wish to celebrate a special occasion, the Brien's serve dinner in their Grand Dining Room with its exquisite Victorian Gothic style and furnishings; the table setting has to be seen to be believed. The Mansion is surrounded by walled gardens and a number of outdoor areas can be used for summer functions. Take a trip to Cleveland and discover old world grace.

CLEVELAND VINEYARD

Address: Shannons Road, Lancefield, VIC 3435
Phone: (03) 5429 1449
Fax: (03) 5429 2017
Established: 1984
Owners: Keith and Lyn Brien
Winemaker: Keith Brien
Principal varieties grown: Pinot Noir, Chardonnay, Cabernet Sauvignon
Ha under vine: 3.5
Average annual crush: 20-50 tonnes
Average no. cases produced: 4000

Principal wines & brands	Cellar Potential
'Cleveland'	
Brut	2-5 years
Pinot Noir	5-10 years
Chardonnay	5-10 years
Cabernet Sauvignon	5-10 years
'Brien'	
Chardonnay	2-5 years
Shiraz/Cabernet/Beverford/	
Macedon	5-10 years

Public & trade tours: By Appointment Only
Hours open to public: 9am-6pm, daily
Points of interest:
Historic Home, underground Cellars, restored 'Woolshed' Restaurant and Bed and Breakfast facilities
Retail distribution:
Select Vineyards

Cope-Williams Vineyard – Romsey

Architect Gordon Cope-Williams, a most successful designer of country houses, moved to the lush rolling Romsey countryside with his wife Judy in the early 70's to breed Welsh mountain ponies and grow a few grapes ñ indulgent hobbies if you like.

The initial Rocky Hill Vineyard was planted on an exposed slope, causing considerable problems with ripening fruit. Gusty winds and a high altitude maintained lower temperatures which resulted in very low grape yields.

Consequently, in 1982 a second vineyard was established in a more protected location close to the winery. Named the Coniston Vineyard, it was planted with pinot noir, chardonnay and small plots of cabernets and merlot.

Construction at Romsey is on a grand scale. The towered manor is large enough to accommodate guests. The construction did not stop there. Gordon, an avid cricket fan, has created an English village cricket ground, complete with a charming pavilion and a large clubroom, furnished with old leather chairs, that can cater for up to 120 guests. The Cope-Williams' son Michael, a Roseworthy graduate who has worked in both California and France specialising in sparkling wines, is now in charge of the winemaking. The coup de grace of the maison is their Romsey Brut. The stalwarts of their table wine range are a pinot noir and chardonnay. The Cope-Williams Estate is surrounded by stately conifers providing a necessary windbreak for the vines and the intrepid cricketers. All in all, Cope-Williams have performed a real hat trick of wine, hospitality and cricket, not necessarily in that order!!

COPE-WILLIAMS - ROMSEY VINEYARD

Address: Glenfern Road, Romsey VIC 3434
Direction: 50km north of Melbourne
Phone: (03) 5429 5428
Fax: (03) 5429 5655
Established: 1977
Owners: Judy, Gordon & Michael Cope-Williams
Winemaker: Michael Cope-Williams
Principal varieties grown: Chardonnay, Pinot Noir, Cabernet Sauvignon, Merlot
Ha under vine: 14
Average annual crush: 100 tonnes

Principal wines & brands	Cellar Potential
Cope-Williams Romsey Brut	5+ years
Cope-Williams Romsey Rosé	5+ years
Pinot Noir	5-10 years
Chardonnay	5-10 years
Cabernet/Merlot	10+ years
Romsey Willow	5-10 years

Public & trade tours: Yes
Hours open to public: 9am-5.30pm, daily
Points of interest: Social cricket in village green setting, day conference centre, sparkling wine cellars under cricket pavilion; gardens, weddings, dinners and lunches
Retail distribution: Extensive in NSW and VIC

The Hanging Rock Winery

anging Rock was made famous by the novel 'Picnic at Hanging Rock', adapted into a superb world-renowned film by Australian director Peter Weir. Like the heroines in this mysterious story, I'm sure you'd like to lose yourself in this truly beautiful part of Australia.

Each year, the racetrack tucked under the awesome granite boulders that form this striking landmark comes to life with that particular Australian phenomenon, the picnic race meeting. Several kilometres away, on a slope of the opposing range, spreads the vineyards of a first class winery, 'Hanging Rock'. The winery is also the home to an extremely hospitable and well credentialled wine family. John Ellis was the first wine-maker for Rosemount Estate in the 1970', and he really put them on the map. One of the most gifted winemakers in Australia and highly regarded by his peers, he was sought out by Dr. Peter Tisdall when he launched his wine enterprise at Echuca. John was most taken by The Tisdall Mount Helen Vineyard in the cool Strathbogie Ranges. The wines he made from this vineyard were

sensational. John married Ann Tyrrell, daughter of legendary Hunter Valley Winemaker, Murray Tyrell. They were searching to put down their roots and establish their own vineyard and winery and chose their stunning site in the extremely cool Hanging Rock Valley in the centre of the Macedon Ranges Region, fast becoming one of Australia's foremost cool climate wine regions. John made wine from other vineyards' grapes until their own vineyards came into bearing, and still buys in some fruit. John also makes a good deal of wine under contract for other wineries.

The innovative winery, which incorporates the family home around it with windows looking down into the fermentation and press room, is truly amazing. The front of the winery, with its incredible view of the weathered extinct volcano that is Hanging Rock, sports a classy tasting room and hospitality area to rival anything world wide. Why not pack your own picnic and head for Hanging Rock? John and Ann's wide range of still and sparkling wines will be the perfect accompaniment.

HANGING ROCK

Address: Jim Road, Newham VIC 3442
Phone: (03) 5427 0542
Fax: (03) 5427 0310
Email: HRW@hangingrock.com.au
WWW: http://www.hangingrock.com.au
Established: 1982
Owners: John and Ann Ellis
Winemaker: John Ellis
Principal varieties grown: Pinot Noir, Chardonnay, Sauvignon Blanc, Shiraz
Ha under vine: 6
Average annual crush: 250 tonnes
Average no. cases produced: 15,000

Principal wines & brands	Cellar Potential
Hanging Rock Macedon (Sparkling)	Cuvee
Hanging Rock Jim Jim Sauvignon Blanc	2-5 years
Hanging Rock "Victoria" Range	
Chardonnay	2-5 years
Cabernet Merlot	5-10 years
Pinot Noir	5-10 years
Riesling Semillon Sauvignon Blanc	2-5 years
Hanging Rock 'Picnic' Range	
Hanging Rock Heathcote Shiraz	10-20 years

Public & trade tours: By appointment only
Hours open to public: 10am-5pm, daily except Christmas Day and Good Friday
Points of interest: Close proximity to Hanging Rock with Picnic Grounds, CafÈ etc.
Retail distribution: Melbourne, Country VIC, NSW, QLD

Knight Granite Hills Wines

vineyards – set amongst the rugged granite strewn hills of Victoria's central Great Divide. Like true Chevaliers of the land, the Knight's battle the adversity of their climate with courage and determination, producing individual wines of character.

The Knight family first planted an experimental vineyard on their grazing property 'Granite Hills' in 1970. Although it is one of Australia's highest vineyards at 550 metres above sea level, and prone to occasional strong winds, the grapes ripened well and further plantings followed. Vineyards now total roughly two hectares each of cabernet sauvignon, shiraz, riesling and chardonnay. There are also some smaller plantings of cabernet franc and merlot, with additional grapes are brought in from neighbouring growers.

The first vintage at Granite Hills winery was in 1979. The Granite Hills Shiraz took the wine world by storm and continues to be a benchmark for the peppery, cool climate versions of this Australian classic red. The cabernet, originally 100% cabernet, is a more generous style with the inclusion of cabernet franc and merlot - a lovely wine. Although renowned for their red wines, Knight's also produce some fine white wines. The riesling exhibits pronounced floral aromas and the interesting spiciness, apparent in all Granite Hills wines. A stylish fruit driven chardonnay with soft, integrated oak is also produced.

Wines are made by Llewelyn (Lew) Knight, and the rest of the family looks after the

KNIGHT GRANITE HILLS
Address: Burke & Wills Track, Kyneton VIC 3444
Direction: 85 kms north/northwest of Melbourne **via Lancefield**
Phone: (03) 5423 7264
Fax: (03) 5423 7288
Established: 1970
Owner: Knight Family
Winemaker: Llew Knight
Principal varieties grown: Riesling, Chardonnay, Shiraz, Cabernet Sauvignon
Ha under vine: 9
Average annual crush: 100 tonnes
Average no. cases produced: 7,000

Principal wines & brands	Cellar Potential
'Knight Granite Hills'	
Shiraz	5-10+ years
Cabernet Sauvignon	5-10+ years
Chardonnay	2-8 years
Riesling	2-10+ years
Knight 'Mica'	
Unwooded White	1-3 years
Cabernet Sauvignon	2-5 years

Public & trade tours: By Appointment Only
Hours open to public: 9am-6pm, Mon-Sat; 12pm-6pm, Sunday
Points of interest: Spectacular views of Central Victoria from the Vineyard and rugged granite strewn hills surrounding
Retail distribution: Melbourne, Country VIC, NSW, QLD and ACT

Mount Macedon Wines

MOUNT MACEDON WINES
Address: PO Box 76, Mt. Macedon VIC 3441
Direction: Banden Road - Half way between Mt Macedon and Woodend
Phone: (03) 5427 2735
Fax: (03) 5427 1071
Established: 1989
Owners: Don and Pam Ludbey
Winemaker: Peter Dredge
Principal varieties grown: Chardonnay, Pinot Noir, Shiraz, Merlot, Cabernet Sauvignon
Ha under vine: 10
Average annual crush: 40 tonnes
Average no. cases produced: 2,400

Principal wines & brands	Cellar Potential
Mount Macedon Reserve	
Chardonnay	5-10 years
Mount Macedon Chardonnay	5-10 years
Pinot Noir	5-10 years
Mount Macedon Hay Hill Shiraz	10 years
Mount Macedon Hay Hill	
Cabernet Sauvignon-Merlot	5-10 years
1994 Mount Macedon Cuvee	
(First Release 1998)	

Public & trade tours: By appointment only
Hours open to public: 10am-6pm, daily
Points of interest: Light lunches on weekends and public holidays. Magnificent views in a rural setting

As one winds around the road on the slopes of Mt Macedon with the lush forest of the conservation park both sides one wonders if there really is a winery somewhere around the corner.

Then all of a sudden above you on the slopes of the mountain in a neatly cut out clearing is a beautifully ordered vineyard with a gorgeous cottage winery and cellar door beneath it.

The view from the tasting room over a sea of gums as far as the eye can see makes one feel much further away than just an hour out of Melbourne.

High profile newspaper executive Don Ludbey is now a very much hands-on vineyard and winery proprietor. As we arrived he was unloading the "cake" of chardonnay skins from the press he and his consultant winemaker Peter Dredge had just operated.

It was a glorious autumn evening, the vines vibrant, leaves catching the golden rays as the sun set.

In the cellar door, reminiscent of a Victorian tea room, furnished and decorated by Don's wife Pam in great style we tasted a range of very good chardonnays and pinot noirs.

Mt Macedon have two vineyards, 12 acres at the winery site and 10 acres at the historic Hay Hill site south of Macedon (first planted in 1859). A further 10 acres are due to be planted at Hay Hill soon.

Pam also serves lunch from an innovative menu on weekends.

An introduction to Sunbury

The Viticultural Region at Sunbury is Melbourne's closest. Ironically it is also one of the oldest, having been first planted in the 1850's.

The renaissance of the area began in 1976 when the Carmody Family replanted the Craiglee Vineyard, first planted with vines in 1864 by James Johnston, a politician, who gained international fame for the region when he won an International Award for his 1972 "Hermitage" at an exposition in Vienna. The Carmody's have restored the old bluestone winery and cellars, which are well worth visiting.

Across the road is the impressive Goona Warra Vineyard Estate of John and Elizabeth Barnier, with its beautiful bluestone buildings, now magnificently restored as vineyard, winery, function complex and

restaurant. James Goodall Francis, an early Victorian Premier, first planted vines on the property in 1858.

These famous historic wineries have since been joined by another winery even closer to Melbourne. Under the flight path of the jets as they fly into Tullamarine Airport is the Wildwood Vineyard of surgeon, Dr Wayne Stott. The even newer Sunbury wineries of Longview Creek and Diggers Rest Vineyard now also have wines on the market.

For a day tripper or a serious wine enthusiast, Sunbury, birth place of the famous cricket ashes, is a great wine region to visit just a cricket ball throw or so from Melbourne's famous Melbourne Cricket Ground.

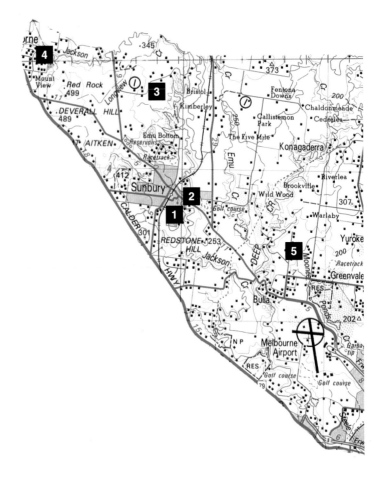

Goona Warra

Former State Premier James Goodall Francis planted vines on his property 'Goona Warra' in 1858. Shortly after the turn of the century, however, the economics of the day forced the vineyard to cease production. The vines were not re-established until John and Elizabeth Barnier purchased the land in 1983.

The original bluestone buildings, including the winery, were still standing, although sorely in need of repair. Appreciating the historical significance of these treasures, Elizabeth's skills as an architect were well used in the restoration of the buildings which now house an excellent winery and a popular restaurant and function centre.

The first small vintage was made at Goona Warra in 1986.

Sunbury is one of Australia's most historic villages, birthplace of the famous 'Ashes' fought for so ardently by the Australian and English cricket teams.

Sunbury is the closest wine region to Melbourne, and by far the easiest to get to. One drives north out of the city on the Tullamarine Freeway and there are only a handful of traffic lights between the wineries and the city centre, it takes little more than half an hour go get there.

Goona Warra Wines are all 100 percent estate grown. The rarely grown cabernet franc is a worthy wine.

The beautiful bluestone buildings houses the cellar and tasting area, which caters for gourmet lunches and afternoon teas on Sundays. The tastefully appointed Great Hall above has become a popular venue for tying the wedding knot and for corporate dinners.

When in Melbourne why not drop in on the delightful cultured couple, John and Elizabeth Barnier. It will be a visit to remember.

GOONA WARRA VINEYARD

Address: Sunbury Road, Sunbury VIC 3429
Phone: (03) 9740 7766
Fax: (03) 9744 7648
Established: Founded 1863/Re-established 1983
Winemaker: John Barnier
Principal varieties grown: Chardonnay, Semillon, Cabernet Franc, Pinot Noir, Cabernet Sauvignon, Merlot
Ha under vine: 5
Average annual crush: 25 tonnes
Average no. cases produced: 2,500

Principal wines & brands	Cellar Potential
Chardonnay	2-5 years
Semillon	2-5 years
Pinot Noir	2-5 years
Cabernet Franc	2-5 years
The Premier (Cabernet Sauvignon/Franc, Merlot)	5-10 years

Public & trade tours: By appointment only
Hours open to public: 10am-5pm, daily
Points of interest: Grand Historic Bluestone Winery now restored offering a popular Cellar lunch every Sunday plus weddings and other functions by appointment
Retail distribution: The Wine Company wholesale - mainly to On Premises (Fine Restaurants - Melbourne & Sydney)

Mt. Aitken Estates is situated in beautiful rolling countryside just north of Melbourne, en route to the famous Mt Macedon, Hanging Rock and Daylesford spa districts. In the early days of Victoria it was reputed to be the playground of the rich, many take advantage of this beautiful area to escape the heat of summer in Melbourne.

Mt. Aitken enjoys a reputation amongst connoisseurs of fine port as one of the world's premier producers of fortified wines and liqueurs. In fact, Mt. Aitken and its dedicated, Proprietor and owner, Roger McLean, enjoy the distinction of having had their wines presented to Royalty on the occasion of Prince Charles and the late Princess Diana's first visit to Australia.

Today, the endeavours and dedication of Roger McLean can be toasted in a superb selection of fine wines, ports and liqueurs which include soft, subtle Chardonnay and Riesling or, if you prefer full-bodied, bold reds from their Heathcote vineyard and of course, their renowned range of Oak Aged Tawny Ports.

Roger's most recent endeavour has resulted in the exciting launch of a unique and exclusive range of Herbal Liquers. The flavour of organically grown, hand picked herbs has been gently extracted using traditional methods, then aged in a specially coopered vat made with selected oak staves from the Kings Forest in England. This process had unlocked some of the ancient secrets of the *'mystical power of herbs'* and resulted in a range of liqueurs which exhibit a magnificent depth of flavour and a taste that in itself is both delicious and euphoric. The elegance and style of these liqueurs are not merely confined to beautifully presented bottles. For the ultimate taste sensation, indulge in a Herbal Liqueur chocolate and enjoy the exotic taste of decadent dark chocolate combined with an exquisite liqueur.

Apart from some of the finest ports in the country, Mt Aitken Estates also boasts a fine collection of barrels dating back in time to the days of kings courts, some still bearing the original carved emblems of famous distilleries from all around the world. This ancient tradition and craft of cooperage is still practised at Mt Aitken today.

Mt Aitken Estates elegant collection of oak-aged ports, sophisticated port liqueurs and exclusive Herbal Liqueurs heralds the beginning of new and tantalising tastes for the connoisseur and provides the perfect gift for all occasions.

Mt. Aitken Estates proudly boasts one of the

finest restaurants in Victoria, set amid lofty bluestone walls, huge wooden beams and slate flooring.... the quality of the food and the ambience has to be experienced to be believed.

Visitors are invited to the vineyard, where warm hospitality combined with an extensive range of Wines, Ports and Liqueurs makes Mt. Aitken Estates a must for everyone.

"Step back in time and enjoy true Australian hospitality"

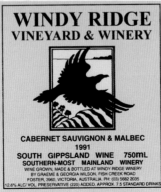

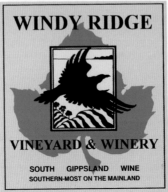

Gippsland - Vic
1 Bass Phillip
2 Coalville Vineyard
3 Lyre Bird Hill Winery
4 Nicholson River Winery
5 Paradise Enough Winery
6 Phillip Island Vineyard & Winery
7 Tarwin Ridge
8 Wa-de-lock Vineyard
9 Westernport Estate Winery
10 Wyanga Park Winery
11 Windy Ridge Winery

Gippsland

Victoria's most isolated wine-producing area is Gippsland in the south-eastern corner of the state. Most vineyards are small, of less than 10 hectares, and are spread over a large area which extends from Lakes Entrance in the far south-east to Phillip Island in Western Port Bay. The southernmost groups of wineries in mainland Australia are the cluster in South Gippsland, between Wilsons Promontory and Phillip Island - Lyre Bird Hill, Bass Phillip, Paradise Enough, Tarwin Ridge and Windy Ridge.

There are a growing number of grape growers in the area, many aiming to make their own wine and open cellar door sales. The first vignerons to plant vines since the nineteenth century were Pauline and Dacre Stubbs at Lulgra Wines of Lakes Entrance, now part of the Wyanga Park Estate. Gippsland is grouped into the three subregions of South Gippsland, Central Gippsland and the Lakes District. The region covers quite a range of territory, topography and climate. Wines generally exhibit the spiciness inherent in cool climate fruit and consist of classic varieties such as pinot noir, cabernet sauvignon, shiraz, chardonnay, riesling and sauvignon blanc. Some of the best pinot noirs in the country have appeared from these tiny vineyards, notably from Lyre Bird, Bass Phillip and Windy Ridge.

Although still largely a cottage industry, winemaking in Gippsland is continuing to develop and the fine wines so far produced are a credit to the far-flung pioneers who created them.

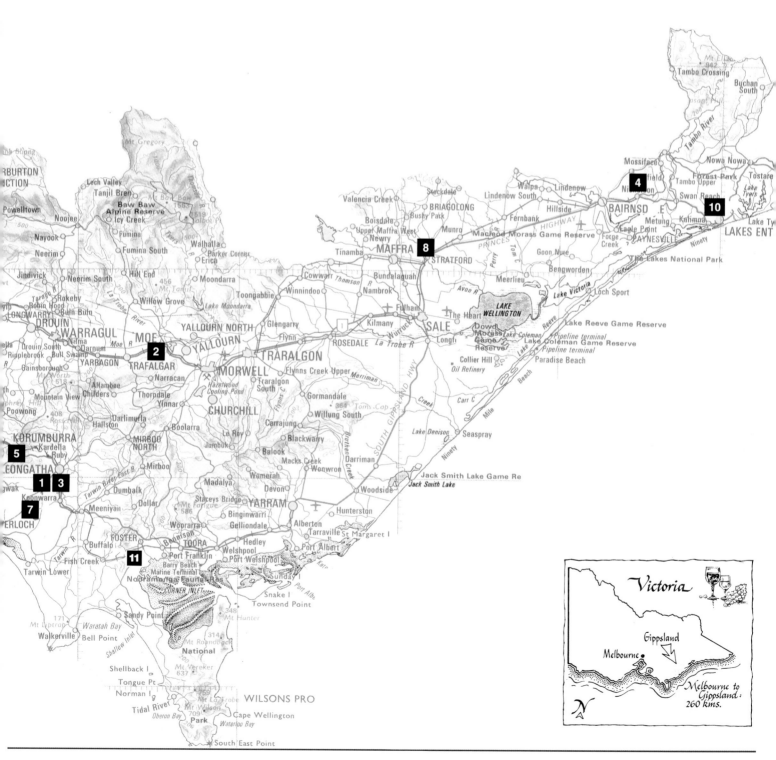

Lyre Bird Hill

Owen and Robyn Schmidt have a deep love for their newly found life style, a passion for their vines, the Lyre Bird Hill Winery and the Country House they have shaped with hard work by their own hands. The property, one of the most southerly vineyards on mainland Australia, is set in the serene bucolic beauty that is South Gippsland. Among the stately gums and ferns which furnish the home for the exquisite, shy lyrebird, they found their little piece of paradise.

Owen had been an accountant at BHP. Although born in Queensland, he travelled Australia, spending a few years in South Australia. Robyn's career was in catering, mainly in the school area, spending a number of years victualling the hungry young students at Melbourne's Wesley College. They decided that they would both give up their careers and set up a winery and provide a hospitality house on their weekend property near Koonwarra in South Gippsland, where they had already planted a vineyard. Guests are welcomed into their home - the guest rooms are tastefully and practically appointed with spacious, yet cosy comfort. All rooms open onto a verandah surrounded by vines and bushland. Dinner is a table díhote affair with Oven and Robyn showcasing their cuisine, wines and delightful company.

Lyre Bird Hill is a wonderfully restorative place to recharge the batteries and get back to nature.

LYRE BIRD HILL
Address: Inverloch Road, Koonwarra VIC 3954
Phone: (03) 5664 3204
Fax: (03) 5664 3206
Email: lyrebird@sympac.com.au
WWW: http://www.sympac.com.au/~lyrebird
Established: 1993
Owners: Owen and Robyn Schmidt
Principal varieties grown: Riesling, Chardonnay, Pinot Noir, Pinot de Jour, Shiraz, Cabernet Sauvignon
Average annual crush: 12 tonnes

Principal wines & brands	Cellar Potential
Riesling	5-10 years
Pinot Noir	3-7 years
Shiraz	5-10 years
Cabernet Sauvignon	5-10 years
Chardonnay	2-5 years
Traminer	2-5 years

Public & trade tours: Yes

Windy Ridge Winery

The most southerly vineyard and winery on mainland Australia is aptly named Windy Ridge, sitting high on a ridge in between the towns of Fish Creek and Foster with spectacular views over Wilsons Promontory and the Shallow Inlet and Corner Inlet Marine and Coastal Parks. Even on the balmy post vintage day of our visit, with the vines in spectacular autumn tones on the green hillsides and the stretches of blue waters in the distance, the wind still had a chill in it.

Graeme and Georgia Wilson are very much hands on, they hand prune and hand pick the grapes from the vines which were planted starting back in 1978 with the first vintage being in 1988.

Small quantities of very individual wines are made with their own hands in their small winery after substantial ageing of many of the wines in oak, they bottle the fruits of their labour again with their own fair hands.

I found their cabernet sauvignon and malbec blends exceptional, they also make a lovely spicy pinot noir, and in some years a traminer.

Generally only open on long weekends and most January weekends they have a cellar club which keeps their members in touch.

WINDY RIDGE VINEYARD AND WINERY

Address: RMB 1852 Fish Creek Road, Foster VIC 3960
Direction: 5km from Foster
Phone: (03) 5682 2035
Email: windyrdg@tpgi.com.au
WWW: http://www1.tpgi.com.au/users/windyrdg
Established: 1985
Owners: Graeme and Georgia Wilson
Winemaker: Graeme Wilson
Principal varieties grown: Cabernet Sauvignon, Pinot Noir, Traminer, Malbec
Ha under vine: 3
Average annual crush: 5
Average no. cases produced: 300

Principal wines & brands	Cellar Potential
Windy Ridge Cabernet Sauvignon-Malbec	3-5 years
Windy Ridge Pinot Noir	6 years
Windy Ridge Traminer	First Vintage
Georgia's Liqueur Pinot Noir	4 years
Graeme's Late Bottled Vintage Port	9 years

Public & trade tours: Public tours by appointment only
Hours open to public: Holiday weekends
Points of interest: Spectacular views of Wilsons Prom.; Boutique Winery, Traditional Winemaking; Australia's Southernmost Mainland Vineyard/Winery
Retail distribution: Cellar Door and Mail Order. South Gippsland outlets

An introduction to Mornington Peninsula

The Mornington Peninsula Vineyards begins 60 kilometres south of the Melbourne C.B.D., near the Dromana area, a one hour drive south of the city.

A few vineyards existed during the 19th century, but due to factors similar to those in the Yarra Valley, viticulture did not continue into the 20th century.

In the late 1940's leading wine judge and Melbourne wine merchant, the late Doug Seabrook, established a vineyard on the slopes of Arthur's Seat, near Dromana. This venture petered out within 10 years however, to be followed by a re-introduction of vines to the area by several winemakers during the 1970's.

The first of these was developed by Baillieu Myer in 1972. Named 'Elgee Park', the vineyard is situated at Merricks North.

A new, technically superb winery was completed in time for production of the 1984 vintage. Nat White was another vigneron to contribute to the early re-development of the Mornington Peninsula's wine industry, with the establishment of Main Ridge Estate in 1975. George and Jacquelyn Kefford followed, founding Merricks Estate in 1977 and Stoniers Merricks vineyard one year later. There are now more than 120 vineyards in the area, covering 1,000 acres, supporting 35 wineries.

By both Australian and European standards, the climate of the Peninsula is very cool, somewhat like the Bordeaux region in France. As the area is virtually surrounded by ocean, vines receive adequate rainfall throughout the growing season, and the high level of humidity in summer prevents vines from suffering stress.

Vineyards of the Mornington Peninsula produce table wines of clean, well-defined varietal characters, and crisp acidity. These features result in refreshing wines with considerable ageing potential.

The predominant varieties are chardonnay and pinot noir, used in both table and sparkling wine-making. Other varieties include cabernet sauvignon, merlot, shiraz, riesling, sauvignon blanc, semillon and pinot gris.

The Mornington Peninsula has produced some excellent wines since the re-establishment of viticulture in the area. Given the expertise and skill of the winemakers, this should continue and currently available wines are of a very high standard. The physical beauty of the peninsula and its tourist pull has been well catered for by such excellent winery restaurants as Dromana Estate, where Margaret Crittenden and her family run a really fine establishment overlooking their lake and vineyards.

Sir Peter and Lady Averil Derham have awesome views of Westernport Bay from their indoor/outdoor restaurant in front of the winery. Hann's Creek have a lovely French-style Sunday lunch with the strains of Piaf pumping through the winery.

Fine Bed and Breakfasts abound, whilst restored mansions such as Glynt are world class. Mornington's rebirth as a wine region is a joy to behold.

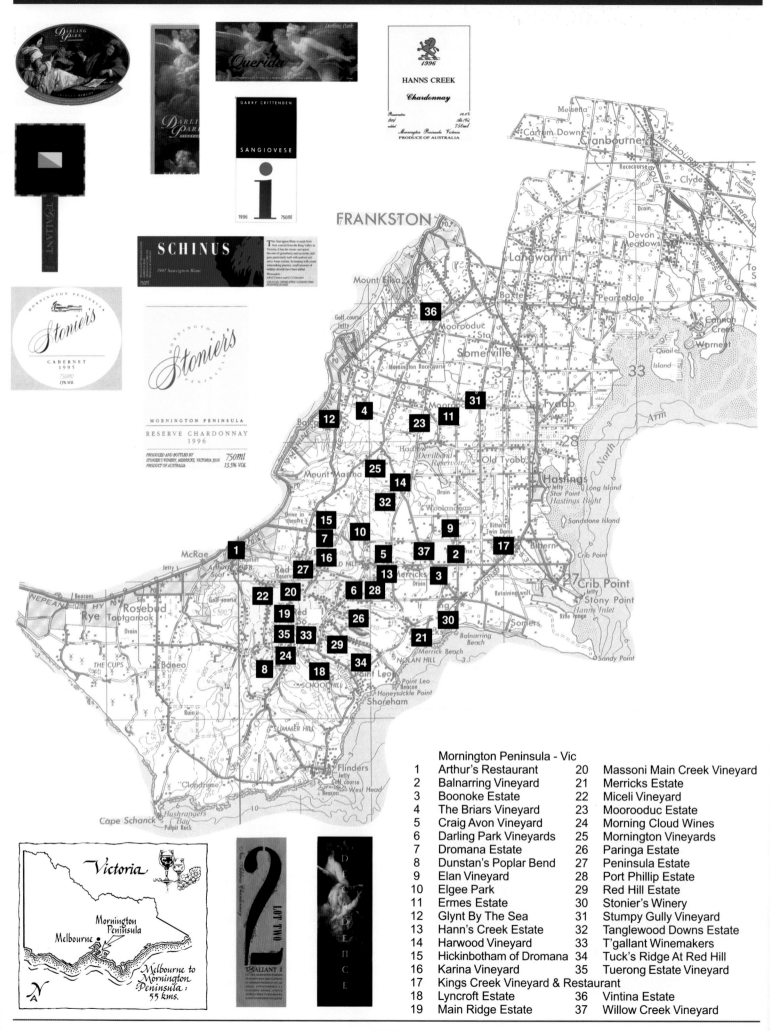

Mornington Peninsula

Mornington Peninsula - Vic

1	Arthur's Restaurant	20	Massoni Main Creek Vineyard
2	Balnarring Vineyard	21	Merricks Estate
3	Boonoke Estate	22	Miceli Vineyard
4	The Briars Vineyard	23	Moorooduc Estate
5	Craig Avon Vineyard	24	Morning Cloud Wines
6	Darling Park Vineyards	25	Mornington Vineyards
7	Dromana Estate	26	Paringa Estate
8	Dunstan's Poplar Bend	27	Peninsula Estate
9	Elan Vineyard	28	Port Phillip Estate
10	Elgee Park	29	Red Hill Estate
11	Ermes Estate	30	Stonier's Winery
12	Glynt By The Sea	31	Stumpy Gully Vineyard
13	Hann's Creek Estate	32	Tanglewood Downs Estate
14	Harwood Vineyard	33	T'gallant Winemakers
15	Hickinbotham of Dromana	34	Tuck's Ridge At Red Hill
16	Karina Vineyard	35	Tuerong Estate Vineyard
17	Kings Creek Vineyard & Restaurant		
18	Lyncroft Estate	36	Vintina Estate
19	Main Ridge Estate	37	Willow Creek Vineyard

232

Hann's Creek

Denise Aubrey-Slocock has a zest for life and astounding energy - it's impossible to be around her and not feel the joy of life flowing over you. Denise's strong and most discerning French accent from her native Brittany. She met her future husband, Tony while running her own little restaurant in Melbourne, earning a living to bring up her children alone, hard work is no hardship for Denise.

On my first visit Denise was busy summer grafting some shiraz, between running the cellar door and packing wine orders, always with a huge smile and a mischievous sense of humour. Tony is equally hard-working and quietly tends the vineyard and makes the wines, which have already won a number of awards.

The vineyard is in a clearing on the lee side of the prevailing winds with a northerly aspect providing a sunny sheltered environment. It produces an excellent cabernet sauvignon. The French influence is obvious, with the winery also providing a crisp rose and burgundian-style pinot noir and chardonnay.

Each Sunday, Hanns Creek really comes to life with a French-style lunch amongst the barrels, complete with gingham table cloths and the strains of Piaf in the air.

It's a three hour affair starting at 1 pm. If you are in need of a little exercise between courses, Tony will instruct you in the art of petanque, the French provincial game of bowls. When on the Peninsula, head for Hanns Creek for a most uplifting experience.

HANN'S CREEK ESTATE
Address: Kentucky Road, Merricks North VIC 3926
Phone: (03) 5989 7266
Fax: (03) 5989 7500
WWW: http://www.ozemail.com.au/~hannscre
Established: 1987
Owners: Tony and Denise Aubrey-Slocock
Winemaker: Tony Aubrey-Slocock
Principal varieties grown: Cabernet Sauvignon, Pinot Noir, Shiraz, Chardonnay
Ha under vine: 4
Average annual crush: 24 Tonnes
Average no. cases produced: 1,500

Principal wines & brands	Cellar Potential
Chardonnay	5 years
Pinot Noir	10 years
Rosé	5 years
Cabernet Sauvignon	10 years
Cabernet Shiraz	10 years

Public & trade tours: By Appointment Only
Hours open to public: 11am-5pm , daily
Points of interest: Restaurant - weekends, public holidays and by arrangement. Petanque played and taught
Retail distribution: By order, phone or mail

Dromana Estate

Garry Crittenden is one of the Australian wine industry's most dynamic and visionary people. Garry sold a chain of plant nurseries to concentrate on his vineyard at Dromana on the Mornington Peninsula. For a number of years, he also operated a viticultural consulting business.

Garry and his wife Margaret are both heavily involved in the Dromana Estate operation and have built a colonial-inspired home on the property which enjoys superb

views over their lake and vineyard. Garry searched a climate where delicate, yet intense flavours could be produced. He found this at Dromana Estate.

I have noticed on a number of visits to the Peninsula that Dromana enjoys its own special micro climate. Whereas it can be cloudy, cold and windy on the Red Hill Ridge, Dromana can be bathed in sunshine. This combination of very cool climate, coupled with loads of sunshine, really makes his wines smile, an attitude he maintains through thick and thin himself.

The pretty gardens surrounding the winery and lake reflect his love of plants. Garry is most innovative; always experimenting, learning and seeking perfection in his wines. Garry has introduced a second label, 'Schinus' under which he makes wines from grapes sourced in other regions. A certain fascination with Northern Italian wines and his penchant for a challenge has seen him produce a range of unusual Italian reds. Garry's hardworking and talented wife Margaret, has a real culinary flair and serves a seasonal menu or simple tasty snack platters, depending on your mood.

If you wish to bring your own tucker, there is a free Barbecue area in front of the winery. Hospitality is the key note of the Crittendens. They see a bright, bright future for the region and it's wines and wineries, with very good reason. Their family are an integral part of this future.

DROMANA ESTATE VINEYARDS
Address: Harrisons Road, Dromana VIC 3936
Phone: (03) 5987 3800
Fax: (03) 5981 0714
Email: devyd@onaustralia.com.au
Established: 1982
Owners: Garry and Margaret Crittenden
Winemaker: Garry Crittenden
Principal varieties grown: Chardonnay, Pinot Noir, Cabernet Sauvignon, Merlot
Ha under vine: 4
Average annual crush: 50 tonnes local and 150 tonnes purchased
Average no. cases produced: 3,500 from own vines for Dromana Estate label, 10,500 for Schinus label, 3,000 for Garry Crittenden 'i' label
Principal wines & brands: Dromana Estate Schinus
Public & trade tours: By appointment only
Hours open to public: 11am-4pm, daily except Christmas Day, Boxing Day and Good Friday
Points of interest: Tasting Centre overlooking the lake with light lunches served daily. Queen's Birthday and Melbourne Cup weekend festivals
Retail distribution: Every Australian State and Territory as well as the USA

Glynt by the Sea

Inspired by a Scottish castle, Glynt was built in the early years of this century as a summer residence for a prominent Melbourne family, entertaining was a priority and the grand ballroom hosted many a gracious soiree. The family's fortunes waned and Glynt fell into disrepair although the superb granite and stucco building was as solid as a rock.

The rebirth of the grandeur of Glynt began when the estate and it's surrounding land was bought by Sir Peter Derham for building development project. Ironically, Sir Peter is now a virtual full time Mornington Peninsula Vigneron at Red Hill Estate. Glynt, which is situated some 100 metres from Port Philip Bay at Mount Martha, was left with an acre or so of it's grounds still intact in the middle of the development. Sir Peter, then Chairman of the Australian Tourism Commission, mentioned Glynt to fellow commissioner, legendary outback tourism pioneer

Bill King. Perhaps it was the glint in his eye that made Bill mention it to his wife Val. Sir Peter suggested they have a look at it. Bill describes their first visit, climbing through a fence, battling the brambles and head high grass, Val was about to turn back, but once they saw the mansion cloaked in it's Virginia Creeper coat, they fell in love with it instantly. Fortunately, among their children and sons-in-law, they had the experts in all the building trades, over several years they pain stakingly restored the building and grounds. To say they are a showpiece would be an understatement. The day of our visit a leading motor company was filming a television commercial at sunset, what a glorious property it is.

Recently the Estate has been taken over by renowned International Television Producer and Director Mark Callan and International Hairdresser William Gilchrist, who managed the salon on the Queen Elizabeth II for many years. They both have great taste, are most hospitable and plan to add further suites and facilities as they get to know the castle better. At present there are four exquisite suites - each with their own drawing rooms and furnished with antiques as well as every modern convenience that would do a 5 star hotel proud. The three Garden View Suites are

magnificent, but the Bay View Suite, with its own spiral staircase leading down the tower to the grand drawing room, will take your beath away.

A full English breakfast is served in the vast garden room, with arched windows overlooking Port Phillip Bay. The licensed dining room is beautifully appointed. It creates an ideal ambience to enjoy a memorable dining experience.

Mark and William will be offering personally guided tours of the Peninsula wineries and world class golf courses. Situated in the centre of the wine growing region, Glynt provides the ideal base from which to explore.

**Glynt by the Sea,
16 Bay Road,
Mt Martha,
Telephone (03) 5974 1216.
Fax. (03) 5974 2546**

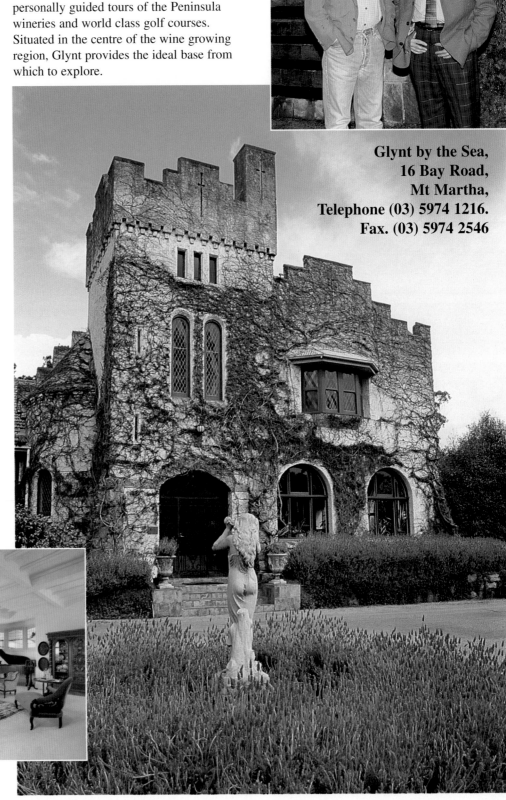

Stoniers

Stonier's can lay claim to being Australia's most successful 'new' winemaker. In 1994, at the prestigious Royal Adelaide Show, they were awarded two trophies for their 1993 Reserve Pinot Noir. One for the best pinot noir in the show and the other for the best varietal red table wine, against the best big reds of cabernet sauvignon, shiraz, merlot and other varieties, on South Australia's home ground. This extraordinary event marked the coming of age of the Mornington Peninsula as a wine region. In 1978, leading publisher Brian Stonier and his wife, Noel, planted 600 vines on their property at Merricks, close to the shores of Western Port Bay.

A year later, far off in the Napa Valley in California, the wine career of Tod Dexter began. Tod, a Melbourne lad and a passionate skier, had been working on the snow slopes of Colorado. He dropped into the Napa Valley and ended up staying there where he worked for Cakebread Cellars across the road from the legendary Robert Mondavi Winery. Tod learnt much in five vintages before returning to Australia in 1985.

Tod credits the vineyards at Stonier's with producing fruit that makes his job rewarding. Tod and his wife Debbi, planted a 15 acre vineyard at Merricks North which now supplies Stonier's Winery with an important 'warmer' climate part of the vintage, adding to the 46 acre estate vineyard production. Stonier's marketing is under the enthusiastic and capable guidance of Brian's daughter Jenny. The produce a wonderful chardonnay and pinot noir, both of which have won many trophies, and a 'cabernet' - a bordeaux-style blend of cabernet savignon, merlot and cabernet franc.

STONIER'S WINERY
Address: 362 Frankston-Flinders Road, Merricks VIC 3916
Direction: Cnr Frankston-Flinders Road & Thompson Lane, Melways 192 F9
Phone: (03) 5989 8300
Fax: (03) 5989 8709
Email: stoniers@peninsula.starway.net.au
WWW: http://www.nepeanet.org.au/stoniers
Established: 1978
Owners: Stonier, Yuill, Hamson and Limb Families
Winemaker: Tod Dexter
Principal varieties grown: Chardonnay, Pinot Noir, Cabernet Sauvignon, Cabernet Franc, Merlot
Ha under vine: 20
Average annual crush: 200 tonnes
Average no. cases produced: 13,000

Principal wines & brands	Cellar Potential
Chardonnay	2-5 years
Pinot Noir	2-5 years
Cabernet	3-5 years
Stoniers Reserve Chardonnay	3-8 years
Pinot Noir - Reserve	2-6 years
Cabernet Sauvignon - Reserve	5-10 years

Public & trade tours: Yes
Hours open to public: 12pm-5pm, daily except Christmas, Good Friday, Boxing Day
Points of interest: Food by prior arrangement, Functions by prior arrangement, childrens' playground, cheese platter available everyday. Festival - Easter, Queens Birthday and Cup Weekend.
Retail distribution: Negociants Australia in every State.

Main Ridge

Nat White, a graduate in oenology from Charles Sturt University, and his wife Rosalie, were the modern-day pioneers who began the rebirth of the Mornington Peninsula as a wine region. In the centre of the Peninsula on the cool, elevated Main Ridge, Nat and Rosalie cleared a sheltered hillside and planted vines more than 20 years ago. The vines today are strong, well established and producing complex wines which are full of character. Nat's commitment to quality includes 'bunch thinning', actually removing some of the bunches and discarding them before the ripening process begins. This lowers the crop, but the noble sacrifice results in greater flavour and colour in the wines. The winery, sculptured into the hillside at the top of the property, has a cool underground cellar with a beautiful tasting room gallery above. The gardens around the winery and vineyard are superb, with more than 100 species of roses planted.

Nat's former occupation as a civil engineer shows through in the pleasing layout of the estate. The Whites' deep love of nature and their estate is well captured in the verse I noticed on the verandah:

"The kiss of the sun for pardon
The song of the bird for mirth
One is nearer God's heart in the garden
Than anywhere else on earth".

MAIN RIDGE ESTATE

Address:
William Road, Red Hill VIC 3937
Phone: (03) 5989 2686
Fax: (03) 5931 0000
Established: 1975
Owners: Nat and Rosalie White
Winemaker: Nat White
Principal varieties grown:
Chardonnay, Pinot Noir, Cabernet Sauvignon, Merlot
Ha under vine: 3
Average annual crush:
12 tonnes
Average no. cases produced:
1,000

Principal wines & brands	Cellar Potential
Chardonnay	3-10 years
Half Acre Pinot Noir	4-10 years
Pinot Noir	3-8 years
Cabernet Merlot	5-10 years

Public & trade tours:
By appointment only
Hours open to public:
12pm-4pm, weekdays; 12pm-5pm, weekends and public holidays
Points of interest:
Garden Walk, Sunday Lunch, Underground Cellar, First Mornington Peninsula Winery

Darling Park Vineyards

One of the most beautifully manicured and tendered vineyards I have ever seen belongs to John and Delys Sargeant of Darling Park Vineyards. Rumour has it that John "Talks" to his vines, by the look of them he's certainly not "paying them out".

The Sargeant's have built a gorgeous cellar door complete with an Alsacienne style wood fired oven producing the exquisite Tortes Flambées they fell in love with on their visits to the Alsace region of France. You can enjoy them as a light lunch or snack with wine or coffee.

The Sargeant's have a different and inventive range of wines which includes pinot coris and tempranillo which used in Northern Italy - they do very well on the Peninsula.

The range also includes a rosé style "Querida" and "Decadence" a blend of cabernet franc and tempranillo bunch pressed and fortified with grape spirit to produce a pale ruby "gloriously seductive" stickie. A chardonnay, pinot noir, merlot and a cabernet merlot rounds off the range. The cellar door in their beautiful vine-valley is open weekends, public holidays, all through January or whenever the gates open – do drop in!!

DARLING PARK VINEYARDS

Address: Red Hill Road, Red Hill VIC 3937
Direction: Follow Red Hill wine region signs. Melways map 191 F3
Phone: (03) 5989 2732
Fax: (03) 5989 2254
Established: 1986
Owners: John and Delys Sargeant
Winemakers: John Sargeant and Kevin McCarthy
Principal varieties grown: Chardonnay, Merlot, Cabernet Sauvignon, Cabernet Franc, Pinot Gris, Pinot Noir, Tempranello
Ha under vine: 2.8
Average annual crush: 20 tonnes
Average no. cases produced: 1,300

Principal wines & brands	Cellar Potential
Chardonnay	4-5 years
Pinot Gris	2-4 years
Querida (rosé style)	2-4 years
Decadence (rosé style)	2-5 years
Pinot Noir	5-8 years
Cabernet Sauvignon Merlot	5-8 years
Merlot	5-8 years
Tempranello	4-5 years

Public & trade tours: By appointment only
Hours open to public: 11am-5pm, weekends, public holidays, all through January and whenever the gate is open
Points of interest: Unique blends of wine (Querida and Decadence) Intimate cellar door, winery visit (by arrangement), with the magic Tartes Flambee cooked in the wood fired oven and served to be enjoyed with in a beautiful valley among vines and roses
Retail distribution: Selected restaurants and cellar door.

T'Gallant

I first met Kathleen Quealy some 12 years ago when she was making wine at the obscure Bungawarra Vineyards in Queensland's Granite Belt as a young enthusiastic Wagga graduate. Her wines shone out in a difficult environment.

At that stage she was engaged to Kevin McCarthy. Today, they are married with children and very happy indeed on their Mornington Peninsula property. Kathleen has lost none of her enthusiasm and she and her trained winemaker husband Kevin make a formidable combination. T'Gallant takes its name from the classic old four-masted barques that made the voyages of discovery around Australia's coastline.

Kevin and Kathleen are keen to make an individual statement with their wines. Their love is pinot gris, a white mutation of pinot noir which needs a very cool climate to produce its rich, yet crystal clean character. That in Kathleen's words "reminds you of oceans and crashing waves, yet holding back a little like a yacht before the line, with unbelievable richness and fatness, length and finesse".

This love affair has led them to plant another four hectares in their 16 hectare property on Mornington Flinders Road. T'Gallant produces a white with a rosy glow from pinot noir, called Holystone, a chardonnay, a big red called Crosstrees and a late harvest dessert wine called Demi Vache from sauvignon blanc as well as their prized Pinot Grigio.

T'GALLANT WINERY & VINEYARD

Address: Mornington Flinders Road, Main Ridge VIC 3928
Direction: Near corner of Mornington Flinders Road & Shands Road, Main Ridge
Phone: (03) 5989 6565
Fax: (03) 5989 6577
Established: 1990
Owners: Kevin McCarthy and Kathleen Quealy
Winemakers: Kevin McCarthy and Kathleen Quealy
Principal varieties grown: Pinot Noir, Chardonnay, Pinot Gris
Ha under vine: 10
Average no. cases produced: 12,000

Principal wines & brands	Cellar Potential
Chardonnay	2-5 years
Holystone	2-5 years
Pinot Gris	5-10 years
Pinot Grigio	2-5 years
Ceclia's White Pinot	2-5 years
Demi-Vache	5-10 years

Public & trade tours: Yes
Hours open to public: 11am-5pm, weekdays; 12pm-5pm, weekends
Points of interest: T'Gallant are at the cutting edge of winemaking. Introducing new winemaking and styles and grape varieties to the Mornington Peninsula & Australia
Retail distribution: Throughout Sydney, Melbourne, QLD

An introduction to Geelong

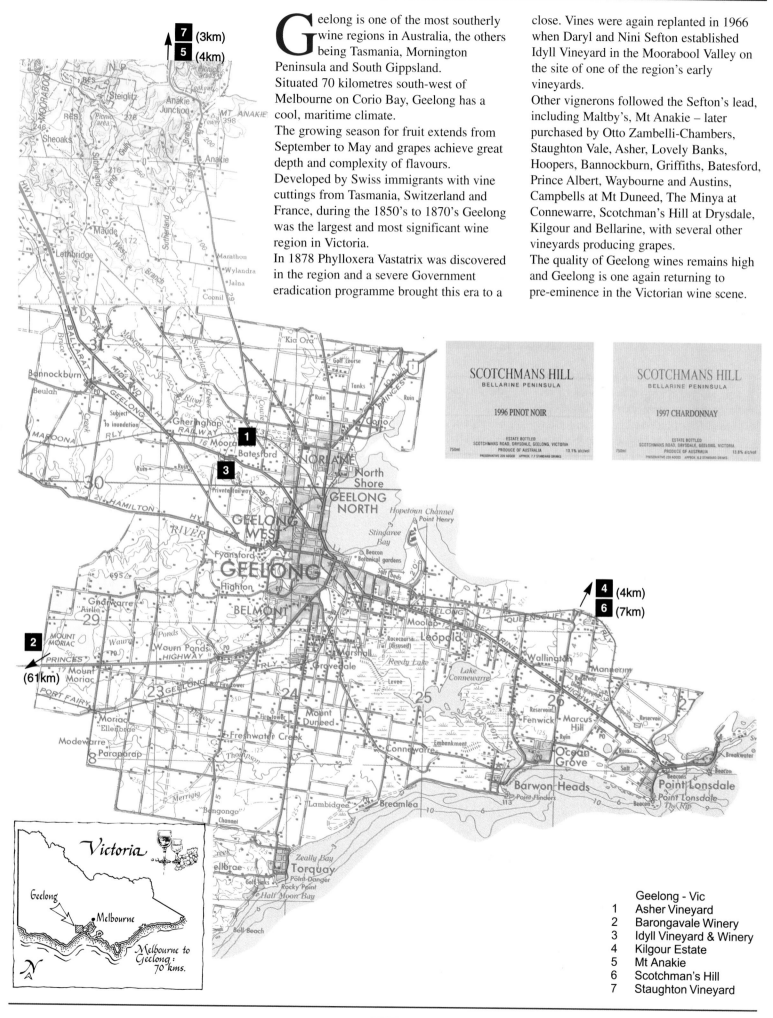

Geelong is one of the most southerly wine regions in Australia, the others being Tasmania, Mornington Peninsula and South Gippsland.

Situated 70 kilometres south-west of Melbourne on Corio Bay, Geelong has a cool, maritime climate.

The growing season for fruit extends from September to May and grapes achieve great depth and complexity of flavours.

Developed by Swiss immigrants with vine cuttings from Tasmania, Switzerland and France, during the 1850's to 1870's Geelong was the largest and most significant wine region in Victoria.

In 1878 Phylloxera Vastatrix was discovered in the region and a severe Government eradication programme brought this era to a close. Vines were again replanted in 1966 when Daryl and Nini Sefton established Idyll Vineyard in the Moorabool Valley on the site of one of the region's early vineyards.

Other vignerons followed the Sefton's lead, including Maltby's, Mt Anakie – later purchased by Otto Zambelli-Chambers, Staughton Vale, Asher, Lovely Banks, Hoopers, Bannockburn, Griffiths, Batesford, Prince Albert, Waybourne and Austins, Campbells at Mt Duneed, The Minya at Connewarre, Scotchman's Hill at Drysdale, Kilgour and Bellarine, with several other vineyards producing grapes.

The quality of Geelong wines remains high and Geelong is one again returning to pre-eminence in the Victorian wine scene.

Geelong - Vic
1 Asher Vineyard
2 Barongavale Winery
3 Idyll Vineyard & Winery
4 Kilgour Estate
5 Mt Anakie
6 Scotchman's Hill
7 Staughton Vineyard

237

Idyll Vineyard

As one of Australia's most beautiful vineyards, Idyll is aptly named. Immaculate rows of vines extend down the valley to the Moorabool River, over gentle green undulations. The site had been planted to vines during the mid 1800's and was chosen by Daryl and Nini Sefton because of family associations with the area. Daryl's great-grandparents, Jacob and Rosina Just, had been among the original Swiss settlers of the district and had also made wines.

The Seftons commenced planting their 20 hectare vineyard in 1966 and Daryl designed and constructed the winery and much of the wine-making equipment.

Idyll's winery is undoubtedly one of the most efficient small wineries in the country. Darylís wife and partner, Nini, has also made considerable contributions to the winery. A tireless promoter Nini is also an accomplished artist who has designed and painted Idyll's Painter's Series of labels. Almost 30% of Idyll wine is exported overseas. Wines are also available through better retail outlets and cellar door. Their gewurztraminer is one of the best wines of this variety in Australia. Idyll range also includes a delightful rose called 'Idyll Blush', usually made from shiraz a chardonnay, shiraz and cabernet/shiraz. The vivacious congeniality of the Seftons,

combined with the winery's superb location and the promise of some fine wines results in Idyll being one of Australia's most popular stops for the wine-lover.

Sadly the Seftons are about to hang up their winemaking boots for a more leisurely life in their beloved Geelong.

Scotchman's Hill

I well remember the newly planted expansive vineyard, just through Geelong on the Bellarine Peninsula, as Milan Roden and I made our first photographic pilgrimage back in 1985. It looked to have all the makings of a well thought out and executed, vinous venture that would create both great wines and gain wide recognition, such has

proved to be the case with Scotchman's Hill. David and Vivienne Browne are perfectionists and made some powerful pinot noirs that made the wine critics and pinotphiles really sit up and take notice with their first vintage in the late 1980's. Nothing was insipid about these full-bodied flavoured and gamey wines – I loved them.

Today they have 130 acres of fine established vineyards. Their son Matthew is now assistant winemaker to chief winemaker Robin Brockett and together they make an exciting range of wines which include a cabernet dominated red, a shiraz, sauvignon blanc and chardonnay as well as their renowned pinot noir. Their cellar door is full of character and a couple of years ago they bought the Historic "Spray Farm" mansion on the shores of Port Phillip Bay with views towards distant Melbourne. This National Trust property will soon become a classy convention centre and already they have a range of "Spray Farm" wines. The Brownes have their act together and their wines reflect their commitment to quality.

SCOTCHMANS HILL

Address: 190 Scotchman's Road, **Drysdale** VIC 3222
Phone: (03) 5251 3176
Fax: (03) 5253 1743
Established: 1982
Winemaker: Robin Brockett

Principal varieties grown: Chardonnay, Merlot, Cabernet Sauvignon, Pinot Noir, Riesling, Cabernet Franc
Ha under vine: 40.5
Average annual crush: 250-499 tonnes

Principal wines & brands   Cellar Potential
'Scotchmans Hill'
'Spray Farm'
'Bellarine Wine Company'

Hours open to public: 10.30am-4.30pm, daily
Points of interest: Winery has views of the Bellarine Peninsula. Cool, maritime climate. Specialises in Pinot Noir and Chardonnay

An introduction to Goulburn Valley

The area known as the Goulburn Valley was first explored and deemed suitable for development by Major Thomas Mitchell in 1836. Many graziers settled the area and despite the emphasis on farming, vines were first planted as early as the 1850's.

In 1860 a successful group of landowners and merchants formed the consortium 'Tahbilk Vineyard Proprietary'. Purchasing 260 hectares of land for the purpose of establishing a vineyard and winery, the group, and in particular, Mr John Pinney Bear, energetically set about creating favourable conditions for making good wines. Mr John Pinney Bear prompted rapid growth of the vineyard by advertising Australia-wide for vine cuttings. Chateau Tahbilk prospered, not only because of the dedication of all those involved, but also because of innovative marketing, a kind climate and ideal topography. Today it is a most significant winery in the area and is the only winery to have remained continuously in production. Although hit by the phylloxera scourge at the turn of the century, some of the company's vineyards survived unharmed, allowing the manufacture of wines to continue. Chateau Tahbilk is now run by the Purbrick family who have utilized the original winery buildings and facilities and thus preserved the heritage of the property. The architectural elegance of the winery coupled with the graceful layout of the surrounding grounds make Tahbilk one of the most beautiful wineries in Australia. Within the last 20 years many other winemakers have planted vines in the Goulburn Valley.

In addition to Chateau Tahbilk the largest concern is the Mitchelton Winery and Vineyards. Mitchelton's 500 acre property is bordered on one side by the Goulburn River and is widely recognised by its distinctive tower which became a part of the landscape in the early 1970's.

In comparison to Chateau Tahbilk, Mitchelton has a more contemporary appearance, bit it too is one of the country's most striking wineries. The Somerset Crossing Winery in the town of Seymour has not only great wines but an excellent winery restaurant.

In total, there are some dozen or so wineries in the region, as well as many small growers who supply high quality fruit, both throughout this area and elsewhere.

As the region includes diverse microclimates, soils and altitudes, wine styles of the Goulburn Valley are many and varied. Both red and white wines are produced and although there are some discrepancies in quality, most are highly regarded.

The Goulburn Valley Winemakers have also taken a wonderful initiative in creating the "Great Australian Shiraz Challenge", an annual judging to find the best Shiraz of any vintage in Australia, graciously sponsored by Qantas. I had the great honour of accepting the inaugural trophy in 1995 on behalf of my brother Geoffrey and his 1993 Kuitpo Shiraz.

Goulburn Valley

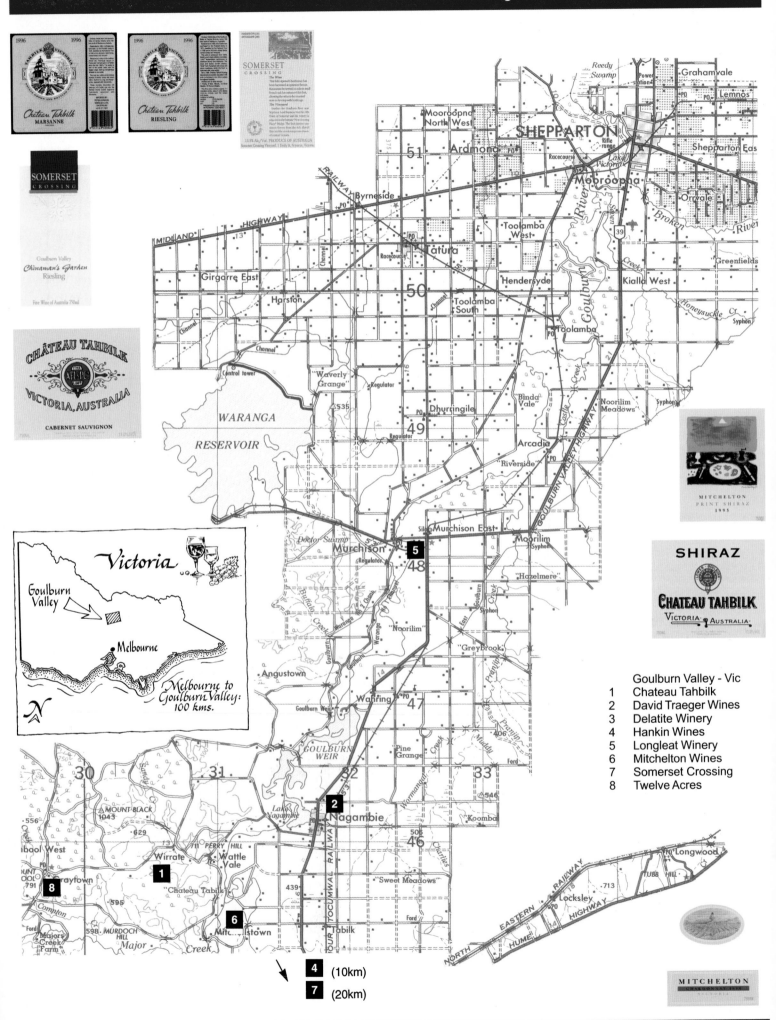

Goulburn Valley - Vic
1. Chateau Tahbilk
2. David Traeger Wines
3. Delatite Winery
4. Hankin Wines
5. Longleat Winery
6. Mitchelton Wines
7. Somerset Crossing
8. Twelve Acres

Mitchelton Winery

The late Ross Shelmerdine, an imaginative and ingenious man, made his mark on the Australian wine industry by creating one of the country's most exciting and unusual winery complexes. In 1969, having purchased a 200 hectare property on a bend in the Goulburn River, he hired Colin Preece, one of Australia's most celebrated winemakers, to assist in planning and planting vineyards. Preece was also retained as a consultant for the first few vintages, giving the winery a solid foundation on which to develop. In late 1972 work began on the winery complex which now includes extensive underground cellars. The complex was named after Mitchellstown, the site where Major Thomas Mitchell set up camp during his exploration of the area in 1836.

The first small vintage was processed at Brown Brothers Winery in 1972. The vines originally planted by Colin Preece continued to bear excellent fruit for the production of high quality wines, by winemaker, Don Lewis, who has now made 26 vintages at the winery. Several years ago the Mitchelton Winery became part of the Petaluma Wine Group and the support and impact of Brian Croser and his team has only enhanced the quality of the already excellent wines.

Mitchelton relies on its own vineyards for about half of its grapes and has contracts with cool climate growers in central Victoria for the rest. Don Lewis's first vintage back in 1973 was only 73 tonnes; in 1997 this was some 3,000 tonnes.

A unique wine in the Mitchelton range is the Wood Matured Marsanne with its distinctive honeysuckle character. It also ages remarkably well.

Mitchelton has an award winning restaurant which focuses on regional produce, an art gallery and accredited nature reserve. In fact, the level of quality afforded to the visitor by Mitchelton gained recognition in 1994 and again in 1995 with the Victorian Tourism Award in the Wineries section.

This is a showpiece winery which also holds occasional concerts and hosts cultural events of various kinds. Things are well in balance at Mitchelton so why not drop in and absorb it great ambience?

MITCHELTON WINES

Address: Mitchellstown via Nagambie VIC 3608
Phone: (03) 5794 2710
Fax: (03) 5794 2615
Email: mitchelton@mitchelton.com.au
WWW: http://www.michelton.com.au
Established: 1974
Winemaker: Don Lewis
Principal varieties grown:
Cabernet Sauvignon, Shiraz, Riesling, Marsanne, Merlot, Chardonnay
Ha under vine: 150
Average annual crush: 3,000 tonnes
Average no. cases produced: 220,000

Principal wines & brands	Cellar Potential
Print Shiraz	20+ years
Michelton Cabernet Sauvignon	15+ years
Michelton Chardonnay	5+ years
Goulburn Valley Marsanne	10+ years
Goulburn Valley Shiraz	10+ years
Blackwood Park Shiraz	15-20 years
Preece	5-10 years

Public & trade tours: By appointment only
Hours open to public: 9am-5pm, daily
Points of interest: Restaurant, Picnic Area, Swimming Pool, Observation Deck, Nature Reserve
Retail distribution: National Distribution - Fesq. Dorado

Chateau Tahbilk

Established in 1860, Chateau Tahbilk Estate is one of Victoria's most beautiful and historic properties. Situated 122 kilometres north of Melbourne, on the east bank of the Goulburn River, at a site the Aboriginals call "tabilk-tabilk".

The property comprises some 1,214 hectares of the richest river flats in the Goulburn Valley, with a frontage of 11 kilometres to the river and approximately 8 kilometres of permanent running back waters and creeks. One of the most interesting and picturesque features of the Estate is the cellars, the main part of which is underground and eminently suitable for the maturation of high-quality table wines. The original cellar and storage, built in 1860 (and surmounted by a tower), which is classified by the National Trust, is 92 metres in length, whereas the "New Cellar", constructed in 1875 and running at right angles, is 60.5 metres long. An idea of the size of the cellars may be obtained from the fact that the roof area alone covers 1 hectare.

Throughout its career, Chateau Tahbilk has obtained over 1000 awards for wines produced on the Estate at all the world's principal exhibitions. These awards include the Diploma of Honour, the highest award obtainable at the Greater London Exhibition of 1899. Also First Order of Merit and Medals in London, Philadelphia, Paris, Bordeaux, Calcutta, Brussels, Amsterdam, Melbourne, Adelaide and Dunedin. More than 60 firsts have been obtained at the Royals Shows of Melbourne, Adelaide, Sydney and Brisbane, and since the introduction of the medals awards in 1965, 4 Trophies, 38 Gold, 133 Silver and 395 Bronze medals have been awarded.

The Estate was purchased by Reginald Purbrick in 1925 and by 1931 his son Eric had taken over management and winemaking responsibilities at Chateau Tahbilk. Eric was joined by his son, John, in 1955 and John's son Alister, a graduate of the Winemaking course at Roseworthy College, took over the role as winemaker and manager in 1978.

The vineyard comprises 156 hectares of vines with classical varieties such as cabernet sauvignon, cabernet franc, shiraz, merlot, malbec, riesling, marsanne, roussanne, viognier, chenin blanc, sauvignon blanc, chardonnay, semillon and white hermitage grown.

The process of vinification at Tahbilk unites traditional winemaking methods with modern, up to date technology. The exquisitely made whites exhibit intense, varietal fruit flavours when young and with bottle age, develop marvellous complexity and character.

The reds are produced with a commitment to the traditional winemaking values held at Tahbilk for over 133 years.

As young wines they show a remarkable balance of complex fruit flavours and natural grape tannins which evolve with considerable bottle age into wines of great power and distinction.

The Chateau Tahbilk Museum was officially opened in October 1995 and is lodged in the "Old Church" built in 1875. This unique building now contains a vast array of fascinating historical pieces and also provides a wonderful setting for exclusive Chateau Tahbilk Wine Club dinners and functions.

CHATEAU TAHBILK WINES

Address: Tabilk VIC 3608
Direction: 8km southwest of Nagambie
Phone: (03) 5794 2555
Fax: (03) 5794 2360
Established: 1860
Owner: Purbrick Family
Winemaker: Alister Purbrick
Principal varieties grown:
Cabernet Sauvignon, Shiraz, Chardonnay, Marsanne, Riesling
Ha under vine: 160
Average annual crush: 1,500
Average no. cases produced: 90,000

Principal wines & brands	Cellar Potential
Chateau Tahbilk Marsanne	5-10 years
Chateau Tahbilk Shiraz	10-20 years
Chateau Tahbilk Cabernet Sauvignon	15-25 years
Chateau Tahbilk 1860 Vines Shiraz	20-35 years
Chateau Tahbilk Reserve Cabernet Sauvignon	30-50 years
Chateau Tahbilk Chardonnay	5 years
Chateau Tahbilk Riesling	5-10 years

Public & trade tours: By Appointment Only
Hours open to public: 9am-5pm, Mon-Sat; 10am-5pm, Sunday and all public holidays except Christmas Day
Points of interest: Original cellars and buildings date from 1840-1880, the most spectacular being the underground cellar
Retail distribution: Tucker Seabrook, National

Somerset Crossing

It is great to see the unique rotunda style building that is now the home of Somerset Crossing come to life as a top classs winery and restaurant.
Built in 1968, at the beginning of the modern renaissance of the Australian Wine Industry, it has a most picturesque location under leafy gums and plane trees on the banks of the Goulburn River.

A syndicate, led by prominent food Industry executive John Ubaldi, also a Goulburn Valley grapegrower, took over the cellars several years ago and have rejuventated the whole enterprise and most tastefully appointed the tasting area and restaurant. Somerset Crossing is the closest Goulburn Valley winery and only just over an hour from Melbourne.

An ideal place to unwind with an early lunch in the restaurant or on the picnic area on the lawns surrounding the winery before leading off to some of the other wonderful wineries further out.
The smartly packaged wines are very well put together by talented Nagambie winemaker David Traeger who has long experience with Goulburn Valley grapes.

An introduction to the Victorian High Country

Some of the most awesomely beautiful country in Australia lies between the towns of Yea Alexandra and Mansfield. The two most striking features being Lake Eildon and Mount Buller whose snow capped peak dominates the vineyards of Delatite Winery, the first winery in the modern day history of this region.

Although there are only four wineries in this region, Delatite whose vineyard planting began in 1968, the Murrindindi Vineyards of the Cuthbertson Family, Hugh Cuthbertson is a young legend of the industry and now works for a major wine company, Antcliff's Chase at Caveat and Plunkett Wines with their large vineyards in the Strathbogie Ranges of the region and their winery with its café near Avenel on the Hume Highway. There are a number of large vineyards in the region also, including the Mount Helen vineyards of Tisdall and Mitchelton's Strathbogie vineyard.

The region is an outdoor persons paradise with skiing, bushwalking, canoeing, ballooning, trout fishing and horseback riding and camel trekking being amongst them. Why not exercise your sense of adventure in this glorious country soon – the wines are worth seeking out.

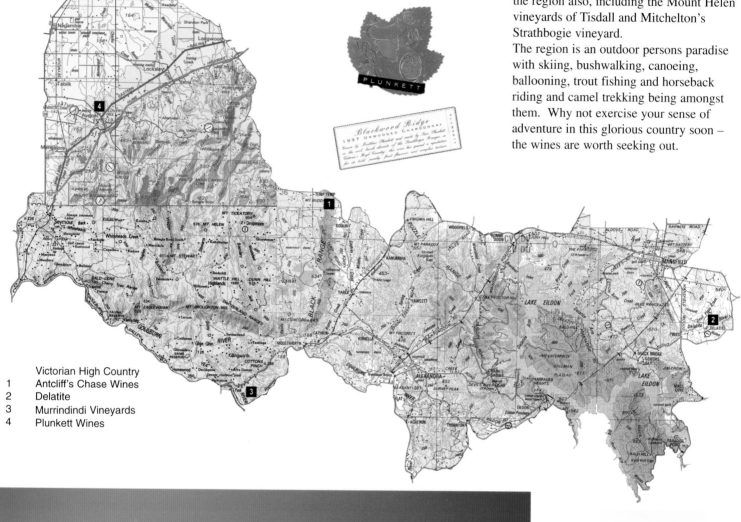

Victorian High Country
1 Antcliff's Chase Wines
2 Delatite
3 Murrindindi Vineyards
4 Plunkett Wines

PLUNKETT

STRATHBOGIE RANGES
CABERNET MERLOT
1995

12.6% ALC/VOL
PRODUCE OF AUSTRALIA   750ML

Victoria

Victorian High Country

Melbourne

Melbourne to Victorian High Country 150 kms.

Delatite

Robert and Vivienne Ritchie first planted vines on their cattle property, Delatite, in 1968. They sold the grapes to Brown Brothers from 1972-1981 and completed the winery at Delatite in time for the 1982 vintage. Their daughter Rosalind returned home to be the family's winemaker in 1982, having completed a degree in oenology at Roseworthy in South Australia. Her brother David manages the vineyards, with his father Robert looking after the farming enterprise. Vivienne is the dynamic and vivacious promoter and marketer of Delatite and makes sure the world knows about these exciting, clean and complex wines which keep winning trophies and awards every vintage.

As well as the famous Delatite Riesling and Gewurztraminer there is also a sensational sauvignon blanc which sells within weeks of its release and an unwooded chardonnay.

The Devil's River, a bordeaux style of cabernet sauvignon blended with merlot, malbec and cabernet franc, is a top class wine with minty and conserve-like fruit intensity plus lovely cassis fruit characters.

Delatite also has a small range of intensely flavoured red varietals – shiraz, malbec, merlot and cabernet sauvignon on their Limited Release range.

The pinot noir and chardonnay – 100% varietal wines – are aged in superb new Alliers, Vosges and Troncais (French) oak and the Demelza is a lovely pinot noir dominated sparkling wine, only available at the cellar door.

The winery has a tasting room with sensational views over Mount Buller and Mount Stirling, underlining its cool mountain location.

Plunkett Wines

The best unwooded chardonnay I have tasted comes from this little known winery with extensive vineyards in the very cool Strathbogie Ranges.

PLUNKETTS WINES
Address: Lamgin Gully Road, Avenel VIC 3664
Phone: (03) 5796 2150
Fax: (03) 5796 2147
Established: Vineyard, 1968; Winery, 1991
Owner: Alan Plunkett
Winemaker: Sam Plunkett
Principal varieties grown: Chardonnay, Sauvignon Blanc, Semillon, Gewurztraminer, Riesling, Shiraz, Pinot Noir, Merlot, Cabernet Franc, Cabernet Sauvignon
Ha under vine: 120
Average annual crush: 150 tonnes
Principal wines & brands
Unwooded Chardonnay
Cabernet Merlot
Wooded Chardonnay
Shiraz
Pinot Noir
Sauvignon Blanc/Semillon
Riesling
Gewürztraminer
Public & trade tours: Trade tours by appointment only
Hours open to public: 11am-5pm, weekdays; 10am-5pm, weekends
Points of interest: Restaurant, Functions
Retail distribution: Bottleshops and Restaurants. Winestock, Melbourne; Alambie, Sydney; Wine2000, Brisbane; Premium Merchants, Perth

Every time I drink this wine under their other label – Blackwood Ridge, its vibrant, fresh fruit flavours and lovely almond like nuttiness just blows me away and I notice all my friends glasses are easily drained, it is moreish in the extreme.

Alan Plunkett began farming at "Whitegate" in the Strathbogie Ranges in 1966. The cool climate enhanced by being 500 metres above sea level seemed ideal for growing premium table wine grapes.

In 1968 Alan pioneered grape growing in the Strathbogie s when he planted 3 acres to 25 varieties. Drought and the demands of a 3,200 acre grazing property during the rural depression shelved this experiment but Alan found which varieties thrived in his lofty environment.

In 1980 25 acres were planted, this is now up to 175 acres. Plunketts also have 9 acres around their winery on the Hume Highway at Avenel which has just been expanded and includes a "Winery Cafe".

I have also been most impressed by the Plunkett Merlot a supple style with lovely cherry and plum overtones.

Alan's son Sam is quietly spoken, but his wines are saying plenty for him!!

The region is located adjacent to the Hume Highway near the rural city of Wangaratta and in view of the Victorian Alps. The major producers of the area are Brown Brothers, Bailey's and Booth, have all had a long history, all being established before 1892. More recently John Gehrig, Rick Morris and Ken Read have established small wineries featuring wines from their own vineyards.

The King Valley, lying south into the Victorian Alps, experiences cooler conditions and a wide range of soil types, making the area one of the most diverse and interesting in Australia. It produces fine sparkling wine fruit grown at more than 800 metres, chardonnay and shiraz in the valleys for table wines and fruit for rich fortifieds on the plains.

Traditionally, the Milawa/Glenrowan area has been renowned for deep complex red wines of great longevity, the rich blackcurrant flavours further enhanced when the wines are cellared for at least 5 years. New growing areas in the King Valley plus the innovation of Brown Brothers has seen an extraordinary range of varietal wines, including gewurztraminer, semillon, sauvignon blanc in white wines, as well as barbera, nebbiolo and dolcetto in reds.

These styles, combined with rich fortified muscat and tokays from Bailey's at Glenrowan, creates great appeal and diversity.

The agricultural produce of the area extends beyond viticulture, with the rich valleys growing an amazing range of produce. The "Milawa Gourmet Region", signposted from the Hume Highway near Glenrowan, makes it easy to find David & Anne Brown's Milawa Cheese, Milawa Mustards and an extensive range of foods, fruits and berries.

The Brown Brothers Epicurean Centre at the winery, generously demonstrates, the regional fare, combining new release wines with the local in season produce.

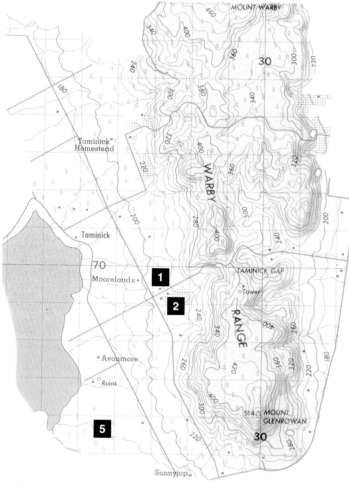

Milawa/Glenrowan - Vic

1 Auldstone Cellars
2 Bailey's Of Glenrowan
3 Brown Brothers Milawa Pty Ltd
4 Ciaverella Wines
5 H.J.T. Vineyards
6 John Gehrig Wines
7 Markwood Estate Winery
8 Milawa Cheese Co
9 Read's

Baileys

Richard Bailey arrived in Melbourne in the 1830's. He spent a decade as a cartage contractor before moving to Glenrowan and opening the towns first general store. Following the gold rush he bought land which his family farmed and planted some vines.

In 1855 Varley Bailey found a strip of deep red granite soil on the slopes below the Warby Ranges giving his red and fortified wines immense colour and strength, muscat was particularly successful.

During the 1970's Harry Tinson became winemaker working hand in hand with Alan Bailey, great grandson of the founder. The Baileys 1920 Block Shiraz (long known as Hermitage) has always been sought after for its big robust colour and flavour. The muscats and tokays under various labels and prices are absolutely top wines in the unique rich Australian style that is taking many of the old world wine markets by storm. Baileys is now part of the Mildara Wine Group but very much maintaining its individual style which has always been its trademark. A range of table wines under the Phantom's Lake (one of the large lakes in the region) label are very good drinking.

BAILEYS

Address: Taminick Gap Road, RMB 4160, Glenrowan VIC 5675
Phone: (03) 5766 3292
Fax: (03) 5766 2596
Established: 1853
Owner: Mildara Blass Limited
Winemaker: Wayne Dutschke
Principal varieties grown: Cabernet Sauvignon, Shiraz
Ha under vine: 288
Average no. cases produced: 28,000

Principal wines & brands	Cellar Potential
Baileys 1920's Block Shiraz	5-30 years
Baileys Touriga	Now
Baileys Tokay	Now
Baileys Muscat	Now
Phantom's Lake Chardonnay	2 years
Phantom's Lake Shiraz Cabernet	5 years

Public & trade tours: Trade tours by appointment only
Hours open to public: 9am-5pm, weekdays; 10am-5pm, weekends and public holidays

Milawa Cheese Company

David and Anne Brown are pioneers of the modern gourmet Australian cheese industry. Inspired by cheese they had experienced in France and Northern Italy they sought out the abandoned butter factory at Milawa. It location close to the famous Brown Brothers Winery, the Snow Road and the tourist attractions of North East Victoria was perfect. Cow's milk was available from the Ovens and Kiewa Valleys and a new industry of milking sheep and goats was about to begin.

The first cheeses made was based on European models, Milawa Blue derived from Dolcelatte from Northern Italy and the pungent Milawa Gold from the washed rind cheeses of France.

Using these foundation stones David Brown has developed a range of uniquely Australian styles, ranging from delicate fresh curd cheeses of sheep and goat's milk to the authoritative blue styles Milawa Roc (sheep's milk) and Mt Buffalo Blue (goats milk). The washed rind range has grown to include the delicate King River Gold as well as washed rind goat and sheep cheeses. The complete range is available for tasting at the factory shop and espresso coffee and ploughman's luncheons are available all day.

MILAWA CHEESE COMPANY

Address: Taminick Gap Road, RMB 4160, Glenrowan VIC 5675
Phone: (03) 5766 3292
Fax: (03) 5766 2596
Established: 1853
Owner: Mildara Blass Limited
Winemaker: Wayne Dutschke
Principal varieties grown: Cabernet Sauvignon, Shiraz
Ha under vine: 288
Average no. cases produced: 28,000

Principal wines & brands	Cellar Potential
Baileys 1920's Block Shiraz	5-30 years
Baileys Touriga	Now
Baileys Tokay	Now
Baileys Muscat	Now
Phantom's Lake Chardonnay	2 years
Phantom's Lake Shiraz Cabernet	5 years

Public & trade tours: Trade tours by appointment only
Hours open to public: 9am-5pm, weekdays; 10am-5pm, weekends and public holidays

An introduction to the King and Ovens Valleys

It is little known that the King Valley has the largest area of vines (some 2,500 acres) of any cool climate grape growing region of Victoria. Situated high in the foothills of the Victorian Alps it supplies many of the top class, large Australian wineries with premium grapes. Brown Brothers still source almost half the crop from the region which is approaching 10,000 tonnes of grapes per annum, planting is continuing at a rapid pace.

The region is very isolated and has few wineries. These include the Darling Estate Winery, Avalon and the Pizzini Family's Lana Trento Winery. The region is very much in two entirely different climates. The plains, close to Milawa and Oxley, I have covered in a separate chapter.

The valley proper is at some 600-800 metres above sea level and some 30-40 kilometres south of Milawa around the towns of Whitfield and Cheshunt on deep volcanic soils. Some problems have been exerpienced with isolated outbreaks of phylloxera aided somewhat by the heavy soils, high rainfall and humidity. These have been contained and most vines are being planted on resistant root stock. The wines from The King Valley have very clean and strong varietal characters and good acid balance. Most vineyards use high vertical trellising and double cordon training of the vines to get maximum leaf exposure to the sun for flavour building photosynthesis and some bunch exposure to the sun to help also with disease control and full ripe characters in the wines.

Recently Miranda Wines have set up a winery and a grower owned crushing facility, 'King Valley Wines', which crushes and supplies juice to about 20 wineries who buy from the region.

1. Avalon
2. Boynton's of Bright
3. Brown Brothers
4. Ciavarella Wines
5. Darling Estate
6. John Gehrig Wines
7. Pennyweight
8. Pizzini-Lana Trento
9. Rosewhite Vineyards

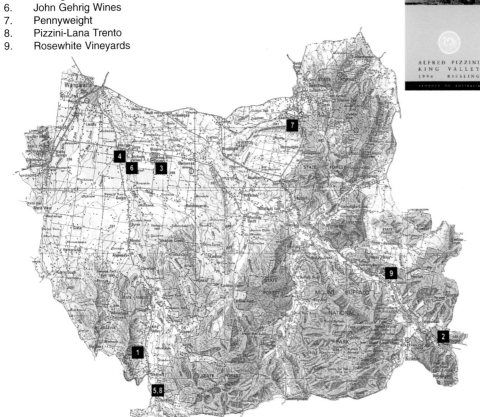

Darling Estate Wines

The Darling Estate is located on 200 acres of lush river flats near Cheshunt in the Upper King Valley. Originally part of the 25,000 acre Glenmore Station of mainly mountainous country south of Whitfield which was taken up by squatter John Bond in 1843, the Darling Family took up their property in 1919 when F.B. Darling returned from World War I. The property had been mostly devoted to tobacco since 1877 and a small portion of the property continues with this usage today. After their fathers death in 1953 his three sons Guy, Harvey and Robin ran the property.

In 1970 Guy Darling bought a property on an elevated bench in the valley some 4 kilometres south near Whitfield. He started the first commercial plantings of vines in the Upper King Valley.

This property, Koombahla for many years, supplied Brown Brothers who used the name on several wines.

Guy also has some pinot noir and chenin blanc on the original family property "Nambucca", aboriginal for 'meeting of the rivers' (The King River and Queen's Creek). An efficient small winery has been built at "Nambucca" in a disused tobacco drying barn.

The first vintage was in 1991. Guy, with the help of his son, makes quite a range of wines using the names 'Darling Estate' or 'Nambucca', for those from Nambucca and 'Koombahla' for those from his Koombahla vineyard.

I found the chenin blancs intriguing with crisp apple and quince characters. All the wines are very well made and good value.

DARLING ESTATE WINES AND KOOMBAHLA VINEYARD

Address: Cheshunt and Whitfield
Phone: (03) 5729 8396
Fax: (03) 5729 8396
Established: Vineyard, 1970; Winery, 1990
Owner: Darling Family
Winemaker: H.G. Darling
Principal varieties grown: Cabernet Sauvignon, Shiraz, Pinot Noir, Cabernet Franc, Chardonnay, Riesling, Sauvignon Blanc, Semillon, Chenin Blanc, Gamay
Ha under vine: 21

Average no. cases produced: 600

Principal wines & brands	Cellar Potential
Cabernet Sauvignon	8 years
Pinot Noir	4 years
Chardonnay	3 years
Riesling	3 years
Gamay	

Public & trade tours: By appointment only
Hours open to public: By Appointment
Retail distribution: Local Area, Melbourne

Pizzini Lana - Trento Vineyard

In 1956 two brothers Robert and Arnold Pizzini migrated to Australia from Northern Italy and began growing tobacco at Myrtleford before moving to the King Valley. Fred (Alfred), Roberts son, and his wife Katrina own a 130 acre property with substantial plantings comprising chardonnay, riesling, shiraz, cabernet and malbec plus the Italian varieties of mebbiolo and sangiovese.

Whilst being involved with grape-growing in the region for 20 years Fred has just began his own wine-making enterprise Lana-Trento and is just launching the Alfred Pizzini Label.

Aiming at "Food" style wines – they have a keen interest in food and hospitality and have recently also taken over the Whitfield Hotel, by all accounts the food there has improved dramatically.

Fred has just won a gold medal for his 1995 Shiraz Cabernet at the 1997 Victorian Wine Show and is naturally very excited about it. Fred's supple sangiovese is a red to enjoy with pasta and the more robust mebbiolo with red meats. He also makes a sauvignon blanc, riesling and chardonnay. Look for the new Pizzini label with a photograph of a thirsty picker imbibing in a little of the produce in the vineyard – it must be good.

Boyntons of Bright

Not far from the head of the Ovens Valley near Mount Buffalo, close by the town of Bright, is the family winery Boyntons of Bright. The impressive looking winery has spectacular views from the spacious cellar door over the pine forest to the imposing Mount Buffalo. Kel Boynton keeps himself very busy as viticulturist in charge of his 40 acres vineyard, winemaker and chief executive as well as earning himself a glowing reputation for his warm cellar doorhospitality.

Kel grows chardonnay, sauvignon blanc, riesling, semillon, cabernet sauvignon, shiraz, merlot and pinot meunier, which he uses in his own Methode Champenoise.

His reds have developed a cult following for their vibrant cool climate fruitiness as have his crisp, impeccably clean, white wines. Right by the turn off from the Ovens Valley Highway to Mount Buffalo at Porepunkah ,and with picnic facilities, it makes an ideal stopping off point on your travels. The Ovens Valley has an illustrious reputation for its reds as Wynns have made use of for years. Kel Boynton is adding to this legend.

BOYNTONS OF BRIGHT

Address: Great Alpine Road, Porepunkah VIC 3740
PO Box 296, Bright VIC 3741
Direction: 10km east of Bright
Phone: (03) 5756 2356
Fax: (03) 5756 2610
Established: 1987
Owner: Kel and Carolien Boynton
Winemaker: Kel Boynton
Principal varieties grown: Shiraz, Cabernet

Sauvignon, Merlot, Chardonnay, Semillon, Sauvignon Blanc
Ha under vine: 16
Average annual crush: 200 tonnes

Principal wines & brands	Cellar Potential
Shiraz	7-10 years
Cabernet Sauvignon	7-10 years
Merlot	7-10 years
Chardonnay	1-3 years
Semillon	2-7 years
Sauvignon Blanc	1-2 years

Public & trade tours: By appointment only
Hours open to public: 10am-5pm, daily except Christmas Day
Retail distribution:
Cellar Door and Mail Order sales. Restaurants and selected Bottle shops, Sydney and Melbourne

An introduction to Mildura/Swan Hill

Most of the wine grapes processed in Victoria are grown in the north-western corner of the state, along the Murray River. The region stretches from Mildura to the east, along the state border to Echuca. Irrigation is necessary as rainfall is very low.

The area was originally developed by the men who initiated the local channel irrigation, the Chaffey brothers. George Chaffey purchased Mildura Station after his arrival from California in 1886. The name 'Mildura' is appropriate to the rich burnt-coloured landscape along the Murray, being aboriginal for 'red rock'. However, even though the soil was fertile, lack of water made the area barren. The South Australian Government, realising the potential of their Murray River region, and the Chaffey Brothers' irrigation successes in California, hired George and his newly arrived brother William to open up the Renmark area. The ensuing success of

this project, saw the Victorian Government hire the pair for a repeat operation in the dry north-western corner of the state. The region quickly became a major fruit-growing area. Although many grape-growers sold their fruit to wine companies, the greater proportion of grapes were used in dried fruit production.

Wine companies were naturally drawn to the Murray Valley. The huge scale of production underway, particularly after the Soldier Settlement Scheme, produced a glut of grapes on the market for attractive development potential. The Murray Valley, concentrating mainly on the production of spirits, prospered during the fortified wine boom. While much fortified wine is still manufactured in the area, the Mildura Region now provides some 25 percent of Australia's wine, involving production in three states - Victoria and several enormous wineries just across the river in New South Wales at

Buronga and grapes which are trucked into South Australia.

Viticultural techniques such as minimal pruning, which sees huge bushy vines producing many small bunches with small tasty berries, has seen wine quality soar. The percentage of excellent bottled premium table wines from the region has grown enormously. Trentham Estate, Alambie, Lindemans, Matthew Lang and the Sunnycliff Wines of Wingara typify this revolution. Further down river, Best's at Lake Boga, Bullers at Beverford and Tisdall at Echuca make excellent premium wines. Australia's competitive position on the world wine market is benefiting greatly from the innovative region. The large Simeon Wine Company had a successful public float and supplies many of Australia's premium wine producers. A trip along the river by riverboat to the lovely Trentham Winery Restaurant is a must when you visit.

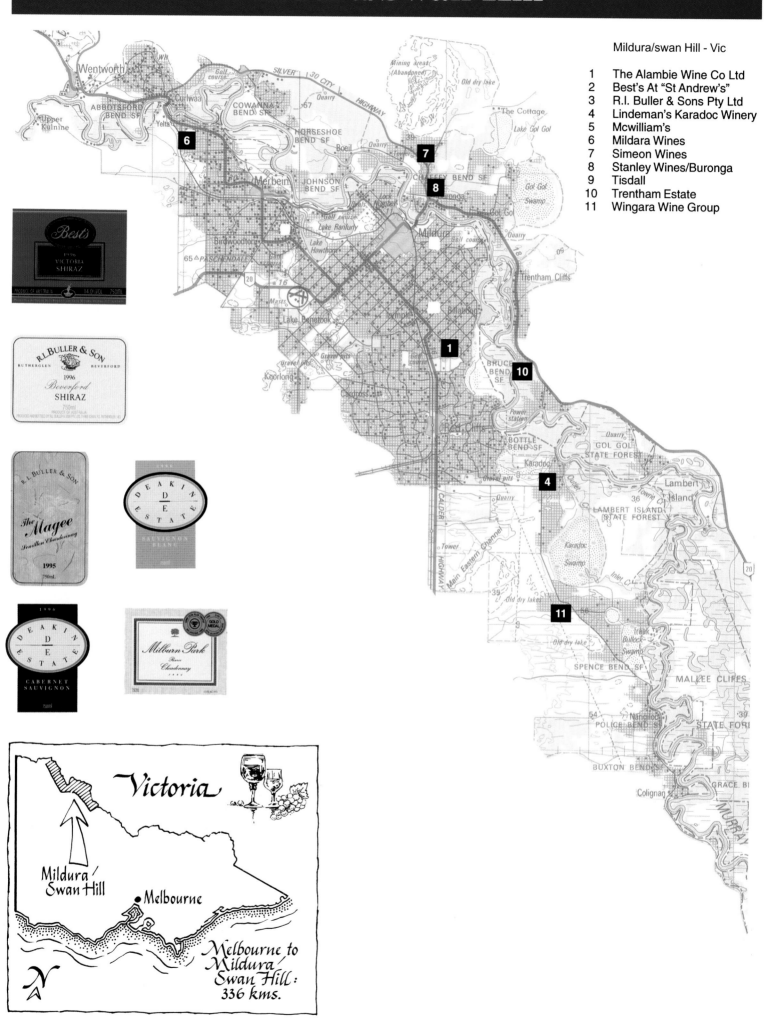

Mildura/swan Hill - Vic

1 The Alambie Wine Co Ltd
2 Best's At "St Andrew's"
3 R.I. Buller & Sons Pty Ltd
4 Lindeman's Karadoc Winery
5 Mcwilliam's
6 Mildara Wines
7 Simeon Wines
8 Stanley Wines/Buronga
9 Tisdall
10 Trentham Estate
11 Wingara Wine Group

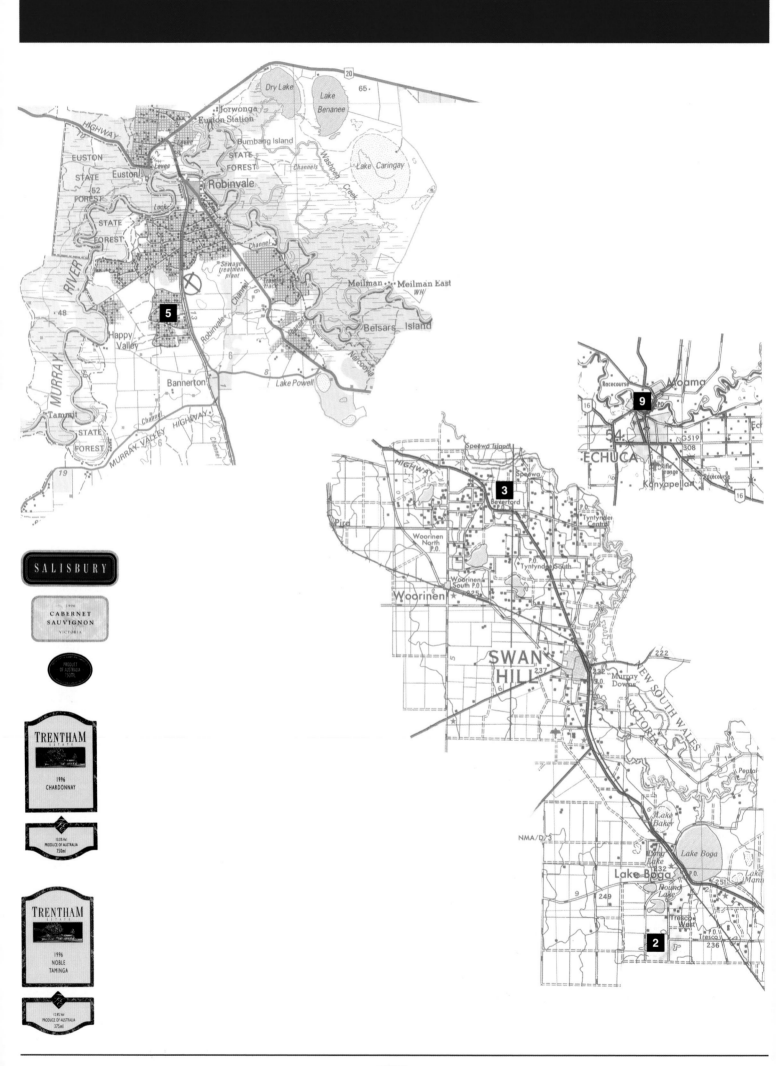

SALISBURY

1996
CABERNET
SAUVIGNON
VICTORIA

PRODUCT
OF AUSTRALIA
750ML

TRENTHAM
ESTATE

1996
CHARDONNAY

13.5% Vol
PRODUCE OF AUSTRALIA
750ml

TRENTHAM
ESTATE

1996
NOBLE
TAMINGA

12.8% Vol
PRODUCE OF AUSTRALIA
375ml

Alambie Wines

Rising rapidly through Australian wine industry ranks, this dynamic company now stands among the nation's top ten wine producers with its Milburn Park, Salisbury Estate and Castle Crossing red and white table wine brands. Established 25 years ago by agricultural scientist, Peter McLaren, Alambie now boasts extensive vineyard areas as well as a large horticultural holding growing premium export quality avocados, citrus and almonds. From origins as a small concern processing grapes to add to its rural value, Alambie today produces premium wines at vintage at its Irymple winery for national and export markets. Company controlled vineyards mean that quality of production is supervised by Alambie's winemaking team from vineyard to bottle.

Chief winemaker, Bob Shields worked previously with Lindemans. At Alambie, he credits the viticultural techniques of minimal pruning to create strong, disease and drought-resistant vines that produce grapes in small berried bunches yielding concentrated flavour. Alambie recently restructured as an unlisted public company. Technological developments have continued each year since the company's inception, assisting in producing critically acclaimed wines. Alambie also has large vineyard holdings in the exciting new vineyard area of Koppamurra in the south east of South Australia.

In value-for-money wine and quality terms, all the Alambie wines are outstanding.

ALAMBIE WINE CO LTD
Address: PO Box 695, Campbell Avenue, Irymple VIC 3498
Direction: Turn off Calder Highway, 2km from Irymple Township
Phone: (03) 5024 6800
Fax: (03) 5024 6605
Established: 1973
Owner: Australian Premium Wines Ltd
Winemakers: Bob Shields and David Martin
Principal varieties grown: Cabernet Sauvignon, Shiraz, Merlot, Chardonnay, Sauvignon Blanc, Semillon, Chenin Blanc, Colombard, Malbec, Mourvedre
Ha under vine: 200
Average annual crush: 20,000 tonnes
Average no. cases produced: 350,000

Principal wines & brands	Cellar Potential
Milburn Park Cabernet Sauvignon	4 years
Milburn Park Chardonnay	4 years
Milburn Park Sauvignon Blanc	3 years
Salisbury Cabernet Sauvignon	3 years
Salisbury Cabernet Merlot	3 years
Salisbury Chardonnay	3 years
Salisbury Sauvignon Blanc	3 years
Salisbury Chardonnay Semillon	3 years
Cattle Crossing Shiraz Malbec Mourvedre	3 years
Cattle Crossing Colombard Chardonnay	2 years

Public & trade tours: No
Hours open to public: 10am-4pm, Mon-Sat
Points of interest: Cellar Door sales and picnic area
Retail distribution: Extensive in all major capital cities. Contact winery for the stockist nearest you.

Wingara Wine Group

The Sunnycliff vineyards were first planted from 1973 with the winery being commissioned in 1980.

Initially all fruit processed at the winery was sold to other wineries as juice or wine.

In 1989 the Sunnycliff range of wines was released. The company has undergone rapid expansion in recent years and in 1995 released its Deakin Estate range.

Today, with the application of new technology in viticulture and winemaking, Wingara Wine Group is at the forefront of value-for-money quality wine in Australia. In both the vineyards and the winery, every effort is directed to maximising the quality of the fruit and wine by preserving fruit flavours and having total control of all stages of production.

DEAKIN ESTATE
Address: Kulkyne Way via Red Cliffs VIC 3496
Phone: (03) 5029 1666
Fax: (03) 5024 3316
Email: wingara@sunland.net.au
Established: 1973
Owner: Wingara Wine Group
Winemaker: Mark Zeppel
Principal varieties grown: Chardonnay, Sauvignon Blanc, Colombard, Cabernet Sauvignon, Shiraz, Merlot
Ha under vine: 360
Average no. cases produced: 200,000

Principal wines & brands	Cellar Potential
Deakin Estate 'Alfred' Chardonnay	5 years
Deakin Estate Colombard	2 years
Deakin Estate Sauvignon Blanc	2 years
Deakin Estate Cabernet Sauvignon	5 years
Deakin Estate Shiraz	5 years
Deakin Estate Brut	2 years

Public & trade tours: By appointment only
Points of interest: Although there is no Cellar Door as such, the public are welcome to picnic on the lawns by our lake
Retail distribution: National Distribution by Tucker Seabrook Pty Ltd

Best's St. Andrews, Lake Boga

The pioneer winery of the Swan Hill district, St. Andrews was established in 1930 by Frederick Thomson and his sons, Eric and Bill. The winery is located five kilometres from the town of Lake Boga, off the Murray Valley Highway. Of the 150 acre property, almost half is under vine. Yields are high and the quality of fruit is consistently excellent. Table wines are vintaged at St Andrews then transferred to Concongella, Great Western, for subsequent maturation, blending and bottling. Best's St. Andrews wines, sold under "Best's Victoria" label, reflect winemaker Viv Thomson's considerable skills. This is most evident in the quality of the chenin blanc and the exemplary cabernet sauvignon. Similarly, the St. Andrews Liqueur Muscat is a wine of great character and is most reasonably priced. Wines from Best's St. Andrews vineyard are most certainly a fine addition to the company's range and represent excellent value-for-money.

BEST'S LAKE BOGA
Address: 'St Andrews', Lake Boga VIC 3584
Direction: Winery Road, 5kms from Lake Boga
Phone: (03) 5356 2250
Fax: (03) 5356 2430
Established: 1930
Owner: The Thomson Family
Winemakers: Vic Thomson and Simon Clayfield

Principal varieties grown: Shiraz, Cabernet Sauvignon, Colombard, Chenin Blanc, Riesling
Average annual crush: 400 tonnes

Principal wines & brands	Cellar Potential
Victoria Shiraz	1-6 years
Victoria Cabernet Sauvignon	1-6 years
Victoria Chenin Blanc	2-5 years
Spaetlese Lexia	2-5 years
Vintage Port	10+ years

Public & trade tours: By appointment only
Hours open to public: 9am-5pm, weekdays; 9am-4pm, Saturday and public holidays; 12pm-4pm, Sunday of holiday periods
Points of interest: Picnic Area, Pot-Still highlight of Tour, Home of Best's Fortified Wines, Brandy & Victoria Table Wines.
Retail distribution: Agents in State Capital Cities with exception of form to

Trentham Estate

One of the best located and prettiest wineries in Australia sits on the elevated banks on a perfect bend of the Murray River. Trentham Estate winery has a large glassed-in cafe`-style restaurant affording panoramic views of the river in both directions over the sweeping lawns.

In front of the winery is a landing where each Thursday the historic paddle steamer Rothbury, built in 1881, pulls in after leaving Mildura at 10.30 am. After a leisurely lunch at the winery, you disembark at Mildura at 3.30 pm. The trip includes a guided tour of the winery by winemaker Anthony Murphy whose family owns the property where they first planted vines back in 1909. Anthony worked at Mildara for some 11 years and while he makes the wine his brother Pat manages the 33 hectares of premium grape varieties. The wines are truly international class. Aside from table wines, they produce both sparkling and fortified wines.

I was particularly impressed by the chardonnay, the shiraz and the vintage port.

TRENTHAM ESTATE
Address: Sturt Highway, Trentham Cliffs NSW 2378
Direction: 15 kms from Mildura on NSW side of Murray River
Phone: (03) 5024 8888
Fax: (03) 5024 8800
Established: 1988
Owner: Murphy Family
Winemaker: Anthony Murphy
Principal varieties grown: Chardonnay, Colombard, Merlot, Shiraz
Ha under vine: 30
Average annual crush: 370 tonnes
Average no. cases produced: 35,000

Principal wines & brands	Cellar Potential
Chardonnay	4-6 years
Sauvignon Blanc	2-4 years
Colombard Chardonnay	1-2 years
Noble Taminga	4-6 years
Merlot	4-6 years
Cabernet Merlot	4-6 years
Ruby Cabernet	2-4 years
Shiraz	4-10 years

Public & trade tours: By appointment only
Hours open to public: 8.30am-5pm, weekdays; 9.30am-5pm, weekends
Points of interest: Restaurant and BBQ's
Retail distribution: Melbourne, Sydney, Brisbane, Adelaide and Perth

An introduction to Rutherglen

Like other Victorian wine-producing areas, Rutherglen's fortunes have fluctuated over the years. Rutherglen has seen so many natural and economic changes throughout its history that one must admire both the courage of the families who continued to persevere with the industry, and the strength and quality of the wines that enabled them to carry on.

The Rutherglen region was first settled by Lindsay Brown, who purchased the large Gooramadda property in 1839. Several of his farm-workers were from Germany and had brought vine cuttings with them, which were duly planted. Under pressure from these workers, Brown was encouraged to plant his own vines, which were also highly successful.

The discovery of gold in Rutherglen in 1860 was an event which greatly increased the local population. Within 10 years, however, the ore had become scarce and people turned to vines to make their fortune. By 1870 a number of large winemaking enterprises were in operation throughout the district. Some of these properties were built on a grand scale and included such magnificent homesteads as Camille Reau's, 'Tuilleries' and Alexander Caughey's 'Mt Prior'. Many family companies were established at this time, some of which are still in existence. Development of the wine industry continued to expand towards the turn of the century, with further companies constructing imposing mansions and wineries. A grand castle was erected by the Sutherland Smith family's company, All Saints, and the Morris family also built a magnificent mansion at Fairfield, with enormous cellars capable of storing three million litres of wine.

The burgeoning popularity of fortified wines was crucial to these developments, particularly as Rutherglen had ideal conditions for the production of Australia's best fortified wines.

Unfortunately the threat of phylloxera became a reality in 1899, when it was identified in the area, temporarily halting the growth of Rutherglen's wine industry. Many vineyards were destroyed but others were replanted with vines of a more resistant nature. This was encouraged by the government who subsidised the price of the new vines. Some vignerons were unable to meet the costs of replanting, however, and by the outbreak of the First World War, these companies had faded from existence. Export of fortified wines to the United Kingdom sustained many companies throughout this time until the market collapsed during the Depression. Wine prices slumped and the government was forced to ration beer supplies to assist the ailing wine industry. Fortified wines again became locally popular and Rutherglen experienced a period of relative growth and prosperity. Public tastes were also veering toward table wines and several companies, including Campbell's, Bullers, All Saints and the Morris family developed new ranges of wines. For the most part red wines were produced but recent years have seen the production of high quality white wines in the area. Both semillon and chardonnay grapes are proving to be very successful and Mount Prior, St Leonards and Campbell's have excellent examples showing the potential of these varieties.

The liqueur muscats, tokays and frontignacs of the Rutherglen area are, without doubt, the best in Australia and are quite probably the best in the world. These wines are truly unique to Australia and are saluted by critics the world over.

Following the success of Rutherglen's table wines and a resurgence of interest in its fortified's, many local winemakers have renovated, new wineries have been built and old ones re-opened. The restoration of the beautiful old All Saints 'Castle' Winery by the Brown Family who purchased it several years ago is fabulous - the gardens and the restaurant function area are really world-class.

Chris Pfeiffer, formerly with Lindemans has done an excellent job restoring and setting up with his wife Robyn, an excellent winery in the old Seppelts distillery at Wahgunyah. Campbell's Winery which has a fine reputation for the wines of four generations, is beautifully presented and provides visitors with the opportunity of walking through their 125 year old winery.

Rutherglen was the first region in Victoria to run a wine festival. These became legendary events during the 1970's. The region now has a number of successful wine events. In March, the Labour Day weekend hosts the Tastes of Rutherglen when the finest restaurants in the region bring their gourmet treasures to the wineries.

The Gourmet Getaway follows on the next week, (which is a long weekend in Canberra). The Queen's Birthday weekend in June sees the famous Winery Walkabout, food and entertainment featuring at all the wineries. Winner of many tourism awards, something for all the family. Rutherglen is back with a vengeance.

Rutherglen

Rutherglen - Vic

1 All Saints Estate/Le Bistro Restaurant
2 Anderson Winery
3 R.I. Buller (Calliope Vineyard
4 Campbell's Rutherglen Winery
5 Chamber's Rosewood
6 Cofield Wines
7 Fairfield Vineyards
8 Gerhig's Winery
9 Jones Winery

10 Morris Wines
11 Mount Prior
12 Pfeiffer Wines
13 St Leonards
14 Stanton & Killeen
15 G Sutherland Smith & Sons

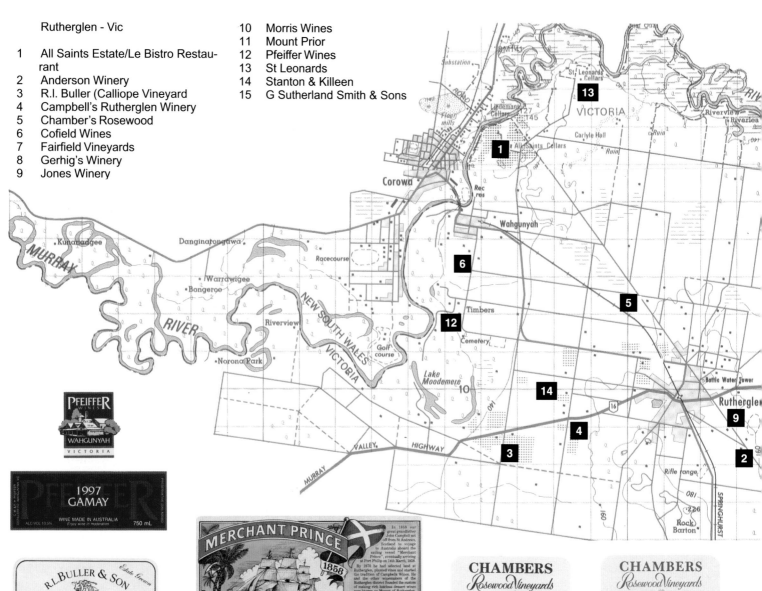

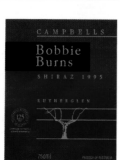

All Saints

All Saints must vie for the title of one of Australia's most imposing and impressive wineries. Its faded glory has been restored and enhanced to a breathtaking degree by the Brown Family of Milawa who purchased the run-down winery and vineyards in 1993. They have created a hospitality centre, beautifully and sensitively blended it into this classic, Scottish Castle inspired winery.

The history of All Saints goes back to 1862 when George Sutherland Smith and his brother-in-law John Banks purchased a 520 hectare property at Wahgunyah on the Murray River. Sutherland Smith had been a tradesman at the castle of Mey in Caithness in Scotland and the winery was built to resemble this building and was named after its Scottish location in the parish of All Saints.

All Saints is one of the premier producers of old fortified dessert wines. Its Museum releases contain predominantly 50-60 year old wines aged in the old oak casks which fill the winery's huge Barrel Hall. The table wines, particularly, have benefited from the impact of the state of the art winemaking equipment of Brown Brothers.

In a separate cellar building which overlooks the splendid formal gardens, there is a special North East Victoria Winemakers Hall of Fame which certainly has more living history and past glory than any other Australian wine region. The indoor/outdoor Terrace Restaurant has an innovative menu featuring local produce and The Great Hall of Fame is a wonderful venue for that special large function. A plan is currently being prepared to construct some accommodation cottages in the vineyards looking towards the Murray River.

ALL SAINTS ESTATE
Address: All Saints Rd, Wahgunyah VIC 3687
Phone: (02) 6033 1922
Fax: (02) 6033 3515
Established: 1864
Owner: Brown Brothers
Principal varieties grown: Cabernet, Shiraz, Chenin Blanc, Chardonnay, Semillon, Marsanne, Tokay, Muscat, Orange Muscat
Ha under vine: 58
Average annual crush: 500 tonnes
Average no. cases produced: 30,000

Principal wines & brands	Cellar Potential
'All Saints' Shiraz	5-10 years
Cabernet Sauvignon	5-10 years
Late Harvest Semillon	5-10 years
NV Sparkling Cabernet	2-5 years
Riesling	2-5 years
Chenin Blanc Marsanne	2-5 years
Chardonnay	2-5 years
Vintage Port	10+ years
Muscat	5-10 years
Tokay	5-10 years

Public & trade tours: By appointment only
Hours open to public: All Saints: 9am-5.30pm, Mon-Sat; from 10am, Sunday except Christmas Day and public holidays. St Leonards: 11am-3pm, weekends except Christmas Day and Good Friday
Points of interest: Terrace Restaurant, picnic baskets, playground, Le Bistro at St. Leonards, Chinese Dormitory, self guided tours, keg factory cooperage, Winemakers Hall of Fame
Retail distribution: Limited to selected outlets in Melbourne

Chambers Rosewood

In a region that boasts many of the true legends of the Australian Wine Industry - Bill Chambers is their Doyen. Bill is not one to stand on ceremony, his bright blue eyes shine with an intelligence that saw him well through the University of Melbourne many years ago. Bill is happiest on his farm, which just happens to have some of the greatest vineyards and wines this great wine nation can boast.

Bill's one that firmly believes a good wine sells itself. A select coterie of knowledgeable wine lovers have beaten a path to his cellar door for many years, but try as he may, he's found fame and fortune hard to avoid.

The Chambers Rosewood Rare Tokay and Muscat in half bottles sells in the United States at $130 each. The Rare Tokay was awarded 98 points out of 100 in a September 1997 Wine Spectator tasting.

The Penfolds Grange Hermitage is the only other Australian wine ever to achieve this incredible feat. The Special Tokay and Special Muscat were not far behind both with 95 points and at $45 a half bottle in the US represent fabulous value.

As I write late at night I am sipping the Special Tokay Bill gave me a few years ago. Its velvety texture and complex nutty and creamy character, it's exquisite liquid gold!! Chambers make some splendid red and white table wines. There is a cellar door where bulk wine and some real bargains can still be found. If your lucky enough to catch Bill in the tasting area - as he just loves to be in the winery or out on the farm - a conversation with him is a most enlightening experience indeed. Seek out this hidden jewel the Chambers have been keeping a secret sine 1858 - your life will be richer for its discovery.

CHAMBERS ROSEWOOD
Address: Barkly Street, Rutherglen VIC 3685
Phone: (02) 6032 8641
Fax: (02) 6032 8101
Established: 1858
Owner: Bill Chambers
Winemaker: Bill Chambers
Principal varieties grown: Shiraz, Cabernet Sauvignon, Blue Imperial, Touriga, Rutherglen Muscat, Muscadelle (Tokay), Chardonnay, Palomino, Riesling
Ha under vine: 53
Average no. cases produced: 10,000

Principal wines & brands	Cellar Potential
Cabernet Sauvignon	10+ years
Shiraz	10+ years
Riesling	5+ years
Chardonnay	5+ years

Muscat (Special and Rare)
Tokay (Special and Rare)
Ports (Tawny, Vintage, Ruby and Late Bottled)
Sherry (Amontillado, Dry, Flor, Oloroso)
Public & trade tours: By appointment only
Hours open to public: 9am-5pm, Mon-Sat; 10am-5pm, Sunday except Christmas Day and Good Friday
Points of interest: Old carved cask imported from Germany in 1888. Chambers is an old fashioned winery, with rows of casks in old buildings. Bill, the winemaker, is acknowledged as one of the world's best winemakers of fortified wines
Retail distribution: Cellar Door. Fine Wine Specialist, Sydney; Walter Seigal, UK; Old Bridge Cellars, USA

Campbells

In 1995, the Campbell clan celebrated their 125th vintage, a significant achievement because the winery, one of the oldest in Australia, has been owned by the Campbell family from the planting of its first vine.

Scotsman John Campbell arrived in Australia in 1858 and immediately set out for the Beechworth goldfields. This stay was shortlived, for a short time later he married and moved to the 'Bobbie Burns' diggings at Rutherglen. When the gold supplies decreased, Campbell decided to stay in Rutherglen and establish a farm. He chose a 75 acre parcel of land adjacent to the gold diggings which he aptly called 'Bobbie Burns', and the following year, he was granted a further 120 acres by the government. Campbell concentrated mainly on grain crops but planted 2½ acres of vines for himself, his family and friends. By 1885, this had increased to 38 acres. This growing concern saw the construction of a winery and the venture into the market place where the wines were very successful, both in sales figures and on the show circuit. In 1898, the vineyard was devastated by the vine louse, phylloxera and by the time John Campbell died, 11 years later, wine production at Bobbie Burns was in a slump. Campbell's son David, determined to reverse the decline of the family wine interests, restored the cellar and replanted vines on resistant rootstock to ensure protection from the phylloxera. In turn, his son Allen carried the business through the difficult years of the Depression.

One of the problems faced at this time was the build-up of wine stocks due to lack of sales. In an attempt to alleviate this situation the Campbellís began the new practice of selling surplus wine at the cellar door; a stop-gap measure that enabled the continuity of the winery. Gradually, the economic climate improved, eventually creating the conditions whereby the Campbellís were able to purchase more land for expansion.

Allenís sons, Malcolm and Colin, currently run the business. Malcolm handles the rural side and the vineyard while Colin, a Roseworthy graduate, manages the wine-making and winery. Colin has proved beyond doubt that the Rutherglen area is capable of producing world class fortifieds and red wines, but can also produce excellent white wines. The successful release in 1995 of the Bobbie Burns Chardonnay adds to the already impressive reputation for whites that Campbellís continue to enjoy. The Bobbie Burns Shiraz has developed a cult following and the recently released super premium, Barkly Durif looks set to go the same way. Campbellís fortifieds including ports, tokays and muscats are marvellous world-renowned wines, demonstrating the incredible style and standard achieved by the very best Rutherglen producers.

Campbell family members are all heavily involved in the business; Mrs Isabel Campbell, Malcolm and his wife Jenny, plus Colin and Prue - even Muscat the cat - can't stay out of the picture. The winery is a picture of beautifully maintained history as can be seen on the self guided tour and in the wines to be enjoyed in the impressive, friendly tasting room. The Campbell's are proud of their past and dedicated to the future.

CAMPBELLS RUTHERGLEN WINES

Address: Murray Valley Highway, Rutherglen VIC.3685
Direction: 3 kms West of Rutherglen on Murray Valley Highway
Phone: (02) 6032 9458
Fax: (02) 6032 9870
Established: 1870
Owner: Campbell Family
Winemaker: Colin Campbell
Principal varieties grown: Shiraz, Muscat, Durif, Cabernet Sauvignon, Riesling, Chardonnay, Semillon, Tokay
Ha under vine: 55
Average annual crush: 750 tonnes
Average no. cases produced: 35,000

Principal wines & brands	Cellar Potential
Bobbie Burns Shiraz	10+ years
The Barkly Durif	10+ years
Chardonnay	5 years
Silverburn	2-5 years
Semillon Chardonnay	2-5 years
Liqueur Muscat	
Liqueur Tokay	
Rutherglen Muscat	
Liquid Gold	
Merchant Prince Muscat	
Isabella Tokay	

Public & trade tours: By appointment only
Hours open to public: 9am-5pm, Mon-Sat; 10am-5pm, Sunday
Points of interest: The Vintage Room featuring re-releases of past excellent vintages. Visitors are able to walk throughout the century old cellars
Retail distribution: National Distribution - Fesq. Dorado and Co.

R L Buller - Calliope Vineyards

Lieutenant Commander Reginald Langdon Buller purchased his vineyard, 5 km west of Rutherglen, in 1921 after returning from active service in the 1914-18 war. He named the vineyard 'Calliope' after the sturdy British warship A.B. (Banjo) Patterson's stirring 'Ballad of the Calliope'.

Having built a winery and established himself in the wine industry, Reginald Buller left 'Calliope' in the hands of his son Richard (Dick), and in 1951 moved to Beverford, north of Swan Hill, to establish a second vineyard and winery.

Reginald Buller retired in 1966 and lived out his days in Melbourne. Dick Buller, who had developed a reputation as a talented wine-maker, carried on the business and developed the Buller label. He also had a distinguished career as a wine show judge and in 1996 was honoured by his peers with the title of a 'Rutherglen Legend'. He died in 1997.

Today R.L. Buller & Son is in the hands of Dick's sons, Richard (Rick) and Andrew. Rick heads up the family company and oversees Beverford while Andrew is winemaker/manager at Rutherglen.

Rutherglen, from its non irrigated vineyard, produces a range of full bodied reds of which the flagship wine is the Calliope Shiraz. It is also here that the famous Buller fortified wines are made - Muscats, Tokays and Ports. The Muscats and Tokays in particular have won medals and trophies in Australia and overseas.

The Beverford range includes a first class wood aged Semillon, a Shiraz which is consistently good, and several varietals offering excellent value for money.

An added attraction at Bullers of Rutherglen is Val Buller's Bird Park, which is open to the public, and was a finalist in the 1997 Victorian Tourism Awards.

R L BULLER

Address:
Murray Valley Highway, Beverford VIC 3590
Phone:
(03) 5037 6305
Fax:
(03) 5037 6803
Established:
1951
Winemaker:
Richard Buller
Principal varieties grown:
Cabernet Sauvignon, Shiraz, Semillon, Muscat, Muscadelle, Gordo, Frontignac
Ha under vine:
27
Average annual crush:
1,000-2,499
Principal wines & brands:
Bullers
Hours open to public:
9am-5pm, Mon-Sat
Retail distribution:
Cellar Door and Mail Order. Harry Williams, ACT; Andrew Waterman, SA; Time Seats, NT; Normans Wines, NSW. Export to NZ, Canada

Morris of Rutherglen

In 1859, George Morris purchased a property at Browns Plains, which he called 'Fairfield'. Morris expanded his vineyard so that by 1872 he had 617 acres under vine.

During the 1880's Morris built the imposing Fairfield mansion, which became one of the showpieces of the area. More than half of Fairfield's output was exported to the United Kingdom.

In fact George Morris had such a reputation that in 1886 he was appointed Wine Commissioner at the Indian Colonial Exhibition in London.

In fact by the 1890's George Morris was in charge of Australia's largest winery. George's son Charles Morris, purchased his own property three kilometres east of Fairfield at Mia Mia in 1887 and also planted vines. The resultant fruit was sold to and processed at Fairfield.

The Fairfield vineyards were attacked suddenly by phylloxera at the turn of the century. Wine production rapidly declined and following the founder's death, the company ceased production altogether. However, at Mia Mia, after the devastation wrought by the vine louse, Charles Morris replanted and continued to make fortified wines.

Today, the winery is run by its founder's great-grandson, David. David carries on the family tradition producing a range of red table wines including Durif which is a wine of great body and character. Likewise his chardonnay is great with both excellent fruit and strong varietal character. The Morris fortifieds are made skilfully and compare favourably with the best in the world. Morris Wines was sold to Orlando in 1970 but fortunately Mick Morris (company winemaker, wine industry legend - and David's father) was retained. Since Mick's retirement David Morris is carrying on the fine family tradition of more than a century.

MORRIS OF RUTHERGLEN
Address:
Mia Mia Vineyard, Rutherglen VIC 3685
Phone:
(02) 6026 7303
Fax:
(02) 6026 7445
Established: 1858
Owner:
Orlando Wyndham Group Pty Ltd
Winemaker:
David Morris
Principal varieties grown:
Chardonnay, Semillon, Shiraz, Cabernet Sauvignon, Durif, Muscat, Tokay, Muscadelle, Blue Imperial
Principal wines & brands:
Morris Old Premium Liqueur Muscat
Morris Old Premium Liqueur Tokay
Morris Canister range
Morris Black Label range
Morris Rutherglen Durif
Morris Rutherglen Shiraz
Morris Chardonnay
Morris Semillon
Morris Sparkling Shiraz Durif
Public & trade tours:
By appointment only
Hours open to public:
9am-5pm, Mon-Sat; 10am-5pm, Sunday
Points of interest:
Picnic and BBQ facilities
Retail distribution: National

Pfeiffers Wines

Chris Pfeiffer was fortified wine-maker for Lindemans Wines, his last position being just across the Murray River from Rutherglen, in Corowa. In 1984 he and his wife Robyn purchased the grand old Seppelt's Distillery in Wahgunyah, and renovated the 19ᵀᴴ Century winery.

The tasting area is full of character, and the scenic picnic area on the banks of the river provides an idyllic location for enjoying Pfeiffer's gourmet lunch hampers.

The original 10 hectare vineyard was planted in 1963 and since 1984 has been expanded to 22 hectares. Chris also has a small planting of the elusive grape variety gamay, which he crafts into an early drinking style of spicy wild berry flavours. The old low yielding pinot noir vines produce a red of great character. Since 1984 Chris has had some cabernet sauvignon, riesling and shiraz vines grown in the cool Kiewa Valley, near Mount Beauty. The lifted aromatics of these grapes enhance the elegance of style and balance for which Pfeiffer Wines are renowned. The delicate dry riesling in particular benefits from this influence.

The Auslese Tokay, is a beautiful dessert wine, and an impressive selection of fortified wines - muscat, tokay, vintage port and a tawny port containing 26 varieties - complete the range.

Pfeiffers have been most successful on the export market with a recently released range of wines made by Chris under the "Carlisle" label representing true regional and varietal character at great value for money prices.

PFEIFFER WINES
Address: Distillery Road, Wahgunyah VIC 3687
Direction: Off Wahgunyah-Rutherglen Road, between Wahgunyah and Rutherglen
Phone: (02) 6033 2805
Fax: (02) 6033 3158
Established: 1984
Winemaker: Christopher Pfeiffer
Principal varieties grown: Chardonnay, Pinot Noir, Gamay, Cabernet Sauvignon, Merlot, Shiraz, Rutherglen Muscat, Rutherglen Tokay, Touriga
Ha under vine: 19
Average no. cases produced: 13,000

Principal wines & brands	Cellar Potential
Chardonnay	5-10 years
Riesling	2-5 years
Chardonnay-Semillon	2-5 years
Cabernet Sauvignon	5-10 years
Shiraz	2-5 years
Old Distillery Port	Enjoy now
Old Distillery Tokay	Enjoy now
Old Distillery Muscat	Enjoy now

Public & trade tours: By appointment only
Hours open to public: 9am-5pm, Mon-Sat; 11am-4pm, Sunday
Points of interest: Picnic Hamper available (ordering essential) to enjoy on bridge.

Fairfield

Melba Morris Slamen is a grand lady of grace and charm. Over the last decade or two she has been restoring "Fairfield", the mansion and imposing winery built by her grandfather George Morris.

George bought the 222 acre property at Browns Plains and by 1872 this had expanded to 617 acres under vines, building the Fairfield Mansion and the grandest cellars in Australia in true colonial Victorian splendour in the 1880's. By the 1890's Fairfield was making Australia's largest vintage.

Today Melba has re-established a boutique winery with the wines being made by Andrew Sutherland Smith, a fifth generation member of the family that founded All Saints Wines.

A strong sense of history and tradition reigns strongly at Fairfield and in the style of their wines. Quite a few of the reds including the imperious Durif have considerable bottle age and are worth seeking out. The historic Fairfield mansion is open most weekends by appointment for a tour guided by the proprietress Melba Morris Slamen. Much of the original furniture and family heirlooms are truly fascinating.

FAIRFIELD
Address: Murray Valley Highway, Rutherglen VIC 3685
Phone: (02) 6032 9381
Established: 1860
Winemaker: Andrew Sutherland-Smith
Principal varieties grown: Cabernet Sauvignon, Shiraz, Riesling, Durif, Muscat, Trebbiano
Ha under vine: 15
Average annual crush: 20-49 tonnes
Principal wines & brands: 'Fairfield Vineyard'
Hours open to public: 10am-4.30pm, weekdays; 10am-5pm, Saturday; 12am-5pm, Sunday
Points of interest: Fairfield House, a lovely old 21 roomed Victorian house has been restored and re-furnished. Tours in Victorian school holidays. Coaches by appointment
Retail distribution: Cellar Door and Mail Order sales

Owing to the dispersed nature of viticulture throughout Victoria and the enormous distances encountered from region to region, this chapter will include the smaller areas of Great Western, Pyrenees, Ballarat and Drumborg near the coast.

The best-known area is Great Western, 218 kilometres west of Melbourne. Centred around a small town of the same name, the district is hilly, of poor soils and is at the mercy of extreme climates, including frosts. Fruit yields are therefore low but, due to the slow ripening period which creates high sugar levels, these yields are of excellent quality.

Since its inception out of the gold rush, the Great Western district has produced long living, high quality wines. Vines were planted in the 1860's by two Frenchmen, Jean Trouette and Emile Blampied and the Best family. In time, the former property faded

from existence, leaving Best family's Great Western vineyards to prosper and expand. Following the death of Joseph Best, the Great Western concern was sold to Hans Irvine who emphasised champagne production. B. Seppelt and Sons bought Great Western in 1918.

Of the 44 district vine growers of 1893, only two, Seppelt Great Western along with the Thomson family, at what was formerly Best's Concongella Vineyard, survive today. Nowadays the Great Western district is part of the region known as Grampians with the two pioneer wineries joined by a number of new ventures, led by Mount Langi Ghiran Vineyards in 1969.

During the 1960's Seppelt decided to expand their operations in Victoria and began a search for suitable land. Owing to quarantine regulations it was not possible to take cuttings from South Australia. As the company wished to continue producing fruit from cool

climate areas, an alternative site in Victoria was required. Karl Seppelt purchased property at Drumborg outside Portland, which he first planted to vines in 1964. The coastal climate is milder than at Great Western and, since Seppelt's successful establishment at Drumborg, other have been encouraged to plant in this area.

The Pyrenees winemaking district, includes Avoca, Moonambel and Redbank. Located north-west of Ballarat in the Pyrenees range, the undulating landscape provides ideal conditions for the manufacture of a wide range of wines. Vines were first planted in the 1840's by Adams on Mountain Creek, closely followed by a Mr Mackereth in 1848. The Mackereth concern was sold and dismantled in 1929, and Mountain Creek closed operations in 1947.

In 1963, John Robb arrived at Avoca and planted extensive vineyards for a consortium of the Remy Martin Company from France

and an Australian wine merchant, Nathan and Wyeth. Although initially established for brandy production, Chateau Remy, now known as Blue Pyrenees Estate, has since changed direction, specialising in fine sparkling wines. During the early 1970's, other vineyards were established in the Pyrenees, including Taltarni, Warrenmang and Dalwhinnie. In 1973 Neill and Sally Robb established the Redbank Winery which have since acquired an outstanding reputation for their red wines.

Winemakers of the Pyrenees region are highly successful at producing a large selection of wine styles, ranging from the excellent sparkling wines of Taltarni and Blue Pyrenees Estate to the minty reds produced by Redbank and others. Local conditions have contributed to their prosperity. Although fruit yields tend to be low and the climate is cold and rainfall moderate, the grapes are first rate.

A smaller winegrowing area centres around Ballarat. Again, like many Victorian 'Born Again' wine districts, the area supported a flourishing wine industry in the 1800s. Ian Home pioneered the new resurgence in 1976 when he established Yellowglen.

Climate and topography vary throughout Western Victoria. So too do the wines produced in each region. For instance, Great Western, although famed for its sparkling wine, is also the origin of highly acclaimed table wines. The Drumborg and Ballarat areas produce cool climate wines of classic styles, while the Pyrenees region seems able to produce any variety of wine desired. While each district is diverse in style and direction, they all share a commitment to the winemaking industry of Victoria and, as a result, produce wines of distinction. Many wineries have hospitality facilities adding to the pleasure of visiting these regions.

GARDEN GULLY

Address: Great Western Highway, Great Western VIC 3377
Phone: (03) 5356 2400
Fax: (03) 5356 2400
Established: 1987
Winemakers: Brian Fletcher and Warren Randall
Principal varieties grown: Shiraz, Riesling
Ha under vine: 7
Average annual crush: 13 tonnes

Principal wines & brands	Cellar Potential
Garden Gully Sparkling Burgundy	5+ years
Garden Gully Shiraz	5 years
Garden Gully Rhine Riesling	2-3 years

Hours open to public: 10.30am-5.30pm, weekdays; 10am-5.30pm, weekends and public holidays
Points of interest: Winery is built on the site of the original Hockheim winery and still remains the original underground wine tanks of hand made bricks, circa 1870. Picnic area and electric BBQ's
Retail distribution: Cellar Door and Mail Order sales. Domaine Wine Shippers, VIC

Western Victoria

Western Victoria

1	Best's Great Western	12	Mountain Creek Vineyard
2	Baroka Vineyards	13	Mount Avoca Vineyard
3	Cathcart Ridge Estate	14	Mount Chalambar Wines
4	Chateau Remy/Blue Pyrenees Estate	15	Mount Langi Ghiran Vineyard/ Winery
5	Crawford River Winery	16	Redbank Winery
6	Dalwhinnie Vineyard	17	Seppelt Drumborg Vineyard
7	Donovan Bottle Outlet	18	Seppelt Great Western
8	Garden Gully	19	Summerfield Vineyards
9	Karra Karra Vineyard	20	Taltarni Vineyards
10	Kimbarra Vineyards	21	Warrenmang Vineyards
11	Montara Vineyard	22	Yellowglen Vineyards

Best's Great Western

Although the Thomson family did not establish Best's Wines, the family have been growing grapes and making wine for more than 100 years in the Great Western region. On 13th November, 1893 at 11.30 a.m. William Thomson became the proud owner of 'St Andrews', a vineyard and winery established by pioneer John Lorimer at Rhymney Reef,. Thomson was a born entrepreneur - in 1888 he was appointed caterer to the Great Colonial Exhibition in Melbourne.

His energy and 'hands' on approach have flowed down five generations of the family. Best's Wines is certainly ranked in the top ten Australian Wineries, with wines of extraordinary quality, ageing potential and, above all, individuality! Much credit must go to their unique vineyard at Great Western, taking its name from the Concongella Creek which flows through the bottom of the property. Most of the original vines are still there, planted from 1866 to 1869. This is no museum piece of recreated history, but a working vineyard which came into the Thomson family's hands in 1920. It must be close to being one of the oldest working vineyard in the world.

Best's also have a vineyard, winery and distillery at Lake Boga, called St. Andrews after William Thomson's original vineyard at Rhymney Reef, which they established in 1930 in the heart of the depression - a word that does not exist in the family's vocabulary.

At St. Andrews they produce superb concentrated fortified wines in the classic North-Eastern Victorian style. The winery also has a Best's Victoria label in the value for money section of the market. These wines are mainly from St. Andrews, but often contain some Great Western material. The Victoria Chenin Blanc and Riesling both have lovely lifted fruit character and the Victoria Shiraz and Cabernet are mouthfilling, great value wines.

The 'piece de resistance' is the Great Western 'Bin O Shiraz'. The Bin O is the best bin, even preceding No.1, and incredibly long living. Viv Thomson and I sat down and drank the 1962 alongside the 1992 released to celebrate the family's centenary in 1993. We agreed the older wine was one of the finest and freshest old reds we had ever tried - its lifted pepper and wild berry flavours with a touch of mint were so seductive and full of the vibrancy of youth.

The Great Western Chardonnay, Riesling, Cabernet Sauvignon, Pinot Noir, Pinot Meunier and the Dolcetto Red, the latter 2 being from 130 year old vines, and their Concongella Cuvee Sparkling are world-beaters. Make sure you beat a path to the door to see the original winery and the historic vineyard, with more than 50 vine varieties, all 100-plus years old.

BEST'S CONCONGELLA VINEYARD
GREAT WESTERN
Address: Great Western VIC 3377
Direction: 1km off Western Highway, Stawell Side of Great Western
Phone: (03) 5356 2250
Fax: (03) 5356 2430
Established: 1866
Owner: The Thomson Family
Winemakers: Vic Thomson and Michael Unwin
Principal varieties grown: Shiraz, Cabernet Sauvignon, Pinot Noir, Pinot Meunier, Riesling, Chardonnay, Merlot
Average annual crush: 200 tonnes

Principal wines & brands	Cellar Potential
Bin No. 0 Shiraz	10+ years
Pinot Meunier	10+ years
Pinot Noir	5-10 years
Chardonnay	5-10 years
Riesling	2-5 years
Cabernet Sauvignon	10+ years

Public & trade tours: Yes, Cellar walk
Hours open to public: 9am-5pm, weekdays; 9am-4pm, Saturday and public holidays; 12pm-4pm Sundays of holiday periods only
Points of interest: Picnic Area, Red Gum Slab Stable, built in the 1860's, used as tasting area; underground cellar
Retail distribution: Agents in State Capital Cities with exception of Northern Territory and Western Australia

Cathcart Ridge

The sense of history and tradition that is uniquely Australian is strong at this unique and characterful winery situated on a ridge surrounded by valleys of vines in the shadow of the majestic 'Mount Ararat'.

The winery is about 5 kilometres out of Ararat on the tourist road to Halls Gap in the Grampians.

In the gold rush days of the 1850's a town of some 5,000 people occupied the site which has returned to a natural bushland setting for the vines, but occasionally relics from the past pop up in the vineyard.

The winery and cellar door and the cutest winery residence in Australia, occupied by winemaker/proprietor David Farnhill, a genuine character, are built out of old railway sleepers and are resplendent with much old historic implements and machinery from the distant past collected by David and his father.

David is currently bouyed up by a remarkable success in the 1997 World Wine Championship in Chicago.

His 1994 Cabernet Sauvignon won a gold medal with an impressive 92 points out of 100. His Rhymney Reef Shiraz and Shiraz Cabernet both won silver medals

At present 25 acres are planted to cabernet sauvignon, shiraz, merlot and chardonnay and 15 acres more will be planted in 1998, with the help of water from Lake Fyans, important in this reasonably avid region with hungry soils.

The Cathcart Ridge Merlot is one of Australia's best and all the wines, like their maker, have very individual character.

CATHCART RIDGE

Address: Moyston Road, Ararat VIC 3777
Phone: (03) 5352 1997
Fax: (03) 5352 1558
WWW: http://www.winetitles.com.au/cathcart.html
Established: 1978
Winemaker: David Farnhill
Principal varieties grown: Chardonnay, Merlot, Cabernet Sauvignon, Shiraz, Riesling, Cabernet Franc, Malbec
Ha under vine: 8.5
Average annual crush: 20-49 tonnes

Principal wines & brands	Cellar Potential
Shiraz	10 years
Shiraz Cabernet	12 years
Cabernet Sauvignon	10 years
Merlot	20 years
Chardonnay	8 years

Public & trade tours: Yes
Hours open to public: 10am-5pm, daily
Points of interest: Winery tours and tastings. BBQ facilities
Retail distribution: Cellar Door and Mail Order. Export to UK, SE Asia, USA

Yellowglen

What has become one of Australia's most successful wine ventures was originally established in 1971 as a hobby vineyard by Ballarat businessman and gastronome, Ian Home. The Yellowglen Vineyard at Smythesdale is situated 18 kilometres south-west of Ballarat.

A number of red and white wines were released under the Yellowglen label. The remainder of fruit was made into sparkling wines by the talented Neil Robb.

In 1982 Ian Home went into partnership with Dominique Landragin, previous sparkling winemaker for Seppelt. Born in the Champagne district of France, Dominique trained at Beaune in Burgundy, working for several major champagne houses before leaving for Australia. The two men decided to concentrate their efforts on the creation of a superior range of methode champenoise wines.

Two years later the classic yellow-labelled Yellowglen Brut Non Vintage was released, followed by Australia's first rosé methode champenoise, and a brut cremant a year later, containing half the gas of other sparkling wines and spends a longer time of yeast lees, creating a classic 'creamy' style. Such was the success of this range that Yellowglen was able to develop from a small concern to one of Australia's leading premium sparkling wine suppliers in little more than a decade. Mildara purchased the company in 1984. Home and Landragin stayed on for a time, but today this hugely successful business is run by the extremely competent Mildara team.

YELLOWGLEN

Address: Whites Road, Smythesdale VIC 3351
Phone: (03) 5342 8617
Fax: (03) 5333 7102
Established: 1971
Owner: Mildara Blass Limited
Winemaker: Adam Eggins
Principal varieties grown: Chardonnay, Cabernet Sauvignon, Shiraz, Pinot Noir
Ha under vine: 69
Average no. cases produced: 270,000

Principal wines & brands	Cellar Potential
Yellowglen Yellow	Now
Yellowglen Pinot Noir Chardonnay	Now
Yellowglen Brut Cremant	Now
Yellowglen Brut Rose	Now
Yellowglen Vintage	2-3 years
Yellowglen "Y" Premium	now
Yellowglen Cuvee Victoria	2-3 years
Wolf Blass Blass Brut	now
Wolf Blass Vintage	2-3 years

Public & trade tours: Trade tours by appointment only
Hours open to public: 10am-5pm, weekdays; 11am-5pm, weekends and public holidays

Mount Langi Ghiran

Langi is aboriginal for 'home of' and Ghiran is the yellow-tailed black cockatoo. Langi is also the home of two of the best red wines in Australia. The Langi Shiraz, with its pepper, mulberry and cedar cigar box character, and the cassis and cedar wood Cabernet Sauvignon are as awesome as the spectacular vineyard location spread across the valley between Mount Langi Ghiran and Mount Cole. This cool isolated location was originally apple country, back in the gold rush days of the 1850's. Vines were first planted in 1880, but saw their demise around 1920, like much of Victoria's other vineyards.

Recently Trevor has found a great partner in European Wine identity Riquet Hess. The development of the vineyards has been astounding. Trevor has always had trouble with wind, birds, kangaroos and other animals in his best shiraz vineyard bring the yields down to as low as 1/4 tonne per acre, absolutely uneconomic.

Late in 1996 an enormous 27 acre permanent net was erected around the vineyard. The 1997 crop of around 3.5 tonnes per acre from the protected vines has been of superb quality.

A huge winery slab, for a huge new winery is now laid and a large vineyard development some 10 kilometres north of the existing vineyards is also underway under Trevor's masterly control. I am sure exciting times and wines lie ahead.

The Mount Chalambar Rhine Riesling is always top class, showing plenty of spice, perhaps due to Trevor's German training.

I have been very impressed with the Mount Chalambar Chardonnay, as well. Also recommended is the Mount Langi Sauvignon Blanc, a superb gold medal standard wine at the tropical fruit end of the flavour spectrum.

MOUNT LANGI GHIRAN VINEYARDS PTY LTD

Address: Warrak Road, Buangor via Ararat VIC 3377
Direction: Western Highway at Buangor, on Warrak Road (26km east of Ararat)
Phone: (03) 5354 3207
Fax: (03) 5354 3277
Established: 1968
Owners: Riquet Hess and Trevor Mast
Winemaker: Trevor Mast
Principal varieties grown: Shiraz, Cabernet Sauvignon, Riesling, Pinot Grigio, Cabernet Sauvignon
Ha under vine: 72
Average no. cases produced: 32,000

Principal wines & brands	Cellar Potential
Langi Shiraz	5-10 years
Langi Cabernet Sauvignon/Merlot	5-10 years
Langi Riesling	2-5 years
Langi Pinot Grigio	0-2 years
4 Sisters Sauvignon Blanc/Semillon	0-2 years
4 Sisters Shiraz	1-5 years

Public & trade tours:
By Appointment
Hours open to public:
9am-5pm, weekdays; 12pm-5pm, weekends
Points of interest:
BBQ facilities, spectacular views of mountains and forest
Retail distribution:
Fesq. Dorado - VIC, NSW, QLD, WA; Porters, SA; David Johnstone, TAS; Lace Wines, NZ

Redbank

Neill Robb worked at various wineries in South Australia before taking a position as Champagne-maker at Chateau Remy in 1970. In 1973 Neill left Chateau Remy to develop his own vineyard and winery at Redbank, in the Pyrenees region of Western Victoria, at the same time consulting on the development of Yellowglen and Bannockburn.

Neill and his wife, Sally, planted eighteen hectares of vines and, using local century-old red bricks, built their steep-gabled winery and colonial-style home. Redbank named after the small town three kilometres to the north, is a credit to the Robb's, being both elegant and distinctly Australian.

As well as their own grapes Redbank processes other high quality fruit, brought in from growers around Central and Western Victoria. It is Neill's policy to process each load of fruit separately. The most well-known Redbank wine from their own grapes is the blend of cabernet sauvignon, shiraz, malbec, merlot and cabernet franc named 'Sally's Paddock'. This is an extremely well-structured red wine, with intense colour, flavour and adequate but soft tannins and ages extremely well. Several years ago, Neill and Sally introduced a range of wines under the Redbank 'Long Paddock' label, sourced from cool regions of south-eastern Australia.

These wines represent excellent value for money and solve the shortage of wine, often a difficulty for the Robb's land provides a valuable export wine alternative.

REDBANK WINERY

Address: Redbank VIC 3478
Direction: 200km northwest of Melbourne on Sunraysia Highway
Phone: (03) 5467 7255
Fax: (03) 5467 7248
Established: 1973
Winemaker: Neill Robb
Principal varieties grown: Cabernet Sauvignon, Shiraz, Cabernet Franc, Pinot Noir
Ha under vine: 20
Average no. cases produced: 55,000

Principal wines & brands
Sally's Paddock
Long Paddock
Goldmine Series
Mountain Forge
Hundred Tree Hill

Public & trade tours: By Appointment
Hours open to public: 9am-5pm, Mon-Sat; 10am-5pm, Sunday
Retail distribution: Australia Wide

Robb Family in "Sally's Paddock". Smokey Pyrenees behind.

One of the most fascinating legacies of Australia's wine industry is Seppelt Great Western. Built by Joseph Best during the mid 1860's, the winery features more than two and a half kilometres of underground cellars which have come to be known as the 'Drives'. Consisting of dug out tunnels, they were excavated by local gold miners originally under the direction from Joseph Best, and serve to house maturing sparkling wines.

Throughout the history of the winery many drives have been opened or visited by contemporary celebrities and as such bear their names. 'Dame Nellie Melba Drive' for example, is named after the famous opera singer who is reputed to have bathed in champagne during her visit. The Drives, classified with an 'A' rating by the National Trust, are still in use, their constant temperature of 15 degrees being well suited to the storage of sparkling wines.

Over recent years, Seppelt has concentrated their efforts on improving their very popular bottle fermented wines, Great Western Imperial Reserve and Great Western Brut. A number of premium methode champenoise wines have also been introduced, starting with Fleur de Lys, released in the early 1980's, followed by the exquisite Salinger.

As part of this program, extensive plantings of new vines have been carried out behind the winery at Great Western, as well as Drumborg near Portland, Barooga in New South Wales and Padthaway and the Coonawarra region in South Australia.

The grape varieties planted are those best suited to sparkling wine production and include chardonnay, pinot noir and pinot meunier. Production of these wines has been radically improved. The base wines are produced and blended in the winery and transferred to the tirage preparation area where sugar and yeast are added prior to tirage bottling. Secondary fermentation and maturation in bottle then occur at the required temperature.

By now the yeast is dormant, its distinctive flavour permeating the wine. This process lasts a minimum of six months, but can take up to three years or more in the case of Salinger and some of the other special limited releases, including the marvellous Show Sparkling Burgundies. The wine is then disgorged (that is the dead yeast or lees removed) using the transfer method for some products and the traditional method (i.e. methode champenoise) for more premium styles. The new complex at Great Western can process a total of 20 million plus bottles, a volume that, going by current sales figures, is necessary to meet popular demand.

The winemaking at Seppelt is in the capable hands of Ian McKenzie and his team, both for sparkling, still whites and reds. The recently released Seppelt Victorian Portfolio wines with their distinctive classy labels have been a big success - the 1991 Harpers Range Red, in fact, won the Jimmy Watson Memorial Trophy for best first year red wine in 1992.

The background of many of the early settlers in the region, including Hans Irvine, was French, which I am sure had much to do with the sparkling wine focus. The cool climate is both ideal, both for the special kind of viticulture needed for sparkling wine grapes and the making and ageing of the wines.

Over the years, Seppelt Great Western, as well as enjoying a fine reputation for both sparkling wines and still table wines, have been blessed with some extraordinary winemakers. Skilled and talented, these men of vision have greatly contributed to the Australian wine scene.

The heritage left by Joseph Best from the early days of the 1860's, through to Hans Irvine and Seppelt's first manager, Reginald Mowatt, paved the way for the great Colin Preece who, having taken over form Reginald Mowatt in 1932, gave Australia such classic wines as Moyston Claret, Chalambar Burgundy, Rhymney Chablis and Arawatta Riesling.

Colin's enormous talents contributed largely to Great Western's establishment as a major winemaking force and this tradition of excellence is today being continued by a professional team of winemakers who are developing exciting wines that will bring credit to the Australian wine industry.

Blue Pyrenees Estate

A renaissance in viticultural activity in the Pyrenees region occurred in 1961 when the French Cognac giant, Remy Martin, teamed with the Australian wine and spirit merchants, Nathan & Wyeth, to form Chateau Remy.

Sited on the open alluvial soils which had attracted thousands of goldseekers a century before and with access to a permanent unlimited water supply the company had chosen perhaps the best and most versatile cool climate location within Australia to conduct its winemaking activities.

Although the focus of operation in the early years was on brandy production the company quickly realised the potential this vineyard site had for the production of premium table and sparkling wines and quickly the Chateau Remy label established itself as a leading Australian brand of methode champenoise.

During the 1980's the French parent company, who are also the proprietors of famous French Champagne Houses of Charles Heidsieck and Piper Heidsieck, took total control of the Chateau Remy operations and consolidated its Australian holdings at this prime Avoca site. Change came quickly with massive vineyard expansion, the erection of a totally new winery, the construction of vast underground cellars and the appointment of a new manager/winemaker, Vincent Gere. With outstanding winemaking qualifications,

and coming from a French wine family rich in pedigree, Vincent embarked on establishing a marque that was generic in concept yet was reflective of the characteristics of this unique Pyrenees location. It was to be called Blue Pyrenees Estate.

To meet this Estate appellation, only sections of the vineyard were used where fruit consistently met strict flavour criteria. This fruit was used as the basis for the original 'Blue Pyrenees' - a Bordeaux style red, the Reserve Chardonnay and the exquisite Reserve Brut Methode Traditionelle which now also appears under this distinctive label. The Blue Pyrenees Estate range of wines undoubtedly represents the pinnacle of winemaking achievement so far in the evolution of this Estate. Their high quality is a reflection of both the nature of the Estate grown cool climate fruit, and the care and expertise with which it has been handled. The beautifully fresh and delicate, 1991 Reserve Brut *'Methode Traditionelle'*, into which Vincent and his team have blended more than 50 different cuvees of Estate grown pinot noir, chardonnay and pinot meunier, has already established a niche for itself in the quality end of the market.

Chateau Remy/Blue Pyrenees Estate will have more than 200 hectares under vine by the end of 1997 and it promises to be one of the most exciting viticultural developments in Australia. Moreover, with its picturesque

location, nearby waterfalls and lookout, and extensive garden surroundings, its visitors centre is also destined to become an increasingly popular visitor and tourist destination.

BLUE PYRENEES ESTATE
Address: Vinoca Road, Avoca VIC 3467
Direction: Off Sunraysia Highway, 66km from Ballarat
Phone: (03) 5465 3202
Fax: (03) 5465 3529
Established: 1963
Owner: Remy Cointreau
Winemakers: Vincent Gere and Kim Hart
Principal varieties grown: Chardonnay, Pinot Noir, Pinot Meunier, Cabernet Sauvignon, Cabernet Franc, Merlot, Shiraz, Sauvignon Blanc, Semillon
Ha under vine: 176
Average annual crush: 1,200 Tonnes
Average no. cases produced: 100,000

Principal wines & brands	Cellar Potential
Blue Pyrenees Estate Red	8-10 years
Blue Pyrenees Estate Chardonnay	3-7 years
Blue Pyrenees Reserve Brut	3-7 years
Blue Pyrenees Midnight Cuvee	3-7 years
Leydens Vale Shiraz	5-10 years
Leydens Vale Chardonnay	5-10 years
Leydens Vale Merlot	5-10 years
Leydens Vale Riesling	3-7 years
Fiddlers Creek Range	2-5 years

Public & trade tours: By appointment only
Hours open to public: 10am-5pm, daily
Points of interest: Restaurant on weekends, Underground Cellars, Petanque Club, BBQ Facilities, Art Displays, Waterfalls and Lookouts
Retail distribution: National

Fiddler's Creek

The Pyrenees region is rich in gold mining history and was a hive of industry in the middle of the 19th century. In fact, from 1852 to 1864, records show that 624,115 ounces of gold were mined, valued at 2,496,000 pounds.

Fiddler's Creek winds its way down across the plains just to the north of the Blue Pyrenees Estate and was named after two musically inclined miners who discovered a significant gold reef. They tried to disguise their find, but were heard in the still of the night playing their fiddles for joy at their new found riches.

Fiddler's Creek has been appropriately chosen to label a second source of wines produced by Blue Pyrenees. Fruit sourced from premium Australian Wine regions supplements that grown on the estate to produce a range of quality varietal wines that are marketed at good value prices. The selection includes semillon, sauvignon blanc, chardonnay, cabernet/shiraz, pinot and an excellent bottle fermented sparkling cuvee brut.

Leydens Vale

John Leyden was one of the original landholders of what is now the reputed Blue Pyrenees Estate Vineyards and Winery near Avoca in Western Victoria.

Seeking to emulate the French tradition of the assemblage of rigorously selected individual batches of various varieties from their own Blue Pyrenees Estate and other highly respected cool climate grape growing regions of Australia.

Highly credentialled French winemaker Vincent Gere, who holds a Phd in viticulture and oenology from the ENSA at Montpellier, selects, assembles and matures these wines with consummate skill.

The varietal range of three wines includes a shiraz made in a vibrant rhone valley style, and aromatic riesling and a burgundian style pinot noir. They all have a definite touch of class and present great value for the premium wine lover.

First and second prizes in the Open Hard Cheese Category at the 1996 World Championship Cheese Contest held in Wisconsin, USA would be a great success for a small specialist cheesemaker, with costs and levels of production of no consequence. But when it is won by a major food processor, with Romano and Parmesan cheeses made at its Simpson plant in Western Victoria, this victory is incredible. This Simpson plant was purchased in 1997 by Dairy Farmers, from Kraft Foods. Dairy Farmers is a farmer co-operative formed by a small group of farmers in 1901. It now

has over 3,000 farmer members around Australia. With such a long history, it is a group that cherishes tradition and recognises the gem it has acquired in the skills, know-how and natural advantages of the Simpson plant.

Simpson is a small town nestled in the foothills of the Otway Ranges. This lush green countryside, just inland from the spectacular Great Ocean Road drive, is ideally suited to producing exceptional milk.

The four cheeses that are produced at the plant, Parmesan, Romano, Pecorino and Pepato are all handmade. The curd is

packed into hoops in cheesecloth, pressed overnight, then placed into a brine bath. The parmesan stays there for 6-8 days until the desired salt content is obtained, the romano, pecorino and pepato for a shorter time.

The rounds of cheese are then dried in racks in a special room with the ideal temperature and humidity controlled.

Following this process they are coated in wax and placed in maturation rooms to age, just like wine. The parmesan for 10-24 months at 12-18 degrees celsius, the romano for 8-15 months, the pecorino and pepato (which has already added green, red, black

and white whole peppercorns) for 6-8 months.

Many of the dedicated local cheesemakers have been working at the plant for 20-30 years. Plant Manager, Bruce Neilson, tells me he has just presented a 25 year and a 30 year award respectively to two of the staff and this sort of experience, combined with traditional recipes, is the secret of success. These cheesemakers can sense the annual and daily differences in the milk and adjust their techniques accordingly.

The plant was opened in the late 1960's. The Spaull Family for instance, have just clocked up 75 years of cheese making between them at Simpson.

The plant's cheeses have also dominated the hard cheese classes at the prestigious Royal Melbourne Show since they began exhibiting in 1993. At the 1996 Show in October

their Romano not only won gold and was best cheese in its class but also won the Supreme Cheese Trophy for the best cheese in the show. The parmesan won a silver award as did the percorino and pepato.

When one considers these cheeses, although all individually handmade, are produced in large commercial quantities, their successes are astounding.

All four of the Dairy Farmers hard cheese range are ideal in cooking but particularly the parmesan and this World Championship winner is the very same cheese you can buy in the Dairy Farmers shredded cheese pack in the dairy cabinet at your local supermarket. When I received a whole wheel of parmesan to try several months ago I thought 9 kilograms would be a lifetimes supply, because properly stored it lasts almost as long as you want to keep it, but already I have used more

than half. I think a true test of great parmesan is if you can enjoy it as an eating cheese on the cheese platter, its texture should be hard but not too dry, but you cannot beat the savoury tang.

Which wine to enjoy with parmesan is difficult to consider because used in various dishes it can be enjoyed with a huge variety of different wines from white to red and delicate to full bodied.

I enjoy a big vintage port with mine but find that a good full bodied wood-aged chardonnay is just right for some of my non-red wine drinking friends.

At Dairy Farmers, the cheesemaker's craft is highly treasured. When they inherited this wonderful place last year, the Board agreed they would change nothing about these cheeses. "Why would we?" asks Managing Director Alan Tooth.

Arnotts Biscuits

Like everything in life, balance is important. Wine and cheese is the perfect marriage but it really needs something to bring these wonderful things together - "voila the water cracker".

I well remember by first stints at wine judging at the Royal Melbourne show some 25 year ago, on every table of wines there were always water crackers to refresh and neutralise the palate to make it all the more receptive to the flavours and textures of the wines.

Impromptu eating and snacking is becoming more a part of our modern lifestyle, but our tastes are becoming more discerning.

We are drinking more and more premium wines, our cheese industry is producing a wonderful array of gourmet cheeses, not to mention the huge range of pates and terrines that are now a part of our diets and "de rigeur" in the aperitif stage of entertaining. When we want to put our best foot forward the water cracker brings all this together both before and after the meal or anytime for that matter.

Arnotts is an Australian institution renowned for top quality in all they do. They have been baking biscuits including water crackers since 1865.

Like wine, water crackers must start with

the best quality natural ingredients. This assured, a fermentation takes place, just as in wine yeast works its magic on the dough and gives it a light sourdough tang.

The dough is then rolled layer upon layer in very fine sheets. Finally it is baked in a furnace hot oven for only two and a half minutes, timing and temperature is critical so that it puffs into crisp, fine, golden crackers.

I have found the Arnotts water crackers have just the right subtle but not overpowering flavour with a perfect crisp texture. The fuller flavour of the wine, cheese or pate the more natural the cracker should be, so the original Arnotts water cracker is perfect. Milder, soft or swiss style cheeses, mild pates, lighter reds and full bodied whites match best with the nutty sesame seed water crackers, whilst creamy fresh cheeses are best accompanied by the Arnotts cracked pepper water crackers and delicate aromatic whites.

I myself adore strong blue cheese and vintage port with the original crackers. So go to it and have a "cracking good" wine and food experience, brought together by Arnotts fine water crackers. **Cheers!!**

An introduction to the Yarra Valley

The history of wine in Australia has an amazing way of repeating itself. Fashions in taste change, economic conditions and the scourges of nature take their toll, but the truly great wines and vineyards that bear them will always re-emerge. Such is the history of the Yarra Valley in Victoria. The district is situated around the towns of Lilydale, Yarra Glen and Healesville with some vineyards in the outer suburbs of Melbourne.

Vines were first planted in the Yarra Valley around 1840 by William Ryrie, a farmer who came south from New South Wales in search of good land. This district, however, blossomed with the Swiss settlers who were encouraged to emigrate to Victoria by Sophie, wife of the first Governor of Victoria, Charles La Trobe. Sophie was the daughter of the Swiss Counsellor of State and was well-connected, mixing in circles which included the brothers Hubert and Paul de Castella, ancestors of our famous marathon runner, Robert de Castella. Hubert founded St. Hubert's Winery in 1854 and another of his countrymen, Baron de Pury, founded Yerinberg in 1862.

These Swiss pioneers were well versed in winemaking and viticulture and had a great influence on the growth and success of the area as a wine producing district.

St. Hubert's Winery won the German Emperor's Grand Prize for the Best Australian Wine Exhibitor in the Great Melbourne Exhibition in 1880, for which the grand Exhibition Buildings in Melbourne were built. The prize reflected the ideal wine-growing conditions of the area. Vineyard areas in the Yarra Valley expanded rapidly and by the late 1860's they covered around 150 hectares.

By 1890, Victoria produced almost 60 percent of Australia's wine - more than all the other states combined. Unfortunately, around this time, tastes changed and fortified wines become the fashion. The lack of knowledge about bacterial spoilage meant, too, that bad wines abounded, as fortification became the norm. Cool climate, low-yielding areas that produced fine table wines, such as the Yarra Valley, died out and by the early part of the

20th century, most vineyards in the Yarra had ceased operating. The last vintage was at Yeringberg in 1921. It is often thought that the vine louse, phylloxera, was responsible for the demise of the Yarra Valley, but surprisingly it was one of the few areas in Victoria not attacked and decimated by this disease. The re-birth of the Yarra Valley came more than 40 years after that last vintage in 1921.

There is a certain rivalry between the new pioneers as to who was actually the first in the renaissance. However, I feel the honour should be shared. In 1963, Reg Egan, a Melbourne solicitor, set up residence and started a small vineyard of several hectares in the outer Melbourne suburb of Wantirna South. Now he crushes about 15 tonnes each vintage. Although a little south of the Yarra region proper, I feel this is rightly classified as a Yarra Valley vineyard. A little north of Wantirna Estate is Kellybrook in the suburb of Wonga Park. Darren Kelly founded his enterprise in 1962 and made both still and sparkling wines from apples grown in his orchard; today the vines vastly outnumber the apple trees. In the 1960's renowned winemaker Dr John Middleton also began growing vines and making wines as a hobby.

The true renaissance started in the Yarra Valley in 1968/69 when St. Hubert's Yarra Yering, Fergussons and Yeringberg all got underway with planting. They were followed closely by Chateau Yarrinya (now de Bortoli's) and Seville Estate in 1971 and more lately by Yarra Burn and Warranmate in 1976. Many other ventures have been successfully launched since. Chief among them is Domaine Chandon, the offshoot of the French Moët and Chandon Champagne company.

Wine tourism has gripped the Yarra, the annual Grape Grazing in March sees this at its zenith with wine, food and music pumping out. Many excellent restaurants and cellar door hospitality areas each week attract thousands of keen wine drinkers, from all corners of the world. The Yarra Valley is once again a wine mecca.

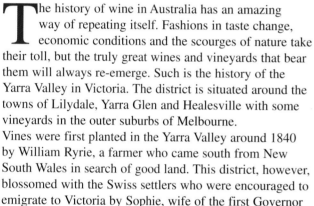

1. Bianchet Winery
2. Broussard's Chum Creek Winery
3. Coldstreams Hills
4. Debortoli Winery & Restaurant
5. Diamond Valley Vineyard
6. Domaine Chandon of Australia
7. Eyton on Yarra
8. Fergusson Winery & Restaurant
9. Kellybrook Winery & Restaurant
10. Lillydale Vineyards
11. Lirralirra Estate
12. Long Gully Estate
13. Lovey's Estate
14. Monbulk Winery
15. Mount Mary Vineyard
16. Oakridge Estate
17. St Huberts Vineyard
18. Seville Estate
19. Shantell
20. Tarrawarra Vineyards
21. Wantirna Estate
22. Warramate Wines
23. Yarra Burn Vineyards & Restaurant
24. Yarra Edge Vineyard
25. Yarra Ridge Vineyard
26. Yarra Valley Hills
27. Yarra Yering Vineyard
28. Yering Station

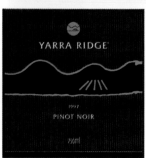

One of the largest and most successful family wine businesses in Australia is De Bortoli. It has risen from virtual obscurity to a prominent respected position in the premium wine industry in less than a decade.

The company's foundation goes back to 1928, four years after Vittorio De Bortoli arrived in the Riverina area of New South Wales from his homeland in northern Italy. Vittorio and his hard working wife, Giuseppina, established a 22 hectare vineyard at Bilbul and eight years later, were making 550,000 litres of wine per year. The original vats and winery are now housed inside the giant complex at Bilbul. De Bortoli really arrived on the wine map when winemaking dynamo Darren, Vittorio's grandson, made a botrytised semillon sauternes-style dessert wine in 1982. It took the wine world by storm, becoming one of the most awarded wines in Australia's history. The *Noble One* is a sensational wine each year. After a long search for a contrasting cool climate vineyard and winery, the family purchased Miller's Chateau Yarrinya vineyard and winery in 1987.

The vineyards have been dramatically expanded by De Bortoli, as has the winery which is partially underground. A separate winery building was constructed in 1995 and the vineyard expansion continues. The winemaking is in the capable hands of Steve Webber, who worked for a time at Rouge Homme in Coonawarra. Steve is married to Chief Executive Deen De Bortoli's daughter Leanne, who runs the showpiece restaurant and hospitality centre on the hill above the winery. The restaurant is large and extremely professionally run, with the feel of a Tuscan bistro and very warm and friendly service. The restaurant also enjoys sweeping panoramic views over the vineyards and the mountain ranges in the distance.

The first crush in 1987 was only 30 tonnes; in 1995 this was elevated to 1,500 tonnes and future growth is planned. There are four labels produced at De Bortoli Yarra Valley.

Melba takes pride of place among the red wines. Blended from the best parcels of red wine from each vintage, the wine is matured in the finest French oak, selection from these barrels ensures that *Melba* is an outstanding wine. *De Bortoli Yarra Valley* is a classic, elegant label with the range featuring Chardonnay, Pinot Noir, Shiraz, Cabernet Sauvignon and Cabernet Merlot. There is a new yarra Valley label Gulf Station which has been produced as a result of the family's involvement with the National Trust. The De Bortoli vineyard was in early times the 'Summer Paddock' of historic gulf Station and the very original label depicts the old homestead. *Windy Peak* is the very popular label which is a selection of wines made from grapes grown in premium Victorian regions. In 1997 De Bortoli was awarded the prestigious Jimmy Watson Memorial Trophy, the second for this vineyard.

De Bortoli is a well-founded, professional family business which does credit to the Yarra Valley and demands a visit.

DE BORTOLI YARRA VALLEY

Address: Pinnacle Lane, Dixons Creek VIC 3775
Phone: (03) 5965 2271
Fax: (03) 5965 2464
Established: 1987
Winemakers: Stephen Webber and David Slingsby-Smith

Principal wines & brands	Cellar Potential
Melba Vineyard Barrel Select	5-10 years
"Yarra Valley"	
Cabernet Sauvignon	5-10 years
Shiraz	5-10 years
Pinot Noir	5-10 years
Cabernet Merlot	5-10 years
Cabernet Franc	4-6 years
Chardonnay	2-5 years
Semillon	4-6 years
"Gulf Station"	
Cabernet Sauvignon Barrel Select	4-6 years
Riesling	4-6 years
"Windy Peak"	
Chardonnay	2-5 years
Rhine Riesling	2-5 years
Spaetlese Riesling	2-4 years
Cabernet Shiraz Merlot	2-5 years
Pinot Noir	2-5 years
Chardonnay Lightly Oaked	2-4 years

Public & trade tours: By appointment only
Hours open to public: 9am-5pm, daily
Points of interest: Restaurant overlooking vineyard featuring northern Italian inspired cuisine
Retail distribution: Available through most fine wine outlets

Coldstream Hills

Coldstream Hills began its life with lofty ideals in a lofty location high on the slopes of Steel Hill with sweeping panoramic views over the vinous enterprises of the Yarra Valley.

Those lofty goals set by the founder of Coldstream Hills, highly respected wine writer and winemaker James Halliday, have more than been met over the 12 years since he planted his first vines in the spectacular north facing amphitheatre that forms the home for the main vineyards of Coldstream Hills.

The financial and marketing demands of a fast growing and successful winery are huge so in 1996 the company formed by James, which owned the winery, sold to Southcorp Wines. James has stayed on and is as ever deeply involved and active on a day to day basis with all aspects of his beloved Coldstream Hills. His home is even higher up the slopes and gives him an ideal perspective and inspiration to oversee the enterprise.

James Halliday turned his keen interest and love for wine into a business interest when he became one of the three founding partners of Brokenwood vineyards and Winery in the Hunter Valley in 1970.

After moving to Melbourne with his legal firm he purchased the Coldstream Hills property and began planting in 1985. The vineyard came into production and a winery was constructed for the 1988 vintage. The 1986 and 1987 vintages were made off-site from the cool climate vineyards grapes selected by James. The 1986 and 1987 vintages amassed 5 trophies, 12 gold, 6 silver and 8 bronze medals from only 39 entries attesting to James Halliday's skill as a winemaker as well as his well evidenced skill as Australia's leading wine writer.

The wines at Coldstream Hills have continued to win huge number of trophies and medals as the vines mature and James, with his viticultural and winemaking team, strive for ever constant improvement.

The vineyards all closely planted on carefully chosen hilly microclimates now cover the various vineyards surrounding the winery, also at Briarston, Gladysdale near Hoddles Creek and the Fernhill Vineyard of Southcorp.

With over 230 acres of vines most of the wines are made from estate grown grapes, a huge quality advantage.

The Coldstream Hills winery, perched above the vineyards with its majestic views over the valley, has just been expanded and includes a classy cellar door that is now open 7 days a week.

Coldstream Hills produce award winning Chardonnay, Sauvignon Blanc, Pinot Noir, Cabernet Sauvignon, Cabernet Merlot, a red Bordeaux blend "Briarston", occasionally a Semillon/Sauvignon Blanc blend and three Reserve Wines, Reserve Chardonnay, Reserve Pinot Noir and Reserve Cabernet Sauvignon. Rigorous selection in the vineyard, full barrel fermentation for the chardonnay and specific attention to the red fermentations and maturation produce some of Australia's finest wines of which James Halliday can be justly proud.

Eyton-on-Yarra

The Eyton on Yarra Winery and Restaurant is situated on Maroondah Highway, Coldstream in the Yarra Valley.

The winery, cellar door, restaurant and surrounding acres of vines are the realisation of the vision of Yarra Valley grazier, the late Newell Cowan and is considered one of the premier winery and restaurant complexes in the country.

The winery took its name from the Cowan's "Eyton on Yarra" property, which was originally established by the Syme Family - of publishing fame - in the 1800's.

In the late 1980's he saw an opportunity to plant vines on the land, and, not a man to do things by halves, subsequently acquired the nearby Coldstream Winery. At this point, shortly after his 80th birthday, he decided to take the grape growing process one step further and produce the wine as well.

Grapes from 120 acres of vines grown on the two Eyton on Yarra properties go to make the stylish wines. With the unique and distinctive regional fruit character of the Yarra Valley. The comprise a pinot chardonnay methode champenoise, a chardonnay, a cabernet merlot, a reserve shiraz, a sauvignon blanc and pinot noir. The Eyton on Yarra Winery and Restaurant is a visitor-oriented winery offering fine food and premium wines in a relaxed and inviting environment. A spiral staircase rises from the centre of the open plan restaurant to a platform giving viewing access over the working winery and Eyton tower which provides magnificent views across the vineyards and the Yarra Valley.

It is an absolute must to visit this Rolls Royce winery. The no expenses spared wines are also top class. Newell's daughter Deidre has assembled a great team under her and runs a very professional operation.

EYTON ON YARRA

Address: Corner of Maroondah Highway & Hill Road, Coldstream VIC 3770
Phone: (03) 5962 2119
Fax: (03) 5962 5319
Email: eytonwines@doncaster.starway.net.au
Established: 1995
Winemaker: Matt Aldridge
Principal varieties grown: Chardonnay, Pinot Noir, Cabernet Sauvignon, Merlot, Sauvignon Blanc
Ha under vine: 50
Average annual crush: 130 tonnes
Average no. cases produced: 10,000

Principal wines & brands	Cellar Potential
Eyton Chardonnay	5 years
Eyton Pinot Noir	5 years
Eyton Cabernets	6-8 years
NDC Shiraz	6-8 years
Dalry Road Chardonnay	Now
Dalry Road Pinot Noir	Now

Public & trade tours: By appointment only
Hours open to public: 10am-5pm, daily
Points of interest: Cafe`, Restaurant (Tourism award winner for 1997), sound shell for outdoor performances, look out tower, self guided tours Retail distribution: Rutherglen Wines, Melbourne, (03) 9646 6666

St. Huberts

St Huberts vineyard and winery was established in 1862 by Swiss wine pioneer Hubert de Castella. The wines achieved worldwide renown in 1881. They won the Emperor's Prize at the International Exhibition of that year. At one point there were 250 acres under vine and it was a premier vineyard of Australia with the cellars able to store over a million litres of wine. The advent of cheaper table wines and the vogue for fortifieds from warmer areas saw the demise of the enterprise and the land reverted to grazing.

St Huberts re-birth came in 1966 as one of the first Yarra Valley Renaissance Wineries. Their reputation and the quality of their wines are once again on the very top rung of wine producers. Through a series of owners the winery is now in the capable hands of Mildara Blass. The wines are consistently winning awards and much of the production is exported.

ST HUBERTS

Address: St Huberts Road, Coldstream VIC 3770
Phone: (03) 9739 1118
Fax: (03) 9739 1015
Established: 1862
Owner: Mildara Blass Limited
Winemaker: Adam Marks
Principal varieties grown: Cabernet Sauvignon, Pinot Noir, Merlot, Chardonnay, Rousanne
Ha under vine: 21
Average no. cases produced: 25,000

Principal wines & brands	Cellar Potential
St Huberts Rousanne	2-4 years
St Huberts Chardonnay	2-4 years
St Huberts Pinot Noir	3-5 years
St Huberts Cabernet Merlot	3-5 years
Rowan Sauvignon Blanc	2-4 years
Rowan Cabernet Merlot	2-5 years

Public & trade tours: No
Hours open to public: 9am-5pm, weekdays; 10.30am-5.30pm, weekends and public holidays
Points of interest: Picnic area and children's playground

Domaine Chandon

The world's largest champagne house, Moët et Chandon, is no stranger to the New World of Wine. It set up a superb champagne cellar and restaurant complex in the Napa Valley back in 1973 and has made forays into other countries. John Wright, who was president of the Californian operation and involved in itís establishment, came to Australia several times in the early 1980's. He was accompanied on some visits by the charming French winemaker, Edmund Maudiere, who bears an uncanny resemblance to the great monk, Dom Perignon himself, who discovered the champagne making process back in the early 1600's quite by accident.

Careful perfectionists in all they do, Moët chose top flight oenologist Dr. Tony Jordan to head up its Australian venture. Tony, at the time, was running the renowned oenological consultancy service Oenotec. As soon as the sites in the Yarra Valley was chosen, vines were planted, but Tony had already made sparkling wine base material in 1986 at wineries using Oenotec Services, such as Mitchelton and Katnook. The resulting sparkling wines were already lying on tirage at Seppelts Great Western, as the contract for the Yarra Valley property was being signed - forethought and planning are a big part of champagne making.

The beautiful buildings housing the winery, sparkling wine tirage cellars, and the stunning tasting and hospitality area were completed on December 1990. The first wine, a 1986, was released to celebrate the occasion and to start the necessary cash flow. Moët at first saw only the local market as of interest and planned a total production of 50,000 cases.

Export (under the Green Point Vineyards label) is mainly to Europe and now accounts for 25 per cent of the production and 100,000 cases is not far away. I am sure the future will see even bigger production.

Even in the days of modern machinery and technology, methode champenoise production is an art form, a mosaic, bringing together an enormous number of pieces like a giant jigsaw, which takes time and a great deal of human skill and effort. Apart from its own extensive Yarra Valley and Strathbogie Ranges vineyards, Domaine Chandon has a network of growers under contract, mainly in the cool regions of Southern Victoria and also sources grapes from as far away as Hobart - Tasmania and Fonty's Farm Vineyard near Pemberton in south-west Western Australia.

The base wines are all made separately, then comes the assemblage, pulling the base wines together to form the cuvees for the secondary fermentation. For this exacting task, an absolutely tranquil environment is needed. The architects (Allen Jack & Cottier of Sydney) designed this assemblage room in a tower above the winery, absolutely isolated, where the winemaking team, under Dr Tony Jordan and Wayne Donaldson, can concentrate 100 per cent on their work to find the perfect matches for the master cuvee for each of the various Domaine Chandon blends.

Needless to say, the finished product celebrates the skill and experience of centuries of champagne-making, combined with the innovation and skill of our Australian winemakers, not forgetting the great grapes that form the base of it all.

When you visit Domaine Chandon, you can sit in the vaulted tasting area with its world class view over the vineyards and mountains, and for a small fee, enjoy a crystal flute of any of the Domaine Chandon range with a delicious gourmet platter. What better way to celebrate a visit to the Yarra Valley?

DOMAINE CHANDON
Address: Green Point Maroondah Highway, Coldstream VIC 3770
Phone: (03) 9739 1110
Fax: (03) 9739 1095
WWW: http://www.domainechandon.com.au
Established: 1985
Owner: Moet Hennessy Group
Winemaker: Wayne Donaldson
Principal varieties grown: Chardonnay, Pinot Noir, Pinot Meunier
Ha under vine: 40
Average annual crush: 385 tonnes
Average no. cases produced: 100,000

Principal wines & brands
Domaine Chandon Vintage Brut
Domaine Chandon Vintage Brut Rosé
Domaine Chandon Vintage Blanc de Blancs
Domaine Chandon Vintage Blanc de Noirs
Domaine Chandon Cuvee Riche
Green Point Chardonnay
Green Point Pinot Noir
Colonnade Chardonnay

Public & trade tours: Yes
Hours open to public: 10.30am-4.30pm, daily
Points of interest: Visitors centre where wines can be purchased by the glass and bottle and accompanied by a complimentary food platter
Retail distribution: Swift and Moore Pty Ltd, National; Rutherglen Wine Co., VIC; Aria Wine Co., QLD, NSW; Chase Agencies, SA

Henkell Vineyards

Whilst Hans Henkell is a newcomer to the Yarra Valley his family's vinous roots go back to the 1830's just before the Yarra Valley's first vineyards were planted.

Hans is the great-great-grandson of Adam Henkell who began the Henkell sparkling wine empire in the heart of the Rhone Valley in Germany ironically, not far from Switzerland where the wine pioneers of the Yarra Valley left for Australia. Hans and his father Otto visited the Yarra Valley in 1980. Plans began which led to the development of Henkell vineyards. The cellar door is resplendent with memorabilia of the Henkellís wine tradition behind the signature gates on the Melba Highway some seven kilometres past Yarra Glen. Henkell produce a range of wines naturally including a sparkling wine and can be tasted along with a range of locally made cheeses and chutneys.

Wine aficionado John Cashen is assisting Hans in the venture which certainly adds another cultural dimension to the Yarra Valley.

Loveys Vineyards and Restaurant

My first contact with Brian Love was an animated phone conversation where Brian described his recent trip through the wine regions of California with my North American Pictorial wine Atlas as his guide. His wife Denise had strongly suggested it was crazy to cart such a heavy book to California, but they were glad they did.

Brian and Denise are old hands at the hospitality game. Starting the first Lovey's Restaurant in Heatherdale in 1979 (Brian's first restaurant was in Little Bourke Street in 1972). A move to a renovated Edwardian house in Wantima in 1985 was a stepping stone to the dream of the Yarra Valley.

In 1989 they bought 50 acres just kilometres out of Yarra Glen at Dixons Creek. Today the renovated Edwardian house, which was relocated from Wantima, is surrounded by a lake and 6 acres of superb gardens with in excess of 200 rose bushes, 100 fruit trees and 450 ornamental trees. Added to this is, one of Australia's largest hedge mazes with 3 kilometres of pathways created by 639 cypress trees modelled on the Hazelhead Park Hedge Maze in Aberdeen, Scotland.

Their "Loveys Estate" (formerly Mount Hope) range of wines, have a revamped label with a stylish gold leaf.

Lovey's Estate is boutique in every way, wines are only available at the cellar door or restaurant, on site accommodation in a 100 year old renovated guest house is also available for restaurant patrons.

The restaurant menu is innovative with a strong hint of French influence.

Lillydale Vineyards

Lillydale Vineyards began its life as part of the second wave of the vinous re-establishment of the Yarra Valley in 1976 when wineyards were planted in the southern part of the Yarra Valley, just off the Warburton Highway at Seville. The soil in this part of the valley is a rich red colour, formed by ancient volcanic action. Pinot noir and chardonnay seem to thrive in a cool climate and this soil type.

The first white wines really made an impact in the early 1980's. An aromatic spicy gewurztraminer and a floral intense riesling became eagerly sought after. This was followed by a classic chardonnay of the finer-boned structure-melons and tropical fruit with a subtle almond nuttiness and a vanilla bean character, enhanced by judicious ageing in French oak.

The pinot noir and the cabernet sauvignon with a touch of merlot were equally as impressive. The quality and style of Lillydale's wines and it's beautiful outlook on the Warburton Ranges did not escape the notice of the McWilliam's family wine company, anxious to expand into premium cool regions.

In 1994 McWilliam's bought Lillydale Vineyards. Max McWilliam moved to live on site and take charge of the operation, which has since been expanded, both for production and a new cellar door and visitors centre added.

The Lilydale wines are, if it is possible, getting even better with the maturing vineyards and the capital input of McWilliam's. The latest sauvignon blanc is a stunner and Lillydale also makes an outstanding botrytised noble riesling.

When on your travels through the Yarra, you must drop in and try these exciting wines.

LILLYDALE VINEYARDS
Address: Davross Court, Seville VIC 3139
Phone: (03) 5964 2016
Fax: (03) 5964 3009
Email: mcwines@mcwilliams.com.au
Established: 1976
Owner: McWilliam's Wines
Winemakers:
Max McWilliam and Jim Brayne
Principal varieties grown:
Chardonnay, Merlot, Cabernet Sauvignon, Sauvignon Blanc, Pinot Noir, Gewurztraminer
Ha under vine: 13
Average annual crush: 100-249 tonnes

Principal wines & brands:
"Lillydale Vineyards"

Public & trade tours:
By appointment only
Hours open to public:
11am-5pm, daily
Retail distribution:
Cellar Door and mail Order sales. McWilliam's Wines Pty Ltd

Long Gully Estate

Reiner Klapp had an extremely successful electronics business. When colour television first came to the Australian market in the early 1970's, Reiner was at the forefront with the top selling German Brands, then the market leaders. At the same time he bought a beautiful property in the Yarra Valley near Healesville at the apex of 'Long Gully', which runs between the Warburton Ranges and a smaller range of hills which divides it off from the main part of the Yarra Valley. Reiner and his delightful wife Irma, built a lovely weekend home in amongst a grove of trees. They ran a few horses and hereford cattle, but Reiner is not an idle person and he had heard of the vineyard revolution that was sweeping the valley, so it wasn't long before he planted vines.

The first vintage was in 1982 with a riesling. Today, Long Gully Estate is like a well-oiled German motor car. The vineyards are lush with substantial vines, but neatly trimmed. The winery is spotless, even during vintage,

and a pretty German-Alsatian Cottage forms and ideal tasting and entertaining area. Long Gully has been extremely successful in international wine shows. In 1993, they pulled off an incredible 'Coup' at Intervin, the New York/Toronto massive wine show held annually. The Long Gully wines entered, were their 1990 Merlot and 1990 Cabernet Sauvignon. 12,000 entries were fined down to 800 odd finalists. After rewarding several hundred gold, silver and bronze medals, 5 only trophies were issued. From this world's best selection, Long Gully won two of the 5, an incredible achievement!

Long Gully Estate make extremely good whites, including a chardonnay, semillon and a sauvignon blanc. Some years a sauvignon blanc/semillon blend is also made. The reds include an award-winning pinot noir, shiraz, merlot and cabernet sauvignon. All the wines have very refined, almost European characters to them. The tannins in the reds are very fine.

Long Gully Estate is a class winery that is well worth seeking out. Look out for the Irma's Cabernet, which has received many gold medals - its great.

LONG GULLY ESTATE
Address: Long Gully Road, Healesville VIC 3777
Phone: (03) 9807 4246
Fax: (03) 9807 2213
Established: 1982
Winemaker: Peter Florance
Principal varieties grown: Chardonnay, Merlot, Cabernet Sauvignon, Shiraz, Sauvignon Blanc, Pinot Noir, Riesling, Semillon, Cabernet Franc, Malbec
Ha under vine: 25
Average annual crush: 100-249 tonnes

Principal wines & brands
"Long Gully Estate"
"L.G.E. Wines"

Hours open to public: 11am-5pm, weekends, public holidays or by appointment
Retail distribution: Cellar Door and Mail Order sales. Export to UK, Germany, Switzerland, Fiji, Singapore, Taiwan, Malaysia, Japan, Thailand, Canada

Yarra Ridge

Yarra Ridge now part of the Mildara Blass Company has had a meteoric rise to fame since its inception in 1988 by Louis Bialkower, who for a number of years worked side by side with celebrated wine writer and fellow Yarra Valley vigneron James Halliday.

The vineyard is located in the foothills of the Christmas Hills, often referred to as the 'Yarra Ridge'. He planted five hectares to cabernet sauvignon, pinot noir and chardonnay and with further plantings the area had grown to 20 hectares by 1994. New varieties included merlot, cabernet franc and sauvignon blanc.

In 1993 Yarra Ridge purchased 40 hectares of land near the Yarra Glen Racecourse in 1994 which by 1995 had been entirely planted.

The soils on all their Yarra Valley vineyards are the grey alluvial podsolic loams so

eagerly sought after by 19th century vignerons such as Hubert-Francois de Costello.

Winemaking is in the hands of affable giant winemaker Rob Dolan, a former league footballer whose winemaking career began at Rouge Homme in 1991/92 under the winemaking legend John Vickery.

Yarra Ridge believe strongly that quality improvements will come from the vineyard and have invested heavily in modern viticultural techniques such as the 'Scott Henry', 'Te Kauwhata two tier', the 'Geneva Double Curtain' and 'U' System trellises aimed at extra fruit and leaf exposure and keeping an air flow through the vines.

The Yarra Ridge wines have had unparalleled success on the Australian Wine Show circuit. The elevated tasting and hospitality area has panoramic views over the valley.

YARRA RIDGE VINEYARD
Address: Glenview Road, Yarra Glen VIC 3775
Phone: (03) 9730 1022
Fax: (03) 9730 1131
Established: 1988
Owner: Mildara Blass Limited
Winemaker: Rob Dolan
Principal varieties grown: Chardonnay, Sauvignon Blanc, Pinot Noir, Cabernet Sauvignon
Ha under vine: 57
Average no. cases produced: 80,000

Principal wines & brands	Cellar Potential
Yarra Ridge Chardonnay	2-4 years
Yarra Ridge Sauvignon Blanc	Now
Yarra Ridge Shiraz	2-5 years
Yarra Ridge Merlot	2-5 years
Yarra Ridge Botrytis Semillon	1-3 years
Yarra Ridge Reserve Pinot Noir	4-8 years
Yarra Ridge Reserve Cabernet Sauvignon	6-15 years

Public & trade tours: By appointment only
Hours open to public: 10am-5pm, weekdays; 10am-5.30pm, weekends and public holidays
Points of interest: Magnificent views of the Yarra Valley

Hoddles Creek Vineyards

The great Methode Champenoise wines under the Sir James Vintage label come from this isolated and scenic vineyard in ranges on the southern and eastern entrances of the Yarra Valley.

The first plantings began in early 1987. The vineyards are situated between 200 and 400 metres above sea level and the temperatures are consistently about 4°c below those in the valley proper. The soils range from red volcanic to yellow and grey granitic types and are friable and loamy giving good drainage.

The more sheltered slopes have been planted and frost does not present a problem as all vines are on the hillsides. Between the Prices Road and Beenak properties almost 200 acres are under vine. Pinot noir and chardonnay dominate with some pinot meunier. Most of these three varieties goes into the premium BRL Champenoise wines including the Yarra Burn Pinot/Chardonnay sparkling. A small amount of sauvignon blanc and 16 acres of cabernet sauvignon are used mainly in the Yarra Burn wines along with some chardonnay and pinot noir.

Trellising and control of crop sizes for quality are state of the art and the wines produced from this vineyard are certainly top class.

Yarra Burn

Founded by Yarra Valley stalwarts and a truly delightful couple, David and Christine Fyffe, in 1976 this winery is now a prized possession of industry leader BRL Hardy following its acquisition in 1995. David and Christine planted their first vines and built a splendid convict stone restaurant during their first year. Christine arranged the catering whilst David turned the giant spit roast on the open hearth in between making and marketing the wines himself. It was a real forerunner of todays Wine Tourism oriented wineries.

The wines are very individual in character with some wonderful pinot noirs in some years. The chardonnay is always a complex fine style with the cabernet sauvignon a substantial wine in warm years. The Yarra Burn Pinot Noir dominated Methode Champenoise is truly excellent.

David has remained on and the resources of BRL Hardy have certainly helped to elevate the wines onto an even higher plane.

The cellar door is original and charming and a bed and breakfast facility now attaches the views on the Warburton Ranges are spectacular particularly at dawn and dusk over the vineyards.

YARRA BURN VINEYARDS

Address: 60 Settlement Road, Yarra Junction VIC 3797
Phone: (03) 5967 1428
Fax: (03) 5967 1146
Established: 1975
Owner: BRL Hardy Limited
Winemaker: David Fyffe
Principal varieties grown: Chardonnay, Merlot, Cabernet Sauvignon, Shiraz, Pinot Noir, Semillon, Cabernet Franc

Ha under vine: 11
Average annual crush: 100-249 tonnes

Principal wines & brands: "Yarra Burn"

Hours open to public: 10am-5pm, daily
Retail distribution: Cellar Door sales. BRL Hardy Wine Company and Yarra Burn Restaurant

Yarra Valley Hills

'Where Quality Means Everything' is the motto of this small family based company, with vineyard interests in a number of areas within the Yarra Valley. This philosophy underpins well their very focussed efforts. In four short years with limited production they have collected 171 show wards awards including 6 trophies and twenty gold medals. Nearly half the awards have been gained in the last 12 months. All four varieties produced, Riesling, Sauvignon Blanc, Chardonnay and Cabernet Sauvignon from the current 1996 vintage have won gold medals recently, a remarkable achievement.

Former School Principal, Terry Hill, also has a masters degree in Educational Administration. In 1992 he took a new tack in life planting a small vineyard on his Healesville property 'Kiah Yallambee'. Terry then embarked on a career contract managing vineyards in various part of the Yarra Valley 'Log Creek' at Gruyere and 'Warranwood' at Warrandyte south on the verge of suburbia.

Terry has been helped in the business by his two sons Marcus and Troy and wife Leah. The family team have recently acquired the excellent small winery 'Bianchet' at Lillydale, nearby 'Warranwood' at Lillydale. The sought after Bianchet Merlot, Shiraz and unique white wine Verduzzo compliment well the Yarra Valley Hills range. Plans are afoot to plant another 5 acres of merlot shortly and top class viti-cultural land surrounding Bianchet may be developed into vineyards by an investment organisation further enhancing this corner of the Yarra Valley.

In 1996 respected winemaker Martin Williams, formerly with Tarrawarra and former Dux of the Enology Master of Science Course at the Davis University in California, joined Yarra Valley Hills. He has designed and commissioned a 300 tonne winery (capable of expansion) which was first operated for the 1997 vintage. Located at the Warranwood Vineyard it is specifically designed to suit Martin's stylistic skills and handle small batches of grapes. Many small vineyard owners have indicated they will be having wines made there by Martin as well as the Yarra Valley Hills and Bianchet wines. Terry is currently finalising the purchase of the balance of the Warranwood property including 20 acres of land and the successful 'La Fontana' restaurant which adjoins the winery and cellar door sales area. A further 8 acres of vines are planned for planting in 1998 to add to the 18 acres currently under vine.

A boutique brewery, the first to be included in a winery in Australia, is also planned utilising the skills of cousin Tim Williams fresh from 4 years in charge of new beer and cider creation for the worlds fourth largest brewer, South African Breweries.

Yarra Valley Hills wines are also making their mark in the export market where their quality has triumphed particularly with the discerning UK Premium Wine Merchants, Oddbins. Qantas are currently using the trophy winning 1996 Sauvignon Blanc as one of only 6 wines on their international flights. Yarra Valley Hills are seeing their lifted vision coming to fruition in so many ways. Watch out for them!

YARRA VALLEY HILLS

Address:
Lot 1, Delaneys Road,
Warranwood VIC 3777
Phone:
(03) 5962 4173
Fax:
(03) 5962 4059
Established:
1993
Winemaker:
Martin Williams
Principal varieties grown:
Chardonnay, Merlot, Cabernet Sauvignon, Sauvignon Blanc, Pinot Noir, Riesling, Cabernet Franc, Malbec
Ha under vine:
19
Average annual crush:
100-249 tonnes

Principal wines & brands:
"Yarra Valley Hills"

Hours open to public:
11am-5pm, weekends and public holidays
Points of interest:
La Fontana Italian Ristorante on site
Retail distribution:
Hill International. Export to Hong Kong, Germany, Switzerland

Otto Wurth

Small goods are like wine, you simply cannot rush quality. There are very few things in this world that improve with aging. Wine is of course one, vintage cheeses another and quality smallgoods of various types another. All share in common, also the best natural ingredients. This takes time and care to put in place.

Otto Wurth's motto is "good is not good enough". Otto arrived in Australia escaping the European depression in 1928 only to be thrown into our own depression.

He managed to find two days a week as an assistant butcher with the firm of Grobbeckers, later to become Austral Smallgoods.

In 1934 he started his own business, Otto Wurth, in Church Street, Richmond producing continental sausages by night and selling them from the basket off his bicycle by day. The "A" Model Ford followed a short time later and his first employee in the same year. His rapid expansion led to larger premises in Johnston Street, Fitzroy. In 1958 Otto Wurth moved to the Watson & Paterson site in Preston where the first smallgoods were made in the 1860's. Otto Wurth's range is wide, encompassing the wursts he first became famous for, continental sausages, salamis, mettwursts, cooked and cured meats of all types.

The most delicate wursts can happily be enjoyed with aromatic whites such as rieslings and sauvignon blancs, whilst the pastrami type meats go hand in hand with the biggest of reds and the multitude of delicacies in between can be matched by the myriad of fine wines Australia produces.

An introduction to Western Australia

The first settlers of the new colony of Western Australia arrived in 1829 on the ship Parmelia, five years before the settlement of Victoria and South Australia.

Even before the official settlement of Perth, cuttings were planted near Fremantle and on Garden Island, but none survived. It was Charles McFaull who planted 300 cuttings at Hamilton Hill and became the state's first successful viticulturist.

In 1834, George Fletcher Moore planted the first vines in the Swan Valley, cuttings from the Cape of Good Hope in South Africa. The oldest winery in Australia, Olive Farm, just near Perth's airport, was established in 1830 and is still going strong today. Olive Farm's founder, Thomas Walters, became the first person to commercially market wine in Western Australia, but was closely followed by fellow Parmelia passenger, John Septimus Roe, the colony's first surveyor general, who founded Sandalford wines in 1840.

Many other areas of the south-west corner of the state were planted with vines in those early years, but commercially only the Swan Valley survived. The Swan Valley industry thrived and by the 1960's Western Australia was second only to South Australia in the number of wineries in the state. It was not, however, until the 1970's when the development boom in the Western Australian wine industry began.

This development was preceded by a report on the viticultural potential of a number of regions in the south west of the state by agricultural scientist, Dr John Gladstones. He highlighted a number of regions with great potential, Margaret River and Mount Barker amongst them.

A new experimental vineyard was planted by the Department of Agriculture at Forest Hill near Mount Barker in 1965.

I well remember tasting two red wines made by Jack Mann at Houghton from the vineyard. That was back in 1972, the wines were several years old and Jack was most enthusiastic about the region's potential. They were certainly memorable wines. Western Australia has seen the greatest growth in wine regions in Australia over the last two decades with six major regions now boasting many vignerons. The Swan Valley has been joined by Margaret River, the Great Southern Region around Mount Barker, the Pemberton/Warren Valley area, the South West Coastal Plains and the Darling Ranges and Perth Hills.

The quality of Western Australian wines and the range of styles is extraordinary and although Western Australia produces less than two per cent of Australian wine production, it accounts for around twenty per cent of the nation's premium bottled wines above $14.00 per bottle. Houghton is a huge Australian premium producer, but others, including Evans & Tate, Vasse Felix, Leeuwin Estate, Goundrey and Capel Vale are significant Australian premium producers.

Wine tourism in Western Australia is a credit to the state, with the Margaret River region having a number of world class winery restaurants and galleries. A wine adventure around Western Australia is a rich experience, indeed. It makes the journey to the West a most worthwhile one.

An introduction to the Coastal Plains of WA

The most fertile coastal soils, both to the north and south of Perth, have been naturally delineated by Western Australia's stately Tuart Gum trees. These massive eucalypts provide very dense timber and are a guide to would-be vignerons as to the location of the best vineyard sites. Temperatures are moderated by proximity to the sea, and overall conditions are ideal for viticulture. The significant wineries to the south of Perth now with their own new geographe appellation - between Bunbury and the Vasse Store at the start of Margaret River are Dr Peter Pratten's Capel Vale, the Killerby Family's Killerby Vineyards and Gill Thomas' Briar Holme. Closer to Perth are Will Nairn's Peel Estate and the impressive Baldivis Estate agricultural property near Rockingham, 180 kilometres south of the city.

Several small wineries and Paul Conti's winery are on the northern outskirts of Perth and the large Moondah Brook Estate of Houghton is the northern-most vineyard of this region.

Table wines produced in this region moderated by the cooling winds off the Indian Ocean share a common trait.

The reds exhibit a beautiful combination of cool climate, berry-like flavours while the whites show good integration of tropical and herbaceous characters with soft acid and the full, round flavours found in wines from a warm climate.

PAUL CONTI WINES

Address: 529 Wanneroo Road, Woodvale WA 6026
Phone: (08) 9409 9160
Fax: (08) 9309 1634
Established: 1958
Owners: Paul and Anne Conti
Winemakers: Paul Conti, ass. Jason Conti
Principal varieties grown: Shiraz, Cabernets, Grenache, Chardonnay, Chenin Blanc, Sauvignon Blanc, Muscat
Ha under vine: 18
Average annual crush: 125 tonnes
Average no. cases produced: 7,000

Principal wines & brands	Cellar Potential
Shiraz	10 years
Cabernet Sauvignon	5 years
Grenache	4 years
Unwooded Chardonnay	4 years
Chardonnay Wooded	8 years
Chenin Blanc	2 years
Late Picked Frontignac	2 years

Public & trade tours: Trade tours by appointment only
Hours open to public: 9.30am-5pm, Mon-Sat
Points of interest: A la carte restaurant
Retail distribution: MGM, Perth; Domaine Wine Shippers, Sydney, Melbourne; Farmstone, Japan; Vertaus and Co., UK

Baldivis Estate

Some sixty kilometres south of Perth on the coastal plains near Rockingham lies the impressive horticultural estate of the Kailis family.

Peter Kailis has overseen the small family business started by his father George, who sold fresh fish door to door, growing into Australia's largest seafood business. His entrepreneurial flair has spilt over into many other industries, including fast food, timber, packaging and construction.

The thirsty black-grey sands of the Serpentine River plains give good drainage and the cooling sea breezes provide an ideal disease-free environment where fruit and varietal flavours shine through.

The Baldivis wines have performed well in local and interstate wine shows, having collected over sixty awards to date. Currently they are available in all Australian states and are exported to Singapore, Malaysia, the United Kingdom and Europe. All have beautiful clean fresh fruit flavours - the Baldivis Estate range comprises of both wooded and unwooded Chardonnays, a Semillon/Sauvignon Blanc blend, a Cabernet Merlot and a lighter early drinking style of red in the Pinot Cabernet.

A special edition of Cabernet Reserve is also produced, and is exclusively packaged in a six bottle box. The other label used by Baldivis is the Lake Kathryn range which is named after Peter's mother and daughter.

The estate also has a large entertainment and hospitality area where functions can be held, adjacent to the Cellar Door Area which sells not only the wines but other fruits grown on the Estate. When you are in Perth why not take a run down to Baldivis to share its bountiful produce?

BALDIVIS ESTATE
Address: Lot 165, River Road, Baldivis WA 6171
Phone: (08) 9525 2066
Fax: (08) 9525 2411
Email: bestate@baldiviswines.com.au
WWW: http://www.baldiviswines.com.au
Established: 1982
Owner: Kailis Consolidated Pty Ltd
Winemaker: Mark Kailis
Principal varieties grown: Chardonnay, Merlot, Cabernet Sauvignon, Shiraz, Sauvignon Blanc, Semillon, Cabernet Franc
Ha under vine: 10
Average annual crush: 50-99 tonnes
Principal wines & brands: "Baldivis Estate" "Lake Kathryn"
Hours open to public: 10am-4pm, weekdays; 11am-5pm, weekends
Points of interest: Major horticultural project including mangoes, avocados, table grapes, limes and olives. Undercover function/BBQ facilities
Retail distribution: National Liquor, WA; Estate Wine Distributors, NSW; Pacific Liquor Co., QLD. Exports to UK, Switzerland, Singapore, Malaysia

---

Killerby Vineyards

The Killerby Chardonnay is rated in Australian and New Zealand Wine Vintages (the "Little Gold Book") as "Gold Five Stars".

For many years, the Gold Book has been the ultimate guide to Australian and New Zealand wine vintages. It rates hundreds of wineries and thousands of different wines. The "Gold Give Star" rating places the Killerby Chardonnay "among the great wines of the world". The book explains the rating: "Each winestyle (label) listed is ranked out of a maximum of five stars...so that the star ranking reflects some of the earned respect for the particular label over the years of its production. A few wines of supreme quality are given "Gold Star" highlighting. In their best years, these wines are among the great wines of the world."

The book goes on to rate every major vineyard in Australia and New Zealand. It pauses briefly at the Killerby Vineyards entry with the comment: "Killerby Chardonnay...one of the country's supreme wines."

The Gold Five Star rating applies not only to the current vintage, but to every vintage of the Killerby Chardonnay.

Killerby Vineyards produces four premium varietal wines, Semillon, chardonnay, Shiraz and Cabernet Sauvignon.

The Killery winemaking philosophy is simple: to produce consistently stylish wines which provide complexity and interest.

KILLERBY VINEYARDS

Address: Lakes Road, Capel WA 6230
Phone: 1800 655 722
Fax: 1800 679 578
Email: killerby@killerby.com.au
WWW: http://www.killerby.com.au
Established: 1973
Winemaker: Paul Boulden
Principal varieties grown: Chardonnay, Cabernet Sauvignon, Shiraz, Semillon, Chardonnay
Ha under vine: 20
Average annual crush: 100-249 tonnes
Principal wines & brands   Cellar Potential "Killerby Vineyards"

	Cellar Potential
Semillon	10 years
Chardonnay	7 years
Shiraz	10 years
Cabernet Sauvignon	7 years

Public & trade tours: By appointment only
Hours open to public: 10am-5pm, daily
Points of interest: Taste the Killerby Chardonnay, rated "Gold Five Stars" in the Little Gold Book and ranked "among the great wines of the world"
Retail distribution: Cellar Door and Mail Order sales. Lionel Samson, WA; The Main Domain, NSW

Capel Vale

Perhaps the staggering number of medical practitioners actively involved in the wine industry says something of the beneficial effects of wine in moderation. Dr. Peter Pratten is a member of this fraternity. In addition to his medical practices he has with his wife Elizabeth, made the time to establish and manage the Capel Vale Winery and Vineyard.

Capel Vale was founded in 1974 and is located on the banks of the Capel River in the Geographe region. Vines produce excellent fruit with good yields. The Capel Vale team has long recognised the different flavours and characters produced from the various cool growing areas in the south west, and their grapes are sourced for each variety from areas where flavours have proven consistently optimal. Thus the Capel Vineyards in "Geographe" produce merlot and chardonnay, the Whispering Hill Vineyard in "Mount Barker" produces riesling and shiraz and the Sheldrake Vineyard produces excellent sauvignon blanc and shiraz in the "Pemberton" region. Capel Vale markets into 10 countries under the "Capel Vale" label and into the U.S.A. under the "Sheldrake" label. During the 1980's, the Pratten's established two other vineyards, one just upstream on the Capel River from their winery at Capel Stirling Estate. They have called this new vineyard Capel Wellington Estate. They also established their Whispering Hill Vineyard,

between Mt. Barker and the Porongurups in the Great Southern Region.

In 1995 a further 100 acres (the Sheldrake Vineyard) was planted in the Lefroy Valley, between Manjimup and Pemberton, in the high country of the south of Western Australia bringing Capel Vale's total vineyard holdings to a substantial 220 acres, covering all the major premium wine areas of the state.

In 1991 Capel Vale made a real coup in securing the talented Rob Bowen who had been making wines for Plantagenet in the Great Southern. In 1993 Krister Jonsson joined the team as winemaker working with Rob Bowen. His fine attention to detail and technique combined with Rob Bowen's expertise has added depth and complexity to all the wine styles in the range.

Capel Vale have won many awards in wine shows. Their 1994 Merlot has just been judged amongst the best 12 Merlots in the World at Vinum, with the 1993 winning gold at Zurich.

Capel Vale produces 4 ranges of wine for the Australian market: The "Layman's Hut" range, is a vintage everyday drinking range of affordable wines, the "C.V." range shows wines with varietal and vintage labelling, ready to drink, the "Capel Vale" range is

premium, high quality varietal wines for cellaring or special occasions and the Black Label "Connoisseur" series are super premium varietal wines, each with a name - "Kinniard Shiraz", "Howecroft Cabernet Merlot", "Frederick Chardonnay" and "Whispering Hill Riesling".

A new winery and visitors centre is under construction at Capel and due to be finished early in 1998. Capel Vale is a premium winemaker on the move which is a credit to its proprietors, Peter and Elizabeth Pratten.

CAPEL VALE

Address: Lot 5, Stirling Estate, Mallokup Road, Capel WA 6271
Phone: (08) 9727 1986
Fax: (08) 9791 2452
Email: primax@ois.net.au
WWW:
http://www.winetitles.com.au/capelvale.html
Established: 1979
Winemaker: Rob Bowen & Krister Jonsson
Principal varieties grown: Chardonnay, Merlot, Cabernet Sauvignon, Shiraz, Sauvignon Blanc, Pinot Noir, Riesling, Semillon
Ha under vine: 90
Average annual crush: 1,200 tonnes

Principal wines & brands:
"Capel Vale"
"CV"
"Shelorake" (USA)

Public & trade tours: By appointment only
Hours open to public: 10am-4.30pm, daily
Points of interest: BBQ facilities. Bus tours for wine groups by appointment
Retail distribution: Cellar Door and Mail Order sales. Haviland Wine Co., NSW; Capel Vale Wines, VIC; Fine Wine Wholesalers, WA; Australian Liquor Marketers, NT; Barrique Fine Wines, QLD; Tasmanian Fine Wines, TAS; Porter and Co., SA. Export to NZ, UK, Europe, USA, Japan, Canada, SE Asia

Peel Estate

<P>eel Estate is only 60 kilometres south of Perth and 3 kilometres inland from the coast at Baldivis.
Will Nairn is a personable character and has built a very personable winery in red brick with huge wooden beams, a viewing mezzanine area with wooden floors forms the characterful cellar door. The entry is via a curved brick path leading to the pergola covered entrance. The lawns and gardens under the giant tuart gums give it a lovely settled rural feel.

The vineyards, which now cover 40 acres, were first planted in 1974 and some of the vines are now very solid citizens indeed and producing wines of great character.
I have always been a fan of chenin blanc with its refreshing apple/quince flavours and honeyed overtones. Peel Estate produce a wood matured version with just a hint of soft vanilla like oak that ages beautifully, its great. The Peel Estate Shiraz is very highly regarded being spicy and supple.
The coastal climate is ideal for Bordeaux

Varieties, red and white, the minty cabernet sauvignon portrays this well. A range of other wines include a full flavoured chardonnay with elegant sweet fruit and chalky tannins from the limestone soil, a tropical style verdelho and a powerful zinfandel with heaps of wild berry flavours. Will does it "his way" and he does it well.

PEEL ESTATE

Address: Box 37, Mandurah 6210. Lot 13 Fletcher Road, Baldivis WA 6171
Phone: (08) 9524 1221
Fax: (08) 9524 1625
Established:

Principal wines & brands	Cellar Potential
Shiraz	10+ years
Wood Chenin	10 years
Cabernet	10+ years
Chardonnay	8 years
Verdelho	4 years
Zinfande	10+ years
Med Dry Chenin	2 years
Vintage Port	10 years

Public & trade tours: Trade tours by appointment only
Hours open to public: 10am-5pm, daily
Points of interest: Jazz day, GT shiraz tasting (annual)
Retail distribution: MGM Wine Dist., WA; Young and Rashleigh, NSW; Ale Pat Taylor, VIC; Barrique Fine Wines, QLD

Moondah Brook Estate

<I>n the late 1960's Houghton Managing Director Ian Smith, began searching for a vineyard site capable of producing grapes for the very successful Houghton White Burgundy, later to become Australia's biggest selling bottled table wine.
Mr. J.M. Clayton, the then co-ordinator of Agricultural Industries, pointed out a site, ideal because of its soil type and the natural spring on the property supplying the Moondah Brook with water at the rate of three million gallons a day, every day of the year.
The property had formerly been held on option by Penfold, under the advice of the late, great winemaker Max Schubert, but Penfold favoured development in the Upper Hunter and let the option drop.
Despite being north of the Swan Valley, its slightly elevated position and the effect of the cooling afternoon sea breezes means its climate is somewhat cooler. The soils are fertile, deep red loams.
Moondah Brook is one of the healthiest and largest vineyards in the state. The vineyard supplied some of Australia's first varietal verdelho, chenin blanc and chardonnay in

the mid 1970's. The verdelho, with its crisp tropical fruit flavours and silky texture is one of Australia's finest examples of its style.
Today the range consists of verdelho, chenin

blanc, chardonnay and cabernet sauvignon. The growth of the verdelho and chenin blanc have been extraordinary, especially with the increased interest in Asian cuisine and as an alternative to chardonnay.

An introduction to the Margaret River

The Margaret River region is centred around the town of Margaret River, south of Bunbury, on a large peninsula. The climate is temperate and rainfall high. Long, dry summers and high rainfall, a yearly average of more than 1,100mm, ensure crops ripen well in soils ideally suited to viticulture. These are well-drained sandy loams, over water retentive clay subsoils.

Irrigation throughout the area therefore is largely unnecessary. Even the State's largest vineyard of 140 hectares operates successfully without any need for irrigation.

This vineyard belongs to Sandalford and contributes to the total area of 500 hectares under vine for the region.

As with other Australian wine-producing areas, Margaret River's wine industry is well represented by the medical profession. The initial development of the region for viticulture was recommended by a report written by Dr John Gladstones in 1965. Margaret River's first vines were planted by Dr Tom Cullity of Vasse Felix two years later. Several other medical men followed suit, including Dr Bill Pannell of Moss Wood and Dr Kevin Cullen of Cullen's.

Red wines from Margaret River have proved very successful; the best of these have been made by various wineries from cabernet sauvignon grapes, as well as cabernet franc and merlot.

Shiraz is not widely grown but has achieved good results, and pinot noir has also produced excellent wines.

Of the white grape varieties, semillon and sauvignon blanc have shown consistently brilliant results, producing fine wines of fresh, crisp styles with pronounced herbaceous and capsicum/asparagus flavours. The palates are rich and mouth-filling, with a frequent hint of tropical fruit, unlike some wines of this type from other regions which can tend towards a flat palate. Semillon particularly shows lifted tropical and herbaceous characters seldom seen elsewhere, with chardonnay and verdelho grapes having produced excellent wines for the region. Riesling however, proved to be less than successful when first introduced, but early problems with the variety now seem to have been overcome. The 1985 Leeuwin Estate Rhine Riesling amply demonstrates the variety's potential, while some of the late-picked rieslings are also very good. The 1984 Auslese Riesling produced by Sandalford has been awarded trophies, and continues to score close to full marks in masked tastings.

Aware of the potential and beauty of their district, the inhabitants of Margaret River have established a series of fine restaurants and accommodation houses.

The cuisine of many cultures can be found in the town of Margaret River and the hotel of the same name has much to offer its guests. Similarly, the Captain Freycinet Motel offers luxurious accommodation and an excellent restaurant at reasonable prices. A number of wineries, both large and small, have constructed restaurants, art galleries and other art and craft establishments.

A trip to 'Flutes' at Brookland Valley is an absolute must - visitors can sit on the decking overlooking the lake and splendid vineyard, and enjoy some sensational cuisine in a truly special atmosphere.

Other restaurants exist at Driftwood, Abbey Vale, Wise Winery Amberley, Leeuwin Estate and Vasse Felix. Cullens and many of the smaller wineries also have great casual eateries, many with exceptional views in this truly beautiful region.

Fishing, surfing, bush walking and some extraordinary caves add an extra dimension to Margaret River, which now certainly vies for the title of the premier wine tourism region in Australia.

During the early 1980's, Leeuwin Estate inaugurated outdoor concerts at dusk, featuring such extraordinary performers such as the London Philharmonic Orchestra, Kiri Te Kanawa and James Galway. Around 7,000 delighted attendees enjoy those magnificent events, many more clamour for tickets but just can't get in. The stature and value of these events for Margaret River are inestimable. Margaret River is a vinous paradise, virtually without equal in the world, and its wines are indeed truly world class.

Margaret River

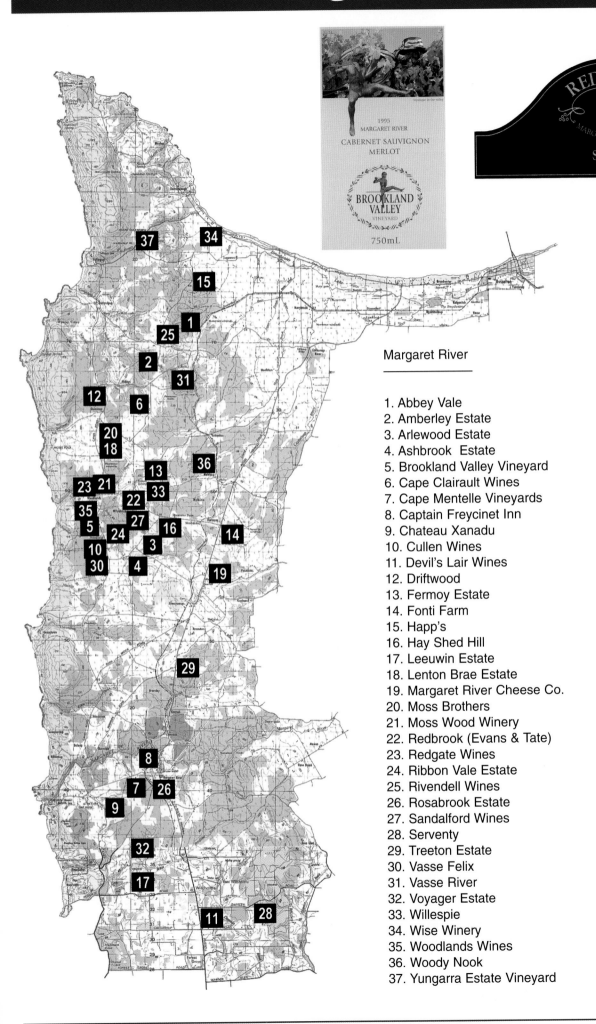

Margaret River

1. Abbey Vale
2. Amberley Estate
3. Arlewood Estate
4. Ashbrook Estate
5. Brookland Valley Vineyard
6. Cape Clairault Wines
7. Cape Mentelle Vineyards
8. Captain Freycinet Inn
9. Chateau Xanadu
10. Cullen Wines
11. Devil's Lair Wines
12. Driftwood
13. Fermoy Estate
14. Fonti Farm
15. Happ's
16. Hay Shed Hill
17. Leeuwin Estate
18. Lenton Brae Estate
19. Margaret River Cheese Co.
20. Moss Brothers
21. Moss Wood Winery
22. Redbrook (Evans & Tate)
23. Redgate Wines
24. Ribbon Vale Estate
25. Rivendell Wines
26. Rosabrook Estate
27. Sandalford Wines
28. Serventy
29. Treeton Estate
30. Vasse Felix
31. Vasse River
32. Voyager Estate
33. Willespie
34. Wise Winery
35. Woodlands Wines
36. Woody Nook
37. Yungarra Estate Vineyard

LEEUWIN ESTATE

1993
Margaret River
Cabernet Sauvignon
PRODUCE OF AUSTRALIA

VOYAGER
ESTATE
MARGARET RIVER

1996
CLASSIC
SAUVIGNON BLANC SEMILLON

Produce of Australia 750ml

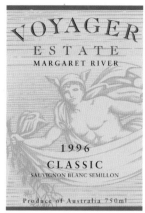

REDGATE
of
MARGARET RIVER

Cabernet Franc
1995

Redgate Wines Pty. Ltd. Boodjidup Road
Margaret River, Western Australia

750ml PRODUCE OF AUSTRALIA

Perth to
Margaret River:
300 kms.

Western
Australia

Margaret
River

Perth •

ABBEY VALE

MARGARET RIVER

Chardonnay

1997

PRODUCT OF AUSTRALIA
750ml   13.5%Alc/Vol

Evans&Tate

1997

MARGARET RIVER
SAUVIGNON
BLANC

750ML PRODUCE OF AUSTRALIA

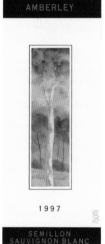

AMBERLEY

1997

SEMILLON
SAUVIGNON BLANC

SANDALFORD

1996
Mount Barker
Riesling

PRODUCE OF AUSTRALIA
PRODUCED BY SANDALFORD WINES PTY LTD
WEST SWAN ROAD CAVERSHAM 6055
750ml   11% Vol

DEVIL'S LAIR
Margaret River

1996
PINOT NOIR

DRIFTWOOD

Margaret River

1997
CHARDONNAY
PRODUCE OF AUSTRALIA
750 ML

SANDALFORD

1995
Mount Barker / Margaret River
Cabernet Sauvignon

PRODUCE OF AUSTRALIA
PRODUCED BY SANDALFORD WINES PTY LTD
WEST SWAN ROAD CAVERSHAM 6055   13% Vol

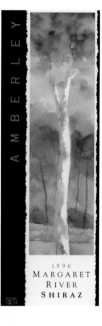

A M B E R L E Y

1996
MARGARET
RIVER
SHIRAZ

VOYAGER
ESTATE
MARGARET RIVER

1993
CABERNET SAUVIGNON
MERLOT
Grown and bottled on the estate

PRODUCE OF AUSTRALIA   750mL

Evans&Tate
E S T A T E

MARGARET RIVER
1994
SHIRAZ

750ML PRODUCE OF AUSTRALIA

Evans&Tate
E S T A T E

MARGARET RIVER
1995
CABERNET
SAUVIGNON
750ML PRODUCE OF AUSTRALIA

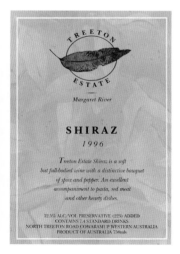

TREETON
ESTATE

Margaret River

SHIRAZ
1996

*Treeton Estate Shiraz is a soft
but full-bodied wine with a distinctive bouquet
of spice and pepper. An excellent
accompaniment to pasta, red meat
and other hearty dishes.*

12.5% ALC/VOL PRESERVATIVE (223) ADDED
CONTAINS 7.4 STANDARD DRINKS
NORTH TREETON ROAD COWARAMUP WESTERN AUSTRALIA
PRODUCT OF AUSTRALIA 750mls

LEEUWIN ESTATE

1994
Margaret River
Chardonnay
PRODUCE OF AUSTRALIA
ALCOHOL 13.5% BY VOLUME

Margaret River

CLAIRAULT

The Clairault
1995

750ml

CAPE MENTELLE

SEMILLON SAUVIGNON 1997

Abbey Vale

One of the prettiest wineries in Margaret River is Abbey Vale. The winery also has a classy restaurant adjoined to the cellar door with views over the large man-made lake and vineyards. Bill and Pam McKay have had an incredible journey leading them to their little piece of paradise.

They left Northern Ireland for Uganda just after their marriage where Bill worked as an engineer. Following this he set up his own electronics business moving on to Vancouver and finally Perth. Following the sale of his electronics business, Bill took a quite different path spending five years "qualifying as a clinical psychologist.

When their son Kevin became interested in viticulture, having assisted in the planting of the nearby Amberley Vineyard, they decided to plant vines on their property they had bought as an investment 10 years earlier in 1975.

The vineyards are looked after by Kevin and he makes the wines with some assistance from legendary winemaker Dorham Mann. On the lawns bordering the lake behind the winery they host a prestigious concert each year as part of the Festival of Perth. 1994 (the first) featured the Budapest Symphony Orchestra and in 1995 the Odessa Philharmonic Orchestra, the tradition continues.I found the wines at Abbey Vale loaded with fruit flavours. I particularly liked the dry verdelho, with its rich tropical fruit salad of flavours and dry finish.

The sauvignon blanc has won a number of awards and the cabernet sauvignon has a lovely rich round plummy character.
I didn't get a chance to eat in the restaurant but it was beautifully set up with a very interesting and innovative menu.

ABBEY VALE VINEYARD
Address: Lot 392, Wildwood Road, Yallingup WA 6282
Phone: (08) 9755 2277
Fax: (08) 9755 2286
Established: 1986
Winemakers: K. McKay and Dorham Mann
Principal varieties grown: Chardonnay, Merlot, Cabernet Sauvignon, Shiraz, Sauvignon Blanc, Semillon, Verdelho, Chenin Blanc
Ha under vine: 34
Average annual crush: 100-249 tonnes
Principal wines & brands: "Abbey Vale"
Hours open to public: 10.30am-5pm, daily
Points of interest: Tourist facility with café "The Barrel Room"
Retail distribution: Cellar Door and Mail Order sales. Export to SE Asia, India, USA

Amberley Estate

Amberley Estate is one of the largest and most important wineries in Margaret River. Since the first planting in 1986 on the Thornton Road property and the first vintage in 1990 Amberley has established itself as a producer of characteristic Margaret River wines. Amberley is blessed with one of the prettiest locations in Australia, a sheltered gully resplendent with stands of imperious red gums. The elegant white winery building is surrounded by manicured gardens and lawns which sweep down to a pond and the vineyards beyond - it looks like they were always supposed to be there and, like the wine, the staff are bright and bubbly.

A considerable area of vineyard is planted with chenin blanc. This truly underrated variety with its lifted apple and quince like flavours has performed marvels under the expert winemaking guidance of Eddie Price, a native of Western Australian, who in 1982 became dux of the Roseworthy oenology course winning the major course prizes.

The philosophy of the Amberley label is to remain a producer of wine from the fruit grown solely in the Margaret River Appellation. The belief of the owners and management is that a steady growth pattern utilising produce from arguably one of the best growing areas in Australia will be far outweighed by the short term gains of outside blending.

The top selling chenin is accompanied by an excellent sauvignon blanc, semillon, semillon/sauvignon blanc, the Margaret River speciality, they also make a superb shiraz. Why not enjoy them as an ideal accompaniment to a delicious lazy lunch under the verandah of the winery. Don't forget to try the rich, wild berry flavoured cabernet merlot with its lifted aromatic characters which typify this top class winemaker.

AMBERLEY ESTATE
Address: Thornton Road, Yallingup WA 6282
Phone: (08) 9755 2288
Fax: (08) 9755 2171
Established: 1986
Winemakers: Eddie Price and Greg Tillbrook
Principal varieties grown: Chardonnay, Merlot, Cabernet Sauvignon, Shiraz, Sauvignon Blanc, Semillon, Cabernet Franc, Chenin Blanc, Cabernet
Ha under vine: 32
Average annual crush: 450 tonnes
Principal wines & brands: "Amberley Estate"
Public & trade tours: By appointment only
Hours open to public: 10am-4.30pm, daily
Points of interest: Luncheons served - reservations advised
Retail distribution: Cellar Door and Mail Order sales. Domaine Wine Shippers, NSW, VIC; Chace Agencies, SA; The Wine Tradition, QLD. Export to UK

Brookland Valley

BROOKLAND VALLEY VINEYARD
Address: Caves Road, Willyabrup WA 6284
Phone: (08) 9755 6250
Fax: (08) 9755 6214
Email: bvwines@netserv.net.au
Established: 1984
Winemaker: Garry Baldwin
Principal varieties grown: Chardonnay, Merlot, Cabernet Sauvignon, Sauvignon Blanc, Cabernet Franc
Ha under vine: 20
Average annual crush: 100-249 tonnes
Principal wines & brands: "Brookland Valley Vineyard"
Public & trade tours: By appointment
Hours open to public: Cellar Door: 10am-5pm, daily. Flutes CafÈ: 11am-4.30pm, Tues-Sun; from 7pm, Saturday Evenings
Points of interest: Flutes Cafe - an award winning Restaurant. Preludes Gallery - Wine & Food - Art & Objects for living well with food and wine.
Retail distribution: BRL Hardy Ltd

Malcolm Jones is a visionary person and his vision is certainly not of the petty variety. Brookland Valley is not just pretty, it is a vinous paradise, with every detail, materially and aesthetically, perfectly in place.
In fact, it is Peter Pan who calls the tune as he plays his flute, happily gazing over the Willyabrup Brook. This beautiful symbol of eternal youth and optimism was one of the last of the wax-moulded bronze cast studies crafted back in 1893.
Malcolm graduated from Lincoln University in New Zealand in 1963 with a degree in Agricultural Science. A successful career as a Farm Management Consultant followed until some 20 years later when the desire to change his life-style led to the search for a rural retreat.

The 50 acre vineyard of close-planted manicured vines surrounding the lake is a real showpiece and produces first-rate fruit.
The wines are all individually styled - the sauvignon blanc is at the tropical fruit end of the flavour spectrum, with a touch of herbaceousness, whilst the chardonnay has subtle melon and grapefruit flavours complemented by toasty hazelnut-like oak from fine French oak barriques.
The cabernet/merlot/cabernet franc red is rich with cherry and plum overtones.
Malcolm and Deidre's daughter Liza was the dux of the diploma course in hospitality and tourism at Perth's Bentley College and 'Student of the Year' in 1989.
Her first project was to create the superb 'Flutes' restaurant, gallery and function facility with her parents. Cantilevered over

the lake, it overlooks the picture book valley and vineyards, it rivals any winery restaurant world wide.
A number of beautiful villas are being built in 95 acres of wilderness bushland surrounding the Willyabrup Brook as it winds down to the Indian Ocean. Bush walking tracks through to the hilltops are now in place.
I can't imagine a more idyllic stay, than at Brookland Valley, it would certainly beat keeping up with the Joneses!

Cape Clairault

The vineyard is towered over by majestic Jarrah and Redgum trees, neatly nestled under a vibrant rainbow on our early morning visit to photograph this picturesque winery in it's wild wooded setting. Everything seemed to say wines of character come from here.
In fact, that's the truth, as the wines of Cape Clairault, particularly the Cabernet Sauvignon and the crisp Sauvignon Blanc with it's delightful tropical fruit flavours have had significant successes. The wines

are balanced, elegant, mouth filling and complex. "The Clairault" is Ian Lewis and his wife Ani's top wine. It is blended from the best red grapes the season has to offer and has been chosen 5 times for Mentelle's Great Cabernet Tasting.
The cellar sales area and cafe are full of character too, making it a worthwhile stop over.
Bite into a homemade loaf with local cheeses, savour a glass of wine while you take in the beautiful natural setting.

CAPE CLAIRAULT

Address: PO Box 360, Dunsborough WA 6281
Direction: Cellar Door off Pusey Road, Willyabrup
Phone: (08) 9755 6225
Fax: (08) 9755 6229
Email: clairalt@compwest.net.au
Established: 1976
Owners: Ian and Ani Lewis
Winemakers: Ian Lewis, Peter Stark
Principal varieties grown: Cabernet Sauvignon, Merlot, Cabernet Franc, Sauvignon Blanc, Semillon, Riesling
Ha under vine: 10
Average annual crush: 100 tonnes
Average no. cases produced: 6,000

Principal wines & brands	Cellar Potential
The Clairault	10-15 years
Sauvignon Blanc	3-5 years
Semillon Sauvignon Blanc	4-8 years
Cape White	Enjoy now
Cape Rosé	Enjoy Now
Cape Red	10+ years
Claireau	(Fortified)
Port	

Hours open to public: 10am-5pm, daily
Points of interest: Café - forest surrounds, terrace or inside dining, children catered for
Retail distribution: Inglewood Wines, NSW; Four Seasons, WA; Select Vineyards, VIC. Export to Malaysia, Fiji, Thailand, Singapore

Cape Mentelle

David Hohnen 'the squire of Cape Mentelle', has expanded the breadth of his squiredom quite considerably in the last decade.

David began his quite remarkable career in the wine industry back in 1968 at Stonyfell Winery in South Australia. David completed his Oenology studies at the Fresno University in California and on returning to Australia in 1970 he, along with brother Mark, planted vines on the family's investment land at Margaret River. David then went to Victoria where he worked with Dominique Portet, establishing the Taltarni Vineyards.

David came back to Western Australian in 1976 and came under the spotlight when he won the Jimmy Watson Memorial Trophy with the 1982 Cabernet Sauvignon.

To prove it was no fluke, David repeated the feat the following year with his 1983 wine. These awards did much to promote the Margaret River region.

In 1985, David established Cloudy Bay in New Zealand and has produced some extraordinary sauvignon blancs. Cloudy Bay now produces a range of wines, including a fine methode champenoise, 'Pelorus'.

In 1990 Veuve Clicquot Ponsardin, the massive French champagne house, obtained a major share in Cape Mentelle, putting an indelible stamp of approval on David Hohnen's enterprises.

The Cape Mentelle range includes a shiraz and cabernet merlot, as well as the cabernet sauvignon. David also produces on of Australia's few zinfandels, a variety grown in California. This makes a huge, black, spicy red - a wine for heroes.

The two Mentelle whites are the region's first semillon/sauvignon blanc blend and a full bodied chardonnay. The new state of the art visitors centre has just been completed and is stunning.

CAPE MENTELLE VINEYARDS

Address: Wallcliffe Road, Margaret River WA 6285
Phone: (08) 9757 3266
Fax: (08) 9757 3233
Established: 1970
Winemaker: John Durham
Principal varieties grown: Chardonnay, Merlot, Cabernet Sauvignon, Shiraz, Sauvignon Blanc, Semillon, Chenin Blanc, Zinfandel
Ha under vine: 80
Average annual crush: 500-999 tonnes
Principal wines & brands: "Cape Mentelle"
Public & trade tours: By appointment only
Hours open to public: 10am-4.30pm, daily
Retail distribution: Cellar Door and Mail Order sales. Tucker Seabrook, Fesq Dorado, Seabrook Tucker Classic, West Coast Wine Cellars. Export to USA, UK, Europe, Hong Kong, NZ, Canada, Singapore, Japan

Evans & Tate Ltd - Redbrook

John and Toni Tate had been great fans of the early wines of Margaret River, and friends of the pioneer vigneron, Tom Cullity. In 1974, two years after establishing their Evans & Tate headquarters in the Swan Valley, they bought 28 hectares of land in Margaret River, planting vines the following year.

At present the vineyard comprises semillon, sauvignon blanc, chardonnay, shiraz, cabernet sauvignon, cabernet franc and merlot which supply a major portion of their grape requirements. In 1994 the company, under the leadership of Chief Executive, Franklin Tate, purchased a further 100 hectares of land at Jindong in the north of the region and the established "Lionel's Vineyard" named after John Tate's late father, the first Tate to enjoy wine in Australia. This site will become the companies new 200 crush winery. Consummate winemaker Brian Fletcher makes the wines.

I have been particularly impressed by the Evans & Tate Margaret River Semillon with its honey and lemon highlights and clean herbaceous flavours, it has been a most successful wine on the show circuit. The Western Australian Classic formerly known as Margaret River Classic, a semillon/sauvignon blanc launched in 1987, has become one of Western Australia's best selling wines and is excellent value. But it is the cabernet sauvignon that has grabbed the limelight; the 1991 in particular had the critics swooning. The delightful cottage with its gorgeous gardens in the middle of the vineyard is a pretty place to drop off for a top-class tasting if you are in the region.

EVANS AND TATE

Address: 38 Swan Street, Henley Brook WA 6055
Phone: (08) 9296 4666
Fax: (08) 9296 1148
Email: et@evansandtate.com.au
WWW: http://www.evansandtate.com.au
Established: 1971
Winemaker: Brian Fletcher
Principal varieties grown: Chardonnay, Semillon, Sauvignon Blanc, Shiraz, Cabernet Sauvignon, Merlot
Ha under vine: 72
Average no. cases produced: 100,000

Principal wines & brands	Cellar Potential
Margaret River Semillon	3-5 years
Margaret River Chardonnay	2-5 years
Margaret River Cabernet Sauvignon	5+ years
Margaret River Merlot	4-6 years
Margaret River Shiraz	4-6 years
Western Australia Sauvignon Blanc	up to 3 years
Western Australia Classic	
Two Vineyards Chardonnay	up to 4 years
Gnangara Shiraz	up to 3 years
Barrique 61 Cabernet Merlot	3-5 years

Public & trade tours: No
Hours open to public: 10.30am-4.30pm, weekdays; 11.00am-4.30pm, weekends
Points of interest: Picnic area
Retail distribution: Nationally and 17 countries worldwide

Chateau Xanadu

The Chateau Xanadu vineyard was established in 1977, by Irish doctors John and Eithne Lagan. As the winery's name suggests, this operation is more than a mere business. John and Eithne share a passion for art and literature, in addition to their love of wine. Their home houses one of the world's most extensive collections of early books and printed works and the name 'Xanadu' is taken from the epic poem by Samuel T. Coleridge.

The winery has been constructed from local stone and boasts beautiful stained glass windows. A love of beauty has been carried over into the vineyard at Chateau Xanadu. There are 50 acres of the 400 acre property under vine and varieties are semillon, sauvignon blanc, chardonnay, cabernet sauvignon, merlot and cabernet franc.

The first wines were made at Xanadu in 1981 and some excellent wines were produced right from the beginning. I well remember tasting the 1985 semillon during a visit to the winery in 1986. Its huge gooseberry flavour and complexity were a knock-out. Today most of the semillon finds its way into the excellent 'Secession', a great bordeaux style dry white. Winemaker since 1990, has been the innovative Swiss, Jurg Muggli. One of his recent additions has been 'Featherwhite', a dry rose, barrel-fermented cabernet sauvignon, drained first and kept cool in the barrels for three months. It is lively, dry and with the complexity often lacking in this style. The Chateau Xanadu Cabernet Sauvignon with a little merlot and cabernet franc is impressive. Of a deep blue mauve colour, the wine displays fresh floral and mint aromas with cassis, fruit flavours. These are well integrated with oak.

The focus today at Xanadu is firmly on innovative quality winemaking and grape-growing with the passionate and talented duo of Conor Lagan and Jurg Muggli who are pushing the frontiers of premium winemaking with outstanding results.

Cullens Winery

Dr. Kevin Cullen and his wife Diana planted the first vines on their property south of Willyabrup in 1971. Their first wines were made three years later and proved very successful. Expansion and development continued and vines now cover more than 28 hectares. The winery consists of two buildings and was constructed from the local red stone by the Cullens' and neighbouring farmers. One of these buildings houses the up-to-date equipment and a laboratory, while the other provides storage space for wines maturing in their oak casks. The latter building, which has just been expanded, also includes a delightful tasting area and kitchen which provides imaginative food for visitors.

This aspect of the business is capably managed by the Cullens' daughter Shelley.

Di is the seemingly tireless manager. Another daughter, Vanya, is the winemaker and is the holder of both a science degree and a diploma of oenology. Vanya has had wide experience which included some time spent at the famous Robert Mondavi Winery in California and Drouhins of Burgundy.

It is not surprising that as the result of such expertise, Cullens wines are consistently excellent. Their semillon sauvignon blanc is of an elegant, grassy, herbaceous style which renders it highly compatible with seafood. Cullens chardonnay is a complex combination of almond, melon and apricot flavours with a hint of smoky oak.

The pinot noir exhibits delicious strawberry and charry flavours with nutty overtones and the cabernet/merlot/cabernet franc blend contains 65% cabernet sauvignon grapes and integrates superb cassis flavours with distinct floral aromas.

Unfortunately Kevin has passed on, but Di has started a special memorial fund in Kevin's memory to help his medical pioneering project, The Busselton Research Foundation. Di, along with her suppliers, have created a red wine, the 'Busselton Research Red', and all proceeds go to the Foundation.

The Cullens' professional approach to wine-making has paid off and Cullens delightful winery has much to offer the visitor, including a warm and friendly welcome.

Devil's Lair

D evil's Lair was the brainchild of Phil Sexton, a very focussed individual. This extraordinarily talented man of great vision has been bewilderingly successful in a number of areas in the hospitality industry.

Phil, in fact, began his career as a trainee brewer at Perth's Swan Brewery in a bid to earn the money to attend the Oenology Course at the Charles Sturt University in Wagga Wagga. His qualifications as a science graduate, majoring in bio-chemistry, stood him in good stead. Through Swan, he went to Birmingham University in England, where he completed a masters degree.

Phil then travelled through Europe where he hatched the idea of a boutique brewery. He later established the remarkably successful Matilda Bay Brewing Co. and purchased a number of hotels and bars, all creatively themed.

His successful hospitality and brewing endeavours allowed him to amass the capital necessary to become a serious vigneron, his long cherished dream. His thoroughness and vision is powerful indeed. He didn't want just any sort of vineyard. He sought a gravelly site where the vines would have to dig deep for sustenance and moisture. In this struggle, as is the case with the world's greatest vineyards, they would produce top quality complex grapes. A particular site appealed to him. He had visited there as an anthropology student in his university days to study the ancient lair of a larger version of today's Tasmanian Devil, now extinct on the mainland. In 1981 Phil purchased the property next door to the devil's lair, which had partly been used as a gravel pit, supplying ballast for the Western Australian railways. The location, some 20 kilometres south of Margaret River and slightly elevated, is definitely cooler than the northerly part of the region and picking occurs some several weeks later. The cabernet sauvignon is often not picked until late April.

The 100 acres of vines are mostly planted on the steep slopes surrounding a massive lake with a surface area of 35 acres. The first red from the property was a 1990 cabernet sauvignon, made at Plantagenet, which also contained a small percentage of merlot and cabernet franc. This wine was instantly successful at the annual SGIO Wine Awards in Perth, where it won the champion prize and a trip to California, also repeating this feat, winning the SGIO Championship award in 1994 with his 1993 Pinot Noir, winning a trip to France. In 1993 a "state of the art" winery was commissioned.

In 1996 Devil's Lair was bought by Southcorp and is now a real jewel in their many diamond studded crown. The unique Devil's Lair label is as individual as its rich and characterful wines. Look out for it.

Driftwood Estate

This impressive imposing winery seems like it has been there for much longer than is the fact. The number of awards they have won with their wines also adds weight to this appearance. In 1987 property developer Tom Galopolous and his wife Helen bought a stretch of land along Caves Road at Willyabrup, with a view to setting up a weekend retreat. Remembering his Greek grandfather's love of his own vines and wines Tom planted a few vines as a hobby. Today he has some 45 acres of beautifully tended vines, a state of the art winery, and a 200 seat brasserie to rival any winery restaurant in the world. In fact, Tom toured California, France, Italy and Greece checking out winery hospitality set-ups and he has certainly done something very special at Driftwood. The high vaulted ceiling with an atrium area overlooking the vineyards is truly spectacular. The large cellar door reception area has a grandeur and class that really impresses. I even noticed a Greek Amphitheatre complete with acropolis like columns mushrooming out of the grounds in front of the vineyards. Maybe a Classic Greek Tragedy or two will play there sometime soon in this magic environment, I hope so. The 1996 Semillon Sauvignon Blanc I tasted at the cellar door was a very stylish polished wine with lifted aromatic jasmine and passionfruit aromas leaping out of the glass. The palate reminded me of ripe honeydew melons and tangerines, quite a wine.

Roseworthy graduate winemakers Maria Melsom and Steven Pester are working wonders in the vineyard and winery. The Driftwood wines are definitely classy and why not enjoy them at lunch or dinner in the restaurant which also has open decking under the verandah for summer and a huge log fire for a cosy winters dining experience.

Moss Wood

Moss Wood was established by Dr. Bill Pannell and his wife, Sandra, in 1969. The first grapes planted on the 10 hectare Willyabrup property were cabernet sauvignon. These have since been followed by pinot noir, semillon and chardonnay. Great care was taken both in choosing the site for the vineyard and the vines to be planted. As a result, fruit has been of very high quality. The first wine, a cabernet sauvignon, was made in 1973. Later wines were made with the assistance of Roseworthy graduate, Keith Mugford. The pinot noir of Moss Wood almost defies description with its complex rich flavours, silky texture and long finish combining to make this one of the best wines of this variety in Australia. Part of the procedure employed to create this magnificent wine involves a considerable sacrifice on the part of the Mugford's in that they thin the bunches before the grapes ripen, to lower the crop and increase the intensity of flavour in the grapes.

The other red release from Moss Wood is their cabernet sauvignon. This intense wine consistently rates as one of Australia's top ten reds, integrating deep flavours of mint and herbs. The last three releases have been outstanding, showing a floral lift in the bouquet. In recent years, the Moss Wood white wines have shown considerable development. The unwooded semillon shows toasty complex flavours echoed by the chardonnay. The latter wine is more complex, however, as a result of varietal differences and the careful wood ageing of half of the wine, prior to blending with the remainder. The reputation established by Bill and Sandra Pannell at Moss Wood has been carried on and enhanced by the hard work and winemaking skill of the Mugfords. Both families have made considerable contributions to the Margaret River region and the best of Moss Wood's wines are comparable to any in the world.

MOSS WOOD WINERY
Address: Metricup Road, Willyabrup WA 6280
Phone: (08) 9755 6266
Fax: (08) 9755 6303
Email: mosswood@netserv.net.au
Established: 1969
Winemaker: Keith Mugford
Principal varieties grown: Chardonnay, Merlot, Cabernet Sauvignon, Pinot Noir, Semillon, Cabernet Franc, Petit Verdot
Ha under vine: 10
Average annual crush: 50-99 tonnes
Principal wines & brands: "Moss Wood"
Public & trade tours: By appointment only
Retail distribution: Tucker Seabrook, WA, VIC; Fesq. Dorado & Co., NSW; Porter & Co., SA; Barrique Wines, QLD. Export to UK, USA, Switzerland, Germany, Hong Kong, Indonesia, Singapore, Malaysia, Japan, NZ

Rosabrook Estate

The cute clinker built bungalow style winery that forms the home for Rosabrook wines began its life as the group settlement Abattoir in about 1930. Just a few minutes south of the Margaret River township it takes its name from Rosabrook Road, so named by local 19th century identity politician and former Mayor of Bunbury, Thomas Campbell Carey, after his second wife, Rose Strickland.

The first vines were planted in 1980 but the estate secured a new lease of life in 1993 when former Cambridge University trained Radiologist/Oncologist, Dr John Sheppard, bought the property.

He immediately initiated work in the vineyards and employed young winemaker Dan Pannell, son of famous district wine pioneer Bill Pannell.

The chardonnay started making a name for itself quickly.

Winemaker and manager is now Wine Science graduate Simon Keall.

New plantings undertaken in 1994 and 1995 are coming into bearing and production will expand over the next few years.

ROSABROOK ESTATE
Address: Rosa Brook Road, Margaret River WA 6285
Phone: (08) 9757 2286
Fax: (08) 9757 3634
Established: 1989
Winemaker: Simon Keall
Principal varieties grown: Chardonnay, Merlot, Cabernet Sauvignon, Shiraz, Sauvignon Blanc, Riesling, Semillon, Cabernet Franc, Malbec
Ha under vine: 14
Average annual crush: 50-99 tonnes

Principal wines & brands	Cellar Potential
Semillon Sauvignon Blanc	0-3 years
Chardonnay	0-5 years
Cabernet Merlot	5-7 years
Shiraz	5-7 years

Hours open to public: 11am-4pm, Thu-Sun, public holidays and by appointment
Points of interest: Cellar door building is a converted 'group settlement' abbatoir built in the early 1930s
Retail distribution: Cellar Door and Mail Order sales. Four Seasons Fine Wines, WA; Winestock, VIC; The Main Domain, NSW; Harbottle Brown, QLD

Leeuwin Estate

As one of Australia's leading producers of high quality varietal wines, Leeuwin has 100 hectares of immaculately tended vines and a state-of-the-art winery.

The guiding philosophy of Leeuwin, since its inception in 1974 has been to produce wines of distinctive character and supreme quality. That this philosophy has been successful is apparent in the recognition and acclaim which Leeuwin has received from experts both in Australia and Overseas.

As one of the five founding wineries in the Margaret River region, the property was identified by eminent American winemaker, Robert Mondavi, as being ideal for the production of premium quality wine.

awarded the Leeuwin 1986 Chardonnay the overall trophy for best Chardonnay in 1992. The wines have also received "Decanter" Magazine's highest recommendation. Leeuwin wines are exported to numerous countries and carried in first class compartments of many international airlines.

Just as the pursuit of excellence manifests

Leeuwin Estate has evolved into a significant tourist attraction. The staging of the concerts has resulted in tourism awards for "Major Tourist Attraction" and recognition as best "Significant Local Event" along with a citation for its contribution to the arts. Housed within the winery is Leeuwin's award winning restaurant. Adorning the restaurant walls is the collection of contemporary Australian art used on the labels featuring paintings from more than thirty prominent Australian artists including Sir Sidney Nolan, Lloyd Rees, John Olsen, Robert Juniper and Arthur Boyd. The restaurant has been a recipient of a Gold Plate Award and has attracted guest appearances from some of Australia's leading chefs.

With Mondavi as mentor, the Horgan family set about transforming their cattle farm into a boutique vineyard and winery. A nursery was planted in 1974 and the vineyards were planted over a five year period from 1975. The first trial vintage was in 1978.

The mild, frost free winters, warm summers and rich soil of the Leeuwin vineyard are ideal for the production of sauvignon blanc, chardonnay, riesling, cabernet sauvignon and pinot noir.

Leeuwin has concentrated on achieving complexity, balance and longevity in its wines through a blend of traditional and modern techniques.

Leeuwin's finest wines are known as the "Art Series" range. Paintings are commissioned from leading contemporary Australian artists to adorn the labels of these wines.

The "Art Series" wines have received much international attention and critical acclaim, with authoritative publications ranking the wines with the top 150 in the world and the top 20 in the "New World". In particular, Leeuwin's Art Series Chardonnays have twice been awarded gold medals in "Wine International Challenges", sponsored by the British publication "Wine Magazine", which

itself in the quality of Leeuwin wines, so too is it expressed in the aesthetic beauty of the winery, which overlooks a meadow, surrounded by a majestic forest of karri trees. Although the building is primarily a modern winery, master architects have created a highly original and uniquely Australian structure than blends harmoniously with its natural environment. The building itself has won a Civic Design Award.

Leeuwin is famous for its annual alfresco concerts, which are performed in the natural amphitheatre in front of the winery.

The tradition of the Leeuwin concerts began in 1985 when the London Philharmonic Orchestra performed alongside the kookaburras in this unique bushland setting. Since then the concerts have featured several international orchestras and leading performers, including Dame Kiri Te Kanawa, James Galway, Ray Charles, Dionne Warwick, Diana Ross, Tom Jones, international soprano star Julia Migenes and tenors, Perrin Allen and George Benson.

The success of these concerts has resulted in an additional annual concert which features Australian talent.

Working on the principle that fine wines, food and the arts are highly complementary,

The Leeuwin Estate is the venue for many art and photographic exhibitions. Leeuwin Estate is truly a vision splendid and it is a moving experience to see everything carried out with such personal care and attention to detail.

As they say in the classics, Leeuwin Estate "have really got their act together".

LEEUWIN ESTATE WINERY
Address: Stevens Road, Margaret River WA 6285
Phone: (08) 9757 6253
Fax: (08) 9757 6364
Established: 1974
Winemaker: Robert Cartwright
Principal varieties grown: Chardonnay, Merlot, Cabernet Sauvignon, Sauvignon Blanc, Pinot Noir, Riesling, Petit Verdot
Ha under vine: 100
Average annual crush: 500-999 tonnes
Principal wines & brands: "Leeuwin Estate"
Public & trade tours: Winery tours: 11am, 1pm and 3pm or by arrangement
Hours open to public: 10am-4.30pm, daily
Points of interest: Restaurant open daily for lunch and Saturday evenings for a la carte dining, weddings and functions. WA Architectural Award. Art collection on display. Winery tours. Annual concerts. Sundowners summer nights
Retail distribution: Cellar Door and Mail Order sales. Fesq Dorado, NSW, QLD; Nelson Wine Co.; VIC. Export to NZ, EEC, USA, Canada, Japan, SE Asia, Hong Kong

Redgate

One of the most extraordinary and pleasurable experiences of my years of travel researching Pictorial Wine books occurred on Anzac Day, 1995. My dear friend, the late Milan Roden, and I were taking some early morning photos at Redgate, making the most of the sunrise, who should appear on the doorstep of the winery but Bill Ullinger on his way to the Anzac Day ceremony in Margaret River. In chatting with Bill, he reminisced on his last bombing raid as a 21 year old pilot in charge of a massive Lancaster bomber, 50 years earlier, in 1945. 50 years to the day, it was on Anzac Day 1945. When we asked to take his photo he said, "do you want me to put my medals on". I replied, "we won't take your photo without them".

As we took Bill's photo, with the Australian Flag flying above the winery's outdoor tank farm, up walked our old friend Andrew Forsell with whom we spent many happy days in California.

Andrew was a winemaker for many years for the high profile Sonoma Winery, Ironhorse.

Bill's son, Paul, was next to appear on the scene. He and Andrew then took us through the wines, from the 1995 vintage just completed, Andrew's first vintage working with Paul. The wines were truly superb and I am sure will win many accolades before they are all consumed, although given their enormous fruit flavours and great balance, you'd better get in quick!

Bill Ullinger established Redgate in 1976 at an age when many would be contemplating retirement. The property's purchase came after a long search of several hundred kilometres of Western Australia's coastline. Early teething difficulties and the first wine tax imposition in 1984 had the Ullingers on the verge of closing the winery's doors. Then came their victory at the 1984 Adelaide Wine Show, winning the prestigious Montgomery Trophy with their 1982 Cabernet Sauvignon.

The winery doesn't have the high flying profile of its neighbours, Leeuwin Estate and Cape Mentelle, but I have a distinct feeling that's all about to change and Bill Ullinger's 'red gate' is about to open and drop a few

bombs to shake up the premium wine market. Watch out!

REDGATE WINES

Address: Boodjidup Road, Margaret River WA 6285
Phone: (08) 9757 6208, (08) 9757 6488
Fax: (08) 9757 6308
Email: redgate@margaretriver.com.au
WWW: http://www.margaretriver.com.au/cope/redgate.html
Established: 1977
Owner: Ullinger Family
Winemaker: Andrew Forsell
Principal varieties grown: Sauvignon Blanc, Semillon, Chardonnay, Chenin Blanc, Pinot Noir, Cabernet Sauvignon, Cabernet Franc, Merlot, Shiraz
Ha under vine: 20
Average annual crush: 110 tonnes
Average no. cases produced: 7,000

Principal wines & brands	Cellar Potential
Sauvignon Blanc Reserve	3-5 years
Classic Semillon-Sauvignon Blanc	0-4 years
Semillon	3-5 years
Chenin	0-4 years
Late Harvest Riesling	1-4 years
Pinot Noir	3-6 years
Cabernet Sauvignon	5-10 years
Cabernet Franc	4-8 years
Shiraz	4-8 years
White Port	0-5 years

Public & trade tours: By appointment only
Hours open to public: 10am-5pm, daily
Points of interest: BBQ facilities
Retail distribution: Cellar Door. Perth, Melbourne, Sydney, Brisbane, Hobart. Denmark, Singapore, Switzerland

Sandalford – Margaret River Vineyard

One of the largest vineyards in Western Australia is the 115 hectares of vines owned and operated by Sandalford Wines at Willyabrup. The vineyard is beautifully situated at the base of a circular valley. This protected site prevents damage to vines by harsh onshore winds, yet allows fruit ample exposure to the sun.

Planting commenced in 1972 under supervision of the then Managing Director, John Roe. The current vineyard manager is the young and enthusiastic Ian Davies and he has overseen a transformation of the property. Retrellising, computer controlled irrigation and the implementation of a strict vineyard regeneration program has given

rise to fantastic improvements to both quality and yield. Davies came to Sandalford in 1993 after five years with Tarrawarra in Victoria's Yarra Valley. Before this he had experience in the Upper Hunter Valley after graduating in viticulture from the Charles Sturt University in Wagga Wagga.

This mixed experience in warm and cool climates and vastly different rainfall patterns prepared him well for his role at Margaret River.

All grapes are machine harvested at night and transported to the company's Swan Valley winery, in the cool of the night in one tonne bins, where the wines are made under the eye of experienced and skilled wine maker Bill Crappsley.

Late in 1985, a delightful rammed earth tasting and cellar door area was constructed. The interior is furnished with polished jarrah (the local timber), and the area offers magnificent views over the vineyard. Sandalford's premium range is available, consisting of wines made from grapes grown in the Margaret River, Mount Barker and Pemberton regions. These are the Mount Barker Riesling, Mount Barker/Margaret River/Pemberton Chardonnay, Margaret River Verdelho, Margaret River Mount Barker Shiraz and Mount Barker/Margaret River Cabernet Sauvignon. These wines represent excellent value for the consumer; their quality is consistently high and prices are very reasonable.

Treeton Estate

Ralph makes your arrival at Treeton something special. This very clever border collie leaps up onto the substantial gate post heralding your entry, it seems only right he should "keep watch" over the estate of his very maritime master, David McGowan, a former mariner and head of the School of Maritime Studies at the Fremantle Technical College. The Margaret River region with its maritime climate seemed to be the ideal spot for David to rest his sealegs, rest probably wouldn't be the word. David and his delightful wife Corinne bought the property in 1981 but spent only weekends and David's 12 weeks of annual leave from TAFE on the

TREETON

Address: PO Box 219, Lot 1 North Treeton Road, Cowaramup WA 6284.
Phone: (08) 9755 5481
Fax: (08) 9755 5051
Established: 1991
Winemaker: David McGowan
Principal varieties grown: Chardonnay, Cabernet Sauvignon, Shiraz, Sauvignon Blanc, Riesling, Semillon, Chenin Blanc
Ha under vine: 15
Average annual crush: 20-49 tonnes

Principal wines & brands	Cellar Potential
Chardonnay	5 years
Shiraz	7+ years
Cabernet Sauvignon	7+ years
Sauvignon Blanc	5 years
Petit Rouge (100% Shiraz)	3 years

Hours open to public: 10am-6pm, daily
Points of interest: Self serve wine and cheese café. Disabled access and facilities
Retail distribution: Cellar Door and Mail Order sales

vineyard over the next 9 years. In 1992 David took a years long service leave from TAFE and returned to the fishing industry skippering, a scallop boat at Shark Bay to raise some capital to be able to build a winery to add to his vineyards. 1998 will see the first crop of sauvignon blanc, 4 acres were planted several years ago.

David makes a light red, Petit rouge, in deference to his French speaking wife, it's lovely chilled. The Treeton Shiraz is a substantial wine full of wild berry flavours. Treeton also have a Chardonnay, a Semillon and make a fine Vintage Port, a favourite of David's and we enjoyed a short snort in the charming Alfresco eating area which forms part of the cellar door. You must not miss the warm hospitality and good wines from this slightly out of the way stopover.

Voyager Estate

In a region with some of Australia's most beautiful wineries, none quite match the stunning symmetry and fresh clean lines of Voyager Estate with its 'Cape Dutch' design, reminiscent of the great wineries in the Cape Province of South Africa. This is all the more fitting as the first vines planted in Margaret River, some 100 years ago, were from South Africa. Voyager Estate also makes an excellent chenin blanc, the grape made famous in South Africa under the name Steen.

In 1991, Michael Wright bought the Freycinet Winery of the Gherardi family, who had named it after the French sea captain who explored the coast of the region. Faced with a legal challenge from the Spanish 'Frexinet' methode champenoise makers, and confusion with the small Tasmanian winery of the same name, Wright named the property 'Voyager Estate' based on his family company name. Michaels father became involved in mining as a partner to Lang Hancock in their massive Pilbara iron mines in northern Western Australia. Michael Wright was looking for a fresh rural challenge and although a teatotaller himself, decided wine was for him.

His Voyager Estate property includes a

substantial 750 acres, of which only 200 acres are suitable for wines. The vineyard covers 60 acres at present and is aided by a 275,000m≥ dam capable of supplying supplementary irrigation to 140 acres. New plantings of 30 acres are planned, comprising semillon and cabernet sauvignon, and by the turn of the century, a production of 25,000 - 30,000 cases of premium wines are anticipated. Already the Voyager Estate wines have made a mark for themselves amongst Australia's best. The range includes a complex barrel fermented chardonnay, a varietal semillon with great palate length. A third of this wine is also barrel fermented, certainly it will age well. The other whites are a fresh unwooded Sauvignon Blanc Semillon, 55% sauvignon blanc and 45% semillon, and finally, the fresh fruit-driven chenin blanc. The only red at present is the cabernet sauvignon with a touch of merlot blended in for softness. A super premium red is planned, but the varietal make-up and style is yet to be determined.

Voyager Estate has not rushed any of the necessary moves needed to make it a leading Australian wine company. I am sure the future will prove the huge investment involved has been worthwhile.

An introduction to Great Southern

Some 400 kms south of Perth, near the Great Southern Ocean, is a wine region of world potential which is already producing some exciting wines. Geographically it is the largest wine producing area in Australia, spreading between the towns of Albany, Denmark, Mt. Barker and Frankland, forming a square of some 2,500 kilometres. That's around 625,000 acres which could provide three times the current Australian wine grape harvest if it were all planted to vines. This, of course would not be possible, but it does show the area's potential.

The climate is perfect, cool with dry summers and wet winters; some supplementary irrigation is necessary, but the country lends itself to the construction of dams. In the east, the Stirling and Porongurup Ranges provide an awesome beauty unrivalled by any other Australian wine region.

Its isolation adds to this feeling of grandeur. The southern coastline is stunning and the stands of eucalypts in the west are breathtaking. Yields are low, but quality is outstanding. The five sub-regions - Albany, Stirling Ranges, Porongurup, Mt. Barker, Denmark and Frankland - support more than 20 producers, all established within the last 25 years. The first winery in the region, Plantagenet, was commissioned in time for the 1975 vintage, with the area's first vineyards being established less than 30 years ago. During the late 1950's the relieving horticultural adviser to the region was Bill Jamieson, later to become Western Australia's Great Southern Government Viticulturist. He was struck by the orchard region's potential for wine and followed this through over the decades. The great Maurice O'Shea from the Hunter Valley was adamant, if he had his time as a winemaker again, it would be near Albany in Western Australia.

The first vines, an experimental vineyard under Bill Jamieson's control at the Pearse family's Forest Hill property at Mt. Barker, was planted in 1965. This was followed by plantings a couple of years later by ex-Adelaide Lord Mayor, John Roche, at his Frankland River property. I tasted the first wine made from the region's grapes at the Houghton Winery Cafe in 1972. A 1972 cabernet sauvignon made by Jack Mann, enjoyed straight from the barrel, it was certainly impressive.

Rieslings from the Great Southern led the way with their limey intense flavours. Pinot noir has been a real star, as has chardonnay. I am sure this could be a great region for methode champenoise. Cabernet sauvignon does well, as does shiraz and even sauvignon blanc. There are so many microclimates and soil types, I am sure that great wines of all varieties are possible. From a wine tourist's point of view this region of natural beauty, freshness and great wines, is well worth the effort to discover.

Cellar doors have always been a little under-developed but during my 1997 visits I have seen this is fast changing. The new Howard Park Winery near Denmark is truly state of the art in every way. Even more impressive is the new Goundrey facility at Langton, a really world class complex. Plantagenet has had a new facade with much improved visitor facilities, Galafrey are opening a new cellar door restaurant and Matildas Meadow has a beautiful restaurant.

Nearly all the small producers have now opened cellar doors or developed their existing ones. It's a real adventure to visit the Great Southern and I always look forward to my visits there.

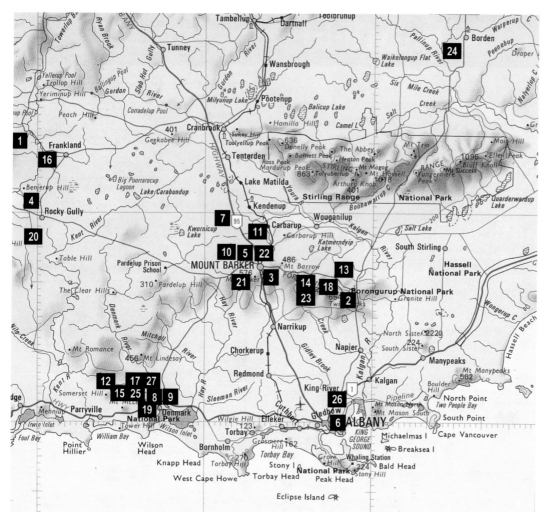

Great Southern

1. Alkoomi Wines
2. Castle Rock Estate
3. Chatsfield Wines
4. Frankland Wines
5. Galafrey Wines
6. Galafrey Wines (Cellar)
7. Gilberts Wines
8. Golden Rise Wines
9. Goundrey Wines (Cellar Sales)
10. Goundrey Wines (Langton)
11. Goundrey Wines (Williams Rest)
12. Harewood Estate
13. Jingalla Wines
14. Karrivale Wines
15. Karriview Wines
16. Marron Creek Wines
17. Matilda's Meadow
18. Millinup Estate Wines
19. Mt Shatforth Estate
20. Old Kent River
21. Pattersons Wines
22. Plantagenet Wines
23. Springviews
24. The Lily
25. Tinglewood Wines
26. Wignalls Wines
27. Yanwirra

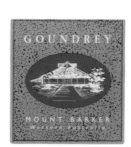

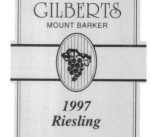

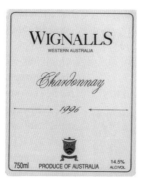

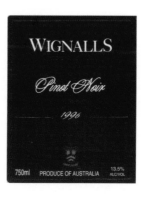

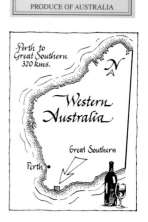

Chatsfield

Dr Ken Lynch's interest in wine began in Dublin as a medical student. He was foraging through a secondhand book shop, specialising in medical volumes, when he found a small book by a French Doctor exploring the virtues of wine in preventing heart and liver disease. Who knows if modern day medico's would agree with his prescription of up to a litre a day.

Nonetheless, Ken's life path eventually took him into an investment in a vineyard planted in 1976 by Ron and Jan Waterman. That was in 1984 and by 1989 Ken and his family had become sole proprietors.

He now commutes between his medical practice in Albany and the vineyards near Mount Barker, which have been expanded to over 40 acres, with some further expansion planned. The wine production of the last couple of vintages has increased significantly and will do so until early in the new century. The rhine rieslings from Chatsfield often have a touch of botrytis giving them some apricot and tropical fruit flavours and added complexity. Both the reds and whites, particularly the shiraz, have won awards and trophies in wine shows.

Ken is not the only doctor from Albany to assist in the vineyard. The cooling "Albany Doctor" sea breeze also helps give a long even ripening season to help wine quality along. Chatsfield is a well integrated wine producer and you will hear much more of them in the future.

CHATSFIELD

Address: PO Box 1417, Albany WA 6330.
Vineyard: O'Neill Road, Mount Barker WA 6324
Phone: (08) 9841 1605
Fax: (08) 9841 6811
Established: 1985
Owners: Dr. Ken and Joyce Lynch
Winemaker: Gavin Berry
Principal varieties grown: Riesling, Gewurztraminer, Chardonnay, Shiraz, Cabernet Franc
Ha under vine: 20
Average no. cases produced: 3,000-10,000

Principal wines & brands	Cellar Potential
Riesling	5 years
Shiraz	7 years
Chardonnay	7 years
Gewurztraminer	5 years
Cabernet Franc	3 years

Public & trade tours: Public tours by appointment only
Hours open to public: 10am-5pm, Tue-Sun and public holidays
Points of interest: Great views of Porongurup Ranges
Retail distribution: Perth, Melbourne, Canberra, Sydney, Wollongong, Brisbane, Hong Kong, Northern Ireland, Singapore, California and Canada

---

Gilberts Wines

The first winery one comes across after several hours driving south on the Albany Highway through the majestic Western Australian landscape is Gilberts Wines, some 18 kilometres north of Mount Barker. The statuesque Stirling and Porongurup Ranges are both visible from the verandah of the rustic brush pole and weatherboard farm cottage tasting room. The vineyards are set amongst a working stone fruit and apple orchard, the produce which you can taste if visiting between January and July.

Jim and Bev Gilbert are a charming country couple, third generation horticulturists, who have a real feel for the fruit they grow naturally including the grapes that go into their wines. A crisp aromatic riesling which has won much acclaim, a full style chardonnay and a peppery shiraz with strong berry flavours.

The barbecue and picnic area is truly delightful and wine loving groups can book for a private function outside or in the cottage.

GILBERTS WINES

Address: RMB 438, Albany Highway, Kendenup WA 6323
Phone: (08) 9851 4028
Fax: (08) 9851 4021
Established: 1985
Winemaker: Gavin Berry
Principal varieties grown: Chardonnay, Riesling, Shiraz
Ha under vine: 5
Average annual crush: 20-49 tonnes

Principal wines & brands	Cellar Potential
Riesling	5+ years
Shiraz	5+ years

Hours open to public: 10am-5pm, Wed-Mon
Points of interest: Restored farm cottage for wine tasting set amidst a working orchard. BBQ and picnic facilities
Retail distribution: Cellar Door and Mail Order sales. The Main Domain, NSW; Sutherland Wines, VIC

Goundrey

From small beginnings, the Goundrey Wines enterprise has become not only by far the largest in the Great Southern region, but also ranks in the top four wineries in the State in terms of size, being bigger than any of the wine producers in the better known Margaret River wine region.

In the early 1970's a small five acre vineyard of cabernet sauvignon and riesling was planted at the original Windy Hill vineyard, just south west of Mt. Barker. The first vintage was produced in 1976 and in 1987 the company Goundrey Wines Limited, was formed, which allowed for the purchase of the Langton property. This magnificent 200 hectare river valley property, is now home to the main vineyard of 145 hectares including a large and modern winery which was completed in time for the 1989 vintage.

The imposing winery is situated high on the valley slopes and beside it lies the historic homestead. In 1996 a magnificent new frontage to the winery has been built housing one of Australia's finest cellar doors with splendid viewing areas overlooking the winery below.

The combination of a cool climate and fertile soils, plus modern and effective viticultural techniques produce a high concentration of aromas and flavours.

Two ranges of wine are now being produced under the quality 'Goundrey' label, and a small volume under the premium 'Reserve' label.

The 1995 vintage saw a record 980 tonne crush at Goundrey's. With the vision and quality to succeed, Goundrey Wines looks set to be a dynamic presence in the Western Australian wine industry in the future.

GOUNDREY WINES
Address: Muir Highway, Mount Barker WA 6324
Phone: (08) 9851 1777
Fax: (08) 9851 1997
Email: info@goundreywines.com.au
WWW: http://www.goundreywines.com.au
Established: 1972
Owner: Mr Jack Bendat
Winemaker: Brenden Smith
Principal varieties grown: Riesling, Chardonnay, Sauvignon Blanc, Semillon, Cabernet Sauvignon, Shiraz, Merlot, Pinot Noir
Ha under vine: 160
Average annual crush: 1,300 tonnes
Average no. cases produced: 115,000
Principal wines & brands:
"Goundrey Range"
Chenin Blanc
Classic White
Unwooded Chardonnay
Cabernet Merlot
"Reserve Range"
Chardonnay
Riesling
Sauvignon Blanc
Cabernet Sauvignon
Pinot Noir
Shiraz
"Fox River Range"
Fox River White
Fox River Red
Public & trade tours: By appointment only
Hours open to public: 10am-4.30pm Mon-Sat; 11am-4.30pm, Sunday
Retail distribution: Goundrey products: Negociants Australia, National. Fox River Wine Company: The National Liquor Company, National. Export to UK, USA, NZ, Malaysia

Howard Park

Howard Park has a wonderful new home. After many years making wine for an extended family of vineyard owners for their own labels, up to 23 separate vignerons in some vintages, John Wade is now concentrating almost solely on his prestigious Howard Park and Mad Fish Bay labels.

John, along with partner Perth businessman Jeff Burch, have constructed a large state of the art winery able to crush at least 1,000 tonnes. Set on a hillside amongst stately gums, with lawns and gardens surrounding the spacious glass conservatory style tasting area with its grand entrance it is impressive indeed.

On the day of our visit the window cleaner was at work. He told us it takes him eight hours at least to clean the lot!!

Howard Park Cabernet Sauvignon is an opulent style in the very top echelon of Australian red and is built for the long haul with careful selection of the fruit and extended ageing in tight grained French Troncais barriques, a touch of merlot adds complexity, it's great wine.

Under the Howard Park label there are also a riesling and a chardonnay. The Mad Fish Bay wines, a red and a white, have unique aboriginal inspired labels. The name comes from a local bay where the fish are often seen madly jumping to avoid the hungry feeding dolphins.

The blended white is crisp and aromatic in a white bordeaux style, the red is soft and generous, both are enjoying spectacular sales in the value for money arena, particularly in the U.K.

John Wade has come a long way from his training as an electrician through the retail wine trade to vintages around Australia and time as winemaker at the famous Wynns Coonawarra Winery before moving to the Great Southern in 1986.

His formal training was in the early days of the Charles Sturt University at Wagga Wagga where he helped build the Winery.

Howard Park is a credit to the region and a sign of the exciting times that are ahead for this great area that has the potential to produce huge quantities of top class premium wines.

Plantagenet

Despite the establishment of an experimental vineyard at the Forest Hill Vineyard in 1965, Tony Smith's 'Plantagenet' was the first commercial vineyard in the Mount Barker area. Tony founded the Bouverie Vineyard at Denbarker in the late 1960's. Partnership plantings followed at Wyjup in 1971 and three years later an old apple-packing shed in Mount Barker was purchased and the Plantagenet Wines partnership was formed. This has since been converted into a functional, well-equipped winery which processes, bottles and provides storage space for number of local vineyards in addition to Plantagenet.

The first Plantagenet wines were made in 1974. Four years later, Roseworthy graduate Robert Bowen was hired as winemaker. The skills and innovative ability of this young Victorian brought great success on the show circuit.

He was replaced by the high profile winemaker John Wade who had been in charge of the wines at Wynns Coonawarra for many years. Gavin Berry is the highly respected current winemaker.

The introduction of the 'Omrah' Unwooded Chardonnay in 1989 proved to be a stroke of genius. It has become one of the biggest selling Western Australian whites, and appeals to those who prefer the more fruit-driven styles which generally taste better with food.

Plantagenet are concentrating more on their own wines with less contract activity now.

The winery has recently expanded and acquired a beautiful stone frontage, complete with a charming and larger cellar door.

In 1993 a Fremantle family company, Lionel Samson & Son Ltd bought ²/₃ of the partnership. Tony Smith retained his ¹/₃ ownership plus the right to manage. At the same time the partnership was transformed into a private company, Plantagenet Wines Pty Ltd.

Plantagenet Wines produced 35,000 cases in 1997. Continued expansion will take the production to 85,000 cases in 2002.

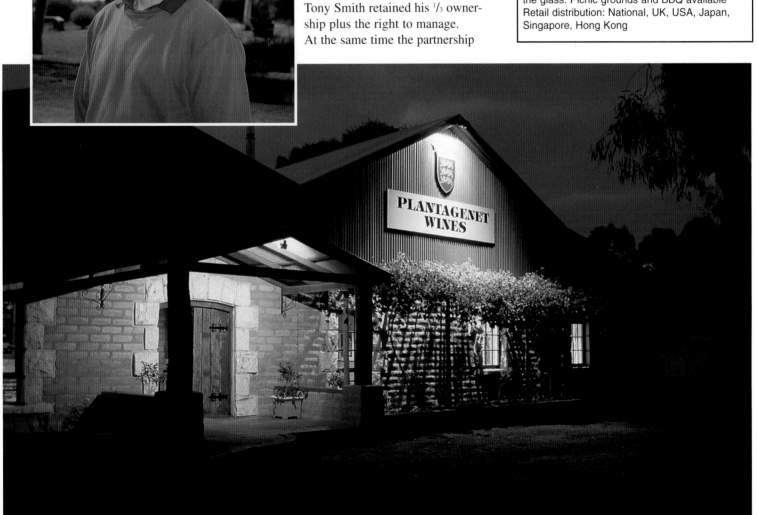

PLANTAGANET WINES
Address: Lot 45-46 Albany Highway, Mount Barker WA 6324
Phone: (08) 9851 2150
Fax: (08) 9851 1839
Established: 1974
Winemaker: Gavin Berry
Principal varieties grown: Chardonnay, Sauvignon Blanc, Riesling, Cabernet Sauvignon, Shiraz, Pinot Noir, Merlot
Ha under vine: 50
Average no. cases produced: 35,000

Principal wines & brands	Cellar Potential
Riesling	7+ years
Mt. Barker Chardonnay	6+ years
Omrah 'Unoaked' Chardonnay	3+ years
Omrah Sauvignon Blanc	2+ years
Omrah Merlot/Cabernet	4+ years
Omrah Shiraz	6+ years
Pinot Noir	5+ years
Cabernet Sauvignon	10+ years
Shiraz	10+ years

Public & trade tours: By appointment only
Hours open to public: 9am-5pm, weekdays; 10am-4pm, weekends and public holidays
Points of interest: Cheeseboards and wine by the glass. Picnic grounds and BBQ available
Retail distribution: National, UK, USA, Japan, Singapore, Hong Kong

Matilda's Meadow

Don Turnbull and his wife Pamela Meldrum-Turnbull both have an ease and grace about them which comes from long successful years in two very different fields a long way from the paradise they have created so beautifully, in the magnificent Karri Country, near the picturesque seaside village of Denmark. Don's family were hoteliers in New South Wales and Pamela a Queenslander, was an oil industry executive for 25 years.

They have painstakingly created a lovely restaurant and home surrounded by vines on sweeping slopes ringed by majestic karri trees. The former apple and pear orchard has proved ideal for vines and on the autumnal morning of our visit the vines were cloaked in golden leaves. Their late picked style Autumn Amethyst is most aptly named indeed. They also produce an unwooded chardonnay, a semillon chardonnay, a pinot noir, a cabernet sauvignon - cabernet franc blend and a late picked riesling.

We did not have time to lunch in the delightful restaurant, play some petanque nor time to take a scenic bushwalk but we were surely tempted! I hope when you visit you will have time to yield to these pleasurable experiences.

MATILDA'S MEADOW
Address: RMB 654, Hamilton Rd, Denmark WA 6333
Phone: (08) 9848 1951
Fax: (08) 9848 1957
Established: 1990, First Vintage 1994
Owners: Don Turnbull and Pamela Meldrum-Turnbull
Winemaker: John Wade. From 1998, Brendan Smith
Principal varieties grown: Chardonnay, Pinot Noir, Semillon, Cabernet Sauvignon, Cabernet Franc, Shiraz, Sauvignon Blanc
Ha under vine: 6.5
Average annual crush: 26 tonnes
Average no. cases produced: 1,200

Principal wines & brands	Cellar Potential
Cabernet Sauvignon-Cabernet Franc Blend	3-5 years
Chardonnay Unwooded	2 years
Semillon-Chardonnay	2 years
Pinot Noir	2 years
Late Picked Riesling	2 years
Autumn Amethyst	2 years

Public & trade tours: By appointment only
Hours open to public: 10am-4pm, Wed-Mon (Dec-Apr), Wed-Sun (May-Nov)
Points of interest: Restaurant, Petanque, scenic bush walks, lovely stands of Karris, friendly Golden Retrievers
Retail distribution: Limited. Ritz Carlton, Sydney; Perth - Porters City Liquors; Whitford City Cellars; Fairways Tavern, Wembley; Beacott Liquor Store, Mt. Lawley. Albany: Ryans Premier Hotel; Charlie Carters; Denmark: Denmark Liquor Store, Denmark Unit Hotel, Denmark Tavern

Wignalls

I well remember riding on the back of a tray top truck through the splendid Wignalls Vineyard with my old mate, Milan Roden, clicking the camera as we passed row upon row of the double "Lyre Bird" trellised vines. So huge and healthy, one could only imagine great wines coming from them.

When we stopped for a look at the dark, perfect bunches of pinot noir, ripe for picking, Bill Wignall was intrigued by Milan's cameras. Many years ago he was a photo journalist before embarking on a career as a vet which led him first to Albany in 1963. Many scoffed at his planting a vineyard "he won't get those grapes ripe".

Bill proved them so wrong, his first Pinot Noir in 1985 won a gold medal and the 1985 Chardonnay was judged the top wine at the 1987 S.G.I.O. Winemakers exhibition which won Bill and his wife Pat a trip to France where they learnt much about viticulture.

Son Robert is also heavily involved in the vineyard which has gradually expanded to 30 acres.

The cellar door created out of the "Chocolate Rock", which underlies the property, is full of character and contains a gallery. The outside areas are beautifully landscaped making a visit even more pleasurable whilst you taste the Wignall family's great wines.

WIGNALLS
Address: PO Box 248, Lot 5384 Chester Pass Road, King River, Albany WA 6331
Phone: (08) 9841 2848
Fax: (08) 9842 9003
Established: 1982
Owner: Wignall
Winemaker: Bill Wignall
Principal varieties grown: Pinot Noir, Chardonnay, Cabernet Sauvignon, Sauvignon Blanc
Ha under vine: 12
Average annual crush: 80 tonnes
Average no. cases produced: 5,000

Principal wines & brands	Cellar Potential
Pinot Noir	2-3 years
Chardonnay	3-5 years
Sauvignon Blanc	2 years
Cabernet Sauvignon	5-8 years

Public & trade tours: Trade tours by appointment only
Hours open to public: 12noon-4pm, daily
Points of interest: Childrens playground, attractive garden setting

An introduction to Swan Valley

The viticultural region known as the Swan Valley includes the Perth suburbs of Guildford, Bassendean and Midland and extends 15 kilometres to the north along the Swan River.

The first vines were planted by Thomas Waters at Olive Farm in 1829, the same year settlers arrived in the state.

Western Australia's first commercial vineyard was Sandalford, planted in the Swan Valley by John Septimus Roe in 1840. Houghton, however, was to become the region's most significant wine producer. The company was established when Dr John Ferguson planted vines in 1859. Following the First World War, the small number of the area's winemaking fraternity were suddenly boosted by the arrival of many Yugoslav and other European immigrants. As a result, hundreds of small family winemaking operations came into existence. Most families sold their wine in bulk from their cellar doors, while some winemakers had become more serious about commercial marketing and packaging.

In addition to these mainly traditional winemakers, and the area's larger concerns of Sandalford and Houghton, the Swan Valley now also hosts a group of winemakers growing in importance. These include Evans and Tate, famous for their red wines and challenging to become the state's second largest vigneron. Another worthy winery is the Jane Brook Estate of Beverley and David Atkinson, which also boasts a casual vineyard cafe. The Lamont Winery of Jack Mann's daughter Corin, also makes traditional full bodies Swan Valley styles along with having a first class restaurant run by Corin's daughter Kate. Westfield Wines, owned and operated by John Kosovich, makes consistently fine reds, whites and fortifieds, including an excellent vintage port.

Without doubt the most significant influence on the wine industry of the Swan Valley was the indomitable and idiosyncratic Jack Mann. Jack began his winemaking career at Houghton in 1922. Fifty one vintages later, in 1972, he retired having made legendary innovations to Australia's wine industry.

In 1937, Jack produced the first vintage of Houghton's White Burgundy. The popular taste of the day was for fortified wines, but the full-bodied flavour of the White Burgundy saw it become Australia's first widely accepted table wine.

The wine has continued to be made, and its great success owes much to Jack's winemaking philosophy and technical developments. The introduction of ideas such as cooling during fermentation and picking fruit only when completely ripe, contributed to the creation of Houghton's full bodied wines. Jack also retained grape skins in fermenting wines to further strengthen flavours.

Another of Jack's developments arose when attempting to crush the shrivelled grapes used in making fortified wines. An ingenious 'Mincer' was created to crush these raisined grapes, and proved very successful in the production of Jack's excellent sherries, muscats and tokays.

Jack unfortunately passed on at the age of 83 years in 1989, but his wines still live on somewhere deep in my cellar.

The Swan Valley of today has much to offer the visitor. A very pleasant way to visit the larger wineries is to take a river cruise up the Swan on either the Miss Sandalford or the Lady Houghton.

These vessels are delightfully furnished, and depart from Perth's Barrack Street Pier at 10.00 am. The trip is completed by 4.00 pm On tours to either the Sandalford or Houghton wineries and vineyards wines are available for tasting and served with lunch.

The highlight of the year for the Swan Valley is the Annual "Spring in the Valley" festival held in October.

This celebration of fine wines, superb food, music, art and theatre involves many of the leading wineries, who all feature at least three different attractions at their premises.

You can enjoy classical, jazz or popular music from live bands, watch magicians and street theatre, participate with potters and painters, see wood carving, tour historic buildings and participate in many other interesting activities, all of course, accompanied by the fine wines and foods of the region. Many wineries choose this time to release their new vintages and some even offer the visitor a taste of wines yet to be released.

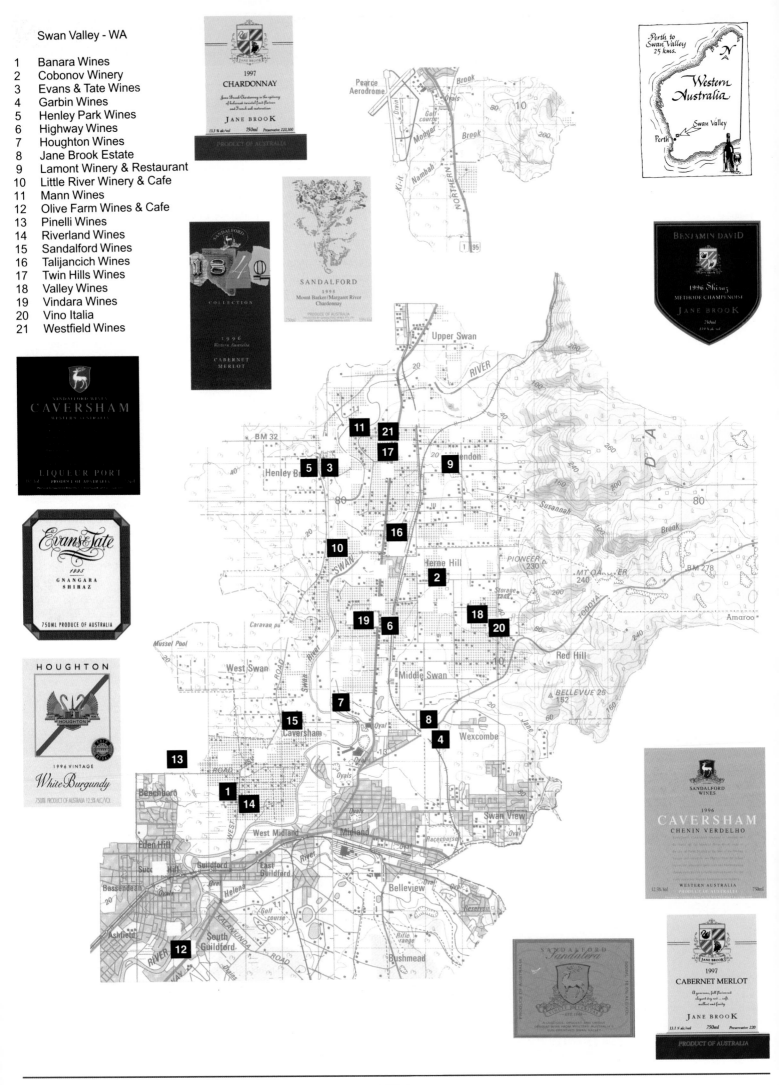

Swan Valley - WA

1 Banara Wines
2 Cobonov Winery
3 Evans & Tate Wines
4 Garbin Wines
5 Henley Park Wines
6 Highway Wines
7 Houghton Wines
8 Jane Brook Estate
9 Lamont Winery & Restaurant
10 Little River Winery & Cafe
11 Mann Wines
12 Olive Farm Wines & Cafe
13 Pinelli Wines
14 Riverland Wines
15 Sandalford Wines
16 Talijancich Wines
17 Twin Hills Wines
18 Valley Wines
19 Vindara Wines
20 Vino Italia
21 Westfield Wines

Houghton

Houghton was established in 1859 by colonial surgeon Dr. John Ferguson. The vineyard was planted at Middle Swan and further developed by the founder's second son, Charles Ferguson. By the time the property was purchased by the Emu Wine Company in 1950 the company had grown to a considerable size. The Emu Wine Company had already purchased the large Valencia Vineyard at Caversham and the addition of Houghton created Western Australia's largest wine company. Staff remaining with the company after the takeover included winemaker Jack Mann. His white burgundy, together with the cabernet sauvignon and fortified wines, were very popular on the Australian market. Much of Houghton's other output was exported and highly successful on the overseas market. Unfortunately, despite the company's financial success, Emu Wines did not re-channel profits into the company, but preferred to maintain a distance with the industry. The ingenuity of General Manager Ian Smith and winemakers Jack Mann and Charlie Kelly at Valencia was tested to the limit. With little but the bare necessities, excellent wine continued to be made at Houghton. Great changes occurred, however, four years after Jack's retirement in 1972. In 1976, the Emu Wine Company was purchased by Thomas Hardy & Sons, who immediately began work on updating winemaking equipment. Bill Hardy and, later, Jon Reynolds were appointed as the new winemakers. Having graduated as dux as the Diploma

D'Oenologique course from the University of Bordeaux in France, and having made several vintages at Hardy's McLaren Vale, Bill was more than qualified to take on this new position. Jon, originally from the Hunter Valley, had made wines at Reynella and came to Houghton.

Without altering the award-winning style of the famous Houghton White Burgundy, Bill and Jon freshened the wine by employing up-to-date winemaking techniques. The Show Reserve Houghton White Burgundies with a blue label, released when fully matured, have shown just how good this Australian classic is. The standard white burgundies are bottle-aged and released under this Show Reserve label; all have won many gold medals and trophies in wine shows.

Currently the popular Blue Stripe range of wines that includes the Houghton White Burgundy also features - Semillon Sauvignon Blanc, Frankland River Rhine Riesling, Cabernet Sauvignon and Cygnet. The Gold Reserve range is the flagship wines and includes a Cabernet Sauvignon, Chardonnay and Verdelho.

In addition to the company's wines, packaging also received a facelift under Hardy's management at Houghton. The new labels are simple yet elegant and the white burgundy has retained its distinctive blue stripe. The classic old cellars at Houghton and Dr. Ferguson's original home have also received some attention. Both have been beautifully restored and additions to the

cellars have been tastefully handled. The Middle Swan Winery is a joy to visit and exudes an air of history.

Houghton wines are popular throughout Western Australia and most releases are marketed Australia-wide. Over the years, the company has done much to further Western Australia's wine industry, particularly in its development of regions outside the Swan Valley.

Like several other medium-sized wine companies, (e.g. Tyrells and Brown Brothers), Houghton have become one of Australia's success stories. As a result of innovative management, the company obtains good financial returns in exchange for its large investments.

Houghton was involved in the merger that formed BRL Hardy in 1992.

The winery has benefited even further from the capital injection this merger provided. In 1994 new vineyards at Pemberton and Mount Barker were added to the collection and fruit from these properties is further enhancing the premium end of the portfolio with additional wines.

Houghton White burgundy still continues to be one of Australia's favourite whites and the 1998 vintage will be the 61st consecutive release for this famous wine.

Winemaker since 1985, Peter Dawson, is now chief winemaker for BRL Hardy based in Adelaide and was succeeded in 1993 by Paul Lapsley. Houghton continues to add lustre to the Western Australian wine industry like a star footballer in a champion team.

Sandalford - Caversham Estate

Sandalford was established by one of the founding fathers of Western Australia - John Septimus Roe, the state's first Surveyor General. Septimus Roe arrived on board the Parmelia in 1829 and quickly set about establishing the site for the beautiful city of Perth. After some ten years he was rewarded for his services with the granting of a tract of land on the banks of the upper reaches of the Swan Valley. The property was named "Sandalford" after the priory in Berkshire at which his father was rector.

Vines were planted on the property but they were made only for family consumption. The Roe Family began commercial production of wines during the 1940's and in 1971 the founders great grandson, John, replanted the vineyards and re-organised the business so that Sandalford became a private company.

The original site is now home to Sandalford's winery and Caversham vineyard which has 15 hectares planted to chenin blanc, verdelho, semillon, shiraz and cabernet sauvignon. There are two table and two fortified wines produced, the chenin verdelho and cabernet shiraz and the enormously popular Sandalera and Founders Reserve Liqueur Port.

In late 1992 the complexion of the company changed dramatically. After a brief period of overseas ownership a group of Western Australian business interests - determined to return the label to its former glory - combined to "buy back the farm".

Under the tutelage of renowned winemaker Bill Crappsley, formerly of Evans and Tate and the dynamic young owner Peter Prindiville the winery and vineyard has been transformed. Vines were re-trained to the Scott Henry trellising system, new stainless steel tanks installed and the winery's cooling system overhauled. Old oak was culled mercilessly and the wines improved dramatically. On my recent visit to Sandalford I was most impressed with the improvements Bill and his team have worked hard to achieve but, above all, I was very impressed with the wines themselves - Sandalford is in good hands, indeed. There is a riverboat that brings visitors to Sandalford's Caversham vineyard and winery every day from Perth's Barrack Street Jetty. If travelling from Perth it's only a leisurely half hours drive.

Sandalford is again a rising star in the Western Australian wine scene - to the benefit of all wine lovers.

Jane Brook Estate

Beverley and David Atkinson are very focussed on their beloved Jane Brook Estate, situated at the base of the Darling Range in the beautiful Swan Valley, less than 30 minutes from Perth. David discovered his passion for wine through a book on Australian wine he came across on his beat in the wheatlands, north of Perth, as Marketing Manager for an oil company. David and Beverley, as newly-weds in 1972, purchased the property known as "Vignacourt Wines". In 1984, after a decade of replanting the vineyard to pre-mium varieties and re-equipping the winery for quality wine production, the Atkinson's changed the winery name to Jane Brook, the name of the brook which runs through the property. The Jane Brook was named by John Septimus Roe, the first Surveyor General of the Swan River colony, during his initial exploration of the upper reaches of the Swan River in September 1829. It was named in honour of Jane Currie, the wife of Capt. Mark Currie, the first Harbour Master of Fremantle.

Beverley and David have continued devel-oping the vineyard and property into a show

piece - a tribute to hard work and commit-ment. The tasting and sales cellars are situated within this traditional rustic winery and there is an attractive vine covered courtyard and timber decking overlooking Jane Brook where lunches are served daily. Lunch comprises a splendid vineyard platter of cheeses, pates, fruit and salads and is a perfect accompaniment to a glass of Jane Brook premium table wine. The welcoming and knowledgable staff at Jane Brook will make any visit a memorable one.

The domain of sales, marketing and export belongs to Beverley, whose energy and enthusiasm is boundless. During recent years she has learnt to speak Japanese to compliment their well funded and researched push into the Japanese market. The Atkinson's are now assisting the Western Australian wine industry to develop a Japanese wine export campaign, a challenge that they find fascinating.

Jane Brook make a classic range of varietal wines, specialising in whites, wood aged chenin blanc, sauvignon blanc, chardonnay and an excellent Mount Barker Rhine Riesling. The cabernet merlot is full bodied with soft tannins and a superb dry red shiraz. Two excellent sparkling wines made by the traditional "methode champenoise" have been produced in the last 5 years. The Elizabeth Jane Chardonnay and Cabernet Merlot B.D.R. named after the Atkinson's daughter, Elizabeth Jane, and son, Benjamin David Robert, have both been scored highly in the prestigious Sheraton Wine Awards in Perth.

An introduction to Pemberton - Manjimup

In virtually no time at all, an important new wine region, now supporting some 20 winemakers and a number of large vineyards of the Goliaths of the wine industry, has sprung to life.

Deep in the karri, jarrah and redgum country, home of the tallest trees in Australia, lies one of the most exciting and beautiful Australian wine regions.

In the 1930's a small amount of wine was made at Middlesex in the heart of the region. Its real birth as a wine region however, came with the urging of Tony Devitt, agricultural and viticultural expert, who proposed vineyard and winemaking trials be undertaken.

It was the recommendation by Dr Gladstones in his viticultural report in the 1960's, that the area was well suited to early ripening vines such as chardonnay and pinot noir, that prompted this move. The results came through a decade later in 1987 with flying colours.

Today, BRL Hardy through Houghton have a large investment in what will become one of the state's largest vineyards; no doubt Sir James Methode Champenoise is in focus for the fruit.

Domaine Chandon are sourcing fruit from a large vineyard at Manjimup. Salitage, the winery of John Horgan, is a splendid operation whose restaurant and planned winery should make it one of Australia's best large boutiques of the next century. Already its wines are world class. Gloucester Ridge have a great little winery near the extraordinary Gloucester Tree park and many other exciting developments such as Chestnut Grove and the renowned Pannell family at Picardy Wines will see this region with huge potential become an important part of premium Australian wine scene.

PICARDY
Address: PO Box 1063, Manjimup WA 6258
Phone: (08) 9776 0036
Fax: (08) 9776 0036
Winemakers: Bill and Dan Pannell
Principal varieties grown: Chardonnay, Merlot, Cabernet Sauvignon, Shiraz, Pinot Noir, Cabernet Franc
Ha under vine: 5
Average annual crush: 40-80 tonnes
Principal wines & brands
"Picardy"
Pinot Noir
Shiraz
Chardonnay
Merlot (50%), Cabernet Sauvignon (25%), Cabernet Franc (25%)
Points of interest: Vineyard situated at Corner Eastbrook Road and Vasse Highway, Pemberton. All unirrigated vines, all wines are grown vintaged and bottled by the Pannell Family at Picardy
Retail distribution: Winery sales and Mail Order. C.C. Taffs, QLD; Sutherland Fine Wines, VIC; Fine Wine Specialist, NSW

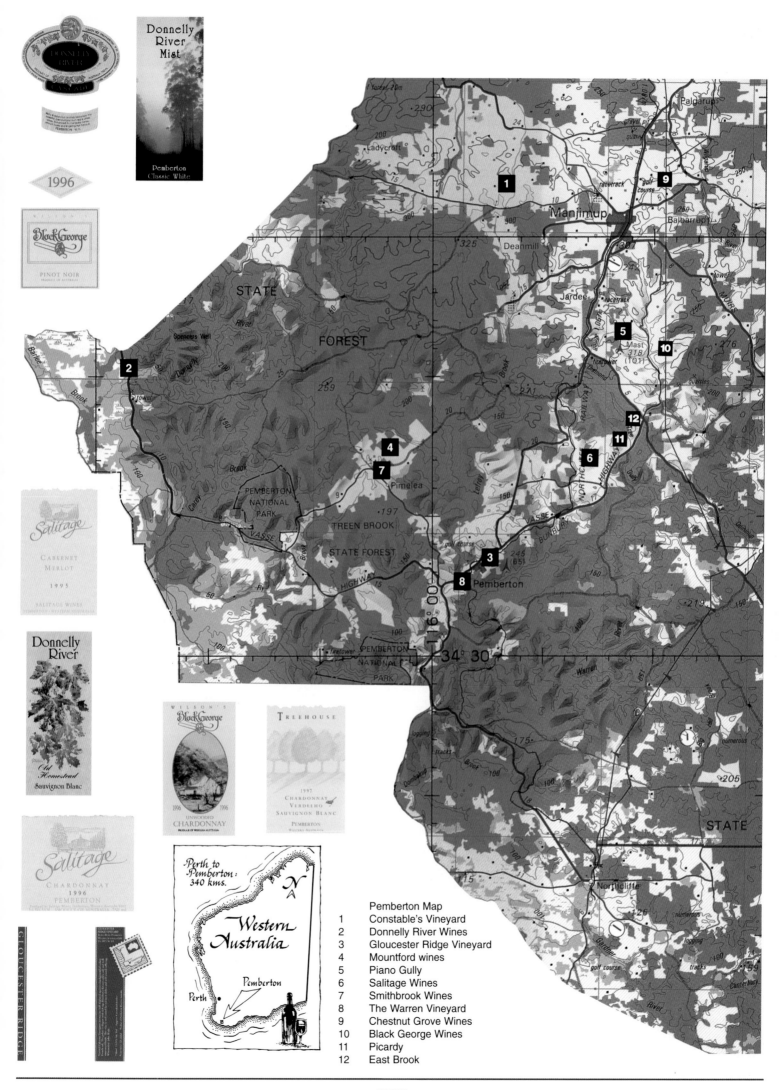

Pemberton Map
1 Constable's Vineyard
2 Donnelly River Wines
3 Gloucester Ridge Vineyard
4 Mountford wines
5 Piano Gully
6 Salitage Wines
7 Smithbrook Wines
8 The Warren Vineyard
9 Chestnut Grove Wines
10 Black George Wines
11 Picardy
12 East Brook

Chestnut Grove

Vic Kordic's tough beginnings in life prepared him well for the future and his now one of the happiest and most contented vignerons I have met, seeing the fruits of his labour flourishing on his Manjimup farm.

During the second world war, as a young man, he was plucked from his native Serbia to work as a forced farm labourer in Germany. Little was he to know, later in his life, farming would become his love and vocation.

In 1949 his chance to escape war-torn Europe came.

He looked at the possibilities in front of him.

He started at A, was it to be Argentina or Australia, happily he opted for the latter.

Arriving at Fremantle by ship through Singapore, with his wife and two children, they saw their suitcases smashed on the wharf. Vic and his family walked away with nothing into their new land.

After a stint in the Lime Kilns at Yanchep Vic moved on to the back breaking work laying railway lines in the south, often living in tents. When the opportunity came to work as a mechanic in Manjimup he jumped at the opportunity. Through his hard work and innovative thinking he built an empire including Real Estate, a Brick-making business and Manjimup's biggest Car dealership, Kordic Holden. Early in his time at Manjimup he bought a farming property north-east of

town which was blessed with a number of natural springs. Whilst mainly raising cattle and sheep he planted chestnuts and olive trees. On retirement in 1981 Vic took a greater interest in his farm.

A lifelong love of wine led to the planting of a vineyard in 1988 and a first vintage in 1991. Today 16 hectares of one of the best tended and managed vineyards I have seen is the result of Vic's labour. When Vic suffered a heart attack in 1992 his friends rallied around him and helped with the vineyards. The Chestnut Grove Wines are made off site and are already making a mark for themselves.

In 1996 Chestnut Grove won a trophy at the Annual Sheraton Wine awards in Perth. The Pinot Noir is complex and full of flavour with lots of strawberry like characters. The chardonnay has loads of stone fruit with nutty overtones.

The Cabernet Merlot, a 50/50 style blend, is rich, round and berry-like with hints of eucalypt and mint. I was most taken with the verdelho which the cool climate has blessed with loads of tropical fruit flavours. Chestnut Grove is an Estate that through Vic Kordic's noble endeavours will become world renowned.

CHESTNUT GROVE
Address: Lot 2227 Perup Road, Manjimup WA 6258
Phone: (08) 9386 3495
Fax: (08) 9386 3325
Email: chestnut@starwon.com.au
Established: 1988
Winemaker: Contract
Principal varieties grown: Chardonnay, Merlot, Cabernet Sauvignon, Shiraz, Verdelho, Pinot Noir, Semillon, Sauvignon Blanc
Ha under vine: 18
Average annual crush: 50-99 tonnes
Principal wines & brands: "Chestnut Grove"
Hours open to public: By appointment
Retail distribution: Cellar Door and Mail Order sales. Selwyn Wines, WA

Black George

"Black George" is a spectacular estate that nestles on a hillside amongst the towering Karri Forests. The original "Group Settlers" Cottage built in the 1920's has been restored and contains the very welcoming cellar door where Doug Wilson dispenses his warm hospitality. Wife Joy runs a herd of Alpacas. These gentle and friendly animals, from Peru, produce a superb fleece, which with knitted garments and many other Alpaca products are available at the boutique adjoining the cellar door.

The 17 acres of vines established on the deep gravelly loams are managed entirely without irrigation, a refreshing rarity these days, and produce wines of distinctive character. The Pinot Noir is particularly good. Doug and Joy's daughter Shelley is a trained Vet and Winemaker and makes the wines in the well-equipped 250 tonne capacity winery, the first to be constructed in Manjimup.

Total control of grape growing and winemaking and the new French barriques being added each year is producing excellent wines which will only get better and forge a great reputation for this fledgling estate.

BLACK GEORGE

Address: PO Box 907, Black Georges Road, Manjimup WA 6258
Phone: (08) 9772 3569
Fax: (08) 9772 3102
Established: 1991
Owner: Wilson Family
Winemaker: Shelley E. Wilson
Principal varieties grown: Pinot Noir, Chardonnay, Sauvignon Blanc, Verdelho, Merlot, Cabernet Franc
Ha under vine: 7
Average annual crush: 53 tonnes
Average no. cases produced: 4,000

Principal wines & brands	Cellar Potential
Pinot Noir	3-5 years
Chardonnay	3-5 years
Late Picked Verdelho	2+ years
Cabernet Franc/Merlot	5-7 years
Sauvignon Blanc	3+ years

Public & trade tours: By appointment only
Hours open to public: 10.45am-5pm, daily
Points of interest: Alpaca Farm - Hand feed Alpacas. Restored settlers cottage. Cellar door and sales of Alpaca products. Picnic grounds

Gloucester Ridge

GLOUCESTER RIDGE VINEYARD
Address: Burma Road, Pemberton WA 6260
Phone: (08) 9776 1035
Fax: (08) 9776 1390
Established: 1985
Owners: Don and Sue Hancock
Winemaker: John Wade
Principal varieties grown: Chardonnay, Cabernet Sauvignon, Cabernet Franc, Pinot Noir, Sauvignon Blanc
Average annual crush: 60 tonnes
Average no. cases produced: 4,000

Principal wines & brands	Cellar Potential
Wooded Chardonnay	3-5 years
Cabernets	4-5 years
Cabernet Sauvignon	4-7 years
Chardonnay - Unwooded	Now-2 years
Sauvignon Blanc	Now-2 years
Semillon/Sauvignon Blanc	Now-2 years

Public & trade tours: By appointment only
Hours open to public: 10am-5pm, daily
Points of interest: Restaurant
Retail distribution: WA Vintners, WA; Fine Wine Specialists, NSW

It's a good thing the massive Gloucester tree does not topple over, as it would certainly add a different meaning to crushing at the pretty little winery in its shadow. At least 250,000 visitors climb this extraordinary Karri tree each year.

Don Hancock's uncle was the well-known Clare winemaker, Mick Knappstein, but Don and his wife Sue, ran a cattle farm in the Margaret River region, ironically surrounded by vineyards. They eventually searched for a vineyard site and in 1981, bought at Pemberton. Vines didn't come until four years later and only a small area was planted.

The results were excellent, so the vineyard has been expanded to 15 acres and plans are to double this. Slowly, the tourists began to drop in and the pretty little cellar door became too small, so they have built a cellar door and restaurant complex mainly using local timbers. It is superb and has patio's looking over the vineyards to the grand Karri Forest.

They are already so busy that further expansion is being envisaged.

The Hancock's son, Michael, is vineyard manager and John Wade is the contract winemaker. Quite a large range of wines are made, including a couple of semi-sweet wines that have proved most successful with the tourists pouring through each day. The two chardonnays I tried, the Reserve and the unwooded version, would be gold medal winners in my book. Gloucester Ridge is obviously serious about its wines and is not just relying on its unique location.

Donnelly River Wines

The first vineyard and winery in the Pemberton-Manjimup region "Donnelly River" began in 1986. Award winning builder, George Oldfield, assisted by his son Kim and son-in-law Blair Meiklejohn, planted the vineyards and in 1990 made the first commercial vintage. Blair went on to study winemaking at Charles Sturt University and has stayed on as winemaker with new owners Ann and Matthew Harsley, who purchased the operation on George's retirement on August 1st, 1997.

Matthew has had a career that has certainly equipped him with innovative skills. He owned and operated an International Diving company, servicing the Oil and Gas Industry, mostly in South East Asia. Donnelly River has a very pretty location on the banks of the Donnelly River as it is crossed by the Vasse Highway. The rich river flats of silty loam have proved ideal for the vines and the pleasant rustic cellar door is about to house a small cafe serving light luncheons early in 1998.

The wines have won more awards than any other producer in the region and I am sure the Harsley's are keen to uphold this tradition.

Mountford Wines

I felt a real kinship with delightful, energetic couple, Andrew and Sue Mountford. They hail from the town of Honiton in Devon, the birthplace of my great-great-grandfather, the Australian Wine pioneer Thomas Hardy.

Andrew attended the Cannington Horticulture College in Somerset where he me an Australian who helped develop his growing interest in wine.

In 1983 Andrew, Sue and their two children migrated to Australia first to the Mudgee area in New South Wales where they established a vineyard. Andrew's brother living in Denmark in the Great Southern region of Western Australia tempted them to the west. Andrew ran a landscaping business in Perth for three years, all the time looking for an opportunity to get back into the wine business.

The Mountford's chose a majestic site in the Karri Country near Pemberton. The views from the hilltop location are spectacular. They have built a substantial winery, gallery and restaurant with their own hands, even making the bricks from the gravelly soils of the property and interspersing it with huge, hard hewn karri beams.

The Mountford's also have a theatrical flair and run the "Knot in the Know" performance, featuring song, dance, music, poetry and prose.

Andrew worked at a 400 year old Cider Barn at Taunton in his homeland and also makes cider at the winery under the Tangletoe label.

John Austin, a talented photographer, is curator for the art and photographic gallery. A visit to Mountford is a must. Mountford have also won many awards including the 1992 S.G.I.O. award for the best Pemberton white wine and the 1995 Sir David Brand award for "Excellence in Tourism Development".

MOUNTFORD WINES
Address: Bamess Road, Pemberton WA 6260
Phone: (08) 9776 1439
Fax: (08) 9776 1439
Established: 1987
Winemaker: Andrew Mountford
Principal varieties grown: Chardonnay, Merlot, Cabernet Sauvignon, Sauvignon Blanc, Pinot Noir, Cabernet Franc, Malbec
Ha under vine: 6
Average annual crush: 50-99 tonnes
Principal wines & brands: "Mountford"
Hours open to public:
Fri., Sat., Sun. 10am-4pm all year round.
Points of interest: Mudbrick cellar sales with art gallery and cafe. Facilities for approximately 100 people. Functions catered for.
Retail distribution: Cellar Door and Mail Order sales. Feq Dorado and Co.; Aria Wine Co., NSW; Prime Wines, VIC

Salitage Wines

John Horgan is a perfectionist who never settles for second best. During the 1970's he set up Leeuwin Estate with his brother Denis, who purchased John's share in 1980. During this time, John developed a strong friendship with, and respect for, the great Robert Mondavi of California. John also had a long-time love affair with the wines of Burgundy. In fact, along with a group of Australians, including two Burgundian enthusiasts, David Clarke and Ross Grant of Sydney, they purchased a French Burgundian Domain, La Pousse d'Or. Pousse in French is a noun meaning to shoot or grow, but also the verb means to drive somebody to do. d'Or of course is gold.

John was driven to find somewhere in his homeland where he could grow the chardonnay and pinot noir vines to make truly Burgundian style wines. He found this land and climate at Pemberton, on the most elevated ridge of the region; the gravelly soil over ironstone provides the wines with a spine, and a distinct flinty character.

John and Jenny Horgan chose the name, a combination of the first two letters of the names of their four children, Sarah, Lisa, Tamara and Gerard.

The winery at Salitage has magnificent, vaulted ceilings, as it has been designed to suit the needs of the future. Considering the already evident greatness of the wines, it was a move of considerable vision.

The wines all see some absolutely top class French oak barriques and they are at once rich and yet complex. So far, the range includes a fresh sauvignon blanc, more at the tropical fruit end of the flavour spectrum, a chardonnay rich with lemon and grapefruit flavours and toasty hazelnut overtones with some pineapple and banana tropical flavours - a real mouthful.

The gamey, racy pinot noir has dark cherries bursting out. It's certainly in the best few examples of the variety in Australia. A cabernet blend is also released and I was most impressed by both the 1994 and 1995 that I tried at the winery. Winemaker is Patrick Coutts, a Roseworthy dux, who has made wine in the south of France at Limoux, in Germany's Rhinephalz, and at Paso Robles in California, as well as the high profile Australian wineries of Brokenwood and Domain Chandon. The winery has a large open restaurant area with tasting facilities featuring many of the local timbers. Alfresco dining is available here and in the beautifully landscaped gardens surrounding the winery. Lunches are simple and classy and are served Friday through Monday. John's son, Gerard, has been involved in the last two years in the marketing. Salitage have made a real impact, not only on the premium Australian Market, but in a number of prestigious International Markets.

In chatting with John Horgan, just prior to going to press, he and wife Jenny have just returned from their second trip in a year hosting wine dinners across the USA.

The Salitage Wines are on the wine lists of many of the most prestigious restaurants in New York, Chicago, Los Angeles and San Francisco, a real feather in their cap, and helping the Salitage export volume which is almost up to 40% of their production.

I take my cap off to their valiant efforts from which all Australian Wines benefit!

SALITAGE WINES
Address: Vasse Highway, Pemberton WA 6260
Direction: 10km east of Pemberton township on Vasse Highway
Phone: (08) 9776 1771 (Winery), (08) 9776 1195 (House)
Fax: (08) 9776 1772 (Winery), (08) 9776 1504 (House)
WWW: http://salitage.iinet.net.au
Established: 1988
Owner: John and Jenny Horgan
Winemaker: Patrick Coutts
Principal varieties grown: Chardonnay, Pinot Noir, Cabernet Sauvignon, Cabernet Franc, Merlot, Sauvignon Blanc, Petit Verdot
Ha under vine: 20
Average annual crush: 200-250 tonnes
Average no. cases produced: 12-15,000

Principal wines & brands	Cellar Potential
"Salitage"	
Chardonnay	2-5 years
Unwooded Chardonnay	0-2 years
Pinot Noir	2-5 years
Cabernet Merlot	5-10 years
Sauvignon Blanc	0-2 years
"Treehouse"	
Chardonnay, Verdelho	0-2 years
Shiraz	2-5 years

Public & trade tours: Yes, trade tours by appointment
Hours open to public: 10am-4pm, daily
Points of interest: Restaurant open weekends
Retail distribution: Mail Order. NSW, VIC, SA, QLD, WA

An introduction to Tasmania

Following the development of a wine industry in New South Wales, the next State to establish viticulture was Tasmania. The state's first commercial vineyard was planted by Bartholomew Broughton in 1823, near New Town, north of Hobart. Other landowners followed suit, developing vineyards around the state, but sadly the industry was short-lived. By the 1890's Tasmania's first involvement with winemaking was over.

A re-birth of the industry occurred during the late 1950's. The first commercial vineyard was established by Claudio Alcorso in 1958, on a beautiful peninsula in the Derwent River. The property is still in existence and is now known as Moorilla Estate. Encouraged by Alcorso's success, other vignerons began to plant vines and there are now four wine producing regions. These are the Pipers River area north-east of Launceston, the Tamar Valley north of Launceston, the East Coast and finally Southern Tasmania - the area around Hobart - comprising the Derwent Valley, Coal Valley and the Huon - d'Entrecasteau Valleys. A large percentage of the production comes from the Pipers River region.

Although the State's production is relatively small, there are more than 50 wine producers and many more vineyards, and the industry is growing fast with the guidance and assistance of a very supportive State Government. The quality of Tasmanian wine has been of such a standard that mainland winemakers have had to take notice. Some wines have been exceptional. It has been widely assumed that Tasmania's cool wet climate would prevent viticulture. This is far from the truth, as many areas of the State experience a mild climate, comparable with some parts of the mainland. All Tasmanian regions can be quite warm in some years, and surprisingly, in some seasons can experience drought conditions. Tasmanian wine styles are many, but the methode champenoise wines are absolutely outstanding, and many mainland wineries are either sourcing grapes or wines in Tasmania to use in their sparkling wine blends. Although Tasmania's winemakers cannot hope to compete with the volume of wine produced on the mainland, their wines are certainly capable of taking on the best in quality terms.

An introduction to Northern Tasmania

There are now two main regions in the north of Tasmania that have vineyards and make wine. The chief of these is the Pipers River region, some 35 kilometres north-east of Launceston. The climate in all Tasmanian wine regions is ideal for viticulture. The soils are generally rich and red, but also drain very well. The country is generally quite hilly and the easterly-facing slopes can be planted to give a better aspect to the sun and protect the vines from at times, severe westerly winds. Many of the vineyards have windbreaks of poplars which provide good growing season protection and add to the magnificent autumn kaleidoscope of colour this region enjoys. The red soils, the green, yellow and amber tones of the vine leaves, the deep blue skies and the fluffy white clouds are truly spectacular.

The region is by far the biggest producer in Tasmania, accounting for about 70 per cent of wine production. One of the first vineyard/wineries established was Heemskerk,

back in 1975, a venture between Graham Wiltshire and the Fesq family wine business in Sydney. For a time the French Champagne House of Louis Roederer were involved, but today, dynamic Tasmanian businessman, Joe Chromy, holds the reins. Dr Andrew Pirie, who has a PhD in viticulture, established Pipers Brook Wines in 1974. Other large players are the Clover Hill vineyards of Dominique Portet's Taltarni Vineyard in Victoria and Rochecombe, Heemskerk's sister winery. Other smaller boutique producers such as Dalrymple make up the balance. In all, around eight wine producers cover the region.

Probably the prettiest viticultural area in Australia, and perhaps the world, is that surrounding the Tamar Estuary. The vineyards generally are planted on the relatively steep slopes of the eastern shores of this estuary which varies from several kilometres to several hundred metres in width. Many of these wineries have hospitality operations

with restaurants and even accommodation. The active bird-life requires netting of the vines (or very active deterrents) to guard the valuable crop. The grapes in this region have a very long ripening period and often achieve high degrees of sugar combined with good acid levels, the winemaker's dream.

Wineries such as Marion's and Strathlynn make the most of their locations. Being less than half an hour from Launceston make a visit essential. The Lake Barrington Vineyard is the first in north-western Tasmania (really more north central). This beautiful vineyard and cute winery and tasting room overlooks the large Lake Barrington. With mountains all around, it's like being in the Swiss Alps. Of the northern Tasmanian wines, chardonnay, pinot noir and methode champenoise stand out but good riesling, sauvignon blanc, shiraz, merlot and cabernet sauvignon can be produced in the various microclimates that the region possesses.

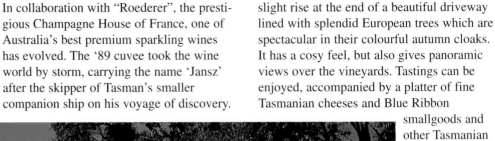

Established in the early 1970's Heemskerk has become one of Tasmania's largest and better known wine producers. The vineyard is located in the heart of the Pipers River region, on rich red soils. The winery has definite seafaring style with its high pitched roof and baltic timbers reminiscent of a stately galleon sailing through a sea of vines. Suitably, the venture was named "Heemskerk" after the ship of Tasmania's discoverer, Abel Tasman. The climate of north east Tasmania is midway between that of Burgundy and Champagne in France. In warmer years this allows Heemskerk to produce rich, soft pinot noir wines, akin to the best of Burgundy, and every year, to produce chardonnay and pinot noir ideal for the splendid 'Jansz' Methode Champenoise Cuvee.

Of the table wines, the cabernet sauvignon, in particular, is extremely well regarded, setting the tone for the cool climate styles eagerly sought after by discerning wine consumers. With its hints of tobacco leaves, green tea and mulberry-like fruit, it has exceptional quality and flavour.

In collaboration with "Roederer", the prestigious Champagne House of France, one of Australia's best premium sparkling wines has evolved. The '89 cuvee took the wine world by storm, carrying the name 'Jansz' after the skipper of Tasman's smaller companion ship on his voyage of discovery.

Heemskerk Vineyards

Normally Jansz has a base wine made predominantly from chardonnay supplied by selected parcels of pinot noir. This results in a superbly dry style, full of citrus/grapefruit characters. Jansz spends a minimum of two and a half years ageing on yeast lees in the bottle.

The other winery in the Heemskerk group is Rochecombe Vineyard which is a picture of beauty and order, with close vines are trimmed in tall hedge-like rows which seem to spread forever over the gently rolling hills of just south of the town of Pipers River. The Vineyard runs down to the river and if you're very quiet you may be lucky enough to spot a platypus (the symbol on the Rochecombe label) playfully cavorting in the stream.

Rochecombe is very well equipped with a multitude of small tanks, with the ability to make many separate batches of wine. A very good restaurant adjoins the winery on a

slight rise at the end of a beautiful driveway lined with splendid European trees which are spectacular in their colourful autumn cloaks. It has a cosy feel, but also gives panoramic views over the vineyards. Tastings can be enjoyed, accompanied by a platter of fine Tasmanian cheeses and Blue Ribbon smallgoods and other Tasmanian produce.

Founded by Swiss winemakers, Bernard and Brigitte Rochaix, Joe Chromy's JAC Group purchased the vineyard and winery complex in 1994.

The vineyard reminds me a lot of burgundy, with the vine training, red soils and undulating slopes. The Burgundian varieties of chardonnay and pinot noir dominate the vineyard, which also grows pinot gris, riesling, sauvignon blanc and the cabernet-related bordeaux varieties. A new methode champenoise sparkling known as RV has recently been added to the range.

The pristine environment which gives clean, fresh and untainted, long-living flavours to the wines is common to both Heemskerk and Rochecombe. Both also source grapes from Joe Chromy's Kayena Vineyards in the Tamar Valley.

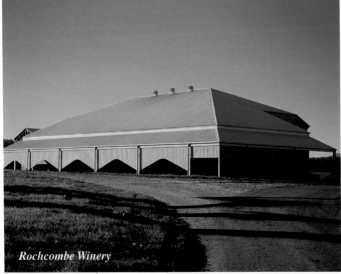

Rochcombe Winery

HEEMSKERK
Address: Pipers Brook Road, Pipers Brook TAS 7254
Phone: (03) 6382 7133
Fax: (03) 6382 7242
Established: 1976
Winemaker: Garry Ford
Principal varieties grown: Pinot Noir, Chardonnay, Riesling
Average annual crush: 114 tonnes
Average no. cases produced: 10,000

Principal wines & brands	Cellar Potential
Jansz Sparkling	5-10 years
Chardonnay	2-5 years
Pinot Noir	5-10 years
Riesling	2-5 years
Cabernet Merlot	5-10 years

Public & trade tours: Yes
Hours open to public: 9am-5pm, daily
Retail distribution: Cellar Door and Mail Order sales. Fesq. Dorado and Co., National

Lactos Master Cheesemakers

Back in 1955 when Milan Vyhnalek arrived as a Czech refugee in Tasmania, with 300 years of cheese-making in his family, he could think of only one word to describe Australian cheese - 'cheddar'. At that time, with our traditional Anglo Saxon based cuisine, very few varieties of cheese were made. So when Milan began the Lactos factory at Burnie on the north-west coast of Tasmania it became Australia's first specialty cheese company making a range of European-style cheeses.

Specialty cheeses are like a regional varietal wine i.e. the Heritage True Blue of Lactos which is made from milk of the Burnie Region only. Lactos is the biggest specialty cheesemaker in Australia. During the peak production period in the summer 320,000 litres of like are made into cheese each day. When you consider that it takes about seven litres of milk to produce one kilogram of cheese, this is still a lot of cheese.

The cheesemaker is middle European Janos Kaldy, a youthful looking vibrant man who surprised me when he said he started working at Lactos back in 1972.

Since then he had a number of years working in America, his last job as cheesemaker at a large family factory in Illinois.

In 1981 Lactos was purchased by Bongrain, a large French Agro Alimentaire (food and beverage) company. Visitors must first don sterilised rubber boots, a hair net, a special coat and gloves. No bacteria can be permitted in a good cheese factory. Visitors then walk through a shallow bath of chlorinated water to sterilise their boots, again these baths are at every doorway. First port of call is the pasteurisation room where the milk is pasteurised overnight.

On day two the milk is inoculated with a culture to start the transformation of the milk sugar into lactic acid, a little like wine fermenting. The milk is now about 12-14° C. The milk also has a coagulant added. The temperature of the milk is raised and it is stirred and 'cut' to a special recipe for each different cheese type. By now quite firm cheese in small cubes is put in various

moulds and enters the drying room where it spends 24 hours on drying and draining trays. It is acid-adjusted to a pH degree of 5.1 which is pleasant to the human palate. The cheese then enters a brine bath; after this it is another day in the drying room. The various cheese styles then age for different lengths of time in curing rooms where the temperature and humidity are strictly controlled. Lactos have spent $1.75 million on a new ultra-filtration plant which can concentrate the strength of the milk by removing water from it without heating it or changing its character at all. In addition last year new equipment was installed in the soft ripened cheese areas. Whilst the process is very much hand crafting the cheeses this has allowed Lactos to increase production in line with increased demand. I was fascinated by the machinery used to 'spike' the Heritage True Blue, inoculating it with lines of the blue penicillin mould which gives it its character. It is unique to Lactos and looks like an ancient torture chamber. Lactos use the name Tasmanian Heritage onthe range of top selling soft ripened cheeses, a Camembert,

Brie and the famous 'True Blue', a soft-ripened blue, plus Camembert with green peppercorns and Camembert with tomato and capsicum are the styles. Then there is the 'Domaine' range - larger, rich, soft-ripened cheeses. The Domaine Red Square, soft ripened with a washed red-orange rind, is a little earthy and pungent. I love it when it is just starting to run inside. There is also the Domaine Deep Blue, a crumbly roquefort style and White Diamond, a classic French style Brie which develops with maturation becoming creamier in texture as it ages for 5-6 weeks but cal also be enjoyed when it is younger, firmer and has more delicate flavours. Lactos make a Swiss style called St. Claire, at least the counterpart to Jarlesberg and also an Edam style under the Cradle Valley brand, which also includes a Gouda and an Havanti style. The final range of Lactos is their matured Club cheddar styles under the name 'Mersey Valley'. Some edam and gouda styles are blended back with the ageing cheddar giving a bitey, crumbly but creamy texture. It is hard to explain but they are superb. Try some soon - in fact, make sure you always have some of the excellent Lactos cheeses styles on hand for when you pull the cork on a bottle of good wine.

Southern Tasmanian wine regions surround Hobart. The first vineyard in Tasmania was planted by fabric baron, Claudio Alcorso, at Berriedale on the banks of the Derwent River, in a northern suburb of Hobart. Further up the Derwent Valley are several vineyards and wineries, including Meadowbank.

The next area planted was the Coal Valley, east of the Derwent, near Richmond and Campania. The fine Domaine A Stoney Vineyard is here and the Victorian Domaine Chandon's expanding Tolpuddle Vineyards, along with several other small wine ventures.

The other Southern Region is the Huon Valley and d'Entrecasteau Valleys, some 30 kilometres south of Hobart on the peninsula between the Huon River and Bruny Island.

Microclimates in these very cold viticultural regions - by world standards - is critical. Long sunshine hours in the summer help the equally long growing season, but the aspect of the slope and protection from the howling westerly winds is essential. The moderating effect of the many estuaries also plays an important role, helping produce some great wines - not without the viticulturist losing a little sleep. A number of wineries now have hospitality adjuncts helping make a visit a complete experience.

MOORILLA ESTATE

Address: 655 Main Road, Berriedale, Hobart TAS 7011
Direction: 10kms north from Hobart on the Brooker Highway
Phone: (03) 6249 2949
Fax: (03) 6249 4093
Established: 1958
Owner: Alain Rousseau
Winemaker: Alain Rousseau
Principal varieties grown: Riesling, Gewurztraminer, Chardonnay, Pinot Noir, Cabernet Sauvignon
Ha under vine: 12
Average annual crush: 170 tonnes
Average no. cases produced: 12,000
Principal wines & brands: "Moorilla Estate"
Public & trade tours: Yes
Hours open to public: 9am-5pm, daily
Points of interest: Vineyard Restaurant (won most popular Tasmanian Tourism Award - 1992). Giftshop and Cellar Door Cafe in the winery. Tasmanian made produce for sale plus wine and cheese tasting for groups or individuals.
Retail distribution: Wines available in selected bottleshops in Victoria, NSW, Tasmania and Queensland. Export - Hong Kong, Japan, Germany, New Zealand, Canada

---

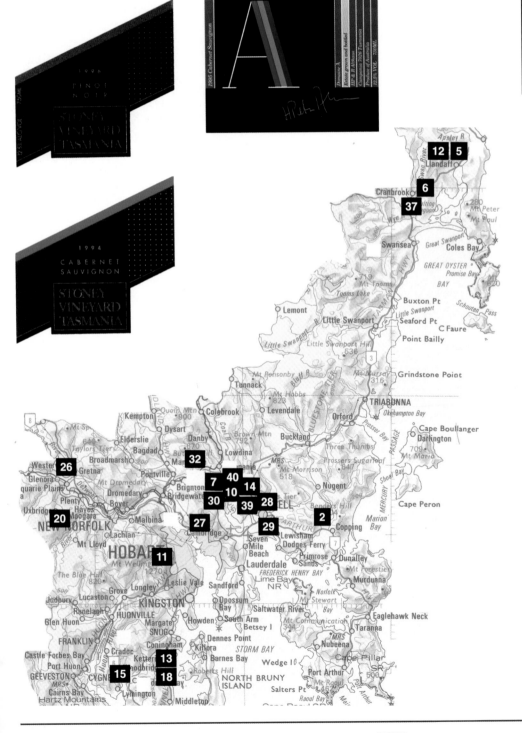

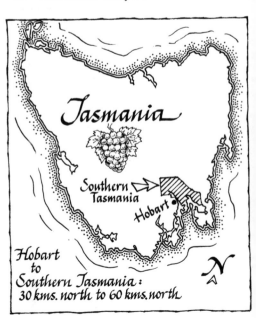

Jasmania

Southern
Tasmania

Hobart

Hobart
to
Southern Jasmania:
30 kms. north to 60 kms. north

Domaine 'A' Stoney Vineyard

Stoney Vineyard began its life as the property of George and Priscilla Park in 1973. In 1988 Ruth and Peter Althaus tasted the wines at a comparative tasting on a trip from their native Switzerland. They fell in love with them and Tasmania.

When they heard the property was on the market a year later they did not hesitate. Peter was a senior executive with IBM in charge of the Customer Engineering Department in Zurich. Peter is a great fan of Bordeaux Wines and 70 per cent of the property is planted to red Bordeaux varieties, cabernet sauvignon, merlot, cabernet franc and petit verdot. A further 20 per cent is pinot noir with only 10 per cent in sauvignon blanc.

The soils are stoney and well-drained with a thin layer of rich black clay. The low rainfall means some supplementary irrigation is necessary. The dry conditions with

loads of sunshine and the north and east-facing slopes produce outstanding fruit. Peter is a fastidious winemaker and his wines are fantastic. A significant addition to the winery has just been completed and includes an area for Functions and

Entertainment. From 15 to 60 guests can be received for set luncheons, dinners and wine appreciation classes. A Swiss trained professional chef takes care that the standard of the food matches the top quality of the wines. This is a winery with its act very much together.

DOMAINE A - STONEY VINEYARD

Address: Tea Tree Road, Campania TAS 7026
Direction: 7km from Richmond towards Campania
Phone: (03) 6260 4174
Fax: (03) 6260 4390
WWW: http://www.view.com.au/domaine
Established: 1973
Owners: Peter and Ruth Althaus
Winemaker: Peter Althaus
Principal varieties grown: Cabernet Sauvignon, Pinot Noir, Sauvignon Blanc
Ha under vine: 10
Average annual crush: 80 tonnes
Average no. cases produced: 5,000

Principal wines & brands	Cellar Potential
Domaine A Cabernet Sauvignon	10+ years
Domaine A Pinot Noir	5-10 years
Stoney Cabernet Sauvignon	5-10 years
Stoney Pinot Noir	3-5 years
Stoney Sauvignon Blanc	2-5 years
Stoney Aurora	2-4 years

Public & trade tours: By appointment only
Hours open to public: 8am-4.30pm, weekdays; weekends by appointment
Points of interest: Chef on property running own catering business. Function facilities available (70 seats)
Retail distribution:
Mail order sales. Major bottleshops. Agent in Melbourne

Wine production first began on a commercial level in Queensland in the unlikely location of Roma, almost 450 kilometres to the north-east of Brisbane. This venture was founded by Samuel Bassett in 1863. Vine cuttings were provided by Bassett's uncle who had an established vineyard in the Hunter Valley. By the time Samuel's son, William, took control of the company in 1912, 'Romavilla' was a thriving business, with more than 180 hectares under vine. William Bassett had received winemaking tuition from the great Leo Buring, and his wines were highly sought-after. Romavilla has remained constantly in production. This seemed in doubt only after William's death in 1973, but a group of Sydney businessmen purchased the property two years later, and production has continued.

While Romavilla is Queensland's longest operating winery, the vast majority of the state's industry is situated around the towns of Stanthorpe and Ballandean, near the border of New South Wales. The region is known as the 'Granite Belt', owing to its location on a small elevated plateau in the Great Dividing Range. Altitudes vary from 800 to 940 metres above sea level, making the area one of the highest wine-producing districts in Australia. Generally therefore, the climate is cool and not dissimilar to that experienced by the Central Highlands of New South Wales. Distance from the sea can result in harsh winters, and even occasional snow. The average maximum temperature during summer months is only 26 degrees centigrade and soils are decomposed granite varieties.

From a small bulk wine industry, began by the early European settlers, wine has now become a fully fledged industry, with larger vineyards and wineries being established. The industry has expanded considerably and the Granite Belt now boasts more than 15 commercial wineries. Winemakers of the region are united in their desire to exploit the unique Queensland climate. Many innovative techniques are being employed and wines released so far show successful evidence of these efforts. In 1985, a light dry red wine was released onto the market by several local vignerons, with favourable results. Called 'Ballandean Nouveau', the wine is delightful served chilled and ideal for the Queensland market.

Every year on the first and second weekend of October the industry has its "Spring Wine Festival" attracting many wine and food enthusiasts to the region. This is followed on the third weekend by the "Australian Small Winemakers Show", attracting 550 - 600 entries involving every State in Australia.

The first Sunday in May boasts the extremely successful "Opera At Sunset", attracting over 1000 opera wine lovers to the wineries.

The Granite Belt region is a unique contributor to Australia's wine industry. Vignerons are highly motivated and justifiably proud of their region. Some of the wines produced are of exceptional quality and are sure to become more widely respected in the near future.

Queensland
1 Bald Mountain Vineyards
2 Ballandean Estate Winery
3 Bassetts Romavilla Winery Pty Ltd
4 Bungawarra Wines
5 Castle Glen

6 Felsberg Winery & Vineyards
7 Golden Grove Winery
8 Granite Cellars
9 Heritage
10 Inigo Granite Country Estate
11 Kominos Wines
12 Mount Magnus
13 Mountview Wines
14 Old Caves Winery
15 Robinsons Family Vineyards
16 Rumbalara Vineyards
17 Stone Ridge Vineyards
18 Winewood

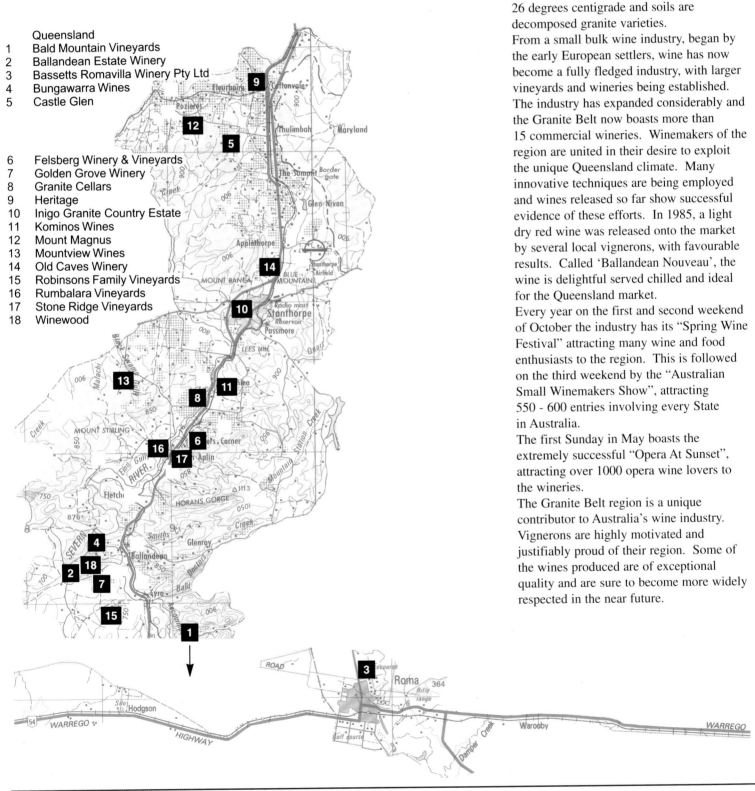

Kóminos Wines

Queensland Grown and Made

New England Highway, Severnlea
P.O. Box 225, Stanthorpe, Qld. 4380
Telephone: (076) 83 4311
Facsimile: (076) 83 4291

**PRODUCT OF THE GRANITE BELT
QUEENSLAND**

Kóminos Wines
Severnlea

National Award-Winning Vintages

Queensland Grown
& Made Wines

New England H'way. Severnlea
Ph: 076 834 311 Fax: 076 834 291

Mountview Wines

As the first long shadows and golden sunrays of dusk were setting on Stanthorpe we arrived at the Red Cedar Barn style winery of Mountview. "Pretty as a Picture" is the slogan David and Linda Price use to describe the "little piece of paradise" they have created. Truer words have never been spoken.

The vineyards are on the site of the original Mountview Vineyards established in 1921, but later to go out of production. David and Linda began planting the property in 1990.

The Cedar Barn contains a cute tasting area cosseted amongst the barrels and stainless steel fermenters and presses, it's a great way for you to immerse yourself in the winemaking process, whilst you taste.

The Mountview Shiraz has received wide acclaim and it certainly got my French photographer, mate, Stephane's attention,

he couldn't stop raving about it for days as we travelled on our wine journey.

Sometimes one finds the greatest wineries and wines in the most unlikely places

because the people who create them care a lot about what they do and put all of themselves into their enterprise. Mountview Wines is such a place.

MOUNTVIEW WINES

Address: Mt. Stirling Road, Glen Aplin QLD 4381
Direction: 2km off New England Highway, 12 km south of Stanthorpe
Phone: (07) 4683 4316
Fax: (07) 4653 4111
Established: 1990
Owners: David and Linda Price
Winemaker: David Price
Principal varieties grown: Shiraz, Cabernet Sauvignon, Merlot, Chardonnay, Semillon, Sauvignon Blanc
Average annual crush: 20 tonnes
Average no. cases produced: 1,200

Principal wines & brands:
Shiraz

Cabernet Merlot
Chardonnay
Semillon
Cerise (sweet red)
Bianco (sweet white)

Public & trade tours: By appointment only
Hours open to public: 9am-5pm, Sat-Wed; 10am-4pm, Sunday; Open all public holidays and school holidays. Other times by appointment
Points of interest:
 Award winning wines every year, tasting room inside winery, picnic and barbeque area, childrens playground, picturesque views
Retail distribution:
Cellar Door and Mail Order sales. Local restaurants, hotels and bottle shops only

Kominos Wines

One of the modern day pioneering wineries in the unique Stanthorpe wine region of southern Queensland is Kominos. The vineyards are located at 850 metres above sea level and even receive the occasional sprinkling of snow in this comparatively cool viticultural area, long known for its top quality stonefruit.

After an extended stay in Greece in 1973 Stephen and Penelope Comino decided they would make their own wine on return to Australia.

They purchased a property near Severnlea naming it "Ambeli Stavrou" "Vineyard of Stephen".

Tony has been involved since the beginning and has put his Bachelor of Agricultural Science degree to good use. He and his personable wife Mary now run the vineyards and the superb new winery they have built in a classic colonial Australian style.

The evening of our visit they put on an impromptu yet classic Greek meal for us, upstairs in the winery, where they were living with their beautiful baby girl, whilst waiting for their new home to be completed. The meal provided a great opportunity to taste their excellent wines - both red and white and chat about the exciting developments, in this often forgotten wine region, which is becoming a real tourist mecca with hundreds of lovely bed and breakfast operations.

They make quite a range of wines from classic varieties and have a beautifully appointed "Natural" tasting room.

Their hospitality is second to none.

KOMINOS WINES

Address: New England Highway, Severnlea QLD 4352
Phone: (07) 4683 4311
Fax: (07) 4683 4291
Established: 1976
Owner: Tony Comino
Winemaker: Tony Comino
Principal varieties grown: Riesling, Semillon, Chardonnay, Shiraz, Pinot Noir, Cabernet Sauvignon, Chenin Blanc, Sauvignon Blanc, Merlot
Ha under vine: 9

Principal wines & brands	Cellar Potential
Cabernet Sauvignon	10 years
Cabernet Merlot	8 years
Shiraz	10 years
Chardonnay	8 years
Sauvignon Blanc	7 years

Public & trade tours: Yes
Hours open to public: 9am-5pm, daily
Retail distribution:
Cellar Door and Mail Order sales. Wholesale sales and export

Settlers Rise Vineyard and Winery is situated in the beautiful highlands of the Blackall Range, a 75 minute drive north of Brisbane. At an elevation of 450 metres, Montville provides a welcome relief to the heat of Queensland summer for the many visitors who come to taste the variety of Settlers Rise wines and enjoy the traditional village atmosphere of Montville. First settled in 1887,

Wine Tasting

Montville began life as a quiet farming town that gradually became a rest point for travellers and holiday makers earlier this century due to its cool summers and mild winters. The basalt lava of the Blackall Range has formed a deep rich red soil that today is producing excellent grapes and other crops for the farmers who still work the soil.

During the 1800s, Southeast Queensland had many vineyards producing excellent quality wines. However, this century saw most of the local industry disappear until the last two decades which has seen a resurgence in local wineries with Southeast Queensland now boasting over 60 vineyards. Settlers Rise is typical of this trend producing fine blended wines that are well rounded and display a splendid bouquet. The winery offers tasting seven days a week throughout the year to select the ideal wine and a

Cellar Tours

The traditional Queenslander and rolling hills of the Blackall Range make an idyllic setting for the vineyard.

Premium Blend Wines

MONTVILLE

well stocked estate vineyard shop for accessories. The art of wine making is revealed by a conducted tours of the estate, cellars and bottling process between 10 am and 6 pm every day.

Rolling hills, ocean views and excellent wine, discover the romance.

Settlers Rise Vineyard and Winery not only has a high standard in wine tasting facilities but provides the perfect balance for good wine - distinctive regional cuisine. The Wine Deck Restaurant provides a la carte dining in a meticulously restored traditional Queenslander nestled among the vineyards. With the full range of Settlers Rise wines to complement any meal, diners can enjoy elegant cuisine on the wide verandas which afford panoramic views over the vineyards, rolling hills of the Blackall Range and the Pacific Ocean.

A La Carte Restaurant

Visitors to the vineyard also discover the unique village life-style of Montville that has not been eroded by the many visitors who come to experience the charm of its idyllic life-style. Since the early 1900s, artisans and artists have established themselves in Montville and display their wares in the beautiful village setting. A pleasant stroll down the main street reveals an incredible range of cottage industries; glass blowing, art galleries, pottery, textiles, paintings, restaurants, sweets, gift shops, wood carving, blacksmithing, leather works, tea houses, traditional German clocks and chocolates. Although many of the visitors are day trippers, many choose to stay longer at the well appointed country inns where the idyllic settings include local lakes and rainforests.

Enjoy the Montville Magic

Rise Vineyard and Winery at Montville is an experience in quality wine, great cuisine, thriving markets and the tranquillity of a village life-style.

Montville Vineyard and Winery Pty Ltd
t/a Settlers Rise Montville
Tel/Fax 075 478 5558
249 Western Ave Montville 4560

Explore Arts & Craft Markets

New Years Eve 1997 was a real grape stomping affair at Chateau Hornsby. The vintage commenced at midnight to the "strains" of the "Grateful Red" band and their "Shiraz Jazz". Australia's most unusual viticultural location is that of Chateau Hornsby. You'll find it at Alice Springs in the Red Centre of Australia, not far from the world's largest monolith, Ayres Rock, the mysterious Olga's Range and Stanley Chasm. Understandably, Alice Springs pharmacist, Denis Hornsby and his wife, Miranda, were reluctant to leave this stunning landscape when they felt the urge to become vignerons, during the early 1970's. Against all odds and much well meant advice, the Hornsby's planted a small vineyard of three hectares in 1974. Grape varieties planted were mainly shiraz, cabernet sauvignon, semillon and riesling. The wines produced from the estate are very good indeed, a testimony to Denis' persistence.

One of the most unusual events at Chateau Hornsby occurred in 1984 with the semillon grapes. As is customary, grapes were harvested in early January. However, owing to the constant heat of the Central Australian climate, vines produced another ripe grape crop by December of the same year. Thus 1984 saw two grape harvests from the same vines. The climate also tends to confuse the vine. During one visit in May of 1986, I noticed new leaf shoots on vines that were still shedding their autumn-toned leaves. Denis explained that they had just received some rain after a dry spell and the vines were indeed confused. It goes without saying that irrigation is absolutely necessary at Chateau Hornsby for all but six weeks of the year. Water is pumped from a bore by submersible pump and delivered to the vineyard by trickle irrigation. A restaurant has been established to provide both indoor and outdoor seating. An entertainment area has been constructed, and a regular performer is 'Foster-phone' virtuoso, Ted Egan. The general atmosphere at the Chateau is worth crossing the desert for.

The beauty of the location, the quality of the wines and delightful facilities ensure that the Hornsby's have many visitors. This unusual venture is bringing them well-deserved success.

CHATEAU HORNSBY

Address:
Petrick Road, Alice Springs NT 0870
Direction:
10kms south east of Alice Springs
Phone:
(08) 8952 6704
Fax:
(08) 8952 9558
Established: 1974
Winemakers:
Denis Hornsby, Gordon Cook
Principal varieties grown:
Shiraz, Cabernet Sauvignon, Chardonnay, Rhine Riesling, Semillon
Ha under vine: 3
Average annual crush:
15 tonnes
Average no. cases produced:
1,000 dozen

Principal wines & brands	Cellar Potential
Hornsby Estate	
Shiraz	2-5 years
Chardonnay	2-5 years
Riesling/Semillon	2-5 years

Public & trade tours:
By appointment only
Hours open to public:
9am-5pm, daily
Points of interest:
Restaurant (inside), Bush Restaurant (outside), Hot Air Ballooning, Music Sunday's
Retail distribution:
Alice Springs only

An introduction to Classic Blends

One of the most complex skills acquired by Australia's most talented winemakers has been the art of blending wine. Among the great blenders in the history of Australia's wine industry I would include Leo Buring; the late Maurice O'Shea from Mount Pleasant in the Hunter Valley (now owned by McWilliam's); Colin Preece from Seppelt at Great Western; Colin Haselgrove and Roger Warren from Thomas Hardy & Sons; Penfolds' great Max Schubert; Yalumba's Rudi Kronberger; and of course, the irrepressible Wolf Blass.

These men and others from today's top winemaking fraternity such as Brian Croser, John Duval, Brian Walsh and Peter Dawson all have in common the ability to recognise compatibility between two or more wines and blend them in the appropriate proportions, so that the end result is superior to any of the single components. Similarly, these winemakers share the responsibility of deciding the regional origin of fruit used. Blending possibilities are therefore virtually infinite and great winemaking skill is required to be successful in this regard. During the varietal table wine boom of the 1970's, the blending wines was often frowned upon. The phenomenal success of Wolf Blass must be attributed then both to his winemaking brilliance and marketing genius. Fortunately, attitudes have now broadened and Australia's great blends are once again receiving the attention they deserve. The great classic Hunter Valley/McLaren Vale and Hunter/Barossa Valley blends have almost vanished. They are being replaced by exciting blends such as Nagambie Victoria/Coonawarra, Coonawarra/Barossa Valley, Coonawarra/Clare and Coonawarrra/McLaren Vale. Fruit from South Australia's Langhorne Creek remains popular with blenders of red wines. Australia's blended wines are among the best in the world and add a fascinating dimension to the country's output.

Queen Adelaide

Queen Adelaide is a regal name from which the beautifully situated and planned city of Adelaide took its name in 1836. This celebrated Queen of England features on one of Australia's most famous wine labels, which has been part of the Australian wine scene for many decades, and could be considered perhaps the best-known of the classic Australian blends. The original Woodley's Winery was situated at Glen Osmond, a suburb of Adelaide on the Hills face some six or seven kilometres from the GPO, and made wine for many years before succumbing to the urban sprawl of Adelaide. Woodley's Queen Adelaide brand became famous for its quality and value for money, the chief varieties being a claret and a riesling.

In the 1980's the company was acquired by Seppelt who added a chardonnay to the Queen Adelaide stable. It proved an instant success, giving extremely good quality at a very reasonable price. Seppelt of course later became part of the giant Southcorp wine conglomerate which produces great wines at often unbelievably low prices. Today, Queen Adelaide is one of Australia's largest selling ranges of table wines. The Queen Adelaide Pinot Noir is an

impressive wines and the expanding range of Queen Adelaide wines, which now includes a recently released Semillon-Chardonnay,

gives the wine-lover a regal choice at a price all her subjects can afford. Why not lift your glass and toast her Royal Highness?

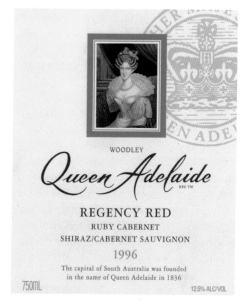

Killawarra

During the premium table wine revolution of the 1970's a new quality and value for money label emerged in Melbourne.

Astute choice of regionally sourced varietal wines red, white and sparkling combined with aggressive marketing saw Killawarra rise to an important position, particularly in the discerning Victorian market.

Today Killawarra is a prestigious label in the Southcorp wine empire and specialising in premium traditional Methode Champenoise Sparkling Wines.

The "Premier Vintage Brut" is a Pinot Noir and Chardonnay Cuvee from one vintage year. It is an elegant style with a fine mousse and long flavours in the mouth, it is made from grapes carefully selected from

the premium cool climate regions of South Australia and Victoria.

The sistership, the Killawarra "Brut", is a top class bottle fermented sparkling that represents great value for money being a cut above the standard sparkling wines available on the market.

Killawarra is a label to trust and drink with confidence.

Cockatoo Ridge

In 1989, outgoing wine personality Geoff Merrill launched a brand in the competitive varietal price bracket. Geoff had a picturesque dam full of birdlife below his historic Mount Hurtle Winery. Strolling around the water's edge one day, Geoff stumbled on a very large egg. Curious, he took it up to the laboratory, wrapped it in a blanket and placed it under a lamp to keep warm. A couple of days later, out popped 'Bruce the Goose'.

Geoff returned him to the dam with a flock of wood ducks who welcomed him into the fold.

This ugly duckling story also has a happy ending - it was indeed 'the goose that laid the golden egg'. Geoff launched the brand name 'Wood Duck Dam', selling several thousand dozen wines in the first year.

Most winemakers would be happy with that, but Geoff had other ideas; he wanted something uniquely Australian and tied in with wine history. This time it was his wife Janet who stepped in. Each dawn and dusk is heralded at Mount Hurtle by the noisy corella cockatoos living in the large gums on the ridge behind the winery, where the vineyard and old crusher which used to feed the gravity flow operation used to be.

Coincidentally, corella comes from Latin and means 'to dig and burrow', exactly what the corellas do in the vineyard.

'Cockatoo Ridge' was born in 1991 and in a few short years, the yearly sales of Cockatoo Ridge have soared.

The chardonnay has led the way, but a red blend and a methode champenoise are selling like hot cakes too.

Overseas demand is strong but there just isn't enough wine to go around at present. However, Geoff is rightly not about to let the quality suffer to keep up supply. Cockatoo Ridge wines are attractively styled, priced and promoted, a winning combination.

Geoff Merrill was certainly no goose when he picked up the egg that hatched 'Bruce the Goose' and began the saga that launched Cockatoo Ridge.

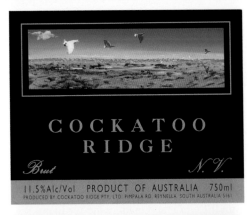

Wolf Blass Foundation

On July 1, 1995 the Wolf Blass Foundation was officially formed. On his 60th birthday in August the previous year, Wolf decided to form a foundation for the betterment of the Australian wine industry to reward achievement in all fields - viticulture, winemaking, wine marketing media promotion and education involving wine. Wolf's generosity in putting A$1 million into this foundation is to be heartily applauded; his foresight is not letting him down. The aim of the Foundation is to reward and provide funds for the award winners to carry out further work and research in their respective fields for the benefit of the Australian wine industry. Wolf has always had the earnest desire to share good wine and the wealth it creates in every way with the industry he loves and the everyday person he relates to so well. He has brought more people to the enjoyment of premium Australian wine through his unceasing and enthusiastic promotion of quality wine and the lifestyle culture it brings.

Fellow board member Guenter Prass A.M. brought about the revolution in sparkling and white wines with his technology in the 1950's, while Wolf revolutionised Australian red wines with his unique handling and barrel ageing in the 1970's, leading to his unsurpassed triple-winning Jimmy Watson wines and refocussing Australians on our great red wines.

Wolf Blass arrived in Australia in 1961 after making the fortunate choice between a sparkling winemaking offer in Venezuela or our own fair country. He took part in the sparkling wine revolution. Wolf's flair and style became quickly obvious when, during an early Kaiser Stuhl pearl wine promotion, he poured sparkling wine out of a petrol pump.

Wolf had a strong family background of wine in his East Germany homeland and as a youngster he worked in his grandfather's vineyard before going to the Wurzburg University where he became the youngest-ever graduate of the Kellermeister Diploma.

Wolf Blass

Ever active and searching for a challenge after three years at Kaiser Stuhl, he became Australia's first freelance winemaker since the great Leo Buring in 1919. For $2.50 per hour and 7 days a week, he travelled in his old Volkswagen beetle from winery to winery around South Australia; his results were legendary. He even sold wine as a consultant broker for 3-5 cents a gallon commission; his fortune was a long way off at this stage.

After consulting to TST Tollana, he was wooed to take on the permanent winemaking role for this new brand. Wolf did a fine job with the quality, style and of course promotion. In 1973, with a $2,000 over-draft, Wolf Blass wines began.

The first vintage release was a 1966 which Wolf had tucked away. The old army shed on 2½ acres of land at Nuriootpa became his headquarters, which he proceeded to get into ship-shape order. His policy right up until merging with Mildara some 15 years later was to crush at wineries selected in each region, bring the juice to his own winery which was superbly set up with many different tank sizes, and make the wines, nurturing them in hisown way.

He is, as many people say, a master blender, but he is much more - he is a master winemaker in every way. In 1991, the year he merged with Mildara, Wolf was honoured by his peers by being named 'International Winemaker of the Year' and received the revered Robert Mondavi Trophy. Wolf's vision for the Foundation is to also assist an interchange of a promising student from Adelaide University's Oenology Course with a student from his old University at Wurzburg in Germany.

In conjunction with the first highly successful "Wine Australia" held in Sydney in 1996 The Wolf Blass Foundation sponsored an "International Wine and Health Conference where the theme was "Medically is wine just another alcoholic beverage".

A panel of 6 overseas Doctors/experts in the field and 6 Australian experts were assembled with the Foundations assistance.

Opened by the South Australian Health Minister, Dr Michael Armitage and Dr Keith Woolard, National President of the A.M.A. Findings were that alcohol in moderation offers cardiovascular protection and wine due to its unique make-up and usually being consumed with food may offer even more health benefits. More research is needed, but findings were encouraging.

The Wolf Blass Foundation is seen by Wolf as an opportunity for all companies in the industry, large and small, to participate and make the Foundation even stronger and more powerful.

To this end, he is focussing on gaining financial support as a top priority. Wolf has a wonderful way with people; he is straight to the point, but I have always found he knows what the point is and more than anything, he is willing to share things with his fellow human beings.

Ein Prosit Wolfgang!

Guenter Prass

Ian Sutton

C. A. Schahinger Pty Ltd

When Wilhelm Schahinger disembarked in Adelaide from his German homeland on the 10th December, 1895 little did he know that almost 102 years to the day later his grandson Geoff and great-grandson Charles, would be celebrating a meritorious achievement as winners, along with their 25 employees, of one of only three "South Australian Enterprize Awards" for "innovation in a continuing enterprise agreement".

At Schahinger's the family are proud to see themselves as top class tradesmen, Geoff Schahinger started with his father Carl in 1949 and like all in the family, including his own son Charles (now in charge of the day to day operations), he did his four year barrel making apprenticeship.

It is easy to see why the team at Schahinger's have such respect for their employers and their unique agreement on

Cooperage is the art and profession of making wooden barrels and vats, an absolutely essential part of todays wine industry.
When Geoff Schahinger started work in

created "Grange Hermitage" and maturation for 18 months to 2 years in American and French oak hogsheads (300 litres capacity) became part of the creation of extra flavours

1949 many said to him he was going into a dying industry. Stainless steel was just coming into the wine industry, replacing in many instances, the large wooden storage vats of 1,500 to 50,000 litres which were the mainstay of the industry (vats stand up, barrels and casks lie on their sides). One of the other key markets, that of wax-lined hardwood barrels for export of fortified wines was also dying out.
However, Geoff hung in there and slowly during the 1950's, when the firm moved from Rose Street, Mile End (near Hardys Wines) to their current site in Hindmarsh, the premium table wine market developed. Max Schubert

bonuses and working conditions has led to such efficiently and first rate quality barrels. I was fortunate to have the honour of hosting the Enterprize Awards and knowing the Schahinger's and their business well, was thrilled to assist in the presentation.

C. A. Schahinger Pty Ltd

and complexity in wines.

Today the business is at least three times the size it was in 1982 and turns out some 12,000 barrels a year, up to 55 in a days work for the "team" of Coopers. The focus in cooperage like wine is more and more in the premium area.

Oak comes from many French forests including Troncais (very dense oak with subtle flavours), Allier, Nevers, Limousin etc. along with German, Russian and the widely used American oak, which seems to have a real affinity with classic Australian shiraz.

Geoff well remembers in the late 1960's when he had to put the price of an American Oak Hogshead up to $50 and thought it would be the last barrel he sold. Today an American Oak Hogshead is around $550 and in French Oak around $850. Fully imported barrels from French Coopers are much dearer but certainly in no way superior to the Schahinger barrels.

around the bottom. The "bung" hole is then drilled and "burnt in". The "heads" (ends) of the cask which have been separately assembled are then added into the grooves cut in each end of the staves. The barrel is then sanded smooth in another machine before having its final hoops added and passing a vigorous inspection and testing. Finally the Schahinger brand and any client specifications are burnt into the barrel and its ready for its many years helping create great wines.

Wilhelm Schahinger started his working life in 1871 as a Cooper in Hamburg and went on to become a ships cooper travelling to South Africa before coming to Australia. Today I am sure he would be pleased indeed to see what the current generations of his family have achieved in their vital role in the hugely successful Australian Wine Industry. Schahinger's are also now exporting to many countries including South Africa, New Zealand and Korea.

Here's a "toast" to the great tradesmen at Schahinger's!!

Toasting of the oak as it sits over the fire used in the bending and construction phase is now considered critical depending on the winemaker and the style of wine he is making, heavy toast (75 minutes over the fire), medium (50 minutes) and light (35 minutes) can be ordered. Schahinger's import only the best seasoned oak from long time suppliers in Europe and America. After the oak has been seasoned from 6 months to 3 years and the moisture content is around 15% it is fed into the shaping machine. These "staves" are then assembled and held together by two hoops at the top whilst it stands over a fire with steam also applied. The barrel then spends some time over the "toasting" fire before going into the trussing machine where, like the ladies of a bygone era, it is pulled into shape by a heavy cable wrapped

It's not every job where you can toast your pie and pastie over a French oak fire!

Travelling with a great photographer is an enlightening experience in everyway. My life has been indelibly coloured and enriched through the twelve years I spent touring the world of wine, through three continents, with a wonderful human being, my great mate, the late Milan Roden. The sunrises and sunsets we shared in some of the most awesomely beautiful places on this planet, are truely memorable. The days of adversity when gods light would not bless us we would travel upwards of a thousand kilometres some days, maybe with nothing between an early or dawn shoot and the uncertainty of where our day would end. It seemed out mercurial efforts were worthy of rewarding because so often we would find ourselves at dusk with a panorama of vines with grapes bathed in golden light.

Today for me the world of light, shade and colour, the forms and movement of clouds,

Milan Roden and Tom Hardy

the moonrise, sunset, sunrise are so much richer, I never ignore them, I never take them for granted, they are a blessing there for all of us.

Milan's philosophies were so profound, it took me many years to fully appreciate them, as we travelled hour upon hour, day upon day, season upon season, year upon year, they subtlely penetrated my skull with his thick Czech accent and unusual use of the English language, it was sometimes a challenge for others to understand him. Many of Milan's masterpieces grace the pages of this book and form a transition to the work of two great photographers who have come into my life these last two years, more of that shortly. I would like to share some of Milan's philosophy with you through the note he wrote in our 1988 North American pictorial Wine Atlas.

"Wine as a living substance of light and happiness has brought me to many places on

this earth. The rich variety of shapes and colours in the landscape, the many happy

Tom Hardy and Stephane L'Hostis

hours with winemakers and growers, the days, the weeks and months became a photographic experience of intense personal joy for me. Wine does not have geographic and ethnic borders. Wine makes its own way as a beautiful gift of mother nature, carefully guided by man and his palate.

As with man, wine can adapt and flourish in the most remote and rugged conditions and create its own character, colours of the sky, clouds and the earth can be found in this liquid form of life.

In my photographs I have tried to capture this ongoing miracle but a mere lifetime is not nearly enough."

In the states of New South Wales, Queensland, Victoria and Western Australia I had the privilege of travelling with a young French photographer, Stephane L'Hostis, ironically born only 30 kms from where I spent 4 years as proprietor/chef at my beautiful Chateau de Fleurac in the Cognac region. Stephane has spent much of his 15 years as a photographer following the Grand Prix circuit around the World, the 1997 Melbourne Grand Prix poster being one of his works.

Stephane is a man of action and movement in the Hunter Valley, he talked me into spending two hours on a hot summers day flying over the vines. He had the pilot remove the door of the plane so he could hang out to get the best angles. He succeeded but I couldn't hear a thing for the next few hours.

His dearest wish was to catch a Kangaroo in the vines and we nearly did so many times, the best he could do was this splendid shot of "The Kangaroo on the Couch" at the Lark Hill Winery in the Canberra region. Stephane's work is "alive" and it has been a great pleasure working with him and "dusting up" my faible French.

Don Brice and I travelled extensively the wine regions of my home state "The Winestate" South Australia.

Don is an optimist and an athlete, he was never phased, occasionally leaping in a single bound onto a vineyard post to capture the angle he wanted. Don is a deep thinker and this depth

Kangaroo on the couch - Stephane L'Hostis - September 1997

comes through in his photography which is always full of life and colour.

Don's sensitivity and empathy with people helped him capture each winemakers individual character with top results. I have been doubly blessed on this wine journey to

Don Brice and Tom Hardy

create this book. I am sure Milan has been looking over me.

"Thomas the Wine is simply a reflection of those who create it, it represents their true character and personality". There was a day when I'd tell Milan to "shut-up" and take the photographs and leave the people and wine to me - no longer - I trust some wisdom has rubbed off on me.

Here's a toast to great photographers and the richness their images bring us!

"Site of an exciting new vineyard venture 'Cathcart Ridge Great Western' overlooking the Grampians in Western Victoria" - Don Brice - December 1997

"Sunset over the Grampians" - Don Brice - December 1997

Index